Advance Praise page for *Solving Latino Psychosocial and Health Problems*

"A 'must read' textbook on the health and overall wellbeing of Latinos in the United States. This updated edition is timely and underscores how our country's health and public health systems of care can more effectively respond to the needs of Latinos. I envision Dr. Organista's text as core reading within numerous health and social welfare disciplines focused on the development of a workforce competent in the provision of healthcare to Latinos."
—**Vincent Guilamo-Ramos**, Duke University

"Since Organista's 1st edition, the Latino population has more than doubled in size and has become the target of policy initiatives purposely designed to weaken its participation in American Society. For his 2nd edition, Organista provides framework to guide members of the helping professions to understand the explosion of Latino-focused research and to apply it in the amelioration of psychosocial and health problems. A Sociocultural Practice Model further guides practitioners in the identification of key social and cultural factors that contextualize Latino-related problems as well as their solutions."
—**David E. Hayes-Bautista**, David Geffen School of Medicine at UCLA

Solving Latino Psychosocial and Health Problems

Theory, Research, and Practice

Second Edition

KURT C. ORGANISTA

OXFORD
UNIVERSITY PRESS

OXFORD
UNIVERSITY PRESS

Oxford University Press is a department of the University of Oxford. It furthers
the University's objective of excellence in research, scholarship, and education
by publishing worldwide. Oxford is a registered trade mark of Oxford University
Press in the UK and certain other countries.

Published in the United States of America by Oxford University Press
198 Madison Avenue, New York, NY 10016, United States of America.

© Oxford University Press 2023

CIP data is on file at the Library of Congress
ISBN 978–0–19–005963–7

DOI: 10.1093/oso/9780190059637.001.0001

Printed by Marquis Book Printing, Canada

*To my wife, Pamela Balls Organista, and to Zena Laura and
Zara Luz Organista, our young adult children, for imbuing my life with love,
joy, hope, and meaning. I am so grateful for who you are and that
we belong to each other.*

Contents

Foreword

Sixteen years is a long time in society; a great deal changes, particularly in advanced economies like the United States. Since the first edition of Kurt C. Organista's book in 2007, the second George W. Bush presidential administration ended and the history-setting election and reelection of Barak Obama followed. Donald Trump surprised the world in 2016 by being elected when so many thought he could not be America's choice. Four stormy years followed, and Joe Biden beat out Trump to become the 46th president in 2020. During the same time, same-sex marriage became legal in the United States, although such couples still face discrimination and microaggressions on a daily basis. Trayvon Martin was killed in 2012 for, in effect, being a young Black man wearing a hoodie. A host of Black men and women seen in witness-recorded videos dying at the hands of police and vigilantes have followed, ceaselessly. Attacks on schools, prayer groups, churches, synagogues, big box stores like Walmart in El Paso and small grocery stores in places like Buffalo, New York, have been all too frequent. Natural disasters such as hurricanes Harvey, Irma, and Maria devastated Puerto Rico and parts of the U.S. mainland, and Latinos have been deeply affected by these. A *Washington Post* (2022) story on October 7, 2022, shows that Latinos, like Blacks, are killed by police disproportionately. But what are the races of the Latinos killed? How many are Afro-Latinos of Dominican, Puerto Rican, Cuban, Honduran, or other national origin? They too "live while Black" and are subject to the poor behavior of police, such as the case of U.S. Army Lt. Caron Nazario, an Afro-Latino who was brutalized by cops in Windsor, Virginia, in December of 2020 while in uniform and trying to obey instructions from the police to pull over. Health care policies changed, the Latino population grew and aged, and immigration policies took on increasingly more mean-spirited attitudes and forms of persecution. That is a lot in 16 years that show many of the factors that need to be considered in a comprehensive examination of the psychosocial and health status of Latinos in the United States, and myriad ways to improve it.

Unchanged across those years was the immigration of Latinos from many Latin American countries, but particularly the Northern Triangle countries of Central America, and the health and health care disparities among Latinos in the U.S. human history shows that migration is inevitable, inexorable, and inexhaustible. There will never be an era without migration. Yet, the United States and many Western countries try to deter rather than sensibly regulate immigration. The unpleasant welcome that many asylum-seekers receive when arriving at the U.S. southern border sends a chilling effect, one that will be remembered for generations to come, and one frequently requiring trauma-informed care as addressed in this book.

A keen observer of the health and social conditions among U.S. Latinos, Organista knows well the changes that have taken place. Organista begins with the obligatory theoretical frames for his understanding and treatment of Latinos. From his own identity definition—*Mexican-American* in the 1960s to a more politically aware *Chicano* in the 1970s and 1980s in California and Arizona, to *Latino* after moving to San Francisco, to having the term *Latinx* find its way into his vocabulary—Organista illustrates the changing nature of the labels that become available for a self-identity and group identity. But it's a naturally changing process with immigration, increased generations of first, second, third, and beyond. While it has always been a matter of examining Latinos by age, gender, and region of the country, we recognize the diversity within and among Latinos, showing the many identities we hold. This intersectionality informs this book.

Organista offers considerable evidence for enhanced *sociocultural understanding* and *sensitivity*, and alights on a refined *Sociocultural Practice Model for Latino Populations*. Included in the description of this multidimensional, multilevel practice model is a refreshing reexamination of *cultural competence* in light of the recent popularity and preference for *cultural humility*.

The above is followed by analysis of major psychosocial and health problems disproportionately affecting Latinos and the most effective systems of care and evidence-based practice, including the incorporation of community health workers currently expanding the health care workforce in culturally effective ways. What's particularly impressive is that Organista does not forget that all of these problems are encountered within a geographic, economic, political, and personal environment that reaches to the policies established by the federal government, impact from global corporations and communication, and regional and local government and service providers. Too often, the forces at work that shape our lives are overlooked, forgotten.

Also underappreciated are the heroic historical and current struggles of diverse Latino populations in the United States to better their lives in ways relevant to practitioner understanding of Latino health, well-being, and social mobility. Organista's book corrects these gaps in the practice literature. The volume will be of exceptional value to teachers and students in the helping professions who seek a comprehensive understanding of the Latino condition in the United States and the many ways to support and advance it.

In the next 16 years, still more will occur that will affect Latinos. Some of the issues will be evolutions of the problems and dilemmas we encounter now. Others that will emerge are, well, yet unknowable and unnamable. But they will be there for providers to tackle. When that time comes, we will have been well served by the insightful theoretical framing of Latino psychosocial and health problems, and by the effective community-based solutions detailed in this masterful second edition.

Luis H. Zayas, PhD
University of Texas at Austin

Works Cited

Washington Post (2022, October 7). Fatal Force. Retrieved from https://www.washingtonpost.com/graphics/investigations/police-shootings-database/

Preface to Second Edition

Integrating the Considerable Accrual of Latino-Focused Outcome Evaluation Research

Completing the second edition of this textbook can be described as an intensive, multi-year, occasionally overwhelming but generally thrilling opportunity to review, critique, and selectively integrate the considerable accrual of Latino-focused outcome evaluation research since publication of the 1st edition in 2007. As compared to 16 years ago, the literature now features several reviews of the literature, including meta-analytic reviews and many randomized control trials evaluating culturally adapted interventions that address Latino health and mental health problems, as well as multilevel practice efforts centering Latino youth and families frequently destabilized by acculturation stress. Hence, this edition maintains its individual chapters on Latino Health, Mental Health, the Latino Family, and Latinx Youth, each now reflecting the current state of effective evidence-based practice, including the expanding role of promotores de salud [community health workers].

More generally, the Latino-focused social science literature continues to broaden and deepen in ways that better capture the sociocultural context of psychosocial and health problem over-affecting Latino populations, either as disparities or non-disparities that nevertheless result in greater morbidity and mortality as compared to non-Latino white (NLW) counterparts. Hence, the book's central practice model is now referred to as the *Sociocultural Practice Model for Latino Population*, given refinements in the ways that it now directs service providers to identify salient social and cultural factors that contextualize Latino psychosocial and health problems during the assessment and intervention phases of service delivery. An additional model refinement is the inclusion of ecological-systems levels (micro-individual, meso-network and community, and macro-social policy) foundational to advancing multilevel practice in the helping professions. Attention to the historical and ongoing need to provide services that are both *available* and *accessible*, as well as *accountable* to Latino clients, communities, and populations, is maintained in the refined practice model.

As with the first edition, a tight set of social science theories (acculturation, social stratification, racial/ethnic identity development, intersectionality) continue to be utilized in the first five chapters of the book to enhance sociocultural understanding and sensitivity to the social and cultural experiences of diverse Latino populations in the United States. While the first edition opened with an analysis of the relation between acculturation and social positionality focusing on the oldest and largest of U.S. Latino populations (Mexican, Puerto Rican, and Cuban American), the second edition features an additional chapter on more recent, smaller but rapidly growing Latino populations (Central Americans and Dominican Americans). Further, while the first edition was forward thinking enough to include a chapter on diversity *within* Latinos along the lines of gender and gender identity, race and skin color, immigration status, and so on, the second edition now updates this chapter by using an *intersectionality* framework to analyze how psychosocial and health problems manifest at various intersections of multiple dimensions of diversity within Latino populations.

The urgency for an updated second edition of this book project is considerable given the auspicious yet uneven pace toward ameliorating psychosocial and health problem over-affecting an increasingly diverse and rapidly growing Latino population. For instance, as of this book's first publication in 2007, the 2000 U.S. Census estimated the Latinos population at 35.3 million or about 12.5% of the U.S. population. Today, the 2020 Census reports a 57% increase in the Latino population to 62.1 million or 19% of the U.S. population, and projected to reach 25% by 2045. Even as early as the 2000 Census, it was documented that Latinos now reside in every state throughout the United States, rapidly forming *new growth immigrant communities* and supplying *essential* labor to vital American industries and markets ranging from agricultural farm work to poultry preparation and meat packing, construction, gardening and landscaping, restaurant services, hotel housekeeping and private domestic work, and numerous other jobs in the vast service sector. Yet, such new growth communities typically lack the supportive services and cultural resources long associated with historical Latino enclaves and anchor communities. Before providing a more in-depth description of the structure, organization, major goals, and intended audiences of the second edition, a brief note on terminology is provided below.

Note on Terminology

Most U.S. Latinos generally refer to themselves based on their historical national origins (i.e., *Mexican-American, Puerto Rican, Cuban American, Nicaraguan*), while also invoking the U.S. government term *Hispanic* in more formal, institutional settings (e.g., when filling out forms) or when referring to U.S. Latinos in the aggregate. Because many Latinos, including the author, have reacted less favorably to the term *Hispanic*, perceived as a top-down government imposed label, they have instead elected to use *Latino* as a general Spanish language population term, in addition to national origins labels. Further, there are many regional variations on preferred terms such as Puerto Ricans who self-identify as *Boriquen* as an assertion of indigenous heritage, or Mexican Americans from New Mexico whose historical mistreatment led to emphasizing their Euro-Spanish heritage through the terms *Spanish* and even *Hispano* long before its English translation became the official U.S. government term. With such a variety of changing terminology, the sensitive service provider simply asks clients what they prefer to be called rather than making assumptions that can be frequently incorrect and off-putting.

As of this writing, the gender-neutral term *Latinx* has begun to replace the Spanish language gendered terms Latino and Latina, at least among some news and entertainment outlets, corporations, local governments, and universities. It is the intent of Latinxs to upend a gendered language so as to be more inclusive and less presumptuous about how people identify with respect to gender and gender identity. This is an admirable yet challenging aspiration considering that, according to the PEW Research Center, 76% of Latinos have not heard of the term *Latinx*; 20% of those that have do not use it, leaving only about 3% of Latinxs that identify as such (Noe-Bustamante, Mora, & Lopez, 2020). Partly based on the author's social positionality (see About the Author), and the predominance of *Latino* in the literature, as well as among Latino clients in the helping professions, I will mainly use *Latino* but also *Latinx* where it feels fitting and reflective of the inclusive efforts of Latinxs (e.g., chapters on intersectionality or Latinx youth).

In my own label-related journey, I came of age in the 1960s with the term *Mexican-American* that was very soon contested (i.e., "We are not hyphenated Americans!") and replaced with *Chicano* and *Chicana* by many politically aware and activist folks in East Los Angeles and Mexican-American communities throughout the southwest. While *Chicano* held in Arizona where I attended graduate school in the 1980s, I added *Latino* and *Latina* to my vocabulary after moving to San Francisco in the late 1980s, given the ubiquity of these terms among the mix of Mexican and Central Americans in the Bay Area. Recently, and especially at UC Berkeley, *Latinx* has found its way into my vocabulary alongside Latino and Chicano. Many of my students assure me that using this mix is OK, and I hope readers feel the same.

Book Structure and Organization

This book is composed of 12 chapters divided into two major sections. Part I contains the first six chapters designed to enhance *sociocultural understanding* and *sensitivity* by applying a tight set of highly relevant social science theories and frameworks to deepen awareness of the historical through current social and cultural experiences of diverse Latino populations in the United States. Given the inseparable nature of social and cultural factors that compose the context of multiple problem levels and solutions, the term *sociocultural* is preferred throughout this book rather than *cultural sensitivity, competence, and humility*, given the way these latter terms over-direct our attention to the cultural at the expense of the social as discussed in Chapter 6. Part I culminates by introducing the book's refined *Sociocultural Practice Model for Latino Populations*. This practice model synthesizes many of the best elements of past and current multicultural and Latino-focused practice models in the social science helping professions such as social work, counseling, and clinical psychology, and other allied disciplines and fields.

Part II, spanning Chapters 7–12, selectively addresses major psychosocial and health problems over-affecting Latinos, either as disparities or non-disparities that nevertheless result in excess morbidity and mortality as compared to NLW counterparts. Detailed descriptions of evidence-based socioculturally competent practices are provided across pressing problem areas and diverse Latino populations and subgroups. Because Latino psychosocial and health profiles are largely a function of lower socioeconomic status (SES) and social positionality, Part I culminates in a pair of chapters addressing Latino political power and, relatedly, Latinx resistance, activism. and social movements—both chapter topics essential to understanding and supporting Latino agency to improve social positionality, and health and well-being in the process. More detailed descriptions of chapters within each of the sections follow.

Part I: Essential Social Science Theories, Frameworks, and Research to Enhance Sociocultural Sensitivity and Practice

Part I grounds the study of U.S. Latinos within a set of interrelated social science theories that illuminate how historical through current social and cultural experiences of Latino populations shape non-random patterns of social positionality and related psychosocial and health profiles. **Chapter 1** (Patterns of Acculturation and Social Positionality in the United States: Mexican, Puerto Rican, and Cuban Americans) uses acculturation theory to compare and contrast the unique histories of the oldest and largest Latino populations in the United States. Differences in social positionality today, and related patterns of psychosocial and health problems, are attributable to degrees of acculturative stress experienced by Mexican, Puerto Rican, and Cuban Americans. **Chapter 2** (Patterns of Acculturation and Social Positionality in the United States: Central and Dominican Americans) is new to the second edition and also analyzes the relationship between acculturation and social positionality by comparing and contrasting the historical experiences of major Central American (i.e., El Salvadoran, Guatemalan, and Nicaraguan) and Dominican American populations in the United States. Historical U.S. involvement in Central America and the Dominican Republic, prior to significant migration from these countries, is emphasized for a more complete understanding of subsequent migration patterns, mixed reception in the United States, acculturation, and adaptation challenges.

Chapter 3 (The Social Stratification of Latino Race/Ethnicity, Power, and Social Positionality in the United States) picks up where Chapters 1 and 2 leave off by using social stratification theory to analyze, describe, and locate Latinos within the American hierarchy or race/ethnicity and power structure, and implications of these locations for general patterns of socioeconomic health and well-being. Current SES data (i.e., median family income, private sector industry concentrations, educational attainment, rates of poverty, and health insurance) are provided to elucidate the stratification of Latinx race/ethnicity and power.

Next, the psychological, individual-level impacts of the above population-level dynamics (i.e., acculturation, social stratification) are addressed in **Chapter 4** (Latino Racial/Ethnic Identity Development: Psychological Impacts of Structured Inequality) by applying Sue et al.'s (2019a) Racial/Cultural Identity Development (R/CID) model to Latinos in the United States to capture the considerable diversity of attitudes, feelings, and behaviors with respect to the racial/ethnic component of self, as well as how other race/ethnic groups are regarded in the American racial hierarchy. A focus on *white racial identity development*, including past (privilege) and current (fragility) developments on the path to a non-racist white identity, is also necessarily included by applying the R/CID to NLW Americans (Sue et al., 2019b).

Chapter 5 (Toward Latinx Intersectionality: From Single to Multiple Dimensional Analysis of Human Diversity) addresses the pressing need to transcend a singular focus on race/ethnicity in our efforts to optimally challenge oppression by understanding its impacts at the intersections of multiple dimensions of human diversity within the Latino population along the lines of gender, gender identity, sexual orientation, skin color and other racial characteristics, and immigration status, to name a few, in order to more fully assess and intervene with problems convoluted in intersectional ways.

Chapter 6 (A Sociocultural Practice Model for Latino Populations), the final chapter in Part I, presents the book's unique practice model for working with Latinos. The refined model features a 4 × 3, four practice dimensions (service availability and access, assessment of key social and cultural factors that contextualize problems, interventions congruent with such assessment, and accountability to clients and communities served) by three ecological-systems (E-S) practice levels (micro-individual, meso-network and community, and macro-social policy). The model's four general practice dimensions derive from a synthesis of past studies, reports, and models developed to promote culturally competent care with people of color. However, these four dimensions represent *socioculturally competent care* given their deliberate attention to interrelated social and cultural factors that contextualize psychosocial and health problems. For example, making services *available* and *accessible* as well as *accountable* to Latino clients is an effective way to mitigate historical obstacles to care by addressing such *social factors*, while identifying such social and interrelated cultural factors (e.g., value-related beliefs, attitudes, and behaviors) that contextualize a problem during the assessment process optimizes interventions congruent with such sociocultural assessment.

Also new to the second edition's updated practice model are eco-systemic practice levels essential to advancing multilevel practice. For instance, while preventing or managing diabetes is necessary at the micro-individual level (e.g., with a client or family), optimal diabetes prevention and care is multilevel and includes meso-network and community level practice (e.g., diabetes awareness and testing at community health fairs, public health media campaigns) and macro-social policy level practice (supporting development of or advocating for diabetes mitigating policies at local and larger levels). Hence, the objective of Chapter 6 is to provide a user-friendly and comprehensive practice model that practitioners, as well as their administrators, can use to evaluate and develop socioculturally responsive services for Latino communities served. The model also serves as a convenient guide for evaluating the many interventions selectively reviewed in Part II.

Part II: Selective Reviews of Psychosocial and Health Problems Over-affecting Latino Populations, and Socioculturally Competent Practices

Part II provides detailed, up-to-date descriptions and illustrations of evidence-based socioculturally competent interventions with diverse Latino populations and subgroups across a wide variety of major psychosocial and health problems. Since the first edition of this book in 2007, there has been a considerable accrual of Latino-focused outcome evaluation research, including many reviews of the literature, and cultural adaptations of interventions. These are reviewed to illustrate effective socioculturally competent care *en acción* [in action].

Part II not only provides illustrations of socioculturally competent interventions, including examples from the author's years of Latino health and mental health research and practice, but also culminates with a primer on Latino political power as well as an overview of Latino resistance, activism, and social movements, past and present, in order to more fully convey how various Latino populations have used their collective agency to empower their communities, make significant gains in civil rights, and elevate their social positionality and psychosocial and health profiles in the process.

As the single most important and enduring cultural institution across diverse Latino populations, even those varying in level of acculturation, *la familia* Latina must be adequately addressed as the site of both acculturation-related problems over-affecting Latino families in the United States and socioculturally competent solutions. Thus, **Chapter 7** (The Latino Family) centers the family in its analysis of frequently destabilizing acculturative stress, its differential impacts on family members, and effective interventions that promote flexible bicultural expansions of *familismo* and other related values and practices. Interpersonal violence, including elder abuse, at the extremes of family destabilization are addressed in this chapter, in addition to youth behavioral problems resulting from generation gaps exacerbated by acculturation gaps.

Flowing from Chapter 7, **Chapter 8** (Latinx Youth) focuses on sociocultually competent ways of addressing the cluster of interrelated psychosocial and health problems over-affecting the rapidly growing Latinx youth population in America: school failure, sexual reproductive health challenges such as unplanned pregnancy and STIs, including HIV; depression and suicidality in Latina youth; alcohol and substance use; delinquency and gang affiliation.

Similarly, **Chapter 9** (Latino Mental Health) provides an overview of Latino mental health followed by a selective review of sociocultural practices for mitigating major problem areas (e.g., depression) over-affecting subgroups (e.g., women), often with the evidence-based assistances of *promotores de salud* [community health workers] effectively supporting and leading mental health care interventions, and often in connection with integrated behavioral health care clinics.

Relatedly, **Chapter 10** (Latino Health) provides an overview of the state of Latino health in America, with attention to pertinent macro level social factors (e.g., need for health insurance and federally qualified health care clinics), cultural factors (e.g., culture-based health-related attitudes, beliefs, and behaviors), and effective culturally adapted interventions to prevent, as well as manage, chronic illnesses over-affecting Latinx health such as diabetes, heart disease, cancer, HIV, and their many correlates and interrelated illnesses. As in Chapter 9, the role of *promotoras* [Latina community health *promotores*] is highlighted as part of an expanded, effective, and needed workforce.

Chapter 11 (Latino Power Primer: Political Participation, Representation, and Policy Benefit) returns to a focus, touched upon in Chapters 1–3, on compromised social positionality, including socioeconomic vulnerability to psychosocial and health problems, and the ongoing need for political empowerment and macro-social solutions. Thus, this chapter grounds the reader in a primer of Latino power in the realm of politics with an emphasis on political participation, representation, and policy benefit, including potential roles for service providers to support macro-political solutions to Latino social problems. The California Latino Legislative Caucus is highlighted to illustrate the historical development of significant political power and policy benefit to the state's 16 million Latinos, and working class Californians more generally, in high-priority areas such as health care, education, employment, and immigrant rights.

From protests by Latino communities during the first half and middle of the 20th century (e.g., Lemon Grove Incident, Mothers of East Los Angeles) through today's robust immigration rights and DREAMers movements, including protesting "crimmigration," former president Trump's separation of families at the border, and his antagonistic handling of Hurricane Maria in Puerto Rico, **Chapter 12** describes salient instances of Latino resistance, activism, and social movements promoting civil rights, social positionality, health, and well-being. Advocated in this final chapter are inclusive frameworks for amplifying the political power and impact of social movements through intersectional collective action (e.g., on the part of diverse DREAMers), and fusing racial and economic justice in order to build movements across race and social class in America. Attention to these matters is foundational to a fuller understanding of how Latinos and other racial and ethnic minority groups improve their lives, at the grassroots level, often in partnership with formal political organizations, community-based nonprofits, and informed practitioners and service providers.

Book Goals and Intended Audiences

Four Interrelated Goals

Now in its second edition, this book project, spanning 15 years since its initial publication in 2007, aspires to achieve four major overriding and interrelated goals:

1. To convey the sociocultural experience of Latinos in the United States, past through present and to provide service providers with an informed and sensitizing background for serving their diverse Latino clients and communities in the practice foreground.
2. To provide a *sociocultural practice model* that directs service providers to the interrelated social and cultural factors that contextualize Latino psychosocial and health problems, as well as congruent, evidence-based, and multilevel practice solutions.
3. To provide readers with a critical review and integration of rigorous outcome evaluation research currently addressing Latino health and

mental health needs, as well as Latino family and youth challenges rooted in acculturation stress.

4. To convey how Latinos have steadily raised their social positionality, and related health and well-being, through resistance, activism, and social movements that have secured civil rights, political power, and policy benefits, and that can be advanced by fusing racial and economic justice in America and hence coalition building across race, class, and other intersectional collective action frameworks.

Intended Audiences

The second edition of this book is designed to be a well-researched and up-to-date resource for students interested in, and professionals already serving, Latino populations in various helping professions such as social work, counseling and clinical psychology, marriage and family therapy, psychiatry, and public health, all of which are deeply committed to providing effective care for a wide variety of psychosocial and health problems over-affecting Latino populations. As such, the book will continue to serve as the primary text for the growing number of Latino-focused graduate and undergraduate courses preparing students for the helping professions (e.g., Social Work with Latino Populations, Latino Mental Health, Latino Health, Latino Children and Families). The nearly 60% increase in the U.S. Latino population, between the first and second edition of this book, from 35.3 to 62.1 million, means that helping professionals and their agencies and institutions are now serving Latino clients and communities more than ever before, and in more diverse geographical locations throughout the United States, now that Latinos live and work in every state in America. Professional service providers and their directors and administrators will find the book's sociocultural practice model an invaluable guide for evaluating their current services and developing new and needed practices for effectively serving their Latino clients and communities.

Selected References Cited

Noe-Bustamante, L., Mora, L., & Lopez, M. H. (2020). About one-in-four U.S. Hispanics have heard of Latinx, but just 3% use it. Pew Research Center (August). www.pewresearch.org

Sue, D. W., Sue, D., Neville, H. A, & Smith, L. (2019a). Racial/cultural identity development in people of color: Counseling implications. In D. W. Sue, D. Sue, H. A. Neville,
and L. Smith, *Counseling the culturally different: Theory and practice* (8th ed.) (pp. 355–
388). New York: John Wiley & Sons.

Sue, D. W., Sue, D., Neville, H. A, & Smith, L. (2019b). White racial identity develop-
ment: Counseling implications. In D. W. Sue, D. Sue, H. A. Neville & L. Smith,
Counseling the culturally different: Theory and practice (8th ed.) (pp. 389–424).
New York: John Wiley & Sons.

Acknowledgments

My family's constant care supported the completion this second edition of a book project close to my heart and one of the reasons for pursuing my career. During our lockstep journey through academia and beyond, my wife **Pamela Balls Organista** has graced my life with her loving, caring, intelligent, and joyful presence for 40 years and counting. **Zena Laura Organista** and **Zara Luz Organista**, now beautiful young adults, continue bringing immense joy into our lives by being exactly the wonderful people that they are.

Regarding my family of origin, my father **Ricardo Rico Organista** continues to enrich my thinking, feelings, and dreams since passing in 2020 at the age of 93, as does my grandmother, **Adela Rico Organista**, who raised me in East Los Angeles along with my father and uncle, **Alex Rico Organista**, who continues to be my loving big brother from Boyle Heights.

Best friend from junior high, **David "T-Bone" Torres**, and his lovely *esposa* **JoAnn Orge Torres**, remain close, as have **Carole Wong** and the late **Danny Alba**, both of whom touched my heart at *Breed Street Elementary School*, and more so in our *viejez*. *Carnal*, **Ruben Funkahuatl Guevara**, of the 70s Chicano rock band *Ruben and the Jets*, continues to enrich the soul of our community as a deeply resonating culture sculptor.

Closer to our Bay Area home, *Compadres* **Celina** and **Pablo Ramirez**, adult children **Quetzali** and **Rubi**, and godson **Diego** continue to ground my family in the best of Mexican *familismo*.

Touchstone colleagues at UC Berkeley's School of Social Welfare have seen me through 33 years at Cal. Receiving the Harry and Riva Specht Chair in Publicly Supported Social Service is especially meaningful given the strong allyship of **Dean Harry Specht** during my years as a junior professor. **Emerita Professor Jewelle Taylor Gibbs** continues embracing my wife and I as part of her remarkable family. Current **Dean Linda Burton**, goes out of her way to lift me up as part of her sound, soulful, and singular leadership at the school. Special thanks to **Paul Terrell**, and *los hermanos* **Joseph Solis**, **Rafael Herrera**, and **Peter Manoleas**, for their enduring friendship, and **Lorretta Morales** for decades of superb administrative support. I have appreciated the soft landing with which you all provided me when beginning at Cal, and

for continued care and support through our many years as *colegas*. Heartfelt
thanks to **Samantha Ngo**, student turned delightful friend and colleague, for
expertly designing many of the figures and tables throughout this book and
for the better part of my academic career.

Outside of my UCB orbit, **Britt Rios-Ellis** has been one of my closest
colegas and friends in the quest to prevent HIV in Latino communities. It's
been a joy getting to know her lovely family over the years: *esposo* **Enrique
Rios**, and young adult children **Quique, Xochitl**, and **Itzel**.

I would also like to acknowledge key mentors: **Manuel Barrera Jr.**, during
graduate school at Arizona State University, who passed in 2020; as well as
Ricardo F. Muñoz, during internship in clinical psychology at San Francisco
General/University of California, San Francisco. Both provided care, guidance, and subsequent decades of *amistad*. I remain grateful to **Lisa I. Gebo**,
editor of this book's first edition, who gracefully blended professionalism,
warmth, and joy with the 2007 publication of this book three years before her
passing. Calm, patient, warm, and understanding editor of this second edition, Oxford University Press editor **Dana Bliss**, held this project within his
editorial grasp despite years of competing priorities and a global pandemic.

Special thanks to the **Latino Community Foundation (LCF)**, for permis-
sion to use photos gracing the cover of this book (Youth from Brown Issues &
Women from KBBF Bilingual Public Radio) by photographer **Bryan Patrick**.
California's only statewide Latino foundation, LCF grows philanthropy by
and for Latinos, and leads with the love our communities deserve. Gracias
Jacqueline Garcel Martinez for your amazing CEO leadership y amistad.

About the Author

Academic Credentials and Professional Experience

Kurt C. Organista, PhD, is Professor, School of Social Welfare, University of California, Berkeley, where his focus is on Latino psychosocial and health problems and solutions. He teaches courses on psychopathology, racial and ethnic relations, and social work practice with Latino populations. He conducts research on HIV prevention with Latino migrant laborers, is editor of the book *HIV Prevention with Latinos: Theory, Research and Practice*, published by Oxford University Press in 2012, and author of *Solving Latino Psychosocial and Health Problems: Theory, Practice, and Populations*, published by John Wiley & Sons, in 2007. He serves on the editorial boards of the *American Journal of Community Psychology*, the *Hispanic Journal of the Behavioral Sciences*, and the *Journal of Ethnic and Cultural Diversity in Social Work*. From 2004–2008, he was appointed to the Office of AIDS Research Advisory Council at the National Institutes of Health, and from 2010 to 2015 was PI of a federal R01 grant from the NIAAA to develop and test a structural environmental model of alcohol-related HIV risk in Latino migrant day laborers in the San Francisco Bay Area. Organista served as trustee of the Latino Community Foundation (2015 to 2022) and as trustee and vice chair of the San Francisco Community Foundation (2008 to 2018). In 2018, he received the Leon Henkin Citation for Excellence in Mentoring Underrepresented Students, and in 2020 he was named the American Cultures Teacher of the Year, as well as inducted as a Fellow into the American Academy of Social Work and Social Welfare. In 2021 he was awarded the Harry and Riva Specht Chair in Publicly Supported Social Services.

Social Positionality Statement

Purpose: To provide readers with a sense of who I am and where I am coming from as the author of this book. Also, to convey my particular Latino background, experience, and motivation for my career path, as well as both the assets and blind spots that accompany my social positionality.

Demographics: I am an older, Latino, heterosexual (cisgender), nondisabled, professional, middle-class, married, male. Pronouns: He, him, *él* & *ese*.

Background: I was born and raised in Boyle Heights, East Los Angeles, in a predominately Mexican-descent community, within an extended Mexican-American family. My father was also born in ELA (first generation), worked as a schoolteacher, and raised me along with my grandmother who was from Sonora, Mexico. My paternal grandfather was from Teocaltiche, Jalisco, Mexico, a town I had the privilege to survey as part of my HIV risk and prevention research. My mother was born in Hatch, New Mexico, a small town famous for its superb long red and green chili. She did not graduate high school.

Interests: My interest in Latino psychosocial and health problems stems from my personal background, participation in the Chicano movement (circa 1965–1975), and from my father's community activism. I am also interested in racial and ethnic relations more generally, including attention to intersectionality, and effective assessment and practice with Latino populations informed by sociocultural contextual factors and solutions.

PART I

ESSENTIAL SOCIAL SCIENCE THEORIES, FRAMEWORKS, AND RESEARCH TO ENHANCE SOCIOCULTURAL SENSITIVITY AND PRACTICE

The purpose of Part I is enhance service provider *sociocultural understanding* of and *sensitivity* to the historical through current lived realities of Latino populations in the United States. This is accomplished by using a tight set of highly relevant social science to analyze the social and cultural experiences of U.S. Latino populations (i.e., acculturation, social stratification, racial/ethnic identity development, and intersectionality), culminating in a sociocultural practice model with Latino populations.

Synthesizing many of the best elements of past and current models of *cultural competence* and *humility*, the current model directs practitioner attention to the interrelated social and cultural factors that contextualize psychosocial and health problems over-affecting Latino populations, as well as to the congruent, evidence-based, and increasingly culturally adapted interventions to mitigate such problems.

1

Patterns of Acculturation and Social Positionality in the United States

Mexican, Puerto Rican, and Cuban Americans

The process of becoming Americanized can result in very different levels of adaptation, adjustment, and social positionality for different racial and ethnic groups historically and today. Why is it that some populations have considerable success achieving the "America Dream" while others do not? That is, why is it that some populations achieve high levels of power and participation in mainstream culture, politics, and the economy, while other groups struggle and suffer toward the bottom or at the margins? Using socioeconomic status (SES) as perhaps the most central indicator of *social positionality* and well-being, it is easy to observe the different levels of SES in the United States, with non-Latino whites (NLWs) overrepresented at the top and most people of color overrepresented at the bottom.

Even focusing only on Latino populations, one can observe considerable differences in SES, with Cuban Americans ranking closer to NLWs, Puerto Ricans ranking much lower alongside African Americans, and Mexican and Central Americans ranking in between. The ways in which we perceive and understand the social positionality of different groups have tremendous implications for how we respond to their psychosocial and health problems. For example, do we view racial and ethnic groups as primarily responsible for their locations in the U.S. hierarchy of resources and power, or do we view social structural and environmental factors as primarily responsible? To be most effective, human service professionals need to think deeply and critically about the origins and perpetuation of psychosocial and health problems over-affecting the various groups they serve.

It is a basic tenet of *cultural sensitivity* to make oneself knowledgeable about the historical and sociocultural experiences of minority groups with whom we work as service providers. Thus, while practitioners should not be expected to become historians, it is important that we obtain

Solving Latino Psychosocial and Health Problems. Kurt C. Organista, Oxford University Press.
© Oxford University Press 2023. DOI: 10.1093/oso/9780190059637.003.0001

sufficient background knowledge with which to better appreciate the current circumstances, problems, and postures of racial/ethnic minority clients. The purpose of this chapter is to apply an acculturation theoretical framework for organizing a brief but salient overview of Latino-relevant American history and sociology. This chapter emphasizes the oldest and currently largest of U.S. Latino groups (i.e., Mexican Americans, Puerto Ricans, and Cubans), comparing and contrasting their acculturation histories and related social positionality. The subsequent chapter covers smaller, more recent and rapidly growing U.S. Latino populations (i.e., Central Americans and Dominicans) for whom scholarly inquiry and literature is finally beginning to accrue.

Acculturation theory enhances human service professional understanding of the historical development of contemporary Latino psychosocial and health problems in ways that help to *depathologize* Latinos without minimizing the gravity of their many health and life-compromising challenges. An acculturation framework can also enhance reader cultural sensitivity by placing Latino problems and issues within a context that considers the dynamics of U.S. race relations, dominance and subordination, and how majority and minority groups co-evolve over time.

The Concept of Acculturation

The classic definition of acculturation dates back to the mid-1930s when anthropologists Redfield, Lipton, and Herskovits (1936) defined it as those phenomena that result when members of two different autonomous cultural groups come into continuous first-hand contact, with subsequent changes in the original cultural patterns and customs of either or both groups (e.g., language, values, lifestyle, attitudes, identity). While many today use the terms acculturation and assimilation interchangeably, Redfield et al. (1936) specified that acculturation referred to cultural changes (e.g., values, lifestyle), whereas assimilation referred specifically to intermarriage between members of groups in contact. They noted that assimilation or intermarriage may or may not be a phase of acculturation for some groups. For example, 30 years ago, the rate of intermarriage for Cuban American women was nearly 50% as compared to 16% for Mexican American women (Gonzales, 1993), quite a difference considering that the vast majority of Cubans had been in the United States only about 30 years versus about 10 years for Mexican Americans. This difference is illuminated by an acculturation framework as described below.

Acculturation American Style

For decades, Canadian psychologist John Berry has studied the process of acculturation by focusing primarily on indigenous peoples and racial/ethnic minority groups in North America and their historical experience with dominant European colonial powers. As such, Berry's conceptualization of acculturation is particularly relevant to major racial and ethnic minority groups such as Native Americans, African and Asian Americans, and Latinos in the United States. For example, in discussing the *nature* of acculturation, Berry notes that while in theory two groups in continuous contact may influence each other, in reality the scenario is usually one in which a larger and more powerful group dominates a smaller and less powerful one (see Figure 1.1). The dominant group typically wields considerably more power to control, influence, coerce, and oppress the non-dominant group, and such dynamics set the stage for a process of acculturation that is typically resistant, stressful, and conflictual for the non-dominant group. Just how stressful is the acculturation process depends on its course.

Berry summarizes the *course* of acculturation as a three-phase process characterized by: (1) contact, (2) conflict, and (3) adaptation. *Contact* refers to the conditions under which two cultural groups encounter each other (e.g., invasion, immigration, seeking refuge). *Conflict* refers to the predictable tension and conflict that results when one group attempts to dominate the other, and *adaptation* refers to the eventual forms of accommodation

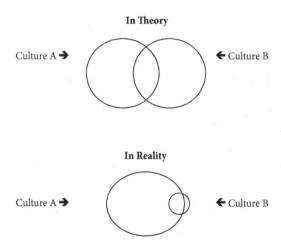

In Theory

Culture A ➡   ⬅ Culture B

In Reality

Culture A ➡   ⬅ Culture B

Figure 1.1. Depiction of the nature of acculturation.

between groups intended to reduce conflict. While it is theoretically possible for conflict not to occur, as indeed some individuals may experience, the all too common dynamics of group level dominance and subordination make conflict a common phase of acculturation. Accommodation can take a variety of forms ranging from assimilation, as when a non-dominant group marries into the dominant group, to separation, as when a non-dominant group exists mostly apart from the dominant group, either by choice but more often by exclusion and marginalization.

Which form of adaptation an ethnic minority group eventually experiences depends on a number of factors including the original conditions of contact, the degree and types of conflict with the majority groups, and the dominant society's tolerance for racial and cultural diversity. All of these factors influence the degree to which the non-dominant group attempts to maintain its culture of origin and the degree to which positive relations between groups is possible. According to Berry, the four major forms of adaptation evident in most societies, depicted in Table 1.1, can be understood by listing all possible combinations of yes/no answers to the following two questions: (1) Does the minority group attempt to retain its culture of origin, and (2) are positive relations between the minority and majority group possible?

For example, the historical experience of Mexican Americans has predominantly been one of segregation due to exclusion and strained relations with the dominant group, and a relatively high retention of Mexican culture. The fact that Mexican American adaptation has slowly been shifting from segregation to integration and degrees of assimilation speaks to the dynamic nature of acculturation and group relations over time, not depicted in Table 1.1. Still, the depiction of the four major forms of adaptation provides us with

Table 1.1. Varieties of Adaptation to Acculturation for U.S. Minority Groups

Significant Effort to Retain Culture?	Positive Relations Possible with Dominant Culture?	Form of Adaptation
No	Yes	Assimilation
Yes	Yes	Integration
Yes	No	Segregation
No	No	Marginalization

From Berry (1990). Psychology of acculturation: Understanding individuals moving between cultures. In A. Brislin (Ed.), *Applied cross-cultural psychology* (pp. 232–253). Newbury Park, CA: Sage. With Permission from Sage Publications, Inc.

a fundamental understanding of how stressful the acculturation process can be for different racial/ethnic groups in the United States. Indeed, the four forms of adaptation can be viewed as a crude gradient of stress in which the scenarios of assimilation and integration are far less stressful than segregation and certainly marginalization. A solid conceptualization of *acculturative stress* is essential for understanding the basis of an ethnic minority group's relative pattern of success and failure or social positionality in the United States.

Acculturative Stress

Berry and colleagues (Berry & Annis, 1974) define acculturative stress as collective confusion and anxiety, loss of identity, feelings of alienation, and striking out against larger society. More specifically, they note that acculturative stress refers to behaviors and experiences generated during acculturation that are maladaptive and disruptive to the individual and ethnic group (e.g., deviant behavior, psychosomatic symptoms, and feelings of marginality). At the macro-level, acculturation stress can be expanded to refer to disparities in SES, health, and quality of life between majority and ethnic minority groups.

The Acculturation Stress Formula

Based on decades of research on both ethnic immigrant and indigenous groups in North America, Berry developed a useful formula for gauging a group's general level of acculturative stress that considers the influential roles of race, ethnicity, culture, and racism embedded in the process of acculturation. According to Berry (2003), acculturative stress will be *highest* when the cultural and behavioral similarity between two groups in contact is *lowest*, and where the minority group is pressured and coerced to acculturate due to the dominant group's low tolerance for racial and cultural diversity. For instance, acculturative stress has been highest for Native Americans and African Americans given their low cultural, behavioral, and *racial* similarity to European Americans, and the tremendous historical coercion placed upon these *involuntary* Americans to relinquish their cultures of origin. Such pressure has been especially stressful considering that the original *contact* experiences of these two groups involved invasion and forced relocation followed by policies of exclusion and separation from mainstream society (e.g., removal and reservations for Native Americans and enslavement followed by legal segregation for African Americans).

In contrast, European immigrants have historically experienced comparatively lower acculturative stress than people of color, given their greater cultural and racial similarity to the dominant group, and because the pressure to acculturate has been buffered by their *voluntary immigration* to America (i.e., their collective inclination to relinquish culture of origin in exchange for American culture and identity). However, this is not to say that European immigrants have not experienced acculturative stress stemming from America's low tolerance for cultural diversity even within European immigrants.

Low tolerance for diversity was exemplified by the famous "melting pot" philosophy that strongly discouraged foreigners from retaining their culture of origin while serving as the guiding philosophy for integrating and socializing European immigrants into American society during the 20th century. Melting pot philosophy made immigration and acculturation overly stressful because it insisted upon conformity to the white Anglo Saxon Protestant/Northern European standard while devaluing dissimilar southern and eastern European cultures, with no vision of healthy functional biculturalism or multiculturalism.

However, as unnecessarily stressful as melting pot–driven acculturation was for many European American immigrant groups, they were eventually accepted as the "right stock" for the melting pot recipe, while non-European people of color were excluded. For example, southern and eastern immigrants (e.g., Jews, Italians, Poles, Hungarians), of the second great immigration stream, were initially perceived as a threat because of their darker Mediterranean features and poverty backgrounds. However, they were eventually accepted by the American majority of northern and western European ancestry, as exemplified by their current SES parity alongside high rates of marital assimilations (Healey, Stepnick, & O'Brien, 2019a).

Berry (1990) notes that acculturative stress is particularly high when countries develop policies that largely exclude certain groups from civic engagement and limit access to power. Thus, herein lies a precarious predicament for people of color who have often been prohibited from practicing their culture yet disallowed from fully participating in American society. Marginality can result from this predicament (see Table 1.1), a scenario most historically evident for Native Americans and African Americans, but also for subgroups of Latinos such as members of Chicano, Puerto Rican, and Central American youth gangs that walk a line between cultures without sufficient grounding in either. See Chapter 8 (Latinx Youth) for extended discussion on gang-affiliated Latino youth.

In response to the double-bind of melting pot pressure to assimilate and forced separation, segregated groups have urgently needed to retain their culture of origin, or if necessary reclaim and even recreate it, in order to survive and validate their humanity in an often dehumanizing and hostile environment. For people of color, group survival has depended on culture-based mutual aid and traditions that have served as an organizing principle for physical and social survival. It is an irony of history that the racist exclusion of people of color from participation in mainstream society has done more to strengthen ethnic culture and identity than any nationalistic movement on their part. Spurts of nationalism, sometimes seen at the fringes of civil rights protest and movements, are more reactions to rejection than proactive efforts to live as a separate nation. The majority of people of color have been and continue to be fiercely patriotic believers in America, willing integrate and assimilate in spite of historical rejection. On a related note, it is a double irony that the most voluntarily self-segregating groups in the United States are of European background (e.g., Amish, Mennonites), and that nationalism has recently reemerged among fringe white supremacist groups.

Acculturative Stress and Social Positionality

In examining the acculturative experiences of different racial and ethnic groups in America, it becomes apparent that degree of acculturative stress is inversely related to a group's overall wellbeing or social positionality. That is, the higher the degree of acculturative stress, the lower overall level of SES and well-being for a group. Given this inverse relation, Berry's three-stage model of acculturation is expanded here to include relative degree of acculturative stress and social positionality, to better connect acculturation dynamics with current levels of well-being in different major race/ethnic groups in America (Table 1.2).

This expanded model of acculturation depicts general historical patterns of adaptation and consequent level of social positionality (i.e., SES) for major U.S. racial and ethnic groups. While no model is comprehensive enough to represent all of the variance within or between groups, the expanded model presented here provides a fundamental framework for beginning to

Table 1.2. Acculturation and Social Positionality for Major Racial/Ethnic Groups in the United States

Race/Ethnic Group	Conditions of Contact	Degree of Conflict	Predominant Form of Adaptation	Degree of Acculturative Stress	Social Positionality (SES)
European Americans	Colonization→ Voluntary Immigration	Low	Assimilation	Low	High
Native Americans	Invasion	High	Marginalization → Segregation	High	Low
African Americans	Forced Relocation	High	Marginalization → Segregation	High	Low to Medium
Old* Chinese Japanese	Voluntary Immigration	Medium	Segregation → Integration → Assimilation	Medium to Low	Medium to High
Latinos	Varies by subgroup	Medium	Segregation → Integration	Medium	Medium

*Refers to oldest and largest Asian (Chinese and Japanese) populations with immigration histories in the United States since the early 1800s.

Note: Arrows indicate change over time.

understand patterns of population-level adjustment or social positionality among major racial and ethnic populations in America.

While it is relatively easy to use the expanded model of acculturation to contrast the general adaptations of NLWs, African Americans, and Native Americans, different Latino groups vary considerably in their conditions of contact with American society and subsequent degrees of acculturative stress, adjustment, and social positionality. The same is true of Asian groups, which is why the examples in Table 1.2 are limited to "old" Chinese and Japanese populations with immigration histories dating back to the early 1800s.

A selective review of salient historical details is necessary to appreciate the conditions of acculturation that undergird current levels of SES and needs of different Latino groups in the United States, as depicted in Table 1.3.

Mexican Americans/Chicanos

Americans of Mexican ancestry comprise about two-thirds of all Latinos in the United States, and their extensive, over a century and a half, history in America predates all other U.S. Latino populations. As such, application of

Table 1.3. Acculturation, Acculturative Stress & Social Positionality (SES) for Major U.S. Latino Populations

Latino Group	Conditions of Contact	Degree of Conflict	Predominant Form of Adaptation	Degree of Acculturative Stress	Social Positionality (SES)
Chicanos	Invasion & Immigration	Medium	Segregation → Integration	Medium	Medium
Cuban Americans	Legal Refugees	Low	Segregation → Integration → Assimilation	Low	High
Puerto Ricans	Colonization	Medium	Segregation	Medium to High	Low to Medium
Central Americans	Mixed Status Refugees*	Medium	Segregation	Medium	Medium

*Undocumented, temporary protected status, delayed expedited departure, etc.

Note: Arrows indicate change over time.

the expanded acculturation model entails considerable analysis and serves as a salient point of reference for understanding Latino acculturation and social positionality in the United States. In this section, the term *Mexican American* is used to refer generally to this population, while also honoring *Chicano*, a term self-selected by civil rights activists, partly as a rejection of the government-imposed term *Hispanic* and the hyphenated term *Mexican-American* prior to that. Used historically by Mexican people as a disparaging term affixed to low class people, Chicano movement activists chose to infuse this term with pride and resistance, much as African Americans turned the term *Black* on its head during the 1960s.

Contact

Although contact for the vast majority of today's estimated 37+ million Mexican Americans is mainly characterized as *voluntary immigration*, it is important to note that Mexican people preceded NLW settlers in what is now the southwestern portion of the United States. They are the only other minority group in U.S. history, besides Native Americans, to be annexed by conquest and subsequently have their rights (supposedly) safeguarded by treaty. As such, the stage for protracted conflict, difficult adjustment, or acculturative stress was set in motion over 150 years ago. Major forms of conflict to understand include war between the United States and Mexico, major loss of land holdings, continuous exploitation of Mexican labor, still highly evident in agricultural labor, and the recent criminalization of undocumented Mexican immigrants, alongside Central American and other undocumented people in the United States.

Prior to America's aggressive westward expansion during the 1800s, Mexico extended north to include a vast area corresponding roughly to what we now know as Texas, California, New Mexico, Arizona, Oregon, Nevada, and parts of Utah and Wyoming—although sparsely populated, as many as 100,000 Mexicans may have occupied this area (McLemore, Romo, & Gonzalex Baker, 2001). Fearful of American encroachment, the Mexican government offered American settlers tracts of land to develop in the 1820s on the condition that they obey Mexican law and eventually become Mexican citizens and members of the Catholic Church. While a few American settlers complied, most did not and entered Mexico illegally, an interesting historical footnote given today's widespread resentment of undocumented Mexicans in the United States.

Conflict

By 1835, American settlers outnumbered Mexicans five to one in Northern Mexico with tensions mounting given Mexico's tenuous control over the region, and the settlers' belief in "manifest destiny" or their god given right to expand American society from east to west or from "sea to shining sea," as we would later learn to sing. Settlers strongly resented the idea of being governed by people they considered racially inferior, as well as policies such as Mexico's anti-slavery law that many settlers violated. Major international conflict soon ensued when settlers declared Texas an independent republic in 1936, resulting in battles with the Mexican army charged with putting down the insurrection of American settlers stealing Mexican land.

Remembering the Alamo(s)

Americans generally imagine the Texas revolt as portrayed in the movie *The Alamo* in which American heroes such as Davy Crockett and Jim Bowie, along with nearly 200 other settlers, occupied the old Spanish mission of the same name and fought valiantly to their deaths in the effort to free Texas from an oppressive Mexican government. It is this Hollywood myth of the Texas revolt that continues to overshadow what many historians consider a calculated effort on the part of American settlers and the U.S. government to take Mexican land by force. Indeed, Mexicans and Americans "Remember the Alamo" quite differently (see Sidebars 1.1 and 1.2).

Sidebar 1.1. The Alamo (1960)

The battle of the Alamo was forever mythologized in 1960 in the nearly 3-hour long, epic-sized production, directed and produced by John Wayne who also played the lead role of Davy Crockett, the legendary coonskin hat wearing frontiersman from Tennessee who was also a savvy congressman. The movie opens to gorgeous oil paintings of the Alamo mission beneath big Texas skies, and the reverent choral sounds of the battle hymn "The Siege of Alamo" (13 days of glory). The stage is quickly set by a pair of written narratives, the first of which tells us that in 1836, Texas was composed of settlers from throughout the United States who had become citizens of Mexico. The next narrative informs us that General Santa Anna "was sweeping north across Mexico toward them, crushing all who opposed his tyrannical rule. They now face the decision that all men in all times must face . . . the eternal choice of men to endure oppression or resist." Much of the film develops the characters of Crockett and Jim Bowie as hard drinking and fighting, yet brave and loyal freedom fighters, and of the equally brave Colonel Travis, a hopelessly rigid and formal military man. While Mexicans in the film are reduced to one-dimensional human props, there is sparse intermittent dialogue about their dignity and bravery and even more dialogue about beautiful Mexican women who are seen dancing flamenco. Even Bowie admits to marrying a Mexican woman, while Crockett defends the honor of a pretty Mexican villager being harassed by the movie's one bad, pro-Santa Anna, Anglo-American. Before the Alamo Mission is eventually overrun by a heavily armed and beautifully uniformed Mexican army of 2,000 men, we are privy to clever night raids led by Crockett and Bowie in which Mexican cannons are destroyed, and soldiers are dispensed with over humorous dialogue. In one amazing scene, several hundred longhorns are stolen out from under the noses of

Mexican soldiers and then run back right through the front door of the Alamo! When it is eventually learned that military back-up will not be coming, and that the battle of the Alamo is a suicide mission, all decide to fight alongside Colonel Travis to their death, despite the Mexican army granting them the option of surrender and allowing women and children to vacate the Alamo.

Sidebar 1.2. The Alamo (2004)

In the 2004 version of the Alamo, little has changed with Hollywood style myth-making. This time two written narratives inform us that: (1) Established in 1718, the mission become a makeshift fort against ma-rauding Indians, rebels, and a succession of conquering armies; and (2) location, proximity to settlements, and perhaps even fate made the Alamo a crossroads for siege and battle. Straight-arrow Colonel Travis claims that "As goes the Alamo, so goes Texas," and is seen defiantly firing a cannon at the massive surrounding Mexican army as they grant the option to sur-render. Slight improvements include Mexican mariachi music instead of Spanish flamenco, and a muttered comment by a Mexican bystander that "Santa Anna may want to rule Mexico, but these wretched creatures want to rule the world!" This time a more understated Davy Crockett, played by Billy Bob Thornton, is seen being executed at the battle's end—unlike John Wayne (in Alamo 1960), who literally goes out with a bang, taking a band of would-be captors with him as he ignites a barrel of gunpowder. In the newer Alamo, Crockett is confronted just before his execution by General Santa Anna himself, and to whom Crockett wisecracks, "I thought you'd be taller!" and "If you surrender, I'll try and protect you." General Santa Anna is portrayed as the consummate egomaniac that he was, but he did have more lines than in Alamo I. For example, in justifying his take no prisoners position, he exclaims that it must stop here, or our grandchildren will be begging the Americans for crumbs. Toward the movie's end, we learn that nine years following the battle of the Alamo, Texas becomes the 28th state, as if preordained.

According to noted Chicano historian, Rodolfo Acuña (2019), Mexican General Antonio Lopez de Santa Anna put down revolts at both the Alamo and the nearby town of Goliad and resumed control of the San Antonio area. The U.S. government responded by sending massive aid into Texas in the form of volunteers, arms, and money, and on April 22, 1836, General Sam Houston coordinated a surprise attack on Santa Anna's resting army resulting in the slaughter of 630 of the 1,000 plus Mexican soldiers. Santa Anna was captured with little choice but to sign away the Texas territory.

From 1836 to 1846, Texas survived as an independent republic, under the Lone Star flag, but in constant conflict with a resentful Mexico over the highly contested border between nations. While Texans regarded the Rio Grande River as the boundary, Mexicans regarded the Nueces River as the proper boundary. As a result, the large tract of land between rivers became a bitter battleground and metaphor for the protracted conflict and resentment that has characterized NLW and Mexican race relations. Authoritative historian Carry McWilliams (1968) notes that "In the bloody zone between the two rivers an uninterrupted guerrilla warfare continued throughout the life of the Texas Republic," and that "Murder was matched by murder; raids by Texans were countered by raids from Mexico. Because a peace treaty was never negotiated, no boundaries could be fixed" (p. 101).

The U.S.–Mexico War

As the Texas Republic prepared to join the Union, the president of Mexico declared that the annexation of Texas would be considered a declaration of war (Healey et al., 2019b). After annexation in 1846, President Polk ordered General Taylor into the disputed land between the Rio Grande and Nueces rivers, provoking Mexico to battle over what it declared an invasion by the United States. Next, President Polk petitioned Congress to declare war claiming that Mexico had invaded the United States. While Abraham Lincoln condemned Polk's petition of war as unconstitutional, international war ensued with far more at stake than the strip of land dividing Mexico and Texas.

By 1848, Mexico surrendered under the terms of the Treaty of Guadalupe-Hidalgo in which approximately half of Mexico (current day Southwest) was ceded to the United States. Mexicans that remained in this region became American citizens by default, constituting the new Mexican American minority group. It is important to note here that like a defeated neighbor,

Mexico has never recognized the moral right of the United States to Mexican land. For example, as late as 1943, maps used in Mexican schools referred to Northern Mexico as "territory temporarily in the hands of the United States" (McWilliams, 1968, p.103).

While the Treaty of Guadalupe-Hidalgo technically granted Mexican Americans full rights of citizenship, white settlers generally considered them a conquered race of inferior people whose rights were to be ignored. In fact, protection of property, under Article X of the treaty, was omitted during its ratification by the U.S. Senate. As a result, Mexicans were rapidly dispossessed of major land holdings through a variety of devious means (del Castillo, 1990).

Seizing Mexican Land

Acuña (2019) describes the "land grab" in New Mexico as a well-organized seizure consisting of the following devious methods: (1) Mexicans were required to register their land, often by inadequately posted announcements in English, and their land was seized when they failed to do so; (2) Mexican lands were heavily taxed and seized when taxes could not be paid (taxes were then lowered after land was acquired by NLWs); and (3) land was seized when Mexicans could not pay for so-called agricultural land "improvements" provided by the government. An estimated two million acres of private land and 1.7 million acres of communal land were lost between 1854 and 1930 in New Mexico alone, in a pattern that repeated itself throughout Texas, California, and the rest of the Southwest (Feagin & Booher Feagin, 1999a). Elite and peasant Mexicans alike quickly found themselves landless laborers subjugated to the bottom of the new American stratification system.

During the 1960s, Chicano activist and Pentecostalist minister Reies Lopez Tijerina formed the *Alianza Federal de Mercedes* [Mercedes Federal Alliance of Land Grants] in New Mexico that sought to recover stolen Mexican land (Feagin & Booher Feagin, 1999a). In addition to marching and presenting grievances to Santa Fe officials, the Alianza boldly occupied Kit Carson National Forest, once part of a Mexican communal land grant. When forest rangers tried to remove the protesters, they were seized and "tried" for violating old land-grant boundaries researched by protesters. Tijerina and other members of the Alianza were eventually arrested following a shoot-out with police. Tijerina served a year in prison in 1970, and later moved to Mexico and eventually to his home state of Texas, passing away in El Paso in 2015.

Bandidos or Folk Heroes?

Like Tijerina, Mexican people in the new frontier resisted and protested their outrage through a variety of methods ranging from strikes and court battles to outright raids on white settlers, who retaliated in return. For example, in the decades between 1850 and 1930, the number of Mexican Americans killed in the Southwest may have rivaled the number of African Americans lynched during this same period (Moquin & Van Doren, 1971). The enduring stereotypic image of Mexicans as *bandidos* [bandits] has an interesting basis in anti-white outlaw activity on the part of Mexicans. While Americans have attempted to create images of these early militants as simply outlaws and as criminals, Mexicans and studied Chicanos see many as folk heroes who revolted against white imperialism, racism, and discrimination. For example, in 1859, Mexico-born Texas rancher Juan Cortina organized a band of outlaws and invaded Brownsville, Texas, to protest violations of the Treaty of Guadalupe-Hidalgo. Known as the Robin Hood of the Rio Grande, Cortina and 1,200 men fought and defeated local Brownsville militia in 1860, set free falsely imprisoned Mexicans, and killed four white settlers who had gone unpunished for killing Mexicans. He also defeated the notorious Texas Rangers, well known for their blatant abuse and killings of Mexicans, who pursued Cortina after the Brownsville battle. As a result, General Robert E. Lee, veteran of the war with Mexico and later leader of the Confederacy during the Civil War, was deployed to Texas to put down Cortina. However, even with the cooperation of the Mexican army, fearing another war with the United States, Cortina evaded Lee's pursuit. When the U.S. army began to get the best of Cortina, he relocated to Mexico to fight alongside Benito Juarez against the short-lived French invasion of Mexico (PBS, 2020).

In New Mexico, the famous Mexican revolutionary Francisco "Pancho" Villa raided the city of Columbus, killing a few NLWs as a protest to the U.S. recognition of the New Mexico state government (McLemore, Romo, & Gonzalez Baker, 2001). General John J. Pershing spent nine long and unsuccessful months perusing Villa in Mexico as Pershing's men sang, "It's a long way to capture Villa/It's a long way to go/It's a long way across the border/Where the dirty greasers grow" (Jacobs, Landau, & Pell, 1971, p. 242). In California, folk heroes Joaquin Murrieta and Tiburcio Vasquez avenged NLW wrongs perpetrated against Mexicans by terrorizing white settlers and robbing white establishments, vigilante style. Outside of *Murrieta's Well*, a winery in Livermore, California, a historical plaque marks the well where Murrieta watered his horses between confrontations with white settlers.

Exploitation of Mexican Labor

Despite the legacy of conflict between Mexicans and NLWs in the United States, significant Mexican immigration to the United States continues to the present day. In the decades following the war with Mexico, hundreds of thousands of Mexicans, "pushed" by the political upheaval and lack of work in Mexico, were "pulled" by the tremendous need for labor in the Southwest that continues throughout the United States today. In the early economic growth and development of the southwestern United States, Mexican labor was *essential* to such major industries as agriculture, canning, mining, and railroads. While less than 30,000 Mexicans "immigrated" between 1820 and 1900, nearly three-quarters of a million immigrated between 1900 and 1930, pushed by the Mexican revolution (1910–1920) and pulled by the rapidly accelerating American industrial revolution and its expanding need for labor (McLemore, Romo, & Gonzalez Baker, 2001).

Most Americans today have little understanding of how *essential* Mexican labor has been and continues to be to American industries, corporations, and vast service sector. Most Americans are also unaware of the historical patterns of exploitation of Mexican labor that continue to fan the flames of intergroup tension and conflict. A decade-by-decade analysis of Mexican labor in the 20th century reveals a distinct cyclical and cynical pattern of exploiting Mexican labor during labor shortages, and then abusing Mexican civil rights during periods of diminished labor need and economic recession.

During the 1910s, federal authorities waived immigration restrictions due to a World War I labor shortage in agriculture, allowing some 70,000 thousand Mexicans to enter the United States. Improved canning and shipping technologies opened new markets during the 1920s, and around 500,000 Mexicans came to supply needed labor. While the federal Immigration Act of 1924 barred most southern and eastern Europeans, in an effort to preserve the WASP core of America, Mexicans were exempt because they comprised the main source of cheap labor for the rapidly expanding southwestern and midwestern United States (Feagin & Booher Feagin, 1999a).

However, when the Great Depression struck in 1929, illegal entry to the United States was suddenly elevated to a felony, and deportation campaigns were initiated against Mexicans who were scapegoated for the country's economic problems. About a half million or 40% of the Mexican American population, both documented and undocumented, was deported or coerced to leave by U. S. authorities in a program called Repatriation (Acuña, 2019). Yet as soon as the World War II labor shortage struck in 1942, the United States initiated a binational agreement with Mexico to import desperately needed agricultural labor.

The Bracero Program

From 1942 to 1964, The *Bracero* [arms] Program, as it was called, brought in approximately five million *braceros* (Healey et al., 2019b) to fill major U.S. labor shortages. The Bracero Program also stimulated a parallel stream of undocumented workers who were extremely desirable to employers who wished to avoid the Bracero Program's bureaucratic red tape, including stipulations of fair pay and treatment of Braceros. It is estimated that since 1920, between six and nine million undocumented Mexicans have entered the United States, many of whom returned to Mexico. Undocumented workers are essential to agriculture, manufacturing, and tourism in Southern California and elsewhere in the United States (Chavez, 1992). Mexican workers and U.S. employees are linked together in one major international labor market. For example, Mexican migrants still comprise more than two-thirds of the nation's migrant farmworkers, estimated by the U.S. Department of Labor (1992) to be between 2.7 and four million people, over half of whom are undocumented. As such, sensible regulation of Mexican labor, benefiting both workers and the U.S. economy, is long overdue and reflects a major strand of ongoing tension between Mexicans and mainstream society.

Zoot Suit Riots

Another historical flashpoint of conflict between NLWs and Chicanos occurred during the so-called Zoot Suit riots in 1943, during which sailors, off-duty police, and other servicemen staged mob style attacks on Chicano street gang members in the barrios of Los Angeles. Gang-affiliated youth wore flashy Zoot Suits consisting of chest-high baggy pants, fingertip length broad shoulder jackets, fedora hats, and pointed dress shoes. In one highly publicized incident, 200 sailors in 20 taxicabs invaded the East Los Angeles barrio, beating and stripping Zoot Suiters. These "riots" made headline news across the country during an all-time high in WWII-fueled patriotism that condemned most things foreign (Mazon, 1984). While primarily second-generation, U.S. born Chicanos, they expressed their marginality and alienation in provocative dress and delinquent activities. These were socioculturally displaced youth looking for a sense of belonging, identity, and power, that made easy targets of what Mazon (1984) called "symbolic annihilation" on the part of American military, local law enforcement, and the press.

Yet, in spite of national anti-Mexican propaganda, disproportionately high numbers of young Chicanos joined the war effort, resulting in disproportionately high deaths, injuries, and medals of valor. In fact, Chicanos were the most decorated ethnic group in WWII, with 39 Congressional Medals of Honor. Sadly, some of these war heroes could not even be served a cup of coffee upon returning to their segregated barrios throughout the Southwest.

Operation Wetback

Partly as a result of the growing number of undocumented braceros during the mid-1950s, President Eisenhower approved of a military style immigration control campaign, known disparagingly as "Operation Wetback," which resulted in the mass deportation of Mexicans with estimates ranging from 300,000 to over a million (Encyclopedia Britannica, 2019). A popular derogatory term, *wetback* refers to Mexicans that cross the border without documentation by wading across the Rio Grande River. As in the 1930s, the civil rights of Mexican Americans were commonly violated as homes and workplaces were raided by police and military for suspected "illegal aliens," much to the chagrin of employers and businesses dependent upon Mexican labor.

The Bracero Program was eventually terminated in 1964 due to glaring gaps between what the program promised to formal program participants, or Braceros, and the exploitation of undocumented workers. In addition to the U.S. Congress and Mexico, Chicano farmworker activist Cesar Chavez also advocated ending the Bracero program because it was antithetical to his efforts to unionize farmworkers in order to gain the bargaining power needed to negotiate fair wages and benefits, with opposed agricultural growers reaping the benefits of decades of labor exploitation. In 1962, Cesar Chavez and Dolores Huerta organized the United Farm Workers Union (UFW) in California. Unlike other Chicano social justice protests, the UFW movement elevated the plight of Mexican and other farmworkers to national and even international attention, partly because of its nonviolent philosophy modeled on the works of Gandhi and Martin Luther King Jr. The UFW was foundational to the Chicano movement of the 1960s and 1970s.

The Chicano Movement

Between WWII and the 1960s, Chicano determination to fight racism and discrimination grew into the climax of the Chicano civil rights movement roughly between the mid-1960s and mid-1970s. Court and street battles pushed this movement forward, culminating in the National Chicano Moratorium of 1970 in which over 20,000 Chicanos from across the country marched on East Los Angeles to protest the war in Vietnam and its disproportionately high death toll of Chicano soldiers. The rally turned violent when busloads of sheriffs in full riot gear attacked the crowd with tear gas and batons, declaring it an unlawful assembly at Laguna Park. A major riot ensued, with millions of dollars in damage to local merchants on Whittier Boulevard, thousands of injuries and arrests, and even a few deaths.

The most high-profile killing was that of Ruben Salazar, *Los Angeles. Times* columnist and director the city's Spanish language television station, KMEX. Salazar had been covering the moratorium when he was killed by an L.A. County Sheriff who negligently fired a 10-inch teargas missile into the Silver Dollar bar on Whittier Boulevard, fatally striking Salazar in the temple. While four of the seven-member judicial inquest recommended pursuing a criminal case, District Attorney Evelle Younger dismissed the case and refused requests from the Latino community and 22 California state legislators for further investigation (Garcia, 1995).

Viewed by many as premeditated, especially in view of Salazar's ongoing investigations of misconduct by the Los Angeles Police Department and L.A. County Sheriffs, at the very least this preventable killing conveys the disregard for Chicano life on the part of local law enforcement too often experienced by community members. It was a harsh blow to the Chicano community to lose its highest ranking Chicano journalist championing *La Causa*

[The Cause, referring to Chicano civil rights] with his superb and persistent investigative reporting. How Chicanos have adapted to life in America, amid such salient examples of ongoing conflict with mainstream society, is addressed below.

Adaptation

The predominant form of adaptation for Mexican Americans, still considerably in evidence today, has been *segregation*. Segregation in residence, work, school, and recreation has historically been the rule for Chicanos, resulting in painstakingly slow yet steady progress toward integration and moderate levels of SES achievement as compared to European immigrants. Segregation continues to be a living legacy of racism and discrimination that compromises the general welfare of most Latinos and other people of color in America. For roughly 75 years after the end of the war between Mexico and the United States, Chicanos faced forced segregation in most public facilities including schools, restaurants, movie theaters, swimming pools, barbershops, primary election procedures, and housing (McLemore, Romo, & Gonzalez Baker, 2001). "Mexican schools" were instituted in Texas in 1902, and by 1940 separate schools for Mexicans existed throughout the state (Montejano, 1987), as well as in California. Insulting signs such as "Mexicans not allowed" were not uncommon in service sector businesses throughout the Southwest (see Figure 1.2).

Figure 1.2. Frequent signage in the South and Southwest during first half of the 20th century.

From Wikimedia Commons (Adam Jones, PhD).

Segregation Index

Based on analyses of U.S. Census data from 1990 to 2010, Frey (2011) reveals entrenched Latino segregation by reporting on the top 10 most segregated metropolitan areas where Latinos are most numerous (i.e., at least half a million in population size). Such segregation levels are based on the Index of Dissimilarity (ID) that measures the degree to which a minority group is distributed differently than NLWs across census tracts. IDs range from 0 (completely integrated) to 100 (completely segregated) where the value indicates the percentage of the minority group that would need to move to be distributed exactly like NLWs. As can be seen in Table 1.4, IDs for Latinos range from the high 50s to mid-60s for the top 10 most segregated cities, with little change across the two decades examined.

More specifically, the ID for Latinos in Los Angeles was 60.3 in 1990 and 62.5 in both 2000 and 2010, indicating that over 60% of predominately Mexican Latinos would need to move out of their residential tracts to produce an even residential distribution of Latinos and whites in Los Angeles.

Table 1.4. Index of Dissimilarity (ID) for the Top 10 Most Hispanic *vis a vis* White Segregated Metropolitan Statistical Areas (MSAs) with Latino Populations Greater than 500,000, 1990–2010

Rank (2010)	Name	1990	2000	2010
1	Springfield, MA	64.3	64.1	63.4
2	Los Angeles-Long Beach-Santa Ana, CA	60.3	62.5	62.2
3	New York-Northern New Jersey-Long Island, NY-NJ-PA	66.2	65.6	62.0
4	Providence-New Bedford-Fall River, RI-MA	57.9	64.5	60.1
5	Boston-Cambridge-Quincy, MA-NH	59.3	62.5	59.6
6	Bridgeport-Stamford-Norwalk, CT	60.3	61.5	59.2
7	Hartford-West Hartford-East Hartford, CT	66.3	63.4	58.4
8	Miami-Fort Lauderdale-Pompano Beach, FL	32.5	59.0	57.4
9	Milwaukee-Waukesha-West Allis, WI	56.4	59.5	57.0
10	Chicago-Naperville-Joliet, IL-IN-WI	61.4	60.7	56.3

Adapted with permission from Frey, W. H. (2011). The new metro minority map: Regional shifts in Hispanics, Asians, and Blacks from Census 2010. 1–18 (August).racial segregation measures for large metropolitan areas: Analysis of the 1990–2010 decennial censuses. Report., University of Michigan Population Studies Center. Washington DC: Metropolitan Policy Program at Brookings chrome-extension://efaidnbmnnnibpcajpcglclefindmkaj/https://www.brookings.edu/wp-content/uploads/2016/06/0831_census_race_frey.pdf

Thus, these IDs indicate moderately high and persistent segregation with the same pattern in other Latino-heavy cities such as New York (62), Boston (59.6), Miami (57.4), and Chicago (56.3).

A more recent analysis of census data between 1990 & 2020 reveals that while racial residential segregation declined an impressive 37% for the major racial/ethnic groups combined (i.e., Latinos, African and Asian Americans) in metropolitan areas, Latino segregation from NLW Americans actually increased 8% (Elbers, 2021). In contrast, Latino segregation from African Americans decreased 36% between 1990 & 2020 indicating that while segregation continues to decline considerably for people of color, it is decreasing more slowly for Latinos in relations to NLWs, while increasing considerably in relation to African Americans.

School Resegregation?

Over two decades ago, Gary Orfield and associates (e.g., Orfield & Yun, 1999) at the Civil Rights Project at Harvard University documented what they call the *resegregation* of American schools, especially in poor Black and Latino communities. They reported that while most NLWs polled believe that equal educational opportunity exists, school data show that the American South is resegregating after nearly three decades of civil rights laws that resulted in some of the highest integration rates in the nation. Further, the data show steadily increasing segregation for Latinos, now even more segregated than African Americans. Finally, the majority of resegregated Black and Latino students are concentrated in poor schools, while the majority of white students are in schools composed of mostly middle class peers. For example, the percent of Latino students in high-poverty schools has increased from 35% in 2000 to 48% in 2004. In contrast, the figures for white students during this same period went from 3% to 8% (Healey et al., 2019b). Residential and scholastic segregation for Mexican Americans, in low-resource communities and schools, signals acculturation stress characterized by the trappings of poverty linked to ethnic minority status, historically through today, and is also in evidence for Puerto Ricans in the United States.

Puerto Ricans

To understand the pride and predicament of Puerto Ricans is to understand the impact of a double legacy of conquest and colonization, the triple blending of races that compose this unique Latino population, and the rather unfortunate timing of Puerto Rican migration patterns to the U.S. mainland over the past century, all of which have contributed to one of the most stressful acculturation scenarios for a U.S. Latino population as described in this section.

Contact

Back in 1493, Spanish conquistadors landed on the Caribbean island of *Borinquen* where they encountered and conquered an estimated 50,000 indigenous Taino people. The name of the island was abruptly changed to Puerto Rico and the native Taino people were soon decimated through a combination of forced labor, disease, and violent suppression of rebellion (Feagin & Booher Feagin, 1999b). African slaves were soon imported to compensate for the diminishing Taino population, and the intermixing of Spaniards, Africans, and remaining Taino created the rich racial and cultural blend of the colorful Puerto Rican people.

After four centuries of Spanish colonization, the new and growing Puerto Rican population pressured Spain for autonomy, eventually granted in 1897. Celebrant Puerto Ricans appointed their own governor, established a house of representatives, and enacted democratic laws. However, this fresh taste of freedom was cut short when Puerto Rico was ceded to the United States in 1898 following the brief war between the Spain and the United States for control of the Caribbean and other Spanish holdings, including the Philippines.

The American warship, the *Maine*, had been stationed in the turbulent waters of Havana's harbor where Cuban revolutionaries had been waging a 30-year fight for their own independence from Spain, much like their neighboring Puerto Ricans. However, when the Maine mysteriously exploded, tragically killing 258 American sailors, the United States quickly blamed and declared war on Spain. Then assistant secretary of the navy, Theodore Roosevelt, quickly assembled his famous "Rough Riders," and with patriotic cries of "Remember the Maine!" drove the Spanish out of Cuba. Within a quick four months, Spain ceded Puerto Rico, as well the Philippines, to the United States, while Cuba won a pseudo independence.

The United States had long coveted the Caribbean islands, and the Philippines in the South Pacific, primarily for their geographically strategic military locations and secondarily for developing agricultural business enterprises. For example, during the 20th century, the United States had as many as 25 military installations, both large and small, much resented by the Puerto Rican people. The small Puerto Rican island of Vieques contained two U.S. military bases that for decades elicited protests by natives who claimed that bombing raids and military maneuvers destroyed their beaches, fishing, and coral industries. During World War II, an estimated 15,000 American troops used Vieques as a military training site. The U.S. Navy finally departed Vieques for good in 2003 after over 60 years of military installations, training, and Puerto Rican resentment.

With such primary military and industrial goals, the United States had little intention of fostering autonomy in Puerto Rico or Cuba, and to date, Puerto Rico remains a controversial U.S. "commonwealth" (a polite term for colony), with the long-term conflict that accompanies such dominant–subordinate relations as reviewed next.

Conflict

Puerto Rico came under U.S. control with no input from autonomy-starved Puerto Ricans. In 1898, U.S. General Nelson Miles invaded independent Puerto Rico while claiming to liberate it from Spanish oppression. General Miles was selected based on his military record that included arresting Indian Chief Geronimo and driving the Nez Perce Indian tribe out of Montana and into Canada. Next, the United States installed an American governor, made English the official language, and reserved the right to veto any locally elected legislature (Feagin & Booher Feagin, 1999b).

Seizing Puerto Rican Land

Puerto Ricans, who were largely subsistence farmers, went from owning virtually all of the island's lush farmlands to less than a third within 30 years (Feagin & Booher Feagin, 1996b). By 1930, absentee-owned U.S. companies controlled almost two-thirds of Puerto Rican sugar and tobacco production, as well as shipping lines. Massive land loss resulted from heavy taxation and credit restrictions imposed by the United States on Puerto Rican farmers, as well as forced devaluations of the Puerto Rican *peso*, compelled small Puerto

Rican farmers to sell off their land. The United States also expelled European competitors in order to monopolize island industries and to relegate Puerto Ricans to low-wage farm laborers on their previously owned lands. Puerto Ricans were segregated from Americans in both private and public spaces on their own island. While most Puerto Ricans favored autonomy during the first half of the 20th century, Puerto Ricans were strategically declared U.S. citizens in 1917 in order to draft men into WWI.

During the 1930s, Puerto Ricans resisted colonization and exploitation by forming unions, staging strikes in the sugar cane fields, and even periodically attacking U.S. colonial government buildings on the island (Feagin & Booher Feagin, 1999b). This decade also saw the rise of the pro-independence nationalist movement. In 1930, Harvard educated Pedro Albizu Campos was elected president of the Nationalist Party. Albizu's passionate and unrelenting anti-U.S. platform was perceived as a threat, and president Franklin Delano Roosevelt appointed Georgia southerner Blanton Winship governor of Puerto Rico with the charge of crushing Puerto Rican nationalism.

Social Control of Island Nationalism

Governor Winship wasted no time militarizing the police force, intimidating and arresting Nationalist Party members. In 1936, four party members and a bystander were murdered by the police at the University of Puerto Rico in Rio Piedras in what became known as the *Rio Piedras Massacre*. In retaliation, two Nationalist Party members killed Winthrop's right-hand man, Colonel Riggs. Rigg's killers were rounded up by the police and executed without a trial. Winthrop had Albizu tried and jailed for 10 years for insurrection and while incarcerated, Albizu was subject to torture by the military that is believed to have used him for radiation experiments.

Conflict also came to a head in 1937 when unarmed Nationalist Party members organized a peaceful march in the capital city of Ponce to celebrate the island's early abolition of slavery. However, on Governor Winship's orders, heavily armed police shot and teargassed marchers, killing 20 and wounding 150. The Ponce Massacre, as it came to be known, marked a turning point for nationalists who would now more broadly incorporate militancy and violence in their anticolonial cause.

Like Albizu, Luis Muñoz Marin also favored independence but pursued his politics by forming the Popular Democratic Party (PDP) and seeking a seat in the U.S. Senate. The United States pressured Muñoz Marin and the PDP to oppose nationalism in exchange for supporting his bid for the senate, which he won in 1938. Muñoz Marin quickly enacted pro-peasant land reform in the late 1930s and early 1940s, promoted voter registration, and earnestly combated island poverty.

In 1948, Puerto Ricans were finally permitted to elect their own governor, and Luis Muñoz Marin was their unanimous choice. Puerto Ricans were also permitted by the United States to draft their own constitution, raise their own flag, and reinstate Spanish as the official language. To this date, island Puerto Ricans have no vote in national U.S. elections, cannot be elected to the U.S. House and Senate, and their sole U.S. Congress representative has only observer status with no vote.

Exploitation of Puerto Rican Labor

The pressure to continue repressing nationalism was highly evident in the controversial "muzzle law" of 1948 that forbade nationalism but which caused anticolonial resentment to smolder. Also, in 1948, Muñoz Marin assisted the United States in enacting a program called Operation Bootstrap, ostensibly to stimulate economic development on the island by attracting more U.S. corporations. Unfortunately, incentives for U.S. corporations included a 10-year local tax exemption and the freedom to pay wages lower than those on the mainland. As such, Puerto Rico's poverty and exploitation wages were the program's primary selling points to U.S. multinational corporations that took full advantage.

According to Feagin and Booher Feagin (1999b), around 1,700 factories came to the island between the late 1940s and the mid-1970s creating over 140,000 new manufacturing jobs in the process. Capital investments grew from $1.4 billion in 1960 to $24 billion in 1970. However, despite these impressive figures, the new manufacturing jobs could never offset the island's loss of agricultural jobs. In addition, the tax exemptions granted to corporations resulted in high personal income taxes for Puerto Ricans in order to pay for basic island infrastructure such as water and electricity, sewer systems, and the like.

Many corporations relocated to the mainland after their 10-year tax-free status expired rather than remain and pay Puerto Ricans a fair wage and contribute to the island's treasury. Thus, this program of exploitation served to consolidate island poverty in the guise of an opportunity for Puerto Ricans to "pull themselves up by their own bootstraps." As such, Operation Bootstrap represents one of the many missed opportunities to earnestly invest in Puerto Ricans for the mutual benefit of both the United States and Puerto Rico.

Militancy and Violence

In 1950, armed revolts broke out in five island cities in which hundreds were killed and thousands wounded and arrested. In 1952, Governor Marin Muñoz urged the Puerto Rican people to vote for commonwealth status, claiming that the island would become an *Area Libre Asociado* [liberated associated area], or one step closer to independence. Despite opposition from nationalists desiring independence, the vote passed.

However, commonwealth status and the repression of pro-independence politics proved to be explosive. In 1954, four armed radical nationalists, led by Lolita Lebron, broke into a meeting of the U.S. House of Representatives in Washington D.C. and open fire, striking five senators in a volley of bullets before being subdued. A year later, pro-independence radicals attempted to assassinate President Truman by shooting up Blair House, his temporary residence across from the White House. These are dramatic and desperate acts of political violence about which most Americans, including most Latinos, have little knowledge.

During the 1960s, Governor Marin Muñoz retired, and the conservative pro-statehood party gained prominence and elected party member Luis Ferrer as governor in 1968, much to the chagrin of pro-independence forces. During the 1970s, divisive pro- and anti-statehood politics resulted in Puerto Rico's bloodiest decade. For example, U.S. military aircraft were bombed in San Juan, and a bus of navy personnel was machine-gunned, killing two and wounding 10. Puerto Rican police retaliated by killing two *Independistas* but were brought to trial and found guilty. To worsen matters, massive unemployment on the island resulted in nearly a third of the population relocating to the U.S. mainland during the 1970s. During this same decade, hundreds of thousands of Puerto Ricans attempted to manage their poverty by traveling back and forth between the United States and Puerto Rico in what has been called "revolving door" migration.

Meanwhile on the U.S. mainland, pro-independence Puerto Rican groups bombed a café in lower Manhattan, killing five and wounding many, and robbed a Wells Fargo armored truck in Hartford, Connecticut. In less violent protests, mainland Puerto Ricans organized dozens of civil rights oriented groups addressing injustice in schools, courts, and communities. In East Harlem, Puerto Rican radicals established the Young Lords Party, a Black Panther styled organization advocating democratic-socialist reform and greater control of Puerto Rican communities.

The Young Lords occupied the admissions building of the McCormick Theological Seminary in Chicago, as well as the First Spanish Methodist Church in New York City. They also organized a march to the United Nations building that was 20,000 people strong. The Young Lords also set up free lunch programs for children and tuberculosis testing clinics for adults in Puerto Rican communities, and a young and then unknown Geraldo Rivera served as the party's lawyer.

In 1980, former Puerto Rican governor Muñoz Marin died, uniting Puerto Ricans in mourning despite the political divisions that colonialism engenders. Poverty reached new heights on the island with as many as 50% needing government assistance in the form of food stamps and health care. Unemployment peaked at 23% in 1983 and leveled off to 17% in the early 1990s (Feagin & Booher Feagin, 1999b). Today, manufacturing wages on the island are about half of those on the mainland, and Puerto Rico's per capita income is less than the poorest state in the United States. In 1993, 37% of Puerto Ricans fell below the poverty line as compared to 10% for white Americans. Thus, the perennial push to the mainland is understandable, but what Puerto Ricans have historically encountered has been traumatic in terms of general adaptation. Puerto Rico remains an impoverished pseudo-colony vulnerable to disasters such as Hurricane Maria in 2017 and an inadequate and even contentious response by former president Trump. While Puerto Ricans remain a people culturally united in their assertion of a unique Latino identity and need for greater control over their fate, they also remain politically divided regarding how to achieve such autonomy: statehood, independence, or status quo commonwealth status?

In 2012, over 60% of Puerto Ricans voted for statehood over commonwealth status. However, the U.S. Congress ignored the vote because over half a million blank ballots were cast, causing confusion about the island's preference. In 2017, a vote for the "Immediate Decolonization of Puerto Rico" resulted in a boycott by all major anti-statehood parties (e.g., Popular Democratic Party). The result was a historic low voter turnout of only 23%, almost all of whom voted for statehood (Wikipedia, 2020)). Hence, while Puerto Rico remains in political gridlock, it also remains vulnerable to the trappings of high poverty and vulnerable infrastructure, as tragically witnessed during Hurricane Maria.

Hurricane Maria

Regarded as Puerto Rico's worst natural disaster, Category 5 Hurricane Maria devastated the island in September 2017, as well as the Virgin Islands and the island of Dominica. A destroyed electric power grid left the island's population of over three million residents without electricity for months, with consequent suffering and deaths compounded by slow relief from the United States. Flooding and lack of emergency resources, most of which were depleted from coping with Hurricane Irma just two weeks prior, also left Puerto Rico especially vulnerable.

In August 2018 (almost a year after the hurricane), Puerto Rico revised its official death toll from Maria from the initially low estimate of 64 to a total of 3,059. The official estimate is based on rigorous analysis by researchers at George Washington University, commissioned by the governor of Puerto Rico, who developed statistical models of *excess mortality* attributable to Maria including both direct and indirect fatalities (Project Report, 2018). Such data regarding the human cost of natural disasters are imperative for adequate emergency and disaster relief planning. However, in September 2018, former president Trump disputed the revised death toll, insisting on Twitter that, "3,000 people did not die in the two hurricanes that hit Puerto Rico" and claiming that the Democrats had inflated the official death toll to "make me look as bad as possible." He added more insult to injury by complaining about the expense of emergency assistance to Puerto Rico and stating that Hurricane Maria did not compare to a "real disaster" like Hurricane Katrina that devastated New Orleans in 2005, killing 1,833 mostly poor and African American people.

Lacking empathy and evidence to support his claim, Trump's cruel denial was immediately denounced by the Mayor of San Juan, Carmen Yulín Cruz, and Florida Congresswoman Ileana Ros-Lehtinen. U.S. relief efforts were also criticized by the international charitable organization Oxfam, which stepped in to compensate by providing relief to Puerto Rico. Hurricane Maria exemplifies one of the most recent and significant instances of continued conflict between Puerto Rico and the United States, and the continued acculturation stress and vulnerability of island Puerto Ricans.

Adaptation

The push of island poverty resulted in the first wave of Puerto Rican migration to the United States during the 1920s, shortly after Puerto Ricans were declared U.S. citizens (Feagin & Booher Feagin, 1999b). By 1940, there were approximately 70,000 Puerto Ricans on the mainland, almost exclusively in New York. However, their "great migration" occurred between 1940 and 1970, resulting in a ten-fold increase in Puerto Ricans to approximately 887,000, concentrated mostly in New York, but with communities also in New Jersey, Connecticut, and Chicago. To understand the creation of today's Puerto Rican underclass is to understand not just colonization but the racialization of Puerto Ricans on the U.S. mainland, and the bad timing of Puerto Rican migration as a result of mid-20th century labor market shifts and restructuring.

Like Mexicans, thousands of poor Puerto Rican migrants came to the United States as contract farmworkers at the bottom of the economic ladder. During the 1950s about 40,000 Puerto Ricans migrated to the mainland annually, often lured by U.S. Department of Labor propaganda films like *Trabajo Para Usted!* [Work for you!] that depicted happy Puerto Ricans, picking crops by day and dancing the Rumba by night while making money in the United States.

The Racialization of Puerto Ricans

Most Puerto Ricans however, poured into labor-intensive, urban-based manufacturing industries such as the textile and garment industry sweatshops of New York. Like European immigrants before them, this new group of working class Latinos hoped to succeed in America through living wage industrial labor jobs. Unfortunately, Puerto Rican migrants soon learned the bitter lesson of racism in America, where they were perceived and treated as African Americans. While the color gradient on the island of Puerto Rico had less implication for marriage and social mobility, Puerto Ricans on the mainland often faced intense anti-Black and anti-Latino discrimination.

Like African Americans, discrimination in work and housing quickly contributed to a poverty scenario difficult for Puerto Ricans to escape. For example, labor unions often excluded Puerto Ricans or greatly restricted their participation (Feagin & Booher Feagin, 1999b). As with African Americans before them, Puerto Ricans faced significant redlining housing discrimination resulting in "hyper segregation" alongside African Americans. For example, U.S. Census data has clearly showed for some time that while both Mexicans and Cubans are mostly segregated apart from Blacks, Puerto Ricans are less segregated from Blacks and more segregated from whites (Tienda & Fuentes, 2014). Underclass experts Massey and Denton (1989) warn that like many African Americans, Puerto Ricans are in danger of becoming a permanent part of the urban underclass, or those lacking employment and other social mobility routes out of poverty.

Poor Timing of Migration to Mainland

Puerto Rican migration to the United States peaked in the 1950s just as the American economy began its major economic structural shift from an industrial giant to more of a post-industrial service oriented economy. Thus, while most Americans have been increasingly affected by this nationwide shift, unskilled and semi-skilled poor people have been most frequently dislocated, increasingly including today's white working class. For example, in New York where most Puerto Ricans have resided, nearly half a million manufacturing jobs were lost between 1960 and 1990 (Feagin & Booher Feagin, 1999b). According to Rodriguez (1989), manufacturing accounted for 60% of the Puerto Rican work force in 1960. Between 1960 and 1970, manufacturing jobs in New York decreased by 173,000, and in the next decade another 268,000 jobs were lost. Unfortunately, this loss was not offset by an increase in lower-level service jobs where the Puerto Rican workforce was also concentrated. Today, almost 25% of Puerto Ricans in the United States live in poverty, with high rates of single female–headed households, patterns similar to the African American experience, as compared to a poverty rate of about 19% for Latinos in general. While there are parallels between Puerto

Ricans and Cuban Americans, in terms of Caribbean history vis a vis Spain and later the United States, the latter has manifested better adaptation in the United States given their unique acculturation scenario.

Cuban Americans

Cuban Americans are often called the Latino "model minority" for their remarkable success in America. While complex, this success story comes down to the predominant elite composition of this relatively recent and legal refugee group, coupled with unprecedented refugee benefits and support provided by the U.S. government for largely self-serving political reasons. Prior to this, however, initial contact between the United States and Cuba was problematic and eventually contentious.

Contact

As mentioned above, Cuba became "independent" in 1898 when the United States drove Spain out of the Caribbean during the brief Spanish-American war. However, the United States continued to occupy Cuba for the next four years, declaring it a U.S. "protectorate" in 1902 (Feagin & Feagin, 1999b). Based on the 1900–1901 Platt Amendment to the U.S. military appropriations bill, the United States also reserved the right to military intervention in Cuba, ostensibly to protect life, property, individual liberty, and the island's independence. In reality, however, the pseudo-colonization of Cuba resulted in major political, economic, and military domination from 1898 to 1959, with the United States continuing to occupy and operate a military base in Guantanamo Bay to this day, despite a cold war-like trade embargo and cessation of diplomatic relations between the two countries.

Conflict

Within 15 years after Cuba's so-called independence from Spain, U.S. investments grew from $50 million to an estimated $220 million. By the late 1920s, the United States controlled three-quarters of Cuba's sugar industry, and by 1960 the United States controlled 90% of Cuba's mines, 80% of its public utilities, 50% of its railways, 40% of its sugar production, and 25% of its bank deposits (Feagin & Booher Feagin, 1999b).

With regard to political domination, no elected Cuban president opposed to U.S. economic interests could remain in office. Both U.S. military and diplomatic interference regulated American-friendly Cuban politics. During the first half of the 20th century, international relations between the United States and Cuba epitomized the general pattern of U.S.–Latin American relations, with the United States instrumental in installing repressive dictators who could be manipulated by U.S. political and business leaders. For this reason, resentment and grass roots rebellions constantly simmered beneath the tenuous Cuban political surface.

Castro's Socialist Revolution

During the 1950s, a young Fidel Castro attempted several times to overthrow president and former army chief Fulgencio Batista, who had assumed power in 1952. By 1958, Batista was losing most battles with revolutionary factions and fled when the United States gave up supporting him in 1959, leaving Castro and his bearded army to claim the country and implement a socialist government. Castro's anti-American platform can be understood as a defiant response to the United States' historical choice to exploit Cuba for its own benefit rather than investing in a mutually beneficial relationship. The upshot is today's miniature 60-year cold war with our Latino neighbor.

To the majority of Cubans, Castro's rise to power was regarded with hope and optimism that was initially validated by land grants to tenant farmers and guaranteed compensation to small sugar growers. Indeed, significant improvements were accomplished in the basic areas of quality universal health care and high educational level relative to international standards. However, the new regime succumbed to oppressive tendencies characterized by mass trials and executions to cleanse former foes and non-supporters of the revolution. Phone tapping and spying also became common.

Next, the stated goal of nationalizing both Cuban and American owned businesses (Feagin & Booher Feagin, 1999b), as well as a no-tolerance policy for U.S. manipulation, greatly threatened U.S. and Cuban business and political interests. Open hostility broke out between Cuba and the United States, as well as between the new government and Cuban elites concerned about persecution and losing their considerable wealth. The United States broke off diplomatic relations with Cuba and established an "open door" policy of welcoming Cuban exiles fleeing "communist oppression" and seeking refuge in the "free world."

Between 1959 and 1962, about a quarter of a million Cuban exiles relocated to the United States, almost all to South Florida where they could live a mere 90 miles from their homeland in the event of Castro's anticipated imminent demise (Garcia, 1996). Today, over half of all Cuban Americans continue to live in South Florida. While they are highly integrated into the economic, political, and social network of their environment, Cubans have also clung tenaciously to their culture given their history as a community in exile with dreams of retaking their beloved country.

The First Wave of Exiles

Not surprisingly, the first major wave of Cuban exiles began with those whose success in Cuba was directly related to their political and economic connections to the United States. These were elite government officials, bankers, and successful industrialists under the Batista dictatorship, followed by middle and upper class professionals, managers, merchants, landlords, and over half of all of Cuba's doctors and teachers (Feagin & Booher Feagin, 1999b). In contrast to Puerto Ricans, the overwhelming majority of first-wave Cuban exiles were also racially white, even though over a quarter of Cubans on the island are Black. As addressed in Chapter 3, Latin America is stratified by SES and race ranging from Spanish European at the top to indigenous and African at the bottom. Castro greatly resented the exodus of such human capital and resources and labeled the exiles self-interested, disloyal traitors.

The Bay of Pigs Fiasco

In the minds of both early Cuban exiles and the U.S. government, Cubans were temporary exiles that would quickly return to their homeland once Castro was somehow overthrown. On this note, President Kennedy and the CIA trained and funded some 1,500 Cuban exiles in a half-baked plan to take back Cuba in 1961. In what has come to be known as the Bay of Pigs fiasco, the poorly conceived plan failed miserably as the well-alerted Cuban army quickly put down the rebellion of the Cuban exile brigade soldiers. In just a few days, 120 exile brigade soldiers were killed and 1,125 were jailed. Castro later ransomed these prisoners of war for millions of dollars in needed products such as medicines, baby food, and pesticides.

The Cuban Missile Crisis

Conflict between Cuba and the United States came to a head in 1962, when the United States staged a showdown with Russia over the presence of mid-range nuclear warheads and facilities on the island. Castro had been cultivating relations with Russia and cleverly declared Cuba a socialist government on the night before the anticipated Bay of Pigs fiasco. Castro's plan was to garner Russian support by exploiting the Bay of Pigs attack as an American invasion on a fellow socialist country. The plan worked well, with Russia supplying billions of dollars in aid to Cuba until the Soviet Union's demise in the 1990s. Russia was also quite interested in establishing an armed communist stronghold in the Western Hemisphere. The American quarantine or interruption of Russian ships into Cuba resulted in negotiations between Kennedy and Khrushchev, leader of the Soviet Union, in which Russia agreed to remove the warheads in exchange for a U.S. promise not to invade Cuba.

The Second and Third Waves of Exiles

Although flights out of Cuba were suspended in 1962, a second wave of 56,000 Cubans, mostly relatives of the first wave, came to the United States between 1962 and 1965, mostly by way of Spain and Mexico. Between 1965 and the late 1970s, a third wave of Cubans relocated to the United States (Feagin & Booher Feagin, 1999b). At a ceremony at the base of the Statue of Liberty, President Johnson guaranteed refuge for this wave of Cubans and arranged for daily "freedom flights" to transport more of them (Garcia, 1996). Prior to flights from Cuba being halted in 1973, over 3,000 flights had transported almost 300,000 Cuban refugees to the United States. Again, this latter group was composed predominantly of white Cubans who were relatives of prior exiles, but also included more working class and small business people than previous waves. The majority of these individuals settled into South Florida, where they quickly integrated into the thriving Cuban ethnic enclave that was beginning to accept America as its permanent home.

As with Puerto Ricans, the timing of Cuban immigration to the United States was not good in terms of labor market shifts. However, unlike Puerto Ricans, poor timing was no obstacle to success, because (1) Cubans were not racialized and treated as Blacks, (2) they were predominantly middle and upper class professionals, and (3) they received major support from public and private sectors of U.S. society. The magnitude of government and private assistance provided to help Cubans resettle into the United States is not only unique among Latino populations, but unprecedented for *any* refugee group in American history (Garcia, 1996).

Investing in Cubans

President Eisenhower (1953–1961) responded to the immediate resettlement needs of first-wave Cubans by allocating $1 million in federal funds to create the Cuban Refugee Emergency Center in Miami. In 1961, President Kennedy established the Cuban Refugee Program and expanded aid to include employment, health services, education, vocational training programs, surplus food distribution, and aid to more than 14,000 unaccompanied children sent by Cuban parents who feared their children being educated in a communist state and being conscripted into Castro's military. Even Pan American Airlines (which closed in 1991) assisted in smuggling these children out of Cuba in what was cleverly named "Operation Peter Pan."

Between 1961 and the mid-1970s, the Cuban Refugee Program provided nearly a billion dollars of resettlement support across a wide array of services (Feagin & Booher Feagin, 1999b). In fact, between 1959 and 1965, government assistance to Cuban exiles actually exceeded what was granted to native-born Americans in the entire state of Florida (Garcia, 1996). In Dade County, Florida, the nation's first federally funded and highly successful bilingual education program was set up for Cuban children as well as their NLW classmates.

One exile problem specifically addressed the significant downward mobility of Cuban professionals whose skills needed to be adapted to the United States. For Cuban doctors, lawyers, and teachers, federal grant monies were poured into universities and community organizations to create intensive retraining programs that enabled Cuban professionals to graduate with American licenses, while others received preparation for licensing exams. This unique acculturation scenario changed in 1980 with the last and unwelcomed wave of Cuban refugees.

Marielito Conflict in the United States

While conflict between the United States and Cubans has been mostly confined to the island, some domestic conflict occurred with the fourth wave of approximately 125,000 exiles that arrived suddenly in 1980. Known as *Marielitos* because they sailed from the Cuban port of Mariel, these exiles received a rocky reception for a number of reasons. Not only did Marielitos arrive during an economic recession, but also 75% were blue-collar workers and up to 40% were dark-skinned, Black Cubans. While some were forced to leave Cuba, most were allowed to leave given their desire to escape growing island poverty. As such, they were initially denied the federal financial support granted to political refugees. However, an amendment to the Refugee Assistance and Education Act of 1980 eventually allowed them to receive full refugee benefits that facilitated their adaptation to the United States (Garcia, 1996).

Still, the reception of *Marielitos* was harsh. They were housed in temporary "tent cities" upon arrival, flown to military detention centers, and screened for dangerousness. American apprehension over the *Marielitos* stemmed from Castro's well publicized "tainting" of this migration stream supposedly with hardened criminals, mental patients, "homosexuals," and others he deemed undesirable. As it turned out, less than 4% of *Marielitos* had committed felonies or had been hospitalized for mental illness, yet exaggerated media attention fueled Americans fears (Garcia, 1996).

Scarface, the Movie

The extremes of America's fear of *Marielitos* was captured by movie director Brian De Palma's 1983 remake of the classic James Cagney gangster film *Scarface*. The updated version begins with footage of the Mariel boatlift, followed by the detention center interrogation of Tony Montana, a *Marielito* criminal played by Al Pacino. The rest of the film depicts Tony's violent rise as a cocaine drug lord who flaunts a buxom NLW American girlfriend, buries his face in a mountain of cocaine piled upon his desk, and who wields a bazooka-sized gun while screaming "You want to fuck with me?!" in a feeble Cuban accent. However, that's not all. Tony is also a pervert who kills his sister's boyfriend (formerly Tony's best friend) in order to incestuously possess her. The film is so absurd that it has become a laughable cult classic in the barrios of America!

But for all of the media hype about Cuban criminals, only 2% of *Marielitos* ever ended up in penitentiaries for serious violations of the law (Feagin & Booher Feagin, 1999b), and by the mid-1980s the majority of *Marielitos* were well absorbed into Cuban American communities. Ironically, it was America's overreaction and restrictiveness that resulted in *Marielito* protest and violence during the 1980s. Angered by their mistreatment and the crowded conditions in detention camps and prisons, several inmates rioted and clashed with National Guard troops. Between 1980 and 1983, a few *Marielitos* also protested by frequently hijacking airliners back to Cuba.

In 1987, riots broke out at the Atlanta federal penitentiary in Georgia and the Oakdale federal detention center in Louisiana where about 3,000 *Marielitos* awaited deportation for committing crimes in the United States. Angry about being jailed indefinitely, these inmates burned several buildings and took over 100 people hostage (Garcia, 1996). They demanded parole board reviews to remain in the United States, but were difficult negotiators. It took Reverend Agustin Roman, Auxiliary Bishop of the Archdiocese of Miami, to negotiate with the inmates, resulting in the parole of the majority of inmates and deportation of 400 back to Cuba.

Six years later, the United States ended its three-decade-long open door policy to Cuba in response to some 30,000 Cuban "boat people" who attempted to enter the United States when Cuba again lifted its ban on emigration. Hundreds of thousands of Cubans tried to escape the disastrous economic crisis in Cuba caused by the break-up of Soviet Union that had supplied Cuba with billions in annual foreign aid. This last wave was returned to Guantanamo Bay, and the United States and Cuba reached an agreement in which the United States would increase its number of visas granted to Cubans to 20,000 annually in return for halting the mass exodus of refugees.

While the rapidly rising social positionality for Cuban refugees, including their U.S.-born family members, has been remarkable, the post-1980 waves of Cuban immigrants noted above have been far less successful. For instance, as of 2006, family income for self-employed as well as salaried Cubans were $105,921 and $82,363, respectively. However, for pre-1980 Cuban refugees, these figures are $94,683 and $75,569, respectively, and a considerably lower $53,545 and $49,410, respectively, for post-1980 Cuban immigrants (Healey, Stepnick & O'Brien, 2019b). Hence, there is more diversity within Cuban American SES than presumed, with need concentrated in the last pair of waves during the 1980s and 1990s.

Adaptation

By the early 1990s, there were over 28,000 Cuban-owned businesses in the Miami area, and in Dade County over 18,000 firms in the areas of finance, construction, textiles, leather, furniture, and cigar production. There were also 16 Cuban American bank presidents and 250 vice presidents, 3,500 doctors, 500 lawyers, 500 supermarket owners, 250 drug store owners, and 60 auto dealership owners (Gonzales, 1993). Cuban adaptation to the United States began with self-imposed segregation and retention of culture born out of the exile dream to reclaim Cuba after a temporary stay in the United States. However, with Castro's 50 + years in power (1959 to 2011), Cuban exiles became permanent Cuban Americans who rapidly integrated into all spheres of American society. While not the original intention, the combination of high Cuban SES and high U.S. government investment in Cuban adjustment resulted in one of the best-case scenarios for a refugee group in America. However, the portrait of Cubans as the Latino model minority is divisive to other U.S. Latino populations that continue to struggle with challenging social positionalities related to harsher acculturation histories as reviewed in this chapter as well as the subsequent chapter on Central Americans and Dominican Americans.

Conclusion

Informed by knowledge about the conditions of acculturation for different U.S. Latino populations, service providers can begin to understand that the various patterns of Latino social positionality, including disparities in SES and related psychosocial and health patterns, are neither random nor simply of their own making. What emerges from a careful analysis of historical conditions of acculturation is recognition of the living legacies of people actively coping with forces of racism and discrimination, partly by resisting and maintaining their life-supporting and self-affirming Latino culture. As such, acculturation knowledge quells naive and derisive questions such as "Why can't Mexican Americans be like Cubans or Asians?" and provides human and social service providers with an empathic understanding of the role of historical through current injustice in the social positionality of U.S. Latinos. This chapter focused on the oldest and largest Latino populations in the United States (Mexican, Puerto Rican, Cuban), while the subsequent chapter will apply the acculturation framework to more recent, smaller, yet rapidly growing Central Americans and Dominican American Latino populations.

References

Acuña, R. (2019). *Occupied America: A history of Chicanos* (9th ed.). New York: Pearson Education.

Berry, J. W. (1990). Psychology of acculturation: Understanding individuals moving between cultures. In A. Brislin (Ed.), *Applied cross-cultural psychology* (pp. 232–253). Newbury Park, CA: Sage.

Berry, J. W. (2003). Conceptual approaches to acculturation. In. K. M. Chun, P. Balls Organista, and G. Marin (Eds.), *Acculturation: Advances in theory, measurement, and applied research* (pp. 17–34). Washington DC: American Psychological Association.

Berry, J., & Annis, R. C. (1974). Acculturative stress: The role of ecology, culture and differentiation. *Journal of Cross-Cultural Psychology, 5,* 382–406.

Chavez, L. R. (1992). *Shadowed lives: Undocumented immigrants in American society* (p. viii). Orlando, FL: Harcourt Brace Janovich.

del Castillo, R. G. (1990). *The treaty of Guadalupe Hidalgo: A legacy of conflict.* Norman, OK: University of Oklahoma Press.

Elbers, B. (2021). Trends in U.S. residential racial segregation, 1990 to 2020. *Socius: Sociological Research for a Dynamic World, 7,* 1–3. https://doi.org/10.1177/23780231211053982

Encyclopedia Britannica (2019). Operation Wetback. https://www.britannica.com/topic/Operation-Wetback

Feagin, J. R., & Booher Feagin. C. (1999a). Mexican Americans. In J. R. Feagin and C. Booher Feagin (Eds.), *Race and ethnic relations* (6th ed.) (pp. 291–335). Upper Saddle River, NJ: Prentice Hall.

Feagin, J. R., & Booher Feagin. C. (1999b). Puerto Ricans and Cuban Americans. In J. R. Feagin and C. Booher Feagin (Eds.), *Race and ethnic relations* (6th ed.) (pp. 336–379). Upper Saddle River, NJ: Prentice Hall.

Frey, W. H. (2011). The new metro minority map: Regional shifts in Hispanics, Asians, and Blacks from Census 2010. 1–18 (August). Washington DC: Metropolitan Policy Program at Brookings. chrome-extension://efaidnbmnnnibpcajpcglclefindmkaj/ https://www.brookings.edu/wp-content/uploads/2016/06/0831_census_race_frey.pdf

Garcia, M. C. (1996). *Havana USA: Cuban exiles and Cuban Americans in South Florida, 1959-1994.* Berkeley, CA: University of California Press.

Garcia, M. T. (1995). *Ruben Salazar: Border correspondent.* Berkeley: University of California Press.

Gonzales, J. L., Jr. (1993). The Cuban American experience. In J. L., Jr., Gonzales (Ed.), *Racial and ethnic groups in America* (2nd ed.) (pp. 275–288). Dubuque, Iowa: Kendall/ Hunt.

Healey, F. F., Stepnick, A., & O'Brien, E. (2019a). Assimilation and pluralism: From immigrants to white ethnics. In J. F. Healey and E. O'Brien (Eds.), *Race, ethnicity, gender & class: The sociology of group conflict and change* (pp. 36–76). Los Angeles: Sage.

Healey, F. F., Stepnick, A., & O'Brien, E. (2019b). Hispanic Americans: Colonization, immigration, and ethnic enclaves. In J. F. Healey and E. O'Brien (Eds.), Race, *ethnicity, gender & class: The sociology of group conflict and change* (pp. 262–311). Los Angeles: Sage.

Jacobs, P., Landua, S., & Pell, E. (1971). *To serve the devil Volume I: Natives and slaves* (pp. 229–249). New York: Vintage Books.

Massey, D. S., & Denton, N. A. (1989). Trends in the residential segregation of blacks, Hispanics, and Asians: 1970-1980. *American Sociological Review, 52,* 802–825.

Mazon, M. (1984). *The zoot-suit riots: The psychology of symbolic annihilation.* Austin, TX: University of Texas Press.

McLemore, S. D., Romo, H., & Gonzalez Baker, S. (2001). Mexican Americans: From colonized minority to political activists. In S. D. McLemore, H. Romo & S. Gonzalez Baker (Eds.), *Racial and ethnic relations in America* (pp. 187–220). Boston: Allyn & Bacon.

McWilliams, C. (1968). *North from Mexico: The Spanish-speaking people of the United States.* New York: Greenwood Press.

Montejano, D. (1987). *Anglos and Mexicans in the making of Texas, 1936-1980.* Austin, TX: University of Texas Press.

Moquin, W., & Van Doren, C. (Eds.) (1971). *A documentary history of the Mexican Americans.* New York: Bantam Books.

Orfield, G., & Yun, J. T. (1999). *Resegregation in American schools.* Cambridge, MA: The Civil Rights Project, Harvard University.

PBS (2020). Juan Cortina. New perspectives on the west (People). https://www.pbs.org/ weta/thewest/people/a_c/cortina.htm

Project Report (2018). Ascertainment of the estimated excess mortality from Hurricane Maria in Puerto Rico. Milken Institute School of Public Health, George Washington University.

Redfield, R., Linton, R., & Herskovits, M. J. (1936). Memorandum on the study of acculturation. *American Anthropologist, 38,* 149–152.

Rodriguez, C. E. (1989). The political-economic context. In C. E. Rodriguez, *Puerto Ricans: Born in the U.S.A.* (pp. 85–105). Boston: Unwin Hyman.

Tienda, M., & Fuentes, N. (2014). Hispanics in metropolitan America: New realities and old debates. *Annual Review of Sociology, 40,* 499–520.

U.S. Department of Labor (1992). Findings from the national agricultural workers survey (NAWS), 1990: a demographic and employment profile of perishable crop farmworkers. Washington DC: U.S. Department of Labor, 89, 97–98.

Wikipedia (2020). Puerto Rican status Referendum. https://en.wikipedia.org/wiki/2017_Puerto_Rican_status_referendum

2

Patterns of Acculturation and Social Positionality in the United States

Dominican and Central Americans

In Chapter 1, Berry's model of acculturation and adaptation illuminated the Americanization of Mexican, Puerto Rican, and Cuban American populations in the United States. This chapter focuses on several Central American populations, as well as Dominicans, for whom Berry's first phase of acculturation, *conditions of contact* with America, actually began with deep U.S. involvement in Central America and the Dominican Republic decades before members of these Latino populations became U.S. minority groups in appreciable numbers. In fact, it is precisely because of such involvement in Latin America that so many Latino minority groups have become a part of the United States.

Briefly, the historical pattern of U.S. involvement in Latin America involves lucrative business investments and partnerships with brutally repressive right-wing military dictatorships, resulting in resistance and revolution on the part of oppressed masses, with the U.S. supporting ruthless dictatorships with massive economic aid and military assistance. One tangible result of such unethical U.S. involvement has been the influx of over a million Central Americans beginning in the 1980s, and hundreds of thousands of Dominican immigrants desperate to escape oppression, civil war, and extreme poverty by seeking refuge in the United States, whether their migration is officially recognized or not.

The United Provinces of Central America?

While volumes continue to be written about Central America, described here for providers of social and human services are salient historical details, events, people, and data for understanding the acculturation of Central

Solving Latino Psychosocial and Health Problems. Kurt C. Organista, Oxford University Press.
© Oxford University Press 2023. DOI: 10.1093/oso/9780190059637.003.0002

Americans to the United States, their consequent social positionality, and hovering questions about America's accountability to these Latino populations. As the U.S. Civil War ended and Abraham Lincoln started his second term as president in 1865, the region that we know today as Central America emerged from over four decades of ambitious, chaotic, and ultimately futile efforts to forge a united region modeled after the United States: *Las Provincias Unidas de Centro America* [The United Provinces of Central America] (Cordova, 2005). Since the region's liberation from Spain in 1821, post-colonial conservative and liberal factions waged numerous wars throughout the region during what is referred to as the Period of Anarchy. What ensued between 1865 and the 1930s was a harsh period of ruthless rule by conservative oligarch families that exploited indigenous agricultural labor, monopolized profits, and hammered down on the slightest instance of resistance, resulting in vicious cycles of repression and revolution throughout each Central American country, as well as the Dominican Republic as profiled later below.

Salvadoran Americans

During the early 20th century, an elite oligarchy known as *Las Catorce* or the "14 families," owned all banks and 60% of farmlands, while 8% of El Salvador's 5 million people earned half of the country's income produced primarily by an impoverished peasant agricultural workforce (Garcia, 2006). The interests of *Las Catorce* were protected by ruthless military generals such as General Hernandez Martinez and the newly formed National Guard that implemented a wave of terror against demands for better working and living conditions on the part of peasants and activists inspired by socialism as an alternative to their authoritarian regime (Cordova, 2005).

La Matanza and Roots of the Frente Martí para la Liberación Nacional

In response to a brief peasant uprising in 1932 spearheaded by Farabundo Martí, founder of El Salvador's communist party, the National Guard slaughtered at least 10,000 peasants in what became known as *La Mantaza* [The Slaughter]. Subsequently, the indigenous population abandoned external markers of their culture and practiced it in secret to avoid being targeted, tortured, and killed as communist sympathizers. However, the spirit of Farabundo Martí would live on in the rise of the *Frente Farabundo Martí para la Liberación Nacional* (FMLN) [Farabundo Martí National Liberation Front], a political party that would spearhead the revolution and civil war in El Salvador for decades to come.

Contact

Between 1932 and the revolution of 1979, a series of military dictators continued to repress the population until a civilian and military junta briefly overthrew the dictatorship of General Carlos Humberto Romero, only to be quickly dissolved by Jose Napoleon Duarte, who assumed the presidency of El Salvador in 1980 and again in 1984 (Cordova, 2005). Between 1979 and 1982, three different junta governments tried and failed to enact modest reforms, again provoking vicious crackdowns by the military government (Garcia, 2006). Despite such turmoil, many U.S. corporations including General Foods, Procter and Gamble, Esso, Westinghouse, Kimberly-Clark, and Texas Instruments established operations in El Salvador in order to take advantage of low-wage labor and lack of worker and environmental protections (Teaching Central America, 2018).

Death Squads in El Salvador

The 1980s marked the emergence of notorious paramilitary death squads, composed of off-duty military and police and leaders of right-wing civilian organizations who supported the Salvadoran government. Death squads harassed, tortured, disappeared, and assassinated opposition politicians, labor leaders, teachers, students, FMLN leftist guerilla groups, priests, and nuns practicing liberation theology on behalf of the poor (see Sidebar 2.1). The 1980s also marked a period of deep and sustained U.S. support of the government of El Salvador despite its expanding record of human rights violations and atrocities condemned around the world.

In 1980, a death squad in the capital city of San Salvador brazenly assassinated Archbishop Oscar Romero, a charismatic vocal critic of government, while he was serving mass. At his funeral procession, attended by thousands, the military fired into the crowd of mourners, killing 30 and wounding hundreds. Also, in 1980, progressive Attorney General

---

Sidebar 2.1. Liberation Theology

On the night before his shocking assassination by the government of El Salvador, Archbishop Oscar Arnulfo Romero said, "In the name of God, in the name of this suffering people whose cries rise to heaven more loudly each day, I implore you, I beg you, I order you in the name of God: stop the repression" (Bonner, 2016). To speak such truth to power reflects Romero's commitment to a 20th-century movement in Christian theology, developed by Latin American Roman Catholics, that emphasizes liberation from social, political, and economic oppression as integral to ultimate salvation. Liberation theology practitioners seek to apply religious faith by aiding the poor and oppressed through involvement in political and civic affairs. It stresses both heightens awareness of the "sinful" socioeconomic structures that cause social inequities and supports active participation in changing those structures. Liberation theologists view the Roman Catholic Church in Latin America as fundamentally different from the Church in Europe, in that the Latin American Catholic Church should be actively engaged in improving the lives of the poor given its post-colonial position in the new world (Encyclopedia Britannica, 2018a).

Mario Zamora was shot 12 times in the face at a dinner party in his home as a warning to socialist sympathizers. Further, three American nuns and a lay missionary church worker in El Salvador were also kidnapped, raped, and murdered in 1980 (see Sidebar 2.2), with an estimated 25,000 people assassinated between 1980 and 1981 by death squads operating with impunity as they terrorized dissenters, often by leaving mutilated bodies as public warning signs. Undeterred, galvanized revolutionary forces mounted counter-offensives, and by the late 1980s close to a million El Salvadorans had fled the country to destinations throughout Central America and Mexico, Europe, and the United States in desperate attempts to escape the crossfire of civil war, often referred to as *La Situación* (Cordova, 2005).

The Reagan Administration and El Salvador

Elected in 1981, and again in 1985, President Ronald Reagan inflamed the civil war in El Salvador (as well as Nicaragua) by infusing massive military

---

Sidebar 2.2. Slain American Nuns in El Salvador, 1980

Maryknoll nuns Ita Ford and Maura Clarke, Ursuline nun Dorothy Kazel, and Roman Catholic lay church worker Jean Donovan were slain on December 2, 1980, after being stopped by security officers as they were driving from the airport to the capital. Their bodies were found two days later in a shallow grave. Several of them (the number was never clear) were raped, and all were shot to death. The women had been running a temporary refugee center, as well as an orphanage, in the civil war-torn Northern Province, and occasionally gave rides to refugees fleeing to the capital. In 1984, for the first time in El Salvador's history, a jury convicted five members of the Salvadoran National Guard for the murders. The United States had been withholding $19 million in foreign aid pending the outcome of the court decision (Ford, 1984).

---

and economic aid (as much as $300 million per year) to the government of El Salvador, with the rationale of containing communism in the region (Cordova, 2005). By the mid-1980s, opposition groups gave up trying to negotiate with the Salvadoran government, joined the revolution, and gained the upper hand until more infusions of U.S. aid enabled the Salvadoran government to maintain a bloody decade-long war resulting in the loss of an estimated 70,000 people from both sides of the conflict by the late 1980s.

El Mozote Massacre

In 1981, 936 villagers of El Mozote, half under the age of 14, where slaughtered by the U.S.-trained Atlacatl, El Salvador's elite military battalion. Despite international condemnation and press coverage, the United States denied the massacre until forensic scientists unearthed mass graves. Despite urgings by the United Nations, as well as Mexico and Canada, to end military aid to the government of El Salvador, the Reagan administration provided an estimated $6 billion, effectively prolonging and exacerbating the 12-year civil war (Garcia, 2006).

In 1989, a pivotal showdown occurred during which President Alfredo Cristiani bombed working class neighborhoods while the FMLN brought guerilla warfare to the rich neighborhoods of the capital, paving the way for a greater balance of power in the elections of 1991, and both sides signing a peace accord mediated by the United Nations. By 1992, the FMLN, National Guard, and various police organizations disbanded, and civilian organizations gained greater control over police, armed forces, and the judicial system. 1992 also saw the election in the United States of President Bill Clinton, who sharply curbed military and economic aid to El Salvador, making such assistance contingent upon ousting military officers guilty of wartime atrocities.

Conflict

At the Comalapa International Airport in El Salvador's capital city of San Salvador, a huge monument honors the *Hermanos Lejanos* [Distant Brothers & Sisters], or Salvadoran immigrants in the United States that send billions of dollars in remittances each year to their families in El Salvador (Cordova, 2005). In fact, these immigrants are referred to as *El Departamento Quince* [15th State], in a 14-state country, to symbolize their continued importance to the government and people of El Salvador. According to the Central Reserve Bank of El Salvador, Salvadoran Americans send about $4.5 billion a year to El Salvador, a major supplement to an economy with an annual output of about $27 billion annually (Gillespie, 2018). Reviewed below are obstacles to Salvadoran adjustment in the United States and related social positionality.

Not surprisingly, mass migration from El Salvador began during the violent civil war years (1979 through 1992) despite numerous legal obstacles posed by the Reagan Administrations (1981–1989). Such obstacles are reflected in the following quote by Cordova (2005): "The United States has traditionally allowed liberal immigration practices when dealing with political refugees from totalitarian communist countries, but not from friendly totalitarian or authoritarian noncommunist dictatorships" (pp. 37–38). Despite protests by the United Nations, the American Civil Liberties Union, and churches throughout America, the United States denied about 97% of applications for refugee or asylum status, leaving Salvadorans to adjust to life in the United States either as undocumented or with temporary immigration status. Fortunately, the marginal status of Central Americans was mitigated by hundreds of religious leaders and churches throughout America that answered to a higher calling by assisting Central Americans in what came to be known as the Sanctuary Movement.

Roots of Today's Sanctuary Movement and Ordinances

During the early 1980s, a quarter of a million desperate Central Americans had little choice but to migrate without documentation into the United States, frequently risking their lives by walking through the Arizona desert because of stepped-up border control at traditional crossing points in California and Texas (Cordova, 2005). When 21 Salvadorans tragically died in the desert heat in 1980, Jim Corbett, a rancher from Tucson, Arizona, appealed to the government to support asylum for this new wave of migrants, only to be met with Immigration and Naturalization Service (INS) deportation campaigns instead. Boldly challenging the federal government, Corbett spent the next few years assisting those crossing the border by delivering them to church-affiliated safe houses and enlisting the support of the Tucson Ecumenical Council and Reverend John Fife, pastor of Southside Presbyterian Council, who publicly declared in 1982 that their churches were sanctuaries for Central Americans escaping civil war. Soon, over 330 churches throughout America joined the movement and pushed for humanitarian public policies.

In 1985, the INS began persecuting sanctuary movement leaders, and a federal grand jury handed down multiple-count indictments against Corbett, Fife, and over a dozen church leaders (Cordova, 2005). While most were acquitted or let off with probation, a few were imprisoned for conspiracy, smuggling, aiding, and harboring illegal aliens. Yet, this early religious movement would ignite today's Sanctuary Movement, or embattled civic movement in which major cities such as New York, Los Angeles, Chicago, Miami, and San Francisco have passed sanctuary laws limiting the role of local law enforcement in federal immigration control. While discussed further in Chapter 12, sanctuary cities oppose enlisting local law enforcement, whose role of fighting crime depends on cooperation with the community, to also police the immigration status of community members, thus jeopardizing trust in local police on the part of undocumented people, their family members and friends, and the larger Latino and other immigrant communities.

Immigration Reform and Control Act (1986)

In 1987, Congress implemented the amnesty provision of the Immigration Reform and Control Act (IRCA) that granted legal status to undocumented people in good standing who had resided continuously in the United States prior to January 1, 1982. While a tremendous opportunity for undocumented Mexicans, IRCA was unhelpful to the vast majority of Salvadorans who arrived between 1982 through 1989 (Cordova, 2005). It was during these same years that Congress debated various types of temporary immigration status for the hundreds of thousands of undocumented Salvadorans and other Central Americans.

Temporary Protected Status/Deferred Enforced Departure

Congress created Temporary Protected Status (TPS) within the Immigration Act of 1990, giving the U.S. Attorney General the discretion to grant TPS to countries experiencing: (1) continuing armed conflict posing danger to citizens required to return, (2) natural disasters or other conditions resulting in the disruption of living conditions, and (3) inability to accommodate the return of its citizens (Cordova, 2005). TPS expired after 18 months, after which the Department of Justice granted another 12-month stay called TPS/Deferred Enforced Departure or TPS/DED. Despite an additional extension through 1994, no further extensions were granted, and those with TPS/DED were expected to voluntarily deport themselves back to a shaky Central America after planting significant roots in the United States.

However, 186,000 Salvadorans with expired TPS became eligible to file for political asylum thanks to a class action suit filed by the American Baptist Churches charging discrimination on the part of the INS with regard to Central American asylum applications (Cordova, 2006). When the case was settled in 1991, TPS was extended to the above Salvadorans through 1996 in order to provide time to apply for asylum. In 1997, the Nicaraguan Adjustment and Central American Relief Act (NACARA) permitted Central Americans to apply for suspension of deportation provided they were registered asylum seekers and had been in the country at least five years. Further, the number of Salvadorans applying for and becoming citizens increased dramatically during the mid to late 1990s as a response to the fear and resentment caused by 1994's California Proposition 187 designed to bar undocumented people from all social and public services, a state proposition struck down as unconstitutional before it could be implemented.

While TPS/DED has alleviated some deportation anxiety and allowed hundreds of thousands of Salvadorans to work legally over the past 25 years, the ephemeral nature of this immigration status was recently demonstrated when former President Trump decided to end TPS in early 2018 for about 200,000 El Salvadorans granted TPS after a pair of earthquakes devastated El Salvador in 2001. The Department of Homeland Security (DHS), now in charge of TPS, stressed the "T" in TPS and declared that El Salvador had recovered from the earthquakes. Ignored in this abrupt decision was the immense poverty, drought, and extreme gang violence to which these 200,000 El Salvadorans were being asked to return. El Salvador's president, Salvador Sánchez Cerén, spoke by phone with Kirstjen Nielsen, then director of the DHS, pleading to extend TPS because his country was unable to accommodate so many returnees and because it also depends on the billions in remittances that Salvadoran Americans send to El Salvador each year (Jordan, 2018).

Further, after nearly two decades of integrating themselves into U.S. society, including families with U.S.-born children and even grandchildren, the threat of suddenly rescinding TPS was shocking to these families and the larger Salvadoran community given the forced choice of either returning to the most violent non-wartime country in the world or remaining as undocumented Latinos during a new era of heightened immigration control and criminalization. Also ignored was America's exacerbation of the bloody 12-year civil war that propelled hundreds of thousands of Salvadorans to the United States, forming Salvadoran communities to which the United States needs to be more accountable. That President Trump referred to El Salvador, as well as Haiti and several African countries, as "shithole countries" as compared to Norway underscores the racism behind his abrupt executive action to eliminate TPS for many that have migrated from those countries. In response to the expiration date for TPS that was set for September 9, 2019, multiple law suits against President Trump and the DHS resulted in injunctions overriding the TPS deadline. With the Biden administration's commitment to immigration reform, El Salvadorans as well as other Central Americans, Haitians, and Africans have had their TPS extended through June of 2024, a reprieve for the time being.

Social Positionality of Salvadoran Americans

Differences between Latino groups in terms of SES in the United States are illustrated in Chapter 1 comparing the acculturation histories and social positionalities of Mexican Americans, Puerto Ricans, and Cuban Americans. Illustrated in this section is the stark contrast between Cuban Americans, who benefited from their higher social capital and full refugee status, and Central Americans that have suffered from lower social capital and obstacles to refugee status. The result has been sub-optimal adaptation to the United States and a generally depressed SES profile as compared to other Latino populations.

Based on Pew Research Center tabulations of the 2013 American Community Survey, and the Pew Center's 2013 National Survey of Latinos, about 60% of Salvadorans are immigrants, 40% have resided in the United States for more than 20 years, and about a third are U.S. citizens (Lopez, 2015a). About half report speaking English proficiently while the other half reports less than well, as compared to 32% of Latinos in general. With regard to education, only 8% of Salvadorans ages 25 or older have earned a bachelor's degree as compared to 14% of all U.S. Latinos and 30% of the entire U.S. population.

Surprisingly, the annual household income for Salvadorans is about $44,000, or somewhat higher than that of all U.S. Latinos ($41,000) but significantly lower than for the overall U.S. population ($52,000) (Lopez, 2015a). About 20% of Salvadorans live in poverty, which while higher than the general U.S. population (16%) is again better than for most Latinos (25%) considering the many obstacles to adaptation reviewed above, as well as mental health challenges stemming from a not so distant violent civil war.

Salvadoran Americans currently number about two million, soon to surpass Cuban Americans to become the third largest Latino population in the United States (Healey & O'Brien, 2015). Rapid growth is reflected in U.S. Census counts of 565,081 in 1990 and 708,741 in 2000, with frequent undercounts of this population (Cordova, 2005). While Salvadorans reside throughout America, they are concentrated in California (especially Los Angeles-Long Beach), followed by Texas (especially Houston), New York (especially Nassau-Suffolk), and the Washington D.C. area (Maryland, Virginia, and West Virginia).

As with Central American immigrants in general, Salvadoran immigrants include political actors from both sides of their home country's civil war. However, the vast majority are considered "crossfire" refugees desperate to escape the immense danger of living in the middle of, and frequently being pulled into, civil war conflict. For example, noncombatants tragically made up the majority of the estimated 75,000 killed, and 9,000 disappeared, during El Salvador's horrendous civil war from 1979 to 1992 (Cordova, 2005). While mental health data are lacking, we would expect PTSD to be above average in this population and a concern for health providers and nonprofit agencies serving the Salvadoran community. However, almost 40% of Salvadorans lack health insurance versus 29% of all Latinos and 15% of the general U.S. population (Lopez, 2016a). Thus, the availability and access to federally qualified health care (FQHC) centers featuring integrated behavioral health care (IBHC) is imperative for the Salvadoran American community.

Salvadorans have formed ethnic enclaves in cities in which they are numerous, typically alongside other Latino groups. Given their mixed SES, Salvadoran enclaves provide multiple forms of formal and informal social support. A variety of political and service nonprofit organizations have evolved to address the unique needs of such Central Americans. For example, since 1981, the Central American Resource Center (CARECEN) has provided legal, health, education, leadership training, and other services mindful of obstacles to community empowerment such as high numbers of undocumented members, trauma and political division carried over from civil wars, and more recently continued poverty, gang violence, and corruption in law enforcement and political leadership in countries of origin.

Religious affiliation is another important area of community support about which service providers need to be mindful. As compared to U.S. Latinos in general, Salvadorans are less Catholic (42% versus 55%) and more Protestant (37% versus 22%) (Lopez, 2015a). These churches, along with CARECEN and other community-based organizations, have challenged former President Trump's executive order to eliminate TPS as noted above. Another topic worthy of continued debate is the Trump administration's, and particularly his former Attorney General Jeff Session's frequent public condemnations of the Salvadoran gang, MS-13, intended more to smear El Salvadoran asylum seekers than to address the gang problem in helpful ways. That the United States helped to create the MS-13 gang problem in El Salvador is never acknowledged (see Sidebar 2.3). See Table 2.1 for a summation of the above details of U.S. involvement in El Salvador and subsequent migration of El Salvadorans to the United States. Such summations are also detailed in Table 2.1 for subsequent Central American and Dominican Latino populations.

Table 2.1. Repetitive Pattern of U.S. Involvement in Central America and Dominican Republic and Consequent Migrations to the United States

	El Salvador	Guatemala	Nicaragua	Dominican Republic
Long-term Dictatorship	La Matanza massacre (1932) • 10,000 peasants killed Civil war (1979–1992) • Death squads terrorize opposition Assassination of Gen. Zamora & Bishop Romero El Mazote massacre (1981)	Colonel Carlos Arana Osorio ("Butcher of Zacapa") Civil War (1960–1996) • 50,000 Maya killed (1966–1976) • Death squads (1980s) • Killed 100,000 (1978–1984) • Disappeared 40,000 • 440 villages destroyed	*Anastacio Somosa & Sons* (1934–1979) • Assassinated 30,000 • Exiled 1000s *Civil War (1961-90)*	Ramon, Baez (1868) • Tries to sell DR to U.S. → rebellion Anti-communist Trujillo's (1930–1960) "reign of terror" • Backed by U.S. until assassinated in 1961 *Civil War (1965–1965)*
Immense Inequality	• 14 families own 60% farms • All banking • 8% had 1/2 national income in early 1900s–1990s	• 2% owned 75% private lands • 66% indigenous worked farmland	• 3 million in extreme poverty • Somosa worth $1 billion • Owned airlines, TV, fishing, meatpacking, construction, radio, 1/3 land, some banking	• Trujillo family owned 1/2 country's wealth
U.S. Backing & Investments	• $6 billion during civil war • U.S. trained military • Almost 1,000 killed El Mazote • 1/2 children	• Economic and military aid • Training death squads • Fear of "Second Cuba"	• Millions in economic/military aid • Trained brutal National Guard • Owned mines, lumber, banking, railroads, fertile land • Extradited Somosa to Michigan • President Reagan (1981) secretly funds Contras to overthrow SNLF	• U.S. gunboats back Baez • Controlled sugar, ports, customs (1893), all finances through 1964 • Declares Monroe Doctrine (1907–1944) • Occupies (1869; 1961; 1924) • Overthrows anti-conservative Constitutionalists (1965) • Helps Trujillo loyalists defeat PRD in 1966

Revolutionary Factions	• Catholic Church Liberation Theology, Bishop Romero, & FMLN (Farabundo Martí Liberación Nacional) became political party (1992)	• URNG (Unión Revolucionario Nacional de Guatemala)	• Sandinista National Liberation Front (SNLF) rise to power (1979) replaced by National Opposition Union (1990) & Violeta Chamorro	• Rise of Constitutionalists (1965) • Partido Revolucionario Dominicano (PRD) & presidential candidate Bosch (1966)
Migration to United States	• > 1 million • Limited asylum, TPS, DED • Los Angeles & Long Beach • Birth of Sanctuary Movement (early 1980s) & today's Sanctuary Ordinances	• 100,000 (1977–1985) • Denied refugee status • 1/2 eventually gaining amnesty • Postville Raid (2008) • Sanctuary Movement support	• 1.2 million Nicaraguans flee to U.S. • LPR status due to NACARA (1997) = better SES/ positionality v. other Central Americans	• 1966 mass migration with defeat of PRD • Well over 1 million migrate

Table by Samantha Ngo, MPH, MSW.

Sidebar 2.3. Why Is MS-13 National News?

In a provocative article entitled "El Salvador's Worst Shitholes are 'Made in America'," Roberto Lovato (2018) asserted: "Most damaging for El Salvador and its shitholes was the way Los Angeles Police Department (LAPD) then broke sanctuary laws designed to protect people fleeing extreme violence and other disasters from deportation. In the early '90s, the LAPD and Immigration and Naturalization Service (INS) began the fatal practice of handing the young gang members over to the then INS for deportation. In the process, these agents of U.S. policy helped create a gang culture in a country with no history of U.S.-style gangs and gang warfare. These gangs have since gone on to fill the mass graves that mark El Salvador as one of the most violent countries on earth." This powerful publication by the North American Congress on Latin America, sponsored by New York University's Center for Latin American and Caribbean Studies, was an indignant reply to President Trump's attorney general, Jeff Sessions' racist crusade to scare the public into believing that undocumented Latinos are dangerous criminals by singling out MS-13 as an international threat. At a 2017 meeting of the International Association of Chiefs of Police in Center City, Philadelphia, Attorney General Sessions announced, "I have designated MS-13 as a priority for our Crime Drug Enforcement Task Forces . . . MS-13 threatens the lives and well-being of each and every family and each and every neighborhood that they infest." Further, "They leave misery, devastation and death in their wake. They threaten entire governments." (NBC 10 Staff, 2017). Without minimizing MS-13 as a social problem in need of remedies, two points need underscoring. First, Lovato's MS-13 backstory checks out. Second, the racist dehumanization of gang-affiliated youth as an "infestation" does nothing to remedy the problem. Regarding MS-13's origin story, Cordova (2006) documents that as Salvadorans arrived in Los Angeles during the 1980s and 1990s, they settled alongside established Mexican American communities where, often perceived as outsiders, some Mexican gang-affiliated youth targeted Salvadoran youth for harassment and worse. In response, some Salvadoran youth formed small gangs that evolved into La Mara-Salvatrucha-13, a name referring to a group of friends or *Mara* that hang out together, *Salvatrucha* a slang word for Salvadoran, and 13 refers to "M" or the 13th letter of the alphabet. What began as self-protection soon grew to extorting local small businesses and residents, and eventually MS-13 recruited in states throughout the United States and back in El Salvador when deported by the INS. Because some of the original MS-13 members had combat or guerilla warfare training from the civil war in El Salvador, the gang gained a notorious reputation for extreme violence. While primarily Salvadoran, other Central and South Americans as well as a few African Americans have joined MS-13. The gang is now deeply networked in El Salvador because of the hundreds of deportations coordinated by the LAPD and INS. Sadly, many impoverished youth in El Salvador were easy recruits, frequently coerced, into local versions of MS-13. In response to this growing problem, El Salvador's ARENA ruling party passed Article 29 or the "anti-Mara" law resulting in the arrest of youth who appear to be gang members, and particularly those deported from the United States. Such so-called crackdowns, whether in El Salvador or the United States, do little to curb the presence and growth of Latino gangs. In contrast, community organizations, such as Homies Unidos and Homeboy Industries in Los Angeles, staffed by former gang members, community activists, social workers, and other nonprofit staff, focus their skills and empathy on rehabilitating gang-affiliated youth through counseling, employment opportunities, tattoo removal, and reincorporation into the community. Because a bad identity is better than none at all, we should strive to help gang-affiliated youth develop healthy prosocial roles and identities rather than reinforce and glorify bad identities in the racist and scapegoating ways former Attorney General Jeff Sessions has done at the national level.

Guatemalan Americans

For the United States, it is important that I state clearly that support for military forces and intelligence units which engaged in violence and widespread repression was wrong, and the United States must not repeat that mistake.

—President Bill Clinton, March 11, 1999

As can be surmised by the above quote, U.S. involvement in Guatemala repeated the same pattern of American self-interest at the expense of

Guatemalan peasants and members of the working class. For instance, revolution broke out in 1954 in response to a U.S.-sponsored military coup that overthrew the democratically elected government of Jacobo Arbenz Guzman following the country's 10-year struggle for agrarian reform (Garcia, 2006). The reform movement was a predictable response to extreme wealth inequality, with 2% of the population owning three-quarters of all private land while two-thirds of Guatemalans toiled in extreme poverty harvesting coffee, sugar, and cotton for export markets. Characteristically, the ruling class responded to any indigenous protest or resistance movements with repressive state-sponsored terrorism supported by the United States.

Contact

Rise of the Unión Revolucionario Nacional de Guatemala

Indigenous Mayas, who composed half of Guatemala's population of eight million, suffered the worst victimization in the form of kidnappings, torture, and murder for forming agricultural cooperatives, unions, and political organizations (Garcia, 2006). Between 1966 and 1976, an estimated 50,000 Mayas were murdered by military leaders such as Colonel Carlos Arana Osorio, who was known as the "Butcher of Zacapa" and was once quoted as declaring, "If it is necessary to turn the country into a cemetery in order to pacify it, I will not hesitate to do so" (Garcia, 2006, p. 27). With Osorio assuming the presidency (1970–1974) the United States, fearing a "second Cuba," supervised the government's counter-insurgency operations and trained the off-duty security officers who formed the same types of death squads that terrorized El Salvador (Jonas & Rodriguez, 2014). However, because such near-genocidal measures engender resistance, by 1982 four major guerilla armies joined forces to create the *Unión Revolucionario Nacional de Guatemala* (URNG) [National Revolutionary Union of Guatemala] demanding agrarian reform, civil liberties, democratic representation, and an end to repression.

Civilian Death Squads

The Guatemalan government responded to the URNG by recruiting and coercing civilians into *Patrullas de Autodefena Civil* [Civilian Self-defense Patrols] to oppose the URNG in exchange for food, guns, and employment.

Trained as death squads, the *Patrullas* grew to 900,000 members and began by destroying the opposition's food supply, scorching farm fields and killing livestock upon which villagers depended. Many Mayan villages were destroyed and villagers brutally tortured and slaughtered through the mid-1980s. According to Garcia (2006), between 1978 and 1984, an estimated 100,000 Guatemalans were killed, 40,000 disappeared, 440 villages were destroyed, and three-quarters of million were displaced internally, while over a quarter of a million fled the country, most heading to *el norte* [the north].

Conflict

Not surprisingly, most Guatemalans migrated to the United States beginning in the late 1970s and early 1980s with 3,600 entering the country with documentation and 5,100 apprehended for undocumented entry (Jonas & Rodriguez, 2014). Jonas & Rodriguez (2014) provide a detailed analysis of Guatemalan migration, divided into various phases from 1970 to 2011, demonstrating how the trickle of Guatemalans from 1970 to 1975 became a stream of predominately undocumented immigrants, averaging about 13,000 annually between 1977 and 1985. The adaptation of these predominantly peasant migrants was hampered by war-related trauma, undocumented status, and denial of refugee status by the U.S. government despite its dishonorable role in the Guatemalan civil war that compelled so many to seek refuge in America.

While Central American petitions for asylum were generally rejected by the United States, some 50,000 Guatemalans gained amnesty under IRCA (1986), followed by settlement of the aforementioned American Baptist Church class action suit against the INS in 1990 that allowed many Guatemalans to successfully apply for asylum, as was the case for El Salvadorans described above. Immediate asylum benefits included moving out of the dead-end secondary labor market to earning living wages in better jobs and being able to petition family members to join their relatives in the United States. However, several thousands of undocumented Central Americans were eventually deported in the late 1990s because of the 1996 federal immigration law that formed the basis of today's immigrant criminalization and deportation regime that primarily impacts Latinos.

Illegal Immigration Reform and Immigrant Responsibility Act (1996)

The Illegal Immigration Reform and Immigrant Responsibility Act (IIRIRA) of 1996 took immigration control to a new level in America by making it easier to deport non-citizens, harder for deportees to return, and by hyper-criminalizing undocumented immigrants, including legal permanent residents, through a variety of pernicious programs and procedures (Jonas & Rodriguez, 2014). In addition to thousands of Mexican and other Central Americans, nearly 7,000 undocumented Guatemalans were deported between 1996 and 2003 because of IIRIRA, separating mixed status families, terminating U.S. employment, and returning immigrants to impoverished and unstable countries of origin. Worse, IIRIRA legalized labeling undocumented people as "criminal aliens" and "felons" for merely being in the country without authorization, placing them in federal prisons with permanent criminal records. Military-style raids by Immigration and Customs Enforcement (ICE), such as the one described below, represent the outcome of IIRIRA and similar laws and policies.

Postville Raid of 2008

On May 12, 2008, ICE agents staked out and staged a military-styled workplace raid, complete with helicopters circling overhead, of the Agriprocessor kosher slaughterhouse in Postville, Iowa. Rounded up and arrested were 389 predominately Guatemalan (75%) and Mexican (25%) workers who were busy butchering and packing meat for American consumers. Shackled and chained like dangerous criminals, they were taken to a nearby cattle facility used as a makeshift detention center/courtroom, where they were rapidly processed for deportation in groups of 10–12 (Jonas and Rodriguez, 2014). ICE agents pressured detainees to plead guilty to "aggravated identity theft," a felony for possessing Social Security numbers that undocumented workers sometimes purchase in order to obtain work, rather than to steal from the bank accounts of citizens to whom some numbers may belong. Shockingly, the penalty for such a plea was five months in federal prison, followed by deportation and a permanent criminal record as having committed a felony.

Most Postville detainees complied in order to avoid the alternative: a minimum of two years in federal prison followed by deportation if they refused to plead guilty to aggravated identity theft. Sadly, the rapidity with which the groups of detainees were court processed, and the presence of criminal defense rather than immigration lawyers, gave these workers no time to ponder their options, which most, and especially the many Mayas arrested, did not understand. After being charged, about three dozen women who were rounded up in the raid were released to be with their babies and children while required to wear ankle shackles with GPS monitoring devices (Jonas & Rodriguez, 2014).

While ICE hailed its Postville raid as a model workplace raid that they were eager to replicate, in 2011 the U.S. Supreme Court unanimously ruled that the above use of a Social Security number did not constitute "aggravated identity theft," particularly when the undocumented workers were unaware that the numbers belonged to actual people (Jonas & Rodriguez, 2014). While discussed further in Chapter 12, this raid exemplifies how hard-working undocumented immigrants, virtually none of whom had a criminal record, are criminalized without due process based on what amount to trumped-up felony charges, void of the harm and danger previously reserved for criminal felony offenses.

Social Positionality of Guatemalans

According to a Pew Research Center analysis of the Census Bureau's American Community Survey, there are an estimated 1.3 million Guatemalan Americans in the United States—two-thirds of whom are immigrants, versus 33% of Latinos in general—a quarter of whom are U.S. citizens, with a third having been in the United States for 20 years or more (Lopez, 2015b). English proficiency is reported by 45% of Guatemalans aged five and older, while the remaining 55% report speaking English less than very well versus 32% of all Latinos. Only 9% of Guatemalans ages 25 and older have a bachelor's degree as compared with 14% of all U.S. Latinos and 30% of the entire U.S. population.

Annual household income for Guatemalans is $38,200 as compared to $41,000 for all U.S. Latinos and $52,000 for the overall U.S. population (Lopez, 2015b). Consequently, 28% live in poverty versus 16% for the general U.S. population and 25% of U.S. Latinos overall. About 45% of Guatemalans lack health insurance, compared with 29% of all Latinos and 15% of the general U.S. population (Lopez, 2015b). Thus, needs related to low-income Latino minority status are considerable for this more recent, small, but growing Latino population.

During the early 1980s, Los Angeles became the most popular destination for Guatemalans as well as other Central Americans, living alongside

Mexican and Asian immigrants, working in the rapidly expanding but low-paying service sector, and living in some of the most rundown parts of the city such as the Pico-Union section of Westlake just west of downtown. Jonas and Rodriguez (2014) provide a detailed study of Guatemalan settlement in Houston, Texas, home to over 31,000 Guatemalans who arrived during the local economic downturn of the 1980s that made cheap apartments and homes unusually available to these new Latino immigrants, including many Maya.

Guatemalan men in Houston found better than average working class jobs (e.g., in a local thriving supermarket chain), while women developed a local market of domestic work including child care for middle class families. Interestingly, the Maya are the most visible Guatemalans in Houston with community organizing revolving around the Evangelical church, soccer leagues, and employment networks. Despite initial resentment by local citizens for being heavily undocumented, hundreds of sanctuary movement churches, several universities, and local governments and nonprofit organizations supported the resettlement of Guatemalans in Houston.

About 11,395 young Guatemalans received deferred deportation status and work authorization in 2013, when President Obama used an executive order to sign Deferred Action for Childhood Arrivals (DACA) into law. However, in 2018 President Trump signed an executive order canceling DACA, leading to court injunctions against that order, with the lives of an estimated 800,000 DACA recipients in limbo. Once the case made its way to the Supreme Court in 2020, Trump's effort to ban DACA were blocked, to the relief of DACA recipients, their families, and communities. On President Biden's first day in office, he ordering DHS to fortify and expand DACA, including a path to legal permanent residency or green cards. However, on July 16, 2021, a U.S. district court in Texas issued an injunction against DACA in *Texas v. United States*, holding that DACA is unlawful. Until this case makes its way to the Supreme Court, DACA benefits will continue for current recipients, including continued renewals, while no new applications are currently being processed.

Nicaraguan Americans

Somoza may be a son of a bitch but he's our son of a bitch.
—Franklin D. Roosevelt, circa 1939

Contact

While disagreement exists regarding the source and authenticity of the above quote, it clearly fits the description of U.S. involvement in Nicaragua that dates back over a century, with the first armed U.S. invasion ordered by President Taft in 1909 to overthrow then President Jose Santos Zelaya. Zelaya is a transitional figure in Central American history with dreams of Central American reunification that included disallowing the United States from building a canal through Nicaragua to connect the Pacific and Atlantic Oceans, which of course eventually happened in Panama. However, what really earned the wrath of the United States is when Zelaya decided to contract with Japan to build his country's own competing canal in Nicaragua that led the United States to encourage Zelaya's conservative opposition to revolt against his government. When two U.S. citizens were executed for participating in the anti-Zelaya revolt, U.S. Marines were rapidly deployed to control the outcome of this civil war, occupying Nicaragua through 1925 while supporting a series of conservative pro-U.S. Nicaraguan presidents, as is the pattern of U.S. involvement in Central America.

As soon as the U.S. Marines exited Nicaragua in 1925, rebellious liberal factions under the leadership of Augusto Sandino immediately rose to challenge the U.S.-supported conservative government, prompting U.S. Marines to return in 1927 to squash the revolt and to support the U.S. choice for president. Interestingly, Sandino had been trained by the Marines to serve in the National Guard under General Anastacio Somoza. However, given Sandino's rising popularity and power, Somoza had him assassinated in 1934 and eventually took over the presidency by rigging the 1937 election.

Thus began the astounding 42-year multi-generational Somoza family dictatorship, embraced and supported by the U.S. government. During these decades, Anastacio senior was eventually assassinated in 1956, with the presidency transferred to his son Luis Somoza Debayle, who also won the contested presidential election in 1957, presiding through 1963. It was in 1961 that Marxist revolutionaries founded the *Frente Sandinista de Liberación Nacional* or FSLN [Sandinista National Liberation Front] in honor of Augusto César Sandino and in direct opposition to the Somoza regime. Although Luis Somoza eventually passed away in 1967, Anastacio Junior, or "Tachito" as he was known, assumed the presidency in yet another rigged election. In 1974 he had the constitution changed in order to continue his presidency again.

As full-scale civil war came to a head in 1979, the U.S.-supported Somoza dictatorship was finally overthrown by the FSLN after decades of revolutionary activity. The Somoza family, Anastacio Sr. followed by Luis and later Anastacio Jr., had ruled Nicaragua with an iron fist since 1937 in partnership with the United States, which provided millions of dollars in economic and military aid, helped Nicaragua secure millions in international banking loans, and earned millions supplying Nicaragua with the majority of its imported U.S. goods. U.S. profits in the hundreds of millions of dollars also derived from its control of thousands of acres of farmland as well as the country's mining, lumber, railroads, and banking industries (Garcia, 2006).

As with El Salvador and Guatemala, the majority of Nicaragua's population of three million lived in extreme poverty while the Somoza family's net worth of a billion dollars derived from controlling the nation's construction, meatpacking, and fishing industries, as well as a third of the country's best farmlands (Garcia, 2006). Naturally, resistance emerged frequently from labor organizers, journalists, students, and the church, and just as predictably the U.S.-trained National Guard hammered down mercilessly on the slightest sign of resistance or protest.

One natural and one manmade crisis during the 1970s were pivotal in finally turning the tide against the repressive Somoza regime (Garcia, 2006). The first was the devastating earthquake of 1972 that destroyed much of the capital city of Managua, giving opposition forces a unique opportunity to step up strikes and protests against a vulnerable government. While not surprised, the public was incensed by the Somoza family pocketing millions of dollars in earthquake relief donations from around the world.

Pedro Joaquin Chamorro, editor of Guatemala's *La Prensa* [The Press], documented government corruption such as the theft of international disaster relief funds, stoking demonstrations. For the remainder of the 1970s the FSLN attacked government offices and military garrisons while kidnapping and ransoming political and business leaders. While the National Guard counter-attacked by torturing, imprisoning, and murdering members of the opposition, including political moderates, the assassination of Juan Pedro Chamorro in 1978 triggered a nationwide strike and insurrection, with the Sandinistas gaining control of most of Nicaragua by 1979. This same year, the United States arranged for Anastacio Somoza Jr. and senior members of the National Guard members to safely flee to Miami, Florida, for a rich and comfortable retirement.

Between 1979 and 1982, cleavages within the new Sandinista government saw moderates lose out to hardline socialists who suspended elections, clamped down on free speech and press, exported arms and advisers to neighboring El Salvador, and began to fortify the military against *contra-revolucionairos* [counter-revolutionaries] or *Contras*, who wanted to take back the government with U.S. backing and support. Key moderates resigned from the new leftist government including Violeta Chamorro, wife of the slain *La Prensa* editor, and *Comandante Zero* (Eden Pastora Gomez), heroic leader of the attack on National Palace in Managua. Many middle and upper class Nicaraguans also chose to leave the country, which may partly account for the noticeably better SES of Nicaraguan Americans relative to other Central Americans in the United States.

During the waning years of the Somoza dictatorship, President Jimmy Carter withdrew U.S. aid for humanitarian rights violations, and he was quick to recognize and support the new socialist Sandinista government. Between 1979 and 1980 the United States provided $100 million in emergency aid and facilitated acquisition of another $200 million in international loans and grants, in the hope of avoiding another cold war Cuban scenario. However, Nicaragua's shipment of arms to El Salvador, along with the presence of Soviet and Cuban advisers, proved intolerable for the Carter administration, and millions in promised aid were quickly cancelled. But the worst in U.S. interference was yet to come.

The Reagan Administration in Nicaragua
Between 1981 and 1990, President Reagan and his administration's aversion to socialist victories in Latin America resulted in massive, scandalous, and illegal military and economic support of the anti-Sandinista Contras, fueling yet another bloody decade of civil war just as was done in El Salvador. According to Garcia (2006), CIA-trained Contras not only bombed industrial and economic targets but also kidnapped and murdered members of the Nicaragua's leftist government. The CIA also violated international law by directly assisting with the mining of Nicaraguan harbors and bombing of oil refineries, actions condemned by the United Nation's International Court of Justice (ICJ) in 1986. The ICJ ruled in favor of Nicaragua and against the United States, awarding reparations to Nicaragua that the United States never paid after refusing to participate further in the U.N. proceedings and blocking enforcement of the U.N. Security Council's judgment (Wikipedia, 2018a).

Despite the U.S. Congress prohibiting further aid to the Contras in 1984, key members of the Reagan administration engineered the illegal sale of arms to Iran in order to funnel profits to the Contras. Despite the scandalous findings of the congressional Iran–Contra hearings of 1987, indicting 14 of Reagan's senior officials, a weakened Sandinista government agreed to free elections in 1989, leading to the victory of Violeta Chamorro, who had become a moderate National Opposition Union candidate in 1990. Chamorro's campaign had been supported by millions in U.S. dollars, followed by millions more to help rebuild a less left-leaning Nicaragua. With regard to the ICJ ruling noted above, Chamorro withdrew the complaint from the U.N. in September 1992, following a repeal of the law that required Nicaragua to seek compensation from the United States. However, the high price paid for regime change in Nicaragua included an estimated 30,000 dead, 50,000 wounded, 300,000 homeless, and over a million Nicaraguans living outside of their country, with the majority choosing the United States with little intention of return (Garcia, 2005).

Conflict

Like other Central Americans in the United States, Nicaraguans faced a loose patchwork of efforts to address their undocumented status, including generally denied applications for asylum despite fleeing a communist government, the very same rationale for providing Cuban exiles with generous refugee status from the 1960s through the 1980s. Yet, when the Sandinistas came to power in 1979, President Carter provided only Extended Voluntary Departure (EVD) to Nicaraguans rather than full refugee status with all benefits included.

In contrast, the Reagan administration during the 1980s created the Nicaraguan Review Program, charged with re-reviewing denied asylum applications, granting thousands in the process, in order to bolster Reagan's request that Congress continue funding the Contra rebels in Nicaragua. However, when Congress eventually refused to support the Contras, the granting of Nicaraguan asylum applications by Reagan's attorney general also declined. Further, when the Sandinista party lost the election in 1990, returning the country to a noncommunist government, over 20,000 pending Nicaraguan asylum applications suddenly lost their political usefulness and thus chance of succeeding.

Nicaraguan Adjustment and Central American Relief Act (1997)

Modeling their Cuban American neighbors in South Florida, Nicaraguans formed dozens of community and political organizations advocating for safe haven, staging hunger strikes for work authorization, raising legal fees for detained compatriots, demanding an end to deportation, and asking to be embraced by the United States as were Cubans from the 1960s through the 1980s. While Nicaraguans may have been more politically divided than Cuban refugees, they understood the potential benefits of being perceived to be in the same historical predicament as Cuban Americans beginning in the early 1960s.

For example, 40,000 Nicaraguans sued the U.S. government in response to the impact of IIRIRA (1996), which limited the cancellation of deportation to only those with 10 or more continuous years in the United States who could prove "extreme and exceptional hardship" if returned to country of origin (Garcia, 2006; p. 117). With the strong support of Cuban American allies, including elected officials such as Florida Congressman Lincoln Diaz-Balart who initiated the bill, Congress passed the Nicaraguan Adjustment and Central American Relief Act (1997) that allowed Nicaraguans in the United States as of December 1, 1995, to adjust their status to Legal Permanent Residents (LPR) or green card holders.

While the Relief Act primarily benefited Nicaraguans, it also benefited some Salvadoran and Guatemalans who became eligible for deportation cancellation under pre-IIRIRA (1996) rules (i.e., in U.S. for seven continuous years, able to prove extreme hardship for self or first-degree family member if deported). One result of the above immigration politics is that Nicaraguans have fared better than most Central Americans in terms of adjusting their undocumented status, and consequently gaining the opportunity to earn an SES profile that compares favorably with other U.S. Latino populations.

Social Positionality of Nicaraguans

By the end of the 1980s, tens of thousands of predominately working class and undocumented Nicaraguans had fled to major U.S. cities such as Los Angeles, Houston, San Francisco, and New York, with almost 200,000 or 40% settling into Dade County, Florida, where the city of Sweetwater became dubbed "Little Managua" (Garcia, 2006c). They are one of the smallest Central American populations in the United States. At 381,000, they are less than a third the number of Guatemalan Americans and a fifth the number of Salvadoran Americans.

Interestingly, Nicaraguans are both highly immigrant (58% versus 35% of Latinos in general) and highly U.S. citizens (56%), and about 60% have been in the country for 20 years or more (Lopez, 2015c). English proficiency is reported by nearly two-thirds of Nicaraguans ages five and older, while the remaining 37% report speaking English less than very well versus 32% of all Latinos. Given their relatively greater success with adjusting immigration status, almost a quarter of Nicaraguans aged 25 and older have a bachelor's degree versus 16% of all U.S. Latinos and 33% of the entire U.S. population, and their annual household income ($50,000) is higher than most Latinos ($41,000) and just below that of the U.S. population as a whole ($52,000) (Lopez, 2015c). Evident in this profile are the social capital benefits of documented immigration status.

Consequently, poverty levels for Nicaraguans (13%) are about equivalent for the general U.S. population (12%) and thus lower than for U.S. Latinos overall (19%) (Zambrana et al., 2021). Given the above data, it is surprising that about 31% of Nicaraguans lack health insurance, similar to Latinos in general (29%), and 15% of the general U.S. population (Lopez, 2015). Thus, Nicaraguans have higher SES than other Central American and Latino populations in general, yet still have unique needs shaped by Latino minority status laced with civil war trauma and continuing limited forms of immigration status for many.

Dominican Americans

The Dominican Republic (DR) occupies about two-thirds of the Caribbean Island of Hispañola, with the other third belonging to Haiti. A brief overview of the DR's tumultuous, nearly 200-year history begins here with its liberation from Spain, for a second time, in 1821, only to be taken over by Haiti three times from 1822 through 1844. The latter provides some insight into historical tensions between Haitians and Dominicans, and atrocities in both directions. Liberation resurfaced from 1844 to 1861 until the DR was annexed back to Spain, but only for four years, after which an insurgency led by Ramon Baez regained independence in 1865. In 1866, Baez assumed the presidency and offered to sell parts of, or the entire DR to the United States, much to the chagrin of the Dominican people, who organized a resistance movement.

Contact

In an act of what came to be known as "gunboat diplomacy" (see Sidebar 2.4), the United States sent battleships to support Baez and his crackdown on resistance, and occupied the DR between 1869 and 1871 (Hollander, 1907). However, in 1871 Congress voted against President Ulysses S. Grant's treaty to annex the DR and his dreams of America owning this island country (Wikipedia, 2018b). Nevertheless, major business deals were struck between the United States and DR president and dictator Ulises Heureaux during the 1890s (e.g., booming sugar industry, management of ports, customs, and all transportation between the DR and New York). However, business dealings came to an abrupt halt when Heureaux was assassinated in 1899, resulting in continued political turmoil, including European debt collectors descending upon the DR, causing the United States to become incensed about continued European involvement in the Western Hemisphere, a region to which the United States now felt strongly entitled (Wikipedia, 2018c).

Sidebar 2.4. Gunboat Diplomacy

Gunboat Diplomacy refers to the use of military threats by a strong country against a weaker one in order to make that country obey it (Cambridge Dictionary, 2018). However, the term is most often associated with the activities of the Great Powers in the second half of the nineteenth century and the early twentieth century. During this period, the construction of steel-hulled vessels of relatively shallow draught (i.e., gunboats) that were heavily armed provided new opportunities for the projection of power on the part of rival imperial powers. In the case of the United States, gunboat diplomacy is historically associated with Washington DC's diplomatic and military interventions throughout the Caribbean during the early decades of the 20th century (Dictionary of American History, 2018).

In 1904, President Theodore Roosevelt invoked the Monroe Doctrine to justify the United States taking control of all DR ports of U.S. customs while training and supporting the U.S. puppet dictator and president, Carlos Morales (1903 to 1905) (see Sidebar 2.5). Between 1907 and 1940, the United States controlled all DR finances despite continuous rumblings of popular resistance. In 1914, President Wilson implemented the Wilson Plan in the attempted to quell feuding DR factions, resulting in the election of Juan Isidro Jimenez, who abandoned the presidency after two years when opposition leader Desiderio Arias staged a coup. The United States responded to the political turmoil by once again occupying the DR between 1916 and 1924 and installing General Horacio Vasquez as president from 1924 to 1930.

During the eight-year U.S. occupation of the DR, many improvements were made in the country's infrastructure in such areas as roadways and transportation, sanitation, health, and public works, while the United States enjoyed the benefit of free trade and saturating the DR market with American products, under the Tariff Act (1919). As a result, poor subsistence farmers lost their land and became hired hands on their previously owned farms, and Dominicans developed an enduring preference for American products and culture (e.g., baseball versus cockfighting) (Torres-Saillant & Hernandez, 1998). Also, during this second occupation, U.S. Marines trained Rafael Trujillo, who rose from army lieutenant in 1918 to commander of the

---

Sidebar 2.5. Monroe Doctrine

Around the time that most Latin American countries were liberating themselves from Spain, United States president James Monroe, in a message to Congress in 1823, put Europe on notice by declaring that any further attempt by a European power to oppress or control any nation in the Western Hemisphere would be viewed as a hostile act against the United States (Encyclopedia Britannica, 2018c). While initially cheered by newly independent Latin American nations, the United States soon claimed the entire Western Hemisphere as its sphere of influence as it emerged as a world power. Thus, the Monroe Doctrine soon included the United States' patriarchal self-proclaimed right to police Latin America and to intervene in the internal affairs of any country it perceived to be unruly, mismanaged, or involved in what it considered wrongdoings. The rest, as they say, is history.

national police (1919–1925) and then to general in 1927, three years before he would take over the country.

President Vasquez proved to be so incompetent and corrupt that revolution broke out and overthrew his presidency. Interestingly, General Rafael "El Jefe" Trujillo ordered the military to stand by and allow the revolution to succeed in ousting Vasquez so that Trujillo could claim the presidency for himself, ushering in what would become one of the longest and cruelest dictatorships in 20th century Latin America.

Trujillo Regime (1930 and 1961)

Under the expert guidance of the U.S. armed forces, Trujillo and his violent military regime ushered in a 30-year reign of terror until his assassination in 1961. In the effort to exercise complete control over the DR, Trujillo commanded the army, installed family members in his cabinet, had political opponents murdered, and created a secret police force to detect the slightest resistance and respond with intimidation, harassment, exile, imprisonment, and brutal murders (Wikipedia, 2018d). The secret police were well known for assassinating members of the opposition by staging thousands of supposed accidents and suicides.

Trujillo renamed the capital city of Santo Domingo, Trujillo City, and erected a continuously illuminated sign broadcasting "God and Trujillo." He also mass-produced statues of himself as monuments throughout the country, and declared his Dominican Party to be the nation's only political party, requiring everyone be card-carrying members or face dire consequences (i.e., visits from the secret police).

While credited with bringing unprecedented peace and even prosperity to the DR, this came at the cost of political and civil liberties as well as multiple millions in kickbacks extracted by Trujillo from virtually all major business contracts throughout the country. Trujillo also openly encouraged anti-Haitian racism and discrimination, and in 1937 ordered the massacre of thousands of Haitians living in the DR. This massacre, ostensibly for crimes committed, was part of Trujillo's racial whitening campaign designed to lighten the complexion of the Dominican population, which also included encouraging immigration from Europe.

Trujillo versus the Butterflies of Freedom

Despite Trujillo's repressive police state, where merely criticizing the government prompted visits from the secret police, underground opposition and activism grew throughout the regime, as best exemplified by the heroic Mirabel sisters. Patricia, Minerva, and Maria Theresa were courageous, college educated, and beautiful middle class sisters committed to freedom, democracy, and the overthrow of Trujillo. Using the codename *Las Marioposas* or *The Butterflies*, the Mirabel sisters began *The 14th of June* movement, named after the date of a massacre witnessed by Patricia (or "Patria" as she was called). A fourth sister, Dedé, was disallowed from participating in political activism by her husband.

Minerva studied law but was denied a license to practice after turning down romantic advances from Trujillo, who preyed on women. Instead, she was followed and harassed by the secret police, as were her activist sisters. Soon the sisters, as well as their activist husbands, were repeatedly jailed for their resistance. In 1960, the Organization of American States condemned Trujillo's retaliation and sent witnesses to the DR, prompting the release of the sisters from prison, but not their husbands. On November 25, 1960, during a trip to visit their husbands in prison, the three sisters, along with their driver, were stopped by the secret police, who strangled and clubbed them to death, returned their bodies to their car, and pushed the vehicle off a cliff as a feebly staged accident.

1960 was also the year that Trujillo mounted a failed assassination attempt on the president of Venezuela, Romulo Betancourt, who he believed was plotting against him. After decades of evading sufficient scrutiny, Trujillo's mounting crimes and human rights violations were finally condemned by the Organization of American States, which also imposed sanctions on the DR, and the United States finally terminated its decades of profitable but unethical support for the cruel dictator (Encyclopedia Britannica, 2018b).

In the aftermath of the Maribel assassinations, the three sisters became national martyrs included in the DR's National Museum of History and Geography, public school curriculum, and monuments throughout the DR. Surviving sister Dedé, who passed away in 2014 at the age of 88, dedicated her life to the legacy of her sisters. She opened the Mirabel Sisters Museum, and wrote the 2009 book *Vivas en su Jardin* [Alive in their garden], *The true history of the Mirabel sisters and their struggle for their freedom*. She also raised Minerva's daughter, now a prominent public figure in the DR, in addition to her own children.

As global symbols of social justice and feminism, many honors have been bestowed upon Las Mariposas including the United Nations General Assembly designation of November 25 as International Day for the

Elimination of Violence against Women in 1999. In the DR, the sisters' native province of Salcedo was renamed *Hermanas Mirabel* province in 2007; their image now graces the 200 peso bill, as well as a commemorative stamp, and a mural honoring the sisters now covers the 137-foot obelisk that Trujillo constructed in 1935 to commemorate the renaming of the capital city after himself. In 1994, prolific Dominican author Julia Alvarez wrote the fictionalized novel, *In the Time of the Butterflies*, in honor of the Mirabel sisters, which became a motion picture in 2001 starring Salma Hayek as Minerva and Edward James Olmos as Rafael Trujillo.

After the assassination of Trujillo in 1961, socialist democrat Juan Bosch won the presidency in 1962 with over 60% of the popular vote, but served only for a mere seven months, after which he was overthrown by a conservative coalition of Dominican elites including industrialists, landowners, members of Trujillo's military, and even the Catholic Church. The right-wing coalition was so unpopular that it provoked a civil war fueled by a liberal faction of the military, demanding the return of constitutionally elected President Juan Bosch. Hence these left-wing revolutionaries became known as the *constitucionalistas*.

Chronic fear of "another Cuba" and the loss of major U.S. business holdings led President Lyndon Johnson to order 42,000 U.S. troops into the DR in April of 1965 to support Trujillo's former army and the conservative right-wing coalition. By September of 1965, the popular rebellion was defeated, a peace treaty was signed and, under U.S. supervision, a presidential election was held in 1966 resulting in the installation of Joaquin Balaguer, the last of Trujillo-related puppet presidents, supported by a DR military trained by American Marines and financially supported by the United States.

Social Positionality of Dominicans

During Trujillo's police state regime, Dominicans were forbidden from traveling outside of the country in order to deter losing workers and to prevent people from denouncing the government abroad. Shortly after Trujillo's assassination in 1961, Dominicans began migrating to the United States in record numbers (Torres-Saillant & Hernandez, 1998). For example, while only 4,603 immigrated to the United States in 1962, the number more than doubled to 10,683 in 1963, with momentum continuing through the 1990s. In the decade between 1962 and 1972, Dominican immigrants averaged 11,445 per year, which increased to 16,000 annually during the 1970s and over 30,000 each year during the 1980s. In 1991 and 1992, over 40,000 Dominicans entered the United States, twice the annual limit of 20,000 per country set by the INS (Torres-Saillant & Hernandez, 1998). Another factor in the dramatic rise in visas granted to Dominicans was the United States' strategic safety-valve role in allowing those outraged by U.S. puppet President Balaguer's government to leave the country, in hopes of avoiding yet another revolution.

The rapidly growing Dominican American population more than tripled from over half a million in 1990 to 1.8 million today. About 55% of Dominicans are immigrant versus 35% of Latinos in general, 50% are U.S. citizens, and about 40% have been in the United States for 20 years or more (Lopez, 2015d). English proficiency is reported by 57% of Dominicans ages five and older, while the remaining 43% report speaking English less than very well versus 32% of all Latinos. Similar to Nicaraguans, 17% of Dominicans aged 25 and older have a bachelor's degree versus 14% of all U.S. Latinos, and 33% of the entire U.S. population. However, their annual household income ($43,000) is lower than for Latinos in general ($49,000), and much lower than for the U.S. population ($52,000) (Lopez, 2015d; Zambrana et al., 2021).

Consequently, level of poverty for Dominicans (22%) is much higher than for the general U.S. population (12%) and slightly higher than for U.S. Latinos overall (19%). About 21% of Dominicans lack health insurance, as compared to 29% of Latinos in general and 15% of the general U.S. population (Lopez, 2015d). Thus, Dominicans have a significant rate of poverty despite slightly better education and health insurance rates. With 80% of Dominicans residing in the northeastern United States, including half in New York alone, they are an especially concentrated population of Latino Americans.

Unfortunately, the massive arrival of Dominicans into New York, especially between 1980 and 1990, coincided with major neoliberal economic restructuring in the city from industrial manufacturing jobs (e.g., apparel) with living wages, to a more service sector economy (e.g., restaurants, bars, retail stores) dependent upon unskilled labor in exchange for poor wages, few benefits, and little if any upward mobility (Torres-Saillant & Hernandez, 1998). For example, Dominicans employed in the manufacturing industry decreased from just almost 50% in 1980 to just over a quarter in 1990. Conversely, Dominicans in New York are underrepresented in better paying professional and managerial jobs as compared to NLW, NLB, and other

Latino counterparts, despite Dominican men having the highest work participation rates among any ethnic group in New York. One visible response of Dominicans to dead-end service sector jobs has been relatively high participation in small ethnic businesses that serve the Dominican communities. Bodegas and independent supermarkets catering to inner-city residents are entrepreneurial examples of Dominicans in New York and New Jersey neighborhoods. Hence, there is considerable urban-based economic agency on the part of Dominican Americans, as well as fair levels of education and health care with which to mitigate the ill effects of poverty. Complementary social and human services can further support this relatively new and growing Latino population in the United States.

Conclusion

In conveying some of the salient details of Central American and Dominican acculturation and adjustment to the United States, this chapter touched upon the post-colonial and 20th-century histories of these countries in order to highlight two major overarching themes. The first is that while Berry's three-phase model of acculturation conceptualizes *conditions of contact* as beginning when minority groups become part of the majority group, for U.S. Latinos conditions of contact typically preceded becoming minority groups, given America's extensive history of self-serving and entitled intrusions throughout Latin America. In fact, Berry's second phase acculturation, *conflict* between minority and majority groups, also appears to occur decades before most Latino minority group members enter U.S. society, albeit in more indirect forms of conflict, as when revolutionary factions fight U.S.-backed military dictatorships. That is, conflict caused or exacerbated by U.S. involvement in Central America and the Dominican Republic, as reviewed in this chapter, as well as U.S. involvement in Mexico, Puerto Rico, and Cuba, as reviewed in Chapter 1. Hence, the boundaries between Berry's three phases of acculturation appears more blurred than originally conceptualized, especially for Latinos in America.

The second take-home theme in this chapter is that it is precisely because of a calculated U.S. pattern of involvement in Central America and the Dominican Republic that so many members of these nations have become Latino ethnic minority groups in our society. Such involvement in Latin America begs a nagging question: If the United States was so concerned about the spread of communism, then why support repressive right-wing dictatorships that foment socialist resistance and revolutions? The missed opportunity that jumps out from this reading is the ignored win–win scenario of conducting ethical business with Latin American governments contingent upon supporting human rights and inclusion of citizens in the economic, political, and social prosperity of such developing nations.

The popular but less uniformed view of Latinos as simply economic immigrants, pushed by poverty and corrupt governments and pulled by opportunities in the United States, is far from the full story, although clearly immigration continues from Latin America. However, it is more accurate and informative to conclude that America's historical self-interest and support of right-wing dictatorships contributed to decades of repression, revolution, civil wars, and the need for millions of Latinos to escape their countries of origin, frequently seeking refuge in America where the probability of surviving and thriving is better than in most other countries. While the United States is unlikely to recognize its accountability to such U.S. Latino populations, it's important that such populations, and their political and practitioner allies, resist and protest the continuation of anti-Latino rhetoric and policies today.

References

Bonner, R. (2016). Time for a U.S. apology to El Salvador. The Nation, April 15. CNN. http://money.cnn.com/2018/01/08/news/economy/el-salvador-remittances/index.html

Cambridge Dictionary (2018). Gunboat Diplomacy. https://dictionary.cambridge.org/us/dictionary/english/gunboat-diplomacy

Ford, W. P. (1984). *A little justice in El Salvador*. New York Times (May 31st). https://www.nytimes.com/1984/05/31/opinion/a-little-justice-in-salvador.html

Cordova, C. B. (2005). *The Salvadoran Americans*. Westport, CT: Greenwood Press.

Dictionary of American History (2018). Gunboat diplomacy. http://www.encyclopedia.com/history/dictionaries-thesauruses-pictures-and-press-releases/gunboat-diplomacy

Encyclopedia Britannica (2018a). Liberation Theology. https://www.britannica.com/topic/liberation-theology

Encyclopedia Britannica (2018b). Dominican Republic/Caudillos. https://www.britannica.com/place/Dominican-Republic/Caudillos

Encyclopedia Britannica (2018c). Monroe Doctrine. https://www.britannica.com/event/Monroe-Doctrine

Garcia, M. C. (2006). *Seeking refuge: Central American migration to Mexico, the United States & Canada*. Berkeley, CA: University of California Press.

Gillespie, P. (2018). Trump clamps down on El Salvador's lifeline. CNNMoney, January 8. http://money.cnn.com/2018/01/08/news/economy/el-salvador-remittances/index.html

Healey, J. F., & O'Brien, E. (2015). Hispanic Americans. In J. F. Healey & E. O'Brien (Eds.), *Race, ethnicity, gender, & class: The sociology of group conflict and change* (pp. 214–249). Los Angeles: Sage.

Hollander, J. H. (1907). The Convention of 1907 between the United States and the Dominican Republic. *The American Journal of International Law*, *1*(2) (Apr., 1907), 287–296.

Jonas, S., & Rodriguez, N. (2014). *Guatemala-U.S. migration: Transforming regions.* Austin: University of Texas Press.

Jordan, M. (2018). Trump administration says that nearly 200,000 Salvadorans must leave. *New York Times.* https://www.nytimes.com/2018/01/08/us/salvadorans-tps-end.html

Lopez, G. (2015a). Hispanics of Salvadoran origin in the United States, 2013. Washington DC: Pew Research Center, September.

Lopez, G. (2015b). Hispanics of Guatemalan origin in the United States, 2013. Washington DC: Pew Research Center, September.

Lopez, G. (2015c). Hispanics of Nicaraguan origin in the United States, 2013. Washington DC: Pew Research Center, September.

Lopez, G. (2015d). Hispanics of Dominican origin in the United States, 2013. Washington DC: Pew Research Center, September.

Lovato, R. (2018). El Salvador's worst shitholes are 'Made in America'. North American Congress on Latin America (NACLA). New York City. https://nacla.org

NBC 10 Staff (2017). AG Jeff Sessions takes aim at 'brutal' MS-13 gang in speech to police chiefs in Philadelphia. National Broadcasting Company (October 23). https://www.nbcphiladelphia.com/news/local/MS-13-Jeff-Sessions-Police-Chiefs-452477613.html

Teaching Central America. (2018). History of El Salvador. http://www.teachingcentralamerica.org/history-of-el-salvador

Torres-Saillant, S., & Hernandez, R. (1998). *The Dominican Americans.* Westport, CT: Greenwood Press.

Wikipedia (2018a). Nicaragua. https://en.wikipedia.orgwiki/Nicaragua_v._United_States

Wikipedia (2018b). Buenaventura. https://en.wikipedia.org/wiki/Buenaventura

Wikipedia (2018c). Biography/Ulises Heureax. https://www.britannica.com/biography/Ulises-Heureaux

Wikipedia (2018d). Biography/Rafael Trujillo. https://www.britannica.com/biography/Rafael-Trujillo

3

The Social Stratification of Latino Ethnicity, Power, and Social Positionality in the United States

The sociological concept of *social stratification* is extremely helpful for understanding Latino social positionality, or where this population is located relative to other race/ethnic groups in the American hierarchy of power and resources needed for social mobility and well-being. This analysis picks up where the study of Latino acculturation and social positionality left off in Chapters 1 and 2. That is, while acculturation theory imparts understanding of the general historical through present day dynamics of group-level dominance and subordination, social stratification elucidates how a group's social location becomes formally and informally institutionalized and justified by mainstream ideologies, core values, and narratives.

In analyzing the social stratification of Latinos in America, this chapter provides socioeconomic profiles of the major Latino groups under study that convey uneven levels of incorporation and integration into mainstream society. These profiles emphasize the socioeconomic dimensions of the Latino experience, with some attention to political participation addressed more fully in Chapters 11 and 12.

The Concept of Social Stratification

According to Marger (2012a), *stratification* refers to the structured inequality of society's power, resources, and opportunities as regulated by the government and, more specifically, by key government institutions such as its political system, economic sector, educational and health care systems, social services, and so on. That is, stratification refers to inequality by design, or how all societies are biased in favor of those groups with the most power

Solving Latino Psychosocial and Health Problems. Kurt C. Organista, Oxford University Press.
© Oxford University Press 2023. DOI: 10.1093/oso/9780190059637.003.0003

and against those with the least. Such glaring social inequities are justified by ideologies, values, and dominant narratives that rationalize and "explain" inequality in ways that stabilize stratification, or the "status quo," partly by impeding progress toward a more just distribution of life-supporting and enhancing power and resources.

Because stratification is the case the world over, it appears that we human beings characteristically monopolize resources and power and organize ourselves into unequal social hierarchies or strata responsible for varying degrees of tension and discord. International comparisons allow some insight into our own stratification system. For example, Central American countries such as El Salvador, Nicaragua, and Guatemala continue to manifest extremely unequal "pyramid shaped" stratification systems in which tiny elite ruling classes, which comprise single-digit percentages of the population, typically own between a third and the vast majority of land, industries, and businesses, resulting in extreme labor exploitation, oppression, and abject poverty seen in developing or least developing countries (Cordova, 1987; Ferris, 1987). By comparison, our own U.S. stratification system has historically insured a better distribution of wealth, resources, and opportunities, resulting in most people achieving middle class status with fewer people at the extremes of poverty or affluence, ideally approximating more of a squat "diamond shaped" distribution. However, dramatically rising wealth inequality, particularly during the past 50 years, has begun to reverse the fairer distribution of wealth in America that peaked during the middle of the 20th century. The result is today's more literal and metaphoric "teardrop" shaped distribution as depicted in Figure 3.1.

For example, stratification data from the 2000 U.S. Census, used in the first 2007 edition of this book, showed that a majority of between 50% and 60% of Americans were middle class, about 28% were working class, a minority or 15% were poor, and a much smaller minority of 1%–2% were super-rich or elite. However, just 10 years later, 2010 Census data reveal that 44% or a minority of Americans are middle class, a quarter are working class, 30%, or twice as many, are poor, and 1% are among the super-elite (Healey et al., 2019a). Such rapidly growing wealth inequality, and relatedly the Great Recession of 2008–2009, motivated 2011's Occupy Wall Street movement throughout the United States, during which protesters blocked or encamped upon public spaces only to be eventually be cleared away by law enforcement.

"Occupy" protested accelerating income inequality and corporate greed stemming from neoliberal economics, an ideology and policy model of

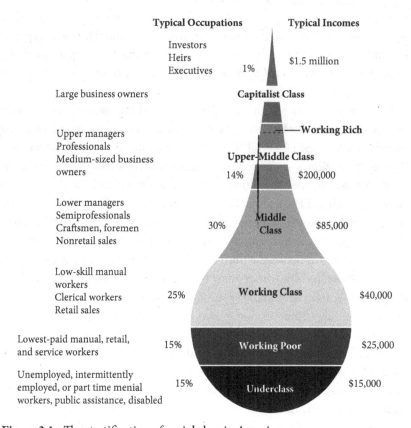

Figure 3.1. The stratification of social class in America.

From Gilbert, D. L. (2011). *The American Class Structure in an Age of Growing Inequality*. Thousand Oaks, CA: Pine Forge Press. Reprinted with permission from Sage.

free market capitalism characterized by the privatization of social services and goods, with minimal government regulation, international free trade, outsourcing work for maximum profit, and excessive faith in the "invisible hand" of the competitive free market to resolve economic as well as social problems (Encyclopedia Britannica, 2019). Embraced by the Reagan administration during the 1980s, neoliberal economics resulted in hollowing out major domestic manufacturing sectors, outsourcing once vital work to cheap exploited labor around the world, and leaving a displaced working class with few safety nets given gutted government programs that were casualties of major tax cuts for corporate America. Despite the failure of Reagan's "trickle-down economics" (profits and savings that were supposed to trickle down to the average consumer), major corporate tax breaks were repeated by the George W. Bush administration (2001–2009) leading up to the Great Recession of 2008–2009, or the worst economic crisis in America since the Great Depression of 1929.

Wealth inequality is most harmful to economically vulnerable populations, disproportionately Latinos and African Americans but increasingly the white working class, and our overtaxed and shrinking middle class (Putnam, 2017). Yet, rather than hold the government responsible for under-protecting displaced workers (e.g., with financial support, retraining, and educational opportunities) that comprise our shrinking middle class, and for over-protecting the corporate sector from paying its fair share of taxes, voters elected an elite corporate president in 2016 that further slashed corporate taxes, exacerbating toxic wealth inequality like the W. Bush and Reagan administrations before him.

Economist, professor of public policy at UC Berkeley, and former Secretary of Labor under President Clinton, Robert Reich (2007) shares several dramatic indicators of wealth inequality in his book on *Supercapitalism*. For instance, between 1936 and 1989, the ratio of CEO compensation to their average worker's pay vacillated between 35:1 and 75:1. However, by the beginning of the 21st century, the ratio accelerated to about 370:1. With regard to the nation's super-elite or richest 1%, Reich notes that by the dawn of the 21st century the approximately 1.5 million families in this elite category owned over a third of the nation's wealth, or more than the bottom 90% combined.

Dimensions of Stratification

With regard to dimensions of stratification, Karl Marx is most famous for his focus on societies divided into those who control the means of production and those who do not (i.e., the famous "haves" and "have nots"). In Marx's classic theory of economic determinism, he views the division between the ruling and working classes as the basis for social-political tension and struggle over access to resources and power. In addition to the central economic dimension of social stratification, there are several other interrelated dimensions that work in concert to influence probabilities of success and failure for different groups in society. Further, Marxism's deep faith in communism to promote equality paid little attention to the role of racism and discrimination in multicultural societies where social class and race/ethnicity are hugely conflated.

Lenski's (1966) classic multidimensional model of stratification is described as consisting of several hierarchical sub-class systems, each of which is based on a key social criterion such as political power, occupation, education, property ownership, and so on. Together, these interacting class systems compose a society's *distributive system* for allocating resources and opportunities to its members. Lenski's distributive model of stratification is important because it reveals the relative importance or interaction of sub-class systems in determining a group's social positionality throughout the entire social stratification system.

Central to the current discussion of Latinos, as well as other racial and ethnic minority groups, is Lenski's insightful inclusion of an *ethnic class system* to illustrate the relation between race/ethnicity and other class systems, or the consistency of locations across class systems for different racial and ethnic groups in multicultural societies as elaborated below.

Ethnic Stratification of Power and Inequality

Lenski's multidimensional model of social stratification, including its race/ethnic class system, is depicted in Figure 3.2 to illustrate various locations of major racial/ethnic groups within the hierarchical U.S. distributive system. As can be seen, four major sub-class systems are included: the political, property, occupational, and ethnic class systems. More class systems can be added to the extent that they are relevant to the discussion at hand (e.g., education). Of utmost importance is the powerful relation between race/ethnicity and a group's position or location across all other class systems—that is, the consistent relation between race/ethnicity, power, resources, and consequent social positionality. As with the acculturation framework, this model of stratification elucidates *non-random* patterns of SES disparities and consequent psychosocial and health problems that continue to be systemically linked to racial/ethnic minority status.

In addition to Lenski's depiction of the racialized U.S. stratification system, adapted in Figure 3.2, he also illustrated social stratification in a fictional yet highly representative Latin American country, including a race/ethnic class system in such a mestizo society, adapted here in Figure 3.3. Hence, while far less multiracial than the United States, this prototypical Latin American

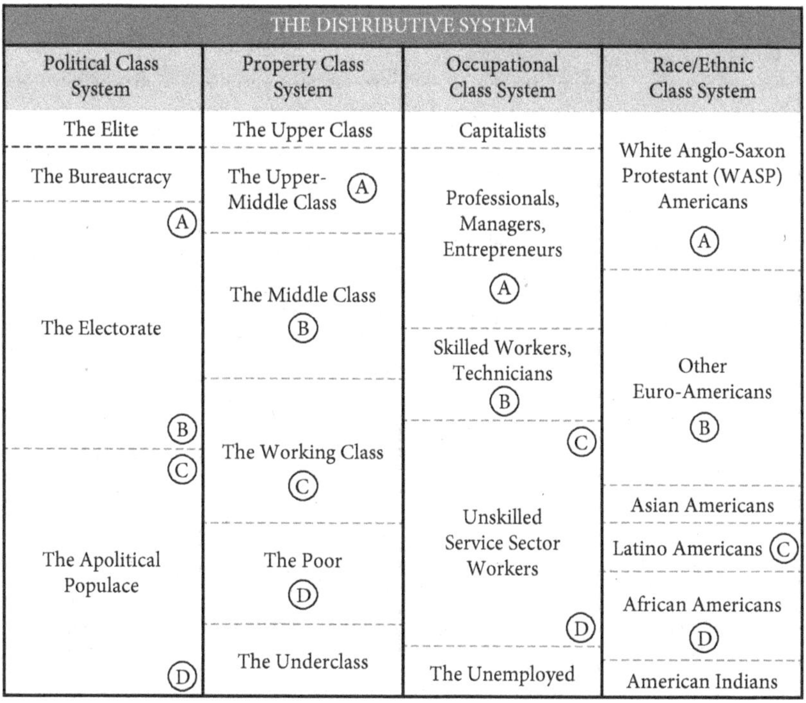

THE DISTRIBUTIVE SYSTEM			
Political Class System	Property Class System	Occupational Class System	Race/Ethnic Class System
The Elite	The Upper Class	Capitalists	White Anglo-Saxon Protestant (WASP) Americans (A)
The Bureaucracy (A)	The Upper-Middle Class (A)	Professionals, Managers, Entrepreneurs (A)	
The Electorate	The Middle Class (B)		Other Euro-Americans (B)
		Skilled Workers, Technicians (B)	
(B) (C)	The Working Class (C)	(C)	
The Apolitical Populace	The Poor (D)	Unskilled Service Sector Workers	Asian Americans
			Latino Americans (C)
		(D)	African Americans (D)
(D)	The Underclass	The Unemployed	American Indians

Figure 3.2. The social stratification of class, race, and power in America. A, B, C, and D represent four individuals or groups.
Adapted from & permission granted by Gerard Lenski.

country also stratifies race/ethnicity and power in ways consistent with racialized stratification systems. As can be seen, more direct descendants of Spanish colonizers predominate at the higher end of the distributive system, with the power to control most resources, while descendants of colonized indigenous people struggle and resist at the lower end, with blended majority mestizos occupying most of the mid-range of this Latin American social stratification system.

Power

It is imperative to underscore the construct of *power* in discussing social stratification as the ability to control the flow of resources in society. Obviously, groups and individuals at the top of a stratification system are the most powerful and influential in this regard, and vice versa. Groups at the top are also highly invested in maintaining and justifying a stratification system

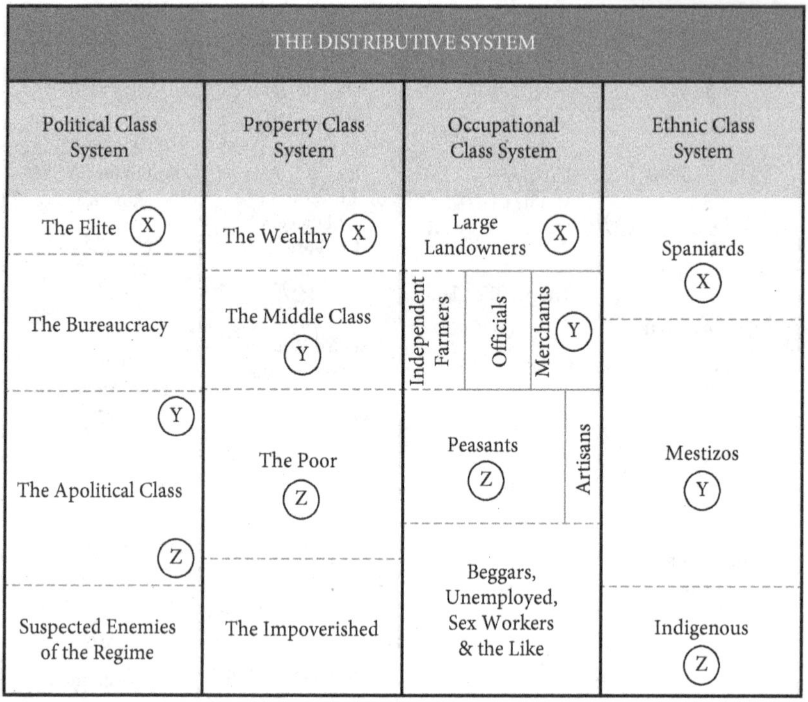

THE DISTRIBUTIVE SYSTEM			
Political Class System	Property Class System	Occupational Class System	Ethnic Class System
The Elite (X)	The Wealthy (X)	Large Landowners (X)	Spaniards (X)
The Bureaucracy	The Middle Class (Y)	Independent Farmers / Officials / Merchants (Y)	
(Y) The Apolitical Class (Z)	The Poor (Z)	Peasants (Z) / Artisans	Mestizos (Y)
Suspected Enemies of the Regime	The Impoverished	Beggars, Unemployed, Sex Workers & the Like	Indigenous (Z)

Figure 3.3. Social stratification of social class and race in a fictional Latin American Country. X, Y, and Z represent three individuals or groups.
Adapted from & permission granted by Gerard Lenski.

that distributes disproportionately greater amounts of resources and favorable life chances to their own group. Complex ideologies, value systems, and cherished national narratives are generated and infused into the socialization process, through mainstream institutions and culture, in order to rationalize and justify a society's particular distribution of precious, life-sustaining, and social mobility enhancing resources.

For example, as we saw in Chapters 1 and 2, historical accounts of American territorial expansion traditionally have been interpreted by historians and depicted in movies as righteous patriotic myths of defending freedom and defeating oppression (e.g., "Remember the Alamo!" in Texas and "Remember the Maine!" in Cuba). Thus, the maintenance of power is accomplished by exercising wide-ranging influence from creating and perpetuating ideologies and attitudes (e.g., via the educational system, media, and popular culture) to the social control of resistance and protest (via law enforcement) that challenge unfair resource and opportunity allocations and attempt to rectify such forms of social injustice.

Immigration

Immigration control is an extremely important dimension of stratification strategically used historically and currently to not only regulate our capacity to absorb immigrants, but also to further consolidate power at the top and to regulate the racial and ethnic composition of American society. Consider, for example, the evolution of policies to restrict immigration that took place when the color and ethnicity of European immigrants went from whiter northern and western Europeans, during the 1800s, to darker southern and eastern European immigrants at the turn of the century and into the early 1900s.

In response to the second great immigration wave, at the turn of the 20th century, Congress passed the Emergency Quota Act of 1921 that limited each European immigrant group to 3% of its U.S. population size based on the 1910 Census. Because northern and western European groups (e.g., British White Anglo Saxon Protestants or WASPs) were of course the largest groups in 1910, this immigration policy strategically allowed far greater numbers of these select groups to immigrate and far fewer numbers of southern and eastern Europeans (McLemore, Romo, & Gonzales, 2001). Then, in 1924, the quota was changed to 2% based on the 1890 census, further restricting the number of southern and eastern European immigrants relative to northern and western. Today, we continue to experience effects of the third major immigration stream, composed this time of even more racially and ethnically distinct people primarily from Latin America and Asia, with fewer immigrants from European countries.

It was not until 1965 that the Immigration and Naturalization Act (INA) abolished the European quota system in order to establish a new immigration policy based mostly on family reunification, as well as extending refuge for those escaping violence and war (History.com, 2019). The INA was partly inspired by the civil rights movement, as well as by earlier protests by discriminated southern and eastern Europeans. As a result, between 1965 and 2000, the largest group of immigrants now came from Mexico (4.3 million), with an additional 1.4 million from Cuba, the Dominican Republic, the Philippines, Korea, Vietnam, and India.

The Western Hemisphere Act of 1976 limited immigration to 20,000 per country, and the Immigration Reform and Control Act (IRCA) of 1986 attempted to curb undocumented Mexican immigration by imposing penalties for employers of undocumented workers. However, IRCA also addressed the high number of undocumented people in the United States by providing a path to citizenship if they could provide evidence of long-term residency, which most did. Sanctions against employers, however, were rarely if ever implemented because of lack of enforcement, a rise in easily obtainable false documents, and because employers easily sidestepped their responsibility as employers by using third-party labor contractors to provide needed work crews (e.g., in farm work). While it took years to pass, IRCA was the last we've seen of urgently needed immigration reform to address our broken immigration system which fails to address undocumented immigration by considering the compatible needs of labor migrants and the U.S. economy.

Recent nativist backlash against predominantly Latino undocumented immigrants includes federal laws to criminalize the estimated 10.5 million such immigrants without authorization to live and work in the United States. Couched in the usual debatable rhetoric of "taking American jobs" and sponging off of social services, along with the new rhetoric of undermining homeland security, these laws have sparked national debates—but this time with the Catholic Church branding such laws as human rights violations, and Latino communities mobilizing locally and nationally to condemn such defamation. An expanded overview of today's anti-immigrant administration, related abuses, and resistance on the part of Latino, immigrant and other pro-immigration rights leaders is provided in Chapter 12.

The Role of Racism

In the context of social stratification, the ideology of racism, or the belief in human hierarchies of inherent racial/ethnic inferiority and superiority, becomes a major driving belief system for justifying discrimination and the unequal distribution across race groups of society's precious resources and opportunity. For example, the colonial conviction that African Americans were genetically inferior subhumans relative to whites justified the practice of slavery for almost two and a half centuries, followed by another 89 years of "separate and unequal" federally mandated segregation and marginalization throughout the country. In the case of Latinos, the belief that Mexicans and Puerto Ricans were an inferior, mixed-race (i.e., mongrel) and docile peasant class was used as a rationale for maintaining exploitative dual wage systems, exclusion from unions, and subduing strikes and attempts to unionize in industries essential to the development of the Southwest (farm work, canning, mining, railroad construction, etc.) and the United States more generally.

Only when stigmatizing and dehumanizing ideologies are challenged can shifts in the stratification system lead to more just distributions of power, resources, and life chances (e.g., civil rights movements). Conversely, when members of various minority groups internalize and believe pervasive racist ideologies, consciously as well as subconsciously, the unchallenged stratification system remains stable, and minorities remain at risk for self-compromising conformity and related racial/ethnic identity problems (addressed in Chapter 4).

Meritocracy and Human Capital Theory

A core American ideology that continues to stabilize structured inequality is the conviction that our society is fair, with opportunity structures open to all that possess sufficient achievement motivation, intelligence, talent, and industriousness to take advantage of such opportunities. This central ideology of *meritocracy* continues to justify the stratification of race/ethnicity and power because it attributes a group's social position to the internal and cultural characteristics of its members, while discounting the external effects of prolonged dominance and subordination and dynamics of stratification.

Similarly, one of the popular socioeconomic theories for understanding gaps in SES between racial and ethnic groups is the meritocracy-friendly *human capital theory* that attributes success to "human capital" or "accrued" assets such as education, job skills, and experience needed to secure well-paying jobs and social mobility. However, while such valuable variables clearly predict SES for everyone, the theory is curiously ignorant of stratification theory and fails to consider how ascribed characteristics, such as race or gender for example, influence the allocation of labor opportunity and rewards, and how dominant groups protect their interests beyond human capital variables (e.g., through exclusive social and professional networks). That is, "fixed" characteristics such as race/ethnicity or gender continue to be rewarded differently.

Thus, human capital theory and meritocracy are *half-truths* that erase or minimize labor history, the disadvantaged starting places of minorities, on-going job discrimination, and the disproportionately negative impact of labor market shifts on Latinos and other economically vulnerable groups. Such labor shifts include neoliberal industrial downsizing and global outsourcing of labor, and the expansion of dead-end service sector work short on living wages, benefits, and vertical mobility.

The political backlash against affirmative action, or merely the consideration of race in college admissions, is emblematic of human capital theory and conviction that people of color should not receive government support because the role of racism and discrimination are minimal or non-existent in determining social positionality. While hard work and experience, skills, and education clearly drive social mobility, the payoff for such social capital is stratified by race/ethnicity and gender. For example, Figure 3.4 dramatically reveals how annual full-time income is stratified not just by education, as we would expect in a meritocracy, but also by gender in ways that reveal socially unjust patriarchy. As can be seen, women continue to receive less financial return on education than men at every equivalent level of education, from less than high school through PhD and professional degrees. Only enforced federal laws can ultimately remedy such sexist manifestations of social stratification.

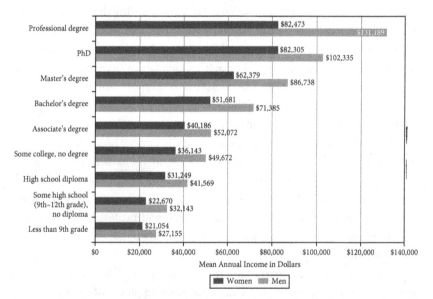

Figure 3.4. Mean annual income by gender and educational attainment for full-time, year-round workers ages 25–64, 2015.

From Healey et al. (2019). Gender. In J. F. Healey, *Race, Ethnicity, Gender & Class: The Sociology of Group Conflict and Change* (pp. 392–429). Los Angeles, CA: Sage. Reprinted with permission.

Interpersonal Prestige and Social Distance

Racial and ethnic stratification also structures our relationships, both personal and work-related, because social prestige and acceptance are stratified or ranked based on a minority group's similarity to the white majority. Biased perceptions of prestige are also shaped by popular culture, formal education, and enduring stereotypes generated about different groups over centuries. Social distance rankings reflect formal and informal interpersonal norms and socialization patterns associated with integration and assimilation. Surveys of social distance norms have been conducted for decades by asking respondents to rank different groups on a seven-point scale ranging from (1) Would marry into group and (2) Would have as a close friend, to (6) Have as visitor only to my nation and (7) Would bar from my country, with (4) Would work in same office as a mid-point (Smith & Dempsey, 1983). Data are compiled from a wide variety of surveys such as the Gallup Poll, National Opinion Research Center, ABC News/Washington Post, University of Michigan's Survey Research Center, and convenience samples of college students from across the country.

Results show that social distance norms not only follow the color gradient evident in our society's ethnic class system, but have remained remarkably stable since 1926 when they were first assessed, through 1977 (Smith & Dempsey, 1983), and again in 2011 when they were once again reassessed by Parillo and Donohough (2013). That is, most favorable ratings are of northern and western Europeans, followed by southern and eastern Europeans, and finally a mix of Asians, Latinos, and Blacks toward the bottom. Only the study by Parillo and Donohough (2013) included Muslims and Arabs, who were ranked lowest given growing Islamophobia since 9/11 and reinforced by the Trump administration's immigration ban on predominantly Muslim countries based on stereotypes of Muslims as terrorists.

Racial and ethnic intermarriage rates are heavily stratified in the United States, given how race/ethnicity is conflated with SESs and hence interpersonal social distance norms as reviewed above. While minority–majority intermarriage rates have slowly increased over the decades, over 90% of whites continue to marry within their own race group, a choice shaped by a historical legacy of self-segregation in residence and work apart from people of color. With regard to intermarriage rates, about 18% of Latinos are married to whites (Choi, 2020) as compared to 11% for African Americans (Healey et al., 2019). In contrast, about 40% of Asian Americans marry outside of their race/ethnic group, primarily to whites.

Racial Privilege

Discussions of "white privilege" and more recently "white fragility" (DiAngelo, 2018) have invigorated the tired national debate about racism in America. Critical white studies aim to de-center white power and privilege by reinserting white people into the analysis of race problems, whereas focusing on "minority disadvantage" not only reifies the deficit model of minorities but also distances whites from their role in race relations, thereby making it easy for them to superficially respond or ignore this immense social problem. Re-engaging whites is partially accomplished by focusing on what they have accrued (e.g., via inherited wealth, influential social networks and contacts) and continue to gain from structural and systemic racism and discrimination, in its many informal and institutionalized forms.

As with the interrogation of all forms of privilege, white privilege is understandably a touchy subject because while most whites are generally willing to admit that racial and ethnic minorities have been discriminated and disadvantaged, they are frequently oblivious to, or only vaguely aware of, the flipside or how whites have been simultaneously advantaged by such conditions of racial inequality. Historically and through today, being racially white has meant significantly better life chances, opportunities, and general well-being in America, and not simply because of meritocracy or returns on social capital. Whites have generally succeeded not only because of their industriousness, skills, and intelligence, but also because their path has been unencumbered by the life-limiting barriers and obstacles faced by those stigmatized and discriminated on the basis of race/ethnicity. While race privilege does not guarantee success, it does allow white people to take fuller advantage of their human potential and capital, or exactly what racial and ethnic minorities desire and continue to demand. But there's another important side to white privilege. In addition to a path free of race-linked obstacles, there are also unearned and hence unfair advantages that frequently provide a conveyer belt to accelerate forward progress regardless of their efforts and social capital. It is this latter dimension of privilege, often invisible or difficult to see, that contradicts how whites have been socialized to view their accomplishments, as rigorously documented below.

Labor Discrimination

Quillian et al. (2017) conducted a meta-analysis of every study of hiring discrimination against Latinos or African Americans (N = 28 studies), with an emphasis on the 24 studies conducted since 1989 that featured more rigorous research methods. Taken together, this group of studies replied to 26,326 job advertisements by submitting 55,842 identical job applications that differed only in the white, Black, or Latino sounding names on the applications. Controlling for gender, education, type of job, and local labor market conditions, results revealed that on average, white applications received 36% more callbacks than African Americans, and 24% more than Latino applications. Quillian et al. conclude that job discrimination against Latinos decreased only slightly, and not at all for African American applicants, over the past 25 years. Thus, white applicants unknowingly benefit from an unearned and mostly hidden advantage when competing with people of color on the job market, in the form of callbacks from prospective employers.

Critical white studies include historical analyses of how various European immigrant ethnic groups (e.g., the Irish, Italians) relinquished their ethnicity and *became white* and thus privileged in America, and distant from people of color, despite centuries of inter-European rivalries, violence, and white ethnic hierarchies in the Old World. An online search reveals a sizable genre of literature about white on white racism and discrimination.

Peggy McIntosh's 1998 seminal article on white privilege was a minor revolution in critical white studies. In her article she states, "I have come to see white privilege as an invisible package of unearned assets that I can count on cashing in each day, but about which I was 'meant' to remain oblivious. White privilege is like an invisible weightless knapsack of special provisions, assurances, tools, maps, guides, code books, passports, visas, clothes, compass, emergency gear, and blank checks" (p. 71). McIntosh discloses that, "For me, white privilege has turned out to be an elusive and fugitive subject. The pressure to avoid it is great, for in facing it I must give up the myth of meritocracy. If these things are true, this is not such a free country; one's life is not what one makes it; many doors open for certain people through no virtues of their own. These perceptions mean also that my moral condition is not what I had been led to believe. The appearance of being a good citizen rather than a troublemaker comes in large part from having all sorts of doors open automatically because of my color." (pp. 75–76). The concept of white privilege is underscored in this discussion of social stratification to remind us that whites even have the privilege to be average or to fail, or even commit crimes, without it being attributed to their race. It also means that average or less qualified whites have benefited throughout history given the circumstances into which they were born (see Chapter 4 for continued discussion).

In contrast, the trickle of people of color who have benefited from affirmative action opportunities cannot be average or fail without it being used as
evidence of their racial/ethnic inferiority and/or as proof that affirmative action is a failure. The irony here is that affirmative action can never advantage people of color in all of the myriad ways that white privilege has and
continues to advantage white people throughout America. Further, because
affirmative action includes women, veterans, and persons with disabilities, as
it should, and not just racial and ethnic minorities, whites continue to be the
numerically largest beneficiary of affirmative action.

The more conscious whites become of race privilege, the more accurately
and fairly they can conceptualize their co-evolution with people of color,
including how whites can personally benefit from advancing racial justice
in America. As discussed further in Chapter 12, the current social divide
over race and immigration in America, stoked by the Trump administration, works as a distraction from toxic wealth inequality that is injuring the
working class, regardless of race/ethnicity, and continuing to squeeze and
shrink the middle class in our stratification system.

While surrendering privilege is challenging because it means limiting unearned resources that accrue to the privileged unfairly, benefits include fuller
overdue human rights for people of color, less distorted sense of self and society on the part of whites, more authentic interpersonal majority–minority
relations, unencumbered by stigma and discrimination, and coalitions
across race and class better positioned to insist upon a government truly responsive to the vast majority of Americans.

Toward Intersectionality

Of course, race and ethnicity are not the only socially constructed
dimensions of humanity singled out for stigma and discrimination and lower
social positionality. Entrenched legacies of sexism, heteronormativity, and
nativism continue to justify discrimination against targeted populations on
the basis of distinguishing characteristics, or those perceived to distinguish
them, from society's more powerful members. The struggle for a fairer distribution of resources, including ways of compensating minorities to address tenacious legacies of discrimination, continues to be an uphill battle
led primarily by discriminated minority groups experiencing the most pain
and urgency. Issues of multiple minority and majority group memberships
or *intersectionality* is addressed in Chapter 5 (Latino Toward Latino
Intersectionality).

Hence, the hierarchy of interrelated race/ethnic, economic, educational, and political class systems has tremendous implications for the social mobility and general well-being of different populations in America, including their concentrations within particular strata or social classes, work sectors, levels of education, degrees of political power, formal and informal relationships between majority and minority groups, and consequent social positionality (e.g., SES).

The Stratification of Latino SES

The Latino community trails the majority non-Hispanic white population in many important indicators of economic well-being, including employment, income and wealth accumulation. The gaps are largest for Latinos born outside the United States. However, Latinos born in this country—although still lagging by some measures—are making progress on many fronts.

Joint Economic Committee of the
U.S. Congress (JECUSC) (2015)

The above quote from the JECUSC (2015) captures the social stratification of Latino social positionality as well as its slow but persistent progress driven by high labor participation rates, the pronounced social mobility drive of immigrants, and rising educational achievement. In addition to an overview of Latino SES, this chapter also touches upon variance between Latino populations, relevant policy issues, and vulnerability to labor market shifts such as the Great Recession of 2007–2009, as well as the uneven impact of Covid-19 on the American economy.

As reviewed in Chapters 1–2, the vast majority of Latino populations have been historically incorporated into the U.S. stratification system at the lowest levels characterized by segregation, economic exclusion, and exploitation, with little collective bargaining power. In particular, Mexican Americans and Puerto Ricans were incorporated into local, distinct labor markets (e.g., farm work, mining, railroad construction, manufacturing) with little advancement opportunities and high vulnerability to structural changes in the labor market. As such, the historical *rate* of Latino progress for the oldest and largest of Latino populations has been painfully slow, with too many compromised lives in the balance.

Latinos generally occupy a space in the stratification system approximately between NLWs and African Americans. A comparison of socioeconomic indicators substantiates this position. For instance, median annual household income for whites, Latinos, and African Americans are $61,354, $44,782 and $37,211, respectively, with variance among Latino populations ranging from a high of $55,082 for Colombians to a low of $37,000 for Dominicans (see Figure 3.5) (Healey et al., 2019b). Respective poverty rates for whites, Latinos and African Americans are 8.2%, 17% and 19.5% for 2020 (Federal Safety Net, 2022).

With the historical exception of Cubans, and more recently Nicaraguans whose median household income ($51,509) is second only to Colombians, Latinos continue to be underrepresented in higher status occupations, and vice versa. As reviewed in Chapters 1–2, historical discrimination has been foundational to this distinct pattern of social positionality, with frequent immigration of low SES workers and families also contributing. The consequent

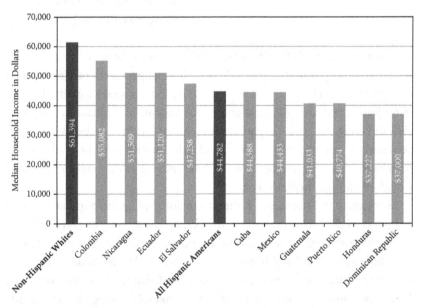

Figure 3.5. Median household income for non-hispanic whites, all Hispanic Americans, and 10 largest Hispanic groups, 2015.

From Healey et al. (2019). Hispanic Americans: Colonization, Immigration, and Ethnic Enclaves. In J. F. Healey, *Race, Ethnicity, Gender & Class: The Sociology of Group Conflict and Change* (pp. 262–311). Los Angeles, CA: Sage. Reprinted with permission.

stratified pattern of Latino job concentration in the private sector can be seen in Figure 3.6 from the JECUSC (2015).

As can be seen, Latinos make up well over a quarter of workers in construction and are also overrepresented in low-paying agriculture, leisure and hospitality, and other service occupations such as food services, groundskeeping, and maintenance. In fact, 27% of Latinos work such low-paying services jobs, as compared to 17% of NLW Americans. Conversely, Latinos are underrepresented in high-paying financial services, information technology, and professional and business services, including rapidly expanding educational and health services. For instance, Latinos comprise less than 1% of professionals in architecture and engineering.

With such stratified positionality in the private industry sector comes a cascade of vulnerabilities such as insufficient income, lack of health

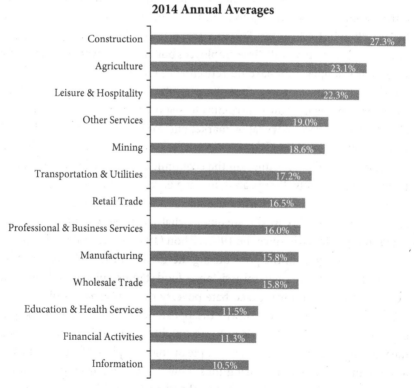

2014 Annual Averages

Industry	Percentage
Construction	27.3%
Agriculture	23.1%
Leisure & Hospitality	22.3%
Other Services	19.0%
Mining	18.6%
Transportation & Utilities	17.2%
Retail Trade	16.5%
Professional & Business Services	16.0%
Manufacturing	15.8%
Wholesale Trade	15.8%
Education & Health Services	11.5%
Financial Activities	11.3%
Information	10.5%

Figure 3.6. Hispanic employment in private sector industries.
From Joint Economic Committee of U.S. Congress (2015). The Economic State of the Latino Community in America.

insurance, and limited job security. For example, while the unemployment rate has always been 1%–2% higher for Latinos as compared to NLWs, during the Great Recession of 2007–2009, unemployment soared to 13% and 10% for Latino and white Americans, respectively (JECUSC, 2015). With regard to income, the average full-time Latino employee earns about $600 weekly as compared to $830 for NLW employees. Further, while Latinos comprise 13% of U.S. households, they make up only 7% of households in the top fifth earning bracket and 15% of the bottom fifth or lowest earning bracket. With an overall poverty rate of about 18%, this means that about 10.8 million Latinos live in poverty.

While declines in manufacturing jobs have been offset by rising service sector work for Latinos, wages and hours in the service sector declined throughout the 1980s and have not kept up with the cost of living since. For instance, corporate restructuring included converting full-time jobs to part-time work that has overly impacted Latinos in the secondary labor market. Early estimates of part-time jobs indicate an increase from 8 million in 1980 to 18 million in 1991 (Torres & De La Torre, 1991). Part-time employees not only earn less pay than full-time employees but have far fewer benefits, if any at all. For example, 70% have no retirement pension, and 42% are without health insurance according Ehrenberg et al.'s (1988) early analysis. Thus, such part-time work now contributes to segmenting much of the working class within the secondary labor market and lower SES strata, regardless of race and ethnicity.

The traditional lower rungs on the economic ladder needed for advancement have practically disappeared, moving us toward the "teardrop" shaped distribution of SES noted earlier. Evidence of this concerning scenario are reflected in worsening wealth inequality that has been widening since the 1960s, but particularly since the 1980s. Zhou (1997) notes that while the economic dislocations of the poor during the 1970s and 1980s were offset by accessible welfare (e.g., general assistance, food stamps, subsidized housing), policies of welfare reform exacerbate poverty by gutting accessible welfare while doing nothing to address the disappearance of living-wage work and extreme wealth inequality. This sink or swim dilemma continues to devastate the working class, white as well as people of color, displaced from what used to be living-wage manufacturing jobs, now outsourced around the globe, and rendered vulnerable to psychosocial and health problems, as evident in the Covid-19 pandemic.

Vulnerability to Covid-19

Risk for Covid-19, the pandemic that took hold in 2020, and the virus' devastating impact on the economy, is also stratified with disproportionate health and economic impacts on Latinos who comprise the majority of immigrants in the United States, a population overrepresented in essential yet high risk occupations. For instance, Figure 3.7 illustrates the outsized role of predominately Latino immigrant workers in the U.S. food supply chain. As can be seen, while immigrants are 17% of civilian employees, they are 22% or 2.1 million of the 10 million of food supply employees (Gelatt, 2020). The latter includes 70% of agricultural workers in California and seafood processors in Alaska, and two-thirds of meat processors in Nebraska. In addition to outbreaks of Covid-19 at meatpacking plants, and lack of protective gear for farmworkers, whose crowded living conditions is conducive to viral spreading, significant proportions of these workers are undocumented without access to health insurance or federal stimulus monies to defray economic hardship.

Stratification of the Power Elite

Another intriguing way of understanding the stratification of race/ethnicity and power is to examine the extreme underrepresentation of racial and ethnic minorities in the upper echelons of elite corporate America. In the most comprehensive study of diversity in the power elite, Zweigenhaft and Domhoff (2018) found that Latinos comprise less than 1% of corporate directors of Fortune 1000 boards, and only 1.4% of executives at vice-presidential levels and above. In fact, the raw number of Latino corporate directors went from a mere 40 in 1990 to 51 in 1995. Currently, 136 Latinos comprise 3.1% of corporate directors of Fortune 500 companies (i.e., the 500 most profitable in America). So, who are they?

Perhaps predictably, an analysis of the backgrounds of the few Latino corporate elite during the 1990s reveals that the majority are Cuban Americans from middle and upper class backgrounds. A subsequent analysis of skin color and facial features, by a pair of independent raters, also reveals this group to be light in complexion and more racially European-presenting than mestizo, indigenous Indian, or Black-appearing. An additional analysis of

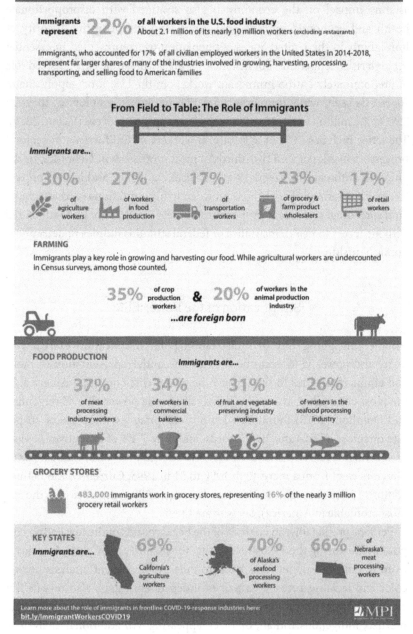

The Essential Role of Immigrants in the U.S. Food Supply Chain

Immigrants represent **22%** **of all workers in the U.S. food industry**
About 2.1 million of its nearly 10 million workers (excluding restaurants)

Immigrants, who accounted for 17% of all civilian employed workers in the United States in 2014-2018, represent far larger shares of many of the industries involved in growing, harvesting, processing, transporting, and selling food to American families

From Field to Table: The Role of Immigrants

Immigrants are...

30% of agriculture workers

27% of workers in food production

17% of transportation workers

23% of grocery & farm product wholesalers

17% of retail workers

FARMING

Immigrants play a key role in growing and harvesting our food. While agricultural workers are undercounted in Census surveys, among those counted,

35% of crop production workers **&** **20%** of workers in the animal production industry

...are foreign born

FOOD PRODUCTION

Immigrants are...

37% of meat processing industry workers

34% of workers in commercial bakeries

31% of fruit and vegetable preserving industry workers

26% of workers in the seafood processing industry

GROCERY STORES

483,000 immigrants work in grocery stores, representing 16% of the nearly 3 million grocery retail workers

KEY STATES

Immigrants are...

69% of California's agriculture workers

70% of Alaska's seafood processing workers

66% of Nebraska's meat processing workers

Learn more about the role of immigrants in frontline COVID-19-response industries here:
bit.ly/ImmigrantWorkersCOVID19

MPI

Figure 3.7. Essential immigrant workers in the American food supply chain.
From Gelatt, J., & Batalova, J. (2020). Center for Migration Studies of New York; with permission.

the racial features of new Latino CEOs of Fortune 400 companies continued to show that they are indistinguishable from NLWs, and almost two-thirds were born in Cuba (6), Spain (3), Mexico (2), or other Latino countries. Hence, Latino corporate elite are not representative of the majority of Latinos in the United States, given their advantaged backgrounds, lighter skin color, and white racial features.

The Cuban Enclave

As intimated above, Cubans have been a notable exception to the stratification of Latino race/ethnicity and SES in the United States. Their historical conditions of acculturation have resulted in a vibrant ethnic enclave sub-economy as a mechanism for economic livelihood and social mobility. An ethnic enclave is a geographically located network of ethnically linked business enterprises that serve both the immediate ethnic market and mainstream markets. Such enclaves typically offer and depend upon subsequent immigrant workers when work in regular labor markets is less available. Ethnic enclaves provide opportunity for advancement, and there is even a sense of solidarity in that workers are expected to be loyal, and employers are expected to provide skills and advancement. The Cuban enclave has been able to take full advantage of its location by working with Caribbean and Latin America businesses. Cubans continue to be the most concentrated Latino population, with almost two-thirds continuing to live in the Miami metropolitan area and nearly 80% in the state of Florida.

By the 1980s, a mere two decades since the arrival of the first wave of Cuban refugees, significant success and rising social positionality was evident in Dade County, Florida, where there were over 18,000 Cuban-owned firms, most in construction, finance, textiles, leather, furniture, and cigar making. There were also 16 Cuban Americans presidents of banks and 250 vice presidents, 3,500 doctors, 500 lawyers, 500 supermarket owners, 250 drug store owners, and over 60 Cuban-owned auto dealerships (Boswell, 1985).

It should be noted, however, that Cuban immigrants today, half of whom arrived in the United States since 2000, have low socioeconomic indicators. For instance, they are less likely to be employed in better paying management, business, science, and arts occupations than immigrants in general (25% versus 33%, respectively), more likely to be employed in lower paying production, transportation, and material moving jobs (20% and

16%, respectively), and about as likely to work in low-paying production, construction, and maintenance operations (14% and 13%, respectively) (Blizzard & Batalova, 2018). Consequently, median family income for Cuban immigrants is $46,000 as compared to $60,000 for immigrants generally, and they now have a poverty rate of 13%.

The Stratification of Latino Education

The stratification of education and race/ethnicity has long been characterized by disparities between NLWs and most people of color that were either denied access to or provided meager forms of segregated education. Today, only about two-thirds of Latinos have graduated from high school as compared to 92.3% of white Americans who also graduate from college at twice the rate (34.2% and 16%, respectively) (Healey et al., 2019b). Much is at stake here, given that Latino families with a college graduate head of household earn twice as much and have over four times more wealth compared to their non-college family counterparts (CIF, 2015). Variance among Latino populations, with respective high school and college graduation rates, ranges from higher rates for Cubans (79.2% and 26%), Puerto Ricans (79% and 18,4%) and Nicaraguans (80% and 19%), to lowest for Hondurans (52.3% and 10.6%), El Salvadorans (52% and 9%), and Guatemalans (47.5% & 8.8%), for reasons related to their acculturation histories as reviewed in Chapters 1 and 2.

Latino persistence in education is reflected in data showing that the percent earning a bachelor's degree doubled from 8% in 1990 to 16% currently. Unfortunately, such a promising trend continues to be hampered by limited access to quality K–12 education. For example, Healey et al. (2019b) report that the percent of Latino youth stuck in high-poverty schools increased from over a third in 2000 to almost half in 2013. In comparison, NLW students trapped in such impoverished schools were only 3% in 2000, increasing to 8% in 2013. Further, the percent of Latino students fortunate enough to attend affluent schools decreased from 16% in 2000 to 8% in 2013. NLW students also experienced a decline from 53% to 30% in affluent schools. Clearly, these educational trends, across race/ethnicity and lower social class, are moving rapidly in the wrong direction and should be addressed together.

Historically, Latino students have scored lower than their NLW counterparts on educational tests and have higher rates of "school delay" (a polite term for flunking). Low performance leads to placement into lower curriculum "tracks" (e.g., vocational versus college preparation) and low expectations on the part of teachers, career counselors, and unfortunately even Latino parents and students themselves.

To better understand the persistent education gap between Mexican and Puerto Ricans on the one hand, and Cubans and NLWs on the other, an early study by Bean and Tienda (1987) assessed the role of social class and cultural variables on school performance. Using Census data between 1960 and 1980, what these researchers found was that cultural factors (i.e., limited English and immigrant status) *did* contribute to school underperformance as expected, *but only in combination with disadvantaged social class* or poverty rooted in the acculturation histories of Mexican and Puerto Rican versus Cuban and NLW students. That is, the effects of limited English and immigrant status on school delay were outweighed by family income and parental education or low SES. In fact, for Cuban students, school delay was higher in children from homes that were monolingual English or English dominant!

Sidebar 3.1. The Richest Latino in America?

Hailing from a wealthy sugar plantation family in Cuba, and of Spanish-Basque heritage, Roberto Goizueta worked for a subsidiary of Coca-Cola from 1954 to 1960, after graduating from Yale with a degree in engineering. But with Fidel Castro threatening to nationalize capitalist enterprises, Goizueta fled Cuba in 1960 with his family to become the senior vice president of Coca-Cola in the Bahamas. Over the next 20 years, he would relocate to company headquarters in Atlanta, where he received a series of major corporate promotions culminating in chairman of the board and CEO of Coca-Cola in 1981 with an annual salary of almost five million dollars. But that was just the beginning! In addition to introducing the ill-fated New Coke (a Pepsi taste-alike) in 1985, Goizueta also gained notoriety in 1992 for arranging a compensation package so immense that it made Johnny Carson's monologue on the *Tonight Show*, ABC's *Nightline* devoted an entire show to it, and David Cay Johnston (2003) devoted a chapter to it in his book, *Perfectly Legal: The covert campaign to rig our tax system to benefit the super rich and cheat everybody else*. On top of his annual income of nearly $5 million, Goizueta arranged to be paid one million shares of Coke worth $81 million, and at federal income tax rate of less than 2%! A heavy smoker, he passed away in 1997.

For Mexican Americans, the probability of school delay decreased 2% for each yearly increment in parental education. Similarly, not persisting in high school was inversely related to family income, yet generally unrelated to speaking Spanish in the home.

Thus, the gap between Mexicans and Puerto Ricans on the one hand, and Cubans on the other, is not explained by Spanish language maintenance or immigration status, because these background factors are shared by all three Latino groups studied. Where these groups differ is in their SES and historical conditions of acculturation and inclusion in the United States. An extreme example of this is provided in Sidebar 3.1. Unfortunately, informative analyses such as these have been routinely overlooked in heated public and partisan debates about immigration and bilingual education.

The Battle of Bilingual Education

During the 1990s, Californians led the nation in their mission to abolish bilingual education by passing Proposition 227 in 1999. The tired rationale was that such programs do not help immigrant children learn English, they retard assimilation, and, even worse, contribute to the "decay of the core parts of our civilization" according to combative former Speaker of the Assembly Newt Gingrich. Just as bold as Gingrich's assertion is the opinion of bilingual education experts such as Kenji Hakuta (1986), who asserted that that such condemnation results from bilingual education affirming the legitimacy of non-English languages and cultures and threatens the high status of English and NLW domination over people of color. The latter assertion is consistent with the definition and history of bilingual education in a society stratified by race/ethnicity.

Californians such as those mentioned could not conceive that the first California state constitution of 1849 was published in Spanish and English and legislated that all state laws, decrees, regulations, and provisions be printed in both languages (Feagin & Booher Feagin, 1999). But shortly afterwards, Spanish was declared foreign despite the fact that it predates English in America. Another irony is that bilingualism has historically been equated with "mental confusion," whereas research now shows that bilingualism promotes academic achievement (Moran and Hakuta, 1995) and may even forestall and lessen the severity of dementia in those affected. The so-called language deficiency of Latino children was a major historical rationale for segregating Mexican Americans in the Southwest and thereby stratifying their inferior education. Viewed in its historical context, the bilingual education movement of the 1960s and 7190s was an effort to protect Latinos, and other non-English speaking children from being pathologized, marginalized, and undereducated.

As early as 1939, the Congress of Spanish Speaking Peoples denounced school segregation as racist and demanded that the bilingual needs of Mexican youth be addressed by Spanish-speaking teachers, materials, and programs. But it took a series of protests, demonstrations, and court cases by Mexican parents to eliminate the segregation of their children in California years before the nation's landmark *Brown v. Topeka Board of Education* decision, which declared segregation illegal nationwide (see Chapter 12 for more detail).

Twenty years after *Brown*, Latino students in California were the beneficiaries of a Supreme Court ruling in favor of non-English speaking Chinese students in San Francisco, who took the school district to court for not providing supplemental language instruction. *Lau v. Nichols* (1974), ruled that inattention to the language needs of English-limited children in California was a denial of their participation in public education. Bilingual education was recommended by the Office of Civil Rights as the best solution to this problem. However, while most Californians viewed bilingual education as a way to transition children from their native language to English, its original intent was to provide instruction in both languages in order to affirm and maintain native language and culture while simultaneously acquiring English and American culture (i.e., additive bicultural model). Unfortunately, the majority of bilingual education programs have been transitional in design, reflecting deep resistance to legitimating languages such as Spanish or Chinese.

A Best-case Scenario for Bilingual Education

Regarding the effectiveness of bilingual education, we need look no further than the early Cuban American refugee experience that involved high U.S. investment in the bilingual and bicultural education of youth from this community. In the early 1960s, the Ford Foundation funded an experimental bilingual education program in which equal numbers of Cuban refugee *and* NLW children, from a middle class school district, were instructed in English and Spanish. Refugee Cuban teachers, highly invested in the success of Cuban children, were re-credentialed and hired to teach. Not only did white children learn a valuable second language, but both groups of children also improved their reading scores (Hakuta, 1986).

In 1982, the Supreme Court ruled that all children be provided an education and cannot be discriminated on the basis of parent immigrant status. This is partly why ex-governor Pete Wilson's ill-fated California Proposition 187, passed by California voters in 1994, was ruled unconstitutional given its intent to deny public education (and nearly all other human services) to the predominantly Latino children of undocumented parents in California (see Chapter 12 for more on Prop 187). As elaborated in Chapter 11, California schools today, populated by a majority of Latino students, now have the legal discretion to implement bilingual education as needed, a victory that was a long time coming, thanks to a powerful Latino Legislative Caucus committed to serving the needs of the state's 16 million Latinos, and working class Californians more generally.

Latino Political (Dis)empowerment

While Latino political power is more fully addressed in Chapter 11, suffice to say here that it is central to overcoming the social stratification of race/ethnicity and power. Historically, Mexicans in the Southwest and Puerto Ricans in New York have been victimized by many of the same racist deterrents to voting as African Americans, including poll taxes, literacy tests, gerrymandering, and outright intimidation. More recent underparticipation is more a function of age, nativity, continuing poverty, and more subtle discrimination. For example, Marger (2000b) noted over 20 years ago that over a third of Latinos are too young to vote, and over half are ineligible non-citizens. Today, about 79% of Latinos are citizens eligible to vote, making the prospect of significant political participation much brighter.

However, continuous immigration from Mexico and Central Americans, and the circular migration of Puerto Ricans, have historically slowed the development of political loyalties, interests, and investments. Further, considering that political participation is primarily a function of SES-related resources (i.e., time and money, relevant work experience, social networks), low levels of Latino political power is predictable although not acceptable nor immutable.

Historically, a series of political crises have spurred Latino activism and political participation in significant ways. Such crises have ranged from small-town to statewide assaults on Latino culture and well-being, including today's barrage of anti-immigrant rhetoric and previous executive orders, laws, and policies, spearheaded by the former president and the enabling Republicans in the U.S. Congress. Such attacks foment racial fear and resentment as well as violent forms of criminalization, persecution, imprisonment, and deportation harmful to undocumented Latinos, their families, and communities. Only recently have political surveys begun to capture Latinos' reactions and related views and political intentions, given that they now comprise 10% of the voting electorate in America.

2020 National Latino Electorate Survey (NLES)

With the goal of capturing "what Latino voters want" during the high-stakes presidential election year 2020, UnidosUS (the organization formerly known as National Council of La Raza) released its 2020 NLES with data from 1,854 eligible Latino voters (1,506 registered and 308 unregistered). UCLA's *Latino Decisions*, a leader in Latino political opinion research, was commissioned to conduct this national survey that provides timely information on voting-related concerns and candidate choices by a national sample of Latinos.

When asked to rank order the top three issues participants would like their presidential candidate to address, three-quarters of Latino participants listed health care, jobs and the economy, and immigration. When asked why, participants stressed the unaffordability of health care and need to be covered; lack of living-wage work; and the need to stop separating families, abusing/ caging children, and deportations. In response to the question, "Which immigration issue do you want a new president address first?" respondents rank ordered the following three top choices: (1) Stop the Trump administration's policy of separating undocumented children from their families at the border; (2) pass comprehensive immigration reform, including a path to citizenship for undocumented people; and (3) protect DACA recipients. Clearly, the vast majority of Latinos are spurned by former president Trump's racist remarks and cruel policies toward Latino and other immigrants, particularly undocumented, while they worry about earning a living and having access to health care as elaborated below.

With regard to top concerns, 78% endorsed the item, "I am frustrated with how President Trump and his allies treat immigrants and Latinos, worry it will get worse if Trump is re-elected"; 63% endorsed, "I am concerned that I may not be able to afford to own a home, or afford to keep the one I have now"; and 61% agreed that, "Sometimes I delay or skip doctor visits or buying medicine because it is too expensive." In response to the question who would they vote for if the election was held today, 62% indicated definitely or probably the Democratic Party candidate yet 21.3% indicated definitely or probably President Trump. Why one in five Latinos would consider voting for Trump has been a topic of much speculation, including possible reasons such as the way Trump's anti-immigration rhetoric faded in 2020 and was partly replaced by his strong position on keeping the economy open during the emerging Covid-19 pandemic. Other reasons include the predictable voting pattern of conservative and higher-SES Latinos (e.g., Cubans and those from South America), as well as Christian-right (i.e., Evangelicals) Latinos that view Trump as a means to their religious ends such as ending abortion rights, turning the Supreme Court conservative, and elevating right-wing Christians to vaunted positions in government (e.g., Vice President Pence, Secretary of Education Betsy Devos).

Given the above recent political survey data, we appear to be witnessing another surge in Latino political participation at the national level, in response to a pernicious political climate for Latinos in the United States. Latino resistance, activism, and political participation, past and present, are addressed in the two following chapters. The election of Joe Biden, partly a function of the Latino vote, has advanced an administration with significant promise for raising responsive Latino representation at the national political level (e.g., appointment of Xavier Becerra to Secretary of Health and Human Services), as well as undoing anti-Latino immigration policies of the Trump administration, some of which has begun to happen. What these recent presidential actions, survey datapoints, and voting patterns portend for the stratification of Latino political power remains to be seen at the dawn of the 2024 presidential election with Republicans still significantly aligned with Trumpism, and predominating the House, while Democrats maintain a razor-thin majority in the senate.

References

Bean, F. D., & Tienda, M. (1987). Hispanics in the U. S. labor force. In F. D. Bean & M. Tienda, *The Hispanic population of the United States* (pp. 280–337) New York: Sage.

Blizzard, B., & Batalova, J. (2018). Cuban immigrants in the United States in 2018. Washington DC: Migration Policy Institute. https://www.migrationpolicy.org/article/cuban-immigrants-united-states-2018

Boswell, T. D. (1985). The Cuban Americans. In J. O. McKee (Ed.), *Ethnicity in Contemporary America: A geographical appraisal* (pp. 95–116). Dubuque, IA: Kendall/ Hunt.

Choi, K. H. (2020). Racial diversity in the marital assimilation of Hispanics. *Journal of Marriage and Family, 82*, 675–690. https://doi.org/10.1111/jomf.12601

Cordova, R. (1987). Undocumented El Salvadorans in the San Francisco Bay area: Migration and adaptation dynamic. *Journal of La Raza Studies, 1*, 9–35.

Ehrenberg, R., Rosenberg, P., & Li, J. (1988). Part-time employment in the United States. In R. Hart (Ed.), *Employment, underemployment, and labor utilization.* (pp. 256–287). Boston: Unwin Hyman.

Encyclopedia Britannica (2019). Neoliberalism. https://www.britannica.com/topic/ neoliberalism

Feagin, J. R., & Booher Feagin. C. (1999). Mexican Americans. In J. R. Feagin and C. Booher Feagin (Eds.), *Race and ethnic relations* (6th ed.) (pp. 291–335). Upper Saddle River, NJ: Prentice Hall.

Federal Safety Net (2022). U.S. poverty statistics. https://federalsafetynet.com/about-us/

Ferris, E. G. (1987). *The Central American refugees.* New York: Praeger.

Gelatt, J. (2020). Immigrant workers: Vital to the U.S. COVID-19 response, disproportionately vulnerable. Washington DC: Migrant Policy Institute. https://www.migratio npolicy.org/research/immigrant-workers-us-covid-19-response

Hakuta, K. (1986). *Mirror of language: The debate on bilingualism.* New York: Basic Books.

Healey, J. F., Stepnick, A., & O'Brien, E. (2019a). Diversity in the United States: Questions and concepts. In Healey et al. (Eds.), *Race, ethnicity, gender & class: The sociology of group conflict and change* (pp. 2–35). Los Angeles: Sage.

Healey, J. F., Stepnick, A., & O'Brien, E. (2019b). Hispanic Americans: Colonization, immigration, and ethnic enclaves. In Healey et al. (Eds.), *Race, ethnicity, gender & class: The sociology of group conflict and change* (pp. 262–311). Los Angeles: Sage.

History.com (2019). U.S. immigration since 1965. https://www.history.com/topics/immi gration/us-immigration-since-1965

Joint Economic Committee of United States Congress (2015). The economic state of the Latino community in America. Washington DC.

Lenski, G. (1966). *Power and privilege: A theory of social stratification.* New York: McGraw-Hill.

Marger, N. N. (2012a). Ethnic stratification: Majority and minority. In M. N. Marger (Ed.), *Race and ethnic relations: American and global perspectives* (10th ed.) (pp. 27–48) Stamford, CT: CENAGE Learning.

McIntosh, P. (1998). White privilege and male privilege: A personal account of coming to see correspondence through work in women's studies. In M. L. Andersen and P. H. Collins (Eds.), *Race, class and gender: An anthology* (pp. 95–105). Belmont, CA: Wadsworth.

McLemore, S. D. Romo, H., & Gonzalez Baker, S. (2001). The golden door. In S. D. McLemore, H. Romo, & S. Gonzalez Baker, *Racial and ethnic relations in America* (pp. 75–107). Boston: Allyn & Bacon.

Moran, C. E., & Hakuta, K. (1995). Bilingual education: Broadening research perspectives. In J. A. Banks and C. A. McGee Banks (Eds.), *Handbook of research on multicultural education* (pp. 445–462). New York: Macmillan.

Putnam, R. (2017). Our kids: The American dream in crisis. New York: Simon and Shuster.

Quillian, L., Pager, D., Hexel, O., & Midtbøen, A. H. (2017). Meta-analysis of field experiments shows no change in racial discrimination in hiring over time. *PNAS*, 114(41), 10870–10875. https://www.pnas.org/content/pnas/114/41/10870.full.pdf

Reich, R. B. (2007). *Supercapitalism: The transformation of business, democracy, and everyday life*. New York: Vintage.

Smith, T. W., & Dempsey, G. R. (1983). The polls: Ethnic social distance and prejudice. *Public Opinion Quarterly*, 47, 584–600.

Torres, R. D., & Del Lá Torre, A. C. (1991). Latinos, class, and the U.S. political economy: Income inequality and policy alternatives. In E. Melendez, C. Rodriguez, and J. B. Figueroa (Eds.), *Hispanics in the Labor Force* (pp. 265–287). New York: Plenum Press.

UnidosUS (2020). The 2020 national Latino electorate survey. June 2019. Washington DC. chrome-extension://efaidnbmnnnibpcajpcglclefindmkaj/https://unidosus.org/wp-content/uploads/2021/07/UnidosUS_2020latinoelectoratesurvey_june2019.pdf

Zhou, M. (1997). Segmented assimilation: Issues, controversies, and recent research on the new second generation. *International Immigration Review*, 31(4), 1–22.

4

Latino Racial/Ethnic
Identity Development

Psychological Impacts of Structured Inequality

It is one of the ironies of anti-racism that we must identify racially in order to identify the racial privileges and dangers of being in our bodies. Latino and Asian, African and European and Indigenous and Middle Eastern: These six races—at least in the American context—are fundamentally power identities, because race is fundamentally a power construct of blended differences that lives socially. Race creates new forms of power: the power to categorize and judge, elevate and downgrade, include and exclude. Race markers use that power to process distinct individuals, ethnicities and nationalities into monolithic races.

—Ibram X. Kendi (2019, p. 38)

Question: When did Latinos in America become a racialized and minoritized population? Answer: When they became part of the United States as described in Chapters 1 and 2. The above quote, from Kendi's (2019) book, *How to Be an Antiracist*, recognizes the necessity of identifying as a racialized and *minoritized* person of color in a society that has methodically constructed a hierarchy of racialized differences in order to stratify power by race as described in Chapter 3's analysis of the stratification of Latino ethnicity/race and power. It is indeed ironic that in order to resist and challenge such oppressive racialized arrangements, it must be done from our racialized positionality, but one imbued with a level of consciousness and identity that rejects racialized hierarchies and insists upon everyone's full humanity. Relatedly, Collins and Bilge (2016), in their primer on intersectionality, assert that identity is strategically essential to struggle politically against

Solving Latino Psychosocial and Health Problems. Kurt C. Organista, Oxford University Press.

disenfranchisement, that identity is inherently collective, coalitional, and transformative with regard to social change in power relations. So how does racial/ethnic identity achieve such consciousness and social justice agency?

The sociological frameworks of acculturation in Chapters 1 and 2, and social stratification in Chapter 3, advance our understanding of the historical and continuing experiences of U.S. Latino populations. These frameworks emphasize the roles of stigmatized and discriminated minority status, strained and frequently conflictual race relations between Latinos and mainstream society, and social-structural forms of biased policies and practices that disadvantage the majority of Latinos. What, however, are the individual-level, psychological and emotional impacts and responses to such structured inequality? In what ways does being Latino affect a group member's self-concept and self-esteem with regard to racial and ethnic identity? Of course, this is a complex question with a wide variety of evolving answers. There has accrued, however, a substantial literature on racial and ethnic identity development, including *critical whiteness studies*, that are informative for conceptualizing key dimensions of racial and ethnic identity for Latino and non-Latino white (NLW) counterparts, and their relation to psychosocial adjustment and well-being.

Racial/Ethnic Identity

Strictly speaking, ethnic identity refers to the culture with which an individual or population identifies and practices, that guides the lives of members with a core set of values and preferred lifeways intended to imbue life with meaning, direction, and affirmation. Thus, culture is less about race and more about shared history and tradition, language and religion, and family and community structures and functioning, all of which reflect to varying degrees key beliefs, attitudes, behaviors, and feelings about ethnic group membership. However, how to achieve a healthy sense of self as a member of a stigmatized and discriminated racialized minority group, historically constructed and treated as an inferior non-white race group, is complicated. It may be easier to imagine how such an experience imparts varying degrees of biculturalism and bilingualism, identity confusion and coherence, and the formidable challenge of developing a healthy ethnic sense of self, imbued with positive self-regard and esteem, with which to function more fully in the world.

The Salience of Ethnic Identity

As one of several dimensions of the self, racial/ethnic identity is clearly important from a sociocultural perspective, but it is also imperative because of the ways that American society has historically socialized us to define, prejudge and perceive, and treat people of different racial and ethnic backgrounds. Given the negative stereotypic content and historical mistreatment associated with people of color, members of these groups often struggle with a mix of feelings and meanings associated with racial and ethnic group memberships. That is, the ethnic/racial component of self is a force with which to reckon.

Author's Social Positionality

As a Chicano child growing up in East Los Angeles (ELA) from the mid-1950s to the mid-1970s, the author can share early years during which Latinos were virtually absent from popular and mainstream culture reflected in media such as television, newspapers and magazines, and textbooks at school. Latinos were also negatively characterized, on the rare occasions that they were portrayed, as gang members, prostitutes, *bandidos* [bandits], and servile *Sí señor* [Yes, sir] peasants. As with most Latino barrios at the time, ELA residents were predominantly working class and frequently challenged by poverty, while teachers, police, firefighters, store owners and managers, and even lifeguards were overwhelmingly white. What is a Latino child to conclude from such a social environment, lacking positive and powerful representation and with too few messages from parents and trusted authority figures needed to explain subordination and power differences, in order to help "inoculate" Latino youth from negative social comparisons and prevent them from internalizing stereotypes about their race/ethnic minority group?

Fortunately, the author also recalls a large, supportive, and caring extended family and neighbors, culturally rich foods, music, cultural celebrations, a supportive Catholic Church, occasional immersive visits to Mexico, and a burgeoning Chicano movement. Thus, being Chicano then, as well as now, is a complex mix of social, cultural, and psychological phenomena from which to develop the racial and cultural component of self. While Latino representation is gradually improving throughout society, it remains uneven and inadequate, with problematic ethnic identity development a frequent outcome as illustrated in the following vignette.

Hank's Ethnic Identity Crisis

Imagine a young Latino adult named Enrique who insists on being called "Hank," which is short for Henry, his name translated into English. He takes pride in speaking English with little if any Latino accent, and of moving out of the barrio into a mostly NLW neighborhood as soon as he could. He works in the software industry, and both his co-workers and friends are predominantly white middle class professionals. He married a NLW woman after years of exclusively dating such women, and they have a beautiful young son. Politically, Hank is a conservative Republican and supports anti–bilingual education and anti–affirmative action initiatives, as well as immigration control and diminishing welfare benefits. When asked about the lingering social problems of Latinos, Hank says that they lack initiative and motivation, that clinging to their culture holds them back, and that they should spend more time learning to be like NLWs and less time complaining and depending on the federal government. Hank encourages his son to work twice as hard as NLW children to prove his worth.

While on the surface, Hank has the right to his political opinions, loving whom he pleases, and living his own law-abiding lifestyle, conversations with him reveal that he considers NLW women to be *more* attractive than Latinas, and all other women of color for that matter. He also believes that marrying a NLW person is a sign of getting ahead, and that his child is better than Latino children because he is half-white and being raised to be American in all respects and Latino in none. Peers with whom Hank grew up, as well as some of his family members, say that Enrique wants to be white and that he is ashamed of his culture and family. Sometimes they feel resentful of him and call him a *vendido*, or sell-out. On the infrequent occasions that he visits his family of origin, he often gets into heated debates about political issues like immigration control or about the best ways for family members to improve their lives.

There is something concerning about the above vignette, not because we don't all have the right to live the life that we choose but because some of our perceptions, feelings, behaviors, and lifestyles may be overly influenced by internalized racism and oppression. At the heart of such internalized oppression is an unnecessary and preventable rejection and dislike of one's own racial or cultural group and self, as well as the consequences of believing in the inferiority of one's ethnic group and the superiority of the dominant NLW group.

While many of us are capable of recognizing ethnic identity problems, they can be subtle, complex, energy draining, and ultimately debilitating. For example, one could imagine the above vignette without the rejection of ethnic group and ethnic self. That is, a Latino marrying a NLW or any person could simply be a matter of mutual love and compatibility, rather than bettering one's self, as could finding NLW women and friends attractive, but not necessarily more attractive or better than women of color and Latino friends. Conservative political views can also be based sincerely on how one weighs both sides of political issues and arguments.

For many progressive Latinos, it is tempting to dismiss conservative Latinos as Latino-rejecting or ignorant, partly because they are sometimes used by conservative leaders to counter Latino protests or movements for greater fairness. For example, much praise is given to high-profile people of color espousing neoconservative views and policies that perpetuate a status quo that blames minorities for their problems, versus holding society accountable for its biased ways of stratifying race/ethnicity and power as reviewed in Chapter 3. Thus, understanding when attitudes, beliefs, and behaviors may reflect ethnic identity problems or not, is important in our professional work with clients, and in personal relationships, and can be informed by theories of racial and ethnic identity development and related research.

Racial/Ethnic Identity Theory

In their pioneering textbook *Counseling the Culturally Different: Theory and Practice*, now in its eighth edition, Sue et al. (2019a) address the issue of racial and ethnic identity by presenting their Racial/Cultural Identity Development model (R/CID), based upon previous stage models developed by and for African Americans and subsequently applied to other populations of color. The R/CID captures the development of racial/cultural identity in oppressed ethnic minority groups, but has also been applied to white racial identity development as discussed below.

As can be seen in Table 4.1, the R/CID model is a matrix of five theoretical stages of minority identity development inferred from four corresponding sets of psychosocial attitudes toward: oneself as a minority, one's own minority group, other racial and ethnic minority groups, and the dominant NLW group. Sue et al. (2019a) qualify that the five stages are continuous

Table 4.1. Racial/Cultural Identity Development (R/CID) Model

Stages of Minority Development Model	Attitude Toward Self	Attitude Toward Others of the Same Minority Group	Attitude Toward Others of Different Minority Groups	Attitude Toward Dominant Group
Stage 1 – Conformity	Self-depreciating	Group-depreciating	Discriminatory	Group-appreciating
Stage 2 – Dissonance	Conflict between self-depreciating and self-appreciating	Conflict between group-depreciating and group-appreciating	Conflict between dominant-held views of minority hierarchy and feelings of shared experience	Conflict between group appreciating and group depreciating
Stage 3 – Resistance and Immersion	Self-appreciating	Group-appreciating	Conflict between feelings of empathy for other minority experiences and feelings of culturo-centrism	Group-depreciating
Stage 4 – Introspection	Concern with basis of self-appreciation	Concern with nature of unequivocal appreciation	Concern with ethnocentric basis for judging others	Concern with the basis of group-depreciation
Stage 5 – Integrative Awareness	Selective appreciation	Selective appreciation	Selective appreciation	Selective appreciation

From: Sue et al. (2019). Racial/cultural identity development in people of color: Counseling implications. In D. W. Sue, D. Sue, H. A. Neville and L. Smith, *Counseling the culturally different: Theory and practice* (8th ed.) (pp. 355–388). New York: John Wiley & Sons, with permission.

and blending, neither strictly sequential nor irreversible, and that many individuals may not experience all five stages in their lifetime. Further, minority individuals may begin at any of the stages depending on their upbringing and socialization (e.g., parenting), and may even skip stages, forward or backward, depending on their life circumstances and experiences. Despite such qualifiers, the R/CID is understandably criticized for being linear and typological. Nevertheless, the model provides an intuitive and user-friendly introduction or handle on the complexity of racial and ethnic identity development in America.

Stage 1: Conformity to the Racial Status Quo

Ethnic identity problems are most evident in the conformity stage in which members of oppressed minority groups are socialized to internalize, consciously and subconsciously, a racialized hierarchy of different groups in society (e.g., via education, popular culture, portrayals, or lack thereof). Historically, stereotypes have assaulted every conceivable dimension of a minority group's humanity (e.g., intelligence, morality, behavior, physical appearance, sexuality) in order to rationalize and justify minority group subordination, exploitation, and even worse at times. Conversely, NLW America is generally idealized through racial socialization.

Melting-pot Philosophy

Conformity is reflected in the traditional melting-pot metaphor of 20th-century America that has served as the guiding philosophy for socializing European immigrant groups for inclusion. Even diverse European immigrant groups were initially viewed as inferior to the original British stock of colonial White Anglo Saxon Protestants (WASPs) and the evolving amalgam of assimilating northern Europeans. Southern (e.g., Italian, Greek) and eastern (e.g., Polish, Russian) European immigrants were negatively stereotyped and mistreated in ways that we have come to stereotype people of color (inferior intelligence and culture, criminal, violent, dirty, clannish, etc.). It was the concerted project of formal and informal American institutions to pressure and coerce European immigrants to discard their inferior cultures of origin, abandon their ethnic ghettos in the United States as soon as possible, and assimilate or "melt" into mainstream American society.

However, the melting pot was conceptualized by and for white Europeans and excluded non-whites, creating scenarios of segregation and marginalization for minority groups, including those groups and individuals open to assimilation had the option been available to them. For instance, Hayes-Bautista (2017a) documents how many Mexicans, during the takeover of California by white settlers, were open to joining the new American California state, only to face concerted racist efforts to exclude their participation (see Chapter 12 for more detail). Thus, people of color were generally the "wrong stock" for the American melting pot, and their racial stigma has been a greater obstacle than the ethnic stigma historically attached to southern and eastern European immigrants who were eventually able to assimilate.

In Hank's vignette above, Mexican cultural and physical markers (e.g., Spanish name, mestizo features and affiliations) are sources of shame and embarrassment to be minimized and avoided. Hank also idealizes NLW people as physically, intellectually, and morally superior to Mexican and other of people of color. Historically, the predominantly positive and normative representations of white people versus the mostly negative and abnormal portrayals (or invisibility) of minorities contributes to a conformity mindset, especially in the absence of contradictory images and messages regarding people of color. It is theorized that conformist minorities may never be fully adjusted because race and ethnically linked reminders and situations are difficult to avoid or conceal. Even if one could hide one's race and/or ethnicity and "pass" for white, there remains the burden of expending energy to hide a dimension of self too frequently salient in our racialized society. For example, Hank's Mexican mestizo features frequently prompt whites in his social networks to ask him, "What are you?" or seek his opinions about Latino issues of the day.

As mentioned above, the problematic social position of Latinos and other people of color is viewed by Hank as a product of their own deficits. Such a belief denies or minimizes past through current social injustice and fails to challenge the status quo, because it does not comprehend or accept how powerful historical and social forces have shaped Latino positionality as documented in Chapters 1–3. Most conformity minorities may not consciously register self-rejection and may have other compensating identities and assets (e.g., Hank is an attractive person with an outgoing personality, good athletic skills, and talented enough to succeed in the software industry). Awareness of internalized oppression would require ethnic identity development beyond conformity, as discussed below.

In a penetrating exposé by Iwata (1991), he reveals how self-rejection as an Asian American led him to undergo blepharoplasty, a form of cosmetic surgery designed to make almond shaped Asian eyes look rounder and more European by removing some of the epicanthic fold of the upper eyelid to simulate NLW double eyelids (see Figure 4.1). Such cosmetic surgery frequently occurs among Asian Americans graduating from college and embarking on careers in mainstream America. Iwata also shares undergoing rhinoplasty or a "nose job" to give his relatively flat Asian nose "more definition."

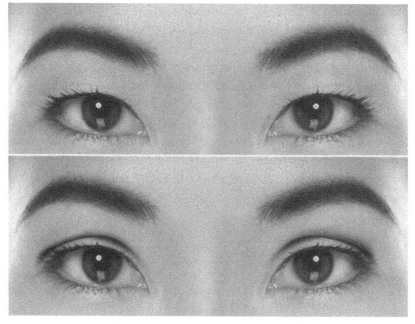

Figure 4.1. Asian eyes before and after blepharoplasty or double eyelid surgery to look more Caucasian.
From iStock by Getty Images.

Such optional surgeries recall the nose jobs pursued by too many Jewish and African American people. As concluded by Iwata, years after his surgeries, ultimately nothing is more attractive than self-acceptance.

Stage 2: Dissonance about Self-Rejection

Cognitive dissonance occurs when people in the conformity stage are exposed to experiences and/or information and insights that contradict their biased socialization. *Disconfirmatory* experiences need not be directly experienced, as in the case of news stories or negative experiences suffered by others in one's social environment. For example, Hank denied accusations of racial profiling until high-profile investigations substantiated and outlawed such systemic police practices. Even then, he reasoned that criminal Latino and African Americans provoke such action by exasperated police—until the day he was pulled over for "driving while Latino." When he complained about being stopped for no apparent reason, he was sternly put in his place under the threat of arrest and harm. This mini-trauma created a dilemma in which Hank's over-valuing of law enforcement competed with his ethnic-linked experience of discrimination. It should be noted that the "dissonance" induced by Hank's disconfirmatory experience can be resolved by either recognizing discrimination previously denied, or by clinging to conformity type explanations (i.e., Hank could blame his misfortune on bad Latinos who make life worse for good Latinos like himself). On the other hand, such unjust treatment can also initiate greater consideration of ways in which racism engenders discrimination, and the need to take a stand on such matters.

Stage 3: Resistance to Racism and Cultural Immersion

The hallmarks of this stage are resistance to and frequent condemnation of the dominant culture alongside a passionate, ethnocentric immersion into one's culture of origin as a way of reinforcing newfound ethnic pride and venting anger at social injustice. Resistance and immersion are frequently reflected in ethnic identity political activism, militancy, an over-valuing of all things ethnic, and devaluation of the dominant group's culture, history, and humanity, even including harsh criticism and rejection of Latinos in the conformity stage, who are viewed as brainwashed *Tío Tacos* [Uncle Tacos or the Chicano version of "Uncle Tom"]. While understandable reactions to oppression, such beliefs can be overly reactive and fall prey to a sense of Latino superiority and what Cornell West (1993) calls counter-racist thinking that makes the knot of racism even more convoluted.

During the 1960s and 1970s, the Brown Berets in the Chicano community and the Young Lords in the Puerto Rican community, both modeled after Oakland's Black Panther Party, represented strong resistance and immersion. These groups embodied organized militant resistance that stirred fears in mainstream society of armed retribution, occasionally provoked by the intense surveillance and provocations of law enforcement, the legal system, and FBI labeling of such youth organizations as threats to national security. Most often, however, these groups organized marches and public demonstrations against discrimination well within their constitutional rights.

While the anger and activism of resistance and immersion can be politically productive and a healthy departure from the self-rejection of conformity or the confusion and paralysis of dissonance, this stage may also result in the problem of over-responding to all manner of provocation and insinuation of injustice versus more selectively *fighting the good fight*. For example, a Latino client once shared a story to his therapist about speeding on a Texas highway with his Stage 3-like brother who overreacted to a highway patrol officer who pulled the client over. Although unhappy to receive a citation, the client did not perceive the situation as racially linked, given that he had been going 80 miles per hour on a rural highway. His brother, however, whose strong dislike for police was rooted in a racist beating by police during his youth, looked menacingly at the officer and began confronting him with angry questions such as "What's the problem here?!", "What law are we really breaking on this empty highway, anyways?!"

The client became quite anxious when the officer harshly reminded the brother that he was speaking to the driver and that he should stop interfering. When the client's brother persisted, the officer stuck his head partially into the driver's window and sternly warned him that if he did not shut up, he would arrest him. The client promptly pleaded with his brother to allow him to handle the situation. Apparently, the brother had an impressive history as a community organizer and activist for Latino rights. However, he was also vulnerable to over-responding to cues and situations perceived as race-linked that may not be worth the fight, depending on the situation.

Stage 4: Introspection into Racial Socialization

This contemplative stage of racial/cultural identity development involves needing to look back, around, and within to question and interrogate the basis of idealizing one's own group, as well as other people of color, and one's devaluation of the NLW dominant group. Such self-analysis typically results in more fair, balanced, and humane assessments of the strengths and weaknesses in *all* groups. For example, the story of NLWs founding and advancing a society primarily by and for themselves, characterized by dominating or rejecting/eliminating other groups perceived as different and undesirable, is the story of humankind throughout history and all around the world. That is, the tendency to "Other" white people in Stage 3, as if fundamentally different from people of color, gives way to the emerging insight that all people share the impulse to dominate others for their own advantage, usually on the basis of some self-serving construction of difference, just as all people have the impulse to resist and challenge oppression in order to share power and resources more fairly.

Hence, despite the racist contradictions built into our evolving American system, in Stage 4, as well as Stage 5 discussed below, there remains appreciation for our constitutional democracy and aspiring vision of government, in addition to a technologically advanced, modern nation that is the most popular destination of people around the globe. The 20th century was the American century, and it is precisely for this reason that Latinos and other people of color continue believing in and contributing to the American dream despite race-linked obstacles. Holding society accountable to its highest ideals is ultimately a patriotic duty designed to advance our aspiration of democracy.

Latinos in the introspection stage recognize that while they have many wonderful culture-based assets, as with any culture there are also elements that need to evolve or be discarded in order to progress in more just and healthier ways (e.g., extreme forms of machismo oppressive to women, heteronormativity rejecting of sexual minority family members). Contemplation is also devoted to shaping one's identity in a less reactive (e.g., Stage 3 Latinos feeling overly obligated to their community) and more proactive manner (feeling free to address causes that transcend the Latino experience). Many successful Latinos are frequently reminded by Latino activists of their "obligation" to "give back" to their community, when perhaps a better motivator is one's own personal desire and commitment to address injustice within the Latino experience and beyond.

Stage 5: Integrative Awareness

An integration of previous stages, typically through some combination of socialization, life lessons, and formal learning, results in a proactive place from which to flexibly operate in a society characterized by *both* democracy *and* racial injustice. Individuals with integrative awareness are described as approaching social justice issues by more broadly addressing all human rights and forms of oppression, as increasingly advocated by an intersectionality perspective.

The example of Martin Luther King publicly opposing the Viet Nam war during the 1960s is instructive for the criticism that it drew from some African American activists who feared that expanding his focus beyond a

Black civil rights agenda would dilute King's time, energy, and impact. While the logic of this criticism makes sense from a resistance and immersion, ethnocentric perspective, it is inherently reactive and limiting. Individuals at this more developed level of consciousness become critical of oppression within their own group, such as sexism and homophobia, viewed as dehumanizing and divisive. There is also faith that NLWs, as fellow human beings, can and do rise to the occasion of fighting racism and discrimination to create a fairer world for everyone.

Proactive personal development at Stage 5 works to integrate a variety of overlapping identities such as being Latino, American, and simply human. Such development manifests in autonomous choices ranging from friends and romantic partners to occupational callings and political leanings. Herein lies the dilemma of trying to gauge someone's level of racial/cultural development by merely observing social affiliations, career paths, and political behavior. While Stage 5 individuals may be viewed with suspicion and confusion, they are empathic and understanding of such perceptions and work to form alliances between factions within their ethnic group, as well as to build coalitions with other minorities and NLWs. For instance, Latino persons with integrated awareness understand that conflict with Latinos at the conformity stage reflects within-group division, rooted in minority group oppression and the convolutions of racism, and as such should be mitigated.

Informative Empirical Model of Chicano Ethnicity

Over 30 years ago, Keefe and Padilla (1987) developed an empirical model of Chicano ethnicity that impressively demonstrates the complex, multidimensional, and nonlinear nature of both ethnicity and the process of acculturation. Based on their review of research, these researchers theorize that ethnic identity and acculturation are related but separate processes, and that cultural change occurs at different rates across different cultural dimensions (e.g., values, language, social affiliations, self-identifications, styles of dress). Keefe and Padilla (1987) theorize that ethnic identity is composed of two distinct developmental dimensions: (1) cultural awareness (CA), which refers to cultural knowledge such as ability to speak Spanish, knowledge of Mexican values, history and traditions, and heroes, as influenced by parents' and spouse's backgrounds; and (2) ethnic loyalty (EL), which refers to the subjective feelings of ethnic-related pride, preferences in social affiliations, and perceived discrimination. These researchers developed a questionnaire to assess CA and EL and administered it to a stratified random sample of 370 Chicanos in Southern California. Factor analysis of questionnaire data revealed that CA and EL did indeed emerge as the two distinct factors or dimensions of ethnic identity.

CA, EL, and Acculturation

Figure 4.2 reveals that over time in the United States, CA drops sharply from first to second generation and then steadily declines from second generation to fourth. In contrast, EL dips a little from first to second generation yet remains stable from second to fourth. Thus, while Chicanos lose much of the content of their Mexican culture from one generation to the next, they retain pride in and preference for own-group members while continuing to perceive racism and discrimination. Thus, the development of ethnic identity may be influenced less by the retention of Mexican culture, as many believe, and more by stigmatized minority status in the United States. This development is typically characterized by segregation (i.e., limited affiliation

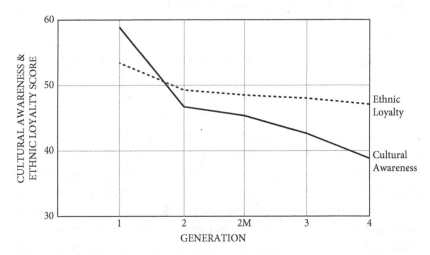

Figure 4.2. Cultural Awareness and Ethnic Loyalty by Generation in Chicanos. *Note*: 2M refers to having one first-generation parent and one second-generation parent.

Adapted with permission: Keefe & Padilla (1987). *Chicano Ethnicity*. Albuquerque: University of New Mexico Press.

choices), discrimination, and the need to transcend the conformity stage of ethnic identity development by accentuating ethnic pride as a defense against stigma, and as a potential vehicle for activism and identity politics promoting group civil rights and advancement.

Results of the above model of Chicano ethnicity are consistent with Hayes-Bautista's (2017b) description of the Chicanx generation, baby boomers interviewed who mourned their loss of Spanish, expressed feeling neither Mexican nor American, but who forged ethnic identities committed to civil rights for their community based on perceptions of racism and discrimination. Further, these members of the Chicano generation also embraced what Hayes-Bautista calls *retro-assimilation* (i.e., Mexican cultural immersion) given the continuous influx of Mexican and Central American immigrants into Chicanx communities in Los Angeles, throughout the Southwest, and beyond (e.g., Chicago), and subsequent changes to local goods, products, and services responding to the needs and preferences of immigrants.

While high EL can help fuel identity politics, as well as "Stage 3" type cultural exploration, ethnic identity void of sufficient cultural content can also be a vulnerability when opportunities for upward mobility are limited, as in the scenario of segmented assimilation discussed in earlier chapters. For example, many gang-affiliated Chicanos claim ethnic pride, loyalty to their *barrio*, and perceive discrimination yet are vulnerable to Latino on Latino hate and violence and self-destruction. Such a contradiction betrays empty cultural assertions void of substance needed to prevent or minimize acting out their psychosocial marginality and frequently traumatic backgrounds. Understanding the relation between ethnic identity and psychosocial adjustment in Latinos has accelerated in the past two decades, some of which is highlighted below.

Ethnic Identity Development and Adjustment

There is ample empirical evidence demonstrating that higher stages of R/CID are associated with better psychosocial adjustment. For example, research shows higher levels of self-esteem in Mexican American, African American, Asian American adolescents (Phinney, 1989), and minority college students (Phinney & Alipuria, 1990) at higher stages of ethnic identity development. "Higher stages" in these studies refers to members of stigmatized minority groups actively grappling with negative racial and ethnic narratives and experiences, resulting in a greater clarity or a firm decision about who they are as racial/ethnic persons. Such promising findings are also corroborated by a review of the literature by Umaña-Taylor, Diversi, and Fine (2002) that examined 21 empirical studies of adolescent Latino ethnic identity and self-esteem. While ethnic identity was conceptualized and measured differently in these studies (i.e., simply identifying as Latino, degree of acculturation and biculturality), the review found general support for higher self-esteem co-occurring with higher Latino ethnic identification, particularly for adolescents living in Latino communities.

A subsequent study by Umana-Taylor et al. (2012) found that ethnic identity affirmation (i.e., positive feelings and attachment for one's ethnic group) protected male Mexican American students, transitioning to middle school, from the negative impact of perceived discrimination on school performance (i.e., teacher reports of externalizing behaviors and deviant peer associations). However, high ethnic identity affirmation was also associated with lower GPA, leading Umana-Taylor and colleagues to wonder if *stereotype threat* might be operating (i.e., anxiety about confirming the negative stereotypes of poor academic ability resulting in less effort as a way of protecting their self-esteem).

Stereotype Threat and Impaired Performance

Let's say you're committed to performing well on a test of ability, but you are also a member of a minority group stereotyped as unable to perform well on the test (e.g., women in math and physical sciences, African Americans and Latinos on standardized academic tests, Asian Americans in non-math or non-science majors). How might such negative stereotypes hurt your performance when you may not believe them to be true, or at least not for you? Well, in his seminal research on what he calls *stereotype threat*, Claude Steele (1997) demonstrates that during important performance situations in which negative stereotypes are *invoked* or become salient, minority performance can suffer. For example, Steele administered a challenging math exam to academically matched male and female math majors at Stanford University. In one experimental condition, the math test is introduced as being able to detect sex differences, while in another condition no such description is provided. Results showed significantly poorer performance on the part of women in the *sex-primed* condition yet no significant differences between men and women in the non-sex-primed condition. Steele and Aronson (1995) demonstrated comparable results when they administered a verbal Graduate Record Examination (GRE) test to African American and white college students, also at Stanford. In the *race-primed* condition, the GRE test was introduced as diagnostic of intelligence, and students were asked to indicate their race on the test form, while in the non-primed condition no such description or instruction was made.

Steele (1997) concludes that institutionalized sexism and racism can undermine identification with school and performance in areas important to even qualified women and minority students. While such school disidentification may protect the self-esteem of minorities who experience low academic preparation and expectations, it can also result in a lack of sustained motivation and effort in important performance situations that become racially primed or charged. Steele also detected greater anxiety (e.g., blood pressure, distracting thoughts) in minorities in race-primed performance situations. His work helps to explain continuing performance gaps between majority and some minority groups in educational settings, even on the part of equally qualified women and minorities.

Latino Stereotype Threat

Rodriguez (2014) demonstrates stereotype threat in Latino students participating in a summer bridge program prior to entering a 4-year university to which they have been admitted. Those in the stereotype threat condition (N = 31) were asked to indicate their ethnic background on a questionnaire, to read two passages from an article about the achievement gap between both Latinos and African Americans as compared to white students, to complete 40 items from the verbal section of the SAT, described as a text of academic ability, and to answer questions about their experience afterwards. As compared to Latino students in the comparison condition (n = 31) that completed the same SAT items but without ethnic and ability priming, students in the stereotype threat condition scored significantly lower (i.e., 2.27 items lower on average for a difference of 9%). Responses to the follow-up questions corroborate the presence of stereotype threat:

> "I was thinking about the gap between whites and Hispanics [during the test] . . . and how we do worse in school."

"I wanted to do [well] but I started getting nervous because I didn't want to add to the achievement gap."

"I felt pressure to do well [on the test] because I wanted to prove that Hispanics can do well in school, too." (pp. 198–99).

Latino Ethnicity and Gender

A study by Gonzales, Blanton, and Williams (2002) also demonstrated ethnic stereotype threat in a sample of 60 Latino college students, evenly divided between male and female, as compared to 60 white college students also divided by sex. Participants were administered a set of problems assessing mathematical and analytic ability, described to half of participants as a test of ability and to the other half as a way of examining the problem-solving process. Interestingly, Latinas also demonstrated gender stereotype threat reflected in their lower performance relative to men (Latino and white), as well as Latinas in the non-primed condition, along with white women (regardless of condition). These results underscore the need to better understand vulnerability in Latinos at the intersection of ethnicity and gender.

White Stereotype Threat?

Surprisingly, white Americans are also vulnerable to stereotype threat even though they are not stigmatized or discriminated on the basis of their race. That is, there are stereotype threats to which whites may succumb when a situation suddenly becomes charged or primed with such threats. For example, Steele (2010) reports on a study in which white and Black male college students are asked to perform on a miniature golf course that requires between 22 and 24 strokes on average to complete, based on prior testing with such participants. However, when participants are told that it is a test of "natural athletic ability," it takes whites an extra three strokes to complete the course while Black performance is unaffected. Steele reasons that white performance is impaired in this race-primed condition when they became anxious about confirming the pervasive stereotype that they have less natural athletic ability than Blacks (e.g., white men can't jump). Conversely, it took Black participants an extra four strokes to complete the course when participants were told that it was a test of "sports strategic intelligence," while white performance was not impaired by this race-primed message that stereotypically favors whites.

How about in a situation in which there is a chance that whites might confirm the stereotype that all whites are racist? To test this, Steele (2010) conducted an experiment in which white undergraduate students are told that they will be conversing with two other students, either about love and relationships or about racial profiling. Next, participants are shown photographs of the two other students with whom they will be conversing, who happened to be African American. Finally, the white participants are asked to arrange three chairs in a room in preparation for the conversation. As predicted, whites expecting to converse with African Americans about racial profiling place their own chair much farther from the other two chairs as compared to a closer placement of chairs when expecting to converse about love and relationships. Further, no differences in chair placements are found between the two conversation topics when white participants were shown pictures of white conversation partners.

Thus, stereotype threat alerts us to the pernicious impact of stereotypes on various important forms of performance and behaviors in situations that can suddenly switch from neutral to primed or charged with a stereotype that is well known in society. That people of color *as well as whites* are negatively affected by stereotype threat underscores the need to recognize, resist, and mitigate it—but how? Steele says that we mitigate stereotype threat by taking measures to support *identity safety* or a sense of trust that our performance is not being evaluated or judged through the lens of stereotypes. The following studies provide insight regarding how to support identity safety.

Supporting Identity Safety

Steele (2010) concludes that stereotype operates in response to, but also transcends, the usual predictors of poor academic performance such as poor segregated backgrounds characterized by low-quality schools, low family income, low professional networks, excessive violence and trauma, and so on. In fact, stereotype threat operates even for the few privileged Black students in predominantly white universities, where minority students sometimes feel they are not expected to do well. One factor found to mitigate such stereotype threat is having Black professors whose presence signals ability and are perceived as less likely to harbor anti-Black stereotypes. However, because faculty of color are still a tiny minority in most colleges (e.g., Latino faculty at UC Berkeley are currently about 7%), the question emerges: how can white faculty help to mitigate stereotype threat? For instance, how can they test and evaluate the work of Black and Latino students without triggering stereotype threat?

To answer this question, Steele and colleagues devised a study in which Black and white Stanford students were asked to write an essay about a favorite instructor, possibly to be published in a new campus magazine depending on critical feedback about the essay's quality. When students returned for the feedback, one type of feedback motivated Black students to revise their essay, while two other types of feedback did not. That is, Black students were motivated to improve their essays when told that *high standards* were used to evaluate their essays for possible publication and that evaluators were *confident* that they could revise and meet those standards. Blacks reported trusting such feedback more than neutral feedback on essay quality or feedback prefaced by positive reassuring statements such as "Great effort on your essay!" or "Please don't feel discouraged by the following feedback." Something about the latter forms of feedback dampened trust and motivation consistent with stereotype threat.

But how might we mitigate stereotype threat at larger institutional levels when, according to Steele, universities continue to generate numerous cues that elicit stereotype threat, including a sense that certain people of color do not belong on campus? To begin to answer this immense question, colleagues of Steele at Northeastern University provided freshmen African American students with two brief narratives. The first described upper-division Black students now comfortable and doing well at the university, even though they admitted not feeling comfortable as freshmen. The second narrative simply shared survey results regarding political attitudes rather than anything about college life. Students receiving the first narrative performed better academically in the subsequent semester than students exposed to the second narrative.

Similar results were found in another study by Steele and colleagues in which they simply hosted late-night "bull sessions" in college dorms that featured open-ended sharing of their college experience (relations with friends, romantic partners, family, professors, how classes were going, etc.). While participating African American students were few in these sessions (between two and four), they subsequently performed better academically than counterparts that did not participate in such discussion. Steele concludes that participating African American students learned that many of their college-related experiences were similar to those of other students and not just a function of their racial background.

In addition to the above tweaks to feedback on performance and student inclusion and sharing, mitigating stereotype threat also depends on conveying a *flexible view of intelligence* as ongoing and expanding versus something "fixed," as most of us have been socialized to assume (i.e., some people are smart and some aren't, some are good at math and some aren't). To remedy this rigid binary, Steele reports on an intervention with low-income and minority students entering junior high school in rural Texas. A random sample of students were each assigned a college student academic mentor that met twice with students over the year and communicated regularly by email. For one group of students, mentors stressed the expandability of intelligence, or how the brain makes new neural connections while learning new things. The latter included website illustrations of how dendrites grow when attempting to solve challenging problems. Mentors for the comparison group of students instead emphasized drug abuse prevention. As predicted, students in the expandability of intelligence condition performed significantly better on the reading section of the Texas Assessment of Academic Skills (TAAS) versus students in the drug abuse prevention condition. Further, girls in the expandability conditions did as well as boys within the same condition on the math section of the TAAS. In contrast, girls in the drug abuse prevention condition performed significantly poorer than boys, reproducing the stereotypic gender gap in tests of math ability.

Implications of the above research include the possibility of mitigating stereotype threat at the institutional level through deliberate yet fairly easy practices that support and promote *identity safety*. Such efforts include diversifying faculty, staff, and administrators; providing trustworthy and motivating feedback; community-building mechanisms that allow diverse students to compare their experiences at school; and conveying the flexible and expanding nature of intelligence in school settings, rather than reifying reductionistic stereotypes of ability.

Additional strategies to support identity safety may include promoting external architectural and interior designs that reflect and welcome racial and ethnic diversity in ways that promote a more secure sense of belonging.

Progress mitigating stereotype threat will depend on understanding its causes, cues, consequences, and solutions, as well as racial identity development on the part of NLWs at university, work and corporate, political, and other settings where power is substantial and minority representation low.

White Racial Identity and Critical Whiteness Studies

We too often forget that when we speak of *minority* identity we automatically imply its counterpart, *majority* identity. Yet, focus on majority or NLW identity is a relatively recent development that opens up needed space to directly analyze who white Americans are in the racial identity mix, and why they lack much of an "ethnic" identity despite our country's insistence on labeling racial and ethnic minority groups as such. In the United States during the late 20th century, *critical whiteness studies* emerged to de-center whiteness as the norm, and yet center white people within discussions of race relations, to highlight the dominant role of white people toward minorities and to render whiteness amenable to study "under the microscope," the same as minorities. What does it mean to be white, given the central linkages of this racial category to power, resources, and privilege?

Listing Privileges

Over 30 years ago, Peggy McIntosh (1988) incited a minor revolution in critical whiteness studies with a revealing article that listed almost 50 different yet common ways, hardly noticed by whites, in which white privilege systematically makes life better for them on average and also worse for Blacks and other people of color. A few telling examples include:

- I can turn on the television or open to the front page of a newspaper and see people of my race widely and positively represented.
- I can be reasonably sure that if I ask to talk to "the person in charge," I will be facing a person of my race.
- I can go home from most meetings or organizations I belong to feeling somewhat tied in, rather than isolated, out of place, outnumbered, unheard, held at a distance, or feared.

- I can worry about racism without being seen as self-interested or self-seeking.
- If my day, week, or year is going badly, I need not ask of each negative episode or situations whether it has racial overtones.
- I can be pretty sure that my children's teachers and employers will tolerate them if they fit school and workplace norms; my chief worries about them do not concern others' attitudes toward their race.
- I can do well in a challenging situation without being called a credit to my race.
- I can be sure that if I need legal or medical help, my race will not work against me.
- I can be late to a meeting without having the lateness reflect on my race.

More important than McIntosh's now famous list, however, is her explanation of how members of the dominant group are socialized, directly and indirectly (i.e., indoctrinated), to be "oblivious" to their race privilege, and how such lack of awareness perpetuates white privilege and a racially biased status quo. McIntosh asserts that the white experience in America is generally one that recognizes, reflects, validates, and supports its members. From the representation and indeed overrepresentation of whites in all positions of power in society, to their predominance in popular culture, theirs is a world that largely elicits comfort, security, and confidence as opposed to the disproportionately high discomfort, alienation, and insecurity experienced by too many people of color. You could say that America generally works as designed and advertised for whites, while minorities must face significantly more false advertising.

Building upon McIntosh, Frankenberg (2000) refers to whiteness as an "unmarked" racial category and to white people as the "unmarked markers of others" for their historical practice of labeling, categorizing, quantifying, defining, and evaluating non-whites while presuming themselves to be the central norm from which people of color are perceived to deviate. Such a common colonial practice reflects the privilege and power to be the unexamined norm (Tatum, 1997)—the power position within a racial hierarchy that allows whites the privilege to view themselves as simply normal individuals, rather than as part of a hegemonic controlling race group. Such white normativity, including obliviousness to white privilege, cultivates immense defensiveness on the part of whites frequently confronted with their role in the dynamics of American racism as described below.

White Fragility?

DiAngelo (2018) uses her white positionality to interrogate racism and privilege in her book, *White Fragility: Why is it so hard for white people to talk about racism?* DiAngelo explains that white fragility refers to the conditioned response of white people to recoil from the slightest insinuation that they are racist, a reaction DiAngelo explains is rooted in the socialization of whites as characterized by:

- Viewing oneself as an individual, shaped by meritocracy, rather than part of a privileged white collective.
- Viewing racism as an individual-level negative trait characteristic of bad individuals and hence highly offensive.
- Viewing oneself as free from historical and current expressions of racism.
- Believing one can exempt oneself from racism via individual-level arguments (e.g., being a descendent of oppressed ethnic ancestors; being poor or having survived poverty; possessing past or present relations with people of color).
- Failing to consider one's individual story alongside their whiteness.
- Resenting people of color for criticizing and protesting racism in the United States when they are viewed as getting what they deserve.

Given such racialization, whites express the above beliefs and attitudes with sincerity, even indignity and outright anger, without the insight that such conditioned defensiveness serves to protect and maintain the racial status quo or racial hierarchy because it reflexively rebuffs any consideration of a system that over-rewards whites at the expense of racial and ethnic minorities. One pronounced example is the rapidly expanding population of poor and struggling working class whites, many succumbing to opiate addition, that balk at the idea of being advantaged by race. Yet, compared to Blacks and other non-whites within the same social class, their lives are better *on average* because they are free of race stigma and discriminatory pitfalls and impediments, while being over-rewarded for being white relative to people of color. As mentioned in Chapter 3's focus on social stratification of race and power, whites are three times as likely as Blacks and Latinos to get call-backs as applicants for non-skilled jobs simply because of their white-sounding names on their job applications.

Given the above, it is ironic that so many whites resent beneficiaries of affirmative action programs that barely mitigate centuries of exclusion and disempowerment. Yet such beneficiaries are resented because many NLWs perceive minorities as receiving an unfair advantage, or precisely the pervasive defining feature of white privilege. Unfortunately, there is little if any awareness of how being privileged by race has historically provided whites with the ultimate unfair advantage, versus how affirmative action has provided minuscule representation of minorities in positions of power without any significant displacement of whites. On the other hand, some whites understand affirmative action as an imperfect yet partial solution to an extreme problem, and count themselves and society as direct beneficiaries of enhanced diversity and fairness. Many also recognize that white women, and hence white families, have been the largest group of beneficiaries of affirmative action designed to support minorities *and* women. Such awareness helps many whites to develop the *racial stamina* necessary to tolerate the struggle to recognize and rectify racial inequality.

How to Build Racial Stamina

White fragility limits the development of what DiAngelo calls *racial stamina*, or the ability to tolerate uncomfortable but potentially insightful learning about links between one's whiteness and racism in America. Sufficient racial stamina maximizes the probability of better understanding and changing our participation in racial hierarchy. DiAngelo strives personally and as a professional diversity trainer to transform white fragility into racial stamina. Transformation is evident in adaptive responses to others who point out inevitable but unnoticed racist patterns: discomfort and guilt mitigated by gratitude, motivation, and humility that promote listening, reflecting, grappling, seeking deeper understanding, and apology. A few beliefs that support racial stamina for whites include:

- We are all socialized into the system of racism.
- Nothing exempts me from the forces of racism.
- It is my responsibility to resist defensiveness and complacency.
- Focus on the message not the messenger.
- Being good or bad is irrelevant.
- The antidote to guilt is action.

- Authentic anti-racism is rarely comfortable. Discomfort is the key to my growth and thus desirable.
- My analysis must be intersectional (a recognition that my other social identities—class, gender, ability—inform how I was socialized into the racial system).
- Racism hurts (even kills) people of color 24-7. Interrupting it is more important than my feelings, ego, or self-image.

Emerging racial stamina is evident in the unprecedented widespread support for Black Lives Matter on the part of whites in the wake of George Floyd's brutal murder by Minneapolis police officers in the summer of 2020. Such support includes the direct participation of whites in protests in urban centers as well as the suburbs, and poll numbers indicating a plurality of whites supporting the need for police reform. Implied in the above transformation described by DiAngelo is increasing white racial identity development as elaborated below.

White Racial Identity Development

Sue et al. (2019b) apply their R/CID model to the analysis of racial identity development in NLW Americans. While the dominant majority group has no U.S. history of *racial* oppression (i.e., stigma and discrimination), Sue et al. maintain that whites can be viewed as experiencing a parallel form of racial identity development, ranging from white conformity to multiculturalist identity.

White Conformity

Whites are viewed as overwhelmingly socialized within Stage 1, where there is little questioning of the status quo (i.e., social stratification of race, ethnicity, and power). Lack of questioning is a function of the generally higher positionality of whites and lower positionality of people of color. This positionality is attributed to individual-level, internal factors such as intelligence, talent and work effort, and cultural values, as opposed to external social factors such as a living legacy of structural racism and discrimination. As such, inequity is viewed as normal and natural, as rationalized by cherished national narratives such as *meritocracy* and the *American dream* discussed in Chapter 3. Indeed, immersion in white culture at this stage is experienced as central and normal, while different cultures are viewed as non-normative deviations. While somewhat aware of past and continuing racism, white Americans in the conformity stage generally minimize the intensity of its structural legacy and do not perceive themselves as personally responsible, even though they have collectively inherited the advantaged side of this legacy.

Tatum (1997) asserts that while it is the task of oppressed minorities to challenge racism and develop positive identities by externalizing stigma and challenging discrimination, it is also the task of whites to develop a non-racist identity by relinquishing a distorted view of themselves as superior and as having earned their generally higher social positionality in a completely fair manner. Such a complex task requires a deeper understanding of racism, not simply as occasional blatant acts on the part of bad actors but as an entrenched social, cultural, stratified institutional system that differentially rewards and punishes a socially constructed racialized hierarchy of people.

White Dissonance

In Sue et al.'s dissonance stage, information and experiences that disconfirm the beliefs and perceptions of conformity-stage whites prompts them to question their socialization around racial inequality and explicit or implicit white superiority. Awareness of one's membership in the dominant and privileged race group often elicits feelings of guilt and shame, although ultimately these are unhelpful emotions in the effort to advance fairness and civil and human rights. While dissonance can set the stage for progression into a white version of resistance and immersion, the subjective discomfort of dissonance can also cause whites to minimize the truth and retreat into their privileged white experience. Such backward movement is reflected in rationalizations such as "It can't be that bad," or "There's really nothing I can do about it" and "It's not really my problem or responsibility." Such retreat is yet another option within the *invisible knapsack* of white privilege. That is, while whites can generally avoid and minimize their interactions with people of color, and related social problems and issues, people of color must deal directly with majority whiteness on a daily basis.

In addition to the privilege of retreating from dissonance, whites at this stage can also run the risk of over-responding to racism all around them and sometimes alienating other whites in the process. In her pioneering book *The Education of a WASP*, Lois Stalvey (Stalvey, 1988), herself a white Anglo

Saxon Protestant, describes how becoming aware of, discussing, and taking action against racism alienated her white friends and neighbors who could not understand why she was bothering with such issues that they viewed as distant from and irrelevant to their racially comfortable lives.

Tatum (1977) also discusses whites at the dissonance stage as sometimes feeling frustrated and even upset with people of color for supposedly contributing to their own problems. There's an urgent sense that people of color should change and "get with the program," as well as an insistence that everybody is an "individual," overlooking that whites are uniquely privileged to make such a claim. Part of the distress that this stage engenders for whites is a gnawing awareness that their prideful well-being and accomplishments are acquired *partly* by race privilege rather than solely by their individual efforts, talents, and abilities. Exposures to such unfair advantage, whether personal, academic, direct, or indirect, sometimes compel whites into their own form of resistance and immersion.

White Resistance and Immersion

In the resistance and immersion stage, whites become upset about their biased socialization and begin to devalue their group while idealizing minorities with whom they sometimes over-identify. While this stage reflects significant growth on the part of whites, Sue et al. caution that some in this stage get caught up in a "white liberal syndrome" in which guilt-driven efforts to help minorities can be unintentionally paternalistic given the white script to "take charge," especially where the affairs of people of color are concerned.

The author recalls that while attending Roosevelt High School in ELA during the early 1970s, a group of white college students from Cal State Los Angeles were invited to enrich our weak public school curriculum. While these talented students did enhance our modest course offerings with advanced art and science classes and activities, we stylish continental dressers were a bit shocked when they arrived on our campus dressed in Mexican guaracha sandals and South American *ponchos*! While we couldn't articulate it at the time, they appeared to be over-identifying with off-putting stereotypes of Mexican-ness and Latino-ness, despite their otherwise good deeds and intentions. As with people of color at this stage who come to question the limits of their reactivity to racism, whites can also come to question how they are expressing their newfound anti-racism activism.

White Introspection

For whites, introspection is a time to pause and question the basis of an often wholesale rejection of whiteness, including themselves, as well as an over-identification and occasional valorization of minorities. It is a time to fairly evaluate both majority and minority groups, to begin to reject racism and privilege in all groups, and distill the best of fair and humanistic elements in each. Tatum describes the need to advance beyond white guilt and shame and the role of victimizer, oppressor, or even colonist. Such growth requires searching for white allies, historical as well as contemporary, fictional as well as real. There can be a need to vent to other whites about how challenging it is to be anti-racist, anti-privilege, and diversity-embracing white person, especially when such expressions of distress fall on the deaf ears of minorities whose larger race-linked pains can make it difficult and even sometimes impossible to hear and validate legitimate white pain and suffering. While ignoring the pain of whites struggling with racial identity development may be viewed as "giving them a taste of their own medicine," such reactions do not advance needed cross-race alliances. One of the fundamental shifts for whites in this stage of development is a refocusing of one's energies from "helping poor minorities" to challenging institutional racism and biased national policies and practices for everybody's well-being.

White Integrative Awareness

This advanced stage of racial/cultural identity development is characterized by an anti-racist white identity that actively explores the best in white culture without denying racism and ending one's paralysis to do something about it. There is also selective appreciation for the humanistic values and actions in all racial and cultural groups. Privilege is accurately viewed as ultimately damaging to whites and society for the distortions that it creates regarding social inequalities, convictions about who merits reward and support and who does not, and how it perpetuates and stabilizes inequality. Tatum describes this stage of development as foundational for authentic cross-racial relationships and alliances capable of promoting human rights in sustainable ways, and reminds us that this stage is an aspirational "work in progress" because salient race-linked situations can unexpectedly trigger primitive, reactionary, and conditioned responses in people. Still, this advanced stage is characterized by fewer negative reactions to uncomfortable race-linked experiences and more productive responses. The bottom line is no denial of the pervasive effects of group memberships in a racialized hierarchy and the need to undermine them for the greater good.

Toward Intersectionality

So how does all of the above R/CID theory and research play out in the lives of women as compared to men, or sexual minorities? How does Latino ethnicity become complicated by diversity within Latinos such as being a racially Black Latino (e.g., from Puerto Rico, Cuba, Dominican Republic, or Panama)? Also, where do Latinos of mixed racial and ethnic heritage (e.g., Latino and Anglo or Latino and African American) fit into the racial and ethnic identity puzzle? Such questions have emerged with increasing frequency, deserving our attention as service providers, researchers, and members of society. Thus, while deeply influential, racial and ethnic identity is ultimately but one dimension of the self-concept at the intersection of many other dynamic and consequential identities and roles in our complex lives. The next chapter will consider how other dimensions and identities such as gender and sexual orientation, racial characteristics, and immigration status play out in the lives of U.S. Latinos.

References

DiAngelo, R. (2018). *White Fragility: Why it's so hard for white people to talk about racism.* Boston, MA: Beacon Press.

Collins, P. H., & Bilge, S. (2016). *Intersectionality.* Malden, MA: Polity Press.

Hayes-Bautista, D. E. (2017a). America defines Latinos. In D. Hayes-Bautista (Ed.), *La Nueva California: Latinos from pioneers to post-millennials* (pp. 1–24). Berkeley: University of California Press.

Hayes-Bautista, D. E. (2017b). Latinos define Latinos. In D. Hayes-Bautista (Ed.), *La Nueva California: Latinos from pioneers to post-millennials* (pp. 67–91). Berkeley: University of California Press.

Frankenberg, R. (2000). Whiteness as an "unmarked" cultural category. In K. E. Rosenblum & T. C. Travis (Eds.), *The meaning of difference: American constructions of race, sex and gender, social class, and sexual orientation* (3rd ed.) (pp. 92–98). Boston: McGraw Hill.

Gonzales, P. M., Blanton, H., & Williams, K. J. (2002). The effects of stereotype threat and double-minority status on the test performance of Latino women. *Personality and Social Psychology Bulletin, 28*(5), 659–670.

Iwata, E. (1991). Race without face. *San Francisco Focus*, May, pp. 51–53, 128–132.

Keefe, S. E., & Padilla, A. M. (1987). *Chicano ethnicity*. Albuquerque: University of New Mexico Press.

Kendi, I. X. (2019). *How to be an anti-racist*. New York: One World Publishers.

McIntosh, P. (1998). White privilege and male privilege: A personal account of coming to see correspondence through work in women's studies. *Peace and Freedom* (July/August), 10–12.

Phinney, J. S. (1989). Stages of ethnic identity in minority group adolescents. *Journal of Early Adolescence, 45*, 1297–1303.

Phinney, J. S., & Alipuria, L. (1990). Ethnic identity in older adolescents from four ethnic groups. *Journal of Adolescence, 13*, 171–183.

Rodriguez, B. (2014). The threat of living up to expectations: Analyzing the performance of Hispanic students on standardized exams. *Journal of Hispanic Higher Education, 13*(3) 191–205. https://doi.org/10.1177/1538192714531292

Stalvey, L. M. (1989). *The education of a WASP*. Madison: The University of Wisconsin Press.

Steele, C. M. (1997). A threat in the air: How stereotypes shape intellectual identity and performance. *American Psychologist, 52*(6), 613–629.

Steele, C. M. (2010). *Whistling Vivaldi: How stereotypes affect us and what we can do*. New York: W. W. Norton.

Steele, C. M., & Aronson, J. (1995). Stereotype threat and the intellectual test performance of African Americans. *Journal of Personality and Social Psychology, 69*(5), 797–811.

Sue, D. W., Sue, D., Neville, H. A, & Smith, L. (2019a). Racial/cultural identity development in people of color: Counseling implications. In D. W. Sue, D. Sue, H. A. Neville and L. Smith (Eds.), *Counseling the culturally different: Theory and practice* (8th ed.) (pp. 355–388). New York: John Wiley.

Sue, D. W., Sue, D., Neville, H. A, & Smith, L. (2019b). White racial identity development: Counseling implications. In D. W. Sue, D. Sue, H. A. Neville & L. Smith (Eds.), *Counseling the culturally different: Theory and practice* (8th ed.) (pp. 389–424). New York: John Wiley.

Tatum, B. D. (1997). The development of white identity: "I'm not ethnic, I'm just normal". In B. D. Tatum (Ed.), *Why are all the Black kids sitting together in the cafeteria?* (pp. 93–113). New York: Basic Books.

Umaña-Taylor, A. J., Diversi, M., & Fine, M. A. (2002). Ethnic identity and self-esteem of Latino adolescents: Distinctions among the Latino populations. *Journal of Adolescent Research, 17*, 303–327.

Umana-Taylor, A. J., Wong, J. J, Gonzales, N. A., & Dumka, L. E. (2012). Ethnic identity and gender as moderators of the association between discrimination and academic adjustment among Mexican-origin adolescents. *Journal of Adolescence, 35*(4): 773–786. https://doi.org/10.1016/j.adolescence.2011.11.003.

West, C. (1993). The pitfalls of racial reasoning. In C. West (Ed.), *Race matters* (pp. 23–32). Boston: Beacon Press.

5

Toward Latinx Intersectionality

From Single to Multiple Dimensional Analysis of Human Diversity

> Intersectionality is a way of understanding and analyzing the complexity in the world, in people, and in human experiences. The events and conditions of social and political life and the self can seldom be understood as shaped by one factor. They are generally shaped by many factors in diverse and mutually influencing ways. When it comes to social inequality, people's lives and the organization of power in a given society are better understood as being shaped not by a single axis of social division, be it race or gender or class, but by many axes that work together and influence each other. Intersectionality as an analytic took gives people better access to the complexity of the world and of themselves.
>
> —Patricia Hill Collins and Sirma Bilge (2016), p. 2

Intersectionality, or the recognition that each of us occupies several dimensions of human diversity simultaneously including related identities, stigmas, and privileges, makes subjective experiential sense in our multiple daily roles. It also follows from such intuition that optimal understanding of social justice–related problems necessitates using intersectionality as an analytic tool with which to achieve better problem assessment and outcomes in practice and society. The overarching rationale for an intersectional approach, evident in Collins' quote above, is that it is insufficient to focus on only one or a few forms of human diversity because doing so can render invisible other relevant forms. The prototypical example illustrated in the original texts on intersectionality is that of being Black and female. That is, it is inadequate to focus primarily on race (e.g., in the civil rights movement) or

Solving Latino Psychosocial and Health Problems. Kurt C. Organista, Oxford University Press.
© Oxford University Press 2023. DOI: 10.1093/oso/9780190059637.003.0005

gender (e.g., in the women's movement) because it renders Black women less visible given their simultaneous oppression at the intersection of racism and sexism. Ideally, we should address being Black *and* female, and other related forms of diversity (e.g., social class), by focusing on the intersection of racism, sexism, and classism for such individuals, along with other relevant dimensions (e.g., sexual orientation).

Indeed, the metaphor of an intersection where two or more roads cross is helpful in visualizing where multiple systems of oppression converge and impinge upon the life of an individual or population. Figure 5.1, for example, can be used to construct several scenarios of Latinx intersectionality characterized by several forms of diversity that vary with regard to degrees of stigma as well as privilege.

Challenges to Intersectionality Thinking

So why does thinking in terms of intersectionality continue to be more the exception than the rule? That is, if it is so logical and intuitive, why don't we utilize intersectionality as much as we should? One compelling reason is that we have been socialized in the United States to think about human diversity

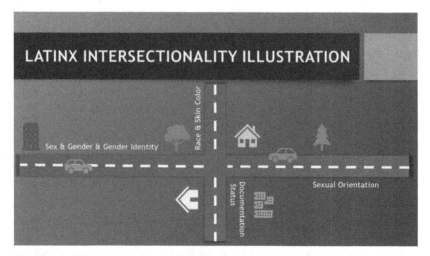

Figure 5.1. Illustration of Latinx intersectionality scenarios.
(PowerPoint Slide by Samantha Ngo, MPH, MSW).

one dimension or oppressed group at a time (e.g., with regard to civil rights movements, within graduate education and training, and in professional practice settings). Historically, there has been a sequential focus on how various civil or minority rights movements have developed and progressed over the decades. For example, while the 1960s witnessed the breakthrough of several major movements, the civil rights movement, primarily focusing on African American liberation, held a certain primacy in proportion to the epic struggle to address anti-blackness in America. In fact, African American resistance and civil rights leadership has long served as the model emulated by smaller racial and ethnic minority movements (i.e., the Chicano and Puerto Rican movements of the 1960s and 1970s, as well as the American Indian and Asian American movements).

While the women's liberation or feminist movement also achieved new footing during the 1960s, it initially struggled to garner support from mainstream institutions and political leaders, as well as from within racial and ethnic minority movements, where it was typically subjugated beneath racial and ethnic liberation. That is, patriarchy within mainstream America and also within racial and ethnic minority cultures slowed the progress of the women's movement and made it seem secondary and subsequent to the racialized civil rights movement.

Similarly, the gay liberation movement of the 1960s, and especially following the pivotal Stonewall uprising of 1969, can seem subsequent and secondary to the women's movement that gained significant momentum through the 1970s and continues through the present. Similarly, the disability rights movement appears to follow the women's movement, culminating in the Americans with Disabilities Act of 1990, the civil rights law prohibiting discrimination on the basis of disability in all areas of public life (i.e., work, schools, transportation, and public and private places open to the general public).

Intersectionality theorists would rightly argue that the above movements need to be integrated because they collectively target various interacting systems of oppression. For instance, a person that happens to be Latinx, female, lesbian, and disabled belongs to all of the above movements. Thus, focusing on a single dimension of oppression is suboptimal and helps to explain the persistence of oppression based on social constructs of hierarchy of human differences. Intersectional thinking advances our understanding of the impact of multiple systems of oppression as well as privilege. For instance, if the above Latinx person happens to male, gay, and non-disabled, they would be differently impacted at the intersection of systems of racism, male privilege, heteronormativity, and able-bodied privilege.

Thus, with an intersectional aspiration in mind, the predominately single dimension–focused literature regarding diversity within Latinxs is reviewed with intersectionality framing in mind. This goal is attempted with respect to pertinent intersectionality-related principles, guidelines, as well as critiques in this still nascent, challenging yet imperative area of inquiry:

- Consideration of multiple identities is insufficient unless considered in terms of structural systems of power.
- We need to shift our focus toward oppressive structures of power rather than individual groups and identities without sufficient attention to the social-structural relational context.
- The common thread across uses of intersectionality is the capacity for an intersectional perspective to render visible how systems of inequality function in overlapping ways, thereby enabling the possibility of transforming matrices of power (National Association of Social Work [NASW], 2021).

Warner and Sheilds (2013) implore us to keep in mind that: (a) Within applications of intersectionality, the act of using categories is itself problematic; (b) applications of intersectionality do not adequately address the fluidity of identities (e.g., non-binary conforming youth); and (c) applications of intersectionality do not sufficiently address the social construction of identity categories that should be acknowledged.

Social Constructionism

Social constructionism posits that what we believe to be true about ourselves, others, and the world can only result from our perceptions and interpretation-driven beliefs that are ultimately bounded by the historical window in which we live, our context of social and political power, networks of social affiliations, latest funds of knowledge, and so on. Thus, what we believe to be true and *real* can be limited by how far knowledge has advanced (e.g., the world is round vs. flat) and/or what powerful social leaders claim to be true, right and wrong, good and bad, and the like. The latter point emphasizes the inevitable relation between power and conceptions of reality, in that those with power have more resources and channels with which to project their typically self-serving view to members of society of what's real and right and what's not.

As was mentioned in Chapter 3's discussion of social stratification, the rich, powerful, and elite are overly invested in maintaining a stratification system that distributes a disproportionately greater amount of power and resources to their own memberships. Thus, status quo maintenance is ac-complished through the production of pervasive narratives and ideologies, value systems, myths, and legends that are infused into the socialization process through mainstream institutions, policies, and culture in order to rationalize and normalize a society's uneven distribution of life-sustaining resources and power (Marger, 2015). Fortunately, counter-narratives are also constructed by the less powerful, more oppressed populations of people resisting and pursuing their fair share of opportunities, resources, and power.

Social constructivists do not deny the world available to our perceptions, including the tremendous biodiversity around and within it, but they do de-fine as arbitrary our interpretations of things or their *social meanings*. For ex-ample, biological sex is considered a social construction not because male and female bodies aren't biologically distinct, but because our culture has devel-oped elaborate constructions of what such differences mean, with immense consequences for how males and females are distinctly socialized. Thus, the fact that we've never had a female president in the United States is rooted in a traditionally patriarchal, albeit changing, conception of women as not biologically (i.e., emotionally, intellectually) suited to the task. Fortunately the women's movement, past and present, has challenged stigmatizing and limiting social constructions of women, resulting in gradual social libera-tion and less oppressive conceptions of gender, albeit with a considerable way to go.

For the purpose this book, the social constructivist perspective can be a liberating and humanistic view that challenges *essentialistic* and stigmatizing constructions of Latinxs and other people of color as solely responsible for their social positionality due to supposed individual and population-wide deficits. Constructivism can inspire those experiencing oppression to question authority and contest the so-called *truth*: "Says who, and based on what evidence?" and "Does this social construction allow some groups to benefit at the expense of others?" (e.g., the monopolization of power by men).

Social constructivism flies in the face of *essentialism*, or the position that an objective reality exists apart from human perceptions and interpretations. But because in our early youth we are raised in an essentialist manner, and because important human enterprises such as science appear to purport essentialist truths (e.g., facts vs. findings), social constructivism can be initially difficult to grasp and is often harshly criticized ("If you think that gravity is a social construction, then try jumping off the roof!"). However, such criticism misses the point.

Zen Buddhists have known for ages that just because you attach a term such as "gravity" to some phenomenon doesn't make the word *gravity* real. This lesson is driven home by the famous Zen koan in which the master displays his fist to a student and asks, "See the fist?" Then, once the student nods, the master quickly un-balls his hand and asks, "Where did the fist go?" It is the student's job to realize that there is no such thing as a fist, merely a label that we invent and attach to a conception of something that we label for useful purposes (e.g., in verbal communication). Thus, the critical questions become, *which* social constructions are more useful and adaptive and which are less so? Also, by whom are certain constructions used and for what purpose?

Shifting our focus to social injustice on the basis of social constructions of human differences makes clearer the links between the many oppressive "isms" in society that privilege some human categories at the expense of others, thus rendering more visible the overarching nature of human systems of oppression within society. Paradoxically, corresponding systems of liberation are also rendered more visible. This chapter attempts an intersectional approach to human diversity within Latinxs by first outlining a social justice framework to deepen understanding of the dynamics of complex systems of oppression that result in variations in problem patterns among subgroups of Latinxs. Following this framework, a selective review of diversity within Latinxs from an intersectional context is ventured.

Diversity, Oppression, and Social Justice

Interestingly, the vast majority of human service providers come from academic and professional trainings with very strong ethics about promoting social justice, fighting oppression, respecting human differences, and providing culturally competent services. For example, in the National Association of Social Workers' (2021) most recently updated Code of Ethics, it explicitly states in the Ethical Principles section:

Value: Social Justice

Ethical Principle: Social workers challenge social injustice

Social workers challenge social injustice. Social workers pursue social change, particularly with and on behalf of vulnerable and oppressed individuals and groups of people. Social workers' social change efforts are focused primarily on issues of poverty, unemployment, discrimination, and other forms of social injustice. These activities seek to promote sensitivity to and knowledge about oppression and cultural and ethnic diversity. Social workers strive to ensure access to needed information, services, and resources; equality of opportunity; and meaningful participation in decision making for all people.

Links between social justice, human diversity, and culturally competent services are further fused:

Cultural Competence

(a) *Social workers should demonstrate understanding of culture and its function in human behavior and society, recognizing the strengths that exist in all cultures.*

(b) *Social workers should demonstrate knowledge that guides practice with clients of various cultures and be able to demonstrate skills in the provision of culturally informed services that empower marginalized individuals and groups. Social workers must take action against oppression, racism, discrimination, and inequities, and acknowledge personal privilege.*

(c) *Social workers should demonstrate awareness and cultural humility by engaging in critical self-reflection (understanding their own bias and engaging in self-correction); recognizing clients as experts of their own culture; committing to life-long learning; and holding institutions accountable for advancing cultural humility.*

(d) *Social workers should obtain education about and demonstrate under-standing of the nature of social diversity and oppression with respect to race, ethnicity, national origin, color, sex, sexual orientation, gender identity or expression, age, marital status, political belief, religion, immi-gration status, and mental or physical ability.*

(e) *Social workers who provide electronic social work services should be aware of cultural and socioeconomic differences among clients' use of and access to electronic technology and seek to prevent such potential barriers. Social workers should assess cultural, environmental, economic, mental or physical ability, linguistic, and other issues that may affect the delivery or use of these services.*

While aspirational professional ethics represent ideals worth striving for, they can be difficult to approximate in practice unless service providers have a firm conceptual grounding regarding the complex nature of op-pression, and how we are all socialized to enact various roles within its matrix-like structure. With deeper understanding of how the dynamics of oppression operate, we can better recognize and respond to oppressive tendencies at structural and individual levels, both outside of as well as within ourselves. As practitioners and members of society, it is our *collec-tive responsibility* to recognize the living legacy of oppression that we all inherit, through no volition of our own, and that must be challenged in order to advance *liberty and justice for all*. Such insight minimizes our fre-quent knee-jerk reaction of denying any personal responsibility for past or ongoing oppression of minority groups ("I'm not responsible for what happened in the past!") and motivates accepting our collective responsi-bility to work for a fairer society.

Defining Features of Op(press)ion

It is helpful to take note of the word *press* embedded in the term *oppres-sion*, given that it refers to a pressing down upon a person or population in order to limit movement, expression, power, freedom, and indeed life itself. Bell (1997) notes five defining features of oppression that capture its com-plexity: (1) *restricting*—of life chances by limiting access to material and struc-tural resources; (2) *hierarchical*—characterized by dominant–subordinate relations of power; (3) *pervasive*—consisting of a complex web of relations in socially structured environments; (4) composed of individuals who occupy complex, multiple, and cross-cutting relations with varying degrees of internalized subordination *and* dominance or *intersectionality*; and (5) consisting of an overarching system composed of several ideologies or "isms" that privilege some categories of people at the expense of others. While most people are aware of the first two of the above defining features of oppression (i.e., that some powerful individuals and groups frequently exploit and abuse the less powerful), they are often less aware of the pervasive and institutionalized nature of oppression and how it structures their daily social experiences, or how we all occupy multiple status dimensions *simultaneously*, some of which are privileged (e.g., being white and middle class) and some of which are stigmatized (e.g., being female and a sexual minority). This latter point reminds us that we are talking about social categories of people and not individuals per se, while the former point stresses the degree to which such categories literally structure our social experience and existence (i.e., the social class and predominant race/ethnic group within which we grow up). Consistent with intersectionality, Bell's fifth dimension of oppression emphasizes the ideal need to address *all* manifestations of oppression because each is part of the same interlocking system of dehumanization.

The Social Oppression Matrix

The above dimensions of oppression can be visualized as a matrix-like social structure within which members of society are socialized to live, work, think, feel, interact, love, and so on. This construct is illustrated in Hardiman and Jackson's (1997) Social Oppression Matrix that contains at least three levels of oppression about which we need to remain aware (see Figure 5.2): (1) *individual*—where conscious and unconscious cognitive, emotional, and behavioral activities are experienced (although we should also include *subconscious* to capture our frequent semi-awareness of oppressive tendencies); (2) *institutional*—where family, community, government, educational, and corporate-industrial-work activities play out (e.g., historical social policies of inclusion and exclusion;); and (3) *social and cultural*—which refers to society-wide cultural norms that serve to bind institutions and individuals (e.g., through values, attitudes, and role prescriptions imbued with rationales and justification for practices of reward and punishment, including

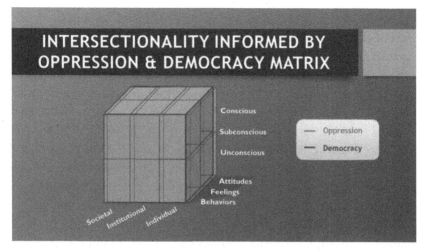

Figure 5.2. Oppression and Democracy Matrix.
(Adapted from Hardiman & Jackson, 1997. Slide by Samantha Ngo, MPH, MSW).

social control of certain groups and individuals that challenge oppressive conditions).

The social oppression matrix helps us to better visualize ourselves immersed within oppressive social structures and cultural forces. As such, we can become more aware and critical of oppressive psychosocial processes such as when privileged individuals and groups perceive their higher social locations within the matrix as *normal* (e.g., the sole result of honest hard work and merit) versus partly resulting from unfair advantages.

The matrix metaphor also helps us understand how we have been socialized in biased ways to perceive and interact (or not interact) with other categories of people. However, the matrix is even more complex if we include living in a democracy, albeit an aspiring and challenged one, with many dimensions of equality and space for resistance and accountability. Hence, a matrix of oppression *and* democracy may better capture the complex and convoluted dynamics of the society in which we live.

Diversity: Can We Talk about It?

Discussing diversity is very challenging yet necessary and can be frequently rewarding. Urgently needed dialogue and critical debates about fairness and human difference continue to be undermined by our socialization around diversity and positionality within the matrix of oppression and democracy. How often have we heard those whom we love and trust while growing up (parents and family members, teachers, clergy, coaches, and neighbors) resort to platitudes about race (e.g., "Everyone is the same," "It doesn't matter if you're black, white, green, or purple") and merit ("Anyone can make it if they try!") in place of more informed critical discussion about how the differential treatment of diverse groups leads to social stratification and different life chances? Within a social matrix of oppression, questions and experiences about stigmatized human differences elicit discomfort and anxiety throughout the life cycle that we are typically not socialized to tolerate and address. Hence, it is difficult to think "outside the matrix," if you will.

Thandeka (2003) offers a helpful explanation of our frequently impaired ability to genuinely think, feel, and talk openly about the categories of human differences that we all occupy with varying combinations of stigma and privilege. With regard to race, Thandeka contends that our development of racial self-awareness frequently emerges through what she calls naïve *transgressions* of the "racial order" that result in punishment (e.g., admonishment or rejection and consequent feelings of shame, guilt, and discomfort). Consider the example of a NLW colleague of the author who shared that as a young child, raised on her family's small farm in California's Central Valley, she recalls inviting the children of Mexican farmworkers into her home to play, only to be sternly reprimanded by her parents and told that they don't socialize with those children whose families are there only to pick crops on the farm. According to Thandeka, the result of such encounters is that normal, *naïve*, and innocent curiosity is quickly transformed into a "transgression" of racist cultural norms, resulting in the child experiencing a harsh lesson about what it means to be white.

On a gut level, such "transgressions," many of them early and even preverbal, may include a sense of something being wrong with one's self for having interests and feelings at odds with powerful, trusted, and loved authority figures (i.e., parents). The author's colleague recalls feeling very sad and unable to understand why it was wrong to want to play with the Mexican children milling around the house while their parents worked the farm. No wonder that feelings about being white and about racially different others frequently become walled off, compartmentalized, and shrouded in vague tension and discomfort. Later in life, racial encounters and experiences can automatically trigger anxiety and avoidance without much insight.

In another example, the author recalls observing the outrage of a father in response to his four-year-old son polishing his nails red while at Montessori day care. When the teacher patiently explained that the children are free to explore all of the available stimuli and activities in the classroom, later discussed for their learning value, the upset father demanded that his son not be allowed to engage in activities *for girls*. As Thandeka (2003) would argue, the little boy learned a harsh lesson about what it meant to be a boy. Other examples include visibly disabled people who note that when out in public, children who innocently stare at them or ask about their condition are frequently admonished by their parents and told not to stare or ask such questions. While such parents justify their actions as curbing rudeness, it often has more to do with the anxiety often experienced around disabled people based on our negative social constructions of the disabled (e.g., as pitiful, miserable, dependent) and hence our need to render them invisible.

Privilege and Stigma

Implicit in the above discussion is the profound role of privilege and stigma in limiting our understanding of human diversity. Whether we are privileged by race (e.g., white), sex (e.g., male), sexual orientation (e.g., heterosexual), or disability status (e.g., able bodied), we are socialized to minimize the experience of those stigmatized by these same domains (i.e., person of color, female, sexual minority, disabled) because such stigmas play no negative role in our lives. Simply put, privilege makes our lives better in a variety of ways on average, while stigma does the opposite. Thus, people mistreated on the basis of race are keenly aware of racism while those not mistreated or treated better on the basis of race are less aware of racism because it doesn't constrain their ability to make society work for them as it should. While this may sound abstract, consider the deadliest terrorist attack in U.S. history prior to 9/11 that killed 168 people and injured 680 when the Oklahoma federal building was bombed in 1995 by former Gulf War veteran and white supremacist, Timothy McVeigh. He was viewed solely as a white individual; there was no backlash or hate crime against white male veteran citizens, because no such stigma exists for these privileged categories. In contrast, a few Americans of Middle Eastern backgrounds were randomly assaulted and even killed in the wake of 9/11 because they belong to a group stigmatized on the basis of race/ethnicity.

The unfair advantages and disadvantages of privileged and stigmatized backgrounds, typically in multiple intersectional ways, have real life consequences that often evade our awareness, despite research designed to raise our consciousness. For example, in one of the earliest large-scale studies of race and treatment decisions made by primary care physicians (Schulman et al., 1999), it was found that when faced with identical videotaped complaints of chest pain by white and Black men and women, doctors were less likely to recommend further cardiac testing for African American women (79% of time) as compared to patients that were either white (male or female) or even Black and male (91% of the time). Such findings do not mean that doctors are necessarily racist and sexist at the *individual level*, but that they are socialized at *institutional* and *cultural levels* to perceive the concerns of white and Black men as more real than the complaints of African American women, who experience discrimination at the intersection of being Black and female. Interestingly, this study controlled for access to medical care by noting that all in the videos possessed health insurance, thereby minimizing the bias of social class, and demonstrating how a pair of intersecting stigmas may work against a person that is Black and female rather than being white and female, as well as male regardless of race.

Given such biased socialization that distorts our perceptions of human difference in consequential ways, it is no wonder that our emotional stamina for genuinely discussing human differences rarely goes beyond the anxiety-provoking, defensive, and superficial rhetoric that leaves social oppression unchallenged. Additional costs noted by Thandeka (2003) include the early suppression of natural diversity-related curiosity, and lowered probability of authentic relationships across race, ethnicity, and gender that mitigate bias and discrimination.

A basic grounding in social injustice on the basis of social constructions of human difference beckons us to explore *differences within differences*, consistent with intersectionality, as we struggle to comprehend the differential effects of oppression on various members of society. Some of these effects within U.S. Latinxs and their unique experiences, problems, and needs are selectively considered below.

Gender and Acculturation

Clearly acculturation has different impacts on Latinx males and females, in part because of patriarchy operative within both majority U.S. and Latinx minority cultures, but also because of resistance to patriarchy and biased gender socialization. Thus, while people of color have been subjugated on the basis of race and ethnicity, females within these populations have been further subjugated on the basis of gender or at the intersection of race/ethnicity and gender. For example, there's a revealing scene in *Chicano! History of the Mexican American Civil Rights Movement*, the 1995 documentary directed by Hector Galan, about the Chicano movement of the 1960s and 1970s, where at the first national conference to discuss political empowerment, Chicanas confront their *compañeros* [male counterparts or companions] for relegating them to the secretarial and coffee and food-serving periphery of the movement despite their consistent activism and support. That is, while the *hombres* [men] were keenly aware of their disempowerment on the basis of race/ethnicity, they were less aware of, or considered less important, their privileged status as males in both Chicano and U.S. cultures. This is why an intersectionality framework is imperative if we are to mitigate a single-dimension focus that erases the links between interacting forms of oppression (e.g., racism and sexism). Such a narrow focus also results in rank ordering oppressions, a tempting yet ultimately derisive endeavor.

In their pioneering work on acculturation in Cuban American refugee families in Miami, Szapocznik et al. (1978) theorized and demonstrated that the degree and pace of acculturation varies with the age and sex of family members as depicted in Figure 5.3. For example, as with most immigrant families, Cuban children generally acculturate much faster to the United

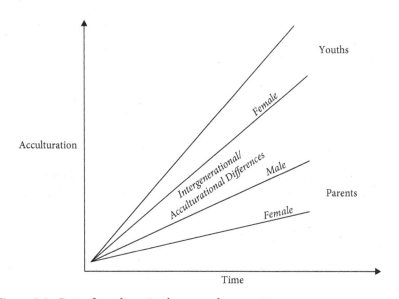

Figure 5.3. Rate of acculturation by sex and generation.

From Scapocznik et al. (1978). Theory and measurement of acculturation. *Interamerican Journal of Psychology, 12,* 113–130. With permission.

States than their parents, and females within both younger and older age groups also acculturate more slowly than their male counterparts, given the cultural bias of granting males more freedom and latitude to explore their environments.

The consideration of sex and age in acculturation became critical in Szapocznik and colleagues' understanding of Latinx family problems. That is, it was found that tensions most often occurred between what they called over-acculturated children and under-acculturated parents adapting to life in the United States. Further, some of the worst conflicts and behavior problems occurred between the most and least acculturated family members (i.e., between male adolescents engaged in delinquent activity and substance use and mothers abusing prescription drugs). Such early attention to intersectionality within the family spawned a prolific line of clinical work, research, and theorizing by Szapocznik and colleagues regarding how to address dysfunctional acculturation gaps within Latinx families that render family members vulnerable to psychosocial and health problems (see Chapter 7 on the Latinx family for more attention to this topic).

Gendered Migration

While traditional Latinx gender roles may slow the acculturation of females relative to males, Espin (1987) asserts that changes in gender roles may actually be more dramatic for Latina versus Latino immigrants, given the pressing need for women to work outside of the home and the consequent larger changes in lifestyle for such women versus their male counterparts. Indeed, Guendleman's (1987) early research on female Mexican migrants to the United States revealed considerable *gender role expansion* in terms of women's earning power and subsequent gains in decision-making in family matters. Relatedly, Hondagneu-Sotelo (1994) conducted an ethnography of a Mexican migrant settlement community in the San Francisco Bay Area, based on the participant observation of 44 men and women from 26 different migrant families. She concluded that the relation between international "push and pull" factors and individual-level decisions to migrate are mediated by gender roles in the family, and broader social networks which serve to constrain or facilitate migration for men and women:

While patriarchal practices and rules in families and social networks have persisted, through migration women and men reinterpret normative standards and creatively manipulate the rules of gender. As they do so, understandings about proper gendered behavior are reformulated and new paths to migration are created. When exclusionary practices persist in the networks, Mexican women have devised their own systems and networks of support (p. 96).

For example, Hondagneu-Sotelo (1994) found that the familiar migratory scenario, in which men leave wives and families behind to seek work in the United States, primes both husbands and wives for greater gender role flexibility. That is, the husband's absence in the family, and inadequate remittances from the United States, push wives to take charge of family matters and to earn wages by working. Meanwhile, husbands fending for themselves in the United States hone domestic skills such as cooking and cleaning. Upon family reunification in the United States, gender role expansion continues, with wives entering the world of work, including its social network, and make further gains in family decision-making, division of household responsibilities, and interests outside of the family including local civic involvement and community activism (see Chapter 12 for more in-depth discussion).

While rapidly shifting gender roles can result in more egalitarian relations in Latinx couples, without sufficient support and insight they can also result in family tension, destabilization, and even dysfunction (e.g., divorce, interpersonal violence, intergenerational conflict). Flexibility and resilience in migrant and immigrant families are strengths than can be supported and used to leverage needed interventions. Understanding intersectionality dynamics in acculturating Latinx families provides insights into adaptive as well as problematic aspects of adjustment to the United States for family members differentially impacted by racism, sexism, and social class (given Latinx poverty rates of around 20%). Attention to immigration status adds another critical dimension of intersectionality to our understanding of the Latinx experience, particularly during a current window of anti-immigration policies, practices, and sentiments in America.

Undocumented Immigration Status

Over two decades ago, Chavez (1998) provided richly detailed and personal case histories of undocumented Mexican and Central American individuals and families living and working in the San Diego area. With regard to the dilemma of seeking a livelihood in a country where one is constructed as an "illegal alien," increasingly vulnerable to legal persecution and deportation, Chavez conveys how undocumented Latinxs generally endure the chronic threat of apprehension, even multiple deportations, in exchange for what they are able to achieve in the United States. While such calculated risks continue, the predicament of undocumented migrants has become drastically worse due to increasingly dangerous push factors in Central America and Mexico (i.e., immense violence, corruption, and poverty) and increasingly cruel and inhumane methods of deterrence in the United States.

Regarding push factors, Honduras, Guatemala, and Nicaragua, known collectively as the Northern Triangle, as well as Mexico, are now frequently ranked among the most violent countries in the world, pushing hundreds of thousands of desperate refugees to seek asylum in the United States. However, contrary to national and international law, the Trump administration discredited the asylum process a "sham" and erected numerous barriers (i.e., fewer applications, longer waiting time, insisting that refugees seek asylum at another country first) resulting in thousands of stranded refugees occupying impoverished tent cities on the Mexico side of the border. While the new Biden administration has ordered a review of a Trump asylum policy resulting in 65,000 asylum seekers waiting on the Mexican side of the border for a hearing, considerable desperation and trauma have ensued, and any undoing of the previous administration's policies will take considerable time.

Deterrents for apprehended undocumented migrants currently include up to six months in federal prison for first-time border crossers, being charged with a felony with up to two years in federal prison for repeat crossings, and the cruel separation of children from their parents in the case of apprehended families during former President Trump's short-lived but violent Zero Tolerance policy of 2018. By the time national and international outrage resulted in the latter executive order's reversal, over 2,500 children had been separated from families, dispersed into detention centers and social welfare agencies throughout the country.

Today's unprecedented criminalization and severe punishment of undocumented migrants creates an intersection of oppression where racism and immigration status impinge upon millions of people seeking refuge and/or better economic opportunities in the United States. While the estimated 10.5 million undocumented migrants in the U.S. compose an about 5% of the American workforce, and 10% in immigrant rich states such as California (Healey et al., 2019), the United States depends upon yet refuses to regulate such labor through sensible immigration reform beneficial to both the

U.S. and immigrant Latino workers. Instead, the Trump administration routinely responded to this humanitarian crisis by declaring a national state of emergency, sending troops to the already militarized border, and baselessly proclaiming such migrants an invading infestation tainted with criminals and even Middle Easterners. There is indeed a crisis of state-level violence aimed primarily at undocumented Latinxs and undocumented people more generally.

Chavez (1998) was among the first Latinx scholars to document the stress and heart-wrenching trauma of mothers whose husbands are deported, of parents whose children are apprehended, and of whole families deported and making subsequent exhausting and dangerous attempts to return to the United States, frequently only to be caught and *felonized*. Sadly, too many Americans dismiss such hardship as the self-imposed consequence of breaking the law and entering the United States illegally, a violation severely punished as if such people pose an existential threat to society as propagandized by the former president.

California Proposition 187

Indeed, the scapegoating of undocumented Latinxs was the central thrust of California's Proposition 187, passed by voters in 1994, attempting to deprive the undocumented families of health care, education, and other publicly funded benefits (an unconstitutional proposition that resulted in an immediate court injunction and eventual demise). Proposition 187 also called on all service providers (i.e., educators, health care workers, social workers) to police the citizenship of clients and deny services accordingly. However, professional service organizations refused to participate in immigration control, filed lawsuits against the state, and continued to provide services for ethical and humanitarian reasons as well as to resist a racist, inhumane, and ultimately indefensible policy.

Interestingly, the nativist, anti-immigrant, and anti-Latino tone of Proposition 187, and the increasingly hostile debates on undocumented immigration, had the unintended consequence of galvanizing unprecedented Latinx political organizing, voting, and participation in the political process that continues to this day. In fact, the current immigration rights movement, with deep professional and advocacy networks across the country, emanated from Latinx resistance to Proposition 187. Authors such as Nicholls (2013) and Terriquez, Brenes, and Lopez (2018) document the pronounced role of intersectionality in re-energizing today's immigrant rights movement following repeated failures to pass the DREAM Act at the national level, based on a political strategy advocating support for "innocent" high achieving youth brought illegally to this country by their parents. While this strategy was partly responsible for President Obama's executive order to enact Deferred Action for Childhood Arrivals (DACA), sexual minority youth in the immigration rights movement resented and eventually resisted being discouraged from showing up as themselves by national immigration rights organizations who feared it would tarnish the image of deserving undocumented youth. As the above authors conclude from their research, recognition of Latinxs discriminated at the intersection of immigration status, sexual minority status, and racism resulted in coalition building that energized the immigration rights movement, which also strategically switched its focus to more attainable local state, county, and city immigration reform as evidenced in states such as California (see Chapter 12 for more description of this increasingly intersectional immigration rights movement).

Sexual Orientation

Scholars writing on the experience of Latinx sexual minorities (e.g., gay, lesbian, bisexual, transgendered, queer, and questioning. or LGBTQ+) also note interesting links with the process of migration and acculturation. For example, Diaz (1998) notes the frequent practice among gay Latino men of immigrating to the United States as a "geographical pseudo-cure" (p. 103) in response to the need to escape their closeted lives in Latin America. But while immigration brings relief, distance from country (and family) of origin does not "cure" the uncomfortable double lives many are forced to endure. As Diaz explains, while *familismo* (i.e., the centrality of the family in the lives of Latinxs) is the central foundational support for Latinx family members, it can also hamper the psychosocial health and well-being of Latinx gay men who feel compelled to live secret sexual and romantic lives in order to avoid family rejection and dishonor on the basis of heteronormativity. In fact, Diaz underscores the link between homophobia within Latinx culture and HIV risk in Latino gay men, whose sexual lives can become relegated to the domain of secretive and impersonal sexual encounters frequently fraught with risk and feelings of shame. In contrast, heterosexual family members can more openly develop and express romantic and sexual interests, in culturally consistent ways, within accepting and supportive families.

With regard to Latinx lesbians, Espin (1997a) conducted an early survey of 16 Cuban Americans and found that while the majority identified as Latina and valued their intersectional Latina and lesbian identities, two-thirds admitted that if forced to choose, they would prefer living among non-Latinx lesbians, with little awareness of Latino culture, as opposed to living closeted lives among Latinxs (indeed, many had already made this unfortunate forced choice). In an in-depth case study of two women from the above sample, both connected coming out as lesbians with immigrating to the United States (Espin, 1997b).

The preventable choice between one's ethnicity and sexual orientation is highly relevant to sexual minority Latinxs given that their sexuality is challenged by heteronormativity within Latinx culture, where traditional gender roles render sexual minority status invisible and to be rejected when it appears. Feeling forced to choose between one's Latino family and community and an open sexual orientation and social life can result in a painfully divided self. For example, Espin (1997a) notes that when a lesbian orientation is known or suspected in the Latinx family, the tendency is to silently tolerate the individual provided that she remains closeted, and to make excuses for her not being married (e.g., too religious, smart, or busy with career). Espin (1997a) also notes that 14 of the 16 lesbians surveyed reported being Catholic, yet only three were practicing Catholics who chose to worship at Dignity, an organization designed to meet the religious needs of sexual minority Catholics estranged from their church.

In intersectionality terms, sexual minority Latinxs face stigma and discrimination at the intersection of racism, sexism, and heteronormativity, the latter system of oppression operative in both Latinx and U.S. cultures, albeit with some hard won progressive reforms. Addressing this intersection necessitates challenging reluctant Latinx families to accept and support sexual minority family members via the same familism intended for all family members. For instance, Espin professes faith in the power of *familismo*, noting that if strong, not even sexual minority status can split bonds between family members. Such family support does happen for some, and such optimism speaks to the promise of expanding familism through public education campaigns about the negative consequences of rejecting sexual minority children and the need for the family to be the central buffer in their lives.

To assist with such work, sexual minority scholars have pioneered models of sexual identity development, based on the logic of the Racial/Cultural Identity Development model reviewed in Chapter 4. For example, one such model by Cass (1990) posits early stages of sexual identity *confusion* and ambivalence, middle stages of exploration, *tolerance*, and *pride*, including resentment of homophobia, and ultimately a more developed and integrated stage of *synthesis* in which public and private lives fit together in a fulfilling manner. How sexual and ethnic identity development co-occur in Latinxs warrants further research to illuminate how such individuals cope with two significant stigmatized identities.

The Transgender Challenge

Resistance to heteronormativity has slowly resulted in greater acceptance and freedom for gay and lesbian members of society (e.g., the right to marry and adopt children, increasing representation throughout popular culture). However, transgendered people continue to be much more stigmatized and discriminated on the basis of gender identity, which we are socialized to perceive, in the words of Thandeka, as a "transgression" of the rigid and reductionistic socially constructed binary of biological sex that categorizes all people as either biologically male or female with matching gender identities and roles. Thus, the struggle for acceptance, respect, and equal human and civil rights for transgendered people continues to set an especially high bar. Part of the challenge resides in the dilemma that transgendered people are not only stigmatized and rejected by heterosexual people, who frequently (mis) perceive them as gay or lesbian, but have also been historically stigmatized and rejected by gays and lesbians, who have frequently (mis)perceived them as renouncing their gayness and attempting to pass as the "opposite sex" in a conformist manner (Green, 2000). Hence, it has taken time to finally add the "T" to "LGB" in the increasingly intersectional movement for sexual minority rights.

At the core of the umbrella term *transgendered* are people who experience a mismatch between their biological and assigned sex and their gender identity. For example, male-to-female (MTF) or female-to-male (FTM) transgendered people feel more congruent with a gender identity, role, and appearance of the so-called *opposite* sex, whether or not they pursue hormonal treatment and/or reassignment surgery to enhance congruence

(Green, 2000). However, even these binary sounding descriptions of trans people may well limit our understanding.

Transgendered people are at considerable risk for the long list of vulnerabilities resulting from pervasive oppression, or what might be called *trans-antagonism* (e.g., physical and sexual abuse, harassment and hate crimes, work and service-related discrimination, and consequent injury to health and mental health). Results from the 2015 U.S. Transgender Survey (USTS) document multiple and pervasive risks and consequent problems for the U.S. transgendered population (James et al.; 2016). The USTS is the largest survey examining the experiences of transgender people, with 27,715 respondents from all fifty states, the District of Columbia, American Samoa, Guam, Puerto Rico, and U.S. military bases overseas. This was an anonymous, online survey for transgender adults 18 years and older, available in English and Spanish. While eight years old, the 2022 survey has been completed with results soon to be released.

As revealed in Figure 5.4, rates of serious psychological distress, including attempted suicide, as well as homelessness are alarmingly high for trans folks lacking family support (50%, 54%, and 45%, respectively), and while family support clearly reduces these rates, they remain unacceptably high (31%, 37%, and 27%, respectively).

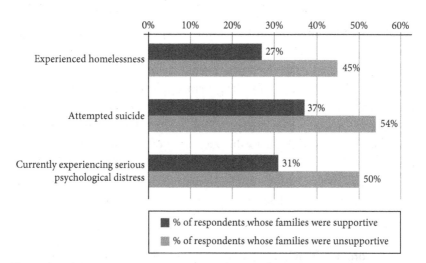

Figure 5.4. Negative experiences among those with supportive and unsupportive families.

From James et al. (2016). The Report of the 2015 U.S. Transgender Survey. Washington, DC: National Center for Transgender Equality. With permission.

EXPERIENCES	% OF THOSE WHO WERE OUT OR PERCEIVED AS TRANSGENDER
Verbally harassed because people thought they were transgender	54%
Not allowed to dress in a way that fit their gender identity or expression	52%
Disciplined for fighting back against bullies	36%
Physically attacked because people thought they were transgender	24%
Believe they were disciplined more harshly because teachers or staff thought they were transgender	20%
Left a school because the mistreatment was so bad	17%
Sexually assaulted because people thought they were transgender	13%
Expelled from school	6%
One or more experiences listed	77%

Figure 5.5. Experiences of people who were out as transgender in K–12 or believed classmates, teachers, or school staff thought they were transgender.
From James et al. (2016). The Report of the 2015 U.S. Transgender Survey. Washington, DC: National Center for Transgender Equality. With permission.

Harsh rejection is also documented throughout the formative K–12 school years, with over half of participants reporting not being allowed to dress in ways consistent with their desired gender expression, and verbal harassment during these developmentally critical years (see Figure 5.5). About a quarter of participants recall being physically attacked for their transgendered appearance, while over a third report being disciplined for fighting back against their bullies. Sadly, but not surprisingly, 17% report leaving school because it was so bad, only to face work-related discrimination.

As can be seen in Figure 5.6, the unemployment rate for trans participants in general is 15% versus 5% for the general public at the time of the survey, and typically worse for trans people of color: American Indian (23%), Latinx (21%), African American (20%), White (12%), Asian American (10%). These findings, in addition to the vast array of chronic stressors further documented in the USTS, sensitize us to the considerable structural vulnerability of trans people. Risk for HIV is a particularly striking example of trans vulnerability as described below.

HIV Risk

Long before the Covid-19 pandemic, the HIV pandemic had clearly demonstrated dramatic differential impacts on diverse populations based on their vulnerability profiles decades ago. For instance, alarming rates of HIV infection, between 25% and 33%, were detected in San Francisco–based

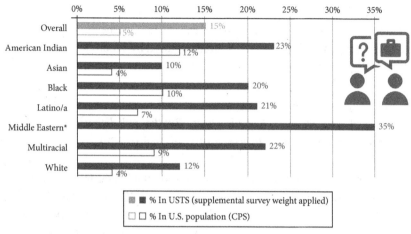

* U.S. population data for Middle Eastern people alone is unavailable in the CPS.

Figure 5.6. Unemployment rate by race/ethnicity.
From James et al. (2016). The Report of the 2015 U.S. Transgender Survey. Washington, DC: National Center for Transgender Equality. With permission.

samples of transwomen (Nemoto et al., 1999; Clements-Nolle, Guzman, & Katz, 2001). To better understand the context of such vulnerability to HIV, the MTF Transgender of Color Study was launched by Nemoto and colleagues (2004a) based on focus groups with 48 MTFs (16 Black, 15 Asian, 12 Latinas, and 5 other) as well as interviews with providers serving this population. Results reveal the repercussions of the multiple vulnerabilities of these women at the intersections of trans antagonism, racism, and poverty. First, significant involvement in *commercial sex work* emerged as one of the few options for economic survival, in which almost all had participated, including about half currently, often beginning in adolescence. Related reasons for sex work include early rejection from families and consequent homelessness, job discrimination, money needed for survival and costly gender maintenance medical procedures, as well as substance use (including injection drugs) often used to cope with the above stressors. Participants even noted that sex work and drug use came to be viewed as a rite of passage among transwomen. It was further found that sex with customers was generally regarded as a business transaction, in which to practice safe sex, while sex with primary partners involved love, trust, and penetration without condoms. However, unsafe sex with customers was reported during economically vulnerable times when more money was offered for not using condoms. The fact that transgendered people are too frequently the victims of violent hate crimes, including murder, is a tragic indicator of their inter-sectional stigma and oppression, so well captured by a focus group member's brutally honest statement:

> No one's going to kill a gay man if he finds a dick between his legs. No one's gonna kill a gay woman if he finds a pussy. But they will definitely put a knife through a tranny's throat if they see breasts and dick (p. 729).

The 2002 conviction of four young men for the brutal murder of Gwen Araujo, an adolescent Latina transwoman, is significant in that following a hung jury the men were retried, and the jury refused to buy their "trans panic" defense which held that they killed Gwen in a fit of panic after discovering that they were sexually involved with an MTF transgendered person rather than a "real woman." That Latinx men were among those convicted underscores the depth of trans-antagonism and rejection within Latinx as well as U.S. culture.

With regard to vulnerability to HIV, Nemoto et al. (2004b) found the following self-reported rates of infection in their MTF sample: 41% for African Americans, 23% For Latinas, and 13% for APIs (Asian Pacific Islanders). Both Latinas and African Americans reported lower incomes and higher rates of sex work, including unprotected receptive anal sex (URAS), and substance use, as compared to API MFTs. HIV-positive MTFs were almost four times as likely as HIV-negative MTFs to report URAS with casual (not customer) sex partners. Also, while only 12% reported URAS with customers in the past 30 days, this risk was 4.5 times more frequent in African American MTFs and in those with the lowest income level (< $500/monthly), hence the role of racial and economic intersectionality among participants.

A unique obstacle to condom use noted in the finding was that rates of URAS were highest with primary partners as compared to casual or commercial sex partners. In the focus groups conducted by Nemoto et al. (2004a), the interpersonal context of (un)safe sex was clarified in that condoms were perceived as undermining intimacy with primary partners, as well as undermining *gender validation* (i.e., attention, affection, and sex for being a woman) with casual sex partners. Also, while most used condoms with commercial sex clients, economic vulnerability did occasionally undermine this intention. These findings underscore unique relationship-based vulnerabilities for MTFs that can leave them at a power disadvantage for negotiating safe sex if protection is secondary to the need for money, intimacy, and gender validation.

Service implications of the above results are many and include transgender competent early intervention to curtail and prevent interpersonal abuse as well as provide alternatives to survival sex and substance use to cope with transphobia, both within Latinx and broader society. A comprehensive approach should also include assisting transgendered clients with work and housing-related discrimination, counseling to prevent the need for *gender validation* from becoming a risk liability, and referring clients to transgender responsive health services. Such thinking and progressive services, often spearheaded by transgendered activists, other sexual minorities, and allies, are sparse, yet exemplify human rights at the core of diversity competent practice. The struggle for such rights continues to play out at the highest levels of our government.

National Transgender Discrimination

In 2017, President Trump announced on Twitter that the country would no longer "accept or allow" transgendered Americans to serve in the military, citing "tremendous medical costs and disruption." The move was intended to reverse the Obama administration's inclusive policy ruling that transgender Americans can serve *openly* in the military and obtain funding for gender reassignment surgery if desired. Trump's then Secretary of Defense, James Mattis, refined the ban to apply only to those with a history of gender dysphoria (GD) and not to those currently serving or willing to service "in their biological sex." GD is a controversial psychiatric diagnosis (i.e., supposedly distress from the incongruence between experienced/expressed gender and assigned biological sex) currently debated within LGBTQ organizations and professional organizations—such as the National Association of Social Workers calling for its removal from the *Diagnostic and Statistical Manual of Mental Disorders* (DSM), similar to how the diagnosis of homosexuality was resisted and eventually removed from the DSM in 1980.

A report by the Palm Center, based on 2017 Department of Defense data, found that the estimated cost of sexual reassignment surgery was $2.2 million for that year, a figure much lower than in the report proposing the ban. This expense works out to less than one-tenth of one percent of the military's annual health care budget. Lead authors of the Palm Center report, including former U.S. Navy, U.S. Army, and U.S. Coast Guard Surgeon Generals, oppose the Trump administration's ban. While several trial judges from around the country issued injunctions blocking Trump's transgender ban, in January 2019 the Supreme Court voted 5–4, along strict conservative–liberal party lines, to grant the Trump administration's request to lift the lower court injunctions blocking the ban while legal challenges continue as expected. However, while out transgendered people were banned from the military for about two years, President Biden immediately repealed Trump's transgender ban in January 2021, asserting that gender identity should not be a ban to serving in the military and receiving medical care.

More recently, Governor Ron DeSantis of Florida has launched an extensive anti-LGBTQ campaign that includes signing laws that limit what teachers can teach about race, sexual orientation, and gender identity in elementary schools. As a long-time Trump supporter, endorsed by Trump while running for governor in 2018, DeSantis imitates the same divisive culture war politics that ultimately render sexual minority people vulnerable to rejection and the dire consequences of dehumanization described above.

Colorismo: Latinx on Latinx Racism and Discrimination

The author recalls meeting with Benito, a dark-skinned indigenous appearing Latinx community outreach worker in Oakland, California, to ask him about his impressive HIV prevention outreach with local *jornaleros*, or Latinx migrant day laborers. On the day we met, I invited Benito for a spicy bowl of *Sopa Azteca* [Aztec soup] at the Otaez restaurant in the Latinx Fruitvale district. Wasting no time sizing me up, Benito asked, "You're such a *guero* [light-skinned, racially white appearing] Latino, do you think that has helped you to become successful?" I swallowed my spoonful of soup and, without skipping a beat, replied, "In a racist society like ours? How could it not be an advantage?" He nodded and smiled approvingly at my quick, honest, and *correct* response and proceeded to orient me to his excellent work with the local day laborers, which included rolling out a cart of *pan dulce* [sweet bread] and *café con canela* [cinnamon coffee] at 7:00 am to the intersection where *jornaleros* wait to be picked up for a day's labor. In exchange for such a welcomed treat, the men listened to Benito's counsel on safe sex and accepted the free condoms that he distributed.

Because Latinxs can be of any racial background, there is considerable variation in skin color and racial features. In racialized Latinx and

U.S. societies, we should expect that phenotypic differences within Latinxs will result in varied perceptions and treatment affecting well-being and social positionality. While colorism has been studied more extensively in African Americans, similar research is emerging for Latinxs. For instance, researchers Hector Adames and Nayeli Chavez-Dueñas are currently advancing the need to understand and address Latinx colorism. Their project includes providing a historical overview of the colonial basis of colorism throughout Latin America, pointing readers to informative cultural renderings of colorism (e.g., novels, movies, non-academic writings), familiarizing readers with its vocabulary, including popular *dichos* or sayings such as, "Oh! *Nacio negrito/ prietito pero aun asi lo queremos*" [Oh, even though he was born Black/dark, we still love him].

Adames and Chavez-Dueñas also review the scarce literature on colorism and practice relevant outcomes, case vignettes, and intervention guidelines for mitigating this pernicious form of internalized oppression. For instance, when a young Latina client insinuates that her family believes she will never get married because she's too dark, the clinician in the vignette gently probes, "Why do you think some Latino families are prejudiced toward darker skinned family members?" Their review of the sparse literature on colorism consistently shows more negative outcomes for Latinxs that are more phenotypically indigenous or African in appearance, including lower SES (i.e., annual income and occupational prestige scores) and greater psychological distress (Adames, Chavez-Dueñas, & Organista, 2016). Related research also shows less social mobility in darker, and especially Puerto Rican, Latinxs as compared to Mexican and Cuban counterparts (South, Crowder, & Chavez, 2005), as well as worse birth outcomes (i.e., low birth weight) in Black as compared to white Latinas, especially those born in the United States versus immigrants (Mydam et al., 2019).

Interestingly, a recent study by Ostfeld and Yadon (2021) examined the relation between skin color and views on racialized political issues in a sample of 495 Latinxs recruited from public events throughout the Detroit and Chicago metropolitan areas. Participants agreed to rate their skin tone, using the authors' skin color scale (Figure 5.7), and also agreed to be machine-rated with a spectrophotometer measure of light reflectance that captures skin color without the biases inherent in self-ratings. Hence, these subjective and objective measures of skin tone allowed the researchers to assess when participants were underestimating, overestimating, or rating their skin color consistently with the spectrophotometer.

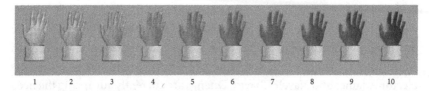

Figure 5.7. Yadon-Ostfeld Skin Color Scale.
From Ostfeld & Yadon (2021). ¿Mejorando La Raza?: The political undertones of Latinos' skin color in the United States. *Social Forces*, 1–27. With permission from Oxford Academic.

Results reveal that over half of the sample overestimated their whiteness by one hand on the Ostfeld-Yadon Skin Color Scale, and that those who over-estimate their whiteness are more politically conservative on racialized polit-ical issues (e.g., support for Trump, view of police treatment of Latinos), and vice versa for Latinxs that overestimate the darkness of their skin tone. The authors end their interesting study of colorism and race-related politics with the following words of caution:

> [P]erceptions of one's own skin color are not simply based on appearance, but are deeply intertwined with one's understanding of power in the con-text of American politics. Political identities may not only be reflecting but also reproducing racialized divisions in American politics (p. 20).

Colorism in the Power Elite

The social stratification of race and color described in Chapter 3 focused on the resulting lower social positionality of most Latinos. However, the role of race and colorism is equally evident in the extremely low representation of Latinxs at the upper echelons of society. In the most authoritative analysis of diversity in the power elite or highest levels of political, corporate, and military power, Zweigenhaft and Domhoff (2017) reveal the glaring lack of diversity at the intersection of race and gender. For instance, at the time of their book's publication, these authors document only just over 3% Latinos on Fortune 500 (i.e., most powerful and lucrative 500 corporations) boards of directors, and find that the majority are racially white Latinxs from Cuba,

Spain, and Latin America, and 80% male. Further, Latinxs elected to the U.S. Congress are just 4% of the 100-member Senate, and 8% of 435 members of the House of Representatives. Sonia Sotomayor is the first ever Latinx U.S. Supreme Court justice. With regard to the coveted 16 presidential cabinet positions, there have historically been only 17 Latinxs appointed through 2017, with President Obama appointing a record six of those 17.

In contrast, Trump, who began with none, eventually appointed two Latinxs to his cabinet after considerable criticism from Latinx organizations. For example, Alex Acosta, a Republican of Cuban American background, was appointed Secretary of Labor in 2017, at which time he was serving as dean of the law school at Florida International University. Acosta also served as the first Latinx Assistant Attorney General before becoming U.S. Attorney in 2005 during the George W. Bush administration. Thus, there not only continue to be too few Latinxs at the highest levels of political power, but also a lack of diversity within these overwhelmingly white foreign and domestic conservatives from elite backgrounds that do not represent the vast majority of U.S. Latinxs. More representative Latinos would include domestic, progressive, darker, and non-white Latinos.

Mixed Racial and Ethnic Heritage

While mixed racial heritage is an inherent part of being Latino, given their history of *mestizaje* or "mixture" of Spanish and indigenous Indian heritage latter blended with the African diaspora during the Caribbean slave trade (early 1500s through late 1800s), the term here refers to the American usage of being from two or more predominant race/ethnic parental backgrounds (e.g., African American and European American, Latino and European American, Latino and African American). Despite the reductionism of such a narrow social construction of racial/ethnic background, its impactful consequences for psychosocial adjustment warrant attention. A few early and informative studies support this need.

In an early 15-family study of biracial children, Winn and Priest (1993) found that over 80% of the 34 children interviewed reported feeling obligated to assume a single racial identification and to feel like traitors to the parent with whom they did not racially identify. These youth also consistently claimed that their parents did not adequately prepare them for the negative reactions of both whites and minority peers, and a third expressed a desire to learn about the cultures of both parents. Interestingly, two of the three Cuban/white adolescents in the study identified as Cuban, the other as white, and all three reported dating both Cuban and NLW partners. The one mixed Puerto Rican/Anglo participant identified as Puerto Rican and socialized mostly with Puerto Rican peers. Thus, this study documents some of the potential problems that mixed youth may experience in a society with rigid constructions of race, and where most people, let alone parents, are not adept at preparing such youth for mixed racial socialization (i.e., inoculation from internalizing stereotypes and biases).

On the encouraging side, Winn and Priest (1993) found that most of the adolescents in their sample indicated feeling good about their racial identity and reported socializing (e.g., dating) with a mix of friends. These researchers end their report by urging counselors and parents to help children explore their dual heritage but stopped short of saying *how*. One obvious key to adjustment in such youth would be close ties to both parents, and mitigating the pressure to identify with only one side of their family. For example, de Anda and Riddel (1991) studied a sample of 70 mixed adolescents (22 Asian/ White; 23 Black/White, 25 Latino/White) who reported identifying as multiethnic, high comfort and acceptance by both majority and minority peers and settings, strong bonds with both sides of their family, and a preference for ethnically diverse friends. Interestingly, of the 23 Latino/White respondents, 15 reported being perceived as white by strangers, yet all but two identified as Latino.

De Anda and Riddel (1991) stressed the importance of not drawing samples of mixed race individuals from clinical settings, where maladjustment is more likely, and also reported that their sample (obtained through both convenience and snowball sampling) was characterized by a high percent of intact homes (61.4%), although with notable differences across the three groups (81.2% in the Asian/White group, 64% in the Latino/White group, and 39.1% in the Black/White group). While these three groups did not differ on the above healthy outcomes, it makes one wonder about the challenges of integrating a dual race/ethnic heritage if one is from a divorced or separated background with access to only or mostly one parent. Also, because participants in de Anda and Riddel's study were all *half white*, it brings up questions regarding how being from two stigmatized minority backgrounds (e.g., Latino and African American) might affect racial/cultural adjustment.

Afro-Latinxs

In the classic Puerto Rican coming of age novel, *Down These Mean Streets*, author Piri Thomas (1967) describes the challenges of growing up in Spanish Harlem as including being perceived and treated as African American. Job discrimination and interpersonal rejections are poignantly detailed, and there's even a chapter titled, "How to be a Negro without really trying." Since Thomas' literary document, there has been a steady trickle of literature about the experience of Black Latinos (i.e., those who are racially Black and culturally Latino) as well as the scholarly literature as noted earlier.

Family therapist, Baptiste (1990), wrote one of the earliest papers on this topic. The author made mention of some of the identity problems faced by adolescent family members trying to figure out who they are in America's color conscious society. A few years later, Comas-Diaz (1996) wrote about the *Latinegra*, or Black Latina of Caribbean background, and the myriad of challenges faced by such women. In addition to identity issues, Comas-Diaz highlights intersectional sex and class issues such as being stereotyped as sexually exotic yet too dark to be suitable for a marriage that can *adelantar la raza* [lift up the race]. She also notes that terms of endearment such as *negrita* [little black one] or *prieta* [dark one] contain ambivalence and often mean something like, "You're black and ugly but we love you anyway!" Also described are ways in which *Latinegras* have begun to empower themselves by forming organizations such as the *Unión de Mujeres Puertorriquenas Negras* [Union of Black Puerto Rican Women] and bringing attention to this derisive intra-cultural manifestation of racism.

While some writings on this sensitive topic may veer close to a "tragic mulatto" portrait of Black Latinos, a shred of empirical support comes from a rare study by Ramos, Jaccard, and Guilamo-Ramos (2003), who compared symptoms of depression in four groups of adolescents grades 7–12: Anglo Americans, African Americans, Black Latinos, and non-black Latinos from the large National Longitudinal Study of Adolescent Health survey of over 20,000 students. What these researchers found was that *Latinegras* had the highest levels of depression, which was attributed to the intersection of race, ethnicity, and gender, and perhaps being less able than male counterparts to negotiate the intersection of race and ethnicity. That Latinas in this study, including Afro-Latinos, were Caribbean and predominantly Puerto Rican in background, corroborates the pioneering writings of Comas-Diaz (1996) above.

While much more research is needed on Latinx intersectionality, service providers need to be better prepared to address potential dilemmas in mixed racial heritage or being Black and Latinx. Because traditional racial/cultural identity models were developed with single race/ethnic groups in mind, they are limited in their application to many Latinos. Still, familiarity with the racial/cultural and white identity models reviewed in Chapter 4 provides a basis upon which to support mixed race and mixed ethnic individuals to resist negative social conceptions of either side of their family backgrounds, and to pursue the objective of selectively sorting out cultural strengths from each particular background with which to create a more integrated multiracial, multi-ethnic, intersectional sense of self.

Addressing Latinx Intersectionality

This chapter scratches the surface regarding the immense human diversity within U.S. Latinxs, and of the differential impacts of oppression, as well as privilege, at the intersections of various social constructions of human diversity such as gender and gender identity, sexual orientation, immigration status, phenotype, and mixed racial/ethnic heritage. The consequences of so many other *intersectionalities* (e.g., those including disability status) await our needed attention. Hopefully we will continue to connect the many dots of oppression and intersectionality affecting Latinx as well as all people in the United States as we continue aspiring to the most just society possible.

References

Adames, H. Y., Chavez-Dueñas, N. Y., & Organista, K. C. (2016). Skin color matters in Latino/a communities: Identifying, understanding, and addressing mestizaje racial ideologies in clinical practice. *Professional Psychology: Research and Practice*, 47(1), 46–55.

Baptiste, D. (1990). Therapeutic strategies with Black-Hispanic families: Identity problems of a neglected minority. *Journal of Family Psychotherapy*, 1, 15–38.

Bell, L. A. (1997). Theoretical foundations for social justice education. In M. Adams, L. A. Bell, and P. Griffin (Eds.), *Teaching for diversity and social justice: A sourcebook* (pp. 3–15). New York: Routledge.

Cass, V. C. (1990). The implications of homosexual identity formation for the Kinsey model and scale of sexual preference. In D. P. McWhirter, S. A. Sanders, and J. Machover Reinish (Eds.), *Homosexuality/heterosexuality: Concepts of sexual orientation* (pp. 239–266). New York: Oxford University Press.

Chavez, L. R. (1998). *Shadowed lives: Undocumented immigrants in American society* (2nd ed.). United States: Wadsworth.

Comas-Diaz, L. (1996). Latinegra [Black Latina]: Mental health issues of African Latinas. In M. Root (Ed.), *The multiracial experience* (pp. 167–190). Thousand Oaks, CA: Sage.

Clements-Nolle, K., Guzman, R., & Katz, M. (2001). HIV prevention, risk behaviours, health care use, and mental health status of transgender persons: Implications for public health intervention. *American Journal of Public Health, 91*, 915–921.

Diaz, R. M. (1998). Family loyalty and sexual silence: Splitting off sexuality. In R. M. Diaz (Ed.), *Latino gay men and HIV: Culture, sexuality, and risk behavior* (pp. 89–111). New York: Routledge.

De Anda, D., & Riddel, V. A. (1991). Ethnic identity, self-esteem, and interpersonal relationships among multiethnic adolescents. *Journal of Multicultural Social Work, 1*(2), 83–98.

Espin, O. M. (1987). Psychological impacts of migration on Latinas: Implications for psychotherapeutic practice. *Psychology of Women Quarterly, 11*, 480–503.

Espin, O. M. (1997a). Issues of identity in the psychology of Latina lesbians. In O. M. Espin (Ed.), *Latina realities: Essays on healing, migration, and sexuality* (pp. 97–109). Boulder, CO: Westview Press.

Espin, O. M. (1997b). Leaving the nation and joining the tribe: Lesbian Latinas crossing geographical and identity borders. In O. M. Espin (Ed.), *Latina realities: Essays on healing, migration, and sexuality* (pp. 186–192). Boulder, CO: Westview Press.

Green, J. (2000). Introduction to transgender issues. In P. Currah & S. Minter (Eds.), *Transgender equality: A handbook for activists and policy makers* (pp. 1–12). Washington DC: National Center for Lesbian Rights and the Policy Institute of the National Gay and Lesbian Task Force.

Guendelman, S. (1987). The incorporation of Mexican women in seasonal migration: A study of gender differences. *Hispanic Journal of Behavioral Sciences, 9*, 245–264.

Hardiman, R., & Jackson, B. W. (1997). Conceptual foundations for social justice courses. In M. Adams, L. A. Bell, and P. Griffin (Eds.), *Teaching for diversity and social justice: A sourcebook* (pp. 16–29). New York: Routledge.

Healey, J. F, Stepnick, A. & O'Brien, E. (2019). Hispanic Americans: Colonization, immigration, and ethnic enclaves. In J. F. Healey, A. Stepnick, & E. O'Brien (Eds.), *Race, ethnicity, gender, and class: The sociology of group conflict and change* (8th ed., pp. 262–311). Thousand Oaks: Sage.

Hondagneu-Sotelo, P. (1994). *Gendered transitions: Mexican experiences of immigration*. Berkeley: University of California Press.

James, S. E., Herman, J. L., Rankin, S., Keisling, M., Mottet, L., & Anafi, M. (2016). The Report of the 2015 U.S. Transgender Survey. Washington, DC: National Center for Transgender Equality.

Marger, M. N. (2015). Ethnic stratification: Minority and majority. In M. N. Marger (Ed.), *Race and ethnic relations: American and global perspectives* (10th ed.) (pp. 27–48). Stamford, CT: Cengage Learning.

Mydam, J., David, R. J., Rankin, K. M., & Collins, J. W. (2019). Low birth weight among infants born to Black Latina women in the United States. *Maternal and Child Health Journal, 23*(4), 538–546. https://doi.org/10.1007/s10995-018-2669-9

National Association of Social Workers (2021). Code of Ethics of the National Association of Social Workers. Washington, DC: NASW.

Nemoto, T., Luke, D., Mamo, L., Ching, A., & Patria, J. (1999). HIV risk behaviours among male-to-female transgenders in comparison with homosexual or bisexual male and heterosexual females. *AIDS Care, 16*(6), 724–735.

Nemoto, T., Operario, D., Keatley, J., Han, L, & Soma, T. (2004b). HIV risk behaviors among male-to-female transgender persons of color in San Francisco. *American Journal of Public Health, 94*(7), 1193–1199.

Nemoto, T., Operario, D., Keatley, J., & Villegas, D. (2004a). Social context of HIV risk behaviours among male-to-female transgenders of colour. *AIDS Care, 16*(6), 724–735.

Nicholls, W. J. (2013). *The DREAMers: How the undocumented youth movement transformed the immigration rights debate.* Stanford: Stanford University Press.

Ostfeld, M. C., & Yadon, N. D. (2021). ¿Mejorando La Raza?: The Political Undertones of Latinos' Skin Color in the United States. *Social Forces, 100*(3), 1–27. https://doi.org/10.1093/sf/soab060

Ramos, B. Jaccard, J., & Guilamo-Ramos, V. (2003). Dual ethnicity and depressive symptoms: Implications of being Black and Latino in the United States. *Hispanic Journal of Behavioral Sciences, 25*(2), 147–173

Schulman, K. A., Berlin, J. A., Harless, W. et al. (1999). The effect of race and sex on physicians' recommendations for cardiac catheterization. *The New England Journal of Medicine, 340*(8), 618–626.

South, S. J., Crowder, K., & Chavez, E. (2005). Migration and spatial assimilation among U.S. Latinos: Classical versus segmented trajectories. *Demography, 42*(3), 497–521.

Szapocznik, J., Santisteban, D., Kurtines, W., Perez-Vidal, A., & Heavies, O. (1984). Bicultural Effectiveness Training (BET): A treatment intervention for enhancing intercultural adjustment in Cuban American families. *Hispanic Journal of Behavioral Sciences, 6*(4), 317–344.

Scapocznik, J. Scopetta, M. A., Kurtines, W. & Arnalde, M. A. (1978). Theory and measurement of acculturation. *Interamerican Journal of Psychology, 12*, 113–130.

Thandeka (2003). The cost of whiteness. In K. E. Rosenblum and T. C. Travis (Eds.), *The meaning of difference: American constructions of race, sex and gender, social class, and sexual orientation* (3rd. ed.) (pp. 254–263). Boston: McGraw Hill.

Terriquez, V., Brenes, T., & Lopez, A. (2018). Intersectionality as a multipurpose collective action frame: The case of the undocumented youth movement. *Ethnicities, 18*(2), 260–276.

Thomas, P. (1967). *Down these mean streets.* New York: Signet Books.

Winn, N. N., & Priest, R. (1993). Counseling biracial children: A forgotten component of multicultural counseling. *Family Therapy, 20*(1), 29–36.

Zweigenhaft, R. L., & Domhoff, W. D. (2017). Latinos in the power elite. In R. L. Zweigenhaft & W. D. Domhoff (Eds.), *Diversity in the power elite: Have women and minorities reached the top?* (3rd ed.) (pp. 118–139). New Haven, CT: Yale University Press.

6

Sociocultural Practice Model for Latino Populations

The theoretical frameworks presented in Chapters 1–5 (acculturation, social stratification, racial/ethnic identity development, and intersectionality) are designed to enhance our knowledge and understanding of the social and cultural or *sociocultural* experience of U.S. Latino populations, past through present. These informative and sensitizing frameworks, selected from relevant social science theory and research, provide an informed foundation for addressing Latino psychosocial and health problems in a contextualized manner that maximizes the probability of effective assessment and intervention. Various terms used to describe such an approach to diverse client populations are discussed below.

Cultural Competence and Cultural Humility

For at least 30 years, the term *cultural competence* has been used to refer to the movement within health and mental health education, training, and practice to more effectively work with our increasingly diverse client population. More recently, the term *cultural humility* has gained popularity, often sparking heated debate about how it differs from cultural competence and which is best. In the spirit of mitigating unnecessary conflict, it is worth keeping in mind that both approaches are committed to the same overarching goal of working effectively with diverse client populations and may differ little in actual practice. One semantic problem with *both* terms is their emphasis on the *cultural* over the *social* dimension of psychosocial and health problems over-affecting Latinos and other people of color. Inextricable, both social and cultural factors comprise the context of problem patterns and solutions.

Solving Latino Psychosocial and Health Problems. Kurt C. Organista, Oxford University Press.
© Oxford University Press 2023. DOI: 10.1093/oso/9780190059637.003.0006

The purpose of this chapter is to present a *sociocultural* practice model for working more effectively with Latino populations that derives from decades of theory, research, and practice in the realm of cultural competence and humility. The current model features four major practice dimensions solidly grounded in the literature. The state of the art in such model development continues to evolve with room for growth that hopefully will flow from increasing research and service attention to Latinos and other diverse populations. The sociocultural practice model advanced here is designed to provide practitioners and service administrators with a comprehensive yet user-friendly approach that can easily be utilized to evaluate service and practice settings. Model presentation is preceded by a foregrounding section on the foundations of diversity-related practice, followed by reviews of the literature on its components and their effectiveness. Given the literature's traditional and predominant use of the terms *cultural sensitivity* and *competence*, working definitions of these constructs are offered briefly below, including the increasingly popular *cultural humility*.

Cultural Sensitivity

Cultural sensitivity refers to becoming sensitized to the cultural and social realities of Latinos, past through present, in ways that render their social positionality in the U.S. hierarchy as overly influenced by stigma and discrimination related to racial/ethnic minority status rather than deficits constructed and perpetuated by racist and dehumanizing ideologies more generally (i.e., deficient racial or cultural make-up, damaged by poverty, etc.). Cultural sensitivity, informed by knowledge and experience, elevates the *sociological imagination* and consciousness needed to better understand how one's own positionality, race, and multiple group memberships shape ways in which we perceive and respond to each other's intersectional backgrounds and experiences. The latter includes analysis of one's varying degrees of intersectional stigma and privilege and corresponding degrees of power in relationships, both personal and professional. One way to begin such a process of enhanced self-awareness is to compose a *positionality statement* (e.g., my own under About the Author) and share with others doing the same (e.g., in the classroom and practice settings) (see Sidebar 6.1).

Sidebar 6.1. Social Positionality Statement as Exercise in Shared Self-Awareness

Also called a reflexivity statement, a *social positionality* statement is an exercise in self-awareness written for a variety of purposes. For example, the author's positionality statement at the beginning of this book (About the Author) has two purposes:

1. To remind himself of the key socio-demographic background experiences and values that guided the writing of this book for its intended audiences and,
2. To give readers insight into where the author is coming from, beyond professional credentials, reflected throughout the book (i.e., what the book includes and excludes, insights and blind spots, tone and emphasis with which information is communicated).

Similarly, it is recommended that students, practitioners, and administrators compose positionality statements for the purpose of enhancing self-awareness and sharpening client understanding of practitioner and the professional relationship. Hamby (2018) offers helpful social positionality guidelines elaborated here:

- List key socio-demographic background characteristics that define your social position (i.e., race/ethnicity, sex and gender identity, age, SES, etc.), and consider the extent to which these are sources of power and privilege and/or stigma, discrimination, and (dis)advantage.
- Note settings where you were raised (e.g., family information, SES, geographical location, religion) and how they have influenced your life course (i.e., childhood, adolescence, adulthood, work and relationships).
- What pivotal events or key individuals have helped to shape who you are?
- What core values inform your worldview?
- What lenses does your academic discipline or profession use to view client problems, situations and solutions? To which problem areas and client populations are you drawn and why?
- Personal disclosure should be *judicious* and *intentional*. That is, be careful not to over-disclose less relevant or distracting details (i.e., details of past traumas, gripes), and make sure to include details that support the *purpose* of your statement (i.e., to enhance own awareness of blind spots, to promote power *with* versus power *over* clients, etc.).

Like cultural competence, developing cultural sensitivity is an ongoing and challenging process when we ponder the ways in which we have been historically socialized to view people of color—first as genetically inferior, later as culturally or morally flawed, even as damaged by discrimination-related poverty, but ultimately to situate responsibility within these populations for their problematic social positionality, hence undeserving of government intervention. Parallel forms of biased socialization around gender and sexual orientation *within all American race/ethnic groups* similarly render women and sexual minorities as inferior and thus deserving of stigma, discrimination, and lower places in the social stratification system. The culturally sensitive practitioner is aware of such dehumanization and is committed to mitigating it in their professional and personal lives. Cultural sensitivity advances commitment to "re-humanize" Latinos and other dehumanized groups via professional and personal lifelong learning. Cultural sensitivity is foundational to developing the engagement, assessment, and intervention skills that compose cultural competence and humility.

Cultural Competence

As originally conceived, cultural competence is an aspirational construct informed by ongoing cultural sensitivity, education, and training necessary to effectively engage, assess, and intervene in ways congruent with the social and cultural realities of Latino clients. Included here is consideration of cultural and other assets and inputs from clients and their communities. Ideally, cultural competence maximizes the probability of being effective in framing and solving problems while minimizing the probability of insensitivity and incompetence that reify the biased socialization with which we frequently struggle to mitigate. Over the past two decades, cultural competence has come under fire for promoting an arrogant sense of presumed mastery over a finite set of knowledge and skills needed to work with diverse client populations. While never the intent of the construct, critics caution us to be aware of such a potential inadvertent consequence of professional education and training. Is there something about the term *competence* that can seduce practitioners into falsely believing they have achieved complete cultural competence? All licensed practitioners are mandated to engage in ongoing education and training as part of professional development, and cultural competence falls squarely under such professionalism.

Cultural Humility

The construct of cultural humility has gained momentum over the past 20 years, advocated as a replacement for *cultural competence*, the latter criticized for presuming possession of all the knowledge and skills needed to work effectively with culturally diverse clients. However, there seems to be a need to better understand both of these overlapping constructs in our ultimate quest to work caringly and effectively with Latinos and other diverse populations. In their seminal article, Tervalon and Murray-Garcia (1998) describe cultural competence in traditional medical training as characterized by a "detached mastery of a theoretically finite body of knowledge" (p. 117) that falls short of being responsive to medical patients of different cultural backgrounds. Thus, these authors assert that, alternatively, cultural humility "incorporates a lifelong commitment to self-evaluation and critique, to redressing the power imbalances in the physician–patient dynamic, and to developing mutually beneficial and non-paternalistic partnerships with communities on behalf of individuals and defined populations" (p. 123). While an aspirational goal, and perhaps most pertinent to health care where power differences between doctors and patients seem most pronounced, cultural competence as originally and currently defined by scholars of color does not appear to be inconsistent with cultural humility. As illustrated below, pioneering scholars of color from psychology, health care, social work, and public health conceptualize cultural competence as infused by cultural sensitivity.

Foundations of Sociocultural Practice

Contextual Ecological-Systems Perspective

Cultural competence is intended to provide a more contextual understanding of minority client problems and solutions as informed, for example, by an ecological-systems (E-S) framework of human beings in the social environment (e.g., Bronfenbrenner, 1979). The bottom line of the E-S framework is to help service providers envision multiple problem levels and solutions and to think "outside of the box" of traditional disciplinary training that is designed to narrowly focus on the individual level of analysis. As such, the E-S framework helps us to visualize how multiple interactions between human

systems of various sizes, over the life cycle and across biological, psychological, and social domains, result in degrees of adaptation and adjustment for
individuals, communities, and populations. Using an E-S map is no small
feat considering the boundaries of disciplinary training that are traditionally firm by design, tending to over-produce practice specialists while under-
producing generalists often better able to grasp the larger human picture.

Even in the field of social work, which subscribes to the E-S perspective
as its general multilevel practice framework, the tendency has been to set
this perspective aside in the process of specialization in areas such as health,
mental health, gerontology, school social work, and so forth. Part of the
problem is that the E-S perspective can be detailed to a fault, overwhelming
in the practice arena, and is ultimately a descriptive rather than prescrip-
tive theoretical framework regarding problem understanding and solutions
(Wakefield, 1996a, 1996b). For this reason, a brief and hopefully *retainable*
overview of an E-S map is provided below upon which this chapter's sociocultural practice model is built.

At minimum, eco-systemic informed practitioners picture the social environment as depicted in Figure 6.1. As can be seen, the individual at the center
is a system of biological, psychological, and social subsystems, reminding
practitioners to ask the overriding assessment question, "How much of the
problem before me is a function of this individual's biological, psychological,

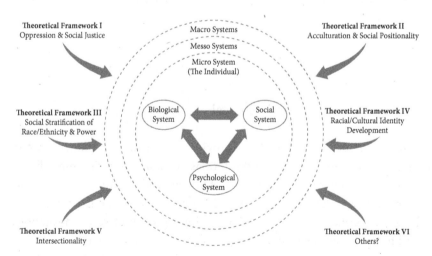

Figure 6.1. The Ecological-Systems Perspective as informed by key social
science knowledge frameworks.

and social make-up?" This *bio-psycho-social perspective* is thus a perspective within a perspective and represents a significant advancement over training to see human problems as overdetermined by any one E-S subsystem.

For example, a former client shared that her son once suffered from terrible headaches as a toddler that baffled the family's medical provider, who referred the child's parents to mental health professionals, who somehow attributed the headaches to marital problems. However, when the child's headaches persisted after weeks of couple therapy the client concluded, despite some initial buy-in to working on couple issues, that couple therapy was not the solution to the problem. Thus, she and her husband took their son to a university hospital where it was discovered that he was suffering from a benign brainstem tumor. Emergency brain surgery followed and fortunately was successful in resolving the problem.

Micro-level Systems

The above story illustrates the semi-porous boundaries between bio-psycho-social and other E-S levels. That is, a problem arising primarily in the biological system of the child dramatically spilled over into the child's temperament and behavior (psychological system), and into the family system in which confused siblings and exasperated parents struggled to understand and remedy the problem. The micro-system in Figure 6.1 refers to any immediate system containing an individual (e.g., the family, day care center, school) or containing the couple or family unit (e.g., places of work, health center, mental health center). Defining the above problem as marital, and treating it at the local mental health center, represents a micro-system containing the couple, as does the initial health care setting where the child was misdiagnosed, and the subsequent university hospital that diagnosed and treated the problem.

Meso-level Systems

Meso-systems refer to interactions between micro-systems that contain an individual, couple, or family (e.g., the family practitioner referring the family to the mental health center). Theoretically, the more meso-systemic activity on behalf of a client, family, or group, the more comprehensive the care because more problem levels can be addressed with more solutions. The interactions between several client micro-systems (i.e., family, neighborhood, school, church, health center, etc.) also imply social networks and communities in E-S frameworks.

The above example reminds us of the need to perform all of our respective jobs well, within our specific domains of service and practice, and to strive for greater continuity between systems of care (e.g., the family practitioner could have better assessed the child before referring the family to mental health professionals, who in turn could have communicated more with the physician about "ruling out" a physical health problem). As discussed further below, integrated behavioral health care is an important step toward meso-level care, given its integration and coordination of health and mental health care within the same clinic setting.

Macro-level Systems

Related to meso-systems are broader norms and social policies, pervasive values, ideologies, and numerous institutions and organizations that influence and govern meso- and micro- human systems within them. In the United States, macro-systems include pervasive American ideologies and practices such as democracy, capitalism and the free enterprise economic system, and dominant values and narratives such as the "American dream," rugged individualism, and meritocracy as discussed in previous chapters. Predominant patterns of national and cultural lifestyle are also included under macro-systems, including predominant social, political, economic, and religious lifeways.

While abstract, macro-systems remind us of the power of overarching social and structural forces to shape social and human service policies, funding streams, and the specific designs of formal and informal helping institutions. They also remind us of ways in which we as a society define and respond to economic, psychosocial, and health problems. For the most part, problem definitions and solutions have historically been generated by and for mainstream Americans in an ethnocentric manner that has ignored or minimized the problems and needs of people of color, attributing them to cultural or individual deficits *within* these groups versus compelling external contextual factors and forces as reviewed in Chapters 1–5.

As the arrows illustrate in Figure 6.1, the purpose of this book is to infuse our E-S framework with several Latino-relevant social science theories, research, and knowledge, organized in Chapters 1–5, to enhance sociocultural awareness and sensitivity. While not definitive, such a set of key frameworks and knowledge lowers the probability of perpetuating past bias and mistakes by providing a foundation for developing and utilizing effective interventions with Latinos that are contextually informed by relevant cultural and social factors. As we progress toward this aspirational goal, it is humbling to keep in mind that mounting research on cultural competence reveals increasing consensus regarding its components but also the continuing need for evaluations of effectiveness.

Deconstructing Cultural Competence

Pioneers in the field of social work, such as Doman Lum (1996, 1999), have provided in-depth descriptions of the three major dimensions of culturally competent practice: knowledge, skills, and lifelong commitment to learning.

Knowledge

The first major dimension of cultural competence consists of formal knowledge (e.g., as conveyed in Chapters 1–5), but also informal knowledge acquired in the daily experiences of committed practitioners outside of work (e.g., in daily interactions with people, consuming various forms of popular culture, casual and intimate relationships). Knowledge refers to both the acquisition of pertinent information and to increasing *awareness* and *sensitivity* to the sociocultural, and historical through current, experiences of Latinos and other diverse groups, including attention to the practitioner's own social positionality. Such specialized knowledge includes a fundamental understanding of oppression and social justice, stigma and privilege, and resistance and social movements to empower oppressed people, including coalition building across race, class, and other intersectional dimensions. Because learning is an ongoing endeavor, knowledge needs to be frequently replenished, formally and informally.

Skills

While knowledge is necessary, it is not sufficient to facilitate needed change with Latino clients and communities. Thus, the skills dimension refers to the ongoing development of engagement, assessment, and intervention skills with which to effectively address pressing problems. Too often, we are socialized and trained to think of such skills as formal and discipline bound, but are learning the value of being open to how our clients think about and respond to their problems and situations, frequently relying upon cultural and community-based assets and alternative ways of knowing. Frankly, it is precisely such indigenous and natural support systems that have primarily been responsible for the survival and adaptation of historically marginalized racial and ethnic minorities in the United States (e.g., development of ethnic communities and extended family systems engaged in mutual support; adherence to or reinvention of cultural practices needed to validate and support the humanity of group members under dehumanizing conditions).

The above is consistent with Tervalon and Murray-García's (1998) classic article in which they assert that *cultural humility* is a prerequisite for physicians in order to relinquish the role of expert to the patient, becoming the student of the patient with a conviction and explicit expression of the patient's potential to be a capable and full partner in the therapeutic alliance. While such flipping of the client–professional relationship is laudable, how to facilitate greater balance in professional–client relationships is challenging given the top-down ways in which professions have been socialized to operate for centuries.

Such facilitation should include not confusing one's professional expertise for "knowing it all" but making the effort to open-mindedly inquire into the patient's understanding of problems and potential solutions within the social and cultural context of their lives. In some cases great insights may be gleaned from clients and applied to interventions, but in others, patients may have internalized maladaptive ways of understanding and coping with their situations (e.g., pathological self-blame, internalized oppression, acting-out problems when overwhelmed). In such cases, informed providers will need to be able to detect, carefully challenge, and transform less than adequate ways of coping while engaging clients as partners in the process as much as possible.

For example, Latino youth that do not persist in high school, experience unwanted pregnancies, become gang affiliated and prison system–impacted, frequently blame themselves for experiencing psychosocial and health problems at the individual level but that are part of larger sociological patterns disproportionately impacting members of their community. Such youth may require guidance in cultivating the *sociological imagination* needed to see their problems not just at the micro-individual-level but also at meso-community and macro-social levels related to social injustice and the persistence of racial hierarchy. Caution also needs to be exercised not to place Latino patients in a pressurized role of educating medical providers about Latino culture or how to best conceptualize and treat complex problems.

In his well-known model of culturally competent social work practice, Lum (1999) goes into great detail in describing skill development that includes the following basic competencies:

- The skill to generate profiles of the communities in which one practices that include socio-demographic data, locations of cultural and community resources that can be tapped to co-address local patterns of psychosocial, health, and economic problems. Ideally, such profiles also include awareness of local history and community struggles to empower itself, some of which may have directly involved the practitioner's place of work! For example, when the author approached a community Latino health center with the idea of evaluating their HIV prevention services for farmworkers, he expected and understood the immediate reaction of staff who complained about the number of times that his university had "used them like Guinea pigs" to collect data from which only the researchers benefited (called "hit and run" research by some community members). The author smiled knowingly and agreed that "I know that can happen," and proceeded to ask how they might work together to mitigate exploitation and maximize benefits to the agency and clients in more of a win–win scenario. The author complied with requests to pay farmworkers for their interview time and to return and share study findings with staff, interested farmworkers, and larger community at the local library. This request also gave the author an added opportunity to see how study results resonated with the community.
- The skill to engage in culturally sensitive *relationship protocols* with diverse clients that enhance initial rapport and facilitate engagement in the professional helping relationship is fundamental. For example, the common mainstream approach of beginning professional relationships by immediately addressing the task at hand (e.g., "What seems to be the problem?" or "How can I help you?") is frequently misperceived by Latinos as impersonal, even cold and rude, if time is not taken to first personalize the relationship (e.g., by introducing oneself with some background information, expressing warmth and care by asking clients how they are doing, whether they are comfortable, if they need a glass of water, cup of coffee).
- The skill to view problems less from a perspective of pathology and more as "unmet needs" or ways of coping that attempt promote survival under trying circumstances. However, from the author's contextual

perspective, optimal assessment skills need to be comprehensive and balanced in identifying strengths *and* weaknesses, health *and* pathology, that frequently coexist at individual and larger social levels. So long as we maintain sight of the full humanity of our diverse clients, including the social and cultural context of unmet needs, then labeling serious problems as pathology need not be dehumanizing. For example, and as discussed in Chapter 8 (Latinx Youth), the *pathological* part of gang affiliation (i.e., violent deaths and injuries, serious crime, incarceration, etc.) should not be minimized but neither should the multiple *unmet needs* and traumas of such marginalized youth (i.e., developmental, familial, community, personal and social power) that leave many vulnerable to the lure of gang activity as a misdirected way of attempting to meet basic human needs.

- At administrative levels, Lum discusses the skill of designing and managing socially and culturally responsive agencies. Taking cultural competence to administrative levels involves incorporating its major dimensions into agency mission statements, policies and objectives, training diverse staff, student supervision, ongoing evaluation of services, and client partnership guided by cultural humility. The sociocultural practice model presented in this chapter can serve as a user-friendly and comprehensive checklist for such services.

- Applying research in an informed manner to client problems involves remaining on top of studies in one's area in order to provide evidence-based treatments if available, versus doing merely what is familiar or comfortable. For example, some clinical practitioners in training frequently express an anti-medication bias despite research evidence showing that antidepressant medications, for example, are as effective as different forms of psychotherapy. Getting beyond such biases frees practitioners to consider more treatment options, educate clients about such choices, and maximizes matching treatments and client preferences.

Commitment to Ongoing Learning

The third major dimension of cultural competence described by Lum (1999) is professional commitment to an ongoing process of formal knowledge and skill acquisition that continues to enhance practice with Latinos and other diverse groups. To a significant degree, mandated continuing professional education and conferences constitute the formal mechanism for keeping professional practitioner knowledge and skills fresh and up to date in both general and specialized ways. Lum (1999) describes the culturally competent practitioner as consistently keeping up with the latest in diversity-related practice knowledge and skills, in addition to generating and passing on such expertise via supervision, program evaluation, teaching, and consultation. In spite of this central component of cultural competence, proponents of cultural humility often assert that those espousing cultural competence falsely believe they have mastered a finite knowledge and skills base. If this is true, at least in some cases, from where might such a misunderstanding of cultural competence arise?

The above represents the author's understanding of the state of art in culturally competent practice. Ongoing refinement of the construct benefits from the many reviews of the literature and evaluations of cultural competence highlighted below.

Evaluating Cultural Competence

Because "there is no consensus regarding the definition or the components of this concept and there is a dearth of empirical proof indicating the benefits of cultural competence" (p. 117), Alizadeh and Chevan (2016) conducted a systematic review of the literature on cultural competence in order to identify its most common dimensions and evidence of effectiveness. Their review of over 1,200 citations yielded 18 publications that included models of cultural competence, 13 of which also included evaluations of effectiveness findings. Results and conclusions of this review confirm emerging consensus in the literature regarding the components and overall purpose of cultural competence, while also raising concerns about the mixed state of outcome evaluations:

- There is general consensus that cultural competence consists of awareness, knowledge, and skills that impart the ability to communicate and work effectively and appropriately with people from culturally different backgrounds. *Appropriately* refers to respecting valued cultural relationship protocols regarding how people should relate and interact (e.g., upon first meeting, expressing care, warmth, respect, assistance).
- Interestingly, two additional components of cultural competence emerged in the review: *Cultural desire* refers to practitioner

motivation to learn about cultural diversity and to raise their own cultural awareness, knowledge, and skills. Such desire would be important in professional settings where practitioners are required to participate in diversity-related trainings and continuing education. Limited desire would be an important starting point for any such trainings. *Cultural encounter* refers to enacting desire by engagement in face-to-face contacts and interactions with people from diverse cultural backgrounds in both work and personal lives (i.e., making it happen!).

• There was general consensus in the literature that cultural competence is an ongoing process, not an endpoint, meaning that competency can and should be continuously enhanced over time, same as all professional knowledge and skill sets. Thus, any practitioners that mistake competency with achieving complete knowledge and ability to work with diverse clients is not adhering to cultural competence as defined and discussed in the literature.

• Effectiveness generally referred to achieving valued goals and outcomes in practice, although authors in the studies reviewed did not specify if these were mutually agreed upon goals derived from practitioner–client collaboration. This suggests the need to work toward mitigating power differences by engaging clients in problem definitions and solutions and greater open-mindedness on the part of practitioners in this regard, consistent with the tenets of cultural humility.

• With regard to the 13 outcome evaluations of models of cultural competence, all were from the United States, and 12 assessed patient satisfaction, two assessed trust in provider, one adherence to treatment, but only one actually assessed health outcomes. While all of these assessments represent important aspects of effective treatment, outcome evaluation needs to be more comprehensive with greater emphasis on health outcomes and adherence to treatment.

• Regarding the quality and rigor of methods used in the 13 evaluation studies reviewed, five were rated as *weak*, five moderate–weak, and three moderate–strong. These ratings were made by two independent researchers using an assessment model focused on adequacy of sampling, outcome measures, and statistical analyses employed in the outcome evaluations. Thus, the rigor of outcome evaluations lean heavily toward the weak side of the evaluation continuum, warranting much-needed improvement.

Regarding improving outcome evaluations of culturally competent practice, it is instructive to review the three studies that Alizadeh and Chevan (2016) rated as most rigorous or moderate–strong in their review. For instance, these three studies used large diverse samples (Ns = 40,723, 1,305, and 465) and assessed cultural competence with published scales of provider self-ratings and/or client satisfaction, across the following outcomes: mental health care, emergency and trauma care, and parent ratings of health care received by their children. While one study found no relationship between provider self-ratings and client satisfaction, the two other studies found associations between provider self-rated cultural competence and client satisfaction, respect for cultural differences, convenient appointments, and engagement of family and community in treatment. Again, while these outcomes are aspects of helpful care, they do not constitute health or mental health outcomes which need to be targeted in such evaluations.

Further, it is also recommended that evaluations assess the six components of cultural competence noted in the literature review (knowledge, skills, commitment, desire, contact/interaction, and engaging clients in assessment and treatment process). Evaluations should also compare services deliberately implementing these components with services that do not, often referred to as *treatment as usual*, while treating the same outcome variables and similar client populations. Many of these more direct evaluations of culturally competent treatment versus treatments as usual are documented in the following chapters of this book focusing on Latino health, mental health, and interventions for Latino families and youth.

Review of Reviews

Another notable publication by Truong et al. (2014) features a systematic review of over 6,830 reviews of the cultural competence literature, between 2000 and 2011, with the goal of evaluating the effectiveness of interventions reviewed. To achieve this goal, the quality of each literature review was critically appraised by two study authors, independently, using a health-evidence tool for assessing evidence-informed principles. This rigorous approach yielded 19 reviews of the literature of which three were rated as *strong*, 10 moderate–strong, five moderate, and one weak. Thus, the rigor of these reviews of the cultural competence intervention literature lean heavily toward the strong side of the evaluation continuum. Reviews of reviews are rare authoritative assessments of the state of the literature in focal areas, in this case culturally competent practice. Major findings are highlighted and elaborated here:

- The majority of literature reviews found *moderate* evidence of improvement in provider competence (i.e., knowledge, skills) as well as improvement of health care access and utilization. The former was the result of diversity training, while the latter were typically related to hiring diverse staff, including bilingual providers, and outreach workers from the community trained to provide health education and helping clients navigate service systems. These encouraging findings validate the need for a workforce, both professional and paraprofessional, that speak client languages and are familiar with their social positionality. Closer matching of provider needs with specific types of training may improve these outcomes above their moderate rating.

- However, there was *weaker* evidence for improvements in patient/client outcomes such as improved health and mental health, adherence to treatment, and adoption of healthier lifestyle changes. Given this ultimate objective, such client outcomes must be prioritized and assessed in multiple ways (e.g., symptom relief, biomarkers, observations of family members) and over various points in time, given the long-term and uneven course of chronic illnesses.

- Evaluations of interventions in the literature reviews were characterized by very few validated/published self-assessment measures of provider cultural competence, client satisfaction and health outcomes, and service agency's cultural competence. In addition to utilizing objective methods of assessment (i.e., by outside professional, consumer, and community member evaluators), the above three dimensions of cultural competence, including interactions between them (e.g., provider–client interactions), should ideally be assessed simultaneously.

- Truong et al. (2014) note some attention to involving clients in treatment in some of the reviews, but without elaboration. This black box needs to be illuminated given the formidable goal of mitigating power differences by open-mindedly facilitating collaboration with clients and community in the project of service delivery.

- The authors note that reviews over-focus on "culture" at the expense of broader socioeconomic factors central to poorer health outcomes (e.g., poor education and work opportunities, the trappings of poverty). This astute criticism may be semantically built into terms such as *cultural competency*, *cultural sensitivity*, and *cultural humility* that over-direct our attention more to the *cultural* rather than the *social* experience of racial and ethnic minority groups facing life-compromising racism and discrimination in the racial hierarchy of America.

The above mixed yet encouraging reviews confirm and expand our understanding of the social and cultural context of practice. While knowledge, skills, and commitment to ongoing training and education have been promoted and practiced for decades, the addition of practitioner *motivation/ desire* and corresponding *contact/engagement* clarifies some of the more personal/subjective dimensions of practice that may promote coherence between knowledge and skills.

Cultural humility represents another dimension for promoting effective practice across human diversity. For instance, consistently inviting client input and collaboration represents a critical first step in mitigating built-in power differences between clients and professionals, partly by deliberately expanding the potential for two-way listening and learning. Such bidirectional learning may reveal culture and community-based assets and practices that complement professional services and help to mitigate psychosocial and health problems. As such, collaborations between professionals and community practices are ways to expand client services. For example, Homeboy Industries in Los Angeles *heals* gang affiliated and system impacted individuals by including them in a spiritual community of boundless love and radical tenderness and compassion, while clinical social worker staff provide therapy for trauma, anger management, couples, and imparting job skills and work opportunities in order for members to support themselves and their families and to reintegrate into society is adaptive ways (see Chapter 8 for more detail on Homeboy Industries).

Mindful of the need for more theorizing, rigorous outcome evaluation research, and professional–community collaboration, offered here is a practice model with Latinos intended to integrate the social and cultural context of psychosocial and health problems, with attention to multiple E-S problem levels and solutions or multilevel practice.

Sociocultural Practice Model for Latino Populations

Bumper sticker wisdom urges us to "Think globally and act locally," and that is exactly what a viable sociocultural practice model can help us do. That is, all of the preceding foundational background information enables us to think more contextually about psychosocial and health problems over-affecting Latino populations so as to more effectively address particular problems and clients in our various professional practices and settings. Thus, the sociocultural practice model presented here is a 4 × 3: four practice dimensions (service availability and access, assessment of key social and cultural factors that contextualize problems, interventions congruent with such assessment, and accountability to clients and communities served) by three ecological-systems (E-S) practice levels (micro-individual, meso-network and community, and macro-social policy).

The model's four general practice dimensions derive form a synthesis of past studies, reports, and models developed to promote culturally competent care with people of color. However, these four dimensions represent socioculturally competent care given their deliberate attention to interrelated social and cultural factors that contextualize psychosocial and health problems. For example, making services available and accessible, as well as accountable to Latino clients, are effective ways to address historical obstacles to care by mitigating such structural social factors. And focusing assessment on identifying key social and cultural factors (e.g., values-related beliefs, attitudes, and practices interrelated to social situations) that contextualize a problem optimizes intervention efforts congruent with such sociocultural assessment.

Table 6.1. Sociocultural Practice Model for Working with Latino Populations

	4 Dimensions of Sociocultural Practice			
Potential Multilevel Practice	Increase Service Availability & Access	Problem Assessment in Social and Cultural Context	Select Socially & Culturally Congruent Interventions	Increase Service Accountability
Micro-Individual				
Meso-Community				
Macro-Policy				

The corresponding E-S practice levels remind and motivate practitioners to construct cognitive maps of the multiple levels of a problem, as well as corresponding solution levels, to more comprehensively address psychosocial and health problems over-affecting Latino populations. For example, while preventing or managing diabetes is necessary at the micro-individual level (e.g., with a client or family), optimal diabetes prevention and care is multilevel and includes both meso-network and community-level practice (e.g., diabetes awareness and testing at community health fairs, public health media campaigns) and macro social policy level practice (supporting development of diabetes-mitigating policies and practices).

General and Specialized Practice
Most practitioners are trained to specialize within a specific practice domain such as health, mental health, child and/or family services, or other social or human service capacity. Even social workers, whose training includes a generalist foundation, typically develop domain-specific expertise around certain client problems and populations (e.g., licensed clinical social worker addressing depression and anxiety disorders in adults or working in child and family services). However, social workers, and increasingly other helping professions, are trained in *multilevel practice* such that they can envision, and often address, multiple problem levels from an E-S perspective, as discussed earlier and depicted along the left-hand column of the model. Across the top row of the model are four general service dimensions that compose what virtually all competent sociocultural services need to address. How the model's generalist practice framework, as well as its attention to multilevel practice, is addressed in subsequent practice-oriented chapters that follow, while model dimensions are described in detail below.

Increasing Service Availability and Access

Latino Underutilization
Back in the 1950s and 60s, mental health service providers concluded that Mexican Americans had better mental health than non-Latino whites (NLWs) because their rates of mental health service use were so much lower (Padilla, 1978). While it was tempting for Mexican Americans to believe that they were less mentally ill than NLWs, pioneering Latino mental health experts began to challenge this assumption, citing the many risk

factors surrounding the racialized ethnic minority experience of Chicanos (e.g., immigration and acculturation stress, poverty linked to stigma and discrimination). Indeed, some of the first prevalence studies to include Mexican Americans documented rates of mental disorders roughly equivalent to the general U.S. population (e.g., Karno et al., 1987). It was eventually concluded that their low rates of mental health service use were primarily due to structural obstacles rather than lack of need.

Initially, Latino underutilization was attributed to factors presumed to be *within* Latino culture and experience, including strict reliance on close family ties to solve problems, mistrust of NLW systems and professionals, and preference for indigenous folk healers (e.g., *curanderos*) and medicine over professional services. It was not until the late 1970s that evidence began to accrue pointing to major social and institutional obstacles to service use well *outside* of Latino culture and experience. For example in 1978, President Carter's Task Force on Minority Mental Health published a landmark report that attributed pervasive underutilization to four major social-structural barriers (Parron, 1982). Because each of these obstacles begins with the letter "A" they compose a convenient checklist to quickly assess the degree to which an agency or service provider may be socioculturally effective at multiple E-S practice levels:

- *Availability*: This obstacle refers to the historical and pervasive lack of mental health services available to racial and ethnic minority populations and communities in need.
- *Accessibility*: This obstacle refers to lack of accessible mental health services due to their inconvenient locations and limited hours of operation, lack of convenient transportation, and lack of affordable service (e.g., due to lack of health insurance and other financial resources), lack of child care, and the like.
- *Acceptability*: This obstacle refers to the pervasive lack of mental health services that are acceptable to ethnically diverse clients. Basic to this obstacle has been the chronic lack of diverse staff and practitioners who are bilingual and bicultural, and have experienced backgrounds similar to client populations served. Other aspects of acceptable services include the sociocultural adaptation of conventional services to better resonate with the experience of diverse clients (e.g., language, values, culture-based interpersonal styles, ways of defining and solving problems, art/

architecture and physical appearance of services). In an early review of the literature comparing culturally responsive to conventional mental health services, Atkinson and Lowe (1995) found the former to be superior in increasing perceived credibility of therapists, willingness to return to treatment, satisfaction with therapy, and depth of disclosure in therapy on the part of ethnic minority clients.

- *Accountability*: This obstacle refers to a lack of accountability to the racial/ethnic minority client and community in terms of providing desired mental health services that include client and community input, and ongoing assessment of treatment response and satisfaction. Rarely have ethnic community leaders and mental health service consumers been consulted about service need, development, and provision. There is also a pervasive lack of formal mechanisms of practice and agency accountability, ranging from outcome evaluation research to exit interviews with clients upon treatment completion, and even simple suggestion boxes with which to inquire about satisfaction and recommendations for improvement. And while satisfaction surveys are fairly common these days (e.g., after receiving services at an HMO), clients are rarely if ever informed about how feedback was utilized.

The Outreach Imperative

Latinos and other populations over-affected by the trappings of poverty (i.e., segregation, overwhelming problems) require concerted efforts by service providers to help clients in need be aware of and encouraged to use available and accessible services. Service providers need to routinely institutionalize multiple forms of outreach, ranging from advertisements in popular media to the use of community outreach workers or *promotores* [health promoters] able to engage Latinos where they live and work to increase their awareness of services and to provide them with on-the-spot health education, service information, and referrals, as well as interventions for chronic illnesses as detailed in subsequent chapters. In general, Latinos at highest risk for serious psychosocial and health problems are also often the most marginal, overwhelmed, and in need of outreach efforts. For example, poor, urban-based, IV drug-using Puerto Ricans are at high risk for HIV/AIDS and require customized outreach efforts to mitigate risk where it hits hardest (e.g., engaged by former IV drug-using outreach workers in the community, where they convene).

Problem Assessment in Social and Cultural Context

Imagine defining Latino client, family, community, and population-wide problem patterns in ways that link such problems to ongoing Latino historical experience of oppression and its living legacies of disproportionate segregation and marginality, poverty, and hence stressful acculturation. While a bit abstract, Lum (1999) would begin such an endeavor with a bias toward defining problems as "unmet needs," coping efforts to survive, and as "psycho-individual reactions" (at the micro level) to environmental impacts (at meso and macro levels). While some problems may seem more amenable to such consideration than others (e.g., gang affiliation versus diabetes), it is a worthwhile exercise for practitioners to use the E-S model in Figure 6.1, and alongside the left-hand column of the practice model, to consider multiple problem levels and whether or not the presenting problems are part of larger *problem patterns* linked to Latino culture and social experience or some other dimension of diversity.

For example, while diabetes as a health problem seems neatly confined to the domain of physical health and biology, why is it disproportionately highest among the poorest of Latinos, African Americans, and Native Americans? Further, why are diabetes risk factors such as obesity, poor diets, and sedentary lifestyles also disproportionately high in these groups? Finally, why do people of color experience more complications and die sooner from diabetes than NLW counterparts? Thus, if links between diabetes and race/ethnicity-related experience can be made, this problem should be understood and addressed as such (e.g., tailored public health campaigns, targeted community-based interventions, policies to reduce poverty and promote healthy lifestyles) as illustrated in Chapter 10 (Latino Health).

Bio-psycho-social Problem Levels

As mentioned earlier, a bio-psycho-social perspective allows us to consider the possible contribution of each of these domains to a problem such as diabetes. For example, in the social-structural domain, research shows that many Latinos with diabetes are less aware of it due to lack of effective public health information, health literacy, and access to health services. In the psychological domain, how Latinos think and feel about this disease bears serious consideration for optimal intervention. For instance, for those who become diagnosed, the prospect of changing a traditional Latino diet, typically tied to cultural lifestyle and economics, can result in pessimism to control the course of this serious medical condition. The bottom line here is that even the most formal of medical diagnoses require a healthy co-construction of the disease, on the part of physicians and patients, in ways that help patients become knowledgeable, skilled, and efficacious in managing such problems within the sociocultural context of their lives. Seeking client input also elevates provider understanding of the role of family in supporting diabetic clients, or food as culture necessitating creative alterations of recipes rather than "cutting them off" of one's diet.

Client Empowerment

Problem assessment is generally improved by actively soliciting the client's or the community's conception of target problems and collaborating in a process of co-defining problems, intervention goals, and methods. This is consistent with an "empowerment approach" to providing services to Latinos and other groups with a history of significant disempowerment. According to Gutierrez, Parsons, and Cox (1998), empowerment practice imbues professional assistance with consciousness raising that makes clients aware of problems on a continuum from the personal to the public, social, and political. That is, while immediate problems require attention to relieve suffering, dialogue between practitioners and clients about links between problems and social and political forces can be gradually pursued. As such, problem definition and understanding are performed more *with* versus *for* clients, as are intervention efforts that increasingly engage clients along a continuum from self-care to helping others affected by community-wide problem patterns. Empowerment is thus both process and outcome and requires deliberate effort on the part of practitioners and agencies to include this theme in service provision. Consistent with *cultural humility*, client empowerment involves inviting and trusting such collaboration in service provision that can also mitigate some of the structural power difference between clients and professional practitioners.

One starting place is to openly discuss power imbalances inherent to professional relationships and to acknowledge that there are informed and legitimate uses of greater power, as when a client is out of control, not capable of assuming a more collaborative role, or in danger of hurting self or others. Even in such crisis situations, clients should be made aware of rationales driving actions and be invited to provide input as much as possible. Attention to these matters within Latino problem themes is illustrated throughout the second half of this book (Chapters 7–12) and outlined below.

Latino Problem Themes

Assessment as described above presumes a historical and ongoing environmental context in which most of the major problems affecting Latino populations form patterns linked to their ethnic minoritized experience in America. As such, several overarching and overlapping problem themes for most U.S. Latinos begin to emerge, ranging from compromised social positionality to individual level identity issues: (1) Immigration, acculturation, and adaptation issues; (2) poverty, segregation, and marginalization issues; (3) consequent destabilization of ethnic community and extended family systems; (4) racial and ethnic identity issues; and (5) variations on these problem themes along the intersectional lines of gender and gender identity, sexual minority status, color and other racial features, immigration status, and so on.

Socioculturally Congruent Interventions

Historically, there has been little research indicating the effectiveness of treatment approaches or services for various psychosocial and health problems over-affecting Latino populations, but this has changed significantly. Since the publication of the first edition of this book in 2007, a considerable amount of Latino-focused outcome evaluation research has begun to accrue, as selectively featured in the subsequent chapters. Hence, we have more evidenced-based or *best practices* to guide services and practitioners than ever before, although more is continuously needed. When evidence-based practices are scarce or missing, we must carefully select, adapt, or design *promising* approaches that are conceptually sound based on the assessment and intervention strategies outlined in this chapter. The overarching goal is to provide interventions that are congruent with the lived social and cultural reality of Latino clients, and are thus more likely to be experienced as relevant and helpful.

Latino Client Needs and Expectations

Much has been written on the service and treatment expectations of less acculturated Latinos (e.g., immigrants, lower income) who continue to comprise considerable portions of U.S. Latino populations (i.e., about one-third of Latinos overall). Because of their social and cultural circumstances, service expectations are likely to include immediate symptom relief, direct attention to problems of daily living, prescriptions for medications, advice regarding how to solve problems, and preferences for practitioners who are active and directive but also warm, personable, well mannered, or *bien educado* [well mannered, cultured, or raised well]. A recent assessment of underserved minority clients (N = 35), utilizing a mobile health clinic found that they prefer practitioners that are well-trained, compassionate, and caring, and that practice cultural humility or cultural awareness, knowledge, skills, and responsiveness to client needs and desires (Moore de Peralta et al., 2019).

From the above description of Latino client expectations, it makes practical sense to begin with interventions that are short-term and that emphasize prevention, psycho-education, coping, and problem-solving skills applied to present circumstances. In the area of mental health, for example, the above expectations provide a rationale for using integrated behavioral health care, a community-based model of culturally and socially responsive care that addresses health, mental health, and social problems within the same agency as discussed in subsequent chapters on Latino health and mental health.

Practitioners should also practice being flexible enough to assist with needs and requests that may not be a focus of professional attention (e.g., a recent immigrant client seeks the provider's help recovering a car that has been towed away, reading a letter from the city that she can't understand, or with the emotional problems of a relative back in El Salvador) while supporting client empowerment (via information, resources, and engagement) to co-address such issues.

Family-centered Services

Given the centrality of the family in the lives of most Latinos, it makes sense to consider service approaches that attempt to involve members of the extended family in the assessment and intervention processes. Family therapy is an obvious mental health example, but virtually any human service can involve more family members who can help by providing greater insight into problems and circumstances, needed support, and participation in problem solving and follow-through.

Community-based Services

The location of most Latino families in heavily Latino communities, and most Latino problems manifested in ethnically linked community and population-wide patterns, compels practitioners to provide community-based services that interact with natural support systems and community resources. For example, Rapp and Winersteen (1989) found that when the *strength model* of case management was used by agencies caring for the chronically mentally ill, social workers performed most client contacts in the community and achieved client goals utilizing community resources. Gutierrez et al. (1998) similarly advocate teaching clients to make connections between personal and social problems and to better address them through informal and formal self-help groups, community organizing, and political action as addressed in Chapters 11 and 12.

The growing popularity of comprehensive school-based services for both students and their families represents needed movement toward community-based and family-centered efforts toward intervening at several points along the problem continuum from private to public as described in Chapter 8 (Latinx Youth).

Attention to Intersectionality

Once viable service approaches have been identified for Latinos affected by specific problems, practitioners also need to consider how such approaches play out over intersectional dimensions of human diversity within the Latino experience (i.e., female versus male versus gender nonconforming; sexual minority versus majority; elderly versus young adults; undocumented versus citizens), as discussed in Chapter 5 (Toward Latino Intersectionality). Such consideration will include challenging Latino cultural values and practices as needed and touched upon below.

Deviating from Culture of Origin?

In their classic article on culturally sensitive mental health service for Latinos, Rogler et al. (1987) note that while it makes sense to work *within* the culture of the client, as the literature often uncritically advocates, it also is in best interest of Latino clients to challenge and work *outside* of culture of origin as needed. This recommendation is consistent with consensus in the literature that bicultural Latinos most likely possess more adaptive skills than their monocultural counterparts. For example, few would question the value of monolingual Spanish speakers learning English in the United States. Thus, the frequent assertion to work *within culture* can sometimes be a well-intentioned overreaction to the historical practice of cultural imperialism or social institutions coercing Latinos to abandon their culture and replace it with mainstream American culture (e.g., the historical practice of punishing U.S. Latinos for speaking Spanish in the classroom).

Thus, the delicate task of the socioculturally competent practitioner is to understand oppressive history and still be prepared to work outside of traditional Latino culture, when necessary, in a *non-oppressive* manner. For instance, Latinos as well as Asians are frequently stereotyped as submissive and passive and hence recommended assertiveness training as a remedy for such deficits. That is, assertiveness is offered as a superior replacement for traditional Latino communication protocol rather than as a different cultural style of communication that can be *added* to the client's repertoire in the spirit of flexible biculturality. Trickier are issues of bias and prejudice within Latino culture, and all cultures for that matter, that need to be addressed when they are damaging to family members and community (e.g., sexist double standards, homophobia, trans-antagonism, colorism, stigmatizing undocumented members).

Increase Service Accountability

As noted above, federally mandated research in the area of minority mental health has long documented the pervasive lack of *accountability* to ethnic and racial minority clients and communities on that segment of service providers nationwide during the 1970s. Thus, the current sociocultural practice model advocates multiple institutionalized methods and mechanisms of frequently involving minority clients and their communities in the development, delivery, and evaluation of well-intended services. On the client side, methods of accountability range from simple suggestion boxes in waiting rooms (to which responses are promptly posted) to exit interviews following service use to elicit critical client feedback. The development of community advisory boards composed of key community players (i.e., leaders, advocates, service consumers) is an excellent way to institutionalize Latino voice and input.

At the service provider and agency level, periodic staff surveys regarding service provision and agency climate and environment is another fairly easy way to implement accountability, as is periodic outcome evaluation research to assess the effectiveness of services provided. HMOs such as Kaiser Permanente now routinely elicit consumer feedback regarding services used via online, as well as regular mail surveys. While probably helpful, consumers still have no indication of how their feedback is received or acted upon, challenging motivation to participate.

While the above recommendations make intuitive sense, service providers sometimes dread mounting evaluations given the lack of internal research infrastructure (e.g., in nonprofit agencies), concerns over fault-finding, and limited capacity to make improvements. The latter are understandable worries and can be addressed by involving providers directly and early in the planning of evaluations (what do they most want to know and why?). Implications of such service assessments range from staff trainings in areas of desired improvement, to improving existing and developing new Latino-focused services. Subsequent chapters offer a selective review of *best* and *promising* practices with various Latino groups and subgroups across a wide variety of psychosocial and health problems in need of competent sociocultural understanding and practice.

Conclusion

While challenging, it has been worthwhile developing and testing conceptually sound practice models that increase the probability of effective interventions with Latinos, and other racial and ethnic minority groups, by assessing and responding to problem patterns within the sociocultural context or lived realities of Latino clients and communities. Since the first edition of this book, published in 2007, a considerable amount of Latino-focused outcome evaluation research has accrued, advancing our understanding, assessment, and treatment of psychosocial and health problems over-affecting Latino populations. In the chapters that follow, the current sociocultural Latino practice model serves as a guiding framework for evaluating *state of the art* as well as *cutting edge* interventions across a wide variety of Latino problems, populations, and diverse subgroups.

More specifically, practice efforts are analyzed with respect to the degree to which they address availability and access, engagement, assessment of client and community problems in a culturally and socially informed manner, and the development or selection of interventions congruent with the cultural and social reality of Latinos, including interventions that deviate from Latino culture as needed to mitigate within-group oppression, and incorporate multiple mechanisms of accountability. The advantage of using a selective review of the *best* (i.e., evidence-based) Latino practice literature to illustrate sociocultural practice is that it reviews actual examples while providing a conceptually grounded critique, versus overwhelming readers with long and impractical wish lists of all the things we should but often can't do. Further, because all psychosocial and health problems affecting Latinos cannot be addressed in a single book, it makes sense to carefully select and describe a few best and promising (i.e., lacking in evidence yet conceptually compelling) practices that not only solve some of the most significant psychosocial and health problems affecting Latino populations today, but also illustrate practice principles applicable to related problems.

References

Alizadeh, S., & Chavan, M. (2016). Cultural competence dimensions and outcomes: A systematic review of the literature. *Health and Social Care in the Community, 24*(6), e117–e130.

Atkinson, D. R., & Lowe, S. M. (1995). The role of ethnicity, cultural knowledge, and conventional techniques in counseling and psychology. In J. G. Ponterotto, J. M. Casas, L. A. Suzuki, & C. M. Alexander (Eds.), *Handbook of multicultural counseling* (pp. 387–456). Thousand Oaks, CA: Sage Publications.

Bronfenbrenner, U. (1979). *The ecology of human development: Experiments by nature and design.* Cambridge: Harvard University Press.

Gutierrez, L. M., Parsons, R. J., & Cox, E. O. (1998). A model for empowerment practice. In L. M. Gutierrez, R. J. Parsons, & E. O. Cox (Eds.), *Empowerment in social work practice: A sourcebook* (pp. 3–23). Pacific Grove, CA: Brooks/Cole.

Hamby, S. (2018). Know thyself: How to write a reflexivity statement: More self-awareness will help you on your path to being a better psychologist. *Psychology Today*, Posted May 22, 2018. https://www.psychologytoday.com/us/blog/the-web-of-violence/201805/know-thyself-how-to-write-a-reflexivity-statement

Karno, M., Hough, R. L., Burnam, M. A., Escobar, J. I., Timbers, D. M., Santana, F., & Boyd, J. H. (1987). Lifetime prevalence of specific psychiatric disorders among Mexican Americans and non-Hispanic whites in Los Angeles. *Archives of General Psychiatry, 44*, 695–701.

Lum, D. (1996). *Social work practice with people of color: A process-stage approach.* Pacific Grove, CA: Brooks/Cole.

Lum, D. (1999). *Culturally competent practice: A framework for growth and action.* Pacific Grove, CA: Brooks/Cole.

Moore de Peralta, A., Gillispie, M., Mobley, C., & Gibson. L. M. (2019). It's all about trust and respect: Cultural competence and cultural humility in mobile health clinic services for underserved minority populations. *Journal of Health Care for the Poor and Underserved, 30*(3), 1103–1118. https://doi.org/10.1353/hpu.2019.0076

Padilla, A. M. (1978). Psychological research and the Mexican American. In C. A. Hernandez, M. J. Haug, & N. N. Wagner (Eds.), *Chicanos: Social and psychological perspectives* (pp. 152–159). St. Louis, MO: C. V. Mosby.

Parron, D. L. (1982). An overview of minority group mental health needs and issues as presented to the President's Commission on Mental Health. In F. V. Munoz & R. Endo (Eds.), *Perspectives on minority group mental health* (pp. 3–22). Washington, DC: University Press of America.

Rapp, C. A., & Wintersteen, R. (1989). The strength model of case management: Results from twelve demonstration projects. *Psychosocial Rehabilitation Journal, 13*(1), 23–32.

Rogler, L. H., Malgady, R. G., Costantino, G., & Blumenthal, R. (1987). What do culturally sensitive mental health services mean? *American Psychologist, 42*(6), 565–570.

Tervalon, M., & Murray-Garcia, J. (1998). Cultural humility vs. cultural competence: A critical distinction in defining physician training outcomes in multicultural education. *Journal of Health Care for the Poor and Underserved, 9*(2), 117–125.

Truong, M., Paradies, Y., & Priest, N. (2014). Interventions to improve cultural competency in healthcare: A systematic review of reviews. *BMC Health Services Research, 14*(99), 1–17. http://www.biomedcentral.com/1472-6963/14/99

Wakefield, J. C. (1996a, March). Does social work need the eco-systems perspective? Part 1. Is the perspective clinically useful? *Social Service Review, 70*(1), 1–32.

Wakefield, J. C. (1996b, March). Does social work need the eco-systems perspective? Part 2. Does the perspective save social work from incoherence? *Social Service Review, 70*(2), 183–213.

PART II

SELECTIVE REVIEWS OF PSYCHOSOCIAL AND HEALTH PROBLEMS OVER-AFFECTING LATINO POPULATIONS, AND SOCIOCULTURALLY COMPETENT PRACTICES

The purpose of Part II is to provide detailed descriptions and illustrations of *socioculturally competent* services and interventions with diverse Latino populations and subpopulations across a broad variety of some of the most compelling health and mental health problems over-affecting Latinos. Family and youth problems, related to destabilizing acculturative stress, are also centered in Section II, as are effective interventions designed to expand *familismo* and related values and practices in flexible bicultural directions. The sociocultural practice model from Part I serves as a guide for evaluating the many services and interventions covered in this section. Part II also provides a primer on Latino political power, as well as an overview of Latino resistance, activism, and social movements, past and present, to more fully comprehend how various Latino populations have used their collective agency to empower their communities and make significant gains in civil rights, elevating their social positionality and psychosocial and health profiles in the process.

7

The Latino Family

As stated in the first edition of this text, no book on Latinos would be complete without a chapter dedicated to the central social-psychological and sociocultural institution of the Latino experience: *La Familia*. Despite the challenge of capturing such a complex, enduring yet dynamically evolving cultural construct, this chapter strives to provide a theoretical framework, description, and empirical overview of the Latino family, followed by a selective review of significant family-related problems and issues and socioculturally competent responses. As a meta-construct, *La Familia* continues to evolve as an increasingly complex set of structured relationships, identities, and sources of direction and meaning within and beyond the extended family.

Early reviews of the literature on Latino families (Baca Zinn, 1982/83; Garcia-Preto, 1996; Ramirez and Arce, 1981; Vega, 1990) capture a variety of organizational structures and functions that derive from a blend of Latino cultures of origin (e.g., from Latin America) combined with adjustments and adaptations to life in the United States, including a diversity of newer and more inclusive forms of family and multicultural social contexts. In her seminal writings on the Latino family, Celia Falicov (2014) uses the term *culture* to refer to a community of people that *partially* share the same meaning systems that describe and ascribe meaning to the world (e.g., preferred values, norms, and practices). Cultural similarities and differences between community members reflect different degrees of inclusion and exclusion across subgroups within the culture (e.g., along the lines of age, gender and gender identity, sexual orientation, immigration status, racial characteristics), as well as outside the culture (i.e., among non-Latino whites [NLWs] and other people of color). Thus, each individual family member develops within a plurality of social and cultural contexts and subgroups that exert multiple influences to varying degrees depending on the salience of subgroup memberships across different situations as well as over time. Such a rich conception of culture helps to free it from static stereotypes by allowing for

Solving Latino Psychosocial and Health Problems. Kurt C. Organista, Oxford University Press.
© Oxford University Press 2023. DOI: 10.1093/oso/9780190059637.003.0007

cultural consistencies as well as contradictions and related dilemmas among families and their members as typically encountered in practice.

In her multicultural eco-systemic comparative approach (MECA) to Latino family assessment and treatment, Falicov asserts that like all families, Latino families in the United States are exposed to and influenced by multiple cultures in addition to their own, including NLW American and other people of color, depending on their social location. Regarding the latter, Falicov stresses assessing the eco-systemic or ecological niche occupied by families that includes social class–related interactions with formal and informal institutions such as the extended family, local and other communities, schools, churches, health care and other social services, and the impacts of social policies that structure such interactions. With such social and cultural contextual knowledge, Falicov's comparative approach examines variations among Latino families with regard to migration and acculturation history (e.g., push and pull factors, related trauma, family separation and reunification issues, years/generations in United States), current ecological context (neighborhood, living and working conditions), family organization (e.g., extended or nuclear, two or single parent) and related family lifecycle stage (e.g., newly formed family, children and their ages, young adult children leaving home, parents retiring or passing away).

Falicov's conception of a family's ecological niche, or unique combination of social and cultural contexts and partial cultural perspectives, helps to conceptualize each family's and each member's variation on major cultural themes and practices. Such niches guide the evolution of values and behaviors (for better or worse) given their link to the social and physical environment (e.g., social class), and crucial issues such as access to the resources and power necessary for survival and healthy development. Latino family values, structures, and functioning during the process of acculturation is briefly touched upon here for their relevance to understanding in the practice and service provision space.

Family Structure, Functions, and Changes

Central Values
Ethnic groups coalesce around a set of central values and their practice. Central Latino cultural values that comprise the basis of norms, beliefs and attitudes, prescribed social roles and behaviors become modified within a

family's particular social niche, and provide a convenient, if over-simplified, way of describing family structure and functioning. For example, while the variety of Latino families continues to expand (single parent, nuclear and extended, immigrant and multi-generational, transnational, sexual minority couples, etc.), they are partially based on the central cultural value of *familismo* that refers to the central significance of the family manifested in strong emotional, relational, and instrumental interdependence between members, within and across generations, over the life cycle. While more mainstream American norms and values generally stress individualism, competition, independence, and even individuation from home and family as offspring become young adults, familism promotes closer contact, loyalty, and a lifelong sense of self-in-family that serves as a psychosocial guide for family members with regard to their values, attitudes and behaviors, and identity in the world.

Reviews of the empirical literature on the Latino family consistently demonstrate greater participation in family networks within and across generations (e.g., social support) as compared to NLWs. For example, Sabogal et al. (1987) studied the effects of acculturation on familism in a diverse Latino sample (N = 452), compared to NLWs (N = 227), and found that perceptions of the family as highly supportive remained constant across Latinos of varying levels of acculturation, and that even the most acculturated were more family oriented than their NLW counterparts. At the same time, other dimensions of familism, such as sense of family obligation and use of family as the reference of central attitudes and behaviors, clearly decrease with acculturation. Similarly, Perez and Padilla (2000) studied a three-generation sample of 203 Chicano adolescents and found that while Mexican cultural orientation decreased across generations, and American cultural orientation increased, participants maintained allegiance to Latino family values described below.

Most Latino families also partially share the central value of *respeto* [respect] that refers to deference given to those of higher hierarchical status in the traditional sense (i.e., by virtue of older age or higher position in the family, community, or society). As such, *respeto* differs slightly from American respect more typically accorded to those admired for their abilities, achievements, or special qualities (i.e., more for what people *do* rather than who they *are*). However, *respeto* is also stratified by SES, as well as by gender (males above females), the latter increasingly contested, particularly in the United States but also throughout Latin America. Thus, you might say that the U.S. notion that one must *earn* respect is contrasted with the Latino notion of *giving* respect to older family and community members, in addition to those who have earned it through valued accomplishments.

Other key Latino values include *colectivismo* or collective cooperation and teamwork, usually stressed in family relations of mutual support rather than individualistic independence. The latter can certainly feel at odds with mainstream society's value for competition and individual accomplishment, with many Latino family members often trying to find the bicultural balance to be able navigate life both within and outside of the family and Latino community.

Simpatía refers to the valuing of smooth and pleasant relationships that overlook, minimize, and even avoid problems and conflict (even when hurt feelings, anger, and resentment are aroused). The refrain, "*No te preocupes*" [Don't worry about it], is the culturally sanctioned response to mistakes and trespasses (e.g., in relationships and social settings) so as not to interrupt the flow of warm and pleasant interaction. While the noble intention of *simpatía* is to let nothing interfere with caring relations, it can be a challenging contrast with the U.S. value of assertiveness that advocates expressing negative as well as positive feelings in response to the actions of others. While not incompatible, a creative hybrid mix is in order for Latinos in the United States negotiating at least two major cultural systems.

Closely related to *simpatía* is the perennial value of *personalismo* [personalism] that refers to emphasizing the personal dimension of relationships over the transactional or task-oriented dimension of relationships, including professional relationships encountered in human and social services. Hence, the social inclination of most Latinos is to engage others as people first, irrespective of their transactional roles (e.g., wanting to know a little about who people are through small talk, or actually expecting a full answer the salutation, "How are you?"). The professional practice of almost immediately focusing on a presenting problem can be perceived as impersonal or cold by Latino clients if it comes at the expense of the social lubrication needed to build *confianza* or trust. It's important to note that *personalismo* should not be confused with informality. That is, it would be a mistake for a service provider to come across too casually or overly friendly, but rather one should strive for a balance between the task-oriented formality of business and warm and caring attention to the client (e.g., asking how the client is and actually listening to the responses to convey care and attention). Engaging in sufficient small talk or *plática* that includes judicious self-disclosure is one way of achieving such balance.

While familiarity with core Latino values can help prepare practitioners for cultural consistencies in most Latino clients, Falicov's framework alerts us to also be open to variations in such values, including contradictions, given the influences of different ecological niches in which families and individual members reside. She even asks practitioners think about how Latino values play out in other cultures to mitigate stereotyping (e.g., machismo reflects patriarchy in the United States as well as the world over). This stance of "Knowing and Not knowing" (Falicov, 2014, p. 26), or having background information while remaining open to information that unfolds in the foreground of practice, is further recommended while contemplating descriptions of Latino family functioning, as described more below.

Child Rearing

Latino child-rearing practices partially reflect the above values, frequently expressed through traditional age and gender hierarchies in which conformity is frequently praised and deviations discouraged. For example, children are commonly socialized to respect and obey parents such that "being right" in an argument can be secondary to respecting elders by not disagreeing or arguing a point. Interestingly, the term *bien educado* [well educated] refers to children (and adults) who have been properly raised and abide by traditional values and interpersonal protocol, rather than to formal schooling. *Mal criado* [poorly raised] means the opposite. But child-rearing practices also partially reflect NLW values and practices, as well as other proximal cultures, resulting in considerable bicultural and multiculturality.

The traditional patriarchal basis of most Latino families can often be challenging to understand in mainstream America that stresses more egalitarian and "friendly" relations within and between generations, and increasing equality between men and women. The frequent clash of values experienced by Latino youth can be especially difficult when there are few if any models of flexible cultural hybridity both within their families and in their communities and larger society. The problem is exacerbated by family destabilization resulting from poverty-linked minority status, and uneven levels of acculturation between family members. While psychosocial and health problems may result, there are also cultural and community-based resources that support Latino families and members. From Falicov's decades of clinical work with Latino families, she is consistently impressed by their strong family and community bonds and supports, maintenance of cultural rituals, capacity for hard work, and pride in good parenting. Hence, she uses a strengths-based and assets model to frame family challenges rather than a deficit model that carries over from the medical model of psychiatry and consequently the field of mental health. This assets-based framework extends to the Latino community.

Cultural and Community-based Resources

Service providers are advised to learn about and tap into community-based resources, assets, and stakeholders, while also being careful not to overtax such supports that have partly evolved to compensate for social exclusion, neglect, and antagonism. Any support that professionals can provide to cultural and community resources can go a long way toward mitigating psychosocial and health problems (e.g., volunteer work, sitting on advisory boards, grant writing and fund raising, connecting community organizations with philanthropic foundations, advocating for policy benefits). The Church is one such community resource that has long provided a range of supports to Latino families.

The Catholic Church

Despite increasingly different religious affiliations, the majority of Latinos continue to be Catholic. Falicov (2014) notes that the Catholic Church provides continuity to families throughout the life cycle and across generations for its central role in rites of passage such as marriage, baptism, children's first Holy Communion, and funerals. The Church also creates community by providing a central location for Sunday mass, Saturday catechism for youth, Catholic school, religious and Latino holiday celebrations, festivals, and other fundraisers. Parochial school continues to provide many Latino youth with a scarce opportunity for a quality private education for about half the price of non-Catholic private schools.

Thus, while the spiritual and supportive dimensions of Catholicism should be assessed and utilized as needed with affiliated clients, we should not assume passive conformity to the Church, nor should we overlook progressive movement on the part of many parishes on behalf of the Latino community, immigration reform, and sex and gender related issues, as noted in Chapter 2 on Central Americans as well as in Chapters 11 and 12 on Latino community resistance, activism, and movements to achieve greater political power and improved social positionality.

While a major cultural resource, *familismo* alone cannot compensate for the Latino family's social-ecological niche, too often characterized by acculturation stress as evident in ethnically linked poverty and related stressors that can often overwhelm family systems and cultural and community resources.

Acculturative Stress and Family Destabilization

The destabilizing effects of acculturative stress on Latino families, as framed above, are increasingly identified by research. For instance, Cook et al. (2009) analyzed six different possible pathways by which increasing time in the United States is associated with increasing mental illness. This study analyzed data from the National Latino and Asian American Survey (NLAAS) which includes a nationally representative sample of 2,554 English- and Spanish-speaking Latinos surveyed between 2002–2003, and designed to approximate the 2000 census profile of Latinos in America. Participants were assessed for prevalence of any depressive or anxiety disorder during the past year, based on the DSM-IV. Given the purpose of the study, Latino participants were divided into four levels of acculturation based on number of years in the United States, in order to first capture the predicted increase in mental disorders with increased acculturation (see Table 7.1). Consistent with past research, increased time in the United States was indeed associated with higher rates of mental illness. That is, rates of any depressive or anxiety disorders are 10.7%, 14.5%, 17.1%, and 19.0% for those living in the United States 0–10 years, 11–20 years, and 21+ years and U.S.-born, respectively.

So, what might be the pathways through which increasing years in the United States result in increasing rates of depression and anxiety for Latinos? The above question was addressed by Cook et al. (2009) by analyzing the relationship between increasing mental illness over time and six different possible pathways well known in the literature to impact Latinos: (1) exposure to discrimination (e.g., being treated with less respect and courtesy than

Table 7.1. The Relation between Acculturation and Mental Disorders in a Nationally Representative Sample of Latinos (N = 2,457) from National Latino and Asian American Study (NLAAS), May 2002–November 2003

Mental Health Outcomes in Past 12 months (%)	Immigrants Living in United States for 0–10 years (n=478)	Immigrants Living in United States for 11–20 years (n=393)	Immigrants Living in United States for ≥ 21 years (n=685)	US-Born (n=901)
Any psychiatric disorder	10.7	14.5	17.1	19.0
Any depressive disorder	5.7	7.2	10.6	9.9
Any anxiety disorder	6.6	8.1	11.4	10.5

Adapted from Cook et al. (2009). Pathways and correlates connecting Latinos' mental health with exposure to the United States. *American Journal of Public Health, 99*(12), 2247–2254.

others); (2) intergenerational family conflict (e.g., arguments with family caused by differences in beliefs, interference with personal goals related to acculturation); (3) ethnic identity (e.g., own group identification, affiliation, shared ideas); (4) satisfaction with one's economic situation; (5) perceived social status relative to others (e.g., in terms of finances, education, job respect); and (6) neighborhood safety (e.g., degree of violence). Analyzed one pathway at a time, results reveal that both *family conflict* and day-to-day *discrimination* are the two pathways significantly related to the rise in mental disorders over time in the United States. These findings help to direct our attention to the need for assessment and intervention efforts that address acculturation-related conflict within the Latino family as described in the studies reviewed next.

Family Care Access and Availability

With regard to access and availability of needed family services, low-income and segregated Latino families have historically accessed care through the advent of bottom-up, community-based efforts on the part of Latino-focused *ethnic agencies* designed to compensate for the lack of access to mainstream services. Community-based family health, mental health, and multi-service centers are examples of such efforts. In addition, many main-stream institutions (e.g., county general hospitals) have gradually developed Latino-focused services as part of their usual array of programs, staffed with bilingual/bicultural staff and professionals. Over the past three decades, community-based federally qualified health care (FQHC) centers have come to provide needed health care to low-income and minority families in America.

Federally Qualified Health Care

During the 1990s, FQHC centers became the major national safety net for poor and underserved populations, specially designed to provide community-based primary health care to uninsured and underinsured populations such as public housing residents, seasonal and migrant farm workers, immigrants, and homeless families and individuals (Visualizations, 2022). As part of the Health Care Consolidation Act of 1996, FQHC was included under Medicare benefits, greatly increasing utilization by those in need, and in 2010 the Affordable Care Act further boosted utilization by expanding access to health insurance to millions of previously uninsured Americans. Today, there are over 1,100 FQHC facilities across the country serving low-income and minority populations. Many FQHC centers have incorporated an integrated behavioral health care (IBHC) model to co-locate and coordinate health and mental health services into a patient-centered team approach to care, increasingly supported by evidence of effectiveness as discussed in Chapter 10's focus on Latino health. Community-based FQHCs in Latino neighborhoods also provide quality care regardless of ability to pay or citizenship status.

Psychosocial and Health Problems
Over-affecting Latino Families

SES and Stability

FQHCs provide a safety net for Latino families given that the majority are large, urban-based, disproportionately poor, and struggling with a cluster of risk factors related to poverty, ethnic minority status, and acculturation.

Table 7.2. Socio-demographic Profiles of Major U.S. Latino Groups and non-Latino Whites

Group	Foreign Born	Median Household Income	No Health Insurance	% Poverty	≥ High School	≥ College Graduation
Latinos	37%	$40,000	31%	25%	66%	15%
Mexican	36%	$38,700	34%	27%	61%	11%
Puerto Rican	1%	$36,000	15%	27%	79%	18%
Cuban	59%	$45,000	25%	18%	79%	26%
Salvadoran	62%	$43,000	41%	20%	52%	9%
Dominican	57%	$35,000	22%	26%	68%	17%
Guatemalan	66%	$38,2000	48%	28%	48%	9%
Nicaraguan	58%	$50,000	31%	17%	78%	19%
Non-Latino Whites	4%	$54,500	11%	10%	88.0	30.9

Pew Research Center 2015 & US Census 2016.

Designed by Samantha Ngo, MPH, MSW.

From Stepler & Brown (Apr. 19, 2016); Lopez (2015a-g, Sept 15).

As can be seen in Table 7.2, as compared to NLW families, Latino families are two and a half times more likely to live in poverty (25% and 10%, respectively) yet earn three-quarters the annual income ($40,000 and $54,500, respectively).

Given such a profile, we should anticipate above average family-related problems linked to poverty, minority status, and consequent acculturation stress. Problem themes frequently discussed in the Latino family literature include role reversals between family members, including (1) women increasingly entering the paid labor force, thereby expanding their gender role and socialization; and (2) children becoming Americanized at faster rates than their immigrant parents, occasionally having to assume parental responsibilities (e.g., translating for or representing the family to social institutions) and absorbing American values and behaviors sometimes at odds with parental socialization. While most Latino families cope admirably with such acculturation-related changes, and view them as part of progressing in the United States, overly stressed and resource-poor families can manifest multiple negative consequences. These are exacerbated by recent persecution of undocumented people in the United States, affecting hundreds of thousands of unauthorized Latinos, their families, and communities.

Impact of Detention and Deportation on Latino Families

A recent problem theme dramatically affecting Latino families and communities is detention and deportation-related family separation as a result of aggressively stepped-up immigration control and the criminalization of undocumented people. Since America's post-9/11 War on Terror and advent of the Department of Homeland Security (DHS), DHS has subsumed the Immigration and Naturalization Service (INS), formerly charged with immigration regulation, and now implements a federal mandate to deport hundreds of thousands of predominately Latino undocumented people each year. Rather than the president and congress enacting long-overdue immigration reform, including regulating labor as a win–win for immigrants desperately needing work and for our vast service economy dependent upon such labor, U.S. administrations have instead defamed and scapegoated the undocumented as dangerous criminals in need of incarceration and removal.

Separating Families at the Border

Extreme forms of immigration control came to a cruel head in 2018 when the Trump administration enacted its infamous "zero tolerance" policy of detaining anyone crossing the U.S.– Mexico border, including families whose small children, including infants, were forcibly taken from parents and dispersed throughout the country in various child welfare organizations. This practice separated over 2,300 children from their families, including nursing infants from their mothers, and incited so much domestic and international outrage that it was quickly rescinded by former president Trump—but not before exacting considerable harm to Mexican and Central American families. Less high profile has been the continuous removal of hundreds of thousands of spouses, parents, and other relatives from their families in communities throughout the country, causing heartbreak, trauma, and economic hardship for undocumented and mixed-status families.

Brabeck, Lykes, and Hunter (2014) examine the state of the literature on the psychosocial impact of detention and deportation on unauthorized migrants, their mixed-status families, and U.S.-born children. These researchers note that approximately 4.5 million children live in mixed-status families in which at least one member is unauthorized and thereby vulnerable to and frequently experiences detention and deportation. Using a social-ecological framework, these authors review research documenting the cascading negative impact of this predicament on the well-being of children, family stability, and deportees—who can be abruptly arrested (e.g., in ICE workplace raids) and frequently detained far from families, unable to contact families for many days, and ultimately faced with the dilemma of arranging for their U.S.-born children to join them in countries of origin or leaving them with relatives or the child welfare system with uncertain family outcomes. Brabeck et al. (2014) assert that the immense trauma inflicted upon undocumented individuals and their families represents a profound change in how undocumented people are now treated (i.e., as criminals persecuted on the basis of federal laws from the late 1990s and early 21st century, discussed further in Chapter 12).

Impact on Youth

In their review of the literature on the impact of deportation-related family separations on the well-being of Latino youth, Lovato et al. (2018) report several negative impacts on youth mental health, psychosocial, and academic outcomes. Of nearly 300 articles screened between 2000 and 2017, 10 peer-reviewed empirical studies are included in this review. Findings regarding the impact of actual deportation of a parent, or increased threat of deportation (i.e., local raids and anti-immigrant policies) on youth are divided into three areas described below.

With regard to behavioral changes, impacted youth demonstrate fear and anxiety, stigma, the burden of hiding the status of undocumented family members, and behavioral acting out with siblings, peers, and in school. Regarding mental health impacts, studies reviewed report elevated symptoms of anxiety, depression, difficulty concentrating and sleeping, excessive fears, hypervigilance, social isolation, worries and/or guilt, and/or trauma. Not surprisingly, negative impacts on school performance include decreased attendance and lower grades, and cruel teasing and comments from peers about deportation. However, schools are also found to be safe havens for these youth, who often distract themselves by delving into school work and activities and who also receive sympathy and support from teachers and staff, including access to mental health and social services. Supportive schools tend to be located in urban, diverse multi-ethnic neighborhoods with large, visible immigrant communities.

Lovato et al. (2018) note that around the time of their publication, 118 school districts and county offices of education in California had declared themselves safe havens that provide safe spaces for all students regardless of documentation status, including plans for assisting children experiencing a parent's deportation. The need for such supports is urgent given that over five million youth live with at least one undocumented parent, and over three million individuals, predominately Latino, had been deported between 2008 and publication of this 2018 review.

Selective Review of Family Responsive Care

Highlighted here is a selective review of significant Latino family-related problems and interventions that illustrate assessment of relevant social and cultural contextual factors resulting in congruent and responsive intervention efforts.

Family Therapy for Latinos

By placing the stresses and strengths tied to migration, culture change, and sociopolitical ecologies at the center of the clinical practice encounter, rather than as an add-on to treatments developed in the mainstream, we are better able to attend to the needs and to honor the wisdom brought by families from different cultures—in this case Latino families in transition. Seeking to incorporate complex sets of cultural and sociopolitical variables into clinical practice requires a clear recognition that clinical practice is, in itself, a cultural and sociopolitical encounter.

—Celia Falicov, 2014, p. 17

Given the centrality of the family in Latino life, and the challenges to family stability and well-being of acculturation and minority status, interventions designed for Latino families hold considerable promise. As a leading light in this area, Falicov (2014) views the primary role of the family therapist to be that of an intermediary of family conflict, whose job is to reframe trouble between family members as "cultural transitions" in need of understanding and greater bicultural flexibility. Frequently, uneven levels of acculturation between parents and children are addressed within the context of migration history and acculturation experience, and remedied by facilitating mutual understanding and appreciation as well as improving communication, negotiation, and compromise skills that expand bicultural flexibility and adjustment to the United States. Tension between parents resulting from shifting gender roles, where women frequently work outside of the home and consequently request more help from husbands with housekeeping and child care, are framed as normal acculturation challenges. In addition to working with whole families, and separately with individual members as needed, Falicov notes that therapists need to be "culture brokers" who help families obtain needed cultural, community, and service-related resources.

Jose Szapocznik is a major pioneering researcher and practitioner in the evolution of Latino family therapy. Over 40 years ago he founded the Spanish Family Guidance Center in Miami, Florida, based on an acculturation sensitive, structural eco-systemic approach to family therapy with Cuban and other Latino immigrant families. Like Falicov, Szapocznik attributes family problems to acculturation gaps that exacerbate normal generation gaps between parents and adolescents, as well as gender role gaps between husbands and wives (e.g., financial responsibilities, household duties, and parenting). Szapocznik and colleagues emphasize the goal of aligning family members to work collectively as a team against acculturation gaps that threaten family stability. The overriding goal of therapy is to foster cross-generational alliances by connecting parents to the positive aspects of American values and practices, while connecting youth to the positive aspects of Latino culture of origin. Hence, their model of bicultural effectiveness training (BET) promotes a flexible hybrid bicultural orientation in Latino families.

Szapocznik and associates were among the first to not only develop and practice a model of Latino family therapy but also to conduct outcome evaluation research, which is challenging when the family is the unit of analysis. For example, in Szapocznik et al.'s (1997) summary of nearly two decades of research, they report that their culture-specific family approaches are as effective in reducing symptoms as non-culturally adapted forms of family therapy (e.g., structural family therapy) and individual psychodynamic therapy, but superior at engaging and retaining Latino families in treatment, promoting bicultural flexibility, and preserving family cohesiveness consistent with *familismo* and adjustment in America. Such work has been foundational to subsequent Latino family-focused practice.

In their 2011 book, *Becoming Bicultural: Risk, resilience and Latino youth*, Smokowski and Bacalao build upon the above works by developing and evaluating *Entre Dos Mundos* (EDM) [between two worlds], their model of family therapy designed primarily with immigrant families in mind. It begins with an acculturation framework for understanding family dysfunction that attributes excessive conflict—between parents, between parents and children, and between families and American society—to acculturative stress. The latter is related to time in the United States, nativity of different family members, linguistic capacities, perceived discrimination, and *acculturation gaps* that are a central focus of EDM given the goal of ameliorating parent–child conflict and enhancing adolescent adjustment. Hence, their evaluation of EDM emphasizes the cluster of psychosocial and health problems that over-affect Latino adolescents: school disengagement, depression and anxiety, alcohol and substance use, behavioral problems including gang affiliation and teen pregnancy: problems that compose the focus of Chapter 8 on Latinx youth.

Smokowski and Bacallao invested considerable time and effort developing EDM, including formative exploratory research with Latino families from Arizona and South Carolina, to refine the acculturation-related content of their eight weekly sessions with 8–10 families per session. EDM sessions feature acculturation-related questions posed to families within and between sessions. For example, "What worries do adolescents have for their parents? What worries do parents have for their adolescents? How can we help each other decrease some of these worries? How can we comfort one another?" Also, "How can we handle discrimination at school and at work? In what ways can family members support each other during or after these experiences?"

EDM evaluation includes assessment of both *proximal* outcomes, measured immediately after eight sessions of treatment, and *distal* outcomes assessed one year post-treatment. Outcomes assessed included parent–child conflict, family cohesion, and numerous adolescent mental health (depression, anxiety) and behavioral (symptoms of conduct and oppositional defiance disorders) outcomes. Interestingly, Smokowski and Bacallao teach a nonlinear model of bicultural development characterized by circular movement from culture of origin to U.S. culture, and vice versa, that reinforces bicultural development versus moving simply from one culture to the other in a straight line. During role plays, different family members are asked to literally position themselves on an enlarged circular model of acculturation, placed on the floor, with regard to where they stand on various issues (e.g., adolescent privileges, discipline) to prompt discussion.

Smokowski and Bacallao mounted a very impressive evaluation by randomizing 81 Latino families living in South Carolina into either a psychoeducational and support version of EDM (N = 25) or a more active psychodrama oriented version of EDM (N = 56). Participating parents were solicited from rural, mid-sized, and urban areas of the state, and had an immigrant adolescent between 12 and 18 years of age participate along with at least one parent. Accessible sessions were conducted locally (e.g., churches, community centers) by bilingual and bicultural Latino social work practitioners. Both transportation and child care were provided, as well as dinner at the start of each three-hour session in order to build community and enhance *personalismo* and *confinaza* via *plática*.

Overall, results revealed good engagement with parents and adolescents respectively attending six and seven of the eight sessions on average. With regard to immediate post-treatment proximal outcomes, there was a significant *dose effect* with more sessions attended correlating with less family conflict and more bicultural support, identity integration, and family adaptability for *both* conditions of EDM. Regarding distal outcomes at one-year follow-up assessment with 62 families, the more active version of EDM was more effective than psychoeducational EDM in terms of the maintenance of moderate gains overall, but especially in reducing parent–child conflict as well as adolescent depression, anxiety, aggression, and oppositional defiance symptoms.

Regarding accountability, post-treatment exit interviews were conducted with participants revealing considerable praise for the opportunity to improve family communication and to learn from the examples of others in the multi-family sessions, including how to not avoid difficult conversations by persisting through difficult emotions despite the value of *simpatía*. This evaluation of EDM took place in a new-growth immigrant state where Latino immigrants are relatively new and growing, and where needed Latinx-focused services are few but slowly beginning to improve.

Supporting Immigrant Families in New Immigrant Growth Areas

Martinez and colleagues (2021) note that over the past 30+ years, there have evolved small but growing communities of Latino immigrants in 22 states with little if any historical concentrations of Latinos. As a result, such Latino families face the challenges of acculturation stress without many of the cultural and community resources more available in established Latino enclaves in states such as Florida and New York, as well as Illinois and in the southwestern United States. Hence, Martinez et al. (2021) replicated an evidence-based family intervention by conducting a community-based, randomized controlled trial (RCT), of a culturally adapted version of an intervention that they call *Nuestras Familias: Andando Entre Culturas* [Our Families: Moving Between Cultures].

Nuestras Familias is a culturally adapted parent management training (PMT) intervention designed to prevent psychosocial and health problems in youth by enhancing parenting knowledge and skills. While the focus on adolescent outcomes anticipates Chapter 8 (Latinx Youth), the careful attention devoted to adapting an evidence-based family intervention to the social and cultural reality of immigrant families in new immigrant growth areas enhances understanding of the effectiveness of this culturally adapted PMT in helping Latino families cope with destabilizing acculturative stress in low-resource communities throughout the United States.

Nuestras Familias utilizes a cognitive behavioral approach that includes psychoeducation, modeling, role playing, and home-based practice to enhance effective parenting skills in key areas such as monitoring, discipline, problem solving, and youth encouragement. PMT was provided during 12 weekly group-based sessions with up to 15 families per group, similar to EDM described above, with all parents in households invited to participate in the spirit of *familismo* and engage more members of family systems. After each 2.5-hour session, facilitators contacted each family by phone to review past session material, check on progress with home assignments, answer questions, and offer support.

Sociocultural competence includes attention to relevant social factors such as providing each family $10 per session to defray transportation costs, free child care and homework activities for children while parents were in sessions, and either private or alternative group make-up sessions when families were unable to attend regular sessions. Attention to relevant cultural factors included sessions delivered in Spanish by providers with children and immigrant backgrounds, sharing a meal at each session, with time for *plática* and *personalismo*, and addressing *familismo*, *respeto*, spousal relationships, gender roles, and different levels of acculturation among family members.

Two-hundred and forty-one families, each with at least one youth in grade five through eight, were randomly assigned to the PMT intervention condition (n = 120) or a no-treatment control group (N = 121). The study was conducted in the Willamette Valley of Oregon, now considered a new dramatic growth immigrant state after a long history of limited Latino immigration and farmworker labor. Families were predominately low-income immigrants from Mexico with an average of just under 14 years in the United States, and mothers comprised virtually all parents participating in *Nuestras Familias*. Auspicious results reveal the benefits of such sociocultural tailoring of the evidence-based practice to mitigate the harmful impacts of acculturation on Latino families.

With regard to feasibility, parents consistently reported high satisfaction and that they would recommend *Nuestras Familias* to others. Regarding parent outcomes, intervention parents reported significantly greater skills encouraging youth and promoting engagement with homework, and effective parenting overall, as compared to control group parents. In terms of youth outcomes, there was significantly lower likelihood to use illicit drugs, including smoking, as well as less depression and anxiety versus control condition youth. This family intervention, as well as BET and EDM described above, help prevent family problems from worsening by enhancing the ability to cope with acculturative stress. Unfortunately, a small percentage of families overwhelmed by acculturative stress, lacking supportive resources and coping skills, may experience extreme problems such as intimate partner violence (IPV), which is addressed next.

Intimate Partner Violence

The pressing and increasingly recognized problem of IPV in Latino families and communities provides an excellent example of how to begin thinking about and responding to such an extreme family problem in a socially and culturally competent manner. For some Latino families, the many challenges discussed above can threaten an already impoverished and strained situation, resulting in increased rates of marital disruption and divorce, family dysfunction, and at the extreme, traumatic problems such as IPV, a term not confined to the realm of the home nor sexual majority relationships.

While more research is needed, Latinos are increasingly included in the IPV literature.

Over thirty years ago, Sorensen and Telles (1991) examined the role of acculturation in their IPV survey and found that rates were clearly higher in U.S.-born Mexican Americans (31%) as compared to Mexico-born Mexican Americans (20%), whose rate was equivalent to NLWs (21.6%) (i.e., one or more incidents of hitting or throwing things at spouse). In an effort to tease out factors related to poverty or culture, Kaufman-Kantor, Jasinski, and Straus (1994) compared Latino (N = 743) and NLW (N = 1025) families regarding the influence of economic stressors and patriarchal cultural norms sanctioning wife assault. Consistent with Sorensen and Telles (1991), Kaufman-Kantor et al. found that wife assault was predicted by being born in the U.S. for Mexican American and Puerto Rican men in their survey. Rates for these U.S.-born Latinos were higher than for Mexican immigrants and the mostly Cuban immigrant subsample. Regarding economic stress, unemployment was also a significant predictor of IPV. With respect to culture, attitudinal norms sanctioning wife assault also predicted IPV, but for *both* Latino and NLW families. In fact, rates of wife assault were the same for these two groups when controlling for economic stressors and pro-wife assault norms. Thus, social factors such as poverty play major roles in IPV, while so-called "cultural factors" are not exclusive to Latinos. In fact, most of the IPV research thus far shows that Latinos most steeped in their culture of origin (i.e., immigrants low in acculturation) are those at lowest risk for IPV.

The above findings are noteworthy in view of the popular idea that traditional Latino culture (e.g., *machismo*) is at the root of IPV. While we should not rule out the role of culture-based patriarchy and sexism, we should not view it apart from social factors such as poverty, which is consistently linked to IPV for *all* race and ethnic groups. For example, in Weinbaum et al.'s (2001) analysis of the 1998 California Women's Health Survey (N = 4006), the major predictors of IPV were participation in the Special Supplemental Nutrition Program for Women, Infants and Children (WIC) during the past two years, unemployment, feeling overwhelmed in past 30 days, and smoking. Prevalence rates of experiencing IPV during the past year were 6% overall in this survey, but a breakdown by race/ethnicity revealed highest rates for Latinas (9.3%), followed by African American women (8.7%), Asian Women (5.4%), and NLW women (4.4%). Weinbaum et al. (2001) found no differences between foreign-born and U.S.-born Latinas in their sample, an analysis of data from this survey in the subsequent years 1997 through 2003 did reveal the expected positive association between acculturation and IPV (Weinbaum & Thorfinnson, 2006).

The Role of Alcohol

The link between alcohol abuse in IPV has been documented for decades, and increasingly for U.S. Latino couples and families. Using data as far back as the 1995 National Alcohol Survey, Cunardi et al. (1999) examined the relation between IPV and alcohol-related problems in African American (N = 358), Latino (N = 527), and White (N = 555) couples and found that in couples reporting male alcohol-related problems, rates of IPV were twice as high in Latinos, three times higher in NLWs, and seven times higher in African Americans, as compared to couples without male alcohol-related problems. Overall rates of male to female (MTF) IPV were 23%, 17%, and 11% for African Americans, Latinos, and whites, respectively; a similar pattern was found for female to male (FTM) IPV: 30%, 21%, and 15%, respectively. While generally not as injurious or lethal, FTM rates are noteworthy in that they are higher than the MTF rates and deserve more attention in all race/ethnic groups.

While Cunardi et al. (1999) found that the presence of male alcohol problems predicted IPV in all three race/ethnic groups, they also found that when predictor analysis controlled for sociodemographic, psychosocial (e.g., experiencing physical child abuse), and alcohol consumption, alcohol-related problems no longer predicted MTF IPV in Latino couples. Rather, economic problems such as unemployment and low family income (less than $20,000 annually) predicted IPV. Thus, while the high rates of problem drinking in Latino couples is concerning and associated with IPV, it may be secondary to stressful poverty-related factors. In fact, Caetano et al. (2007) found no relationship between alcohol and IPV in their analysis of data from a national randomized household survey that included 387 Latino couples and that assessed both MTF and FTM abuse. What these researchers did find is that both forms of IPV are predicted by higher levels of acculturative stress, which was assessed by items measuring conflicts with family members and friends because of changing values, problems with communication in

English, and adjustment problems associated with participants' ethnic culture. Caetano et al. conclude that stressful scenarios of acculturation rather than acculturation per se appear to be related to IPV, with or without alcohol.

Socioculturally Responsive IPV Interventions

In their review of the literature to identify effective IPV interventions for Latinas, Alvarez et al. (2016) report that of the 1,132 related articles identified, only four are intervention studies while the remaining 99% of these articles are either exploratory and/or identify correlates of IPV for Latinas. While the interventions are described below, Alvarez and colleagues summarize documented IPV-related risk factors (e.g., low SES, immigration status, acculturation stress, and machismo), and discrepancies disfavoring Latinas as compared to NLW women, such as more severe IPV consequences (i.e., depression, low self-esteem, physical ailments), minimizing abuse severity, less use of IPV services, or service use after prolonged experience of abuse. Clearly, there is urgent need to address IPV in Latinas in ways that address the above social and cultural factors.

While generalizations are limited across the four intervention studies identified by Alvarez et al. (2016), the three reporting reduced IPV in intervention versus control conditions are all grounded in a theoretical framework (e.g., social learning theory), mitigate stress within spousal and other family relationships, and are delivered in multiple (e.g., group) sessions conducive to increasing self-awareness, empowerment, and peer support. One study demonstrates the underestimated power of simply providing Latinas with information about available IPV-related resources.

With regard to limitations, Alvarez et al. (2016) note that none of the four studies describe how their interventions are tailored to Latinas (e.g., only two note providing Spanish language materials to participants). There is no mention of integrating cultural values/practices (e.g., *familismo*), and family members are not included in any of the interventions. Fortunately, a more recent review of the literature on IPV and immigrant Latinas illuminates many of these puzzling shortcomings by describing how relevant social and cultural factors are integrated into the interventions reviewed. Sidebar 7.1 below also offers a case study of IPV treatment steeped in cultural assets and adaptations.

Sidebar 7.1. Latino IPV Case Study

The following case study by Yvette Flores-Ortiz, a pioneering clinician and academician in the Latino IPV space, reflects efforts to build upon culture-based assets and implement cultural adaptations to family therapy to help expand the bicultural repertoire of Latino families adjusting to life in the United States. In this case study, Flores-Ortiz et al. (1994) describe three broad phases of family therapy for IPV: (1) Assessing legacies of intergenerational violence and framing them as painful patterns of injustice to family members that are possible to change (rituals are sometimes prescribed, such as making altars to abusive parents and forgiving them for their abusive shortcomings); (2) conducting couple sessions for parents in order to review desired relationship, including model couples whom they admire, and discussion of Latino cultural prescriptions of a healthy family as well as NLW models of more egalitarian relationships; and (3) teaching fair argument and negotiation skills.

Immediate treatment goals address urgent issues such as the symptoms and lethality of abuse, stopping the violence, a safety plan for the woman, sobriety requirement for the man, psychoeducation about domestic violence, assessing the mental health needs of each family member, and reviewing steps involved with a non-destructive temporary or permanent separation if necessary. Multiple modes of treatment are recommended to accomplish the above, such as individual and group therapy for the man and woman, couple therapy, and family therapy. If progress is made early, treatment continues and focuses on "unfreezing" rigid cultural scripts by increasing respect, direct and healthy communication, problem-solving skills, and rebuilding trust and forgiveness. The couple is also taught the ways in which their seemingly private problems are reinforced by historical and cultural patterns of colonization, patriarchy, and gender oppression in both the United States and the culture of origin.

The first phase of therapy typically involves constructing a family genogram, likened to an *espejo* [mirror]. In the case study, the genogram revealed intergenerational IPV on both sides of the couple's families of origin (i.e., violent fathers abused both their wives and children). The couple married young, and the man drank excessively and began hitting the woman shortly after marriage. He also journeyed alone to the United States, where he lived with an *amante* or lover until he was later joined by his wife and children. After a couple of arrests (neighbors called the police) for physically assaulting his wife, the man was given the option of jail or treatment, and he participated in 18 months of group therapy for violent Latino men. The group for Latino men was helpful in helping him with sobriety, reducing violence, preparing for family therapy, and for reflecting on destructive versus responsible male cultural scripts.

The couple was reinforced for their disclosures and for attending therapy. The man had an exaggerated macho self-image, and the woman passively resigned herself to the situation like a martyr. Therapists challenged the couples' disbelief in the possibility of change and their view of their behaviors as "normal." Therapists stressed how unfair their legacy of violence was to *all* family members, followed by processing emotional pain.

In the second phase, the couple's own daughter's marital relationship was discussed as a happier, violence free, and fairer relationship to emulate. The advantages of acting a little more like NLW couples with the intent of "unfreezing" their rigid gender roles and increasing their bicultural repertoire was discussed. The couple was also encouraged to go out more alone, and to function as a team where child care was concerned. Interestingly, the man had little to do with the children and sometimes felt isolated as a result. The couple was also helped to negotiate desired changes, which included the man helping more with household responsibilities. The third phase continued the practice of couple negotiation and extended it to negotiations with children and discussions of proper child discipline, with attention to intergenerational issues of acculturation, such as BET and EDM described in this section.

IPV Interventions for Immigrant Latinas

Marrs Fuchsel and Brummett (2021) recently conducted a review of the literature on the characteristics and effectiveness of IPV prevention and treatment groups for immigrant Latinas in which they located 10 such interventions published during the last 25 years. While the sample sizes in these studies are typically small (6–8 participants), and the methods (e.g., support, psychoeducation, empowerment groups) and theoretical frameworks (empowerment, feminism, CBT) vary, the vast majority of groups were available in community-based clinics serving immigrant families, incorporated Latino values and practices as well as immigration-related resources, and all 10 interventions reported auspicious results. The five mixed-methods studies reported significant pre- to post-improvement on measures of PTSD, depression, self-esteem, self-perceived leadership, and knowledge of wellness, while qualitative studies reported improvements in IPV knowledge, self-esteem, social support, communication with children, and coping skills. These findings clearly warrant providing such effective IPV interventions to low-income, immigrant Latinas in need. As addressed below, IPV within families also includes the abuse, neglect, or exploitation of elderly family members, referred to as elder abuse.

Elderly Latino Issues

Elderly Latino family members have unique age-related assets and challenges that deserve greater attention. In the introduction to their recent special issue of *Latino Studies* entitled, "The art of Latina and Latino elderhood," Martinez and Rua (2021) note that, "The growing research and advocacy on behalf of older adults seldom regard the needs and concerns of aging Latinas and Latinos, while Latinx/a/o studies scholarship and advocacy have seldom attended to older adults' circumstances and needs" (p. 419). While research on elderly Latinos remains limited, some progress has been made since the first edition of this textbook in 2007, as selectively reviewed in this closing section of the Latino family chapter.

Falicov (2014, p. 427) conveys that elderly Latinos face physical and psychosocial adjustment tasks similar to their NLW counterparts, including grandparenthood, retirement, illness, and of course death and dying. However, she also underscores the "multiple jeopardy" experienced by many elderly Latinos as a result of acculturation and ethnic minority status that can exacerbate age-related challenges. For example, elderly Latinos lack pensions and health insurance relative to their NLW counterparts, and immigrants retain varying degrees of culture of origin values and expectations about illness, retirement, and death that are not always in alignment with more acculturated family members. Falicov further asserts that it is simply wrong to stereotype the Latino family as ready to meet all of the needs of its elderly members. While there are cultural norms prescribing extended family care of elderly parents and grandparents, such norms change with the sociocultural context of acculturation, as do the nature and quality of family relations and circumstances.

Thus, the trick is to assess actual and potential elderly resources within and beyond *la Familia*, broker needed supports, and to the extent possible help older family members establish mutually beneficial relationships with family, community, and programs. Below is a brief overview of elderly Latino social positionality followed by general and more topical issues pertaining to their unique age-related social and cultural needs.

Overview of Elderly Social Positionality

The 2020 Profile of Hispanic Americans aged 65 and Older is the most recent report by the Administration for Community Living (2021), which includes the Administration on Aging and is a division of the U.S. Department of Health and Human Services. The profile provides a handy snapshot of demographic characteristics and other important age-related indicators for the elderly population in America. The report begins by documenting that there are over 54 million Americans aged 65 and older, including 6.6 million aged 85 and older. The former are expected to increase to 94.7 million by 2060, while the latter will nearly triple to 19 million by that same year. With regard to elderly Latinos aged 65 and older, Figure 7.1 displays similar dramatic

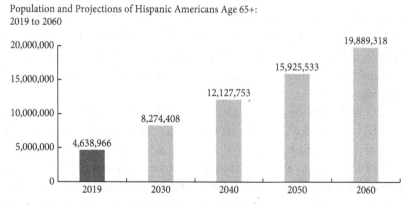

Population and Projections of Hispanic Americans Age 65+: 2019 to 2060

Figure 7.1. Dramatic population growth of elderly Latinos in the United States.
Source: U.S. Census Bureau, Population Estimates and Projections, 2017 (revised).
Note: Increments in years are uneven. Lighter bars indicate projections.

growth projections from 4,638,966 currently to almost 20 million by 2060, or from 9% of today's older U.S. population to a projected 21% by 2060.

Impressively, almost 90% of people age 65 and older in the United States are high school graduates and one-third have a bachelor's degree or higher. In contrast, these rates are 63% and 18%, respectively, for Latinos aged 65 and older. Over half of older Latinos are married, 20% are widowed, 20% are divorced or separated, and 8% never married. With regard to poverty, families headed by elderly Latinos aged 65 and older report a median income of $50,553 as compared to $70,254 for such families in general. Median annual personal income for older Latino men is $21,357 and $14,701 for older Latina women as compared to $36,921 and $21,815, respectively, for elderly men and women in general in the United States. These figures translate to economic hardship for just over 17% of elderly Latinos as compared to 9% for older Americans in general. Taken together, these data speak to significantly lower social positionality, complicated by old age, for many elderly Latinos struggling with functioning and lack of support.

Elderly Latino Poverty, Functioning, and Supports

Expected links between problems related to poverty, functioning, and familial and community connectedness in elderly Latinos were documented over three decades in the 1988 National Survey of Hispanic Elderly People (NSHEP), which included 2,299 elderly Latinos aged 65 and older, from the east coast and Florida, with all major Latino populations represented. Comparisons of NSHEP data with national data on the elderly show lower life satisfaction and peace of mind related to multiple economic, health, and social problems such as higher poverty rates, medical bills, sick spouses, loneliness, and dependency on others (Andrews, Lyons, & Rowlands, 1992).

Tran and Williams (1998) used NSHEP data to examine poverty and health status and concluded that the widespread poverty among elderly Latinos (i.e., ranging from 50% in Cubans to 63.7% in Puerto Ricans at the time) negatively impacts activities of daily living (ADLs) such as getting in and out of bed, light housework, and bathing. Factors that protect elderly Latinos from impairment include being married, more educated, and bilingual. Not surprisingly, elderly Cubans were the least impaired, while Puerto Ricans were the most consistent with their acculturation histories and consequent social positionalities, reviewed in Chapter 1. Given such substantial needs, what kinds of supports are available to elderly Latinos?

Formal and Informal Supports

With respect to formal service use, Deitz, John, and Roy (1998) used NSHEP data to show little if any use, across all major Latino groups including Central and South Americans, of the following: senior center services (e.g., meals, social gatherings), in-home services (e.g., health aide, housekeeping and meal preparation), and low use of federal entitlement programs such as Medicaid and Medicare (e.g., health services and hospitalizations). Cubans and Puerto Ricans were higher in use of entitlement programs, while Mexican and other Latinos were less integrated into such federal programs.

Deitz (1997) also compared formal and family support and found that while Latino elderly did receive *some* family support for ADLs (e.g., food shopping), their needs were not adequately met this way. That is, two-thirds of participants reported difficulty with at least one of eleven ADLs assessed, yet less than half received family assistance. In addition, between 21% and 43% of participants paid for help with things like housework, eating, and bathroom assistance, despite meager incomes. Dietz (1997) also noted the following low rates of formal assistance use by participants to supplement their low incomes: 36% used SSI, 15.4% food stamps, 12% senior centers, and only 4.1% used home health care.

Thus, early survey research on elderly Latinos documents considerable poverty and functional needs exacerbated by inadequate formal and family assistance, problems especially pronounced in the poorest of elderly Latinos without spouses, low in education and English fluency, and of Puerto Rican background. From this profile, we should expect pronounced psychosocial and health problems in elderly Latinos with less than adequate coping resources. For example, using NSHEP data to examine how the elderly cope with depression and family problems, Starrett et al. (1992) found that less than 10% of participants utilized mental health professionals or physicians, 17% used the church, and 36% indicated that they used nothing. Such findings intimate the frequent limitations to eldercare on the part of Latino families despite the central value and practice of *familismo* and obligation to older members.

Familismo and Eldercare

Early literature shows that Latino elders are more likely than NLW counterparts to live with their families, and less likely to be institutionalized in long-term care facilities, including nursing homes (Johnson et al., 1997; Zsembik, 1996). However, the determinants for such living arrangements, as well as questions regarding what is optimal for the elderly and their families, have only sporadically surfaced. Reports from the NSHEP (Zsembik, 1992; 1996) show that the cultural norm of caring for the elderly within the family changes with acculturation and the availability and willingness of family, economic resources, and elderly health challenges and dependency needs. For example, elderly Latinos with retirement incomes were much more likely to live on their own than those with smaller and less stable incomes. Puerto Rican elderly were found to be most likely to live alone and to prefer it this way due to greater poverty, dependency on restrictive public housing, and having children unable to afford to take in their parents.

A more recent study by Angel, Rote, and Markides (2017) addresses eldercare issues by analyzing data from the Hispanic Established Population for Epidemiologic Study of the Elderly (H-EPESE), the first large-scale epidemiologic study of elderly Mexican-origin adults and their caretakers from the southwestern United States. This landmark longitudinal study includes an initial sample of 3,050 elderly adults, aged 65 and older, surveyed in their homes in 1993–94 and re-interviewed in 1995–96, 1998–99, 2000–01, 2004–05, 2006–07, and 2010–11, for seven waves of data collection. In addition to adding 902 new participants aged 75 and older at wave five, over 900 caregivers (upon whom elderly participants depended the most) were added to the H-EPESE in 2010–11. These caregivers, two-thirds of whom were the adult children of the elderly participants, were interviewed about the health, finances, and general situation of their elderly care recipients. Further, questions about traditional Mexican values, including obligation to care for the elderly, were asked of the elderly in wave 2, resulting in over 300 caregiver/elder dyads with complete data on all study variables, an unprecedented sample. Finally, the H-EPESE also examines the role of immigration and acculturation by including elderly participants born in the United States as well as Mexico-born participants that arrived in the United States either early or late in their lives, which of course strongly affects adaptation.

While H-EPSES findings are limited to Mexican origin Latinos in the Southwest, they confirm what the literature has been gradually concluding about how eldercare is impacted by family financial strain, deteriorating elderly health, and diminishing family obligation with rising acculturation, underscoring the need for greater resources including frequently resisted long-term care facilities. Such need is especially pronounced in late-life arriving elderly immigrants and their families, because they report greater limitations to ADLs. Further, late-life as well as early-life arriving elderly immigrants more strongly endorse traditional cultural values than U.S.-born elderly Latinos (i.e., family closeness and obligation to the elderly, traditional sex-role adherence). Thus, caregiving burden may be especially concentrated in the families of immigrant elderly members that manifest greater health challenges and fewer resources, yet greater cultural expectations of support as compared to their U.S.-born counterparts.

Further, while over half of the elderly Mexican participants in the H-EPSES are responsible for most of their own personal care such as bathing, dressing, and using the toilet, only 40% of late-life immigrants are able to complete most of these tasks as compared to almost 60% of U.S.-born and early-life immigrants. Late-life immigrants are more dependent upon a single adult family member for help with household tasks, like meal preparation, transportation, and financial matters versus more acculturated U.S.-born and early-life immigrants that rely more often upon themselves, other family members, and larger networks of caregivers.

Angel et al. (2017) conclude that caregiver burden is concentrated in poorer Mexican-origin families, especially the adult children of late-life or the least acculturated elderly immigrants, who then have little choice but to care for aging parents at home. Given that such late-life immigrants endorse familial obligation to care for the elderly, additional strain on both caregivers and elderly family members is predictable and needs to be addressed (e.g., by assessing needs and exploring family supports, including recommending and assisting with long-term care outside of the family as needed). In addition to uneven family support, some elderly Latinos find themselves isolated and lonely, risk factors for increased health problems and premature death.

Isolation

Because loneliness and isolation are associated with greater morbidity and mortality in older adults, they are now considered public health problems in need of greater attention. In the recent and first ever review of the literature on loneliness and social isolation in older Latino adults, Tibiriçá, Jester, and Jeste (2022) find that loneliness is associated with greater morbidity, including greater risk for metabolic and cardiovascular disorders, and that social isolation is predicted by worse physical health, being male, unmarried, lower in SES, higher rates of smoking, frailty, and cognitive impairment. Tibiriçá et al. (2022) conclude that routine assessment of loneliness and isolation in elderly Latinos is warranted, particularly in those manifesting the above correlates found in their review. Cognitive impairment in particular signals the need to address increasing rates of dementia and caregiver burden in Latino families.

Dementia and Caregiver Burden

According to the Alzheimer's Association (2017), Latinos are 50% more likely to develop Alzheimer's disease (AD) than NLWs, and it is projected that the number of elderly Latinos with AD and related dementias will increase from less than 200,000 today to about 1.3 million by 2050. Key risk factors for Latinos include (1) greater risk for vascular diseases (i.e., mainly diabetes but also high blood pressure and cholesterol), risk factors for AD and stroke-related dementia; (2) low educational levels that limit the protective benefits of formal education against dementia; as well as (3) greater life expectancy projected to surpass all other groups in the United States by 2050 (it is well documented that the prevalence of AD doubles every five years beyond the age of 65, reaching an astounding 50% for those 85 years or older).

Regarding the role of vascular diseases, in the first representative population-based study of dementia in older Mexican Americans (N = 1,789), Haan et al. (2003) found that over 40% of dementia cases was attributable to Type 2 diabetes mellitus, stroke, or a combination of both—major chronic illnesses over-affecting Latinos as addressed in Chapter 10. Haan et al. (2003) conclude that at a minimum, screening for dementia needs to be combined with screening for diabetes, given that a third of their sample had diabetes. Further, even though 90% of their sample had medical insurance and 88% had a regular doctor, the vast majority was diagnosed with dementia for the first time in the study!

Thus, it is important to understand and address the under-detection of dementia in elderly Latinos including the role of social, cultural, and service-related factors. For example, Ortiz and Fitten (2000) studied barriers to health care access in a sample of 65 cognitively impaired elderly Latinos, who reported the following three most frequent obstacles: (1) personal beliefs about aging and illness (38%); (2) language (33%); and (3) economic problems (13%). Personal beliefs that interfere with seeking needed health care include viewing memory problems as normal in old age, not feeling sick, feeling too old to be helped, fear of discrimination and the effects of medication, and believing that God is more helpful than medications. These findings are rich with implications for improving assessment and addressing treatment obstacles beyond health care access, especially in view of the growing prevalence of dementia in Latinos and related disparities.

Prevalence and Disparities

Moon et al. (2019) reported on the prevalence of dementia and its risk factors in adults 65 years and older stratified by race/ethnicity as well as immigration status. These researchers analyzed the first round of data collected in 2011 for the National Health and Aging Trends Study (N = 7,609), a nationally representative sample of Medicare beneficiaries. With regard to prevalence, 10% of participants have *probable dementia* (i.e., as ascertained by a medical professional, usually involving neuropsychological testing), which increases with older age and lower education, cardiovascular conditions, and their respective risk factors. Prevalence for U.S.-born Latinos (12.7%) and NLBs (15.7%) is higher than for U.S.-born NLWs (8.1%), most likely reflecting SES disparities.

Interestingly, all immigrant groups in the study had higher rates of dementia than their U.S.-born counterparts, with the exception of NLB immigrants, whose rate of 10.4% is much lower than for U.S.-born blacks and closer to the overall prevalence of 10%. Moon et al. (2019) reason that greater racism experienced by U.S.-born blacks, and higher levels of education on the part of Black immigrants, may help explain this discrepant finding with regard to immigration and dementia. With regard to Latinos, the rate of 20.6% for immigrants is 8% higher than for U.S.-born Latinos, leading Moon et al. to observe that while the *Latino paradox* generally shows initially better health in immigrant versus U.S.-born Latinos, this advantage decreases over time and may not pertain to elderly Latinos. Data from this study warrant enhanced screening for dementia in elderly Latinos in general, immigrants in particular, and the need to connect cognitively impaired individuals and their families to needed resources given their underutilization as detailed below.

Related Disparities

A review of the literature on the prevalence of Alzheimer's disease, published by the U.S. Department of Health and Human Services (Lines & Weiner, 2014), reports disparities in prevalence similar to those above but also disparities in related morbidity, mortality, use of medications, long-term services and supports, health care expenditures, quality of care, and caregiver burden. For instance, Lines and Weiner report that people of color are 40% less likely to enter a long-term care facility than NLWs because of less insurance yet greater poverty and dementia impairment, with caregivers shouldering the burden of needed support. As can be seen in Figure 7.2, rates of nursing home use are much lower for Latinos and Asians as compared to NLBs and NLWs, with very little change in these rates from 1999 to 2008. Underutilization of nursing homes, for both economic and cultural reasons,

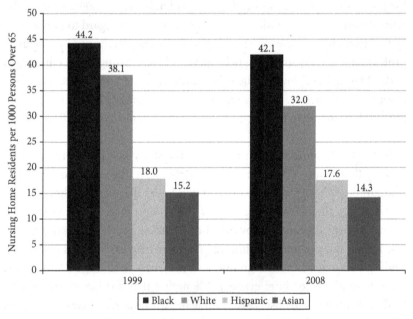

Figure 7.2. Underutilization of nursing homes by elderly Latinos as compared to non-Latino whites and Blacks and Asians per 1,000 persons aged 65 and older in the United States.

From Lines, L.M., & Wiener, J.M. (2014). Racial and ethnic disparities in Alzheimer's disease: A literature review. Office of Disability, Aging and Long-Term Care Policy Office of the Assistant Secretary for Planning and Evaluation. U.S. Department of Health and Human Services.

suggests excessive burden on the Latino family in need of attention and as documented below.

Addressing Dementia Caregiver Burden

> The typical Latino CG [caregiver] is a woman between 35 and 60, caring for parent(s) or parents-in-law. Latino CGs are typically younger, care simultaneously for more children under 18 in the home and have lower household incomes than non-Latino Whites. Reports of unmet needs and problems in accessing available resources are frequently noted, and continued efforts to remedy this problem are warranted. These CGs provide significant hands-on care: 58% assist their care recipient (CR) with getting in and out of beds and chairs; 53% help with feeding; 47% with getting dressed; and 50% with toileting. On average, Latino CGs spend more time on caregiving tasks (approximately 30 hours per week) and more likely to experience high burden from caregiving than non-Latino whites (Gallagher-Thompson et al., 2015, p. 2).

The typically immense burden of dementia caregiving, related to increased morbidity and mortality, is exacerbated in Latinos due to their lower SES yet higher practice of family obligation for both cultural and economic reasons. Thus, service providers need to be prepared to support higher than average caregiver distress in Latino families. For example, in their review of the literature on race and dementia, Lines and Weiner (2014) report that as compared with NLW caregivers, Mexican American caregivers report greater distress and depression, poorer self-rated health, more somatic complaints, and greater sensitivity to the memory and behavioral problems in their care recipients. They also document that the burden of dementia care is gendered, with most of it falling upon Latina family members such as an adult daughter or daughter-in-law, a practice that needs to be assessed and remedied.

Renowned geriatric psychology expert on elderly mental health, Dolores Gallagher-Thompson has devoted decades of her career evaluating interventions for dementia caregiver distress with substantial focus on Latinos. She and her colleagues published a pair of randomized, controlled evaluations of group-based CBT-related coping skills as compared to a community-based-like support group (Gallagher-Thompson et al., 2003) and to a telephone based control group (Gallagher-Thompson et al., 2008) provided to Latina and NLW caregivers. In these group-based interventions, the CBT condition featured three to four months of psychoeducation and adaptive coping skills strategies, and results consistently showed that this skill-building CBT approach was the most effective in reducing depressive symptoms as well as caregiving and general life stress, and increasing adaptive coping strategies in both Latinas and NLW caregivers. Gallagher-Thompson and colleagues attribute results to ample preparation, adapting the intervention to Latinas by addressing Spanish language needs and tailoring CBT techniques to fit with Latino culture (e.g., urging stressed caretakers to take some restorative time out for themselves as a way to provide better care for their relative).

Fotonovela-driven Dementia Care

Subsequently, Gallagher-Thompson and colleagues (2015) evaluated the effectiveness of a Spanish language *fotonovela* designed to mitigate distress and depression in Latino dementia caregivers (CGs), as well as to raise dementia health literacy by teaching coping skills, how to recognize one's own depression, and encouraging the utilization of available resources to mitigate family burden. A *fotonovela* is a comic book form of entertainment, long popular in Latin America, typically using staged photos of real people and bubble dialogue to convey a dramatic, soap opera-like storyline. These are increasingly used to raise health literacy (see Figures 7.3 and 7.4).

To evaluate the effectiveness of their *fotonovela*, *¡Unidos Podemos! Enfrentando la pérdida de memoria en familia* [Together We Can! Facing memory loss as a family] 110 Latino dementia caregivers were randomly assigned to the *fotonovela* condition (N = 55) or the usual dementia information condition (N = 55). Participants were 82% female, and 72% were born in Mexico, 23% born in the U.S., and of generally low-SES backgrounds. Results show that participants in the *fotonovela* condition demonstrated significantly greater reductions in depressive symptoms as compared to participants provided the usual dementia information by medical staff. Participants in both conditions reported significantly less stress in response to the memory and behavioral problems exhibited by their care recipients. *Fotonovela* participants also reported that the format was helpful and that

Figure 7.3. Sample pages from Spanish language *Fotonovela* addressing dementia and caregiver stress.

With permission from the Alzheimer's Association.

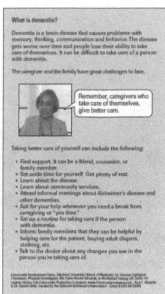

Figure 7.4. Sample pages from English language Pages from *Fotonovela* addressing dementia and caregiver stress.

With permission from the Alzheimer's Association.

they referred to it more often than participants in the information condition referred to their informational materials.

Gallagher-Thompson and colleagues conclude that a culturally tailored *fotonovela* is an effective tool for Latino dementia caregivers given their high unmet needs for assistance and various obstacles to accessing needed resources. The effective tailoring of *¡Unidos Podemos!* is rooted in a preliminary study conducted by Gallagher-Thompson and colleagues to better understand how Latino families cope with dementia behavioral problems (Turner et al.; 2015). In this study, focus groups were conducted with 42 Spanish-speaking Latino caregivers recruited from organizations affiliated with the Alzheimer's Association near San Diego, California. Findings identified several helpful ways of coping with dementia-related behaviors: (1) acceptance (e.g., "But as we are talking here, the patients who are doing these things, it's not for us to criticize or scold them, but rather to understand them and learn how to treat them."); (2) love ("Even though she's no longer aware that I am her husband, unconsciously she knows I am someone who is always there for her . . ."); (3) patience ("There are persons whose talk is purely sexual. This can't be easily changed . . . because of the Alzheimer's or dementia . . . [W]ith patience, we were able to distract him."); (4) adaptability (e.g., when a caregiver's mother repeatedly and anxiously insists on going home, despite being home, the caregiver takes her for a car ride and returns home); and (5) establishing care routines ("We want information about how to establish routines for toileting, bathing, eating, dressing, exercise, and [how] patients can keep busy and enjoy themselves.") (pp. 7–8). Also identified were persistent challenges that frequently undermined the above coping strategies, such as problems with providers and family members, low knowledge of resources, financial strain, and emotional distress. In addition to these *fotonovela*-informing findings, a review of interventions for dementia caregivers also provides insights into the impacts of caregiver stress and effective ways to mitigate it.

A review of interventions for ethnically diverse family dementia caregivers from Latino, NLW, NLB, and non-Latino Asian backgrounds was conducted by Napoles et al. (2010). The review shows that for Latinos, the most frequent differences in their caregiving experience include worse psychosocial health yet more positive appraisals of coping, greater spirituality, a stronger belief in family obligation, and greater aversion to the institutionalization of relatives. These socioculturally patterned differences represent an interesting mix of assets and obstacles to utilizing services that could mitigate well-documented dementia caregiver distress.

With regard to interventions, the review located 11 studies that integrated cultural factors into their services. Eight of these 11 culturally tailored interventions are from the Resources for Enhancing Alzheimer's Caregiver Health (REACH) initiative, a multisite project designed to evaluate interventions in ethnically diverse family caregivers. Impressively, REACH studies demonstrate the effectiveness of in-home, telephone, and small group support on depression, quality of life, and adaptive coping strategies. In the case of Latinos, bilingual and bicultural interventionists addressed *familismo* (i.e., collective family over individual needs), language, health literacy, service advocacy, elder protection, and other logistical service-related barriers. REACH, as well as the subsequent REACH II, demonstrate effectiveness in reducing caregiver distress and depression while improving adaptive coping and quality of life. Taken together, the above studies demonstrate multiple effective ways of mitigating dementia caregiver stress in overly stressed Latino families via culturally adapted approaches. While infrequent, the problem of elder abuse can sometimes result from such overstressed family circumstances as discussed below.

Elder Abuse in Latinos

Research suggests that over 10% of adults aged 60 and older are victims of elder abuse each year, yet only a small proportion of the estimated five million cases of non-institutional elder abuse are reported to Adult Protective Services each year (DeLiema et al., 2012). In an effort to improve upon estimates of prevalence as well as correlates, Acierno et al. (2010) conducted a national survey of 5,777 community-residing adults aged 60 years and older, with two goals: (1) to assess one-year prevalence of physical, sexual, emotional, or financial mistreatment or potential neglect (i.e., an identified yet neglected need for assistance); and (2) to identify correlates of each form of mistreatment. Results reveal that one in 10 elderly respondents reported emotional, physical, or sexual mistreatment, or potential neglect during the past year. More specifically, results reveal a one-year 4.6% prevalence for emotional abuse, 1.6% for physical abuse, 0.6% for sexual abuse, 5.1% for potential neglect, and 5.2% for current financial abuse by a family member. The most consistent correlates of mistreatment across types of abuse are low social support and previous traumatic event exposure, leading Acierno et al. to recommend addressing low social support with preventive interventions to help mitigate abuse. With such baseline data in mind, Latino-specific data are briefly reviewed next.

Immigrants

Given the many obstacles experienced by immigrant Latinos to participating in elder abuse research, DeLiema et al. (2012) recruited and trained *promotores* to interview a sample of 200 Spanish-speaking immigrant Latino adults aged 66 and older living in low-income communities. *Promotores* conducted door-to-door interviews in randomly selected census tracts in Los Angeles to assess the frequency of psychological, physical, and sexual abuse, as well as neglect and financial exploitation. This low-SES Latino sample was 56% female and with a good representation of major Los Angeles. Latino populations: Mexican (64.1%), El Salvadoran (15.7%), Guatemalan (10.6%).

Concerning results from this unique survey revealed that 40.4% of participants reported experiencing some form of abuse during the past year: Almost 25% reported psychological abuse, 10.7% physical abuse, 9% sexual abuse, 16.7% financial exploitation, and 11.7% neglect by their caregivers. These exceedingly high numbers are quite concerning given that they may reflect a particularly vulnerable subgroup of older Latinos assessed by local *promotores* in a culturally congruent manner, as compared to conventional prevalence survey methods (e.g., phone call surveys). While much more research is warranted, results of this study strongly suggest that service providers keep immigrant Latinos on their radar for deeper assessment of elder abuse. With regard to intervention, again, *promotores* (community health workers) represent a particularly viable way of providing psychoeducation about elder abuse and helping abused members of their communities connect with and navigate needed services.

A recent review of the literature on the assessment and treatment of elder abuse in Spanish-speaking Latinos could only locate 13 articles during the 30-year period between 1989 and 2019 (Hincapie et al., 2021). Only five of these articles include assessment information, and only one of those focused on Latinos. Regarding intervention, only seven studies met the review inclusion criteria, and of these, two present theoretical frameworks while five are qualitative studies recommending ways to modify existing interventions for abused elderly Latinos. Thus, the state of the literature, as well as service provision to elderly Latinos experiencing abuse, is quite nascent and in need of considerable attention beyond the usual recommendations for bilingual staff, cultural competence, and collaboration between agencies serving elderly Latinos, their families, and community stakeholders (e.g., leaders of churches and nonprofit centers).

Conclusion

As the enduring yet evolving central sociocultural institution of Latinos, *la familia* will continue to be studied as a major site for understanding and responding to various family-related problems and issues. Given the immensity of this topic, only a selective review of timely, complex, and increasingly important problem areas are addressed in this chapter, with the overriding objective of illustrating how to better understand and respond to Latino family-related problems in a socioculturally competent manner. These illustrations can be extrapolated to the myriad of other family problems and issues of interest and importance. While psychosocial and health problems affecting Latino youth typically occur within a family context, the subsequent chapter opens space for their unique age-related social and cultural experience in the United States.

References

Acierno, R., Hernandez, M. A., Amstadter, A. B., Resnick, H. S., Steve, K., Muzzy, W., & Kilpatrick, D. G. (2010). Prevalence and correlates of emotional, physical, sexual, and financial abuse and potential neglect in the United States: The National Elder Mistreatment Study. *American Journal of Public Health, 100*(2), 297–319.

Administration for Community Living (2021). *The 2020 profile of Hispanic Americans aged 65 and older*. Washington DC: U.S. Department of Health and Human Services.

Alvarez, C. P., Davidson, P. M., Fleming, C., & Glass, N. E. (2016). Elements of effective interventions for addressing intimate partner violence in Latina women: A systematic review. *PLOS ONE, 11*(8), 1–13. | https://doi.org/10.1371/journal.pone.0160518

Alzheimer's Association (2017). 2017 Alzheimer's disease facts and figures. *Alzheimer's & Dementia, 13*(4), 325–373.

Angel, J. L., Rote, S., & Markides, K. (2017). The role of the Latino family in late-life caregiving. In J. M. Wilmoth, and M. Silverstein (Eds.), *Later-Life social support and service provision in diverse and vulnerable populations: Understanding networks of care* (pp. 38–53). Abingdon, UK: Routledge.

Andrews, J. W. Lyons, B., & Rowland, D. (1992). Life satisfaction and peace of mind: Comparative analysis of elderly Hispanics and other elderly Americans. In T. L. Brink (Ed.), *Hispanic Aged Mental Health* (pp. 21–42). New York: Haworth Press.

Baca Zinn, M. (1982/83). Familism among Chicanos: A theoretical review. *Humboldt Journal of Social Relations, 10*(1), 224–238.

Brabeck, K. M., Lykes, M. B., & Hunter, C. (2014). The psychosocial impact of detention and deportation on U.S. migrant children and families. *American Journal of Orthopsychiatry, 84* (5), 496–505.

Caetano, R., Ramisetty-Mikler, S., Caetano Vaeth, P. A., & Robert Harris, T. (2007). Acculturation Stress, Drinking, and Intimate Partner Violence Among Hispanic Couples in the U.S. Journal of Interpersonal Violence, 22(11), 1431–1447. 10.1177/0886260507305568 http://jiv.sagepub.com

Cunardi, C. B., Caetano, R., Clark, C. L., & Schafer, J. (1999). Alcohol-related problems and intimate partner violence among White, Black, and Hispanic couples in the U.S. *Alcoholism: Clinical and Experimental Research, 23*(9), 1492–1501.

Cook, B., Alegria, M., Lin, J. H., & Guo, J. (2009). Pathways and correlates connecting Latinos' mental health with exposure to the United States. *American Journal of Public Health, 99*(12), 2247–2254.

Deitz, T. L. (1997). Family and formal assistance with activity limitations: Who helps the Mexican American elderly? *Hispanic Journal of Behavioral Sciences, 19*(3), 333–352.

Deitz, T. L., John, R., & Roy, L. C. (1998). Exploring intra-ethnic diversity among four groups of Hispanic elderly: Patterns and levels of service utilization. *International Journal of Aging and Human Development, 46*(3), 247–266.

DeLiema, M. Gassoumis, Z. D., Homeier, D. C., Wilber, K. H. (2012). Determining prevalence and correlates of elder abuse using promotores: Low-income immigrant Latinos report high rates of abuse and neglect. *Journal of the American Geriatrics Society, 60*(7), 1333–1339. https://doi.org/10.1111/j.1532-5415.2012.04025.x

Falicov, C. J. (2014). MECA: A meeting place for culture and therapy. In C. J. Falicov (Ed.), *Latino families in therapy* (2nd ed.) (pp. 17–50). New York: The Guilford Press.

Falicov, C. J. (2014). Young, middle, and late adulthood transitions. In C. J. Falicov (Ed.), *Latino families in therapy* (2nd ed.) (p. 410–437). New York: The Guilford Press.

Gallagher-Thompson, D., Coon, d. W., Solano, N., Ambler, C., Rabinowitz, Y., & Thompson, L. W. (2003). Changes in indices of distress among Latino and Anglo female caregivers of elderly relatives with dementia: Site-specific results from the REACH National Collaborative Study. *The Gerontologist, 43*(3), 580–591.

Gallagher-Thompson, D., Gray, H., Dupart, T., Jimenez, D., & Thompson, L. W. (2008). Effectiveness of cognitive/behavioral small group intervention for reduction of depression and stress in non-Hispanic white and Hispanic/Latino women dementia family caregivers: Outcomes and mediators of change. *Journal of Rational Emotive Cognitive Behavioral Therapy, 26*(4): 286–303. https://doi.org/10.1007/s10942-008-0087-4

Gallagher-Thompson, D., Tzuang, M., Hinton, L., Alvarez, P., Rengifo, J., Valverde, I., Chen, N., Emrani, T., & Thompson, L. W. (2015). Effectiveness of a fotonovela for reducing depression and stress in Latino dementia family caregivers. *Alzheimer Disease and Associated Disorders, 29*(2), 146–153. https://doi.org/10.1097/WAD.0000000000 0000077

Garcia-Preto, N. (1996). Latino families: An overview. In M. McGoldrick, J. Giordano, & J. K. Pearce (Eds.), *Ethnicity and family therapy* (2nd ed.) (pp. 141–154). New York: The Guilford Press.

Haan, M. N., Mungas, D. M., Gonzalez, H. M., Ortiz, T. A., Acharya, A., & Jagust, W. J. (2003). Prevalence of dementia in older Latinos: The influence of type 2 diabetes mellitus, stroke and genetic factors. *JAGS, 51*(2), 169–177.

Hincapie, D., Gilmore, M., Lenox, M., & Stripling, A. (2021). Assessment and treatment of elder abuse in Spanish speaking Americans: A scoping review. *Aggression and Violent Behavior, 57*, 1–6. https://doi.org/10.1016/j.avb.2020.101480

Johnson, R. A., Schwiebert, V., Alvarado-Rosemann, P., Pecka, G., & Shirk, N. (1997). Residential preferences and eldercare views of Hispanic elders. *Journal of cross-Cultural Gerontology, 12*, 91–107.

Kaufman Kantor, G., Jasinski, J. L., & Aldarondo, E. (1994). Sociocultural status and incidence of marital violence in Hispanic families. *Violence and Victims, 9*(3), 207–222.

Lines, L. M., & Weiner, J. M. (2014). Racial and ethnic disparities in Alzheimer's Disease: A literature review. Washington DC: Office of Disability, Aging and Long-Term Care Policy Office of the Assistant Secretary for Planning and Evaluation; U.S. Department of Health and Human Services.

López, Gustavo (2015a). Hispanics of Cuban Origin in the United States, 2013. Washington, D.C.: Pew Research Center, September 15.

López, Gustavo (2015b). Hispanics of Dominican Origin in the United States, 2013. Washington, D.C.: Pew Research Center, September 15.

López, Gustavo (2015c). Hispanics of Guatemalan Origin in the United States, 2013. Washington, D.C.: Pew Research Center, September 15.

López, Gustavo (2015d). Hispanics of Mexican Origin in the United States, 2013. Washington, D.C.: Pew Research Center, September 15.

López, Gustavo (2015e). Hispanics of Nicaraguan Origin in the United States, 2013. Washington, D.C.: Pew Research Center, September 15.

López, Gustavo (2015f). Hispanics of Puerto Rican Origin in the United States, 2013. Washington, D.C.: Pew Research Center, September 15.

López, Gustavo (2015g). Hispanics of Salvadoran Origin in the United States, 2013. Washington, D.C.: Pew Research Center, September 15.

Lovato, K., Lopez, C., Karimli, L., & Abrams, L. S. (2018). The impact of deportation-related family separations on the well-being of Latino children and youth: A review of the literature. *Children and Youth Services Review, 95*, 109–116.

Marrs Fuchsel, C. L., & Brummett, A. (2021). Intimate partner violence prevention and intervention group-format programs for immigrant Latinas: A systematic review. *Journal of Family Violence, 36*, 209–221. https://doi.org/10.1007/s10896-020-00160-6

Martinez Jr., C. R. Eddy, J. M., McClure, H. H., & Cobb, C. L. (2021). Promoting strong Latino families within an emerging immigration context: Results of a replication and extension trial of a culturally adapted preventive intervention. *Prevention Science, 23*(2), 282–294. https://doi.org/10.1007/s11121-021-01323-7

Moon, H., Badana, A. N. S., Hwang, S-Y, Sears, J. S., & Haley, W. E. (2019). Dementia prevalence in older adults: Variation by race/ethnicity and immigrant status. *American Journal of Geriatric Psychiatry, 27*(3), 241–250.

Napoles, A. M., Chadiha, L., Eversley, R., & Moreno-John, G. (2010). Developing culturally sensitive dementia caregiver interventions: Are we there yet? *American*

Journal of Alzheimer's Disease & Other Dementias, 25(5) 389–406. doi:10.1177/1533317510370957

Ortiz, F., & Fitten, L. J. (2000). Barriers to healthcare access for cognitively impaired older Hispanics. *Alzheimer Disease and Associated Disorders*, 14(3), 141–150.

Perez, W. & Padilla, A. M. (2000). Cultural orientation across three generations of Hispanic adolescents. *Hispanic Journal of Behavioral Sciences*, 22(3), 390–398.

Ramirez, O., & Arce, C. H. (1981). The contemporary Chicano family: An empirically based review. In A. Barron (Ed.), *Explorations in Chicano psychology* (pp. 3–28). New York: Praeger.

Rodriguez, M. A., Bauer, H. M., & Flores-Ortiz, Y. (2001). Domestic violence in the Latino population. In A. G. Lopez and E. Carrillo, (Eds.), *The Latino psychiatric patient: Assessment and treatment* (pp. 163–180). Washington DC: American Psychiatric Publishing.

Sabogal, F., Marin, G., Otero-Sabogal, R., Marin, B. V., & Perez-Stable, E. J. (1987). Hispanic familism and acculturation: What changes and what doesn't? *Hispanic Journal of Behavioral Sciences*, 9(4), 397–412.

Smokowski, P. R., & Bacallao, M. L. (2011). Entre dos mundos/between two worlds: A bicultural skills training prevention program to help immigrant families cope with acculturation stress. In P. R. Smokowski & M. L. Bacallao (Eds.), Becoming bicultural: Risk, resilience, and Latino youth (pp. 186–216). New York: New York University Press.

Sorensen, S. B., & Telles, C. A. (1991). Self-reports of spousal violence in a Mexican-American and non-Hispanic white population. *Violence and Victims*, 6(1), 3–15.

Starrett, R. A., Rogers, D., & Decker, J. T. (1992). The self-reliance behavior of the Hispanic elderly in comparison to their use of formal mental health helping networks. In T. L. Brink (Ed.), *Hispanic aged mental health* (pp. 157–169). New York: The Haworth Press.

Stepler, R., & Brown, A. (2016). 2014, Hispanics in the United States Statistical Portrait. Report. Washington D.C. PEW Research Center (April 19).

Szapocznik, J., Kurtines, W., Santisteban, D. A., Pantin, H., Scopetta, M., Mancilla, Y., Aisenberg, S., McIntosh, S., Perez-Vidal, A., & Coatsworth, J. D. (1997). The evolution of a structural ecosystemic theory for working with Latino families. In J. G. Garcia & M. C. Zea (Eds.), *Psychological interventions and research with Latino populations* (pp.166–190). Boston: Allyn & Bacon.

Tibiriçá, L., Jester, D. J., & Jeste, D. V. (2022). A systematic review of loneliness and social isolation among Hispanic/Latino older adults in the United States. *Psychiatry Research*, 313(6), 1–31.https://doi.org/10.1016/j.psychres.2022.114568

Tran, T. V., & Williams, L. F. (1998). Poverty and impairment in activities of living among elderly Hispanics. *Social Work and Health Care*, 26(4), 59–78.

Turner, R. M., Hinton, L., Gallagher-Thompson, D., Tzuang, M., Tran, C., & Valle, R. (2015). Using an emic lens to understand how Latino families cope with dementia behavioral problems. *American Journal of Alzheimer's Disease Other Dementias*, 30(5), 454–462. https://doi.org/10.1177/1533317514566115

Vega, W. A. (1990). Hispanic families in the 1980s: A decade of research. *Journal of Marriage and the Family*, 52(Nov.), 1015–1024.

Visualizations (2022). The history of federally qualified health centers (FQHC's). https://www.visualutions.com/blog/the-history-of-federally-qualified-health-centers/

Weinbaum, Z., Stratton, T. L., Chavez, G., Motylewski-Link, C., Barrera, N., & Courtney, J. G. (2001). Female victims of intimate partner physical domestic violence (IPP-DV), California, 1998. *American Journal of Preventive Medicine*, 21(4), 313–319.

Weinbaum, Z., & Thorfinnson, T. (Eds.). (2006). Women's health: Findings from the California Women's Survey, 1997-2003. Sacramento, CA: California Department of Health Services, Office of Women's Health.

Zsembik, B. A. (1992). Determinants of living along among older Hispanics. Research on Aging, 15(4), 449–464.

Zsembik, B. A. (1996). Preference for co residence among older Latinos. *Journal of Aging Studies, 10*(1), 69–81.

Zsembik, B. A., Drevenstedt, G. L., & McLane, C. P. (1997). Economic wellbeing among older Latinos. *International Journal of Sociology and Social Policy, 17*(9/10), 34–54.

8

Latinx Youth

Psychosocial and health problems over-affecting most Latinx youth are framed here as generally resulting from unmet developmental needs due to the destabilization of conventional social and cultural resources and controls within the family, ethnic/local community, and greater society (e.g., health, educational, economic, and legal systems). These often render too many Latinx youth vulnerable to a clustering of related problems, especially in the poorest of barrio-dwelling youth, which need to be assessed and remedied as effectively and comprehensively as possible. Burt, Resnick, and Novick (1998) articulate an ecologically comprehensive framework for understanding adolescent development, including risk, relevant to vulnerable Latinx youth: "The presence of harmful existing conditions (antecedents) in the absence of sufficient protective factors create vulnerabilities. These vulnerabilities, combined with the presence of specific early signs of difficulties (system markers), institutional inabilities to help children and youth who evidence such markers, and the absence of positive behaviors or competencies, may lead in time to problem behavior that will have more serious long-term consequences (negative outcomes)" (p. 38) (see Table 8.1).

For many Latinx youth, antecedents include the several trappings of acculturation stress linked to ethnic minority status and poverty that too often include family destabilization, with deficient community resources and institutions. As described below, vulnerability in Latinx adolescents is generally higher in more acculturated youth who are experiencing family breakdown and disconnections from traditionally stabilizing social institutions such as school, church, prosocial peers and activities, and employment. Psychosocial and health problems are most evident for Mexican American (i.e., Chicano) and Puerto Rican youth, from the oldest and largest of U.S. Latinx populations whose histories reveal ongoing tension and conflict with mainstream society and consequent acculturative stress (e.g., segregation, poverty, lack of resources and opportunities, and offensive social policies). Previously scarce but now growing literature reveals what appear to be parallel problem patterns for Central American and Dominican youth that

Solving Latino Psychosocial and Health Problems. Kurt C. Organista, Oxford University Press.
© Oxford University Press 2023. DOI: 10.1093/oso/9780190059637.003.0008

Table 8.1. Risk Antecedents, Markers, Behaviors, and Outcomes: A Conceptual Framework for Thinking about Youth Vulnerabilities and Assets

Antecedents	Protective Factors	System Markers	Problem Behaviors	Positive Behaviors	Negative Outcomes
Family dysfunction	Individual competencies/abilities Parental competencies, resources	Poor school performance Child protection/out-of-home placement	School-related problem behaviors (truancy, absenteeism, violence) Early sexual behavior	Good school attendance, attachment to school, good performance Postponing sexual behavior	Dropping out of school, poor credentials for economic self-sufficiency Pregnancy, too-early parenthood, poor pregnancy outcomes Sexually transmitted diseases, including chlamydia and AIDS
Poverty			Use of tobacco, alcohol, other drugs		Abuse of or addiction to alcohol or other drugs, and associated health problems
Neighborhood and local institutions	Other adults Neighborhood resources Effective schools and other institutions with responsibility for children and youth		Running away from home, foster home Associating with delinquent peers	Positive interactions with family Participation in community and religious institutions Social, problem-solving, and peer skills High self-esteem and achievement motivation	Homelessness Physical abuse, battering Prostitution Sexual abuse, rape, incest Death or permanent injury from guns, knives, and other violent behavior; automobile accidents; other accidents Other morbidity/mortality outcomes (e.g., hepatitis, tuberculosis, pneumonia, AIDS complications) Depression, suicide Criminal convictions

From Burt, Resnick, & Novick (1998). *Building supportive communities for at-risk adolescents: It takes more than services.* Washington DC: American Psychological Association. With Permission.

typically live alongside urban-based Mexican and Puerto Rican youth, re-spectively. While Cuban youth are not immune to psychosocial problems, literature reviewed here reveals generally better adaptation given their unique acculturation history and better social positionality, as reviewed in Chapter 1.

While protective factors include individual, family, and community assets, as noted in Burt et al.'s (1998) framework, it is important to keep in mind that such precious protective factors are precisely those undermined by the very risk factors listed in that framework. As a result, early system markers (e.g., records of school problems, juvenile court and police records, incarcer-ation) are disproportionately high in Latinx youth, as are more serious and long-term psychosocial and health problems. The most prominent cluster of psychosocial and health problems affecting Latinx youth includes school failure, depression and suicidality, alcohol and substance abuse, delinquency including gang affiliation and incarceration, and sexual reproductive health challenges resulting in unplanned pregnancies and sexually transmitted infections (STIs), including HIV.

The overlapping nature of Latinx youth problems and needed multilevel interventions warrant addressing several problem areas simultaneously through comprehensive, micro-individual and family-centered strategies, and meso-community-based approaches supported by macro-social policies. As if such a charge weren't formidable enough, the recent and growing pre-dicament of undocumented youth and members of their families adds yet another layer of complexity to the above cluster of problems that includes legal limbo, detention and deportation, family separation, and trauma.

Clustering of Psychosocial and Health Problems Over-affecting Latinx Youth

The Centrality of School Adjustment

Whether referred to as dropouts or pushouts, school failure historically has been an entrenched problem for significant numbers of Mexican American and Puerto Rican youth, and more recently for Central American and Dominican youth. As such, school merits special attention for its central role in influencing and exacerbating psychosocial and health problems, including its potential role as a site, system, and optimal location for intervening with youth, families, and communities. Past reviews of the literature have delivered devastating profiles of schools failing Latinx youth, resulting in about a third leaving high school by the 10th grade, with some of the most concerning data revealing even higher dropout rates for Puerto Rican youth in cities such as New York.

Fortunately, high school completion rates have improved dramatically for Latinxs over the past two decades. According to the PEW Research Center, dropout rates for Latinxs have decreased from the past's persistent one-third figure to an all-time low of 10% in 2016 (versus 6% for the nation). Speculation regarding this welcomed trend includes the closing of poor-performing schools that graduate less than two-thirds of students, school principals implementing *every student counts* type schools with accountability, and federal mandates now requiring schools to report non-completion rates by racial/ethnic student populations (Gerwertz, 2017). These strategies are part of the federal government's Every Student Succeeds Act (ESSA), signed into law in 2015, giving states discretion in responding to the results of mandatory school testing in grades three to eight, and during the junior year of high school.

While the ESSA replaces the harshness of No Child Left Behind (2002–2015)—the federal act that punished schools, principals, and communities for poor test results—it cannot ameliorate the entrenched problems that continue to plague the academic performance of many Latinx students in resource-poor public schools. This problematic profile has been summarized by Gándara and Mordechay (2017): Almost two-thirds of Latinx children live in or near poverty, and less than 20% live in a home in which someone has a college education. These children also have at least one immigrant parent, indicating that Spanish is likely spoken at home, while 20% to 30% live in a home in which no adult speaks English very well. For the children of Mexican immigrants, almost half have fathers with less than eight years of education, and two-thirds have mothers without a high school diploma.

As has been documented for decades, Latinx youth in the western United States continue to be the most racially segregated of all student groups, by poverty and often by language. At both elementary and secondary school levels, Mexican American youth are more likely to attend segregated schools with low-quality curricula, less qualified teachers, greater teacher turnover, overemphasis on remedial studies, rigid ability placements and "tracking" into non-college preparatory courses, low-quality programs for limited English proficiency students, and curricula too often irrelevant to their Latinx experience (Solórzano and Solórzano, 1995). Thus, theories of Latinx school failure must focus on the role of school funding, structure, and resources as opposed to the long-standing bias of looking for cultural deficiencies within Latinx students, families, and communities.

For example, there is a persistent misconception that poor Latinx parents place little value on education, as if any population could afford to do so. What research does show is that while Latinx students and parents are similar to non-Latinx white (NLW) counterparts in educational values and aspirations, Latinxs have fewer and smaller social and professional networks. Such networks impart resources, connections, and practical knowledge regarding requirements and preparation for college, and the courses and majors needed to prepare for desired professional careers (Behnke, Piercy, & Diversi, 2004; Garcia, 2001). Low-income Latinx parents are also less able than higher income counterparts to provide direct guidance to help their children with homework and vocational aspirations, with lack of English proficiency continuing to play a significant role in this problem area.

The more Latinx parents are involved in school activities (Quian & Blair, 1999), homework, and monitoring their children (Plunkett & Bamaca-Gomez, 2003), the higher the children's school engagement. Thus, it is imperative that schools support Latinx students *and their parents* to realize their educational values and aspirations through engagement and knowledge-enhancing strategies. Without the information, resources, and skills to achieve educational dreams, it should not surprise us that so many young Latinxs disconnect from school, as reflected in apathy, self-blame for failure, and occasional resistance and anti-school postures.

Gándara and Mordechay (2017) also remind us of the growing lack of school capacity and resources in new Latinx growth communities in the South and Midwest, including the high demand and low supply of certified bilingual teachers. Lack of the latter is also the result of anti-bilingual education policies such as California's Proposition 227 that has decreased the number of certified bilingual teachers by two-thirds since its passing in 1998. Fortunately, schools in California now have the discretion to implement bilingual education as needed thanks to a recent assembly bill designed to respond to the needs of Latinx youth, who comprise the majority of K–12 public school students (see Chapter 11 on Latinx political power for more detail). The combination of school failure and family problems at home can be a depressing proposition for many Latinx youth.

Depression and Suicidality

The breakdown of traditional stabilizing forces within the Latinx family, community, and larger social context, linked to acculturation stress and poverty, can render many Latinx adolescents, and especially girls, vulnerable to depression, suicidality, and related problems. For example, almost 30 years ago Swanson et al. (1992) found higher rates of depression, suicidality, and substance use in 1,775 Chicanx high school students as compared to 2,383 *poorer* high school students in Mexico, suggesting that depression in Chicanx youth may have less to do with poverty per se and more to do with acculturative stress. For instance, the destabilization of the Latinx family appears central in the relation between acculturative stress and mental health problems over-affecting Latinx youth. An early study by Hovey and King (1996) examined depression and suicidality in low-SES Latinx high school students and found that both were predicted by high acculturative stress and low family cohesion.

According to the CDC's (2018) national Youth Risk Behavioral Survey (YRBS), published every two years, there has been a concerning upward trend in symptoms of depression among U.S. high school students from 2007 to 2017, reflected in those endorsing the following survey items: experienced persistent feelings of sadness or hopelessness during the past two weeks (from 28.5% to 31.5%); seriously considered attempting suicide (14.5% to 17.2%); made a suicide plan (11.3% to 13.6%); attempted suicide (6.9% to 7.4%); and injured in a suicide attempt (2% to 2.4%). High rates of depression have been documented for Latinx youth over the past 25 to 30 years, although not as uniformly as in the 2018 YRBS nationally representative survey of junior high and high school students. YRBS comparisons of race/ethnic groups corroborate past research and concern about higher than average depression in Latinx youth: The percentage of high school students experiencing periods of persistent feelings of sadness or hopelessness during the past year is highest for Latinxs (33.7%) as compared to NLW (30.2%) and African American (29.2%) students, also a source of concern.

Suicide attempts in Latinx girls in particular have been on the radar of clinicians and researchers concerned with their pronounced rates relative to girls of other racial and ethnic backgrounds. An examination of suicide attempts by gender in the 2018 YRBS shows a higher rate for Latinx girls (11%) compared to white (7%) and Asian American girls (8%), but slightly lower than for African American girls (12%). While these current rates are slightly better than those reported by Zayas and colleagues over the past decade and a half, they continue to be a source of concern in Latinx families in need of sociocultural assessment and congruent intervention strategies.

Suicidality and Latinx Girls

In 2005, Luis Zayas and colleagues published a signal article entitled, "Why do so many Latina teens attempt suicide? A conceptual model for research." That article emerged from Zayas' concern about the high rates of suicide attempts on the part of Latinx girls from various Latinx populations, as reported by different clinics, studies, and reports. For instance, YBRS data from the CDC (2000a) revealed a 19% one-year prevalence of suicide attempts by Latinas as compared to African American (7.5%) and NLW girls (9%). These suicide attempts by Latinas were also twice as likely to require medical attention as compared to their NLW and African American counterparts.

A couple of years later, the National Household Survey on Drug Abuse (NHSDA), conducted annually by the SAMHSA (2003), reported that approximately 283,000 Latina girls between the ages of 12 and 17 years were at risk for suicide. As would be predicted by acculturation theory, U.S.-born Latinas are at higher risk than immigrant Latinas, with suicide attempts peaking during ages 14–15 (22.6%), followed by 16–17 (17.2%) and 12–13 years (13.2%). The NHSDA also showed no differences by Latinx population, suggesting a national mental health disparity for Latinx girls in general. Based on such data and clinical experience, Zayas and colleagues developed a model to better understand and respond to this concerning problem.

Role-Captivity

Zayas and colleagues advance a theory of *role-captivity* in which some Latina girls come to feel trapped by overly rigid cultural mandates of *familismo* characterized by strict adherence to traditional gender roles, obedience to parents, and subordinating individual needs to family responsibility just as these girls are experiencing adolescent development with external pressures and need for greater autonomy and independence. These intergenerational struggles typically center upon choice of friends and outside activities, dating, romantic partners, emerging sexuality, and identity. Within such vulnerable family scenarios, suicide attempts occur in response to precipitating stressors such as an intense argument about not being a good daughter, hanging out with the wrong friends, or breaking up with a romantic partner. The probability of such a family crisis is increased by family dysfunction, often due to acculturative stress and economic disadvantage, that influences how *rigidly* parents engage girls struggling with a culturally patterned, bicultural crisis of *familismo*, autonomy, and emerging young adult sexuality and identity in the United States.

Support for the theory of role-captivity comes from several studies by Zayas and colleagues that compare and contrast the relationships of adolescent Latinas and their parents in families with and without a daughter that has attempted suicide. For example, Gulbas et al. (2011) studied 24 such families, while Zayas et al. (2009) compared 65 mother–daughter dyads in which a daughter attempted suicide with 75 mother–daughter dyads in which a daughter had not made such an attempt. Overarching findings and implications for intervention included the following:

> Based on a family-level analysis approach that categorizes relationships as reciprocal, asymmetrical, or detached, clear differences are identified: Families of non-attempting daughters primarily cluster in reciprocal families, whereas families with an adolescent daughter that had attempted suicide exhibit characteristics of asymmetrical or detached families (Gulbas et al., 2011, p. 317).

> Both mothers and daughters in attempter dyads report less communication and mutuality than non-attempter counterparts. Mutuality refers to reciprocity of feelings, thoughts, and activities that include mothers' capacity to be caring and an inspiring mentor. Small increments in one measure of mutuality were found to decrease the probability of a suicide attempt by 57% (Zayas et al., 2009, p. 10).

> Programs for treating Latina adolescents at risk for suicidal behavior should focus on enhancing the interdependent negotiation of parent–child expectations, particularly surrounding issues of dating, sexuality, and family responsibilities (Gulbas et al., 2011, p. 317).

Bicultural Expansion

Reciprocal families manifest mutually supportive family roles, expressions of care, togetherness, and *two-way respeto* between parents and daughter (e.g., supporting a daughter's choice in a romantic partner even if parents do not care for the choice). The latter represents a needed expansion of the core Latinx value of *respeto* that usually refers to how children are socialized to regard parents, elders, and authorities within and outside of the family (e.g., teachers, clergy) with deference, and not vice versa. Such bicultural expansion of Latinx values is needed to facilitate caring flexibility during rapid acculturation to U.S. society.

In contrast, *asymmetrical* family relationships stress commitment to the family and respect but primarily in a *one-way* authoritarian direction, often leaving girls feeling frustrated, voiceless, and excessively restricted. Impasses, distance, and resentment between parents and girls are frequent outcomes of asymmetrical relationships. *Detached* families appear to be the most dysfunctional, often lacking in sufficient care, support, and *respeto*, and in which authority is either missing or overly enforced through emotional and sometimes physical violence and abuse at the extremes.

As previously discussed in Chapter 7, supporting bicultural flexibility (e.g., *Entre Dos Mundos* intervention) in the Latinx family is imperative for mitigating excessive family conflict emerging from intergenerational acculturation gaps. This frames acculturation as the problem, rather than under-acculturated parents or over-acculturated adolescents, and stresses that adaptation to the United States requires new and expanded ways of practicing *familismo* and care for all family members. Without such bicultural flexibility, acting out role-captivity can result in suicide attempts as well as unplanned pregnancies on the part of Latina girls feeling trapped.

Sexual Reproductive Health

Teen Pregnancy and Births

Adolescent sexual reproductive health (SRH) continues to be a long-standing public health priority for its connection to unintended pregnancy and births, STIs including HIV, and several life-compromising consequences such as greater health risks for mother and child, less education and career choices for adolescent mothers, higher poverty and divorce rates for teen parents, unemployment, incarceration, and increased risk for IPV and child abuse (Berry et al., 2000; Evans et al., 2020; Franklin & Corcoran, 2000). Given such consequential scenarios, the need to understand recent improvements in adolescent SRH, as well as continuing challenges, is imperative.

With regard to encouraging trends, rates of teen pregnancies and births have been steadily declining for all adolescents in the United States—yet concerns for Latinx adolescents remain. As can be in seen in Figure 8.1, during the 30-year period between 1990 and 2020, birth rates for females

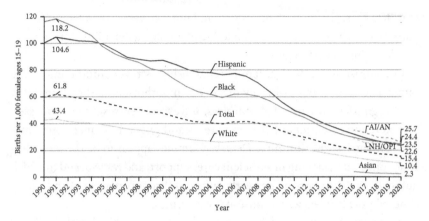

Figure 8.1. Birth rates for females ages 15–19, by race and Hispanic origin of mother, 1990–2020.

Note: AI/AN = American Indian/Alaska Native; NH/OPI = Native Hawaiian/Other Pacific Islander.

Source: Office of Population Health (2022).

ages 15–19 declined from 62 per 1,000 females in this age range to 15.4 in 2020, a dramatic 75% decrease in teen births over the past 30+ years (Office of Population Health, 2022). However, as can also be seen, this decline is most favorable for NLW adolescents (from 43.4 to 10.4 per 1,000) and least so for Latina adolescents (from 118.2 to 23.5 per 1,000), whose current rate of teen births is more than twice that of NLW counterparts.

According to the Office of Population Health (2022), the downward trend in teen pregnancies and births is due both to delays in sexual intercourse (i.e., abstinence) and increased use of effective contraceptives. Elaboration on SRH risk and protective factors is provided by the CDC's 2020 Youth Risk Behavior Survey (CDC, 2020a) highlighted in Table 8.2.

Risk and Protective Factors

As can be seen, Table 8.2 conveys a mix of encouraging and concerning trends for the recent decade between 2009 and 2019 with regard to SRH outcomes most disruptive to the lives of adolescents, their families, and communities. These data help explain the dramatic decrease in teen pregnancy noted by declines in the percent of high school students that ever had sex (from 46% to 38.4%), had four or more lifetime partners (13.8% to 8.6%), and that were currently sexually active when surveyed (34.2% to 27.4%). There is also an increase in the use of effective hormonal birth control (25.3% to 30.9%) between 2011 and 2019. However, disaggregating these data by race/ethnicity reveals continuing

Table 8.2. Progress at a Glance for Sexual Behavior Variables*

THE PERCENTAGE OF HIGH SCHOOL STUDENTS WHO:	2009 Total	2011 Total	2013 Total	2015 Total	2017 Total	2019 Total	Trend
Ever had sex	46.0	47.4	46.8	41.2	39.5	38.4	
Had four or more lifetime sexual partners	13.8	15.3	15.0	11.5	9.7	8.6	
Were currently sexually active	34.2	33.7	34.0	30.1	28.7	27.4	
Used a condom during last sexual intercourse[†]	61.1	60.2	59.1	56.9	53.8	54.3	
Used effective hormonal birth control[†]	–	–	25.3	26.8	29.4	30.9	
Used a condom and effective hormonal birth control[†]	–	–	8.8	8.8	8.8	9.1	
Ever been tested for HIV	12.7	12.9	12.9	10.2	9.3	9.4	
Tested for sexually transmitted diseases during the past year[‡]	–	–	–	–	–	8.6	–

LEGEND

 In wrong direction

 No change

 In right direction

Source: National Youth Risk Behavior Surveys, 2009-2019
*For the complete wording of YRBS questions, refer to Appendix.
[†]Among students who were currently sexually active.
[‡]Variable introduced in 2019.

YOUTH RISK BEHAVIOR SURVEY DATA SUMMARY & TRENDS REPORT: 2009–2019

disparities disfavoring high school students of color. For instance, while Latinxs and African Americans have only slightly higher rates of current sexual activity than NLW high school students (29.7%, 29%, and 27.5%, respectively), they report less than half the rate of effective hormone birth control use (18.2%, 19.7%, and 39.5%, respectively). While there are improvements in some SRH outcomes for Latinxs (i.e., increased condom use), greater understanding of risk and protective factors is needed to continue improving their SRH.

The Office of Population Affairs (2022) also reviews well documented SRH protective factors that adolescent programs need to assess and address as needed: at the micro-level, adolescents who feel engaged with school and do well, and that feel supported by their families, are less likely to have sex and become pregnant. Living with both parents rather than in other arrangements also protects against having a baby during adolescence. Family risk factors include having mothers with low education and a history of giving birth during adolescence. At the meso-level, teens multiply engaged in their communities (e.g., church, sports and recreation, arts, access to coaches and mentors) are less likely to engage in sexual activity, while those living in high-crime areas characterized by greater rates of substance abuse, violence, and food insecurity are more likely to initiate sex early and to have a child. Implicit in the above is the role of social positionality and access to resources and power in the prevention of SRH problems, as well as STIs including HIV/AIDS.

Sexually Transmitted Illnesses and HIV/AIDS

As can be seen in Table 8.2, data from the YRBS (2020) reveal low rates of testing for both STIs (9%) and HIV (9.4%) in high school students, which is concerning given the steady rise in STIs over the past few years that disfavors youth of color. For instance, rates of STIs in the United States (i.e., chlamydia, gonorrhea, and syphilis) increased from 1.9 million in 2014 to 2.5 million in 2019, with adolescents and young adults ages 15 to 24 accounting for half of these infections, despite comprising just 13% of the U.S. population (CDC, 2020a). In addition, STI rates in this age group are also twice as high for Latinxs as compared to NLW counterparts.

HIV

Fortunately, cases of HIV in the United States appear to have declined 17% from just under 40,000 cases in 2016 to 30,635 cases in 2020 (CDC, 2020b). While encouraging, this CDC report cautions that 2020 data collection faced disruptions because of the start of the Covid-19 pandemic. Further, these data continue to reveal disparities in need of diversified HIV assessment, prevention, and care. Men continue to comprise the majority of cases (80%), resulting primarily from sex between men, while women comprise 18% of cases, primarily from sex with men; transwomen are 2% of cases. Data by race/ethnicity show highest risk in African Americans (42%), comparable risk in Latinxs and NLWs (27% and 26%, respectively), and a low rate of 2% for Asian Americans. Data for the adolescents and young adult group, ages 13 to 24, show that they make up 20% of current cases of HIV infection in the United States and that Latinxs comprise a quarter of these younger age group cases. Hence, considerable need for HIV and STI prevention remains, and fortunately can be simultaneously addressed through SRH promotion and problem prevention interventions. HIV transmission by way of sharing needles can similarly be mitigated by substance use prevention and intervention efforts.

Alcohol and Substance Use

Monitoring the Future (MTF) is a long-term study of alcohol and substance use among U.S. adolescents, college students, and adult high school graduates through age 60, which collects representative annual data and is supported by the National Institute on Drug Abuse. While MTF data are available for 2021 and 2020 (Johnston et al., 2020), drops in substance use during these years are probably due to disruptions in data collection caused by the Covid-19 pandemic. Hence, 2019 MTF data most likely provide current best estimates of alcohol and substance use among U.S. adolescents. As such, these data convey that Latinxs in the eighth grade continue to have the highest rates of nearly all classes of illicit drug use as compared to their NLW and NLB counterparts, and that 12th grade Latinx students have the highest rates of several substances including cocaine, crack, crystal methamphetamine, and synthetic marijuana (Johnston et al., 2019). The same pattern of racial/ethnic group differences is also evident for alcohol use during the past 30 days, including binge drinking (i.e., 5+ drinks at a sitting) during the past two weeks.

While YBRS data for 2019 (CDC, 2020a) corroborate the above, they also convey important declines in adolescent substance use between 2009 and 2019: (1) from 20% to 14.8% for high-risk illicit drugs (i.e., cocaine, inhalants, heroin, methamphetamines, hallucinogens, or ecstasy); and (2) from 2.1% to 1.6% for illicit injection drug use. Misuse of prescribed opiates (i.e., codeine, Vicodin, OxyContin, Hydrocodone, or Percocet) has only been assessed by the YBRS since 2017, where it stands at a concerning 14%. Further, disaggregating these data by race/ethnicity reveals that Latinx adolescents report higher substance use rates than NLB and NLW counterparts with regard to high-risk illicit drugs (15.5%, 14.6%, and 14.2%, respectively); misused prescription opiates (16%, 15.3%, and 12.7%, respectively) and rates of illicit injection drug use, which is slightly lower than African Americans but three times the rate of NLWs (2.5%, 2.9%, and 0.8%, respectively). Hence, despite overall declines in alcohol and substance use among adolescents, continuing disparities disfavoring Latinx adolescents warrant better understanding and congruent interventions to mitigate this problem area.

Risk and Protective Factors

Over 20 years ago, Felix-Ortiz and Newcomb (1999) studied a broad range of substance use risk and protective factors in over 500 Chicanx high school students in Los Angeles, selected from well substantiated central adolescent domains: family (e.g., parental support and substance use), peer and community (e.g., peer substance use, availability of substances, tolerance for substances in the community), education (e.g., grades, aspirations), conventionality (i.e., obeying the law, religiosity), health and mental health (i.e., psychological distress, history of physical/sexual abuse, and suicidality), and beliefs about self and substances (e.g., self-acceptance, perceived harmfulness of substances). Substance use assessed included cocaine/crack, PCP, marijuana, inhalants, alcohol (beer/wine/liquor) and cigarette use during the past six months.

Interestingly, the pattern of results that emerged reveals that risk factors predicted substance use more strongly than did protective factors, but that protective factors *mediated* the relation between risk and substance use for both male and female high school students in this Chicanx high school sample. That is, at high levels of risk, protective factors predicted less substance use, while at low levels of risk they did not. This finding is part of a pattern in subsequent literature and is important because it conveys that protective factors mitigate substance use for Latinx youth most at risk. Thus, developing and reinforcing multilevel individual, family, peer, and community protective factors can help these adolescents cope with stressors related to use. Family and peer factors in particular have been a central focus of adolescent substance use research.

Family and Peers

It is well documented that family (and especially parental) and peer factors strongly influence alcohol and substance use. While hardly surprising, close examination of these central factors has only recently begun to be documented for Latinx populations in complex ways that deepen understanding and implications for interventions. For instance, Pereya and Bean (2017) tested a model of relationships among several influential factors, including conflict between parents, deviant peer associations, parenting behaviors (i.e., support, monitoring, coercive control), and alcohol and sub-stance use in 508 Latinx students, grades 9–12, from a West Texas school dis-trict. Students ranged in age from 14–18 years with a mean of 16 years, were from low-SES, two-parent families, and judged to be moderately to highly acculturated based on their enrollment in high school-level English courses (where they were surveyed) and low classification as limited English profi-ciency (2.6%).

Not surprisingly, results reveal that deviant peer associations are positively associated with substance use, but also that maternal (rather than paternal) parental monitoring is negatively associated with substance use and also partially mediates (i.e., mitigates) the relationship between delinquent peer associations and substance use. Unfortunately, results also show that con-flict between parents is associated with less parental monitoring and support, and more parental coercive control—the latter a risk factor for adolescent substance use. Also, deviant peer associations are associated with less ma-ternal monitoring and support and more maternal coercive control. Thus, while maternal monitoring is an important protective factor, it appears to be undermined, along with parental support, by parental conflict, resulting in greater parental coercion and deviant peer associations, resulting in substance use in participants. These model-like findings shed light on the dynamics of family destabilization related to acculturation stress, and behav-ioral risk in adolescents as detailed in Chapter 7, with specific implications for mitigating disproportionately high substance use in Latinx youth.

Practice implications include supporting parental, and especially ma-ternal, monitoring and support, by providing education about the role of pa-rental protective factors as well as the role of coercive parenting as a risk factor for adolescent substance use in addition to the influence of deviant peers. Addressing parental conflict is also highly warranted (e.g., in family therapy as described in Chapter 7), especially given its role in undermining parental protective factors needed to mitigate adolescent alcohol and substance use, as well as other risky behaviors including gang affiliation, addressed next.

Gang Affiliation

Readers interested in studying youth gangs must navigate a long yet lim-ited literature and sources characterized by classic sociological theorizing, a few small and local studies, occasional deep and insightful qualitative book projects, with law enforcement and government agencies (Department of Justice) asserting dubious expertise in the name public safety. The little that we know about Latinx gangs has come mostly from coverage of Mexican American street gangs that date back a century. While Puerto Rican gangs also have a long and concerning history, little coverage has been available, even in books about gangs in America.

Even less information is available on newer Latinx youth (i.e., Central Americans and Dominicans) who join gangs. However, as mentioned in Chapter 2, MS-13 was cast into national news by former president Trump's vociferous criminalizing of Central American immigrants and refugees as harboring gang members from El Salvador. The full story is that MS-13 originated in Los Angeles during the 1980s and spread to El Salvador courtesy of the Los Angeles Police Department's MS-13 deportation campaign. This is not to minimize the lethality of MS-13 to themselves and others, but rather to underscore ways in which our administration's and law enforcement agencies' frames, contribute to, and exacerbate gang problems rather than address the sociocultural roots and context in a more informed and productive manner.

While only a minority of Latinx youth become gang affiliated, this historically entrenched phenomenon has been a painful and destructive part of the Latinx experience since the early 20th century, ranging from multigeneration barrio-dwelling gang families to large groups and subgroups, varying in degrees of organization. About 30 years ago, Goldstein and Soriano (1994) noted that gang data are imprecise because no national level agency was responsible for its systematic collection. Further, gangs have loose sets and subsets that occasionally alter and change names, with a few disappearing on occasion. Using mostly local police and other criminal justice agency records, Goldstein and Soriano estimated 2,000 gangs in the United States with 20,000 members back in the early 1990s. They also noted that the age range for membership had expanded from 12–21 years of age to 9–30, and that the ratio of male to female gangs has decreased from 20:1 to 15:1, with increasing activity and autonomy in the later.

Since the above report, varying estimates of the number of gangs and related characteristics continue, including an accrual of information by the National Gang Center (NGC), funded by the Office of Juvenile Justice and Delinquency Prevention (OJJDP) and the Office of Justice Programs (OJP), both under the U.S. Department of Justice (DOJ). On its website, the NGC claims to "inform, equip, and train communities to prevent gang violence, reduce gang involvement, and suppress gang-related crime." This makes sense from a law enforcement perspective and in view of concerning trends described by Yablonsky (1997) 25 years ago: (1) increased access to more lethal guns and assault rifles; (2) greater availability of drugs; (3) increased interracial violence; and (4) increased multipurpose and sophistication of gang organizations and structures. While crime prevention and intervention are necessary, addressing the complex social problem of gang affiliation from primarily a criminal perspective is reductionistic and limited in the social theorizing needed to more effectively understand and address this ongoing social problem.

Gang Guesstimates

As described in its website, The NGC conducted an annual survey of law enforcement agencies between 1996 and 2011 to assess the extent of gang problems by measuring the presence, characteristics, and behaviors of local gangs in jurisdictions throughout the United States. In addition to aging data, gangs are also loosely defined in the survey as "a group of youths or young adults in your jurisdiction that you or other responsible persons in your agency or community are willing to identify as a 'gang.'" Survey respondents are instructed to exclude motorcycle gangs, hate or ideology groups, prison gangs, and exclusively adult gangs, described in the survey as characteristically distinct. While NGC attempts to document needed much gang-related data, it is worth keeping in mind that the goal of law enforcement is to prevent, intervene with, and investigate crime, rather than theorize about the sociocultural context of this vexing social problem. As such, the NGC's overly subjective definition of gangs, supplied to surveyed law enforcement, is vague and overly inclusive as reflected in the following quote from a participant in a study of Latinx students in an alternative high school:

> I think they pulled us over because my friend Jesus, he kind of looks like a *cholo* [gang member] but he doesn't. It's just the goatee that makes him look like it . . . And I was in a wife beater [white tank top undershirt] and right when I got out of the car they said, "What do your tattoos mean?" Just because I have tattoos on my arm. I bet you anything if they saw an old couple or something, they wouldn't pull them over. But it was two teenagers in a car looking like gang bangers with tattoos when they didn't even know us. It's alright though, it happens all the time . . . you get used to it after a while. (Cordova et al., 2014, p. 9).

With the above limitations in mind, the NGC survey estimates a national average of 27,000 gangs with 770,000 members, between 1996 and 2011, and over 30,000 gangs with 850,000 members in 2011, the last year of the survey. While dated and fuzzy, these data suggest a rise in gang numbers despite law enforcement suppression efforts. Over 92% of gang members are male, and most are 18 years and older, the latter increasing from a low of 50% in 1996 to 65% in 2011. With regard to race/ethnicity, law enforcement agencies report that gang members are 46% Latinx, 35% percent African American/Black, over 11% percent NLW, and 7% other race/ethnicity; and that gangs predominate in urban (41.6%) and suburban (25.8%) settings as compared to small towns (27.1%) and rural areas (5.5%). Regarding gang-related homicides, the NGC surveys conveys nearly 2,000 a year on average, or about 13% of the 15,500 homicides estimated by the FBI for roughly the same time period. Police gang units are correspondingly common within law enforcement agencies in urban (54.2%), suburban (34.8%), and small town (16.7%) locations.

Foundations of Latinx Gang Theory

The foundation for a socioculturally insightful understanding of Latinx gangs was developed in the pioneering works of scholars such as Vigil (1988), Morales (1992), and Moore (1980), who conceptualized gang affiliation as an extreme response to the extreme failures of family, community, and traditional social systems to meet the developmental needs of Latinx youth. Such youth are viewed as struggling with poverty-related risks linked to minority status, including histories of abuse and neglect within families destabilized by acculturative stress as discussed in the previous chapter. Resulting multiple vulnerabilities undermine healthy development and leave frequently neglected, abused, and traumatized youth with an epic struggle to meet their basic and essential needs (i.e., security, care, belonging, visibility, fun and play, status and power). However, trying to meet such needs without healthy cognitive and emotional maps of self, family, culture, and community, developed within caring and resourced families and communities, is fraught with danger and risk of seduction by street culture and gang-affiliated peers who are struggling with and acting out the same problem pattern.

Family Dysfunction

Belitz and Valdez (1994, 1997) build upon the above works by zeroing in on family dysfunction and the psychological crisis of adolescent and ethnic identity development under conditions of family destabilization and adolescent alienation from family, school, and larger society. These authors add that in immigrant families, parent and child role reversals (e.g., negotiating in English) and the low-prestige jobs of parents can create images of parents as weak and irrelevant in contrast to neighborhood gang members that appear powerful, confident, defiant, and aware of what's going on. In multigenerational Latinx families, the long-term effects of poverty and crime erode the healthy family functioning needed to guide youth through the task of identity development, including ethnic identity as discussed in Chapter 4.

Dysfunction can push youth outside of the family to struggle with exceedingly complex issues of belonging, identity, purpose, role, and power on the streets. The pull of gang culture with its defiant power, rigidly defined hierarchy, roles and prescribed activities for members, and symbols of group and cultural identity can be alluring for vulnerable youth. Gang-affiliated members invariably refer to their gang as their *neighborhood* and *familia*, to gang members as *carnales* or blood brothers, and to the *respeto* and sense of protection and security they are accorded as members. Members frequently adopt or are given caricature-like gang names (e.g., *Payaso* or clown, *Sleepy*, and the like.) as well as roles (e.g., soldier, artist, shot caller).) and use a mix of gang and Latinx symbols and images to project individual and collective identities (e.g., tattoos, graffiti, hand signs). Thus, the use of gangs to achieve personal, interpersonal and social, and cultural goals is considerable for otherwise marginalized outsiders, and suggests interventions that meet such basic, normal human needs and motivations in healthy, adaptive, and prosocial ways.

However, while gang members claim their "homies" as family and are capable of occasional displays of deep and genuine care, their distorted maps of love, *familismo*, and friendship typically limit healthy, supportive, and adaptive relationships. For example, in a rare empirical study of incarcerated Chicano and NLW gang members, Lyon, Henggeler, and Hall (1992) found that peer relationships were characterized by more aggressiveness and social immaturity as compared to non–gang member incarcerated youth. Chicano gang members also had more extensive criminal records and hard drug use than non-gang incarcerated counterparts. More recent studies of Chicano gangs in Texas (Valdez, 2007) and Latinx and African American gangs in Los Angeles (Leap, 2012) similarly details the dysfunction and interpersonal violence prevalent in adolescent and adult relationships of gang-affiliated males and females across multiple partners and children from various fathers and mothers.

Belitz and Valdez (1997) note that the following factors typically fuel gang-related family dysfunction: alcohol and substance abuse, interpersonal violence, and physical and/or sexual abuse of children and adolescents. The pent-up rage and violence frequently manifested (and valued) by gang-affiliated youth has many roots, including modeling and identifying with an aggressive and abusive parent, or street role models such as shot callers or *veterano* [veteran] gang members. The fact that Latinx gang member violence is primarily directed at rival Latinx gang members, who mirror each other in almost all sociocultural respects, may reflect deep-seated self-rejection linked to negative images of self and ethnic culture. Violence is also a way of creating real consequences to gang realities that members construct from their limited environments and resources. For example, while the role of protecting one's turf or *barrio* is at odds with lacking property ownership, the price to be paid for crossing the imaginary line is quite consequential.

To illustrate their theorizing, Belitz and Valdes (1994) offer the case study of 17-year-old Benito from an urban, barrio-dwelling, three-generation Chicano gang-involved family paraphrased here:

> Benito's father was dominating, aggressive, and physically abusive toward his wife and children. Growing up, Benito avoided, helplessly tolerated, and eventually imitated his father's violence. Benito loved his mother but saw her as weak and unable to protect him. School failure and disciplinary action at school resulted in hanging out with gang members and eventually joining a local gang of similarly affiliated peers. Benito took on the role of an extremely crazy or *locote* gang member with regard to alcohol and drug use, run-ins with the law, damaging property and fighting. Multiple legal and mental health contacts followed with frequent incarceration where Benito would be victimized by stronger, and would himself victimize weaker, incarcerated youth. Despite the costs, Benito considered his gang his real family and professed his lifelong loyalty and willingness to die for it. *Mi barrio primero!* [My gang-above all!] is a frequent claim of such gang members. For Benito, the gang was also a location in which he could claim his Chicano identity, albeit a distorted one characterized by a crazy, violent, defiant, high risk-taking male macho image.

Unfortunately, schools frequently exacerbate gang affiliation by implementing zero tolerance policies or exclusively disciplinary actions such as detention and suspensions, academic tracking and remedial courses, and alternative continuation schools, all of which serve to further stigmatize, marginalize, and alienate gang members from school and non–gang affiliated peers (Vigil, 1999). Outside of school, the over-criminalization of gangs, and suppression activities by police, further push gangs to the margins of society.

Law Enforcement and the Youth Control Complex
If you Google something like, "School police officer body slams young student to the ground," several links from across the country will emerge, often accompanied by viral videos. There is one of 12-year-old Janessa Valdez, a sixth grader attending public school in San Antonio in 2016. She is seen outside of class being grabbed by Officer Joshua Kehm, raised into the air, and body slammed face first onto the ground of the school as a chorus of onlooking students collectively gasp "Ohhhhhh!" Janessa and another girl were exchanging words when the so-called Resource Officer intervened to prevent a potential fight.

The image of Janessa lying motionless on the ground, and later claiming "I wasn't going to do anything" with a swollen face in subsequent videos captures a part of what Victor Rios (2011) calls the Youth Control Complex (YCC) now governing the lives of Latinx and African American youth. Rios' compelling theory describes how Black and brown youth, particularly in segregated low-income communities, live under regular surveillance and harassment by police, who increasingly occupy spaces in their schools, community centers and playgrounds, job sites, welfare offices, and so on. Under the guise of keeping communities safe, pervasive police surveillance in search of crime and gang activity, combined with zero tolerance school policies, results in youth being watched, followed, stopped for suspicion, provoked, and degraded. Police strongly encourage teachers, parents, and coaches to call them when youth are resistant or disruptive, rather than have caring adult figures intervene with reasoning, fair discipline, second chances, and the life lessons youth need as they grow up. Probation officers in particular often police their young charges at odd hours and at home, too often looking for violations that can send them back to juvenile facilities or prison.

The YCC takes particular aim at gang-affiliated youth such as those studied by Rios within the impoverished flatlands of Oakland, California, where Rios himself grew up gang-affiliated. In his deep three-year ethnographic study, between 2002 and 2005 Rios follows 20 Latinx and 20 Black youth whose risky gang-affiliated lives were regularly exacerbated by police and the YCC.

Embedded with the boys, Rios frequently experienced the harassment first hand, sharing stories in his book and many public presentations. For example, while they were standing in front of a liquor store sipping cans of Arizona brand iced tea, police pulled up on Rios and several of boys who were made to sit on the ground while they were questioned, searched, and had their cans of tea examined. Even on the UC Santa Barbara campus where Rios is a professor of sociology, he and several of the boys who were visiting were stopped by campus police who questioned their presence and ordered them off campus. University police also refused to believe that Rios was a University of California, Santa Barbara, professor.

When surveyed, 30 of the 40 boys in Rios' sample reported prior arrests; 22 had spent a week or more in a juvenile facility; 30 had probation officers; 14 had a parent in jail or prison; and 19 were gang affiliated. All 40 reported negative interactions with the police and rated their chances of becoming incarcerated *within the next few months* as four out of five on average, with five being highly likely. Because they felt treated like criminals, some reasoned, why not act the part and even reap the benefits of crime? While not adaptive, the latter reasoning provides some insight into the oppositional attitudes and behaviors that derive from stigma and provocation. Rios ends his book by advocating for a Youth Support Complex that provides care, resources, and opportunities to learn from mistakes—an experience more typical of youth from stable families. He notes that only three of the 40 boys studies had connections to healthy adult mentors, an important asset, outside of law enforcement and punishing systems.

Gang-Affiliated Latinas
Females have always been actively involved with predominately Latinx male gangs, but primarily as girlfriends of gang members, often mirroring distortions of traditional gender roles as well as pushing back against them. However, tough and autonomous gang-affiliated Latinas appear to be a growing population with potential for violent acts similar to male counterparts. Early interviews with *Cholas* from Southern California (Felkenes & Becker, 1995; Harris, 1994) found them to be very similar to *Cholos* in terms of why they affiliate with or join gangs, involvement in substance use, violence (e.g., fights, feuds with rival gangs), and other prized *loca* behavior. Girls interviewed had weak ties to family, school, and local community, and many had experienced significant abuse within their families. For example, Felkenes and Becker (1995) found that 41.2% of the 40 Los

Angeles-based *Cholas* interviewed had dropped out of school, and less than a quarter were employed either full or part-time.

In his book *Mexican American Girls and Gang Violence: Beyond Risk*, Valdez (2007) provides data and richly detailed descriptions of 150 Chicanas affiliated with 27 local male gangs from San Antonio's oldest and poorest Westside barrios. A rigorous mix of longitudinal qualitative and quantitative research methods yield very concerning empirical data, illuminated by personal narratives, of destructive entanglement in crime, violence, and alcohol and substance abuse. Valdez's research team began with trusted community members who spent months establishing rapport with and enumerating 519 girls affiliated with male gangs, from which 150 were sampled for this informative study.

The girls averaged 16 years of age, 9.6 years of education; almost a third had been expelled from school, just under half had been pregnant, 21% had children, and only 29% lived in a two-parent family, the majority residing with a single mom. Sadly, family member (parents, siblings) involvement in crime, alcohol, and substance abuse was considerable and frequently translated to serious physical and sexual abuse (i.e., resulting in police and medical intervention). These families also evidenced weak ties to community institutions (e.g., school, church, community based organizations or CBOs, political groups), deepening the vulnerability of the girls under study as detailed below.

With regard to delinquency and violence, between two-thirds and 95% of the girls had engaged in alcohol and substance use, fighting, and running away; 40% had committed more serious beatings and assaults, including drive-by shootings, grand theft auto (20%), and carrying weapons (12%). Over 80% reported male friends in gangs, 43% had boyfriends in gangs, and average age of initial affiliation with male gangs was 11.7 years. Such close and sustained affiliations spelled considerable trouble for the girls, with three-quarters having served time in juvenile detention/incarceration— three times, on average, generally beginning at age 14.

Three-quarters of the girls reported being in romantic relationships, over 80% sexually active, beginning around 14 years of age with problematic consequences including high rates of pregnancy, with a quarter having given birth and 16% reporting a history of STDs. As foregrounded above, relationships were characterized by extreme gender inequality and sexual exploitation. A few girls were "sexed into" gangs by submitting to several gang members at the same time, while others were similarly abused when intoxicated beyond resistance. Patriarchal narrative accounts by male gang members and affiliated girls alike blamed the above girls (i.e., "She knew what she was getting into." "It's her fault for getting wasted with those guys.").

Romantic relationships revealed significant sexual coercion (i.e., forced sex, or hitting for not submitting) and IPV. These violent encounters were precipitated by real and imagined jealousy ("I heard you were talking with some guy."), as an assertion of control (e.g., disobeying orders regarding how to dress, where to be, with whom to associate), and because of perceived disrespect (via arguing, facial expressions, embarrassing boyfriends in front of others). Instances of sexual and physical abuse are described in detail by the girls, regardless of length of relationship, with many remaining in such relationships consistent with the cycle of IPV.

While Valdez's study conveys an entrenched tangle of pathology in need of attention to strengths and assets, results are a sobering reminder of worsecase scenarios for Latina girls affiliated with Latinx male gangs and their struggles within *cholo* and non-*cholo* families, both destabilized by postindustrial poverty that can erode *familismo* when most needed. Maladaptive relationship dynamics, familial and romantic, reflect Latinx gang theory's emphasis on abused and traumatized youth, searching for care and belonging, without a compass. Such beginnings forebode negatively for the female and male gang-affiliated youth in Valdez's longitudinal study, which has generated followed-up reports underscoring unfortunate but predictable consequences.

In one follow-up study on 125 of the 150 girls, now women in their 30s, lab tests revealed an alarming 57% rate of herpes simplex virus type 2 (HSV-2), which is almost five times the national rate (Nowotny et al., 2019). The researchers attribute this extreme rate of genital herpes to its comorbidity with injection heroin use, hepatitis C, sexual violence, incarceration, and mental illness. Given the low use of sexual reproductive health services on the part of the women who tested positive for HSV-2, the authors recommend integrated behavioral health care (IBHC), including preventative care, for this multiply disadvantaged and vulnerable subgroup of young Latinas. IBHC can also provide warm handoffs to collaborating mental health specialists within the same health facility as described in Chapter 10 (Latino Health).

In another follow-up study of 40 gang-affiliated males from the San Antonio study, Valdez et al. (2018) report findings from in-depth interviews exploring how these men fare outside of prison, with an emphasis on relationships. The pattern that emerges consists of men with children from different women, current and former female partners with children from different men, and considerable difficulty trying to be good fathers/partners due to serial incarceration, lack of work and stable housing, and continued involvement in substance use and crime. In some cases, connecting with female partners engaged in crime quickly led to the same for these released men. A few were also able to connect with women with assets such as housing and employment, supportive family networks, and government assistance. While the latter sometimes compensated for the men's limited work options and lack of eligibility for government assistance, the majority struggled with "barriers to bonding and fulfilling parenting responsibilities" (p. 12), as well as with dysfunctional relationships reflected in this raw but revealing quote from the study:

> I think that's why a lot of my relationships never worked out. Growing up in a gang it was always, "Fuck that bitch. Don't let her tell you what to do. Never really let your heart hold too much. Don't really care for a chick too much." Stuff like that. I guess it kind of messed me up with women. (p. 9)

Addressing the Cluster of Psychosocial and Health Problems Over-affecting Latinx Youth

Comprehensive, family-centered, community-based, social policy–supported interventions, at multiple ecological practice levels, are urgently needed to address the clustering of psychosocial and health problems over-affecting, compromising the well-being, and frequently endangering the lives of our Latinx youth. The school site represents an optimal space for socioculturally sound prevention and intervention efforts with Latinx youth, beginning with one of the most effective deterrents to the interrelated psychosocial and health problems addressed in this chapter: successful engagement with school.

Scholastic Engagement, Achievement, and Adjustment

Regarding promoting Latinx scholastic engagement, achievement, and adjustment, Gándara and Mordechay (2017) advocate several overarching and proven effective approaches at multiple practice levels in order to promote general youth adjustment and mitigation of the clustering of psychosocial and health problems over-affecting Latinx youth:

- Strong magnet schools enrich curriculum and decrease isolation due to poverty and language. Relatedly, dual language programs that recruit half Spanish-speaking and half native English-speaking students with a goal of producing bilingual and biliterate students have been shown to produce exceptional academic results *for all enrolled students.*
- Counselors that can teach families how to navigate the education system, and help students understand both the demands and rewards of higher education, are critical to preparing students to graduate and go on to college.
- Funding for college in view of research showing that the primary reason why Latinxs quit school is to work and support their families, something they strive to do even while enrolled in college.

The Communities in School Model

An auspicious example of a scholastic intervention addressing many of the above multilevel needs is the Houston Communities in School (CIS) program that coordinates a broad range of child, family, and community services within the Houston public school system with the coordinated goals of increasing persistence, improving academic skills, decreasing delinquency, engaging parents/families in the education of their children, and preparing students for adult work roles. Now in its 40th year of operation, CIS operates its Integrated Student Supports Model to assess the needs of pre-K through community college students and their families in order to maximize school adjustment and success by providing three service tiers: (1) school-wide services for family and community (e.g., health fairs, career days); (2) school-based targeted programs (e.g., healthy relationship groups for girls; assertiveness training); and (3) individualized support (e.g., basic need provision, counseling services). Within each of these three tiers, six core services are provided: (1) individual and group counseling responsive to local problem themes; (2) academic support; (3) comprehensive health and human services; (4) hands-on career and college preparation; (5) parent and family engagement in child's education; and (6) extracurricular cultural and academic activities.

Students vulnerable to clustering problems over-affecting Latinx and other youth are identified and referred to the CIS caseload, while less vulnerable and well-functioning students are simultaneously invited to participate in extracurricular school activities as a way of mitigating program stigma and promoting needed and adaptive interaction between peers at varying levels of vulnerabilities. With over 400 public and private community partners, CIS functions as a broker for local community, city, and county-based services that partner on behalf of students on 140 school campuses.

Regarding impact, for the academic year 2017–2018, CIS succeeded in reaching 118,000 students through campus-wide events, over 33,500 through targeted intervention services, almost 6,000 with intensive case management, 859 home visits to promote family engagement, and almost 200,000 referrals to community partner agencies. Such impressive numbers translate to maintaining 99% of students in school with equivalent rates of academic improvement, grade promotion (K through 11), and an impressive 92% high school graduation rate. With regard to college preparation, over half of CIS engaged students go on to complete college.

Burt et al. (1998) describe a CIS program at Edison Middle School in a community known as "Little Mexico" that featured a "club" approach to attracting Mexican American students to fashion modeling, *Mariachi* [traditional popular Mexican string and brass band], and ESL (English as a second language) clubs. These clubs were found to be particularly attractive to gang-affiliated Chicanas such as those profiled in Valdez's (2007) study of San Antonio's Westside barrios mentioned above. The CIS program at Edison also involved 40 tutors from the University of Houston, two caseworkers, an alcohol and substance counselor, and a community youth service crisis worker. *Padres con Poder* [parents with power] was a program for parents designed to enhance parenting skills with special attention to Latinx family themes, as well as community substance abuse and violence prevention. Burt et al. (1998) also described a collaboration between CIS and county juvenile probation in which staff from both provide intensive coordinated student and family services to adjudicated youth. The school-based programs described above resemble what are called "full service schools" designed to address children-within-families-within-communities by consolidating multiple services within school settings.

Full Service Schools in Latinx Communities

In the informative book, *Full Service Schools: A Revolution in Health and Social Services for Children, Youth, and Families*, Dryfoos (1994a) describes school centers where health, mental health, and social and/or family services are co-located depending on local school and community needs. Dryfoos (1994b) also describes an impressive pair of "full service" schools in two Latinx communities that exemplify what is possible on behalf of Latinx students, families, and communities.

Dominican American Community

Dryfoos (1994b) refers to IS 218, a predominantly Dominican middle school in New York's Washington Heights, as a "settlement house" in a school, given the school's unique development and spectrum of school-based services tailored to the Dominican community. The development of IS 218 began with an extraordinary collaboration between New York City schools and Children's AID Society (CAS), one of the city's oldest and largest nonprofit social services whose budget of over $30 million was being used to operate 26 social service agencies (e.g., community centers, adoption services and foster care, housing for homeless, medical and dental care, jobs programs).

In the late 1980s, CAS began addressing the social service needs of Washington Heights, and during consultations with local school officials the idea of school-based community services arose. The timing was auspicious because the city was planning to replace outdated school buildings, and the new collaboration worked on an architectural plan to create a full service school that would be open seven days a week, from early morning to late evening, as well as during the summer. CAS simultaneously partnered with the community organization *Alianza Dominicana* [Dominican Alliance] by securing grants to train its staff to work in after-school programs in the new "Beacon school" (i.e., schools linked with community agencies). Grants were also obtained to address a number of issues articulated by *Alianza* staff and community members (e.g., mobile medical and dental care, program for disabled students).

After four years of planning, IS 218 opened in 1992 complete with a family resource center, medical suite, and security guards given the late hours. Social workers and community volunteers at the family center help with public assistance and housing, immigration and citizenship needs, crisis intervention, alcohol and drug prevention, and adult education (e.g., uniformed parents earn certificates in dental assistance). Salomé Ureña Middle Academies (SUMA) was named after the trailblazing Dominicana poet who in 1880 opened "Instituto de las Señoritas," the first center of higher education for women in the Dominican Republic.

Upon opening, SUMA served 1,200 students enrolled in one of four academies: (1) Math, Science, And Technology; (2) Business; (3) Expressive Arts; and (4) Community Service. Each academy consists of five classes and five team teachers who meet frequently with advisory groups, each composed of 15 students, to discuss career plans, school, and family problems and issues. After-school programs build upon the academies (e.g., business students develop and operate a school store that can involve family members and family business plans). There's even a Spanish class for local police taught by students and family members! Regular meetings between the school principal, the CAS director, and the superintendent of schools are essential to the administrative management of such a rich and complex venture. Interestingly, Dryfoos (1994b) noted that the school cost about $800,000 a year to operate, and that the annual cost per student of $7,500 was actually *below* what is spent on local suburban school students.

Today, SUMA is one of 22 community schools founded by CAS, all of which provide after-school academic and extracurricular clubs and activities, school and community-based health, behavioral health and dental services, parent and caregiver engagement in child's academic and social-emotional learning, and summer camps for 3,000 children each year. Regarding impact, 100% of enrolled children receive health and vision screening, food boxes containing affordable fruits and vegetables provided to families, and 60 children were placed in adoptive homes as needed.

While the overrepresentation of Latinx youth in resource-poor schools means that innovative school programs continue to be more the exception than the rule, programs reviewed in this section demonstrate the reimagining of schools as multipurpose spaces committed to supporting youth-within-families-within-communities in ways responsive to their sociocultural reality. Healthy outcomes include thriving engagement, achievement, and adjustment within school as an overarching protective factor along with specialized psychosocial and health care as needed—particularly in view of the need to address school disengagement and related problems such as depression and suicidality in Latinx adolescents, which is addressed next.

Addressing Depression and Suicidality

The seriousness of depression during adolescence is reflected in concerning lifetime (11%) and one-year prevalence (7.5%) of major depression disorder in U.S. adolescents according to the National Comorbidity Survey Adolescent Supplement (NCS-A) based on a representative sample of N = 10,123 teenagers between the ages of 13 and 18 (Avenevoli et al., 2015). The NCS-A also documents that Latinx adolescents are at higher risk than NLW and NLB counterparts. Fortunately, there is a robust literature on the treatment of depression in adolescents that documents several effective approaches that can be culturally tailored to the needs of Latinx adolescents.

For instance, at the University of Puerto Rico at Rio Piedras, Guillermo Bernal and colleagues randomized 112 depressed Puerto Rican adolescents into individual and group therapy formats of cognitive behavioral therapy (CBT), as well as interpersonal therapy (IPT), given their interest in comparing these two culturally adapted, evidence-based practices (Rosello, Bernal & Rivera-Medina, 2008). These researchers note ways in which both of these therapies are a good fit with Latinx clients: CBT is a didactic, problem-solving approach to mood management that reduces the stigma of psychotherapy; and IPT focuses on decreasing depression by improving interpersonal relationships in ways consistent with the values and practices of *familismo* and *personalismo*. Other cultural adaptations include making sure to meet with parents before, during, and after 12 weeks of treatment to convey *respecto* for their position in the family while fostering their engagement and collaboration with therapy for their adolescents, especially in view of stigma related to mental illness and its treatment as described earlier in this chapter.

Participants between 6th and 12th grades were recruited from public and private schools in San Juan, Puerto Rico, and results reveal that both forms of therapy, in either format, were effective in reducing depression, although CBT emerged as the most effective in reducing depression and improving self-concept. This finding is consistent with a recent review and evaluation of clinical trials for depression in adolescents between 1980 and 2020, which ranks CBT as the *preeminent* evidence-based treatment, IPT as *well established*, family therapy as *possibly effective*, and short-term psychodynamic therapy as *experimental* (Méndez et al., 2021, p. 1). Despite the lower ranking of family therapy is this review, *la familia* remains an advantageous site for addressing adolescent depression, especially in view of problems such as role-captivity addressed earlier.

Family Therapy
Given the central role of *familismo* within Latinx culture, as well as the role of family destabilization and dysfunction in the psychosocial adjustment

of Latinx youth, family therapy represents an advantageous treatment modality for any of the problems addressed in this chapter. As reviewed in Chapter 7, Latinx family therapists emphasize restoring stability, partly by expanding bicultural flexibility to better comprehend and cope with generation gaps exacerbated by acculturation gaps. More specifically, Falicov (2014) views the family therapist as an intermediary of family conflict tasked with reframing youth problems as the result of *nervios* [nerves] rather than being *mal criados* [poorly raised], and reframing family problems as "cultural transitions" in need of deeper understanding and remediation. Regarding depression, Falicov shares a case study that captures Zayas' concept of role-captivity addressed earlier and paraphrased here:

> Falicov describes a Latinx immigrant family in which a U.S. born 15 year old daughter makes a suicide attempt precipitated by her over-protective father's refusal to let her take a cross town bus trip to visit a friend that has moved out of the neighborhood. As Zayas explains, seemingly minor precipitants to a suicidal gesture signal the larger bind of *role-captivity* for many young Latinas. Therapy focused on helping parents to understand their daughter's struggle for greater autonomy in the U.S., while trying to be a good Latina daughter, and the negative consequences from this bind that are preventable. Simultaneously, the daughter was helped to see the positive intentions behind her father's strictness (i.e., protection from their high-crime, urban environment). Father and daughter were guided through a series of increasingly larger negotiations and compromises such as permission to stay out a little later provided that she call home to check-in, and permission granted to daughter to express her disagreements in a two-way respectful manner.

This classic example of *role-captivity* is remedied by bicultural expansion and flexibility in which the traditional value and practice of *respeto* is expanded bidirectionally, so that parents and adolescent daughter open space within which to express their typically caring emotions and intentions while also supporting the daughter's need to achieve the culturally adaptive hybridity that will enable her to better negotiate her bicultural reality as an emerging young adult in the United States. Without role expansion, depression and its many correlates, including suicidality as well as acting out sexually, can compromise the lives of Latina girls and their families.

Promoting Sexual Reproductive Health

An early review of teen pregnancy programs, serving mostly Latinx and African American youth, found that providing contraceptive knowledge *and* access was superior in increasing contraceptive use and decreasing rates of pregnancy, even though they had no effect on sexual activity (Franklin and Corcoran, 2000). Despite such results, only one in five of 32 programs reviewed provided contraceptives to adolescents, and programs designed to delay sexual activity were effective *only for young adolescents*. This latter point is imperative to understand if we want to avoid the common mistake of one-size-fits-all abstinence-only approaches to diverse adolescents, as was advocated through the George W. Bush administrations during the first decade of the 21st century.

Ideally, SRH promotion for Latinxs youth would include the prevention of STIs, including sexually transmitted HIV, and pregnancy; and such programs would be integrated into families, schools, and churches, given research demonstrating that stability in these domains protects against premature sexual activity (DuRant et al., 1990) and pregnancy (Baumeister et al., 1995) in adolescent Latinas. Moving in this direction is challenging for many reasons, including the Catholic Church's hard line on premarital sex and contraceptives, and the tendency for Latinx parents and children to avoid discussing sexual matters. Such conservative approaches need to better understand the current reality of problematic SRH in Latinx youth and the increasingly effective and creative ways to address it. For example, churches can continue advocating delaying sexual activity, especially in younger adolescents and less acculturated immigrant adolescents more responsive to such a recommendation, but would need to be more realistic about the social experiences of older and more acculturated Latinx adolescents if they wish to be effective in preventing unwanted pregnancies and births, as well as STIs including HIV. Further, given research demonstrating that Mexican American girls who discuss sexual matters with parents are less likely to become pregnant, interventions addressing *sexual silence* are needed to mitigate the well documented discomfort that Latinx parents frequently express about discussing SRH with their children (Baumeister et al., 1995). Fortunately, effective SRH interventions are increasingly documented for Latinx youth.

For instance, Evans et al. (2020) recently published the first ever meta-analytic review of the literature on SRH interventions for Latinx adolescents in which they synthesize findings from 12 rigorous experimental interventions designed to decrease behavioral risk and improve knowledge and self-efficacy, while also exploring the influence of parental behaviors. Results reveal that these interventions, which collectively included 4,673 participants, produced small but significant improvements in abstinence and moderate improvements in condom use, reducing number of sex partners, and improving sexual health knowledge, as compared to participants in the control conditions of the 12 studies reviewed. Evans et al. also found that the relationship between the interventions and improved outcomes was moderated by parental monitoring of their adolescent's peers, and that the eight culturally tailored interventions produced greater improvements than the four non–culturally adapted interventions, although no description of adaptations are included in this review.

However, Evans et al. did note that studies with moderate to large effects on SRH outcomes (e.g., increased condom use) came from evaluations of *Familias Unidas* [Families Together], a program designed to decrease sexual risk as well as alcohol and substance use in Latinx adolescents. A description of *Familias Unidas* by Prado and Patin (2011) provides insights into the effectiveness of this Latinx-specific, family-based intervention developed through community-based participatory research during which parents and other community stakeholders identified sexual risk and substance use as major concerns related to acculturation. Based on such preliminary inquiry, *Familias* is designed to support *familismo* and *respeto* by positioning parents as the experts of their adolescents' needs and development while also addressing acculturative stress as detailed below.

Familias Unidas consists of eight weekly two-hour multi-parent sessions, and four one-hour family visits to support implementation of knowledge and skills acquired in group sessions and to problem-solve potential obstacles. Group sessions utilize Paolo Friere's practice of *participatory learning*, which poses problems of concern to marginalized populations and generates learning through dialogue rather than instruction per se. Roleplays and other types of behavioral rehearsals enhance skill acquisition supported in the home. Elements of *Familias Unidas* are reflected in other effective Latinx-tailored interventions for mitigating problematic SRH outcomes, as well as alcohol and substance use.

Vincent Guilamo-Ramos has spent much of his career researching SRH promotion and the prevention of pregnancy and STI/HIV in Latinx adolescents. As such, he and his colleagues strongly advocate evidence-based parent–adolescent–provider collaborative SRH partnerships, as well as mass-media campaigns informed by best practices in health communication. For instance, parental communication about sex is effective when it conveys the clear expectation that adolescents should not have sex prematurely and teaches youth refusal skills if pressured to have sex, but also promotes correct and consistent condom use and effective contraception more generally, along with use of community SRH services including vaccines. Such communication is also most effective in the context of satisfying parent–adolescent relationships that feature parental monitoring and supervision of dating and peers, including older partners—all family practices that are shown to promote healthy adolescent SRH outcomes.

A recent study by Guilamo-Ramos et al. (2020) demonstrates the effectiveness of the above strategies in a randomized clinical trial to evaluate the effectiveness of *Families Talking Together* (FTT) with 900 families (73.4% Latinx, 20.4% African American, and 6.2% mixed race) randomized into either FTT or one of two other control conditions. Families in this study consisted of adolescents aged 11 to 14 and their female caregivers (mothers primarily) recruited from a community-based federally qualified health care pediatric clinic located in a low-income urban area with high incidence of teen pregnancy, STIs, and HIV.

FTT consists of a 45-minute face-to-face session for mothers, including health care provider endorsement of intervention content, printed materials for families, and a booster call to mothers from the research team. SRH outcomes evaluated are ever having had vaginal intercourse, sexual debut during the past year, and condom use at last sexual intercourse, assessed at baseline, three months, and 12 months post-treatment. Impressive SRH results at one-year follow-up include the following: 5.2% of adolescents in the FTT condition reported having had sexual intercourse as compared with 18% in the control groups; 4.7% of FFT adolescents reported sexual debut within the past 12 months versus 14.7% of control adolescents; and three-quarters of FFT adolescents reported using a condom at last sexual intercourse versus half of control group adolescents.

In addition to these impressive adolescent gains, parent–adolescent relationship gains for supporting SRH include the fact that at 12-month follow-up, FTT adolescents, as compared to control group participants, reported significantly higher levels of parent–adolescent communication about delaying sex, STIs and HIV, and using contraception and/or condoms. FTT participants also reported significantly increased maternal monitoring of SRH knowledge and behavior, including whereabouts after school, plans with friends, consequences of breaking a rule or previous agreement, checking in regularly, and being expected to call when late from an outing. These rigorously derived results, supporting Latinx youth SRH in socioculturally sound ways, illuminate flexible family-based pathways in need of continued implementation. Sidebar 8.1 describes the disparate impact of Dobbs v. Jackson on Latinas in America.

Sidebar 8.1. Supreme Court Ruling on *Dobbs v. Jackson Women's Health Organization* and Latina SRH

In view of the Supreme Court's recent ruling on *Dobbs v. Jackson Women's Health Organization* overturning *Roe v. Wade* and the constitutional option to obtain an abortion, the Latino Policy and Politics Institute (LPPI) at UCLA issued a report on the impact of this ruling on cisgender Latinas (Flores Morales & Hernandez Nierenberg, 2022). Using data from the U.S. Census Bureau's American Community Survey, the report concludes that Latinas will be disproportionately impacted, especially in states with restrictive abortion laws, because they are far more likely to be of childbearing age than NLW women. More specifically, the figure below displays the percentages of Latina and NLW Women of childbearing age (ages 13 to 44) in abortion-restrictive states. As can be seen, the percentages for Latinas is dramatically higher than for NLW women across all of these states. Potential negative consequences for Latinas include self-induced abortions, having no choice but to carry a pregnancy to term, mortality risk, and having to travel to less restrictive or no-restriction states. Policy solutions offered in the report include enshrining the right to an abortion in state constitutions, expanding federal Medicaid coverage, increasing funding for community-based clinics and state hospitals, prohibiting false and misleading medical advice from crisis pregnancy service centers for women seeking care for pregnancies, and protecting transgender and non-binary persons' reproductive rights. While all of these recommendations are politically charged, they are based on principles of choice and equity regardless of how derisively they are used by politicians to divide the country.

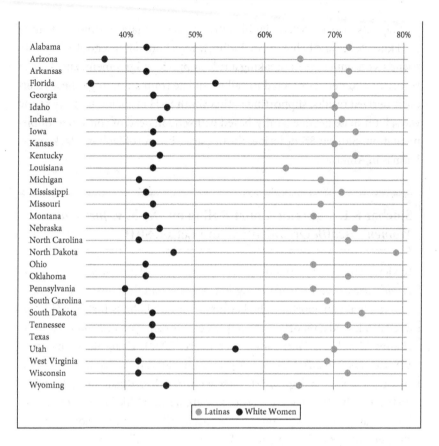

HIV Prevention

While the above SRH programs prevent sexually transmitted HIV, *Cuidate!* [Take care of yourself!] is an evidence-based practice that effectively reduced HIV risk when compared to a health-promotion comparison intervention, based on a sample of 684 adolescents, 80% of whom were Puerto Rican from the northeastern United States (Villarruel, Jemmot & Jemmot; 2006). Participants were recruited from community-based agencies and three high schools in Philadelphia, from 8th through the 11th grade (9th grade median) and 15 years of age on average. Over the post-intervention assessment periods (3, 6, and 12 months), *Cuidate!* participants reported significantly less sexual activity, multiple partners, and unprotected sex, and greater condom use as compared to control participants. Further, Spanish-speaking students in the *Cuidate!* condition were more likely to have used a condom at last intercourse and more likely to engage in safer sex as compared to Spanish speakers in the control condition.

Regarding content, both conditions involved a relatively short eight hours of small-group discussions, videos, interactive exercises, and skill-building activities delivered over two Saturdays, for several successive groups run over a six-month period. *Cuidate!* also integrated the importance of family, gender role expectations, and framed both abstinence *and* condom use as effective *and* culturally acceptable and effective ways to prevent HIV and STIs. In contrast, the health-promotion intervention focused on Latinx adolescent-relevant behaviors such as diet, exercise and physical activity, alcohol and substance use including cigarettes, with Latinx cultural values presented as an important context that supports positive health behaviors. This primarily HIV prevention intervention demonstrates effective SRH promotion approaches beyond family-centric interventions, hence broadening helpful options.

Addressing Problematic Alcohol and Substance Use

After decades of alcohol and substance use programs under-serving youth of color, enough Latinx-focused studies have been conducted and evaluated for the first ever meta-analytic review of the literature on culturally adapted substance use interventions for Latinx adolescents, published between 1990 and 2014 (Hernandez Robles et al., 2016). This review reports small (6%) positive effects on substance use outcomes at post-test, with larger (25%) effects at follow-up, across the 10 studies synthesized in this review, which collectively included 12,564 participants, ages 11 to 18 from across the United States. Review authors conclude that while *promising*, these interventions are only slightly better than non–culturally adapted substance use interventions, and that future studies need to improve upon methodological shortcomings found in the studies reviewed (e.g., high attrition, selection bias, rare assessment of acculturation, limited descriptions of cultural adaptations that deserve more attention).

Cultural Adaptations

Similar to cultural adaptations described thus far in this chapter, nine of the 10 studies reviewed by Hernandez Robles et al. (2016) report integrating cultural values such as *familismo* and *respeto* into to their interventions;

six modified intervention content (i.e., using ethnic actors, *telenovelas* or Spanish language soap operas); four provided interventions in English and Spanish, two modified service delivery (i.e., by including family members during recruitment, engagement, or retention of participants), one provided therapist/participant ethnic matching, and one Latinized the name of the intervention.

Interestingly, one of the 10 studies reviewed was a pilot study that found a culturally adapted version of group CBT to be equally effective as its non–culturally adapted equivalent in the treatment of substance use in 35 Latinx adolescents randomized to one treatment condition or the other (Burrow-Sanchez & Wrona, 2012). Cultural adaptations in this pilot study included adding a module on ethnic identity and adjustment to the treatment manual, changing hypothetical examples in the treatment to fit the experiences of Latinx adolescents, and increasing communication with parents to convey proper respect and keep them frequently updated about their adolescents. More specifically, results revealed significant decreases in substance use from pretreatment to 12-week post-treatment assessment for participants in *both* treatment conditions. However, substance use was found to be lowest for participants in the culturally adapted condition who scored highest on measures of familism and ethnic identity, motivating Burrow-Sanchez to pursue a subsequent larger test of their central hypothesis that culturally adapted versions of treatment should outperform non-adapted versions, a ubiquitous yet rarely tested belief.

Thus, Burrow-Sanchez and Hops (2019) recently published results of their larger follow-up study, comparing culturally adapted group CBT with its non–culturally adapted equivalent—this time with a larger sample of 70 Latinx adolescents, ages 13–18, meeting DSM IV-TR criteria for substance use disorders. Participants averaged 15.2 years of age, were 90% male, with almost two-thirds born in the United States to parents primarily from Mexico (74.3% of mothers and 81.4% of fathers). Three-quarters of these participants were court-mandated at the time of recruitment and referred by either probation officers (63%) or case managers (33%) from the juvenile justice system. These background characteristics convey precisely the vulnerabilities and negative consequences of Latinx youth urgently in need of socioculturally competent care.

Participants were randomly assigned to one or the other treatment condition and followed over four post-treatment assessments, with the last at 12 months. Impressively, results reveal a significant difference at the 12-month post-treatment follow-up, this time in favor of the culturally adapted group CBT (i.e., about 12 days of substance use during the past 90 days versus about 33 days of use for participants in the non-adapted treatment condition). Interestingly, there were no differences between the two treatment conditions (as with the above pilot study) during the first three post-treatment assessments preceding the *striking difference* at one-year post-treatment. This pattern of results suggests that treatment effects may become evident months following the intervention—which was an urgently needed scenario for the participants in this study struggling with significant substance use disorders and related legal problems. Such problems are even more evident in gang-affiliated Latinx youth in need of conceptually similar sociocultural understanding and care.

Addressing Gang Affiliation

Department of Justice Efforts

For years, Vigil (1999) has recommended use of schools as a base of prevention and intervention work with Chicano youth at risk for gang affiliation. While perhaps not exactly what Vigil had in mind, the DOJ, and more specifically its OJJDP, implements several gang-prevention intervention and *suppression* programs in schools and other community settings throughout the United States. Howell (2018) most recently reviewed these programs beginning with a description of their four-level approach: (1) primary prevention for all school children; (2) secondary prevention for high-risk students evidencing early signs of trouble (i.e., in school, neighborhood); (3) intervention for early gang-affiliated youth; and (4) targeted suppression for serious chronic and violent offenders. The following are specific programs for which Howell claims there is evidence of effectiveness, although little evidence is provided in the report:

- Gang Resistance Education and Training (G.R.E.A.T.) is a 13-week *primary prevention* curriculum implemented by police officers in middle schools that describes the dangers of gang involvement and teaches cognitive-behavioral training, social skills development, refusal skills, and conflict resolution. There are elementary school, summer, and family training versions of G.R.E.A.T.
- Aggression Replacement Training (ART) is a *secondary prevention* program for highly aggressive and delinquent youth consisting

of a 10-week, 30-hour cognitive behavioral program administered to groups of eight to 12 adolescents. Youth typically attend three hour-long sessions per week on self-management skills, anger control, and moral reasoning training. Howell notes that ART showed positive results when tested with gang-involved youth in Brooklyn, New York.

- Operation Cease Fire (OCF) Chicago is a community-level, gun-related violence prevention program that provides alternatives to violence when gangs and individuals on the street are deciding whether to engage in violent actions. Predominately formerly incarcerated outreach workers called *violence interrupters* operate on the street and in hospitals to mediate conflicts between gangs by focusing on individual members in the effort to stem the cycle of retaliatory violence. Outreach workers also broker services, assist with employment, acquiring a GED, and peer counseling and support.

While the above programs may do some good, they also raise concerns from the sociocultural perspective that drives this textbook. First, they represent a federal government *top-down* approach by the DOJ, whose primary purpose is to enforce the law and administer justice. As such, the programs are delivered by or with police in predominately Latinx and African American schools and communities, where police have mixed credibility and are subject to Rios's criticism of implementing a Youth Control Complex as discussed earlier. Further, the skills taught (e.g., cognitive-behavioral training, refusal skills) are focused at the micro-individual level and likely to be out-competed by substantial peer, family, and community risk factors as articulated earlier in this chapter. Hence, they fall short of more *bottom-up* community-focused interventions responsive to the sociocultural context of gang affiliation.

Operation Cease Fire (OCF) described above does represent a top-down implementation of a community-based collaboration between law enforcement and local community stakeholders, including formerly incarcerated gang interventionists empowered by their street credibility and motivation to help their communities. As noted by Leap (2012), such gang interventionists are a vital part of best efforts, but there is considerable variance with regard to how much they are trusted and supported by local police, city government, and even some gang members. Support for gang interventionists in the form of salaries provided by city government, foundations, and nonprofits is also quite variable.

Regarding the effectiveness of OCF, Skogan et al. (2009) describe multiple methods and analyses in an unpublished and long 461-page report. While it is challenging to assess the impact of an intervention such as OCF, the authors report findings from comparisons of the seven sites in Chicago where OCF was implemented with seven comparable non-OCF sites, over a five-year period. While an exhausting list of comparisons are described, estimates of killing trends reveal negligible results. That is, four of the seven comparisons revealed insignificant differences, with killing trends actually declining more in three of the non-OCF comparison sites. Of the three remaining comparisons, killings were down in *both* OCF and non-OCF comparison sites, and in only one of the seven comparisons were killings lower in the OCF site. Such results do not support OCF, and earlier evaluations of DOJ-supported gang interventions similarly convey little return on the efforts of law enforcement to address gang affiliation and related problems in Latinx and Black communities.

In their report, *Findings from the Evaluation of OJJDP's [Office of Juvenile Justice & Delinquency Prevention Program] Gang Reduction Program*, Cahill and Hayeslip (2010) present results from their evaluation of several gang-reduction programs (GRPs) implemented across the country. While this report provides few data points and does not appear to have undergone peer review (the standard in academia), it is an independent evaluation of the impact of the GRP on gang-related crime in four major cities. The report emphasizes the implementation process over results, but also highlights *promising* trends in crime reduction despite many bureaucratic challenges on the ground, such as DOJ pressure to implement programs rapidly, laborious subcontracting with partnering but competitive local service providers, and lack of sustainability once federal funds ran out.

Regarding impact, comparisons of gang-related crimes in high gang activity sites, with and without GRP implementation, revealed best results in Richmond, Virginia, as well as Los Angeles, the latter long considered to be the gang capital of America with decades of anti-gang police efforts. Focusing here on Los Angeles, comparison of the GRP implementation and non-GRP control sites revealed significant pre- to post-intervention declines—for *both* sites—for serious, violent gang crime and calls reporting shots fired, but with steeper declines in the GRP target areas. However, no declines were detected for calls reporting vandalism and overall gang crimes, including "serious violent incidents," which seems to contradict the reporting of less "violent gang crime." Again, such findings do not support the efficacy of the GRP, and the five-year follow-up evaluation concludes that *some* improvements continued in three of the four city intervention sites.

Overall, top-down bureaucratic DOJ interventions involve considerable expenditures of time, energy, and expense for minimal if any impact on gang violence and related harms to gang members and the public. While perhaps a positive departure from the historically predominant suppression-only efforts of law enforcement, alternative bottom-up, community-based, non-law enforcement efforts are urgently needed. Fortunately, we have a superb example/model in Homeboy Industries in Los Angeles.

Homeboy Industries: Radical Inclusive Community in Action

Master speaker, storyteller, and author, Father Gregory Boyle, founder and director of Homeboy Industries, Inc. in Los Angeles since 1988, recalls a brief encounter with a Latinx gang member who insisted that his *barrio* (i.e., gang) made him who he is. Father G, as he is called, replies, "No, it has kept you from being who you are!" Father Greg insists that it is goal of Homeboy Industries to return gang-affiliated and formerly incarcerated individuals to their real selves. Further, while gang theorists specify all of the characteristics of gangs that attract vulnerable youth, Father G emphasizes, often in horrendous detail, the severe abuse and neglect from which such youth are fleeing on their misguided paths toward gang affiliation. His many examples are consistent with those already described in this chapter.

The methods of rehabilitation are many at Homeboy (e.g., mental health counseling, tattoo removal, job training and employment, parenting classes, anger management, leadership roles at Homeboy and affiliated work settings), all unified by the lived Jesuit Catholic mission of being in community with those at the margin, the despised and demonized, until the margins and demonization disappear. Boyle and Homeboy staff—composed of *homies* given empowering opportunities to work—lead and practice what they call "radical kinship" or "boundless compassion" for those able to avail themselves to Homeboy's community, underscoring the frequent redemption-related reminder that "nobody is as bad as the worst thing that they've ever done."

Having buried over 200 slain homies over the past 30 years, there is no minimization of the devastation that gang affiliation can wreak among members, their families, communities, and larger society. There are life-correcting rules to follow at Homeboy (i.e., no substance use or gang banging, responsibility on the job, cooperating and supporting fellow homies, including former rival gang members) with which homies struggle. Yet, unlimited faith in each individual is expressed and demonstrated even if jobs are lost and some are asked to leave until they are ready to try again.

Homeboy holds that healing and redemption come from inclusion in a community of care and faith in these severely challenged men and women, versus the hyper-punitive criminal justice system that is largely a failure in rehabilitation. Participants in Homeboy's many programs receive the second and third chances they should have received from caring adults while growing up, and are reminded of their worth and ability to improve their lives, partly through unwavering acceptance and opportunity that many are experiencing for the first time in their abuse and trauma filled lives.

Rather than live out society's stereotypes of coldblooded psychopathic criminals, many participants come to revel in honest work and legitimately and caringly supporting their families, as well as brothers and sisters at Homeboy struggling with leaving gangs and incarceration, or the only life they've known and feel they deserve. Healing transformations, constantly on display in speaking engagements throughout the country and through Father Boyle's poignant storytelling and writings, are awe-inspiring, powerful medicine for a powerful problem.

With regard to cultural relevance, Boyle not only speaks fluent Spanish but also *barrio* slang, and maintains a wicked sense of humor, indispensable for connecting with the homies and pursuing his calling. Because most Latinxs are raised Catholic, Father G has always had a foot in the community's door. An estimated 10,000 come through Homeboy's doors each year as it continues to thrive and expand its operations. On the website, it says:

> Currently employment is offered for more than 180 men and women through a thoughtful, strategic 18-month program that focuses on healing just as much as it focuses on developing work readiness skills. Our overarching goal is to see individuals heal from trauma, allowing them to contribute fully to their family and community. The five key outcomes we strive for as an organization are: 1) Reduce recidivism, 2) Reduce substance abuse, 3) Improve social connectedness, 4) Improve housing safety and stability, and 5) Reunify families.

In her book, *Jumped In: What Gangs Taught Me about Violence, Drugs, Love, and Redemption,* gang researcher and UCLA professor of social work Jorja Leap (2012) concludes her deep ethnographic study of Los Angeles' Black and brown gangs by praising Homeboy as the model for effective, practical, and relevant gang intervention. In her evaluation of Homeboy's effectiveness, Leap documents a recidivism rate of 33%, or half that of our current prison system. Throughout the country, dozens of community-based interventions for gang-affiliated youth, frequently staffed by formerly incarcerated personnel, have taken Homeboy's lessons and Father Greg's mission to heart as they engage such youth in their communities, prosocial work, and relationships.

The hundreds of transformed lives, conveyed through testimonies and Father G's narratives, profound and moving, impress by touching the heart rather than by publishing the results of rigorous outcome evaluation studies. Father G seems to be less interested in researching or replicating Homeboy's effectiveness and more interested in its transformative powers, perhaps concerned that the former might detract from the latter (i.e., becoming overly invested in success via empirical analyses of data, as he has insinuated in his writings). This is similar to Aloholics Anonymous, which is bottom-up, community-based, and non-professional by design, coexisting alongside professional alcohol use disorder interventions and clinics. Such is the perhaps necessary tension between evidence-based professional practice that *treat*, and bottom-up community-based practices that *heal*, both of which are needed.

Family Therapy
Consistent with Homeboy, Belitz and Valdez (1997) begin family therapy for gang-affiliated Latinxs by reviewing each family member's unmet needs and trauma history with the goal to decrease blame and increase understanding of each other's behaviors within the family system. The goal of therapy is to reduce the gang member component of identity by teaching about healthy ethnic identity development. Gang-affiliated clients learn that alienation from both Mexican and American cultures factors into the push toward gangs as a way of compensating for lack of family stability and belonging, ethnic identity, and power. Such clients are also engaged in healthy prosocial activities and affiliations to displace the pull of gangs (e.g., community organizations, education programs at school, probation plans).

Belitz and Valdez (1994) discuss a case study in which two years of group, family, and individual therapy were used to help a Latinx gang member who joined a gang at 12 years of age following years of neglect by a substance abusing mother, sexual abuse by a stepfather, and being shuffled between the homes of mother and grandparents. At 15 years of age he attempted suicide after threatening to kill his pregnant girlfriend for breaking up with him. Individual therapy focused on processing childhood traumas, related vulnerability and rage, and behavioral consequences (substance abuse, gang involvement, suicidal and homicidal impulses). Simultaneous group therapy with other gang-affiliated peers focused on exploring adolescent "gang banger" and Chicano identities. Members were helped to critically examine how their *cholo* identities, *vato loco* [crazy guy] role models, and gang activities were used to cope with inadequate families, roles, and identities, as well as a way of venting pent-up rage. Consistent with an ecological model, members were helped to distinguish the attractive and harmful aspects of gang membership and to move into more adaptive roles and identities outside of the gang (e.g., acquiring a job, being a responsible father, helping the community). The client did not quit the gang for some time, but increasingly felt permission to move into other fulfilling roles. Family therapy included helping him to express his highly ambivalent feelings toward his mother (resentment for lack of protection, yet fantasy of being properly mothered by her), helping the mother to apologize while expressing appropriate concern about his gang involvement, and involving extended family in treatment to construct a more cohesive and supportive traditional Latinx family.

Supporting Latinx Youth Now and in the Future

The pernicious cluster of problems over-affecting large numbers of Latinx youth is unlikely to abate soon, considering the persistent parallel clusters of risk factors that undermine protective factors—vulnerabilities that have their roots in historical through current legacies of racism and subordination, poverty, and segregation, making acculturation more stressful than it need be. Emerging trends toward eco-systemically comprehensive, community- and school-based, child- and family-centered, culturally adapted prevention and intervention programs represent viable ways of addressing the formidable challenges of Latinx youth in America.

As asserted over two decades ago, Burt et al. (1999) refer to comprehensive, integrated youth and family services as "an idea whose time has come" and make several recommendations based on their early study of existing programs. At the individual program level, the most effective were those that worked with community stakeholders to identify gaps in the local service delivery network. Such agencies also evolved to broker services for clients and families, often by working in the gray areas between service boundaries that defined catchment areas, clients served, and particular problems addressed. Burt et al. also note that key players in this arena were successful coalition builders who often mirrored the ethnic and racial characteristics of the communities they represented.

Comprehensive community-based approaches—whether bottom-up or community-based collaborations with other human and social services institutions, including university-based researchers and community foundations—offer evidence-based as well as conceptually sound promising solutions to the cluster of psychosocial and health problems over-affecting Latinx youth that are detailed in this chapter. The recent growth in Latinx-focused reviews of the literature and rigorous evaluation studies of prevention and interventions programs, many culturally adapted, forebode well for continued progress. As discussed in the next chapter on Latinx health, IBHC is another excellent example of an evidence-based approach to co-locating and coordinating needed health and mental health services within the community, and in some cases within public schools.

References

Avenevoli, S., Swendsen, J., He, J.P., Burstein, M., & Merikangas, K.R. (2015). Major depression in the national comorbidity survey-adolescent supplement: Prevalence, correlates, and treatment. *Journal of the American Academy of Child Adolescent. Psychiatry, 54*(1), 37–44. doi:10.1016/j.jaac.2014.10.010.

Behnke, A. O., Piercy, K. W., & Diversi, M. (2004). Educational and occupational aspirations of Latinx youth and their parents. *Hispanic Journal of Behavioral Sciences, 26*(1), 16–35.

Belitz, J., & Valdez, D. (1994). Clinical issues in the treatment of Chicano male gang youth. *Hispanic Journal of Behavioral Sciences, 16*(1), 57–74.

Belitz, J., & Valdez, D. (1997). A sociocultural context for understanding gang involvement among Mexican-American male youth. In J. G. Garcia and M. C. Zea

(Eds.), *Psychological interventions and research with Latinx populations* (pp. 56–72). Boston: Allyn & Bacon.

Berry, E. H., Shillington, A. M., Peak, T., & Hohman, M. M. (2000). Multi-ethnic comparison of risk and protective factors for adolescent pregnancy. *Child and Adolescent Social Work Journal, 17*(2), 79–96.

Burrow-Sanchez, J. J., & Hops, H. (2019). A randomized trial of culturally accommodated versus standard group treatment for Latina/o adolescents with substance use disorders: Posttreatment through 12-month outcomes. *Cultural Diversity and Ethnic Minority Psychology, 25*(3), 311–322. https://dx.doi.org/10.1037/cdp0000249

Burrow-Sanchez, J. J., & Wrona, M. (2012). Comparing culturally accommodated versus standard group CBT for Latinx adolescents with substance use disorders: A pilot study. *Cultural Diversity and Ethnic Minority Psychology, 18*(4), 373–383. https://doi.org/10.1037/a0029439

Burt, M. R., Resnick, G., & Novick, E. R. (1998). *Building supportive communities for at-risk adolescents: It takes more than services.* Washington DC: American Psychological Association.

Cahill, M., & Hayeslip, D. (2010). Findings from the evaluation of OJJDP's gang reduction program. Juvenile Justice Bulletin (December). Office of Juvenile Justice and Delinquency Prevention, Office of Justice Programs, U.S. Department of Justice. https://www.ojp.gov/pdffiles1/ojjdp/230106.pdf

Centers for Disease Control (2000). Youth risk behavior surveillance—United States, 1999. *Morbidity and Mortality Weekly Reports, 49* (SS05), 1–96.

Centers for Disease Control (2018). Youth risk behavior data summary & trends: 2007–2017. 1–66. https://www.cdc.gov/healthyyouth/data/yrbs/pdf/trendsreport.pdf

Centers for Disease Control (2020b). HIV surveillance report, 2020, Vol. 33, 1–142. https://www.cdc.gov/hiv/library/reports/hiv-surveillance.html

Centers for Disease Control (2020a). Youth risk behavior data summary & trends: 2009-2019 (2020). 1–108. https://www.cdc.gov/healthyyouth/data/yrbs/yrbs_data_sum mary_and_trends.htm

Cordova, D., Cioful, A., Park, K., Parra-Cardona, J. R., Holtrop, K., & Cervantes, R. (2014). The role of intrapersonal and ecodevelopmental factors in the lives of Latinx alternative high school youth. *Journal of Ethnic and Cultural Diversity in Social Work, 23*(2), 148–167. https://doi.org/10.1080/15313204.2013.809510

Dryfoos, J. (1994a). *Full-service schools: A revolution in health and social services for children, youth, and families.* San Francisco: Jossey-Bass.

Dryfoos, J. (1994b). Realizing the vision: Two full-service schools. In J. Dryfoos (Ed.), *Full-service schools: A revolution in health and social services for children, youth, and families* (pp. 99–122). San Francisco: Jossey-Bass.

Evans, R. Widman, L., Stokes, M. Javidi, H., Hope, E., & Brasileiro, J. (2020). Sexual health programs for Latinx adolescents: A meta-analysis. *Pediatrics, 146*(1), 1–4. https://doi.org/10.1542/peds.2019-3572

Falicov, C. J. (2014). *Latinx families in therapy: A guide to multicultural practice* (2nd ed.). New York: The Guilford Press.

Felix-Ortiz, M., & Newcomb, M. D. (1999). Vulnerability for drug use among Latinx adolescents. *Journal of Community Psychology, 27*(3), 257–280.

Felkenes, G. T., & Becker, H. K. (1995). Female gang members: A growing issue for policy makers. *Journal of Gang Research, 2*(4), 1–10.

Flores Morales, J., & Hernandez Nierenberg, J. (2022). Differential rights: How abortion bans impact Latinas in their childbearing years. Latino Policy & Politics Institute. University of California, Los Angeles.

Franklin, C., & Corcoran, J. (2000). Preventing adolescent pregnancy: A review of programs and practices, *Social Work, 45*(1), 40–52.

Garcia, E. E. (2001). *The education of Hispanics in the United States: Raices y Alas.* Boulder, CO: Rowen & Littlefield.

Gerwertz, C. (2017). High school dropout rate among hispanics reaches all-time low, study finds. *Education Week's Blogs.* https://blogs.edweek.org/edweek/high_school_and_bey ond/2017/10/high_school_dropout_rate_hispanics_reaches_all_time_low.html

Gándara, P., & Mordechay, K. (2017). Demographic change and the new (and not so new) challenges for Latinx education. *The Educational Forum, 81*(2), 148–159. http://dx.doi. org/10.1080/00131725.2017.1280755

Goldstein, A. P., & Soriano, F. (1994). Juvenile gangs. In L. D. Eron, J. H. Gentry, & P. Schlegel (Eds.), *Reason to hope: A psychosocial perspective on violence and youth* (pp. 315–333). Washington DC: American Psychological Association.

Guilamo-Ramos, V., Benzekri, A., Thimm-Kaiser, M., Dittus, P., Ruiz, Y., Cleland, C. M., & McCoy, W. (2020). A triadic intervention for adolescent sexual health: A randomized clinical trial. *Pediatrics, 145*(5), 1–10. e20192808

Gulbas, L. E., Zayas, L. H., Nolle, A. P., Hausmann-Stabile, C., Kuhlberg, J. A., Baumann, A. A., & Peña, J. B. (2011). Family relationships and Latina teen suicide attempts: Reciprocity, asymmetry, and detachment. *Families in Society: the Journal of Contemporary Social Services, 92*(3), 317–323. https://doi.org/10.1606/1044-3894.4131

Hernandez Robles, E., Maynard, B. R., Salas-Wright, C. P., & Jelena Todic, J. (2016). Culturally adapted substance use interventions for Latinx adolescents: A systematic review and meta-analysis. *Research on Social Work Practice, 28*(7), 1–13. https://doi.org/ 10.1177/1049731516676601

Hovey, J. D., & King, C. A. (1996). Acculturation stress, depression, and suicidal ideation among immigrant and second generation Latinx adolescents. *Journal of the American Academy of Child and Adolescent Psychiatry, 35*(9), 1183–1192.

Howell, J. C. (2018). What works with gangs: A breakthrough. *Criminology & Public Policy, 17*(4), 991–999.

Johnston, L. D., Miech, R. A., O'Malley, P. M., Bachman, J. G., Schulenberg, J. E., & Patrick, M. E. (2019). Demographic subgroup trends among adolescents in the use of various licit and illicit drugs, 1975–2018. *Monitoring the Future Occasional Paper* (No. 92). Ann Arbor, MI: Institute for Social Research, University of Michigan.

Johnston, L. D., Miech, R. A., O'Malley, P. M., Bachman, J. G., Schulenberg, J. E., & Patrick, M. E. (2020). *Monitoring the Future national survey results on drug use 1975-2019: Overview, key findings on adolescent drug use.* Ann Arbor: Institute for Social Research, University of Michigan.

Leap, J. (2012). *Jumped in: What gangs taught me about violence, drugs, love, and redemption.* Boston: Beacon Press.

Lyon, J. M., Henggeler, S., & Hall, J. A. (1992). The family relations, peer relations, and criminal activities of Caucasian and Hispanic-American gang members. *Journal of Abnormal Child Psychology, 20*(5), 439–449.

LATINX YOUTH 301

Méndez, J., Sánchez-Hernández, Ó., Garber, J., Espada, J. P., & Orgilés, M. (2021) Psychological treatments for depression in adolescents: More than three decades later. *International Journal of Environmental Research in Public Health, 18*, 4600. https://pub med.ncbi.nlm.nih.gov/33926111/

Moore, W. J. (1980). *Homeboys: Gangs, drugs, and the prison in the barrios of Los Angeles.* Philadelphia, PA: Temple University Press.

Morales, A. T. (1992). Therapy with Latinx gang members. In L. A. Vargas and J. D. Koss-Chioino (Eds.), *Working with culture: Psychotherapeutic interventions with ethnic minority children and adolescents* (pp. 129–154). San Francisco: Jossey-Bass.

Nowotny, K.M., Frankeberger, J., Rodriguez, V.E., Valdez, A., & Cepeda, A. (2019). Behavioral, psychological, gender, and health service correlates to herpes simplex virus type 2 infection among young adult Mexican American women living in a disadvantaged community. *Behavioral Medicine, 45*(1), 52–61. https://doi.org/10.1080/08964 289.2018.1447906

Office of Population Affairs (2022). Trends in teen pregnancy and childbearing. U.S. Department of Health and Human Services. https://opa.hhs.gov/adolescent-health/reproductive-health-and-teen-pregnancy/trends-teen-pregnancy-and-childbearing.

Pereya, S. B., & Bean, R. A. (2017). Latinx adolescent substance use: A mediating model of inter-parental conflict, deviant peer associations, and parenting. *Children and Youth Services Review, 76*, 154–162.

Prado G., & Pantin H. (2011). Reducing substance use and HIV health disparities among Hispanic youth in the U.S.A.: the Familias Unidas program of research. *Psychosocial Interventions, 20*, 63–73.

Plunkett, S. W., & Bamaca-Gomez, M. Y. (2003). The relationship between parenting, acculturation, and adolescent academics in Mexican-origin immigrant families in Los Angeles. *Hispanic Journal of Behavioral Sciences, 25*, 222–239.

Rios, V. M. (2011). The coupling of criminal justice and community institutions. In V. M. Rios (Ed.), *Punished: Policing the lives of black and Latinx boys* (pp. 74–94). New York: New York University Press.

Rossello´, J., Bernal, G. & Rivera-Medina, C. (2008). Individual and group CBT and IPT for Puerto Rican adolescents with depressive symptoms. *Cultural Diversity and Ethnic Minority Psychology, 14*(3), 234–245.

Substance Abuse and Mental Health Survey Administration. (2003). National Health Survey on Drug Abuse (NHSDA). Retrieved from https://www.datafiles.samhsa.gov/dataset/national-survey-drug-use-and-health-2003-nsduh-2003-ds0001

Skogan, W. G., Hartnett, S. M., Bump, N., & Dubois, J. (2009). Evaluation of Cease Fire-Chicago (Document No. 227181). Office of Justice Programs; U.S. Department of Justice.

Solórzano, D. G., & Solórzano, R. W. (1995). The Chicano educational experience: A framework for effective schools in Chicano communities. *Educational Policy, 9*(3), 293–314.

Swanson, J. W., Linskey, A. O., Quintero-Salinas, R., Pumariega, A. J., & Holzer, C. E., III. (1992). A binational school survey of depression symptoms, drug use, and suicidal ideation. *Journal of the American Academy of Child and Adolescent Psychiatry, 31*(4), 669–678.

Vigil, J. D. (1988). *Barrio gangs: Street life and identity in Southern California.* Austin: University of Texas Press.

Vigil, J. D. (1999). Streets and schools: How educators can help Chicano marginalized gang youth. *Harvard Educational Review, 69*(3), 270–288.

Villarruel, A. M., Jemmott, J. B., & Jemmott, L. S. (2006). A randomized controlled trial testing an HIV prevention intervention for Latinx youth. *Archives of Pediatric Adolescent Medicine, 160,* 772–777.

Zayas, L. H., Bright, C. L. Álvarez-Sánchez, T., & Cabassa, L. J. (2009). *Journal of Primary Prevention, 30*(3–4), 351–369. https://doi.org/10.1007/s10935-009-0181-0

Zayas, L. H., Lester, R. J., Cabassa, L. J., & Fortuna, L. R. (2005). Why do so many Latina teens attempt suicide? A conceptual model for research. *American Journal of Orthopsychiatry, 75*(2), 275–287.

9

Latino Mental Health

A historical overview of Latino mental health research and knowledge reveals decades of early neglect, misguided and biased assumptions, followed by sporadic local community studies lacking in methodological uniformity given their focus on different Latino populations and various mental health problems in a variety of geographical locations. Fortunately, over the past 40 years, improved Latino-focused research has begun to accrue, initially as a trickle during the 1980s and acceleration during the 1990s through the present. Such informative research spans a broad range of projects including large local and national psychiatric prevalence studies, randomized control clinical trials, a vast number of quasi-experimental, qualitative, and mixed methods studies. Findings now elucidate patterns of mental health problems, correlates and contextual factors, *evidence-based* and *promising* practices for alleviating the suffering and dysfunction accompanying mental disorders that affect Latino individuals, families, and communities. Attention to intersectionality is also increasingly evident in the Latino mental health literature, with emphasis on important dimensions of diversity such as race/skin color and immigration status.

However, even before reviewing the literature, we should be able to venture a couple of informed predictions about Latino mental health based on the theoretical frameworks presented in Chapters 1 through 5. For example, given how stressful acculturation has been for most Latino populations, we should expect to find an inverse relation between acculturation and mental health, such that as time in the United States increases, across years and over generations, mental health problems also increase, especially those particularly sensitive to stress such as depression, anxiety, and alcohol and substance use disorders. Relatedly, we can also predict differences between Latino populations based on their unique acculturation histories and consequent acculturative stress and social positionality. Such predictions are based on acculturation for Latinos characterized by racialized minoritized status overly conflated with poverty, the latter inversely related to mental health in the United States and around the world.

Solving Latino Psychosocial and Health Problems. Kurt C. Organista, Oxford University Press.
© Oxford University Press 2023. DOI: 10.1093/oso/9780190059637.003.0009

With regard to acculturative stress, Puerto Ricans have historically been among the most impoverished and segregated Latinos in America, with Cuban Americans attaining SES levels approaching non-Latino whites (NLWs), with the social positionalities of Mexican and Central Americans located at various points between. Similar to Cubans, Central Americans are mostly relatively recent refugees but differ with regard to the frequent impermanence of their various immigration statuses and mixed support by the U.S. government. Most Central Americans also lack the predominant professional backgrounds and lighter skin privilege of most Cuban Americans, which results in the poorer, more segregated, and urban working-class backgrounds resembling Mexican immigrants. Dominican Americans, also one of the newer, smaller, but steadily growing Latino populations, are closer to Puerto Ricans in socioeconomic profile given their conditions of acculturation and more African-presenting features. Awareness of such general patterns of acculturation makes it easier to visualize the relationship between acculturative stress, as described in Chapters 1 and 2, and consequent risk for distress and mental health challenges.

Acculturation Stress and Mental Health Problems

There is a small but growing number of epidemiological, population-based prevalence studies of Latino mental health featuring methodologically uniform survey methods, including large and representative samples, carefully translated and adapted Spanish-language assessment instruments, measures of acculturation, and consistent diagnoses of mental disorders based on the *Diagnostic and Statistical Manual of Mental Disorders* (DSM). The first major surveys of Latino mental health in the United States were reviewed in the first edition of this book and are summarized below for the compelling story they began to tell when reviewed alongside each other. The punchline is that mental health declines with increased acculturation as predicted above, especially disorders with more apparent links to distress such as depression, anxiety, and alcohol and substance use. These particular disorders may exemplify the impact of acculturative stress on mental health for most Latino populations, whose stigmatized and discriminated ethnic minority status has resulted in lower social positionality (i.e., disproportionate poverty and segmented assimilation). More recent and vastly improved surveys of Latino mental health, selectively reviewed below, expand upon this unfolding story with greater complexity, insight, and implications for intervention.

Hispanic Health and Nutrition Examination Survey

Administered by the Centers for Disease Control, the Hispanic Health and Nutrition Examination Survey (HHANES) was the first major prevalence study of Latino health in America, conducted between 1982 and 1984, and included the following large samples of adult Latinos: 7,462 Mexican Americans in the five southwestern states; 2,834 Puerto Ricans in the New York Area; and 1,357 Cubans in Miami, Florida. The HHANES included a DSM-III–based assessment of major depression disorder (MDD), fully translated and administered in Spanish and English as needed. Regarding the lifetime prevalence of MDD, results revealed the highest rates in Puerto Ricans (8.9%) and the lowest in Cuban (3.9%) and Mexican Americans (4.2%) (Moscicki et al., 1987). The similar rates for Mexican and Cuban Americans were later explained by acculturation differences within Mexican Americans that must be assessed in survey research such as that illustrated below.

A follow-up study on the HHANES Mexican American sample found that symptoms of depressions were predicted by an "Anglo orientation," as assessed by being born in the United States, preference for English versus Spanish, and self-identifying as Mexican American or white versus Chicano or *Mexicano*, even after controlling for SES (Moscicki et al., 1989). The relation between depression and self-reported health in the HHANES was also investigated by Angel and Guarnaccia (1989), who also found an inverse relation for Mexican Americans but especially for Puerto Ricans who were rated by their doctors as less healthy that Mexican American participants were rated by their doctors. These findings underscored the comorbidity of health and mental health problems, anticipating the need for integrated behavioral health care as discussed later in this chapter.

Lee, Markides, and Ray (1997) used HHANES data to compare rates of heavy drinking (i.e., in excess of guidelines for safe alcohol consumption) and found greater prevalence in Puerto Rican (35%) and Mexican American (36%) men compared to Cuban American males (17%), with the same but lower pattern for female counterparts (15%, 17%, and 5%, respectively). Puerto Rican men and women also had the longest periods of past heavy drinking (Ms = 6.2 and 4.4 years, respectively) compared to Mexican

American men and women (Ms = 4.6 and 2.8 years, respectively) and Cuban American men (M = 4.4 years, and not enough Cuban American women to calculate years). Past heavy drinking was also related to current heavy drinking and various health risk factors and chronic medical conditions. For instance, Mexican American females who were past heavy drinkers had higher rates of smoking, depression symptoms, and chronic medical conditions compared to Mexican American women with no history of heavy drinking. This same pattern was found for Puerto Rican men for smoking and chronic medical conditions, and for Mexican American men for smoking.

In sum, the HHANES provided rare comparisons between the three major Latino groups in America, revealing a pattern of mental health problems consistent with their different acculturation stress profiles. Puerto Ricans were at highest risk, Cubans lowest, with Mexican American risk closer to that of Puerto Ricans but evincing a clear positive relation between acculturation and mental health problems.

Puerto Rican Youth

A recent longitudinal study on Puerto Ricans transitioning from childhood and adolescence (ages 5 to 13) to young adulthood (ages 15 to 29) demonstrates the link between minority status and mental illness for this Latino population. The purpose of this study by Alegria et al. (2019a) was to examine the relation between minority status and mental health in the South Bronx (N = 848) as well as in San Juan, Puerto Rico (N = 1,015). Based on longitudinal data from their Boricua Youth Study, results reveal associations between minority status and higher rates of lifetime and past-year generalized anxiety disorder, depression and anxiety symptoms, and past 30-day psychological distress, with a marginal trend for MDD, even after controlling for socio-demographic background variables. Despite greater poverty in Puerto Rico (43.5%) versus. the Bronx (28.4%), U.S.-based Puerto Ricans had worse mental health outcomes overall, a greater number female-headed households, and less residential stability during the past five years—differences underscoring the impact of Puerto Rican minority status in the United States versus the majority status of Puerto Ricans on the island.

An examination of several potential mediators by Alegria et al. (2019a) reveal that childhood social support and peer relationships partially explain the relation between minority status and mental illness, in addition to parent–child intercultural conflict, neighborhood discrimination, and unfair treatment in young adulthood. Minority-related stress reported by both youth and their parents (also interviewed in this study) also contribute to mental health problems, while healthy ethnic identity (i.e., pride, ethnicity of peers) is an inversely related protective factor. This unprecedented longitudinal study of Puerto Rican mental health corroborates many of the central tenets and predictions of this book project, aiming to convey psychosocial and health problems within the context of historical through current anti-Latino racism, stigma, and discrimination in the United States, including the destabilization of the family and related supports and protective factors during the acculturation process.

Epidemiologic Catchment Area (ECA) Study

Also during the 1980s, the National Institute of Mental Health sponsored the largest psychiatric prevalence study in America at the time (Robins & Regier, 1991). The ECA study was conducted with population-based probability sampling, stratified by catchment areas, in five major Americans cities, and included DSM-III–based diagnoses. The ECA included a representative sample of Mexican Americans from Los Angeles (N = 1,244), but Puerto Ricans composed only 2% of the New Haven ECA site.

Reports comparing Mexican American and NLW mental health are based on the Los Angeles ECA (LA-ECA) study that was conducted in 1983–1984. Although LA-ECA reports reveal comparable lifetime (Karno et al., 1987) and six-month (Burnam, Hough, Escobar, et al., 1987) prevalence of mental disorders in Mexican Americans and NLWs, important acculturation differences within the former were identified. That is, immigrant Mexican Americans had lower overall lifetime prevalence than NLWs (i.e., less MDD, obsessive-compulsive disorder, and drug abuse/dependence) while U.S.-born Mexican Americans had higher lifetime prevalence (i.e., more alcohol abuse/dependence, dysthymia, and phobia) (Burnam, Hough, Karno, et al., 1987).

Based on a scale of acculturation included in the ECA, Burnam, Hough, Karno, et al. (1987) found that acculturation was positively associated with higher lifetime prevalence of several mental disorders (i.e., alcohol abuse and dependence, substance abuse and dependence, and phobia) even after controlling for age, sex, and marital status. More specifically, U.S.-born Mexican Americans higher in acculturation had higher rates of the above disorders in addition to the affective disorders, MDD, and dysthymia. The fact that immigrants had lower prevalence of mental disorder than their U.S.-born counterparts is intriguing given their generally lower SES and the stress of migration and adjustment. A popular explanation for this finding is the *selective migration hypothesis*, which holds that Mexicans that immigrate to America are healthier compared to those who do not immigrate. In contrast, the *social stress hypothesis* explains the lower mental health of U.S.-born Mexican Americans as the result of their longer and generally stressful experience in America as a devalued, discriminated, and disproportionately low-SES ethnic minority group. The social stress hypothesis is more conceptually consistent with this book's earlier predictions about Latino mental health and is supported by a seminal study by Vega et al. (1998) to be reviewed shortly.

The National Comorbidity Survey (NCS)

The NCS was the first congressionally mandated mental health prevalence study, based on a national probability sample of adults (N = 8,098) that included representative percentages of Latinos (9.7%), African Americans (11.5%), NLWs (75.3%) and Other (3.5%), based on DSM-III-R–based diagnoses. Results published by Kessler et al. (1994) reveal generally comparable mental health profiles across race/ethnic groups, with Latinos evincing higher rates of current affective disorders and comorbidity, the latter term referring to diagnoses of two or more simultaneous mental disorders. Thus, the NCS was helpful in indicating higher risk in Latinos for comorbidity and affective disorders, the most common of which is MDD. Unfortunately, the NCS represented a step backward in failing to account for the role of acculturation in Latino mental health. That is, the NCS included only English-speaking (i.e., more acculturated) Latinos. The fact that about half of Latinos participating in earlier prevalence studies (reviewed above) elected to do interviews in Spanish underscores the enormity of this omission.

A decade after the NCS, the NCS-R (Replication) was conducted with a nationally representative sample of 10,000 in order to document trends in mental illness between these two national prevalence surveys. Overall rates of lifetime prevalence of mental disorders are very similar between the two surveys with slight variations.

Mexican American Prevalence and Services
Survey (MAPSS)

Fortunately, more inclusive prevalence studies on Latinos have advanced our understanding of the relation between acculturation and mental illness. Notably, the MAPSS was a landmark psychiatric prevalence study conducted by William Vega and colleagues (1998) that methodically illuminated the relationship between acculturation and mental illness for Mexican Americans. While not a national study like the NCS, these researchers conducted a stratified random sample survey of 3,012 noninstitutionalized adults of Mexican background from households in Fresno County, California. As with the NCS, DSM-III-R–based diagnoses were assessed, with the emphasis on more common disorders frequently related to stress: anxiety, affective disorders, and alcohol/substance use disorders rather than rarer disorders such as schizophrenia, which tends to have a low and stable prevalence in the United States and globally of about 1%.

In order to conduct a strong test of the relation between acculturation and mental illness, the MAPSS was designed to sample and compare participants from three different levels of acculturation: short-term immigrants (less than 13 years in the United States), long-term immigrants (13 years or more in United States), and U.S.-born Mexican Americans. Further, MAPSS prevalence rates were compared to those of the NCS, including its English-speaking Latino participants, as well as to psychiatric lifetime prevalence rates assessed in a Mexico City survey.

Like the NCS, initial results from the MAPSS reveal comparable prevalence rates between Mexican Americans and the general U.S. population (i.e., a lifetime prevalence rate of nearly 50% for any of the disorders assessed). However, and also like the NCS, this prevalence rate was only the case for U.S.-born and predominately English-speaking Mexican Americans in the MAPSS sample. In contrast, rates of mental disorders among immigrant Mexican Americans were about half those of the U.S.-born Mexican Americans, and closer to rates of mental disorders found in the Mexico City survey. Thus, a dramatic positive relation between acculturation and mental illness emerges from the MAPSS by comparing short- and long-term immigrants and U.S.-born Mexican Americans across all mental disorders assessed. For instance, examining "Any mental disorder" assessed in the study reveals a prevalence of 18.4% for short-term immigrants, 32.3% for long-term immigrants, and 48.7% for U.S.-born Mexican Americans, the latter rate nearly identical to that of the NCS total sample (48.6%) and slightly less than its English-speaking Latino subsample (51.4%). Also noteworthy are the roughly similar rates between short-term immigrants and the Mexico City sample (18.4% and 23.4%).

More specific results from the MAPSS demonstrate the dramatic positive relationship between acculturation and mental illness for categories as well as specific mental disorders when comparing short-term immigrants, long-term immigrants, and U.S.-born Mexican Americans, respectively: (1) any affective disorder (5.9%, 10.8%, and 18.5%); (2) any anxiety disorder (7.6%, 17.1%, and 24.1%); and (3) Any alcohol/substance disorder (9.7%, 14.3%, and 29.3%). Examples within these categories include MDD (3.2%, 7.0%, and 14.4%), agoraphobia (3.0%, 7.5%, and 11.8%), and alcohol dependency (8.6%, 10.4%, and 18%). Clearly, more time in the United States is related to increased risk for mental illness and disorders particularly reactive to stress.

Stressed or Super Mexicans?

With regard to interpreting the MAPSS, Vega et al. (1998) conclude that their findings do not support the *selective migration hypothesis*, given the roughly comparable prevalence rates for Mexico-born immigrants in the MAPSS and their *paisanos* in the Mexico City survey. Instead, the dramatic rise in mental illness with increasing acculturation allowed Vega et al. to conclude that, "Mexican immigrants share the lower risk status of their national origin, but acculturation has deleterious effects on many aspects of their health at the population level" (p. 777). In other words, acculturation may be hazardous to Latino mental health! But how so?

Vega et al. (1998) end their report with a series of questions addressed here. The first question is, "Why does socialization into American culture and society increase susceptibility to psychiatric disorders so markedly, what are the risk factors, and is this process generalizable to other ethnic groups?" A final question posed by Vega and colleagues is, "What components of Mexican culture are protective against mental health problems, and can these be conserved?" (p. 777). While addressing Vega's intriguing question requires ongoing study of the Latino experience, as reviewed in Chapters 1 through 5, their predominant experience has involved significant acculturative stress characterized by stigmatized and discriminated ethnic minority status, conflated with poverty, resulting in what has been called *segmented assimilation* or obstacles to social mobility under debilitating conditions that render a population segmented or stuck within their social strata or lower social positionality. While limited mobility is possible, the upward climb can be excessively prolonged for too many lives in the balance, across generations, decades, and even centuries.

Regarding protective cultural factors, much has been theorized and studied about close and supportive extended family systems as reviewed in Chapter 7. As a core characteristic of Latino culture, *familismo* is likely to be an important buffer of acculturative stress, racial discrimination, and the trappings of poverty. However, *familismo* is not invulnerable to destabilization and dysfunction under excessive challenges and too few resources, as demonstrated in the study below that begins to answer Vega et al.'s key questions.

National Latino and Asian American Survey

Regarding whether the relationship between acculturation and mental illness is generalizable to other Latino populations besides Mexicans, the answer appears to be *yes* as was evinced in the study conducted by Cook et al. (2009) reviewed in Chapter 7. It will be recalled that these researchers analyzed data from the National Latino and Asian American Survey (NLAAS) with its nationally representative sample of English and Spanish speaking Latinos (N = 2,457), surveyed in 2002-03, for lifetime and one year prevalence of anxiety and depressive disorders based on DSM IV diagnoses. This diverse and representative sample replicates the 2000 census profile of Mexican, Puerto Rican, Cuban and other Latinos with regard to age, gender, SES, and geographical location. As can be seen in Table 7.1 from Chapter 7, Cook et al. (2009) demonstrate that increased time in the United States is associated with risk of psychiatric disorders during the past year, as predicted for this diverse and representative sample of Latinos. More specifically, recent immigrants with 10 years or less in the United States had significantly lower rates of all psychiatric disorders assessed (10.7%) as compared to immigrants with between 11 and 20 years in the United States (14.5%), 21 years or more (17.1%), and U.S.-born Latinos (19%). Interestingly, these differences by acculturation disappeared after controlling for socio-demographic background variables, with the exception of anxiety disorders that remained higher for immigrants with > 21 years in the United States as compared to U.S.-born Latinos. Background control variables included age, gender, marital status, employment status, education and parent education, English proficiency, health insurance, and citizenship. Hence, these socio-demographic variables appear to mediate the relation between acculturation and mental disorders in ways that we continue to study and better understand.

Central American Mental Health

As described in Chapter 2, the presence of Central American populations in the United States today is rooted mainly in their historical need to flee countries of origin under the duress of civil war and subsequent corruption and violence, with adaptation to the United States frequently hampered by a mixed reception that includes frequent denial of refugee status and related entitlements, and due to limited ability to provide direct evidence of political persecution. The denial of political asylum and impermanence of immigration status continues to be a chronic stressor in the lives of many Central American families and communities threatened with detention and deportation (e.g., former President Trump's 2020 executive order to terminate Temporary Protective Status affecting over a quarter of a million El Salvadorans currently living in the United States).

Early studies of Central American community samples documented elevated symptom levels of depression, anxiety, somatization, and interpersonal sensitivity compared to American norms (Plante et al., 1995); higher rates of migration-related stress and depression (Salgado de Snyder, Cervantes, & Padilla, 1990); and post-traumatic stress disorder (PTSD) (Cervantes, Salgado de Snyder, & Padilla, 1989) as compared to Mexican immigrants. Subsequent research is scarce but continues to document significant vulnerability to mental health problems in recent immigrants and refugees now fleeing immense corruption and violence in Central America, especially the Northern Triangle countries of El Salvador, Guatemala, and Honduras.

A more recent study by Keller et al. (2017) assessed pre-migration trauma and current mental health in Northern Triangle migrant families settling into McAllen, Texas. Also assessed were reasons for leaving their countries and whether participants met criteria for legal asylum. Of the 232 adults interviewed, over 80% cited violence as a reason for fleeing their country, and a third of these individuals avoided reporting violent events to Central American police for fear of police corruption and gang-related retaliation. More specifically, a third of these participants reported that a family member had been murdered, and about half reported death threats toward themselves

(45.4%) or their family (51.9%). More common were threats of violence (other than death) directed at themselves (57.8%) and family members (66.2%). Not surprisingly, 90% of participants reported being afraid to return to their native country.

Of the 157 participants that completed DSM IV-based mental health measures, a third met diagnostic criteria for PTSD (N = 51), 24% for depression (N = 36), and 17% for both disorders (N = 25). Examining these mental health data against the criteria for asylum revealed that 70% met criteria: 80% from El Salvador, 74% from Honduras, and 41% from Guatemala. Keller et al. (2017) conclude that the majority of Central American migrants arriving at the U.S. border come with significant mental health symptoms in response to violence and persecution, warranting careful consideration for asylum status and mental health services. Given the significant needs of Central American refugees and immigrants, past and present, much more mental health research is needed to assess and intervene with Latinos from these countries.

Mental Health Service Utilization: Facilitators and Obstacles

It has been known for some time that Latinos have historically underutilized mental health services despite mental health needs that we now know increase with acculturation to the point of becoming equivalent to those of the general U.S. population. It is also now known that underutilization is due primarily to a number of structural obstacles, reviewed briefly in Chapter 6, as opposed to culture-related attitudes and practices, as is too often presumed. While excessive emphasis in the past has been placed on the latter, it is certainly worth exploring and understanding obstacles and facilitators to service use for Latinos.

Racial and Ethnic Matching

Underutilization has historically been true for language minority groups such as Latinos and Asian Americans. For example, over 30 years ago, Sue et al. (1991) conducted a major early study of the Los Angeles County Mental Health System and found that Latinos and Asians were underrepresented in proportion to their population sizes, NLWs were proportionately

Table 9.1. Mental Health Service Utilization Patterns for Los Angeles County by Major Ethnic/Racial Groups

Race, % (n≈3,000/group)	% Los Angeles County	% County Patient Population
Latino Americans	34	26
Asian Americans	9	3
Anglo Americans	44	43
African Americans	13	21

Adapted from Sue et al. (1991). Community mental health services for ethnic minority groups: A test of the cultural responsiveness hypothesis. *Journal of Consulting and Clinical Psychology, 59*, 533–540.

represented, and non-Latino Blacks (NLBs) were overrepresented (see Table 9.1). In addition to low service availability and accessibility, the low number of bilingual/bicultural mental health professionals continues to be problematic, especially in view of Sue et al.'s finding that racial/ethnic matching makes a difference for language minorities such as Latinos. Sue and colleagues studied the impact of linguistic and ethnic matching of therapists and clients by reviewing the mental health charts of 12,000 Los Angeles County mental health patients. More specifically, these researchers examined the charts of 3,000 Latino, 3,000 Asian, 3,000 African American, and 3,000 Anglo American mental health patients. Results revealed that linguistic and/or ethnic matching improved treatment outcome, decreased drop-out from therapy, and increased the total number of therapy sessions, but only for Latinos and Asians who were low in acculturation (i.e., recent immigrants, less likely to speak English, and less familiar with the mental health system).

Thus, the presence of bilingual and/or bicultural mental health professionals is important for the huge numbers of Latinos low in acculturation (e.g., immigrants) who benefit from such matching the most, as they confront increasing mental health problems during the acculturation process. Another continuing obstacle to seeking treatment is stigma attached to mental illness and its treatment.

The Persistence of Stigma

Misha et al. (2021) recently published the first ever systematic review of empirical studies assessing cultural aspects of various forms of mental illness stigma among Latinos, African Americans, and Asian Americans. Overarching themes that emerged from this review of both quantitative and qualitative studies included the following: (1) *self-stigma* is expressed in attributions of mental illness to personal weakness and consequent shame, resulting in negative coping such as denial and isolation; (2) *affiliative stigma* is strongly influenced by family experience that includes concealing mental illness and fear of both being a burden and extending stigma to the entire family; (3) *public stigma* arises from lack of knowledge about mental illness and specific cultural beliefs including perceptions of antidepressants as addictive on the part of Latinos, stereotypes of African Americans as strong and independent, and the value placed on work for Asian Americans; and finally, (4) *structural stigma* emerged from perceptions of mental health services as low in accessibility and quality (i.e., lack of responsiveness to the immigrant needs of Asians and Latinos; historical and current racism and disenfranchisement for African Americans). The authors add, "Further, these findings intersected with cross-cutting cultural concerns such as losing face by failing to fulfill lineage obligations for Asian Americans, wariness of reinforcing stereotypes for Black Americans, and dishonoring familial sacrifices for Latino Americans" (p. 21).

The above review included 27 studies on Latinos, from which several stigma-related themes and examples were examined separately. In addition to the themes of stigma noted above for participants of color, Latino-specific forms of stigma documented in the review include the following:

- The need to adhere to personal responsibility emerged as a major crosscutting theme, related to many types of stigma and leading to discouragement of help-seeking.
- Concerns about service cost and immigration status, as well as the double stigma of being Latino and mentally ill.
- Conviction that close others have negative views of mental illness and treatment (i.e., that it is a personal weakness, one's fault, and a source of personal and family shame). Fear of gossip and being perceived as *loco* results in concealment. Family members often discouraged depression treatment, resulting in delayed help-seeking, poor adherence, and efforts to cope alone, the latter especially preferred by older adults who also prefer coping within the family.
- Disclosing mental illness elicits mixed reactions from close others; *familismo* is both a source of support (i.e., recognizing symptoms,

reducing isolation, and decreasing psychological distress and stigma, encouraging treatment) as well as a source of disappointment and burden when the family endorses many types of stigma and discourages seeking help.

- Caregivers described being blamed for mentally ill family members, breakdowns of family relationships, social isolation from the community, and sacrifice due to the demands of caring (e.g., for those with schizophrenia and autism).

Studies designed to decrease stigma are very few in Misra et al.'s (2021) literature review, with only two—a brochure on suicide, and the use of a *fotonovela* designed to raise depression literacy in Mexican immigrant women at high risk for depression. The latter study, by Hernandez and Organista (2013) is described in detail below as an example of an effective socioculturally competent intervention to mitigate stigma related to mental illness and encourage pursuing treatment.

Somatization

Early research supported the widespread belief that Latinos and other immigrant and less acculturated groups tend to express emotional problems through their bodies (i.e., somatization) more so than NLWs, and thus seek help from medical rather than specialty mental health providers (Padilla, Carlos, & Keefe, 1976). The tendency for Latinos to somaticize is especially true for those lower in acculturation and for females. For example, Escobar et al. (1987) used the Los Angeles ECA data to compare somatization disorder in Mexican Americans (N = 1,242) and NLWs (N = 1,309) and found that whereas prevalence for men did not differ, the rate among Mexican American women over 40 years of age was higher than for their NLW counterparts. Somatization in Mexican American women was also found to be positively correlated with age and negatively correlated with level of acculturation. Further, looking just at women who met criteria for depression or dysthymia in the ECA sample, Escobar et al. found that about 50% of Mexican American women also met criteria for somatization disorder, as compared to 20% of NLW women. Thus, medical staff serving Latino communities need to be vigilant regarding the mental health needs of such Latino patients and screen accordingly.

It should also be noted that the diagnosis of somatization disorder is extremely rare (e.g., prevalence of 0.1% in the ECA study), partly because of the complex criteria required in the DSM. Thus, to better capture somatic symptoms in community and clinical settings, Escobar et al. (1987) developed an abridged index of the most common somatic symptoms, requiring only six or more symptoms for women and four or more for men. Using this abridged index, they found a prevalence of 4.4% in the Los Angeles ECA data in addition to the results just enumerated on Mexican American women.

Interpreting Somatization

It is worth mentioning the historically negative bias toward somatization related to Freud's conceptualization of it as a primitive defense mechanism used by those who are not psychologically minded and thus not amenable to psychotherapy. Here's where cultural sensitivity compels us to be critical of any perspective that pathologizes what may be a cultural difference. For example, some researchers have forwarded the idea that somatization may also be viewed as a culturally adaptive *idiom of distress*, of which the culture-bound syndromes *nervios* (nerves) and *ataque de nervios* (nerves attack) are well known Latino examples (Hulme, 1996). As idioms of distress, somatic symptoms communicate emotional distress in a cultural context rather than simply defend against it, but such meaning can be lost upon, and even devalued by, culturally insensitive practitioners.

In the author's mental health work with somatic Latino patients, he learned to emphasize that *pain is pain*, and that the distinction between mental and physical distress is a convention of the modern Western world that too often insists on dividing physical, mental, and even spiritual domains within people in the name of specialization. As such, it may be just as (un)fair to view modern U.S. and European cultures as "psychologizing" physical pain as it is to accuse less acculturated cultures of "somaticizing" mental and emotional pain.

Latino Folk Healers: Facts and Fiction

The Latino mental health literature frequently insists that we understand the importance of folk healers and practices such as *Curanderismo*, in the case of Mexican people, and *Santería* in the case of Puerto Ricans and other Caribbean peoples. Practitioners are told that the use of such folk healers is common, beneficial, and that practitioners should consider collaborating with these culture-based healers—huge assertions given the lack of evidence. Given that folk healing is now considered part of what's referred to as complementary and alternative medicine (CAM), pertinent questions that can be explored with clients utilizing folk healers include, when are folk healers practicing treatments that are complementary or alternatives to professional services and, most importantly, are clients benefitting or not from such utilization? While a substantial literature has accrued about folk doctors and medicine (e.g., in anthropology or sociology), there is very little literature pertinent to direct practice with Latinos that adequately addresses that question.

A study by Hoskin and Padron (2017) elucidates the philosophical framework and practices of *Curanderismo* according to eight *curanderos* interviewed for this small qualitative study. A couple of initial participants were referred by the director of a mental health service in Los Angeles, and subsequent snowball sampling was used to recruit the rest, meeting the following criteria: trained by a *curandero*, at least five years of experience, and practice during the past five years. Their philosophical framework is summarized as follows: (1) help clients heal themselves by attending to the spiritual root of problems; (2) assess client connection to elements of the universe; (3) bring individuals back into balance; and (4) assess the body to trace back the origins of presumed trauma. Practice themes that emerged included holistic attention to emotional, physical, and spiritual dimensions; reading and using body energy; *curandero* self-spiritual practice in order to be an instrument between the natural and supernatural; and not charging for services. More specifically, the *curanderos* identified with providing at least one, and often several, of the following treatments: *yerberos* heal through herbs, *sobadores* heal through touch and massage, *parteros* are midwives in the birthing process; *hueseros* are bonesetters, and *espíritus* call upon the supernatural to heal clients. The *curanderos* shared treating virtually any malaise presented by clients, and frequently using prayer and *pláticas* (talks), *sobadas* (massage), and other rituals such as chanting and using drums, rattles, and burning *copal* (Nahuatl term for incense made from resin).

While Hoskin and Padron claim that as many as 84% of Latinos use *curanderos*, early research does not support widespread utilization and clearly does not support its use as an alternative to formal health and mental health services. For example, in the MAPPS study described earlier, Vega et al. (1998) assessed mental health service utilization in an epidemiological survey of 3,012 Mexican Americans in Fresno County, California, and found that only 3% of the 508 participants who met criteria for one or more psychiatric diagnoses during the prior year had used "informal help," including *curanderos*. Similarly, Higginbotham, Treviño, and Ray (1990) found that only 4.2% of 3,623 southwestern Chicanos reported consulting a *curandero*, *yerbero*, or other folk healer during the prior year.

The limited utilization of folk doctors documented above was predicted by low income and dissatisfaction with conventional medical services recently received, suggesting use of *curanderos* as perhaps a secondary source for the few that utilize it. Finally, an early survey of 666 Chicanos from Los Angeles found that only 2% had consulted a folk healer or *curandero* for emotional problems during the prior year, and only 8% had ever done so in their life time (Padilla et al., 1976). When these participants were asked who is the first person they would recommend to someone with an emotional problem, 0% indicated a *curandero* as opposed to a doctor (25%), relative or *compadre* (20%), priest (17%), friend (14%), mental health clinic (14%), or psychiatrist or counselor (9%).

Despite the above data, the Latino mental health literature continues to insist on the pervasive use of folk healers as a valid culture-based alternative to professional health care, without evidence or critical examination of such practices and benefits (e.g., Harris et al., 2004). It may be that folk healer use in Latinos is similar to the utilization of astrologists, fortune tellers, or even witchcraft on the part of very few NLWs: a real yet small number and with unknown impact. While more research is needed to better capture who *curanderos* are, what they do, and to assess effectiveness, we need to remain aware of CAM while continuing to promote accessible, affordable, and socioculturally effective services such as the integrated behavioral health movement discussed below.

Hopefully, more scholarly research will continue to clarify culture-based folk doctors and medicine as CAM. For example, Becerra and Iglehart (1995) conducted a fascinating study of folk medicine and home remedies in an urban Los Angeles sample of nearly 500 participants from public housing projects in the downtown Chinatown area. The sample was almost evenly divided among Mexican, African, Anglo, and Chinese Americans. Results revealed that (a) all racial/ethnic groups used folk medicine and home remedies; (b) such practices were *complementary* to conventional health care; and (c) folk medicine remedies were used primarily for minor illnesses or to prevent major illnesses, but not to treat chronic illnesses such as diabetes.

Compared to non-users, folk medicine users were found to use *more* self-care strategies in general, suggesting that use of folk medicine may simply reflect part of a more expansive range of health behaviors.

Unfortunately, comparable survey data on use of Caribbean folk doctors do not appear to exist, although we might also expect low use of *santeros* (Caribbean folk healers practicing *Santería*) in Latinos of higher SES (e.g., Cuban Americans whose higher SES affords them more rapid acculturation and high levels of health insurance and access to care). With regard to Puerto Ricans, much descriptive literature has noted their use of *Santería*, but with little detail or critical inquiry.

Selective Review of Effective Mental Health Care with Latinos

The above review of the prevalence of mental disorders in various Latino populations makes clear the compelling link between acculturative stress rooted in challenging histories, ethnic minority status, and poverty, and hence the need for socioculturally responsive mental health assessment and services. Fortunately, we are witnessing the accrual of considerable empirical research illuminating best practices for Latinos for several mental health problems. With the sociocultural practice model presented in Chapter 6 as a guide, we can also better evaluate the promise of outcome evaluations reviewed below, many of which fall under the broad category of community-based approaches.

Community-based Approaches

Pioneers in minority mental health have long advocated community-based approaches to more comprehensively address the needs of racial and ethnic minority groups, given that such interventions strive to integrate many different sectors and services in order to address multiple related problems with the goal of illness prevention and treatment and health promotion. To be effective, community-based approaches must be responsive to the cultural and social realities and related needs of Latinos by hiring bilingual/bicultural providers, including *promotores de salud* [lay health promoters] that expand both the reach of needed services and workforce. Empowering clients and communities also involves community-based services that share service-related power and control (e.g., through community advisory boards, client input, and other forms of accountability reviewed in this book's practice model). While this book's first edition concludes that the literature was limited to descriptions of community-based approaches void of outcome evaluation, a recent review reveals auspicious outcomes alongside continuing challenges to providing urgently needed community-based health and mental health services.

Castillo et al. (2019) review the literature on community-based interventions seeking to promote mental health and social equity by involving multi-service partnerships, actively engaging community members, and attempting to be mindful of the social ecological context of health and mental health problems. Several problem areas were covered in the review, including some especially relevant to this chapter such as the need for school-based interventions for youth and integrated behavioral health care (IBHC) for communities. In fact, IBHC, which mainly serves low-income and minority clients, emerged from Castillo et al.'s (2019) review as one of the most rigorously evaluated and effective community-based interventions for the treatment of depression. Castillo and colleagues also highlighted a review of lay health worker (LHW) interventions, showing that they elevate demand for needed services by increasing awareness, mental health literacy, and reducing barriers to care such as stigma. LHW interventions also increase the supply of services in under-resourced areas by enlarging the workforce of culturally effective providers.

Not included in the Castillo et al. (2019) review is a noteworthy study by Alegria et al. (2019b) that evaluated a community-based approach to multiple mental health symptoms in Latino immigrants in both the United States and Spain, the latter an increasingly popular migration destination. Adult participants (ages 18 to 70) were recruited from 17 primary care clinics or emergency departments and 24 Latino serving community-based organizations in Boston, Massachusetts, as well as in Madrid and Barcelona, Spain. Participants were randomized into either an enhanced treatment as usual control condition (N = 169) or the IIDEA (Integrated Intervention for Dual Problems and Early Action) intervention condition (N = 172), the latter a 10-week manualized treatment that integrates cognitive behavioral therapy, motivational interviewing, and mindfulness practice to address substance misuse (e.g., strategies for reducing cravings, preventing relapse, strengthening coping skills), and concluding with the creation of a self-care plan, practice of learned skills, and booster sessions as needed. IIDEA was delivered in the participants' preferred language and offered at home if there were child care or illness constraints. In contrast, treatment as usual received in primary care was enhanced by visits from a research team member checking in with participants every three weeks for six months in order to conduct assessments and to monitor health and well-being of participants and to refer them for extra care as needed.

At six-month follow-up evaluation, participants in the IIDEAs condition had significantly lower symptoms of depression, anxiety, and PTSD—improvements that were especially pronounced for participants with moderate to severe pre-intervention symptoms. While no between-group differences were found for alcohol and substance misuse, subsequent exploratory analyses found that IIDEA was effective for patients whose pre-intervention drug misuse was moderate to severe as assessed by urine drug test results. This study is noteworthy for its implementation of a transdiagnostic intervention to address a broad range of co-occurring mental health problems that rise during the acculturation of Latino immigrants. Further, Latino immigrants in two different host countries benefited from the IIDEA intervention. Both the broad treatment approach and cluster of mental health problems targeted is highly consistent with the IBHC approach highlighted next.

Integrated Behavioral Health Care

IBHC is a health care model of service delivery that seeks to reduce stigma and promote access and utilization by co-locating and coordinating health and mental health services in the heart of Latino and other low-income and minority communities. In addition to having bilingual staff, IBHC routinely screens broadly for psychosocial and health problems (e.g., interpersonal violence and other trauma) and addresses frequently comorbid conditions (diabetes and depression, heart disease and anxiety) in client and family centered ways that promote needed healthy lifestyle changes.

An article by Bridges et al. (2014), entitled "Does integrated behavioral health care reduce mental health disparities for Latinos? Initial findings," explored whether IBHC service referrals, utilization, and outcomes were comparable for Latinos and NLW primary care patients. Data were collected from just under 800 consecutive patients, two-thirds of whom were Latino with a mean age of 29, a third under 18 years of age, 65.3% female, and well over half of whom were uninsured. These clients were seen for behavioral health services in two primary care clinics during a 10.5-month period. The most common presenting problems were depression (21.6%), anxiety (18.5%), adjustment disorder (13.0%), and externalizing behavior problems (9.8%). As compared to NLW clients, Latinos had significantly lower self-reported psychiatric distress, higher clinician-rated global functioning, and fewer psychiatric diagnoses at initial visit. With regard to mental health treatment, both Latinos and NLWs had comparable service utilization rates, clinically significant improvements in symptoms, and high satisfaction with IBHC. These early findings suggest that integrating behavioral health services into primary care clinics helps to better address pressing Latino mental health needs.

During the past decade, an increasing number of rigorous outcome evaluation studies have demonstrated impressive health and mental health benefits to low-income Latinos—particularly in much needed care for depression and diabetes, addressed separately as well as together. For instance, Ell et al. (2010) conducted a randomized controlled trial (RCT) of 387 diabetic patients (96.5% Hispanic) with clinically significant depression, recruited from two public safety-net clinics in East Los Angeles and followed for 18 months (August 2005 to July 2007). The intervention condition included problem-solving therapy and/or antidepressant medication, based on a stepped-care algorithm that steps up treatment intensity as needed. Clients are also provided with their first choice of treatment options, telephone-facilitated treatment response monitoring, adherence support, relapse prevention follow-up over 12 months, and medical care systems navigation assistance. The comparison condition included usual standard clinic care or "treatment as usual" for diabetic patients, enhanced by depression educational pamphlets and lists of community resources and referrals.

As compared to patients receiving enhanced treatment as usual, intervention patients had significantly greater depression improvement at six, 12, and 18 months follow-up. Intervention patients also reported significant decreases in symptoms of diabetes and anxiety, along with improvements in emotional, physical, and pain-related functioning, disability, financial situation, and number of social stressors. While there were no intervention group improvements in HbA1c levels (a biomarker of blood glucose levels), diabetes complications, self-care management, or BMI, a recent multisite evaluation of IBHC along the U.S.–Mexico border found significant improvements in HbA1c levels and depression symptoms at the population level, as described next.

The *Sí Texas: Social Innovation for a Healthy South Texas* project is a portfolio of studies conducted by eight organizations within the 12-county region along the US–Mexico border, an area with higher poverty rates, poorer health outcomes, and more limited access to primary care and mental health services as compared to the rest of the United States. To evaluate the collective effectiveness of IBHC on the 12-county sample, data were pooled from each of the participating eight organizations that employed rigorous study designs, including four RCTs and four quasi-experimental designs (Wolff et al., 2021).

Collectively, a final sample of 2,955 participants (1,559 intervention group and 1,396 comparison group) was obtained that was over 90% Mexican descent, 70% female, and over 60% Spanish speaking, consistent with the border region. In addition to significant improvements in HbA1c levels and depression symptoms in IBHC patients versus non-IBHC treatment as usual participants (assessed at 12 months), subgroup analyses found that IBHC was especially effective in improving HbA1c levels for participants that were female, older, and who suffered from diabetes, depression, and persistent mental illness at baseline as compared to non-IBHC counterparts. Despite lack of intervention effects on BMI and blood pressure, this is a remarkable large-scale evaluation of IBHC for Latinos of particularly low social positionality and multiple high disparities in health and mental health.

Trauma Assessment

In addition to addressing comorbid health and mental health conditions, IBHC's extensive approach to screening is also helping to reveal the extent of trauma in the lives of low-SES Latinos and particularly immigrants. For example, a study by Mancini and Farina (2019) analyzed the clinical records of 120 Latino adults referred for mental health assessment during a primary care visit to an IBHC clinic in the Midwest during a one year period between 2012–2013. The purpose of this study was to underscore the importance of mental health screening in primary care settings, while contributing to the literature on trauma and comorbid mental health problems in a convenience sample of low-income, mostly immigrant, help-seeking Latino adults in an urban community health clinic serving uninsured and underinsured adult clients regardless of immigration status. Findings revealed that an alarming

44% of the sample met criteria for full, and 19% for partial, PTSD, signifi-cantly associated with symptoms of depression, anxiety, and perceived stress.

Regarding gender differences, symptom severity was significantly greater for the 74 women in the sample for PTSD symptom severity, depression, and stress, reinforcing the need for gender sensitive and trauma-informed assess-ment and care for Latino clients in IBHC settings. Regarding the types of trauma experienced, half of the sample reported physical assault, 43% sexual assault, and almost 30% reported community violence or war. Over half of the women in the sample reported experiencing both sexual and physical assault.

The above sobering findings are consistent with an increasing number of studies examining trauma in immigrant Latinas. For instance, Labash and Swartz (2018) reviewed the charts of 153 predominately Latina immigrants that had received behavioral health assessment at an IBHC clinic in Chicago. These researchers found that nearly three-quarters reported ex-posure to one or more traumas, with IPV by far the most prevalent, but sexual and emotional abuse also common. Cleaveland and Frankenfeld (2019) interviewed Latina immigrants from the Northern Triangle coun-tries of Central America who shared trauma related to gangs in countries of origin that extorted, beat, and killed community members, including friends and relatives of the women interviewed while awaiting primary care appointments.

One study assessed treatment preferences for trauma in a small sample of 27 Latina low-income immigrants from Mexico and Central and South America (Kaltman et al., 2014). More specifically, this study assessed pre-ferred treatment modality, type of psychotherapy, provider, and setting, as well as barriers and facilitators of help-seeking in this sample of trauma-exposed Latinas that met screening criteria for PTSD and/or depression who were currently receiving health care in a primary care clinic. Results revealed preference for individual therapy (especially supportive psychotherapy and cognitive behavioral therapy) delivered in a primary care clinic by a mental health specialist. Despite this study's small sample size, findings corroborate the need for IBHC, where client preferences are frequently met and where the obstacles shared by these women are also mitigated. These obstacles are cost, first and foremost, followed by unfamiliarity with mental health serv-ices and concerns about confidentiality related to immigration status. IBHC clinics in Latino communities provide services regardless of immigration status or ability to pay, and utilize *promotores* to do neighborhood outreach to familiarize residents with services, in addition to escorting and directly assisting clients with navigating services. They are well suited for providing much needed trauma-informed care.

Trauma-informed Care

In their chapter titled "Tools for Treating Trauma-Related Disorders Among Latinos," Torres and Rivera-Maldonado (2017) provide an overview of trauma-informed care (TIC) noting that, "The greatest number of studies has been conducted on exposure-based treatments, which involve having survivors repeatedly re-experience their traumatic event. There is strong evidence for exposure and of the various approaches; prolonged exposure has received the most attention although many clinicians report preferring titrated, gradual exposure . . ." and that "outcomes of such approaches leave room for improvement, with approximately 20–50% of treatment completers continuing to be diagnosed with PTSD after treatment." These writers convey that TIC typically features two key phases: (1) promoting safety and reducing distressing symptoms through psychoeducation about trauma, assessment of harm to self/others, teaching emotion regulation techniques; and (2) reviewing and reappraising trauma by exposure and processing techniques while maintaining emotional engagement with trauma recall and remaining physically, emotionally, and psychologically regulated to achieve reorganization and integration of the trauma into one's memory. In addition to providing TIC-related techniques such as deep breathing, progressive muscle relaxation, and emotion grounding techniques, Torres and Rivera-Maldonado (2017) cite three meta-analyses documenting the superiority of culturally adapted forms of TIC for Latinos.

Depression Care Continuum for Latinos

As has been reviewed, large epidemiological surveys document dramatic increases in depression with acculturation, and this is especially evident in Latino immigrants in general and females in particular. Fortunately, a creative continuum of evidence-based and culturally adapted care has been documented to address this significant mental health problem. Such interventions range from raising depression literacy to conventional therapies, including *promotora*-driven interventions, and RCTs, and are instructive for addressing mental illness in Latinos in socioculturally sound ways as described below.

Depression Literacy

As structural obstacles to mental health care continue to be mitigated by IBHC, enhanced understanding of mental health problems and their treatment also motivates clients to seek care, especially when such literacy is achieved in culturally compelling ways. An excellent example is demonstrated by Hernandez and Organista (2013), who evaluated the effectiveness of a Spanish-language *fotonovela* designed to raise depression literacy with a sample of 142 Latina immigrants experiencing significant symptoms of depression.

As described in Chapter 7, the *fotonovela* is a popular form of entertainment throughout Latin America in the form of a comic book composed of posed photographs of real people, bubble dialogue, and over the top soap opera-like drama and humor. *Sentimientos Secretos* [Secret Feelings], the *fotonovela* used in this study, reads at a fourth grade literacy level and features the story of Sophia, a middle-aged Latina struggling with depression, who learns, along with her family, what depression is and ways to treat it, even in the face of her husband's initial resistance. *Sentimientos* was carefully designed and tested by a Latino-led research team (Cabassa et al., 2010) who found it more effective than depression brochures in a nonclinical sample of Latino night school students.

A pretest–posttest randomized control group experimental design was used randomize 142 immigrant Latinas into either the experimental *fotonovela* condition, in which women took turns reading through the *fotonovela* in a group format, or the control group condition in which participants discussed ways to improve family communication and intergenerational relationships. Both conditions were facilitated by the first author, Maria Hernandez, Ph.D., LCSW, with recruitment support from *promotoras* at the IBHC clinic where the study was conducted in Oakland, California. A compelling set of results revealed significant posttest improvements in knowledge of depression and its treatments, self-efficacy to identify the need for treatment, decreased stigma toward antidepressant medication, and intention to seek treatment, as compared to control group participants.

Recently, the role of *promotoras* has expanded in auspicious ways beyond outreach, psychoeducation, and supporting intervention projects, with implications for greater support and utilization, as described next.

Promotora-driven Interventions

While the supplemental role of *promotores* enhances community-based health and mental health care by providing information, navigation, and psychoeducation through outreach into surrounding neighborhoods, its role in providing direct services is increasingly being evaluated with auspicious results. In an impressive pilot study to reduce depression and stress in recent Latina immigrants, Tran et al. (2014) trained 48 *promotoras* to deliver a "comfort basket" of support and resources to enhance healthy coping in *compañeras*, or women in new immigrant growth communities of North Carolina, where Latinos now make up between 10% and 13% of the community but where services struggle to meet their needs.

Promotoras in this study received 12 to 18 hours of pre-intervention training before reaching out to and engaging with two or three women they perceived as needing care. *Promotoras* were directed to conduct at least three contacts with their *compañeras* and to report on the resources discussed and types of support provided (e.g., emotional, tangible, informational, companionship). A total of 58 women were engaged by the *promotoras*, 32 of whom completed the pre- and post-intervention assessments of depression symptoms and attitudes toward treatment, stress and acculturative stress, social support, and coping.

While intervening with the *compañeras*, *promotoras* met monthly as a group with the training curriculum facilitator for four to nine booster sessions and completed a monthly log of their outreach efforts. These sessions reinforced *promotoras'* skills and provided the opportunity to process their experiences disseminating information and supporting their *compañeras*. So, how did these *promotoras* do? Auspiciously, results revealed a significant decrease in clinically significant depression symptoms and improved attitudes toward treatment (e.g., perceptions of treatment effectiveness). Findings further revealed significant reductions in both stress and acculturative stress (i.e., the most endorsed forms included being away from family and friends, concerns about drug and alcohol use in their community, lack of stores nearby, and difficulty communicating in English, all reported by over three-quarters of the sample). This latter finding corroborates the construct of acculturation stress in this book, which for most Latinos is viewed as conflated with racialized ethnic minority status and poverty. With regard to support and coping, perceived social support increased significantly at posttest, including several forms of heathy coping such as self-distraction, active problem solving, emotional support, positive reframing, and planning. The across the board positive results of this pilot study warrant expanding research on the effectiveness of training *promotoras* to deliver health and mental health care in Latino communities.

Culturally Adapted Cognitive Behavioral Therapy (CBT) for Depression

Latino Immigrants

Pineros-Leano, Leichtly, and Piedra (2017) conducted a systematic review of intervention studies, published between 1995 and 2016, using CBT to treat depressive symptoms among Latino immigrants in the United States They identified 11 studies that met rigorous inclusion criteria. The majority of adult clients in these studies were female from Mexico, secondarily Central American, with a few from South America. Nine of these studies used group treatment, and nine of the 11 studies reported significant reductions in depressive symptoms. Maintenance of treatment effects were also reported at three, four, and six months post-treatment across the eight studies that conducted follow-up.

All of the studies reviewed made at least one cultural adaptation, with Spanish language and literacy level adjustments being the most straightforward. Also important was making sure to address typically stressful migration experiences viewed as related to depression and trauma. Socially responsive adaptations to the local immigrant experience included flexible hours, child care, and bus tokens. Cultural adaptations to CBT varied but included incorporating Latino values (e.g., *personalismo, familismo,* and *respeto*) and *dichos* [sayings], and the *Sí, pero*[Yes, but . . . "] method of restructuring cognitions as an easier alternative to the often challenging A-B-C-D method as discussed below.

Overall, this systematic review suggests that CBT is an effective approach to reducing the burden of depressive symptoms among Latino immigrants, and that cultural adaptations may be needed to serve this population. However, there is insufficient evidence at this time to draw definitive conclusions about the relative effectiveness of specific components of treatment such as length of treatment and type of cultural adaptations (p. 575).

Latina mental health pioneer Lilian Comas-Diaz (1981) was among the first to document the effectiveness of CBT, as compared to a no treatment control condition, in the treatment of depression in Puerto Rican clients. CBTs appear consistent with the expectations of many Latino clients new to therapy, which include immediate symptom relief, guidance and advice, and a problem-centered approach. Such sort-term, directive, problem-solving therapies are also more consistent with the expectations of low-income groups whose pressing life circumstances frequently demand immediate attention and can interfere with long-term treatment.

In a subsequent article focused on Puerto Rican women struggling with problem drinking, Comas-Diaz (1986) details ways in which group therapy was culturally adapted for these women. Comas-Diaz describes incorporating drama into therapy by way of Puerto Rican music, poetry, literature, and *Espiritismo* [spiritism, or Caribbean-based folk healing beliefs and practices] as a more effective alternative to conventional forms of group therapy such as rational emotive therapy. For this *Grupo de Mujeres* [women's group], Comas-Diaz (1986) describes initial aggressive outreach to emergency rooms, police, schools, and churches, followed by group therapy addressing alcoholism within the context of acculturation and conflicts created by shifting gender roles. Further, the cultural stigma attached to women with drinking problems is addressed, and older women are enlisted to communicate their experiences to younger group participants. In a rare (and too short) note on the utilization of folk healers, Comas-Diaz mentions psychologically charged sessions led by *Espiritistas* [spiritualists, or folk healers] who relay messages to group members while professing to be inhabited by spirits. Unfortunately, such messages or their benefit to group members went undescribed in this article.

Puerto Rican *Salsa* and *Bolero* music conveying emotions and struggles similar to those of group members are carefully selected and played as a way of facilitating group process. Because so many Latinas follow *novelas* [soap operas] on Spanish television, Puerto Rican plays that mirror the struggles of the people are also used to facilitate self-examination. Comas-Diaz notes that such media was also found to be helpful in getting Puerto Rican male group members to discuss their problems and issues in mixed groups. All are excellent ideas in need of further exploration.

The Depression Clinic, San Francisco General Hospital: An Illustration

Years before IBHC, and before reviews of the literature supporting the efficacy of CBT with Latinos struggling with depression, between 1985 and 2010 the Cognitive-Behavioral Depression Clinic at the San Francisco General Hospital (SFGH) pioneered integrating mental health services within a primary care setting in ways consistent with this book's sociocultural practice model. Needed services were located at SFGH, where low-income and minority folks from the city's Latino Mission District received their primary care and family medicine services. Access and availability were also maximized by providing free or low fee (affordable) hospital-based treatment provided by linguistically and ethnically matched Latino therapists. In terms of outreach, medical staff was trained to recognize and refer patients presenting with sad affect and/or multiple somatic complaints to the Depression Clinic. Patients were offered an evaluation for depression based on their physician's recommendation, which facilitated the acceptance of mental health services. The clinic received about 300 referrals a year, around half of whom were Spanish-speaking Latino primary care patients, predominantly adult immigrants from Mexico and Central America.

Outpatient group CBT was offered to patients meeting criteria for MDD; however, patients with concomitant anxiety disorders (e.g., generalized anxiety, panic disorder), PTSD, or somatization disorder were not excluded. They were offered 16 weeks of standardized, manual-driven, group CBT provided by bilingual, bicultural Latino therapists. Groups met weekly for two hours, and the treatment protocol addressed three major areas (Muñoz et al., 2000): (1) activity schedules designed to break the vicious cycle of depression leading to low activities and vice versa; (2) assertiveness training to improve interpersonal effectiveness; and (3) cognitive restructuring to identify and change depression-related thinking and beliefs.

The psycho-educational style of CBT quickly orients patients to treatment by sharing how a diagnosis of major depression is made and how CBT conceptualizes and treats this disorder. The use of therapy manuals, homework assignments, and chalk board–aided teaching resulted in patients referring to therapy as *la clase de depresión*, which further helped to alleviate stigma attached to therapy. Each participant was given a copy of the manual that included outlines of each of the sessions, and weekly homework assignments consisting primarily of daily mood ratings in relation to activities, interpersonal contacts, and thoughts. Homework was reviewed at each session to illustrate relations between thoughts, behaviors, and mood.

Pre-treatment Preparation

To help reduce drop-out, patients were invited to a pre-treatment orientation session, over coffee and cookies in a caring and personalized manner, in which they met bilingual, bicultural Latino staff and therapists and learned about the structure and process of group therapy.

Personalized Engagement

Engagement was further enhanced during the first group therapy session by incorporating the salient Latino value of *personalismo* into a culturally sensitive relationship protocol. Hence, time was allotted for *presentaciones* in which therapists and patients share personal background regarding where they are from, their families, work that they have done, personal interests, and so on. Similarities among patients regarding countries of origin, types or work, and interests typically elicit questions and small talk or *plática*, which helps to build trust, or *confianza*. Following presentations, patients were oriented to the diagnosis of major depression and the CBT treatment model.

As a preliminary assessment of depressed thinking, patients are asked to speculate about the causes of their depression. For example, a middle-aged Central American woman attributed her depression to the death of her son, who had been killed years earlier in El Salvador where young men were frequently the targets of either government or guerilla forces during that country's civil war (described in Chapter 2). The woman recalled the trauma of having to identify her son's bullet-riddled body at the local morgue. After ample empathy was expressed, the woman was delicately asked to help group members understand what she felt was most difficult about the loss of her son or why it made her so depressed. The object here is to never to assume but to solicit the personal meanings clients ascribe to traumatic events. Interestingly, this depressed woman blamed herself, because she and her son had engaged in an argument on the morning of his death during which he stormed out of the house, never to return (i.e., "If I had not argued with him, he would not have been killed."). This case illustrates the sharp difference between normal bereavement and distorted, guilt-ridden self-blame resulting in a complicated major depression against a backdrop of the kinds of trauma that Central American refugees often bring into therapy.

Cognitive Restructuring

In the above case, it was imperative to empathically restructure the woman's belief that she was responsible for forces outside of her control. Utilizing the "Yes, but . . ." technique, the woman eventually learned to think, "*Yes*, it's true that my son and I argued, and that he left the house in anger on the day he was killed, *but* that doesn't mean that his death was my fault." The woman was also reminded that her son's life need not be defined only by his tragic death. Hence, she was asked to share her son's interests and characteristics, including that he had a good sense of humor, was quite a joker, and she even recalled a few of his pranks that made her laugh for the first time in a long time.

The above is an example of a streamlined approach to cognitive restructuring that the author refers to as the "Yes, but . . . technique" in which clients are taught that much of problematic thinking amounts to "half-truths" about problems that need to be made into "whole truths." Rather than provoking defensiveness by labeling patient beliefs as irrational a la Albert Ellis, or distorted a la Aaron Beck, patients feel understood when therapists communicate that their thoughts are understandable in view of their circumstances, but problematic in their current form.

The "Yes, but" approach also helps to address another common problem in middle-aged Latinas who must often limit or stop working because of chronic medical problems, disabilities, and depression. For example, in a sample of 176 Depression Clinic patients, 52% had chronic medical conditions (Organista, Munoz, & Gonzales, 1994) that frequently led them to conclude, *No sirvo para nada!* [I'm good for nothing!] because self-worth is too often over-invested in providing tangible support to family. Again, we teach cognitive restructuring by asking patients to complete statements such as, "Yes, my health problems limit what I can do, but . . ." to which patients respond with something like, ". . . but, that doesn't mean I'm worthless," or "but I can still do some things for my family."

Restructuring Prayer?

Because the majority of Latino patients are Catholics, religion is regarded as a relevant domain to which practitioners may need to attend. For example, churchgoing and prayer are reinforced as behavioral and cognitive activities, respectively, that usually help patients cope with negative mood states. However, it is often necessary to assess and even challenge forms of prayer that may lessen active problem solving. For example, when patients report that they "just prayed" as a way of coping, they are asked to share their prayers during group. They often reply that they simply asked God to alleviate their suffering or to solve their problems. In such cases, patients are helped to shift prayers in a more active coping direction by discussing relevant *dichos* such as *Ayudate, que Dios te ayudará* [God helps those who help themselves]. Therapists also model for patients and ask them to recite prayers in which God is asked for support in coping with depression by trying out new behaviors when unmotivated (e.g., God, please give me the strength to increase my daily activities, or to try being more assertive).

On a more serious note, some patients discontinue recommended diets and prescribed medications for medical problems because they put their fate in the hands of God. For example, an elderly Latino man from Mexico, who had stopped following his diet and medication for diabetes, claimed that it was God's will if he lives or dies. We discussed with him the possibility that rather than trusting he seemed to be testing God's will: it was as if he were putting a bullet into the chamber of gun, spinning the chamber, holding the barrel to his head, and saying, "Let's see if it's God's will that I live or die." Further, such patients are told that if they really want to learn God's will, they should make use of the many resources that God has provided them (e.g., doctors, medicines) and then see what happens.

Activity Schedules

Activity schedules and behavioral contracts to increase reinforcing activities are used to break the vicious cycle of depression and loss of interest in things leading to low activity levels that in turn maintain depression. Activity schedules are also helpful in countering agoraphobia related to panic disorder affecting some patients (Organista, 1995).

When applying cognitive-behavioral techniques it is important to be aware of underlying mainstream American cultural assumptions. For example, an implicit assumption underlying activity schedules emphasizes the need to "take time out for one's self" based on the value that this need precedes taking care of others. While such an assumption is undoubtedly adaptive in our individually oriented society, it may run counter to the emphasis in Latino culture, especially for women, to place the needs of family before one's own. This cultural contradiction is further complicated by the fact that while traditional Latino female gender role expectations may be more realistic within intact extended families and community systems (with their many compensating resources), such gendered expectations become unrealistic in the United States, where Latino families become more nuclear with fewer traditional resources.

Consider, for example, the excessiveness of one of our female clients who had the bulk of homemaker and parenting responsibilities in addition to working full-time outside of the home. For this client it was important to balance her responsibilities with some time for restorative relaxation—but how? It was also important to teach this patient how to set limits with her husband and other family members regarding excessive housework and child care.

Usually, Latino patients can be persuaded to do pleasant activities with family members. For instance, the woman in the above example began increasing pleasant activities by taking her children to the park after work and by visiting a co-worker who also had children. The two women talked about work over coffee while their children played together.

Interestingly, Depression Clinic patients frequently expressed a willingness to increase pleasurable activities in order to *distraerse* or distract themselves from problems. This view of pleasant activities as a way of temporarily escaping problems provides practitioners with an opening for encouraging this effective intervention strategy. In addition, because Latino patients are disproportionately poorer, lists of local activities costing little or no money (e.g., free admission to museums and zoo on the first Wednesday of the month, crocheting, preparing a favorite meal) can be generated by group members. Next, obstacles to such activities are addressed (e.g., *falta de ganas* [loss of desire] due to depression). Because Latino patients are fond of *dichos*, we discuss sayings such as, "You can lead a horse to water but you can't make it drink" as a way of increasing motivation.

Finally, teaching patients to assertively set limits on excessive demands from family members or friends is another helpful way of decreasing obstacles to doing activities. For instance, the women in the above example practiced asking her husband to spend more time with the children after school while she shopped. However, getting a traditionally oriented Latina to make such assertive requests requires a culturally sensitive approach to assertiveness training.

Assertiveness Training

In traditional Latino culture, communication is frequently governed by traditional institutions such as the extended family, community, and the church, as well as by values such as deference to those of higher status based on age, gender, and social position. As such, assertive communication can run contrary to the culture's emphasis on *simpatía*, or relations and communication that should be polite, non-confrontational, deferential, and even intentionally indirect (e.g., asking one relative to speak to another on one's behalf). Such communication can be especially true for women who are taught to defer to and even obey men and to subordinate their needs to the family (Comas-Diaz, 1985). Unfortunately, such a patriarchal system of communication is subject to breakdown in U.S. society, where the mediating functions of traditional Latino institutions deteriorate. As such, the need for members of our society to assertively convey their needs and desires is imperative for optimal adaptation in the United States

Despite the dilemma of teaching a Western and particularly American style of communication to traditionally oriented individuals, the compelling argument to do so with Latino patients was documented long ago. For instance, Soto and Shaver (1982) studied a sample of nearly 300 Puerto Rican women and found that women highest in gender-role traditionalism were the least assertive and the most psychologically distressed. So, how can practitioners facilitate assertiveness training in a culturally sensitive manner?

Encouraging descriptions of assertiveness training with Latinos have long been reported, complete with culturally sensitive guidelines for Latinas in particular (Comas-Diaz & Duncan, 1985). These guidelines deemphasize the concept of "personal rights" as a way of motivating assertiveness because it can seem foreign to the less democratic, less egalitarian family and friendship systems of traditional Latinos.

Thus, the trick is to sensitively deviate from traditional Latino culture as needed by encouraging clients to expand their bicultural capabilities by adding assertive communication skills to their usual communication style. That is, we *biculturate* patients by describing assertiveness as an effective communication skill in mainstream American society. Thus, an *additive* model of therapy is emphasized in which the goal is to add mainstream communication skills to the patient's current repertoire rather than replacing traditional communication styles.

Care is taken to stress culturally compatible aspects of assertiveness such as the emphasis on communication that is not just direct but also honest, respectful, a way of improving family relationships, and teaching one's children how to be socially competent in mainstream society. Based on Comas-Diaz & Duncan's (1985) guidelines, Latino cultural factors that may mitigate developing assertiveness are discussed, as well as strategies for dealing with predictable negative reactions from parents or spouses and other higher status individuals. For example, Comas-Diaz and Duncan trained Puerto Rican women to preface assertive expressions with phrases like "*Con todo respeto*" [With all due respect] and, "*Me permite expresar mis sentimientos?*" [Would you permit me to express my feelings?]. In addition, clients are taught to respond to negative reactions to their assertiveness with explanations such as "Expressing my feelings makes me less upset and better able to handle things."

One unassertive woman at the SFGH Depression Clinic learned how to respond more assertively toward her overly critical mother. On one occasion, the patient was hurt because when she shared her desire to look for a job, her mother responded by saying, "And just how do you expect to work a job when you can't even speak English!" When the patient was asked in group why she didn't share her hurt feelings with her mother, she said that she did not want to be rude or disrespectful. This latter point is noteworthy because while Latinos are as likely as anybody else to be passive, the patient's reason for enduring her mother's insensitivity stemmed from her culture-based practice of respectful behavior toward parents, and not passivity per se.

With the help of modeling by therapists and role-play, the woman finally learned to say to her mother, "With all due respect, mamá, could you please be more supportive of my efforts to get a job? It hurts my feelings when you are so discouraging." Both surprised and irritated, the patient's mother quickly accused her daughter of "talking back," even calling her *mal criada* or "poorly raised" (i.e., a child without manners). However, role-playing and group discussion had prepared our client for this response, to which she replied, "Would you permit me to say something about that?" to which the mother could hardly refuse, and the patient continued, "If you don't let me express my feelings to you, I'm going to feel bad and resentful when I'd prefer to feel close to you." In this case, group discussion was helpful in differentiating honest and respectful assertive communication from acting out or the rude and disrespectful expressions of a *mal criada*.

Another way of motivating Latino clients is to ask what happens when they hold in upset feelings. Almost without exception, clients describe the exacerbation of physical illness such as high blood pressure, diabetes, heart disease, or gastrointestinal and other somatic symptoms. This question is important because Latino clients frequently report a tendency to *aguantar* [tolerate] or *guardar* [hold in] anger rather than express it to those with whom they are upset. The tendency to *guardar* is part of a larger culture-based style known

as *controlarse*, or disciplined self-control of negative thoughts and feelings
leading to either resignation or efforts to overcome hardship.

Evaluation

A randomized clinical trial at the Depression Clinic compared group CBT
with and without social work case management (Miranda et al., 2003).
Clinical case management (CCM) was integrated to enhance treatment by
addressing the multiple needs of patients. Case managers also co-facilitated
CBT groups and reinforced clinical work during case management sessions. Participants in this study were 199 patients (77 Spanish-speaking
Latinos, 112 mostly NLWs, and some NLB patients). Results showed less
drop-out in the CBT + CCM condition versus CBT alone for all patients.
However, the combined condition was also more effective in decreasing depression and improving functioning—*but only for Spanish-speaking Latino
clients*. This latter finding is consistent with the aforementioned study by
Sue et al. (1991), which showed that linguistic and ethnic matching in
therapy improves retention and outcome, but only for Latinos and Asians
low in acculturation and not for their higher acculturation counterparts
nor for NLW and NLB patients. Miranda et al. (2003) concluded that Latino
clients were most responsive to group CBT + CCM because of their special linguistic and acculturation-related needs that were directly addressed
in socioculturally adapted CBT and case management. This conclusion
is consistent with the goal and success of IBHC today, and interventions
like it reviewed above, in mitigating mental illness and related problems in
Latino populations.

Conclusions

The purpose of this chapter is to review Latino mental health and its relation to acculturative stress characterized by racialized ethnic minority status,
conflated with poverty, for most Latinos in the United States. This book's *sociocultural practice model* is used as a guide to selectively review the expanding
number of conceptually sound and evidence-based studies that effectively
intervene with mental health problems over-affecting Latinos. This review
demonstrates ways to consider salient social and cultural factors that contextualize mental health problems, including how practitioners can work both
within and outside of Latino culture as needed in culturally sensitive and

effective ways. *Promotores* represent an especially effective human resource from within Latino culture capable of expanding understanding and integration of health resources that are sometimes outside of Latino culture. It is encouraging that the Latino mental health literature is rapidly expanding, complete with informative outcome evaluations, including RCTs, and reviews of the literature that inspire us to continue learning the many ways to best serve Latino populations in order to mitigate excessive suffering and dysfunction.

References

Alegria, M., Falgas-Bague, I., Collazos, F., Carmona Camacho, R., Lapatin Markel, S., Wang, Y. et al. (2019a). Evaluation of the integrated intervention for dual problems and early action among Latino immigrants with co-occurring mental health and substance misuse symptoms: A randomized clinical trial. *JAMA Network Open, 2*(1). e186927. https://doi.org/10.1001/jamanetworkopen.2018.6927

Alegria, M., Shrout, P., Canino, G., Alvarez, K., Wang, Y., Bird, H., et al. (2019b). The effect of minority status and social context on the development of depression and anxiety: Evaluation of the integrated intervention for dual problems and early action among Latino immigrants with co-occurring mental health and substance misuse symptoms: A randomized clinical trial longitudinal study of Puerto Rican descent youth. *World Psychiatry, 18*, 298–307.

Angel, R., & Guarnaccia, P. J. (1989). Mind, body, and cWulture: Somatization among Hispanics. *Social Science Medicine, 28*, 1229–1238.

Becerra, R. M., & Iglehart, A. P. (1995). Folk medicine use: Diverse populations in a metropolitan area. *Social Work in Health Care, 21*(4), 37–53.

Bridges et al. (2014). Does integrated behavioral health care reduce mental health disparities for Latinos? Initial findings. *Journal of Latino Psychology, 2*(1), 37–53.

Burnam, M. A., Hough, R. L., Karno, M., Escobar, J. I., & Telles, C. A. (1987). Acculturation and lifetime prevalence of psychiatric disorders among Mexican Americans in Los Angeles. *Journal of Health and Social Behavior, 28*, 89–102.

Burnam, M. A., Hough, R. L., Escobar, J. I., Karno, M., Timbers, D. M., Telles, C. A., & Locke, B. Z. (1987). Six-month prevalence of specific psychiatric disorders among Mexican Americans and non-Hispanic whites in Los Angeles. *Archives of General Psychiatry, 44*, 687–694.

Castillo, E. G., et al. (2019). Community interventions to promote mental health and social equity. *Current Psychiatry Reports, 21*(35), 1–14. https://doi.org/10.1007/s11 920-019-1017-0

Cervantes, R. C., Salgado de Snyder, V. N., & Padilla, A. M (1989). Post-traumatic stress disorder among immigrants from Central America and Mexico. *Hospital and, Community Psychiatry, 40*, 615–619.

Cleaveland, C., & Frankenfeld, C. (2019). "They kill people over nothing": An exploratory study of Latina immigrant trauma. *Journal of Social Service Research, 46*(10), 1–17. https://doi.org/10.1080/01488376.2019.1602100

Comas-Diaz, L. (1981). Effects of cognitive and behavioral group treatment on the depressive symptomatology of Puerto Rican women. *Journal of Consulting and Clinical Psychology, 49*, 627–632.

Comas-Diaz, L. (1985). Cognitive and behavioral group therapy with Puerto Rican women: A comparison of content themes. *Hispanic Journal of Behavioral Sciences, 7*(3), 273–283.

Comas-Diaz, L. (1986). Puerto Rican alcoholic women: Treatment considerations. *Alcoholism Treatment Quarterly, 3*(1), 47–57.

Comas-Diaz, L., & Duncan, J. W. (1985). The cultural context: A factor in assertiveness training with mainland Puerto Rican women. *Psychology of Women Quarterly, 9*, 463–476.

Cook, B., Alegria, M., Lin, J. Y., & Guo, J. (2009). Pathways and correlates connecting Latinos' mental health with exposure to the United States. *American Journal of Public Health, 99*(12), 2247–2254. doi:10.2105/AJPH.2008.137091

Ell, K., Katon, W., Xie, B., Lee, P. J., Kapetanovik, S., Guterman, J., & Chou, C. P. (2010). Collaborative care management of major depression among low- income, predominantly Hispanics with diabetes: A randomized controlled trial. *Diabetes Care, 33*(4), 706–713.

Escobar, J. I., Golding, J. M., Hough, R. L., Karno, M., Burnam, M. A., & Wells, K. B. (1987). Somatization in the community: Relationship to disability and use of services. *American Journal of Public Health, 77*, 837–840.

Harris, M., Velasquez, R. J., White, J., & Renteria, T. (2004). Folk healing and curanderismo within the contemporary Chicana/o community: Current status. In R. J. Velasquez, L. M. Arellano, & B. W. McNeill (Eds.), *The handbook of Chicana/o psychology and mental health* (pp. 111–125). Mahway, NJ: Lawrence Erlbaum.

Hernandez, M. Y. & Organista, K. C. (2013). Entertainment-education? A fotonovela? A new strategy to improve depression literacy and help-seeking behaviors in at-risk immigrant Latinas. *American Journal of Community Psychology, 52*(3-4), 224–235. doi:10.1007/s10464-013-9587-1

Higginbotham, J. C., Trevino, F. M., & Ray, L. A. (1990). Utilization of curanderos by Mexican Americans: Prevalence and predictors: findings from HHANES 1982-84. *American Journal of Public Health, 80* (supplement), 32–35.

Hoskins, D., & Padrón, E. (2017). The practice of curanderismo: A qualitative study from the perspectives of curandera/os. *Journal of Latina/o Psychology, 6*(2), 79–93. https://dx.doi.org/10.1037/lat0000081

Hulme, P. A. (1996). Somatization in Hispanics. *Journal of Psychosocial Nursing, 34*, 33–36.

Kaltman, S., Hurtado de Mendoza, A., Gonzales, F. A., & Serrano, A. (2014). Preferences for trauma-related mental health services among Latina immigrants from Central America, South America, and Mexico psychological trauma. *Theory, Research, Practice, and Policy, 6*(1), 83–91. http://dx.doi.org/10.1037/a0031539

Karno, M., Hough, R. L., Burnam, M. A., Escobar, J. I., Timbers, D. M., Santana, F., & Boyd, J. H. (1987). Lifetime prevalence of specific psychiatric disorders among Mexican Americans and non-Hispanic whites in Los Angeles. *Archives of General Psychiatry, 44*, 695–701.

Keller, A., Joscelyne, A., Granski, M., & Rosenfeld, B. (2017). Pre-migration trauma exposure and mental health functioning among Central American migrants arriving at the US border. *PLoS ONE, 12*(1): e0168692. https://doi.org/10.1371/journal.pone.0168692

Kessler, R. C., McGonagle, K. A., Zhao, S., Nelson, C. B., Hughes, M., Eshleman, S., Wittchen, H., & Kendler, K. S. (1994). Lifetime and 12-month prevalence of DSM-III-R psychiatric disorders in the United States. *Archives of General Psychiatry, 51*, 8–19.

Labash, A. K. & Swartz, J. A. (2018). Demographic and clinical characteristics associated with trauma exposure among Latinas in primary medical care. *Journal of Ethnic & Cultural Diversity in Social Work*, doi:10.1080/15313204.2018.1449691

Lee, D. J., Markides, K. S., & Ray, L. A. (1997). Epidemiology of self-reported past heavy drinking in Hispanic adults. *Ethnicity and Health, 2*(½), 77–88.

Mancini, M. A., & Farina, A. S. J. (2019). Co-morbid mental health issues in a clinical sample of Latino adults: Implications for integrated behavioral health treatment. *Journal of Ethnic & Cultural Diversity in Social Work, 30*(4), 326–340. https://doi.org/10.1080/15313204.2019.1702132

Miranda, J., Azocar, F., Organista, K. C., Dwyer Valdez, E., & Arian, P. (2003). Treatment of depression in disadvantaged medical patients. *Psychiatric Services, 54*(2), 219–225.

Misra, S., Jackson, V. w., Chong, J., Choe, K., Tay, C., Wong, J., & Yang, L. H. (2021). Systematic Review of Cultural Aspects of Stigma and Mental Illness among Racial and Ethnic Minority Groups in the United States: Implications for Interventions. *American Journal of Community Psychology, 68*(3-4), 486–512. https://doi.org/10.1002/ajcp.12516

Moscicki, E. K., Locke, B. Z., Rae, D. S., & Boyd, J. H. (1989). Depressive symptoms among Mexican Americans: The Hispanic Health and Nutrition Survey. *American Journal of Epidemiology, 130*, 348.

Moscicki, E. K., Rae, D. S., Regier, D. A., & Locke, B. Z. (1987). The Hispanic health and nutrition survey: Depression among Mexican Americans, Cuban Americans, and Puerto Ricans. In M. Garcia and J. Arana (Eds.), *Research agenda for Hispanics* (pp. 145–159). Chicago: University of Illinois Press.

Muñoz, R. F., Ghost Ippen, C., Rao, S., Le, H., & Valdes Dwyer, E. (2000). *Manual for group cognitive-behavioral therapy for major depression: A reality management approach.* San Francisco: Cognitive-Behavioral Depression Clinic, Division of Psychosocial Medicine, San Francisco General Hospital, University of California, San Francisco.

Organista, K. C. (1995). Cognitive-behavioral treatment of depression and panic disorder in a Latina patient: Culturally sensitive case formulation. *In Session: Psychotherapy in Practice, 1*, 53–64.

Organista, K. C., Muñoz, R. F., & Gonzalez, G. (1994). Cognitive behavioral therapy for depression in low-income and minority medical outpatients: Description of a program and exploratory analyses. *Cognitive Therapy and Research, 18*, 241–259.

Padilla, A. M., Carlos, M. L., & Keefe, S. E. (1976). Mental health service utilization by Mexican Americans. In M. R. Miranda (Ed.), *Psychotherapy with the Spanish-speaking: Issues in research and service delivery* (Monograph No. 3; pp. 9–22). Los Angeles: Spanish-Speaking Mental Health Research Center, University of California.

Piernos-Leano, M., Leichtly, J. M., & Piedra, L. M. (2017). Latino immigrants, depressive symptoms, and cognitive behavioral therapy: A systematic review. *Journal of Affective Disorders, 208*, 567–576. http://dx.doi.org/10.1016/j.jad.2016.10.025

Plante, T. G., Manuel, G. M., Menendez, A. V., & Marcotte, D. (1995). Coping with stress among Salvadoran immigrants. *Hispanic Journal of Behavioral Sciences, 17*(4), 471–479.

Robins, L. N., & Regier, D. A. (Eds.) (1991). *Psychiatric disorders in America: The Epidemiologic Catchment Areas Study.* New York: The Free Press.

Soto, E., & Shaver, P. (1982). Sex-role traditionalism, assertiveness, and symptoms of Puerto Rican women living in the United States. *Hispanic Journal of Behavioral Sciences, 4*, 1–19.

Sue, S., Fujino, D. C., Hu, L., Takeuchi, D. T., & Zane, N. W. S. (1991). Community mental health services for ethnic minority groups: A test of the cultural responsiveness hypothesis. *Journal of Consulting and Clinical Psychology, 59*, 533–540.

Torres. A. & Rivera-Maldonado, M. (2017). Tools for treating trauma-related disorders among Latinos. In L. T. Benuto (Ed.), *Toolkit for Counseling Spanish-Speaking Clients: Enhancing behavioral health services* (pp. 39–69). New York City: Springer.

Tran, A. N., Ornelas, I. J., Kim, M., Perez, G., Green, M., Lyn, M. J., & Corbie-Smith, G. (2014). Results from a pilot promotora program to reduce depression and stress among immigrant Latinas. *Health Promotion and Practice, 15*(3), 365–372. https://doi.org/10.1177/1524839913511635

Vega, W. A., Kolody, B., Aguilar-Gaxiola, S., Alderete, E., Catalano, R., & Caraveo-Anduaga, J. (1998). Lifetime prevalence of DSM-III-R psychiatric disorders among urban and rural Mexican Americans in California. *Archives of General Psychiatry, 55*, 771–782.

Wolff, L. S., Flynn, A., Xuan, Z., Errichetti, K. S., Tapia Walker, S., & Brodesky, M. K. (2021). The effect of integrating primary care and mental health services on diabetes and depression a multi-site impact evaluation on the US-Mexico border. *Medical Care, 59*(1), 67–76.

10

Latino Health

After a prolonged history of neglect and a glaring lack of baseline data, the study of Latino health in the United States has finally achieved the momentum necessary to better understand and address vexing health problems either over-affecting Latino populations or that are simply exacerbated by low access to adequate care. Such knowledge production includes major national, state-level, and local epidemiological surveys, analysis of health disparities, and intervention evaluations across a broad variety of health problems in Latino populations and subgroups. Simultaneously, surprisingly good Latino health on several important indicators has also been documented and analyzed for what we can learn about healthy cultural practices and resilience under frequently stressful conditions of acculturation that are too often conflated with poverty and the trappings of racialized ethnic minority status as reviewed in previous chapters.

This chapter provides an overview of Latino health in the United States, followed by a selective review of major Latino-related health problems, in order to situate this immense topic within the context of sociocultural understanding and congruent and responsive health care. It's worth mentioning that the traditional professional convention of separating physical and mental health is rapidly dissolving for the better. That is, health is increasingly viewed more holistically with regard to both assessment and treatment, as reflected in the integrated behavioral health care (IBHC) movement discussed below. Other innovations in Latino health care will also be emphasized, such as the expanding and effective role of *promotores de salud*, or nonprofessional community health workers committed to Latino community health and well-being.

Overview of Latino Mortality and Morbidity

Top 10 Causes of Death in America

The National Center for Health Statistics (NCHS) provides mortality and morbidity data for the U.S. population, most recently for 2019. Table 10.1

Solving Latino Psychosocial and Health Problems. Kurt C. Organista, Oxford University Press.
© Oxford University Press 2023. DOI: 10.1093/oso/9780190059637.003.0010

Table 10.1. The 10 Leading Causes of Death in the United States among Hispanics, Whites, and African Americans (2019)

Cause of Death	Hispanic			Non-Hispanic White			Non-Hispanic Black		
	Rank	Deaths	% Total Deaths	Rank	Deaths	% Total Deaths	Rank	Deaths	% Total Deaths
All causes	—	170,447	100.0	—	1,744,261	100.0	—	277,364	100.0
Diseases of heart	2	41,794	24.5	1	512,600	29.4	1	81,306	29.3
Malignant neoplasms (cancer)	1	43,079	25.3	2	460,950	26.4	2	70,513	25.4
Chronic lower respiratory diseases	8	5,700	3.3	3	136,136	7.8	6	11,446	4.1
Accidents (unintentional injuries)	3	18,874	11.1	4	125,151	7.2	3	21,615	7.8
Cerebrovascular diseases	4	11,959	7.0	5	110,804	6.4	4	20,003	7.2
Alzheimer disease	6	8,221	4.8	6	100,371	5.8	9	9,208	3.3
Diabetes mellitus	5	10,166	6.0	7	57,168	3.3	5	15,415	5.6
Influenza and pneumonia	11	3,808	2.2	8	38,066	2.2	12	5,363	1.9
Intentional self-harm (suicide)	10	4,331	2.5	9	37,428	2.1	15	3,115	1.1
Nephritis, nephrotic syndrome and Nephrosis	9	4,488	2.6	10	35,081	2.0	8	9,740	3.5
Chronic liver disease and cirrhosis	7	6,877	4.0	11	31,881	1.8	13	3,421	1.2
Septicemia	14	2,701	1.6	13	28,143	1.6	11	6,347	2.3
Essential hypertension and hypertensive renal disease	13	3,030	1.8	14	24,962	1.4	10	6,605	2.4
Assault (homicide)	12	3,122	1.8	—	—	—	7	9,951	3.6
Certain conditions originating in the perinatal period	15	2,297	1.3	—	—	—	14	3,316	1.2

Adapted from the National Center for Health Statistics (NCHS), as well as data compiled by Curtin (2019). Suicide rates for females and males by race and ethnicity: United States, 1999 & 2019. Health-E Stats; with permission.

lists NCHS mortality data regarding the percentage of total deaths for the top 10 leading causes of death by race and what the federal government terms *Hispanic origin* (note that up to 15 causes are listed, given variance between comparison groups). In this chapter the term *Latino* will continue to be used, as well as non-Latino white (NLW) and non-Latino Black (NLB), when making comparisons, given that Latinos can be racially white as well as Black.

The NCHS lists the top 10 causes of death for NLWs to which other race and Latino populations are compared. As can be seen, heart diseases and cancer remain the two main causes of death in the United States, which combined account for 55.8% for NLWs, 54.7% for NLBs, and 49.8% for Latinos, the latter indicating a slight mortality *advantage* for these two main causes of death. Unintentional injuries (e.g., car accidents) remain in the top four for all groups in Table 10.1, and Alzheimer's disease, which has increased with longevity in recent decades, is now the sixth leading cause of death for Latinos and NLWs and ninth for NLBs. The latter is interesting, considering that African Americans have higher rates of dementia in general as compared to NLWs and Latinos (Moon et al., 2019).

The fourth leading cause of death for Latinos, cerebrovascular diseases (e.g., stroke), which is fourth also for NLBs and 5th for NLWs, is related to diabetes, which is the fifth leading cause of death for Latinos and NLBs and seventh for NLWs. Hence, there is a slight disadvantage for Latinos with regard to stroke, for which risk factors include diabetes, obesity, and high blood pressure. While high blood pressure is significantly lower for Latinos relative to NLWs and NLBs, Latinos are less likely than NLWs to have hypertension under control (Cirulgea & Ta, 2016). Chronic lower respiratory diseases (CLRD) are the third leading cause of death for whites as compared to the sixth and eighth for NLBs and Latinos, respectively. CLRD refer to a category of respiratory illnesses that include asthmatic conditions and chronic obstructive pulmonary disease, or blocked lung respiration due to what used to be called chronic bronchitis and emphysema, the latter most often the result of smoking. While rates of smoking are lower for Latinos relative to whites, they increase with acculturation and are under-addressed by health professionals.

Sadly, suicide continues to increase over time in the United States and remains in the top 10 for NLWs (#9), and Latinos (#10), while NLBs continue to be more protected by comparison (#15). It is fortunate that this particular health disparity favors NLBs, but interesting that suicide was not in the top

10 for Latinos when the first edition of this book was published in 2007. Rates of suicide per 100,000 in year 2019 do remain significantly lower for NLBs (7.1) and Latinos (6.9) as compared to NLWs (18.05) (Curtin et al., 2019), underscoring differences in rates *between* groups as compared to causes of death *within* each population as listed in Table 10.1.

Today, it's interesting to see influenza and pneumonia as the eighth leading cause of death for NLWs—and 11th and 12th, respectively, for Latinos and NLBs in 2019—in view of the disparate impact on people of color of the Coronavirus or Covid-19 since 2020. Tragically, this global pandemic continues to reveal major holes in our ill-prepared health care system, as well as the long-standing structural vulnerability of people of color whose SES-related living and working conditions rendered them more exposed to infection and consequent hospitalization and death as compared to their NLW counterparts.

Covid-19 Pandemic

In so many ways, Covid-19 serves as a cracked mirror of minority health, reflecting living legacies of accrued stigma and discrimination, exclusion, and marginalization, rendering people of color overexposed to natural and human-made epidemics that endanger their health, as well as that of society, given the intricately interconnected nature of human relations underscored by an airborne virus. As with health disparities in general, underlying causes of racial/ethnic disparities in Covid-19 infection and death are embedded in social and structural determinants of health. These include racism and discrimination, economic and educational disadvantages, poor health care access and quality, individual behavior, and biology according to Webb Hooper, Nápoles, and Pérez-Stable (2020), who elaborate as follows: (1) people of color have a disproportionate burden of underlying comorbidities including cardiovascular disease, asthma, HIV, morbid obesity, and liver and kidney disease (as reviewed above); and (2) concentrated in urban settings, people of color are disproportionately poor, live in crowded housing and neighborhoods, and work in public-facing service and transportation jobs— all conditions that limit physical distancing.

As can be seen in Table 10.2, data on the uneven impact of Covid-19 on racial and ethnic groups in America are sobering. According to the CDC

Table 10.2. Risk for COVID-19 Infection, Hospitalization, and Death by Race/Ethnicity

Rate ratios compared to White, Non-Hispanic persons	American Indian or Alaska Native, Non-Hispanic persons	Asian, Non-Hispanic persons	Black of African American, Non-Hispanic persons	Hispanic or Latino persons
Cases[1]	1.70	0.70	1.10	1.90
Hospitalisation[2]	3.40	1.00	2.80	2.80
Death[3]	2.40	1.00	2.00	2.30

From the Centers for Disease Control (2021).

(2021) summary table of *rate ratios* used to compare people of color to NLWs, Latinos experience two times the rate of infection, 2.8 times the rate of hospitalization, and 2.3 times as many deaths as compared to NLW counterparts, whose rates are set to 1.0 for ratio comparisons.

In California, where Latinos make up 39% of the state population, they compose up 46.4% of Covid-19 deaths (California Department of Public Health, 2021). Webb Hooper et al. (2020) conclude that research is "needed to guide the science of community engaged intervention development, implementation, and evaluation and lay the foundation for a system-wide goal of decreasing health disparities beyond the detrimental effects of COVID-19" (p. 2467). This chapter elucidates such research regarding major health disparities affecting Latino populations (e.g., diabetes), and non-disparate health problems that continue to escape awareness, timely treatment, management, and control, and hence over-affect Latinos.

Latino Health Obstacles and Facilitators

While several challenges to health promotion and disease prevention and treatment in Latino communities persist, health care accessibility via health insurance remains a major obstacle necessitating micro- through macro-level systemic change (e.g., more inclusive health policy at local and larger levels), including increasing the availability of quality health care regardless of ability to pay or immigration status.

Lack of Health Insurance

The fact that many Latinos are likely to lack health insurance clearly has a major impact on their overall health outcomes. It is difficult to imagine how a patient without insurance can get the necessary battery of preventive examinations such as mammography, pap smears, and screening for diabetes and colon and prostate cancer, among others; or how a patient with hypertension can be examined and treated regularly to prevent cardiovascular complications that result from this condition (Carillo et al., 2001, p. 65).

Despite various forms of morbidity and mortality over-affecting Latino populations as documented above, they remain the most underinsured of any racial or ethnic group in the United States. As reported by the Office of Minority Health (in 2019), 18.7% of Latinos are not covered by health insurance, as compared to 6.3% of NLWs. Lack of health insurance coverage by Latino populations is 20.3% for Mexicans, 8.0% for Puerto Ricans, 14% of Cuban Americans, and 19.4% of Central Americans. Further, 9.2% of Latino youth under the age of 19 lack health insurance as compared to 4.3% of NLWs. The consequences for such low rates of health insurance were spelled out over two decades ago by Carillo et al. (2001), who documented that half of uninsured Latinos (1) had not seen a doctor when last sick; (2) had gone without a prescription for needed medication, (3) had gone without recommended medical tests and treatments, and that (4) two-thirds reported trouble paying bills or being contacted by collection agencies for medical expenses. Lack of health coverage through employment is the main explanation for the above lack of insurance, given high concentrations of Latinos in non–white collar occupations (e.g., construction, small firms, agriculture, mining, as reviewed in Chapter 3), in addition to lack of citizenship for some.

California
Even in one of the most progressive states for providing health insurance, and access regardless of income and immigration status, Latinos continue to be the least insured among all Californians (e.g., 13.7% versus 5.3% for NLWs). According to findings from the California Health Inventory Survey (2015–2016), uninsured rates for Mexicans, who comprise about 80% of Latinos in the state, is 19.1%, while the rates for Central Americans, who generally comprise the other 20% of Latinos, range from 16.6% for "Other

Central Americans" all the way to 36% for Guatemalans, with Salvadorans at 23.6% (Becker, Babey, & Charles, 2019). Again, low employer-based health insurance in Latinos as compared to NLWs (34.1% & 61.5%, respectively), as well as the limitations of immigration status, are directly related to low rates of health insurance, as follows: undocumented (44.7%), legal permanent resident (16.5%), naturalized citizen (11.6%), U.S.-born citizen (10.5%).

Despite available insurance options, 21.6% of Latinos ages 0 to 64 (a total of 410,000 people) who are currently eligible for Medi-Cal (what Medicare is called in California) remain unenrolled, despite California extending eligibility to this population in 2016. Further, over three-quarters of Medi-Cal eligible Latino children (0–18 years) also remain unenrolled despite eligibility for *all* children that qualify based on need regardless of citizenship status. As of January 2021, Medi-Cal eligibility has been extended to young adults without citizenship, between the ages of 19 and 26, and youth 19 years and younger have been eligible since 2015. Becker et al. (2019) note that county and hospital eligibility workers can enroll the eligible, as can almost any service provider that takes the time to assess such need. The above numbers should improve significantly in 2024 when *all* undocumented people will be eligible for state-subsidized health care insurance, projected to cover about 700,000 undocumented residents, making California the first state in the nation to provide universal health care for its 40 million residents (Ali, 2022).

Covid-19 is a bracing reminder that disallowing needed health care to millions of people in the United States is a threat to all in the United States. Minus health insurance and affordable health care more generally, low-income and disproportionately minority people throughout the country find themselves depending on safety net programs such as federally qualified health care (FQHC) centers, and overlapping IBHC providers as described below.

Integrated Behavioral Health Care

IBHC is a model of service delivery designed to promote health and the prevention and treatment of illness by promoting health care access and utilization by co-locating and coordinating health and mental health services, often in the heart of Latino and other low-income communities. In addition to bilingual staff, IBHC routinely screens for psychosocial and health problems (e.g., interpersonal violence and other trauma) and addresses frequently comorbid conditions (diabetes and depression, heart disease and anxiety) in client- and family-centered ways that promote needed healthy lifestyle changes and adherence to treatment and medication.

IBHC uses a graded or *step-care* model to provide services ranging from low intensity/least intrusive (e.g., providing information; *watchful waiting.* or monitoring the course of apparently minor distress) to moderate intensity/moderately intrusive (e.g., group or short-term individual therapy emphasizing coping skills; medication) in order to address the vast majority of health care needs, leaving highly intensive/most intrusive care (e.g., inpatient care, *red flags* such as acute suicidality, homicidal intent, gravely disabled status) to referrals outside of IBHC that specialize in such crises.

Chronic Illness

Cirulgea and Ta (2016) describe how IBHC addresses prevention and treatment of chronic illnesses over-affecting Latinos, namely coronary vascular disease (CVD) and related disorders such as hypertension (HTN), stroke and diabetes, and several forms of cancer. Community-based and increasingly FQHC-affiliated IBHC strives to provide care with attention to the sociocultural context of health promotion and disease prevention and treatment. There are currently over 1,400 FQHCs in the United States providing care to more than 20 million patients, over a third of whom are Latino (Whittmore, 2007), regardless of ability to pay or immigration status.

IBHC is informed by evidence-based practices and has been frequently evaluated with auspicious results as reviewed below. Part of IBHC's success, and that of community-based services more generally, is the frequent inclusion of community health workers (CHW) or *promotores de salud* [health promoters], as they are referred to in Latino communities and throughout Latin America. Many of the outcome studies reviewed below also describe CHW recruitment, training, increasing employment, and how they have been effectively employed to support and sometimes lead interventions that improve Latino health.

How Do You Say Community Health Worker in Spanish?

In their review of the literature on community health worker–supported diabetes care for Latinos (described below later), Little et al. (2014) offer the following description of a complex population operating between the boundaries of informal and formal health care:

> Encompassing various terms including lay health workers, peer leaders, or *promotores(as) de salud* (health promoters), CHWs are defined as "individuals who serve as bridges between their ethnic, cultural, or geographic communities and health care providers, and engage their community to prevent diabetes and its complications through education, lifestyle change, self-management and social support" (p. 557).

For the past two decades, the CHW model of care has been supported the American Public Health Association, the Centers for Disease Control and Prevention, and the American Association of Diabetes Educators, given its effectiveness in health promotion, disease prevention and treatment, and expanding the health care workforce, along with its ability to provide socioculturally competent care in response to health problems over-affecting Latinos.

Health Problems Over-Affecting Latinos and Emerging Solutions

Given the major health problems over-affecting U.S. Latinos, either as disparities (e.g., diabetes) or neglected non-health disparities (e.g., heart disease), the remainder of this chapter will selectively review major health problems with necessary attention to sociocultural context, best (i.e., evidence-based) and promising (socioculturally sound) approaches to health promotion, disease prevention, and intervention, by reviewing state-of-the-science research.

Cardiovascular Diseases, Related Disorders, and Risk Factors

Balfour et al. (2016) provide an excellent state-of-the-science review of cardiovascular diseases (CVDs) among Latinos, including recent epidemiological evidence, rates of risk factors, and critique of the quality of available data. While they caution that more research is needed, their review covers findings from two major Latino-focused epidemiological surveys in addition to numerous local Latino-focused surveys across the country. CVD refers to a class of related disorders such as coronary heart disease (narrowing of arteries or blockage due to blood clots), heart failure (slow decline in heart muscle ability to pump blood), and peripheral vascular diseases (disorder of the circulatory system outside heart and brain). Balfour et al. include cerebrovascular disease (e.g., stroke) in their review, given its related pathology (i.e., insufficient vascular blood flow, clots or vascular breakage in the brain). While Latinos are at lower overall risk for CVD compared to NLW and NLB counterparts, a consequential problem pattern persists. As compared to NLWs, Latinos have lower CVD awareness, leading to delayed treatment, insufficient management and control, and thus greater morbidity and mortality.

This same problem pattern holds for hypertension (HTN), a major risk factor for CVD. While lower in Latinx men and women aged 20 and above (29.6% and 29.9%, respectively) as compared to their NLW counterparts (32.9% and 30.1%, respectively), CVD is also less controlled by Latinos than by NLWs (41% and 56%, respectively) due to less awareness, health care, and consequent negative outcomes (Balfour et al., 2016). In the case of diabetes, the other chronic disease and major risk factor for CVD, risk for diagnosis is about 66% higher for Latinos compared to NLWs, yet the same cascading problem pattern persists.

The above findings underscore the interrelated nature of CVD, HTN, diabetes, and stroke, as well as variation in how these top 10 chronic diseases play out in the lives of Latino populations. The same is true for the remaining CVD risk factors for which Latinos are also at greater risk compared to NLWs: BMI (body mass index), cholesterol, lower physical activity, and discrimination. While Latinos are at much lower risk for smoking, this pernicious CVD risk factor increases with acculturation and is under-assessed by health care professionals attending to Latino patients compared to other patients (Balfour et al.; 2016). Given how pervasive the above risk factors are for CVD as well as HTN, diabetes, and stroke, many of the solutions for preventing and treating this cluster of chronic illnesses overlap, as reviewed below. Diabetes is emphasized, given its devastating consequence for Latinos. Cancer, for which Latinos are at even lower overall risk, is also reviewed below, given the preventable suffering and unnecessary deaths resulting from lack of awareness, detection, and treatment.

CVD Prevention and Treatment

Prevention Efforts

Health Literacy Promotion

CVD health literacy among Latinos remains lower than for NLWs, and this is particularly the case for immigrants. For instance, Gore et al. (2021) assessed CVD risk factor knowledge in monolingual Spanish-speaking Latinos, because immigrant Latinos experience higher levels of risk factors and related mortality than U.S.-born Latinos yet are less likely to be screened. The study took place at a community health fair in Denver, CO, where Latinos are now over 20% of the state, or about 1.1 million people. Primarily low-income and uninsured participants were screened for and educated about CVD risk factors, prevention, and management.

High-risk participants presenting with uncontrolled risk factors were connected with bilingual medical professionals providing onsite counseling and education that included discussion of health care access, medication adherence, and resources for healthier lifestyle practices. Contact information was collected from those willing to participate in a subsequent telephone survey assessing awareness of the 10 documented CVD risk factors shared at the health fair (i.e., high cholesterol, high blood pressure, poor diet, overweight/obesity, lack of exercise, diabetes, smoking, family history of premature CVD, older age, and male gender). Gore et al. (2021) report that the 174 self-identified monolingual Spanish-speaking participants could only identify an average of 2.3 of the 10 risk factors. High cholesterol was the most commonly identified risk factor (56%), followed by high blood pressure (34%), poor diet (32%), and overweight/obesity (30%). Only 16% identified smoking, and 17% diabetes. None identified male gender as a CVD risk factor, and 10 participants were unable to identify any of the risk factors.

Analysis of the data shows that higher risk identification scores are predicted by having a high school education or more, and enrollment in an indigent health care program (e.g., FQHC), underscoring the larger structural vulnerability to low health literacy and care. Interestingly, high scores were not predicted by discussion of CVD at the community health fair, leading the authors to advocate greater outreach to improve CVD health literacy and prevention through *promotores de salud*, mobile health technology, radio, and TV. For instance, despite the slightly lower risk for HTN in

Latinos versus NLWs, the problematic cascading pattern of low HTN literacy and lethal consequences warrants immediate screening and management.

Hypertension Management

As documented by Balfour et al. (2020), Latinos are less aware of their HTN than NLWs (78% versus 81%) and NLB adults (87%). They are less likely to be in treatment even when diagnosed (70%) compared to NLW and NLB adults (77% and 80%, respectively) and are the least likely to achieve HTN control (41%) as compared to NLB (48%) and NLW adults (56%). To address screening and treatment disparities, Schoenthaler et al. (2020) evaluated the effectiveness of a medication adherence intervention, delivered by medical assistants (MAs) working with primary care providers, to enhance blood pressure management and control in a diverse sample of 112 non-adherent Latino patients, randomly assigned to the intervention and usual care control conditions. Equal numbers of male and female patients were recruited from a community-based clinic in New York. The intervention included nine 15-minute MA-delivered health coaching sessions provided in person or by phone. The intervention was culturally adapted with input from Latinos with HTN, a university/community advisory board, and from the literature on brief interventions with Latinos. Participants were randomized into this MA intervention or the treatment as usual control condition where they received the standard health coaching procedures followed at their clinic along with BP checks and health education.

Interestingly, HTN medication adherence, as measured by an electronic monitoring device (EMD), declined for both groups with no between-group difference. However, BP improved in both groups overall, and participants in the intervention group self-reported greater medication adherence. The authors note several problems with the EMD (i.e., 20% of participants had no data because they mistrusted, misunderstood, or elected not to use the device), the need for multiple outcome measures, and that their intervention demonstrated significant improvements in self-reported adherence among high-risk Latinos with uncontrolled HTN. These mixed yet auspicious findings warrant improving HTN management and CVD prevention research.

Weight Reduction

A pioneering study to prevent CVD in Latinos, *Cuidando el Corazón* [Caring for the heart] is instructive for its focus on long-term weight loss by comparing three approaches: family-oriented, group intervention, and an information-only control condition. *Corazón* was designed for low-income, married Mexican American women 20% above ideal body weight, with one or more children between the ages of three and six. Multiple benefits derive from this program's focus on overweight/obesity, a mega risk factor not only for CVD but also for HTN, stroke, diabetes, and cancer.

As can be seen in Figure 10.1, between 1976 and 1980 and 2017–2018, rates of obesity have steadily climbed for Mexican Americans and their NLW counterparts, but most dramatically for Mexican American women (from about 27% to over 50%) and men (about 16% to over 50%), with lower yet still concerning rates for white females and males that have recently begun to taper and converge. These data underscore the obesity crisis in America, especially for Latinos, for which interventions such as *Corazón* are urgently needed.

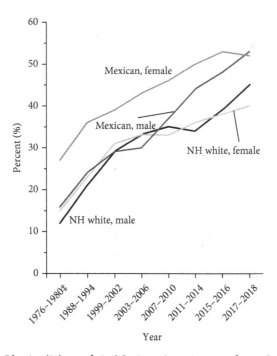

Figure 10.1. Obesity (%) trends in Mexican Americans and non-Latino whites, adults aged 20 to 74 years, 1976 to 2018.

From Miller et al., (2021). Cancer Statistics for Hispanics/Latinos, 2021. *CA: A Cancer Journal for Clinicians*, 71(6), 466–487. With permission from Wiley.

Women in the *Corazón* control group were provided a manual on preventing CVD through behavior change, nutrition, exercise, and modifying the fat content of traditional Mexican recipes. Women in the intervention group received the same manual but also attended a series of 90-minute weekly meetings for a total of 24 meetings throughout the year. These meetings included extended behavioral education, food demonstrations, and six monthly maintenance classes to enhance follow-through by teaching problem-solving strategies to cope with slips and high-risk situations such as holidays and social events. Child care was available for women attending the groups.

Corazón's family-oriented condition matched the above group condition but was composed of married couples learning techniques for supporting each other's efforts to promote healthy habits in children, who attended their own children's group. Culturally congruent weight reduction strategies began with brisk couple and/or family walks, and framing mother's weight loss as beneficial to *la familia* versus just to her individually. Participants were assessed every three months throughout a one-year period for weight loss and other measures. Just over half of the 168 Latina participants completed the multiple assessments, and results showed that participants in both the family and group interventions lost significantly more weight than those in the information-only control group. While a shorter intervention duration may have mitigated patients lost to dropout, it is instructive to note that *collective efforts* via the family or groups of patients struggling to reduce weight together appears to be more effective than individual efforts.

Treatment Efforts

CHARLA [chat] (Community Heart Health Actions for Latinos at Risk) is a community-based, health worker–led program, integrated within primary care, to reduce CVD in low-income urban Latinos. CHARLA consists of 12 weeks of lifestyle education that was evaluated by Krantz et al. (2017) with a sample of 768 Latinos assessed pre-treatment as well as three months post-intervention. There was no control group. Of the participants, 86% were at risk for CVD, including 41% with uncontrolled risk factors. Program content includes CVD risk factor testing and counseling with a nurse or physician, and referrals to medical care for participants with uncontrolled risk factors. Local bilingual CHWs assisted participants primarily with healthy lifestyle improvement, but also follow-up care and health insurance enrollment, meeting with patients at a variety of community venues such as churches, recreation centers, and senior living centers.

For participants with uncontrolled risk factors at baseline, results revealed significant reductions in systolic blood pressure, low-density lipoprotein cholesterol, glucose, triglycerides, and a 10-year global risk score. Completing eight or more sessions also predicted reductions in cholesterol and blood pressure, especially in participants newly prescribed lipid lowering drugs. While this study could be improved by comparing CHARLA to a no-treatment or treatment as usual control condition, it provides auspicious findings warranting further utilization of a *promotora*-led, IBHC-consistent program, urgently needed to treat CVD in Latinos. Related chronic illnesses also benefited from CHARLA, yet deserve their own direct attention given the high rates of HTN (36.3%) and diabetes (28.1%) in study participants.

Diabetes Prevention and Treatment

Type II Diabetes (T2D) accounts for 90%–95% of all cases and increasingly exacts a major toll on the American public, especially people of color. Over the past 60 years, diagnoses of T2D have increased almost 20-fold from a mere 1.5 million cases in the late 1950s to 29 million in 2016, and it remains in the top 10 causes of death for Americans (Heron, 2019), as reviewed earlier. According to the Office of Minority Health (2021), based on 2018 data Latinxs are 70% more likely than NLWs to be diagnosed with diabetes, and 30% more likely to die from it. Relatedly, Latinxs experience twice as many lower extremity amputations than NLWs (25.4 per 1,000 persons with diabetes versus 12.5, respectively), and over three times the rate of end-stage renal (kidney) disease (307.6 versus 100.7 per 1,000 persons with diabetes)— all preventable complications resulting from the pernicious pattern of lower awareness resulting in later detection and treatment.

Sneiderman et al. (2014) note that while reliable diabetes prevalence data are available for NLWs and NLBs 20 years of age or older (10.2% and 18.7%, respectively), they have historically been less reliable for Latinos. Hence, the Hispanic Community Health Study/Study of Latinos (HCHS/SOL) was launched by the National Heart, Lung, and Blood Institute and the National Institutes of Health to document the prevalence and development of chronic diseases, including diabetes among diverse Latino populations in the United

States. The HCHS/SOL is a study of 16,415 women and men aged 18–74 years at screening, from randomly selected households recruited during 2008–2011 in Bronx, NY; Chicago, IL; Miami-Dade County, FL; and San Diego, CA. The HCHS/SOL cohort was selected through a stratified multistage area probability sample of four communities from diverse regions of the country, or four of the 11 urban metropolitan areas with the largest Latino populations. While the survey sample does not represent the entire U.S. Latino population, the high concentrations of specific Latino backgrounds from four communities allows for good estimates of diabetes prevalence and risk factors for each Latino population described.

Results reveal a diabetes prevalence of 17% in Latinos aged 18–74 years with an unweighted (i.e., raw) prevalence of 19.6%, or 3,211 of the 16,385 survey participants having diabetes. After controlling for age, BMI, Latino backgrounds, location of assessment, and years lived in the United States, the prevalence for men and women decreases to 15.3% and 14.2%, respectively. These concerning rates of diabetes locate Latinos between NLW and NLB Americans, with much variation between Latino populations now documented in the HCHS/SOL. These diverse Latino data represent an overdue response to past research in this area, such as that by Pérez-Escamilla and Putnik (2007) who conclude in their article, "The role of acculturation in nutrition, lifestyle, and incidence of Type 2 diabetes among Latinos":

> The process of acculturation among Latinos is associated with subop-timal dietary choices including lack of breast-feeding, low intake of F&V [fruit & vegetables], and a higher consumption of fats and artificial drinks containing high levels of refined sugar. Similarly, acculturation has been positively associated with PA [physical activity] and the likelihood of obesity and type 2 diabetes among Latinos. However, findings have been inconsistent across Latino subgroups and nutrition outcomes of interest. One limitation of available data is that most studies and surveys have concentrated on Mexican Americans and not on other Latino subgroups such as Puerto Ricans, Cuban Americans, Central and South Americans. (p. 867).

Diabetes by Latino Population

Rates of diabetes among different Latino populations are now available thanks to the HCHS/SOL. Schneiderman et al. (2014) examined these rates, as well as T2D awareness and control, among different Latino HCHS/SOL groups and found that rates are lowest among South Americans (10.2%) and Cubans (13.4%), and highest for Central Americans (17.7%), Dominicans (18%), Puerto Ricans (18%), and Mexicans (18.3%)—a pattern consistent with variation in the acculturation histories and related SES backgrounds of these U.S. Latino populations.

Among HCHS/SOL participants meeting criteria for diabetes, less than 60% were aware of their condition; 48% displayed adequate diabetes control, and 52.4% reported having health insurance. Predictably, health insurance was related to being aware of one's diabetes and having diabetes under control in this study (52.4%). Not surprisingly, diabetes was found to increase with age and BMI.

Interestingly, rates of diabetes were positively related to acculturation yet negatively related to education and income (i.e., SES). That is, rates of diabetes steadily increase across four of the five-year "time in the U.S." intervals, as follows: 0-- years (12.3%), 6–10 years (14.84)%, 11–15 years (16.8%), and 16 or more years (18.75%). However, rates for U.S.-born Latinos (14.52%) were comparable to those in the United States for a period of 6–10 years.

These findings generally support acculturation stress theory, with a slight variation in need of replication and further study. While Schneiderman et al. (2014) do not speculate on the slight inconsistency in the relation between acculturation and rates of diabetes, the fact that it is positively related to acculturation and negatively related to SES may suggest a segmented assimilation scenario for most Latinos. That is, most Latinos continue to struggle with attaining social mobility despite increasing time in the United States. At the same time, some Latinos (e.g., U.S.-born) that manage to attain greater SES during the acculturation process, may also acquire more protection against diabetes given the many benefits of better social positionality (e.g., health insurance, healthier foods and exercise options, better working conditions and lifestyle). Increasingly, interventions demonstrate effective strategies for preventing and treating diabetes and mitigating its harmful consequences for Latinos as described below.

Prevention Efforts

According to the Centers for Disease Control (CDC), the risk profile for someone succumbing to diabetes is as follows: 45 years of age or older, overweight, family history of T2D, high blood pressure, physically active fewer than three times a week, history of gestational diabetes or gave birth to a baby that weighed more than nine pounds. Research shows that modest weight loss and regular physical activity prevent or delay T2D by up to 58% in people with prediabetes (up to 71% for people 60 or older). Modest weight loss means 5% to 7% of body weight, or 10 to 14 pounds for a 200-pound person. Getting at least 150 minutes of physical activity each week, such as brisk walking, is also important (i.e., 30 minutes of physical activity a day, five days a week). While this at-risk profile is important for addressing diabetes prevention in adults, such efforts ideally begin in childhood, especially for Latino youth who have a 50% chance of succumbing to diabetes later in life due to factors such as overweight and obesity, and relatedly, *insulin resistance or insensitivity* (Soltero et al.; 2018). The latter refers to cells in the body under-responding to insulin and thereby weakening this hormone's role in reducing and controlling blood glucose and preventing diabetes.

Primary Prevention with Youth

In their intervention to prevent obesity in low-income Latino preschool children, Heerman et al. (2019) remind us that over the past decade, hundreds of behavioral randomized control trials (RCTs) have addressed childhood obesity prevention and treatment with limited success, especially for low-income and minority youth, who remain under-studied. RCTs are among the most rigorous types of research because they reduce bias by randomly assigning participants to two or more conditions, including a control condition that does not receive the intervention. In response to the challenge of preventing obesity, Heerman and colleagues conducted an RCT to evaluate *COACH* (Competency-based Approaches to Community Health) by recruiting Latino parent–child pairs from community settings in Nashville, Tennessee, where Latinos are now 10% of the city (60,400), 20% of its public school children, and 5% of the state population. Children in this study are boys and girls three to five years of age (M = 4.2 years), at risk for obesity (i.e., a BMI ≥ the 50th percentile). Fifty-nine parent–child pairs were randomly assigned to COACH, which consisted of 15 weekly 90-minute sessions, followed by three months of twice-monthly health coaching calls. Fifty-eight parent–child pairs were assigned to the control group, a twice-monthly school readiness curriculum for three months.

COACH sessions were conducted by a health coach in local community centers, with groups of eight to 11 parent–child pairs. BMI, the main outcome, was assessed four times over 12 months, as well as several related outcomes: child and parent diet and physical activity, parent BMI, parent self-efficacy to impact child health behaviors, and parenting practices encouraging/discouraging child physical activity. Deliberate efforts were made to infuse COACH with a personalized family focus with tailored learning plans, assessment of competency in targeted health behaviors, and allowing participants to select which content to spend extra time on during the group sessions.

The standout finding from this study is that over the one-year follow-up period, COACH resulted in significantly slower linear BMI growth for children in this condition as compared to their counterparts in the control condition. Further, at four months follow-up, there were significant improvements in the following related outcomes for parent–child pairs in the COACH program versus pairs in the control condition: time parents spent in moderate to vigorous physical activity and walking; parent self-efficacy to impact child consumption of sugar, juice, fruits/vegetables, and to improve physical activity; improvements in snack and vegetable consumption; and degree to which parents encouraged children's physical activity. While these improvements did not last through subsequent follow-ups, this study represents an auspicious effort to prevent obesity in Latino preschool children, in necessary collaboration with parents given the high degree of difficulty in this type of intervention.

Secondary Prevention with Youth

Regarding secondary prevention (i.e., early detection and treatment to prevent worsening), Soltero et al. (2018) addressed diabetes prevention in obese Latino adolescents, ages 14 to 16, by randomizing a sample of 136 adolescents, from Phoenix, Arizona, into either a culturally grounded and community-based three-month lifestyle intervention (n = 67), or control condition (n = 69), with a one-year follow-up. Youth were recruited from schools, community centers, and health centers, with the intervention taking place at the local YMCA. The intervention consisted of weekly nutrition and health classes delivered to groups of families, and engaging groups of adolescents in exercise sessions three days per week. Control condition teens received general health information and lab results. Main outcomes were insulin sensitivity and weight-related quality of life (i.e., concerns about weight and self, relationships, and the environment), BMI percentile, percent body fat, and waist circumference. Soltero et al. (2018) describe integrating salient social and cultural factors as follows:

> The construct of *familismo* is leveraged by encouraging the entire family, including extended members living in the household, to attend the program and make healthy lifestyle changes as a family. The construct of *respeto* is leveraged to discuss roles and responsibilities of parents and children for making decisions about health, modeling healthy behaviors, selecting, preparing, and consuming healthy foods, communicating within and outside of the family, and honoring traditional gender roles as well as cultural and religious celebrations. The program is delivered by bilingual and bicultural health educators who appreciate the cultural norms within the local community and use examples from their lives to establish rapport, foster dialogue, and discuss challenges and opportunities around health. (p. 2)

At three months assessment, youth in the intervention group exhibited significant increases in insulin sensitivity, weight-related quality of life, and reductions in BMI, percent body fat, and waist circumference, as compared to those in the control condition. Improvements in weight-related quality of life and reductions in BMI and percent body fat remained significant at 12 months follow-up, while changes in insulin sensitivity did not. Analysis of a subsample of youth with prediabetes at baseline assessment revealed significant improvements in insulin sensitivity, weight-related quality of life, and BMI reductions at three months assessment.

Soltero et al. (2018) conclude that their lifestyle intervention improves cardiometabolic and psychosocial health in an obese population of Latino adolescents at very high risk for developing T2D. Together with the above study by Heerman et al. (2019), this pair of studies demonstrates both the ongoing challenge and the promise of primary and secondary prevention efforts with Latino youth vulnerable to developing diabetes. Such efforts with adults are also increasingly underway with similar challenges and promises.

Secondary Prevention with Adults

With regard to secondary prevention in Latino adults, Babamoto et al. (2009) recruited 318 newly diagnosed Latino patients from three inner-city family health centers in Los Angeles to participate in *Amigos de Salud* [Friends of Health]. *Amigos* is a prospective randomized design to evaluate the effectiveness of a *promotora*-delivered intervention as compared to treatment as usual (i.e., routine appointments, medication, lab work, other referrals as needed), as well as a case management condition (i.e., treatment as usual enhanced with a case management plan, monthly meetings with nurses, and follow-up calls). Predominately Mexican-descent patients, diagnosed with T2D during the previous six months, were randomly assigned to the above three conditions.

Three *promotoras* were recruited as paid staff, requiring a high school diploma or GED, and two had been educated in Mexico or Central America. All received formal training: six-week curriculum that included diabetes standards of care, self-management strategies incorporating patient cultural and spiritual beliefs, health behavior change theory, and clinic policies and procedures. Over the six-month intervention period, *promotoras* conducted individual educational sessions with patients and family members tailored to their needs (in-home sessions, problem solving around obstacles, follow-up calls).

For the 189 patients that completed the study, results overwhelming favored the *promotora*-led intervention with regard to significant improvements in knowledge, self-reported health status, fewer emergency room visits, improved diet (increased fruit and vegetables, decreased fatty foods) and exercise, and greater medication adherence. Interestingly, blood glucose (HbA1c) levels significantly decreased in *all* three study conditions, underscoring the importance of general health care access. Considering this study's 40% attrition rate, it is worth noting the significantly lower dropout rate in the *promotora* condition (25%) as compared to treatment as usual (50%) and case management (43%). Hence, secondary diabetes prevention, tailored to the sociocultural reality of newly diagnosed Latino adults, can improve disease management and disrupt the pernicious pattern of low awareness and care resulting in excessive morbidity and mortality, still too common in Latino populations.

Treatment Efforts

Whittemore (2007) conducted one of the first systematic reviews of the literature on culturally competent care for Latinos with T2D. Of the 11 studies that met criteria for inclusion in this review, eight were RCTs and four were single group pre- and post-intervention designs. Most were community-based education programs, with the rest delivered in health clinics. Most were delivered to Mexican-descent Latinos in rural areas and two to Puerto Ricans in the urban northeast, by a mix of nurses, dieticians, diabetes educators and

CHWs. With regard to sociocultural elements, more than half of the studies utilized *promotores de salud*, included family members, were delivered in the community, and addressed Latino food consumption and health beliefs.

Eight of the 11 studies assessed blood glucose or HbA1c, seven of which reported significant improvements, thus supporting the effectiveness of culturally informed care for uncontrolled diabetes in Latinos. However, Whittemore cautiously concludes, "improvements were modest and attrition was moderate to high in many studies. Addressing linguistic and cultural barriers to care are important beginnings to improving health outcomes for Hispanic adults with type 2 diabetes" (p. 157). Fortunately, an increasing number of socioculturally adapted interventions are addressing Whittemore's concerns with auspicious results as described below.

LUNA-D (Latinos Understanding the Need for Adherence in Diabetes) is designed for low-income Spanish-speaking Latinos with T2D, receiving care at a FQHC serving mostly immigrant Mexican-descent patients in San Diego. Essentially, LUNA-D brings a strong IBHC approach to this FQHC worthy of replication across the country. LUNA-D was evaluated by Talavera et al. (2021) by conducting a RCT with 456 Latino adults with diabetes, 23–80 years of age and 63.7% female, over a six-month period, targeting the centrally important biomarkers, HbA1c, blood pressure, and cholesterol.

Participants were randomized into a treatment as usual control condition at the FQHC (i.e., standard primary care diabetes care, with referrals to health education and behavioral health as needed), or an enhanced IBHC-like intervention that included: (1) co-location of medical and behavioral health providers; (2) *warm hand-off* from the medical to the behavioral health provider; (3) provider–client shared treatment plan; (4) up to four medical visits for management of diabetes, related chronic medical conditions, and a behavioral health provider for coping with psychosocial and behavioral factors; (5) care coordination to facilitate the shared treatment plan; and (6) six culturally appropriate group health education classes led by a CHW.

Results showed that LUNA-D significantly decreased blood glucose as compared to treatment as usual and was marginally significant in reducing cholesterol. In addition, both conditions were successful in significantly reducing blood pressure. Hence, this study supports IBHC and its integration into FQHCs. It's worth noting that in addition to including nurses and dieticians in LUNA-D's team approach, *promotores de salud* assisted with the program throughout the six-month period of implementation. *Promotoras* continue to figure more centrally in IBHC, FQHCs, management of diabetes, and other health and mental health illnesses challenging Latino communities as underscored below.

Promotora-supported Diabetes Management

Research increasingly documents the effectiveness of *promotores de salud* in providing diabetes care to Latinos in need. In fact, Little et al. (2014) conducted a systematic review of the literature on *promotora*-supported HbA1c management and control, rigorously evaluated in several RCT studies. Such interventions serve as a reminder that adherence to medication is important, but so is regular monitoring of one's blood glucose levels. The review also describes the background, training, and supervision of CHWs in these rigorous evaluation studies, as well as the diversity of Latino populations served. Study participants were predominately low-income, Spanish-speaking Latinas with uncontrolled diabetes. Seven studies focused exclusively or primarily on Mexican-descent Latinos from Texas and California; one study focused on Dominicans in New York, another primarily on Puerto Ricans in Massachusetts, and three did not specify. CHWs led the interventions alone, in pairs, or as part of teams, and received payment in half of the studies reviewed. Most of the studies described CHWs as racially/ethnically and linguistically matched to participants, including three with a personal history of diabetes and one with diabetes in the family.

While duration and intervention strategies varied, the majority were of good methodological quality as rated by the reviewers. Ten of the 12 studies reported that CHWs were formally trained in delivery of the intervention, although only six of these 10 studies provided training details such as diabetes and medication education, and behavioral intervention strategies such as communication skills, group instruction, behavioral self-management and change techniques, cultural and spiritual sensitivity, CHW roles and responsibilities (i.e., home visiting, advocacy and service coordination, leadership, managerial skills, and clinical employee standards). Six studies indicated that a health care professional (e.g., nurse) or a project investigator supervised the CHWs. Only one study reported unsupervised CHWs.

Of the 12 studies that met the inclusion criteria of Little et al.'s (2014) review, seven report statistically significant improvements in HbA1c at one-year follow-up, and at two-year follow-up in the three studies that conducted such longer assessment. Five of these seven studies also report lower attrition compared to studies unsuccessful at lowering blood glucose. No improvements in blood pressure or cholesterol are reported for studies assessing HTN, and only one study improved BMI while four had no success reducing weight. Hence, *promotora*-supported glucose management remains viable despite continuing challenges with other important biomarkers.

Pérez-Escamilla et al. (2015) evaluated the effectiveness of Diabetes Among Latinos Best Practices Trial (DIALBEST), an intervention for improving glycemic control among adult Latinos with *uncontrolled* T2D that was also not just supported but *led* by CHWs. Two hundred eleven adult Dominican and Puerto Rican Latinos were randomly assigned to the DIALBEST intervention (N = 105) or to treatment as usual (N = 106). DIALBEST consisted of 17 individual sessions conducted at home by CHWs over a period of 12 months with quarterly assessments, as well as an 18-month assessment. CHWs addressed T2D complications, healthy lifestyles, nutrition, healthy food choices and diet for diabetes, blood glucose self-monitoring, and adherence to medication.

Impressively, results reveal that compared to treatment as usual, CHWs had a positive impact on net HbA1c improvements at three months, six months, and especially 12- and 18-month assessments. Interestingly, DIALBEST did not reduce weight, hypertension, or cholesterol as hoped for, similar to findings in Little et al.'s (2014) review of the literature on *promotora*-supported HbA1c control. Despite such ongoing challenges, the effectiveness of *promotora*-led glucose management for Latinos with uncontrolled diabetes, is very encouraging in regard to controlling dangerous glucose levels.

Blood Glucose Control

Between 2006 and 2008, the Institute for Family Health (IFH), a network of FQHCs in New York State, transformed their diabetes care program to address long-term outcomes for high-risk patients as defined by poor glycemic control (i.e., HbA1c >9%). The transformed primary care services now include certified diabetes educator visits, case management services, diabetes group sessions, electronic health record-based clinical support, establishment of a diabetes medical director and system-wide diabetes registry, onsite HbA1c testing and depression screenings, and outreach to patients for missed or overdue visits. Marquez, Calman, and Crump (2018) evaluated the effectiveness of the IFH's transformed diabetes care program by comparing the electronic medical records of 3,259 high-risk Latino and NLW patients enrolled in IFH before (2003–2008) and after (2009–2015) implementation of the enhanced primary care program. Results revealed significant pre to post decreases in HbA1c levels for both groups, but significantly more so for Latino patients. Thus, enhanced primary care services directed at high-risk patients appears to both improve glycemic control and reduce this particular health disparity between Latinx and NLW counterparts. The extra time, care, and integration of salient social-cultural contextual factors continues to expand, including needed attention to the Latino diet in disease prevention and control.

Improving the Latinx Diet as Needed
Upon receiving the results of a blood test indicating that the author's blood glucose crossed into the pre-diabetic range, and that his cholesterol was also just over the line, his doctor suggested a number of dietary improvements including eliminating or limiting corn. The author did a quick mental calculation of the role of corn in delicious and comforting Mexican food (e.g., chips, tortillas, tacos, enchiladas, tamales, pozole, menudo), leading to the snap judgment that cutting out corn was not going to happen! However, limiting consumption and reducing portions of the above foods, stepping up daily exercise, reducing meat and dairy, and increasing plant-based foods has been a feasible trade-off for preventing diabetes and illnesses related to high cholesterol. Hence, because diet and eating habits are central to social, cultural, and emotional developmental experience, they can be very resistant to change even when the goal is to prevent and control numerous chronic diseases and their related suffering and death. Thus, deeper understanding of how to address bicultural Latino diets is warranted, with some insightful research providing guidance.

Buena Alimentación, Buena Salud [Good Nutrition, Good Health] is the name of an early, small but auspicious study that succeeded in improving the diet of overweight Latinos struggling with diabetes (Vasquez et al., 1998). At three months post-intervention, the 18 experimental participants reduced total and saturated fats and increased fiber and carbohydrates, as compared to 20 participants in the control condition. Each of 12 intervention sessions contained three components: active discussion to clarify health information, behavioral skills acquisition, and demonstrations of how to shop for and prepare healthier meals, including in-session cooking and tasting, and trips to the supermarket where participants learned how to decode food labels. The intervention framework used was a social learning theory-based analysis of the antecedents and consequences of food/eating behavior, with emphasis on identifying and coping with high-risk situations (e.g., holidays, eating out, cooking for the family), healthy alternative behaviors, sustaining healthy behaviors, and how to cope with inevitable relapses.

Table 10.3 lists the program contents, skill objectives, and methods for *Buena Alimentación* that were carefully developed from three phases of

Table 10.3. *Buena Alimentación, Buena Salud* [Good Nutrition, Good Health]

Diabetes Management Program in Overweight Latinas (N = 38) Struggling with Diabetes

Week	Content	Skills	Demonstration
1.	Program goals, Diabetes risk in Latinos	Identify realistic outcomes from program participation.	Prepare and taste low-fat recipe.
2.	Diabetes and complications	Identify factors that contribute to diabetes complications. Evaluate food records for fat content.	Low-fat recipe*
3.	Dietary fat and cholesterol	Examine the amount and type of fat in traditional foods.	Analysis of low-fat menu.
4	The role of portion control in diabetes management	Describe appropriate portion sizes of different foods.	Practice measuring portions in a variety of foods.
5.	Label reading	Analyze food labels for fat and calorie content.	Practice reading labels.
6.	Inexpensive and healthy low-fat foods at the market	Identify barriers to low-fat food selection.	Attend supermarket tour.
7.	Review label reading and supermarket idea	Examine food labels.	Low-fat recipe*
8.	Role of weight reduction in NIDDM	Identify problem-eating behavior. Problem solving in situations at high risk for inappropriate eating.	Low-fat recipe*
9.	Psychological lessons– relationship between food, emotions, thoughts, and behaviors	Analyze impact of stress on food choices and eating habits.	Low-fat recipe*
10.	Psychological lesson– stress management	Examine sources of stress. Develop coping strategies for dealing with stress.	Practice relaxation techniques.
11.	Importance of exercise for weight management	Develop realistic exercise plan.	Exercise practice. Monitor glucose before and after activity.
12.	Planning for holidays and vacations	Develop and implement coping strategies.	Problem solving – situations during holidays.

*A traditional low-fat recipe was prepared and taste tested in every class.

From Vasquez et al. (1998). Buena Alimentación, Buena Salud [Good Nutrition, Good Health]: A Preventive nutrition intervention in Caribbean Latinos with Type 2 Diabetes. *American Journal of Health Promotion*, *13*(2), 116–119. With Permission from Sage.

background research and preparation: (1) Convening a local advisory multidisciplinary team; (2) development and implementation of a patient population survey to assess knowledge and attitudes about diabetes management; and (3) conducting focus groups to discuss obstacles to diabetes management. This background research revealed high rates of poverty, considerable lack of compliance with diabetes management, high daily consumption of traditional foods, and the belief in nearly half of participants that they were not overweight. Despite these obstacles, over 90% of survey participants agreed that it is possible to avoid the complications of diabetes—just the opening needed to improve Latino diets. The hands-on nature of the intervention, preparing and tasting healthier versions of traditional Mexican foods, provided participants with a *tasting is believing* opportunity to motivate healthier alternatives to favorite dishes. For example, the author now enjoys Soyrizo and egg whites as a surprisingly delicious, healthy alternative to the classic Mexican breakfast, *chorizo con huevos!*

Diabetes-related Attitudes

Not discussed in the above studies are the specific types of beliefs and attitudes among Latinos with diabetes that compete with disease management. For example, Hunt, Pugh, and Valenzuela (1998) conducted qualitative interviews with 51 Mexican Americans with diabetes revealing that while all expressed concerned and practiced self-care, none fully complied with recommended management because of the following competing beliefs, attitudes, and behaviors in need of modification:

- *Over-estimation of the power of medications to compensate for poor diet.* Half of participants reported using their diabetes medications *in place of* exercise and improved diet, namely as a safety-valve to be used when eating poorly.
- *Strong desire to feel normal.* Almost 80% of participants found it difficult to accept "Never eating/drinking normally again." Men found it distressing to give up favorite fatty dishes such as *tamales* and *enchiladas*, and claimed that low-fat foods were too light and not filling. Men also generally continued to drink alcohol and discounted it as a problem. Women said it was difficult to diet *and* prepare meals for the family, and that taking care of family members left no time for exercise. Some

women tried to eat smaller portions of normal family foods, but then found it difficult to resist eating more.

- *Problems dieting during social events.* Participants reported the bind of either ignoring dieting during social events or avoiding such events.
- *Misconceptions about blood glucose and desire to avoid side effects of medication.* Medication side effects (e.g., acute dizziness, disorientation, sweating, palpitations) sometimes scared patients and caused them to discontinue medications and to eat sweet and heavy foods. Some patients actually expressed fear of low blood glucose!
- *Limited economic resources.* Many low-income participants said that recommended diet and exercise are expensive (i.e., price of blood glucose strips, syringes; preparing separate meals for self and family) and needing to eat what's available when finances are low.
- *Poor recognition of the relation between glucose control and the above factors.* None of the above beliefs and behaviors were seen as affecting control of blood glucose!

Related studies by Hunt and colleagues also found that some Mexican American patients with diabetes lost motivation to manage their diabetes when inconsistencies arose between their efforts and health outcomes (Hunt, Valenzuela, & Pugh, 1998)—that is, when careful diabetes management did not result in controlled glucose levels, and vice versa. Such patients need education about the *process* of disease management, including the need for consistent management despite occasional counterintuitive outcomes.

Interestingly, Hunt, Hamdi Arar & Akana (2000) also examined the use of culture-based practices (e.g., herbs, prayer, fatalistic religious beliefs) as possible competitors to the biomedical management of diabetes in 43 low-income Mexican Americans with T2D. They found that such practices were few and *complementary* to standard medical care. For example, none of the participants reported using *curanderos* [Mexican folk healers] for diabetes; use of herbs was infrequent and *supplemental* to medication; and prayer was viewed as enhancing medicines and not as a substitute. As mentioned in Chapter 9 (Latino Mental Health), prayer and other religious activities are generally faith- and health-promoting but it is worthwhile to examine how the contents of prayer may or may not promote health behaviors (e.g., God give me the strength to follow through with managing my diabetes versus if God wants me to die then I'll die).

The growing focus on cancer prevention and control with Latinos offers further auspicious illustrations of increasingly socioculturally responsive primary and secondary prevention interventions.

Cancer

In their overview of IBHC and major chronic illnesses over-affecting Latinos, Cirlugea and Ta (2016) convey that while Latinos are at lower overall risk for cancer as compared to NLWs, it remains the number one cause of death among Latinos. Among Latinas, breast cancer is the leading cause of cancer-related death, while for Latino men it is lung cancer. Cirlugea and Ta go on to describe how IBHC is designed to addresses psychosocial factors to which cancer is highly sensitive (i.e., fear, anxiety, depression, social isolation), as well as behavioral factors (e.g., prevention screening, smoking), and to support ongoing medical care.

Unfortunately, the same vexing problem pattern reviewed above also exacerbates cancer in Latinos: lower literacy -> later detection and treatment -> consequent excessive morbidity and mortality, mainly due to lack of health insurance and poverty more generally. Latinos are also vulnerable to cancer risk factors such as obesity and T2D as reviewed above. Fortunately, recently improved data on cancer prevalence, morbidity, and mortality in Latinos have begun to accrue in ways needed to better inform prevention and treatment priorities. For instance, Miller et al. (2021) review such data collected by the National Cancer Institute's Surveillance, Epidemiology, and End Results program, and the CDC's National Program of Cancer Registries. An overview of their findings are described below.

Prevalence and Mortality

For 2021, there were an estimated 176,600 new cancer cases and 46,500 cancer deaths among Hispanic individuals in the continental United States and Hawaii, an incidence rate 25% lower than for NLWs. The lifetime probability of developing cancer among Latino men and women was 37% and 36%, respectively, as compared to 41% and 30%, respectively, among NLW men and women, although probabilities vary by specific types of cancer. Compared to NLWs, Latino men and women had 25% to 30% lower incidence (2014–2018) and mortality (2015–2019) rates for all cancers combined, and lower rates for the most common cancers, although this disparity favoring Latinos appears to be diminishing. A closer examination of the data allows for the identification of patterns and priorities for cancer prevention and control in Latinos.

Gender Differences

As can be been in Figure 10.2, over half of the most commonly diagnosed cancers in Latino men include, in descending order, prostate (22%), colon and rectum (11%), lung and bronchus (7%), kidney and renal pelvis (7%), and liver (6%). Relatedly, almost half of cancer-related deaths in Latino males result from four of five of the following diagnoses: lung and bronchus (13%), colon and rectum (11%), liver and related (11%), and prostate (10%), with the addition of pancreatic cancer (8%). For Latinas, almost 60% of cancer diagnoses result from, in descending order: breast (29%), uterine corpus (8%), colon and rectum (8%), thyroid (7%), and lung and bronchus (6%). Relatedly, over half of cancer-related deaths for Latinas result from breast (14%), lung and bronchus (10%), colon and rectum (9%), pancreas (8%), and liver cancer (6%).

Breast Cancer

According to Miller et al. (2021), both incidence and death from breast cancer are about 30% lower for Latinas as compared to NLW counterparts, mainly due to the protective reproductive patterns of these generally younger women (i.e., younger age of first birth, number of subsequent births or what is referred to as *parity*). Such parity is especially true for Mexican immigrant women in California, whose rate of breast cancer is almost 30% lower than for their U.S.-born Mexican counterparts. Thanks to improved detection and treatment since 1990, rates of breast cancer and related deaths have decreased for Latinas and NLW women alike (29% and 42% lower, respectively). Nevertheless, Latinas continue to experience lower rates of early-stage detection and consequent problems. Hence, there is considerable room for primary and secondary prevention.

Cervical Cancer

While cervical cancer is about 32% higher in Latinas as compared to NLW women, incidence has been steadily declining over the past 30 years—by 50% for Latinas (i.e., from 17.8 to 9.4 per 100,000) and by 33% for NLW women (i.e., from 9.4 to 6.8 per 100,000). Such improvement also translates to declining deaths by more than 30% for both groups of women, attributed

Estimated New Cases*

Males

Prostate	17,600	22%
Colon & rectum	9,000	11%
Lung & bronchus	6,000	7%
Kidney & renal pelvis	5,900	7%
Liver & intrahepatic bile duct	4,800	6%
Non-Hodgkin lymphoma	4,700	6%
Leukemia	3,700	5%
Urinary bladder	3,300	4%
Pancreas	2,800	3%
Oral cavity & pharynx	2,500	3%
All sites	80,200	100%

Females

Breast	28,100	29%
Uterine corpus	7,900	8%
Colon & rectum	7,500	8%
Thyroid	6,300	7%
Lung & bronchus	5,800	6%
Non-Hodgkin lymphoma	4,200	4%
Kidney & renal pelvis	3,800	4%
Leukemia	2,900	3%
Pancreas	2,900	3%
Urinary cervix	2,700	3%
All sites	96,400	100%

Estimated Deaths

Males

Lung & bronchus	3,200	13%
Colon & rectum	2,700	11%
Liver & intrahepatic bile duct	2,600	11%
Prostate	2,400	10%
Pancreas	1,900	8%
Stomach	1,200	5%
Leukemia	1,000	4%
Non-Hodgkin lymphoma	1,000	4%
Kidney & renal pelvis	800	3%
Brain & other nervous system	800	3%
All sites	23,800	100%

Females

Breast	3,100	14%
Lung & bronchus	2,300	10%
Colon & rectum	2,000	9%
Pancreas	1,900	8%
Liver & intrahepatic bile duct	1,500	7%
Ovary	1,200	5%
Uterine corpus	1,200	5%
Stomach	1,000	4%
Leukemia	800	4%
Non-Hodgkin lymphoma	800	4%
All sites	22,700	100%

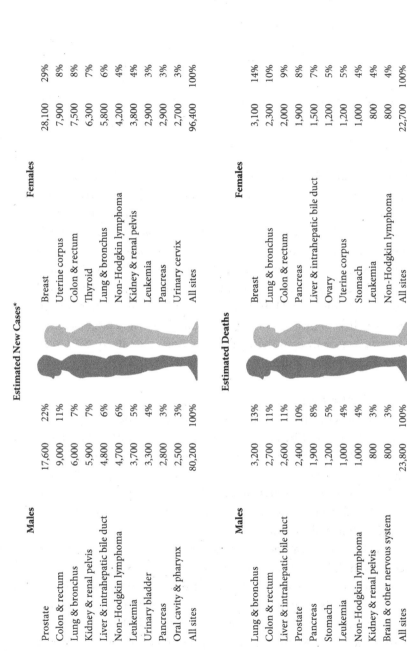

Figure 10.2. Most common types of cancer and related deaths among Latinos in the United States, 2021 estimates.

From Miller et al. (2021). Cancer statistics for Hispanics/Latinos, 2021. *CA: A Cancer Journal for Clinicians, 71*(6), 466–487. With permission from Wiley.

mainly to update of preventive screening or pap smears. Relatedly, Latinos are more willing to receive the human papillomavirus (HPV) vaccine (about 70% in Latinx youth versus 55% in NLW youth), which is capable of preventing almost 90% of all HPV-related cancers (Miller et al., 2018). Hence, providers can feel reasonably confident in supporting Latino openness to cervical cancer screening and vaccine update more generally (e.g., for Covid-19).

Lung Cancer

Lung cancer incidence and death rates are approximately 50% lower in Latino men and 65% lower in Latina women, as compared to NLW counterparts, reflecting long-standing lower rates of smoking. Currently rates of smoking for Latinos are 40% lower than for NLWs (9% and 16%, respectively). Lung cancer death rates have also been declining for Latinos over the past two decades (5.1% decline for men, and 4.6% for women between 2010 and 2019). Nevertheless, lung cancer remains the number one cancer-related cause of death in Latino men (13% of deaths by cancer), and number two in Latina women (10% of deaths by cancer), making it a prime target for prevention efforts, especially considering that smoking accounts for 80% of all lung cancer deaths in the United States

Updates on Other Cancers

While prostate cancer is the most commonly diagnosed type in Latino men, it now accounts for only 10% of cancer deaths thanks to early diagnosis in both Latino and NLW men. In fact, incidence and death have been rapidly declining for all men of color and white counterparts (42% and 49% lower, respectively) since the mid-1990s (Miller et al., 2018). Regular assessment in middle-aged to older men is recommended to continue this welcomed trend in cancer prevention and control.

The incidence of liver cancer is twice as high in Latinos versus NLWs, and twice as high in U.S.-born Mexican men in California versus their immigrant counterparts (21.6 per 100,000 and 11.8 per 100,000, respectively). While more research is needed, such risk appears related to risk factors that rise during acculturation: alcohol use, obesity, T2D, and the Hepatitis C virus (HCV). Miller et al. (2018) note that the long-term increase in U.S. rates of liver cancer appear due in part to the HCV epidemic that began in the 1960s and peaked during the late 1980s. Thus, addressing the above set of risk factors will produce multiple positive health consequences.

Cancer Prevention and Control

Prevention Efforts

En Acción [In Action]: The National Hispanic Leadership Initiative on Cancer (NHLIC) was a pioneering program of research and action to prevent and control cancer in major U.S. Latino populations (i.e., Mexican, Puerto Rican, Cuban American, Central American) in eight major Latino urban centers: San Francisco, San Diego, Houston, San Antonio, Laredo, Brownsville, Brooklyn, and Miami. This initiative consisted of three major components: (1) conducting a large-scale survey to assess cancer screening behaviors and related background and risk factors; (2) promoting cancer prevention and control at the community level by connecting national and regional experts with grass-roots groups to mount media campaigns and peer network support efforts; and (3) evaluating prevention efforts. A series of published reports from the NHLIC documents ethno-regional differences in cancer risk and correlates, and evaluations of NHLIC's socioculturally congruent prevention intervention model. *Acción's* three dimensions and evaluation are highlighted below to underscore the components of effective cancer prevention in Latino communities throughout America.

The NHLIC Risk Survey
With regard to generating cancer risk prevention data, the NHLIC survey was conducted in the early 1990s and consisted of 1,200 telephone interviews per each of the eight key city sites, stratified by sex (male, female) and age (under and over 40) (Ramirez et al., 1999). Areas assessed included degree of health care, fruit and vegetables consumption, smoking, various forms of cancer screening for women (i.e., history of pap smears and mammograms) and men (i.e., digital rectal exams for screening prostate cancer), and other risk factors. Reports from this database provide insights into many of the dynamics of cancer risk in Latino populations across the country, and provide the basis for implementing NHLIC's prevention intervention model.

The NHLIC Prevention Model
Education and advocacy are based on a *social modeling* approach in which *behavioral journalism* is used to create local "role model" stories of actual community residents preventing and controlling cancer that are disseminated through mass media (i.e., television news, radio, newspapers) and small local media

(e.g., print material distributed by grass-roots volunteers). These stories include how the role models acquired information, changed attitudes, and picked up the skills needed for cancer prevention or control. Following the media campaign, local peer networks of CHWs, composed primarily of volunteer housewives and in some places *promotores* connected with community health services, were trained to reinforce the media messages with friends, neighbors, and others in the community, in an effort to prevent cervical and breast cancer specifically.

Preventing Cervical and Breast Cancer

At the time of this study, Latinas had twice the rate of cervical cancer than NLW women (4.2 and 2.1 per 100,000 respectively), both of whom have half of these prevalence rates today. Then as now, Latinas were least likely of all groups of women in the United States to receive pap smear screening. This means that Latinas have been suffering and/or dying needlessly, because cervical cancer screening can save the lives of women of childbearing age who acquire regular pap smear screening so that pre-cancer lesions can be quickly treated. Breast cancer screening is also lower for Latinas than for NLW and NLB women (Ramirez et al.; 2000a).

Ethno-regional Differences in Latina Cancer Screening
NHLIC survey data reveal considerable ethno-regional differences in cancer screening. For example, screening for cervical (Ramirez et al., 2000b) and breast cancer (Ramirez et al., 2000a) was consistently lower for Mexican American women in Texas (especially in the South Texas border region), while cancer screening was highest among Central Americans in San Francisco and among Cuban Americans in Miami. More specifically, for Latinas over the age of 40, use of pap smear screening during the past three years was lowest in Texas (from about 48% in Laredo to 60% in Houston), compared to between 63% (Puerto Ricans in New York) and 74% (Central Americans in San Francisco) for other Latina groups.

Not surprisingly, the same pattern as above was found for mammogram screening during the past two years for Latinas over 40: lowest in Texas (from approximately 42% in Laredo to 59% in San Antonio) as compared to between 60% (Mexican American women in San Diego) and 83% (Central American women in San Francisco) for other Latina groups. Informed by these geographical data, the NHLIC went about conducting analysis to better understand the social and cultural context of cancer prevention screening in these Latino communities, and to test their prevention intervention model.

Social Integration and Cancer Screening

The NHLIC team investigated the relation between cancer screening and social integration for Latinas over the age of 40 (Suarez et al.; 2000) and found that those with more friends and relatives, more social contacts, and higher church membership and attendance were almost twice as likely to have had a recent pap smear than Latinas low in social integration. In fact, church involvement emerged as the strongest predictor of cervical cancer screening. Social networks were generally large and active for these middle-aged and older Latinas, and the impressive link between social integration and cancer screening was strongest for Mexican Americans and weakest Puerto Rican women. In fact, there was no relation between social integration and screening for Puerto Ricans for whom social networks were smallest, indicating greater isolation. The results support the NHLIC's prevention intervention model that is designed to mobilize naturally occurring peer support networks in Latino communities to help prevent cancer.

Deploying the NHLIC Model

The NHLIC team decided to promote cervical cancer screening where it was most needed by implementing their prevention model in the U.S.-Mexico border region of South Texas (Ramirez et al.; 1999). In Brownsville, *Salud en Acción* consisted of a predominantly Spanish-speaking media blitz that included over 80 TV segments, over 60 newspaper stories, and nearly 50 radio programs featuring local role model stories. Embedded in these personalized accounts of cervical cancer prevention were the knowledge, attitudes, and skills involved with acquiring pap smears, as well as ways that spouses and family members supported such behavior for the sake of the entire family. Following the media blitz, peer networks were mobilized by identifying and training 175 predominantly homemaker volunteers to incorporate cancer prevention into their daily communications with community residents.

To evaluate *En Acción*, a panel of just over 100 Brownsville women, who had participated in the NHLIC baseline survey mentioned above, were re-interviewed following several months of the intervention, and their data were compared to both their pre-intervention baseline Brownsville data as well as to the data of a control comparison panel of over 100 women from Laredo, where *En Acción* was not implemented. As can be seen in Table 10.4, impressive intervention effects were reported only in Brownsville, where the percentage of women in the highest pap smear adherence condition increased from a little over half at baseline to nearly two-thirds in this panel of women. Further, the percent of Brownville women in the lowest adherence condition decreased from almost a quarter at baseline to under

Table 10.4. Percent of Mexican American Women in Highest and Lowest Pap Smear Adherence Rates by NHLIC Intervention (Brownsville) and Control (Laredo) Sites

Site	Adherence	Baseline (1994)	Follow-up (1996)
Brownsville	Highest[1]	54.2	60.7
(Program)	Lowest[2]	23.4	13.1
Laredo	Highest[1]	46.8	47.1
(Campaign)	Lowest[2]	27.6	25.0

[1]Within past year or two years (at baseline) and strong intentions (at follow-up).
[2]Never or more than three years late and no intentions (at follow-up).
Adapted from Ramirez et al. (2000a) Cervical cáncer screening in regional Hispanic populations. American Journal of Health Behavior, 24(3), 181–192.

10% in the panel. In contrast, no such positive changes in cancer screening rates were evident for women at the Laredo control site.

Promotora-driven Cervical Cancer Prevention
More recently, Mann et al. (2015) conducted a review of the literature on interventions to increase cervical cancer screening in Latinas that yielded 32 interventions, 12 of which significantly increased screening. Focusing on these 12 studies, the authors conclude that the most successful efforts utilized community-based participatory approaches (e.g., collaborative, tailored), were theory-driven (e.g., behavioral, social cognitive), and utilized *promotoras* to support and lead the interventions. In fact, 75% of all interventions reviewed utilized *promotoras*, whose roles included providing education, serving as role models with screening experience, assisting participants navigating the health care system, and providing transportation and child care.

Breast Cancer Prevention

Telenovela-driven Cancer Prevention
Wilkin et al. (2007) evaluated the effectiveness of inserting a breast cancer prevention storyline into the popular *telenovela* [soap opera] *Ladrón de Corazones* [Thief of Hearts], designed to increase breast cancer knowledge and intention to seek a mammogram. True to the telenovela format, the storyline depicted the dramatic struggles of a woman and her family confronted with breast cancer (avoidance, misinformation, pregnancy, surgery, etc.). The effectiveness of this

intervention was assessed by calls made to 1-800-4-CANCER, as encouraged by the *Ladrón* actress on broadcast days, and by participants in a national viewer telephone survey conducted by *Telemundo*, the Spanish-language television network, that compared 293 regular *Ladrón* viewers with 207 non-reviewers. Subsequent focus groups with viewers also explored their viewing experience. Results revealed significantly greater calls to the 1-800 cancer information number on broadcast versus non-broadcast days, and significantly greater breast cancer knowledge in viewers versus non-viewers, including a significant increase in intention by male viewers to recommend that a family member seek a mammogram. Interestingly, there was no such intention effect for female viewers, because their baseline rate of intentions to seek a mammogram were high to begin with. This study represents a creative culture-based way to reach millions of Spanish-language viewers with potentially lifesaving health information for themselves and family members.

Health Care System–driven Prevention

A Su Salud [To Your Health] *Breast Health Program*, is designed to promote breast cancer screening in Latina women 40 years of age and older, enrolled in a financial assistance program for the uninsured, and who have never been screened for breast cancer, or not during the last five years. Evaluated by Li et al. (2019), this program was implemented by University Health System, Bexar County Hospital District, a historic Texas county that is home to the city of San Antonio, the Alamo, and a Latino population of 60%. *A Su Salud* is a long-term, comprehensive program that includes a health promotion media campaign, educational outreach, patient navigation, and mammography screening services. The media campaign and educational outreach are designed to change behavior through mass-media education, disseminating breast cancer prevention messages that are reinforced by peer role models, and by employing an outreach coordinator to educate small businesses, churches, and local community groups in the program's catchment area. Both patient navigation and mammography service are intended to mitigate social, cultural, and economic obstacles by supporting and guiding Latinas through screening services, free for eligible patients.

Between 2013 and 2016, about 2,100 predominately Latina women, age 40 and older, were successfully navigated through this health care system-wide program, with mammography screening increasing from 60% to 80% for these women with little if any previous breast cancer screening. Five subsequent focus groups with a total of 30 program participants showed that *A Su Salud* improved knowledge, attitudes, and breast health behaviors. This study documents the effectiveness of health care system meso-level innovations tailored to the needs of an especially vulnerable Latina patient population.

Smoking Prevention with NHLIC Model

While rates of smoking are much lower for Latinos than NLWs, it certainly makes sense to build upon their historically low rates of smoking considering that 16% of cancer-related deaths in Latino men, and 13% in Latina women, result from lung cancer. Hence, McAlister et al. (1992) used the NHLIC model, described above, to prevent smoking in a Texas-Mexico border community with auspicious results. Over a period of five years, these researchers implemented four smoking cessation campaigns, advertised as *Programa a Su Salud* [Program for your health], in the South Texas city of Eagle Pass. The nearby town of Del Rio was selected as the no-intervention control comparison. To evaluate *Su Salud*, a panel of 135 participants from Del Rio was compared to a panel of 160 residents from Eagle Pass. The Eagle Pass panel also included a subsample of 70 residents who received intensive counseling for smoking cessation (N = 70) in addition to the community-wide intervention. That is, 70 Eagle Pass residents accepted an additional offer of more individualized counseling for quitting smoking that ranged from telephone consultations to face-to-face meetings with outreach workers, as well as enrollment in the American Cancer Society's Latino-focused telephone-based smoking prevention intervention.

With regard to results, self-reported rates of smoking cessation for Eagle Pass were 17% with half verified though breath samples into a portable carbon monoxide analyzer. In comparison, only 8% of the Del Rio panel reported cessation, with only 1.5% verified through carbon monoxide analysis. Interestingly, no differences were found between 70 Eagle Pass participants who received additional intensive counseling and those exposed only to the NHLIC prevention campaign. Thus, use of the NHLIC model to prevent smoking appears to result in moderate reductions in smoking for border-area Mexican Americans, and appears to be as effective as more intensive individual counseling to prevent smoking. The broad impact (i.e., community or region-wide, TV audiences in the hundreds of thousands) underscores the urgent need for multi-level health promotion and disease prevention and treatment, not only at the micro-individual level but also the meso-community and macro-social levels in order to achieve optimal impact. Such are the approaches described with regard to the persistent global pandemic, HIV/AIDS.

HIV/AIDS

As a highly contagious *airborne* virus, Covid-19 continues to demand our attention and resources as a shape-shifting global pandemic that has claimed the lives of well over six million globally, including one million in the United States, and counting. Fortunately, the advent of effective vaccines, along with public health guidelines, have provided the needed handle on this devastating pandemic despite continuing challenges of increasingly contagious variants of Covid-19, the need for booster vaccinations, and of course citizens divided by an unnecessarily politicized public health crisis that demands unity for optimal control. Overshadowed by the coronavirus, is the *bloodborne* HIV that has claimed the lives of over 36 million people globally and about 700,000 domestically since 1981.

In the United States today, about 1.2 million are infected with HIV, nearly a quarter of whom are Latino (CDC, 2021). Like Covid-19, HIV is also a study in structural vulnerability, exploiting global and domestic inequality along the lines of race/ethnicity, gender and gender identity, and sexual orientation, each conflated with stigma, discrimination, and low SES. According to the CDC (2021), although Latinos compose 19% of the population, Latino adolescents and adult combined comprise 27% of the 38,000 new HIV cases in 2018. Nearly 88% of these Latino HIV cases occur in men that have sex with men. While infection from heterosexual contact (7%) and IV drug use (4%) is low for Latino men, these modes of transmission account for 87% and 12%, respectively, of new HIV cases in Latina adolescents and women combined. While significant advances in AIDS care have evolved since the first case in 1981, Latinos lag slightly behind non-Latinos with AIDS in terms of receiving *some* AIDS care (61% and 65%, respectively), *being retained in* AIDS care (49% and 50%), and *viral suppression* (53% and 56%). Lack of health insurance and immigration status mitigate HIV testing and consequent care if HIV positive, and an estimated 17% of Latinos with HIV are unaware of their status. These data reveal the stratification of risk for HIV along different dimensions of human diversity illustrated below through a lens of *structural vulnerability*.

Structural Vulnerability: The Case of Latino Migrant Laborers

The author has dedicated over 30 years to studying HIV risk in Latino migrant laborers that live and work in the United States, for extended periods of time, providing *essential labor* to lucrative American businesses and industries such as construction, the vast service sector, and agricultural labor. Reviews of the literature over the past 25 years or so (Organista, Carrillo, and Ayala, 2004; Organista and Balls Organista, 1997) document concerning vulnerability to HIV in this population that includes high numbers of sex partners, including sex between men and with female sex workers, high rates of STDs, consequent risk to female partners in Mexico and Central America, and worrisome rates of alcohol and some substance use. Such risk factors are exacerbated by work that is typically difficult, dangerous, inconsistent and low paying, easily exploitable, lonely, and disruptive of social, familial, romantic, and sexual relations in the country of origin. Background characteristics of Latino migrants that also influence vulnerability include low formal education and literacy, limited English, undocumented status, traditional gender roles, and very limited access to health care.

Latino Migrant Day Laborers

Over the past 20 years, the author's own research on Latino migrant day laborers (LMDLs) led to the development and testing of a structural-environmental model of vulnerability to alcohol-related sexual HIV risk in this especially marginalized Latino population. Indeed, this theoretical model formed the basis of his book, *HIV Prevention with Latinos: Theory, Research and Practice*, the first-ever compilation on this topic published over a decade ago (Organista, 2012). All authors contributing to this book project considered their own work in relation to the structural-environmental model described in the book's first chapter. Results from recently testing this model with LMDLs are described here, with larger implications for how HIV/AIDS in Latinos can be better conceptualized and responded to from a structural vulnerability framework that transcends the predominant behavioral and biomedical models of risk, by examining multiples levels of risk with implications for multilevel practice.

After years of surveying Latino labor migrants, both in Mexico as well as the United States, including qualitative individual interviews and focus groups, the author and his research team developed a compelling conceptual model of alcohol-related sexual HIV risk in LMDLs. For this they were awarded a federal grant from the NIAAA (National Institute on Alcohol Abuse and Alcoholism) to refine and test their model in the San Francisco Bay Area. Between 2010 and 2015, the research team partnered with LMDL-serving community-based agencies to access and engage a purposive sample of 51 LMDLs in semi-structured interviews about their lives as day laborers, including alcohol and substance use, and sexual relations, in the United States. *Purposive* refers to deliberately sampling for a specific purpose, in this case to obtain a fairly diverse and representative sample of LMDLs (i.e., from Mexico and Central America, younger and older adults, varying length of time in the United States). This phase of the study centered the voices of the men and proved invaluable for refining ideas about the role of environmental risk factors (i.e., too little work, poor living conditions, discrimination), indirectly leading to sexual risk by way of distress-related risk factors (i.e., problem drinking, depression, anxiety) as well as by way of protective cultural (contact with family in country of origin, *paisanos* at work and in the community, access to Latino festivals, food, music, soccer at the park) and community resources (i.e., services to help mitigate the impact of psychosocial and health problems).

La *Desesperación*

For instance, from the ethnographic interviews, we learned that the Latino cultural idiom of distress, *desesperación* [desperation], was frequently used by participants to express their frustration and dissatisfaction with their lives in the United States, as well as the distressing context of vulnerability or falling into *vicios* [vices] such as problem drinking and unsafe sex:

> En la desesperación, puede ser que se siente uno solo, deprimido y triste y lleva el momento en que uno caiga. [In a state of desperation, one can feel alone, depressed, and sad, and therein lies the moment when one falls].

Thus, the research team developed and validated a scale of *desesperación* to include among the model's distress-related factors depression, anxiety, and problem drinking. After deciding upon the most salient model variables, researchers either created or located existing scales to measure them for the next phase of the study involving the administration of a survey questionnaire to 344 LMDLs from San Francisco and Berkeley. To test the theoretical model of structural-environmental vulnerability to alcohol and substance-related sexual HIV risk in LMDLs, structural equation modeling (SEM) was used to assess the hypothesized relationships among model variables. SEM is a statistical package for testing theories or the predicted relationships between variables in a theoretical model.

384 SOLVING LATINO PSYCHOSOCIAL AND HEALTH PROBLEMS

Testing Structural Vulnerability

The results of model testing, reported elsewhere in detail (Organista, Jung, & Neilands, 2020), are displayed in Figure 10.3. As can be seen, the environmental risk factor *Discrimination* (e.g., day-to-day disrespect, unequal treatment), is positively and significantly related to four of the five distress-related risk factors of depression, anxiety and *desesperación* (divided into its two subscales, or two-factor structure, *frustration* and *dissatisfaction*). Also, the environmental risk factor *Living Conditions* (e.g., degree of trust and getting along with roommates) is negatively and significantly related to *desesperación*/dissatisfaction. Of the distress-related risk factors, only problem drinking is positively and significantly related to the sexual risk outcome index composed of the frequency of alcohol and substance use before or during sex, frequency of condom use, and sexual relations with sex partners vulnerable to HIV (i.e., with sex workers, between men, and with occasional casual sex partners). Monogamous sexual relations with a regular partner was not included this syndemic index of sex especially vulnerable to HIV.

Regarding the role of protective cultural and community factors in mitigating risk, results also show that *Contact with Family* (e.g., sending money or packages of goods back home, phone calls and texting) is negatively and significantly related to all five distress-related risk factors, while accessing local *Latino Cultural Resources and Community Services* (e.g., that solve problems, know how to treat Latinos in the words of participants) is negatively and significantly related to *desesperación*/dissatisfaction and depression. Hence, the more contact with families in Mexico and Central America the less overall distress, including problem drinking which is strongly related to the index of sexual risk. The protective effects of contact with family are pivotal given remaining findings that *Discrimination* is also significantly and negatively related to *Contact with Family* and use of *Cultural Resources and Community Services*. That is, as discrimination increases and contact with family decreases, problem drinking increases and so does sexual HIV risk. Similarly, the positive and significant relation between *Working Conditions* and *Contact with Family* means that when working conditions are typically low or poor (e.g., low earnings during past week, time working/waiting for work), *Contact with Family* is also low, and both *Problem Drinking* and sexual HIV risk increase. Indeed, this latter pair of findings support and specify the hypothesized indirect relations between risky environmental factors (discrimination and working conditions) and

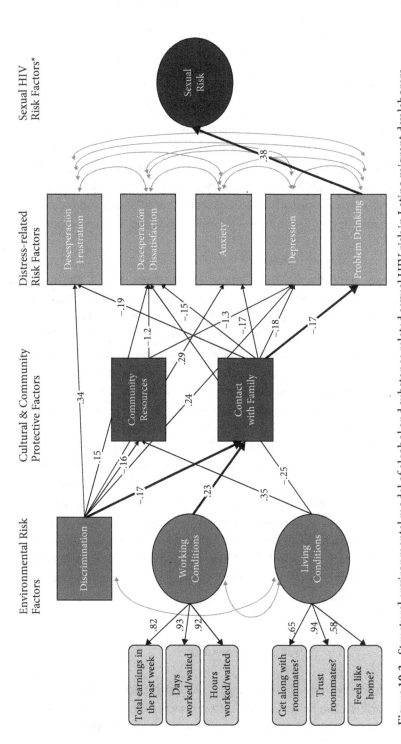

Figure 10.3. Structural environmental model of alcohol and substance related sexual HIV risk in Latino migrant day laborers (N = 344): Significant standardized direct path coefficients and factor loadings.

Note: *Alcohol before/during sex + substances before/during sex + condom use less than always.

From Organista, Jung, & Neilands (2020).

sexual risk, by way of environmentally induced distress (problem drinking), as well as by way of under-utilized protective factors (contact with family) capable of mitigating distress (problem drinking) and sexual HIV risk.

Insights gained from the qualitative phase of the study aid in interpreting study findings. For instance, when discussing contact with family, men mentioned not wanting to burden their family with their problems, often noting that "they wouldn't understand" what they faced in the United States. Further, because these men averaged earnings of only $200/week on average, sending money and goods home was very limited. Also, inability to fulfill their gendered roles as providers most likely further inhibited communication with family despite the protective effects of this central cultural resource.

Implications for Multilevel Practice
Several implications for multilevel practice follow from study findings. At the micro-level, encouraging and facilitating contact with family (e.g., via FaceTime), especially during duress, can help remind men that family support is strongest when it runs in both directions (i.e., that sharing problems in the United States is not simply a burden but a way to garner support while keeping family members informed). At the meso-community level, Latino cultural resources and Latino-focused community services should be supported considering their distress-mitigating qualities. The measure of community services developed for this study was derived from what the men shared about helpful services used, In addition to speaking Spanish, these helpful services know how to treat Latinos, do not keep them waiting for long periods of time, and help to solve problems. At the macro-level, findings strongly suggest mitigating anti-Latino, and especially anti-undocumented, discrimination by pursuing sensible immigration reform that creates a win–win scenario for migrant workers and American businesses and industry that depend on such essential labor. Other illustrations of HIV-prevention strategies that include sociocultural and structural-environmental elements are described below.

Male Farmworkers

A collaboration between the University of California Irvine and a health clinic in Northern San Diego County, with experience serving farm workers, resulted in an intervention designed to increase condom use with female sex workers among 193 Mexican male farmworkers (Mishra & Connor, 1996). HIV prevention information was provided to participants in the culture-friendly form of both *fotonovelas* and *radionovelas* [radio soap operas], the latter broadcasted daily on a local Spanish-language station (participants were given radios, program times, and encouraged to tune in). *Tres hombres sin fronteras* [three men without borders] was both humorous and dramatic and depicted three scenarios in which the three men respectively engage in the following scenarios: (1) one decides to use a condom with a sex worker; (2) another abstains from sex with sex workers; and (3) the third, as a consequence of unprotected sex with a sex worker, infects his wife with HIV, who gives birth to an HIV-positive baby.

All participants were pre- and post-tested, and results showed significant gains in HIV/AIDS knowledge and related attitudes and in reported condom use with sex workers. Of those men who had such sex during the course of the study, 20 of 37 reported condom use at posttest versus only one of 32 at pretest. A more rigorous replication was conducted by Sañudo (1999) with the same auspicious pattern of results: of the 20 out of 85 farmworkers reporting sex with sex workers at baseline, only four reported having used condoms. However, at post-intervention, of the 24 reporting sex with sex workers, 16 reported condom use. Further, in the non-intervention control group, 22 of 90 farmworkers reported sex with sex workers at baseline, and of the 26 of 90 that reported sex with sex workers at post-intervention, none reported any condom use. Replication of this effective intervention is warranted, including illustrations of other vulnerable situations such as excessive drinking before and during sex, unprotected sex between men, including transgendered individuals, and resuming sex with partners in countries of origin following time in the United States.

Latino Men Who Have Sex with Men

Sex between men remains the most vulnerable form of transmission for acquiring HIV in the United States, and this is true throughout Latin American and the Caribbean. Thus, prevention efforts need to address sex between men regardless of sexual identity, and promote prevention efforts responsive to the structural-environmental, sociocultural, and sexual contexts of such vulnerability. Rafael Diaz's pioneering HIV prevention research with

Latino gay men stands out for its tight sociocultural integration of theory, research, and practice.

Oppression versus Self-regulation

Diaz (1998) asserts that while Latino gay men neither wish nor intend to engage in unsafe sex, their sexual self-regulatory processes are vulnerable to breakdown in sexual situations because such regulation is frequently undermined by internalized oppressive social factors such as homophobia, racism, and poverty. These forces include patriarchy embedded within values and practices such as *familismo* and *machismo* that are typically oppressive to sexual minority family members. For example, while familism is generally *the* central cultural source of lifelong support among Latinos, it can increase vulnerability in Latino gay males when it is rejecting of deviations from the traditional heterosexual norm.

Gay male family members are too often faced with the dilemma of having to choose between *la familia* or living one's life openly. For those that remain in the family by concealing their sexual orientation, Diaz believes that their sexuality can become compartmentalized within a forbidden domain of secrecy and shame. Thus there can be dissociation from one's sexuality, leaving many Latino gay males with too little opportunity during their early psychosocial development to have the kinds of normative experiences needed to develop a healthy and meaningful sense of self, especially with respect to sexual, gender, and cultural roles. An unfortunate consequence of this psychosexual and cultural predicament is seeking expression of sexual and romantic feelings in limited, secretive, impulsive, and other unpredictable ways that render Latino gay males vulnerable to risk (e.g., cruising for anonymous sex, secret relationships, being vulnerable to sexual manipulation and abuse).

This is not to say that traditional families can't be supportive of sexual minority family members, especially in view of changing cultural norms such as the legalization of gay marriage in the United States, as well as Mexico five years earlier! However, such family support has been far less available than needed and is more likely to come from a key family member or two (e.g., a mother or sister) that can make a considerable difference. The lack of broader support is unfortunate given the powerful role that family acceptance can play in the lives of sexual- minority members faced with continuing society-wide stigma and discrimination, as evidenced recently in Florida where Governor DeSantis' "Parental Rights in Education" bill now bans state public school teachers from providing classroom instruction about sexual orientation or gender identity through grade three or in a manner claimed to be age-inappropriate—as well as in Texas, where Governor Abbott has ordered child welfare officials to launch child abuse investigations into reports of transgender kids receiving gender-affirming care. While Abbott's directive is blocked by injunction at the time of this writing, numerous other states have also filed or are considering filing similar directives.

Machismo as Oppressor

Machismo is a well-known traditional patriarchal value and practice that gay Latino men often internalize early in maladaptive ways. Diaz (1998) notes that because Latino culture has traditionally confused sexuality with gender, gay men have been popularly likened to women inside of men's bodies. Thus, gay men who internalize this stereotype may be prone to think of themselves as inadequate or "failed men," resulting in either submissive or overly macho gay men with something to prove in the bedroom (e.g., submitting as expected or prioritizing sexual prowess over affection, communication, and safer sex strategies such as condom use).

Racism and poverty can also undermine the sexual and interpersonal lives of gay Latino men, who are frequently stereotyped as sexually exotic in the predominantly NLW gay community, and because they are often at a vulnerable economic disadvantage relative to white counterparts. Rather than risk rejection, some gay Latino men may succumb to the pressure to live up to sexual stereotypes or to not disappoint partners upon whom they may be economically dependent.

The bottom line in Diaz's psycho-cultural theoretical framework is that healthy self-regulation becomes undermined in challenging sexual situations where scripted and automatized behaviors, shaped by oppressive social and cultural forces, take over in unconscious and emotionally charged ways. Repeated experiences of failing to practice safer sex as intended can quickly lead to hopelessness and fatalism about contracting *el premio gordo* [the grand prize], as some gay men refer to HIV/AIDS. Thus, oppressive social and cultural regulators of interpersonal behavior become internalized psychological regulators of sexual behavior, experienced not simply as unsafe and risky but as meaningful scripts. While such a bold theory is not without its critics (e.g., does it lend itself to pathologizing gay Latino men?), it is a compelling theorized effort to conceptualize sexual HIV risk within a sociocultural context that oppresses Latino gay men on the basis of sexual orientation, race/ethnicity, and low SES.

Evidenced-based Practice

Diaz has conducted research to support his theory by connecting HIV risk, in a large and diverse urban sample of gay Latino men, to their personal experiences of homophobia (i.e., verbal and physical harassment during childhood for being gay), racism (i.e., rude treatment and police harassment linked to race/ethnicity), and poverty (i.e., running out of money for basic necessities, needing having to borrow money, having to look for work). Based on a probability sample of 912 gay Latino men, recruited from Latino and gay-identified bars, clubs, and social events in Los Angeles (N = 301), New York (N = 309), and Miami (N = 302), Diaz and Ayala (2000) found that men with high levels of HIV risk (i.e., unprotected sex with a recent non-monogamous partner) reported more of the above oppressive experiences compared to those with lower levels of HIV risk. Such findings led to a conceptually congruent HIV prevention intervention that has received national attention (i.e., supported by CDC, with funds and technical assistance, to disseminate across the country).

Hermanos de Luna y del Sol (HLS) [Brothers of the moon and sun] was designed by Diaz and Latino gay health educators in San Francisco's Latino Mission District, based on Diaz's adaptation of Bandura's (1994) theory of self-regulation and Freire's (1993) principles of empowerment education for the oppressed. HLS is designed to: (1) Break the frequent sexual silence among gay men by providing safe venues for serious and deep communication about their sexuality and sexual experience; (2) provide an experience of commonality and pride in which men feel part of a larger supportive gay Latino community; (3) provide opportunities for critical self-reflection and self-observation about forces that regulate sexual and other behaviors; (4) collaborate in the construction of group and individual strategies to address perceived obstacles to safer sex; and (5) create opportunities for social activism.

Outreach

Participants are recruited into HLS by outreach workers who visit Latino and gay-identified social venues and distribute attractive calling cards advertising *Encuentros de comunicación y amistad* [friendship and communication encounters] *para hombres Latinos 'de ambiente.'* The latter term literally means "for Latino men of the ambience," which according to Diaz (1998) "is a popular Latino expression referring collectively to all those who are homosexually active or self-identify as homosexual, even if only privately (p. 162).

He goes on to say that, "*De Ambiente* is thus a code phrase that denotes (in-group) knowledge about sexual orientation and behavior, but does so in a private, self-referenced way, without the implications of being out publicly within a viable gay community" (p. 162).

The carefully crafted calling cards feature an attractive logo composed of the HLS name around a composite drawing of a Latino man's face, partially eclipsed by a crescent moon on one side, both of which are encircled by the corona of the sun. On the card's backside is a carefully worded description of the program above a photo of smiling Latino men, including contact information and list of incentives ($10 and dinner per meeting, T-shirt). Consistent with *personalismo*, the invitation is warm and culturally familiar (e.g., *La cena ya esta servida* [dinner is already served] and *Solo faltas tu!* [the only thing missing is you!].

HLS HIV Prevention Groups

Interested participants attend four group sessions with the following goals: (1) to facilitate communication resulting in self-observation and critical self-reflection; (2) to enhance a sense of community and gay pride; and (3) to co-construct strategies to combat social and cultural "oppressors" to promote more satisfying and safer sex. Methods to achieve goals include discussions guided by key questions ranging from "What's the most difficult thing about being a Latino gay man?" and "How have you been affected by the HIV/AIDS epidemic?" to "What makes safe sex difficult for you?"

Participants also keep a safe sex journal guided by questions they are asked to answer within 24 hours of a sexual episode. For example, rate how positive or negative the sexual encounter was and why. Answers are discussed in the group to reveal personal and situational factors that hinder or facilitate safer sex, how self-regulation is enhanced by sex journal discourse, and ultimately how having a healthy, satisfying sex life is a *heroic struggle* against the many forms of oppression faced by Latino gay men.

Auspicious Results

A pilot study of 78 HLS participants revealed promising findings. The majority felt better about themselves, more connected to the Latino gay community, more able to understand their sexuality and risk for HIV, more capable of practicing safer sex and avoiding situations that make it difficult to practice safer sex (Diaz, 1998). From a structural vulnerability perspective, these men participated in a liberating, cultural and community-based experience that contextualized and facilitated the unlearning of internalized oppression to promote the proactive, healthy, satisfying, and safer sexual lives to which all people are entitled.

Puerto Rican Vulnerability to HIV/AIDS

Since the early days of the HIV pandemic, infection from injection drug use (IDU) continues to be overrepresented among Puerto Ricans both in the United States and Puerto Rico. Over 20% of new HIV infections result from IDU on the island, a higher rate than for any other group in the United States, with consequent higher morbidity and mortality (Deren et al., 2014). Relatedly, lower availability of syringe exchange programs (SEPs), drug abuse treatment, and anti-retroviral treatment for IDU, especially in Puerto Rico, continues to be a problem. Despite improvement over the past 40 years (e.g., in New York, rates of IDU-related HIV have decreased from about 50% in the mid-1980s to about 12%), Deren et al. (2014) advocate a *regional* approach to prevention and treatment aimed simultaneously at Puerto Rico and the northeastern United States where the majority of U.S. Puerto Ricans reside, where the highest rates of HIV from IDU occur (16%), and where half of all HIV+ Latino cases in the country are located. Further, this regional approach advocates greater access to SEPs which is not only a CDC-certified evidence-based HIV prevention practice but also increases the likelihood of injection drug–using people entering drug treatment. Unfortunately, SEPs are illegal in Puerto Rico and vary on a state to state basis in the U.S.

Research has long documented the IDU-related HIV/AIDS crisis for Puerto Ricans in the United States as well as in Puerto Rico, where the problem is exacerbated by an extremely high rate of poverty (43%) as compared to the United States (13%) and even Mississippi (20%), the most impoverished U.S. state. Multiple publications on this problem have been generated from the most comprehensive and long-term study on the topic. The Alliance for Research in El Barrio and Bayamón (ARIBBA) compared rates of HIV risk, infection, and mortality in 800 Puerto Rican IV drug users and crack smokers in East Harlem, or *El Barrio*, New York, with 399 of their counterparts in Bayamón, Puerto Rico, between 1996 to 2004 (Mino, Deren, & Colon, 2011). Concerning findings reveal that drug users in Puerto Rico became infected almost four times as often as those in New York, and also died three times as often. As compared to New York drug users, those on the island had significantly higher rates of all types of risky IDU behaviors assessed, including sharing needles.

Further, as compared to New York counterparts, drug users in Puerto Rico are also more vulnerable to engaging in IDU and sexual behaviors resulting in HIV infection. Unfortunately, not only are HIV prevention programs scarce in Puerto Rico, but their availability actually declined about 30% during the eight-year study period! While prevention research has benefited from ARIBBA findings, much more is needed to stave off this continuing HIV/AIDS crisis.

Preventing IDU-related HIV

Over 25 years ago, Colón et al. (1995) reported on an HIV prevention effort aimed straight at the heart of the IDU-driven Puerto Rican HIV/AIDS crisis on the island. Former IDUs were trained to conduct HIV prevention outreach education to over 1,100 IDUs in San Juan, Puerto Rico, that were actively injecting drugs, not enrolled in drug treatment programs. They were approached at shooting galleries and "copping areas" where drugs are scored, on the street corners of 10 different neighborhoods. Participants were 80% male, almost half HIV+, and had been injecting drugs for an average of 13 years. Outreach included education about sexual and IDU-related HIV transmission, demonstrations of proper condom use, and how to clean needles with bleach. Outreach workers spent an average of 12 weeks in the community and successfully post-tested almost 90% of the 1100 participants.

Results revealed significant decreases in sharing cookers, and increased needle cleaning with bleach. Also documented was less injecting in galleries, borrowing or renting needs, and sharing cookers. While encouraging, there was no impact on needle-sharing nor on related vulnerable sexual risk behaviors. Imagine how much more effective this unique intervention could be with adequate SEPs that Deren et al. (2014) describe as too few and underfunded to be maximally effective in Puerto Rico. Colón et al. (1998) also advocate specialized interventions for non–IV drug using female partners, who comprised the majority of the sex partners of IV drug using Puerto Rican men in their study. This gender-specific recommendation is consistent with Deren et al.'s advocacy for a policy-supported regional approach to the HIV/AIDS crisis impacting Puerto Ricans in the northeastern United States and Puerto Rico that would coordinate resources, programs, and outcome evaluation research where this pandemic is most impactful in the United States and its Latino territory.

Latino Health Prognosis

An immense amount of Latino-focused health research has accrued since the first edition of this textbook published in 2007, when the overall prognosis of Latino health in American was deemed *mixed* at best. Indeed, there continue to be too many Latinos, and lower-income Americans more generally, without health insurance given its tie to quality jobs that provide such benefits. There are still millions without such employment, ultimately rendering society exposed to public health crises such as the persistent Covid-19 pandemic. A recent analysis of the Affordable Care Act's progress toward significantly decreasing the uninsured in America reports that between 2012–13 (pre-ACA implementation) and 2015–16 (post-ACA implementation), rates of uninsured decreased by 10.5% for Latinos, 7.5% for African Americans, and 10.2% for NLWs and other low-income Americans in general (Lines et al., 2021). While an encouraging dent, multiple millions of Americans remain uninsured. Lines et al. (2021) also report wide variance between states in ACA-related coverage, underscoring that in some states, half of Latinos, over a quarter of African Americans, and almost half of low-income Americans overall remain uninsured despite full implementation of the ACA in 2014.

Further, well over 10 million undocumented residents, at least two-thirds of whom are Latino, remain ineligible for ACA coverage. Fortunately, FQHCs and IBHC more generally have significantly expanded health care access to all lower-income residents regardless of ability to pay or immigration status. Many states have also improved both their economy and public health and safety by taking it upon themselves to insure as many of their residents as possible, with California as a prime example. No doubt the expanding amount of prevalence data, increasingly disaggregated by diverse Latino populations, combined with the increasing number of rigorous and socioculturally informed outcome evaluations of urgently needed health services, will continue to improve the prognosis of Latino health beyond its current *mixed-plus* status.

References

Ali, S. (2022). California will offer health insurance to all undocumented immigrants. *The Hill* (June 29). https://thehill.com/changing-america/well-being/prevention-cures/3541196-california-will-offer-health-insurance-to-all-undocumented-immigrants/

Balfour, P. C. Jr., Ruiz, J. M., Talavera, G. A., Allison, M. A., Rodriguez, C. J. (2016). Cardiovascular Disease in Hispanics/Latinos in the United States *Journal of Latino Psychology*, 4(2), 98–113. https://doi.org/10.1037/lat0000056

Babamoto, K. S., Sey, A., Camilleri, A. J., Karlan, V. J., Catalasan, J., & Morisky, D. E. (2009). Improving diabetes care and health measures among Hispanics using community health workers: Results from a randomized controlled trial. *Health Education & Behavior*, 36(1), 113–126. https://doi.org/10.1177/1090198108325911

Bandura, A. (1994). Social cognitive theory and the exercise of control over HIV infection. In R. J. DiClemente & J. L Peterson (Eds.), *Preventing AIDS: Theories and methods of behavioral interventions* (pp. 25–59). New York: Plenum Press.

Becker, T. L., Babey, S. H., & Charles, S. A. (2019). Still left behind: Health insurance coverage and access to care among Latinos in California. Los Angeles, CA: UCLA Center for Health Policy Research.

California Department of Public Health (2021). COVID-19 Race and ethnicity data. Sacramento, CA. https://www.cdph.ca.gov/Programs/CID/DCDC/Pages/COVID-19/Race-Ethnicity.aspx

Carillo, J. E., Trevino, F. M., Betancourt, J. R., & Coustasse, A. (2001). Latino access to health care: The role of insurance, managed care, and institutional barriers. In M. Aguirre-Molina, C. W. Molina, & R. E. Zambrana (Eds.), *Health issues in the Latino community* (pp. 55–73). San Francisco: Jossey-Bass.

CDC (2021). Risk for COVID-19 infection, hospitalization, and death by race/ethnicity. https://www.cdc.gov/coronavirus/2019-ncov/covid-data/investigations-discovery/hospitalization-death-by-race-ethnicity.html#print

Cirlugea, O., & Ta. J. (2016). Chronic disease management and integrated care among Hispanic populations. In L. T. Benuto & W. O'Donohue (Eds.), *Enhancing behavioral health in Latino populations: Reducing disparities through integrated behavioral and primary care* (pp. 267–296). Springer International.

Colón, H. M., Sahi, H., Robles, R. R., & Matos, T. D. (1995). Effects of a community outreach program in HIV risk behaviors among injection drug users in San Juan, Puerto Rico: An analysis of trends. *AIDS Education and Prevention*, 7(3), 195–209.

Curtin, S. C. (2019). Suicide rates for females and males by race and ethnicity: United States, 1999 & 2019. Hyattsville, MD: NCHS Health-E Stats. https://www.cdc.gov/nchs/data/hestat/suicide/rates_1999_2017.htm

Deren, S., Gelpí-Acosta, C., Albizu-García, C. E., González, A., Des Jarlais, D. C., & Santiago-Negrón, S. (2014). Addressing the HIV/AIDS epidemic among Puerto Rican people who inject drugs: The need for a multiregion approach. *American Journal of Public Health*, 104(11), 2030–2036.

Diaz, R. M. (1998). *Latino gay men and HIV: Culture, sexuality, and risk behavior*. London: Routledge.

Diaz, R. M., & Ayala, G. (2000). *Social discrimination and health: The case of Latino Gay men and HIV risk*. Washington DC: The Policy Institute of the National Gay and Lesbian Task Force.

Pérez-Escamilla, R., & Putnik, P. (2007). The role of acculturation in nutrition, lifestyle, and incidence of Type 2 diabetes among Latinos. *The Journal of Nutrition*, 137, 860–870.

Pérez-Escamilla, R., et al. (2015). Impact of a community health workers–led structured program on blood glucose control among Latinos with type 2 diabetes: The DIALBEST Trial. *Diabetes Care*, 38, 197–205. doi:10.2337/dc14-0327

Freire, P. (1993). *Education for critical consciousness*. New York: Seabury.

Gore, M. O., Estacio, R. O., Dale, R., Coronel-Mockler, S., & Krantz, M. J. (2021). Cardiovascular risk factor knowledge among monolingual Hispanics. *Journal of Health Care for the Poor and Underserved, 32*(2), 688–699.

Heerman, W. J., Teeters, L., Sommer, E. C., Burgess, L. E., Escarfuller, J., Van Wyk, C., et al (2019). Competency-based approaches to community health: A randomized controlled trial to reduce childhood obesity among Latino preschool-aged children. *Childhood Obesity, 15*(8), 519–531. https://doi.org/10.1089/chi.2019.0064

Heron (2019). Deaths: Leading causes for 2017. *National Vital Statistics Reports, 68*(6), 1–76.

Hunt, L. M., Hamdi Arar, N., & Akana, L. L. (2000). Herbs, prayer, and insulin: Use of medical and alternative treatments by a group of Mexican American diabetes patients. *The Journal of Family Practice, 49*(3), 217–223.

Hunt, L. M., Pugh, J., & Valenzuela, M. (1998). How patients adapt diabetes self-care recommendations in everyday life. *The Journal of Family Practice, 46*(3), 207–215.

Hunt, L. M., Valenzuela, M., & Pugh, J. (1998). Porque me tocó a mi? Mexican American patients' causal stories and their relationship to treatment behaviors. *Social Scient and Medicine, 46*(8), 959–969.

Krantz, M., J., Beaty, B., Coronel-Mockler, S., Leeman-Castillo, B., Fletcher, K., & Estacio, R. O. (2017). Reduction in cardiovascular risk among Latino participants in a community-based intervention linked with clinical care. *American Jornal of Prevention Medicine, 53*(2), e71–e75.

Li, Y., Carlson, E., Hernandez, D. A., Green, B., Calle, T., Kumaresan, T., Madondo, K., et al. (2019). Patient perception and cost-effectiveness of a patient navigation program to improve breast cancer screening for Hispanic women. *Health Equity, 3*(1), 280–286. https://doi.org/10.1089/heq.2018.0089

Lines, G., Mengistu, K., Carr LaPorte, M. R., Lee, D., Anderson, L., Novinson, D., Dwyer, E., et al. (2021). States' performance in reducing uninsurance among Black, Hispanic, and low-income Americans following implementation of the Affordable Care Act. *Health Equity, 5*(1), 493–502. https://doi.org/10.1089/heq.2020.0102

Little T. V., Wang M. L., Castro E. M., Jiménez J., & Rosal, M. C. (2014). Community health worker interventions for Latinos with Type 2 diabetes: A systematic review of randomized controlled trials. *Currrent Diabetes Reports, 14*(558), 1–6. https://doi.org/10.1007/s11892-014-0558-1

Mann, L., Foley, K. L., Tanner, A. E., Sun, C. J., & Rhodes, S. D. (2015). Increasing cervical cancer screening among US Hispanics/Latinas: A qualitative systematic review. *Journal of Cancer Education, 30*(2), 374–387. https://doi.org/10.1007/s13187-014-0716-9

Marquez, I., Calman, N., & Crump, C. (2018). Using enhanced primary care services in high- risk Latino Populations to reduce disparities in glycemic control. *Journal of Health Care for the Poor and Underserved, 29*(2), 676–686.

McAlister, A. L., Ramirez, A. G., Amezcua, C., Pulley, L., Stern, M. P., & Mercado, S. (1992). Smoking cessation in Texas-Mexico border communities: A quasi-experimental panel study. *American Journal of Health Promotion, 6*(4), 274–279.

Miller, K. D., Goding Sauer, A., Ortiz, A. P., Fedewa, S. A., Pinheiro, P. S., Tortolero-Luna, G., et al. (2018). Cancer statistics for Hispanics/Latinos, 2018. *CA: A Cancer Journal for Clinicians, 68*(6), 425–445.

Miller, K. D., Ortiz, A. P., Pinheiro, P. S., Bandi, P., Minihan, A., Fuchs, H. E., et al. (2021). Cancer statistics for Hispanics/Latinos, 2021. *CA: A Cancer Journal for Clinicians, 71*(6), 466–487.

Mino, M., Deren, S., & Colon, H. M. (2011). HIV and drug use in Puerto Rico: Findings from the ARIBBA study. *Journal of the International Association of Physicians in AIDS Care, 10*(4), 248–259.

Mishra, S. I., & Conner, R. F. (1996). Evaluation of an HIV prevention program among Latino farmworkers. In S. I. Mishra, R. F. Connor, & J. R. Magana (Eds.), *AIDS crossing borders: The spread of HIV among migrant Latinos* (pp. 157–181). Boulder, CO: Westview Press.

Moon, H., Badana, A. N. S., Hwang, S, Sears, J. S., & Haley, W. E. (2019). Dementia prevalence in older adults: Variation by race/ethnicity and immigrant status. *American Journal of Geriatric Psychiatry, 27* (3), 241–250. https://doi.org/10.1016/j.jagp.2018.11.003

Office of Minority Health (2021). Diabetes and Hispanic Americans. https://www.minorityhealth.hhs.gov/omh/browse.aspx?lvl=4&lvlid=63

Office of Minority Health (2019). Profile: Hispanic/Latino Americans. https://www.minorityhealth.hhs.gov/omh/browse.aspx?lvl=3&lvlid=64

Organista, K. C., & Balls Organista, P. (1997). Migrant laborers and AIDS in the United States: A review of the literature. *AIDS Education and Prevention, 9*, 83–93.

Organista, K. C., Carrillo, H., & Ayala, G. (2004). HIV Prevention with Mexican Migrants: Review, critique, and recommendations. *Journal of Acquired Immune Deficiency Syndrome, 37* (Suppl. 4), S227–S239.

Organista, K. C., Jung, W., & Neilands, T. B. (2020). A structural-environmental model of alcohol and substance-related sexual HIV risk in Latino migrant day laborers. *AIDS and Behavior, 24*(11), 3176–3191. https://doi.org/10.1007/s10461-020-02876-4

Ramirez, A. G., Suarez, L., McAlister, A., Villarreal, R., Trapido, E., Talavera, G. A., et al. (2000b). Cervical cancer screening in regional Hispanic populations. *American Journal of Health Behavior, 24*(3), 181–192.

Ramirez, A. G., Talavera, G. A., Villarreal, R., Suarez, L., McAlister, A., Trapido, E., et al. (2000a). Breast cancer screening in regional Hispanic populations. *Health Education Research, 15*(5), 559–568.

Ramirez, A. G., Villarreal, R., McAlister, A., Gallion, K. J., Suarez, L., & Gomez, P. (1999). Advancing the role of participatory communication in the diffusion of cancer screening among Hispanics. *Journal of Health Communication, 4*, 31–36.

Sañudo, F. (1999). The effects of a culturally appropriate HIV intervention on Mexican farmworkers' knowledge, attitudes, and condom use behavior. Unpublished Master's Thesis. San Diego State University, Department of Public Health.

Schneiderman, N., Llabre, M., Cowie, C. C., et al. (2014). Prevalence of diabetes among Hispanics/Latinos from diverse backgrounds: The Hispanic Community Health Study/Study of Latinos (HCHS/SOL). *Diabetes Care, 37*(8), 2233–2239.

Schoenthaler, A., de la Calle, F., Pitaro, M., Lum, A., Chaplin, W., Mogavero, J. & Rosal, M. C. (2019). A systems-level approach to improving medication adherence in hypertensive Latinos: A randomized control trial. *Journal of General Internal Medicine, 35*(1), 182–189. https://doi.org/10.1007/s11606-019-05419-3

Soltero, E. G., et al. (2018). Effects of a community-based diabetes prevention program for Latino youth with obesity: A randomized controlled trial. *Obesity,* 00, 1–10. doi:10.1002/oby.22300

Talavera, G. A., et al. (2021). Latinos understanding the need for adherence in diabetes (LUNA-D): A randomized controlled trial of an integrated team-based care intervention among Latinos with diabetes. *TBM,* 1–11. doi:10.1093/tbm/ibab052

Suarez, L., Ramirez, A. G., Villarreal, R., Marti, J., McAlister, A., Talavera, G. A., et al. (2000). Social networks and cancer screening in four U.S. Hispanic groups. *American Journal of Preventive Medicine, 19*(1), 47–52.

Vazquez, I., M., Millenh, B., Bissett, L., Levenson, S. M., & Chipkin, S. R. (1998). Buena alimentacion, buena salud [Good Nutrition, Good Health]: A preventive nutrition intervention in Caribbean Latinos with Type 2 Diabetes. *American Journal of Health Promotion, 13*(2), 116–119.

Webb Hooper, M., Nápoles, A. M., & Perez-Stable, E. J. (2020). COVID-19 and racial/ethnic disparities. *JAMA, 323*(24), 2466–2467.

Wilkin, H. A., Valente, T. W., Murphy. S., Cody, M. J., Huang, G., & Beck, V. (2007). Does entertainment-education work with Latinos in the United States? Identification and the effects of a telenovela breast cancer storyline. *Journal of Health Communication, 12*(5), 455-469, https://doi.org/10.1080/10810730701438690.

11

Latino Power Primer

Political Participation, Representation, and Policy Benefit

A basic understanding of Latino political power, including how service providers may play important roles, is key to promoting Latino social positionality and mitigating psychosocial and health problems currently over-affecting Latino populations in the United States. Traditionally, the idea of political support, advocacy, and activism on behalf of a client group has been confined to public and political domains, or professional activity channeled through national, state, and local professional organizations that take positions on social issues and lobby elected officials on matters of importance to the profession. While the latter is imperative, service providers often run up against blurred boundaries within their professional roles regarding how to resist harmful polices and engage in forms of political support and activism on behalf of communities served.

Indeed, political activity has historically been discouraged and looked down upon at the professional public agency and institutional level, leaving many providers to experience a disconnect between political engagement on behalf of clients and their supposedly neutral professional roles. Again, this doesn't mean that national professional organizations, such as the National Association of Social Workers, American Psychological Association, and the American Public Health Association don't weigh in on important client-relevant political matters, but it can mean that practitioners too often possess only a vague sense of how to advocate on behalf of client groups such as Latinos, or even how to resist policies detrimental to communities served.

Human Service Providers and Political Advocacy

In their book *Affecting Change: Social Workers in the Political Arena*, now in its 7th edition, Haynes and Mickelson (2019) remind social and human

Solving Latino Psychosocial and Health Problems. Kurt C. Organista, Oxford University Press.
© Oxford University Press 2023. DOI: 10.1093/oso/9780190059637.003.0011

service professionals that while they may lack training in politics, they do possess a variety of skills and assets for operating in the political arena on behalf of clients and communities. At a minimum, such skills include expertise on specific client, community, and social problems; knowledge about service gaps; and best and promising practices. Service providers also possess access to agency and institutional records and data, as well as compelling case studies that can be highly relevant to policy development and advocacy.

Mindful of vague legal restrictions on the political activities of human service professionals, Haynes and Mickelson (2019) summarize what is allowed while on the job and what isn't according to the Hatch Act, enacted in 1939 to prohibit partisan political activity on the job (see Table 11.1). The Hatch Act was amended in 1993, as well as in 2012, to allow limited partisan political activities on the part of government employees (i.e., federal executive branch and employees of state and local executive agencies):

Table 11.1. Limits on Partisan Political Participation of Federal Government Employees While on the Job

Permitted	Not Permitted
Register people to vote	Register voters for only one party
Assist in voter registration drives	Campaign for/against candidates in partisan elections
Express opinions about candidates and issues	Collect contributions, sell tickets for political fund raising
Contribute funds to political organizations	Campaign activities to elect partisan candidates
Sign nomination petitions	Distribute campaign materials in partisan election
Wear political buttons and political messages *while off duty*; support nonpartisan organizations	Organize or manage political rallies
Campaign on referendum, constitutional amendments, and municipal petitions	Circulate nomination petitions
Be a candidate for nonpartisan elections (e.g., independent party candidate), or local offices such as school board or city council, which do not involve fund raising	Be a candidate in partisan elections

Haynes and Mickelson (2019) admit that exactly to whom the Hatch Act applies is not always clear, and service providers should seek such information from their professional organizations, bylaws, and agency administrators. For example, service providers working for nonprofit, tax-exempt organizations may still be subject to the above restrictions because of government funding streams received. Of course as citizens, service providers have the same rights as all citizens to participate in partisan politics *while off duty*. However, the frequent extremes of questionable and unjust policies often confront providers with the need to resist—as when, for example, California's infamous Proposition 187 required providers to not only deny human services to undocumented clients but to also report them to federal authorities. While Proposition 187 was met with immediate injunctions, and eventually declared unconstitutional by federal courts, many service providers at the time asserted that they would neither abdicate their care for clients in need nor police anybody's immigration status as if they were federal agents. Such resistance is even more relevant today, given the unprecedented persecution of undocumented people discussed in Chapter 12.

Political Participation

In Garcia's (2003a) analysis of Latino politics in America, the authors note that political participation, or actions to get desired officials elected in order to influence the policymaking process, depends heavily on a group's resources and incorporation into the political process. Not surprisingly, SES, with its related skills, networks, and resources, is the most powerful determinant of political participation (e.g., time, money, education, and work-related skills that transfer to the political arena). Related determinants include socialization into the political process (e.g., via parents, other adult and peer role models, workplace, college, and social networks), and generally positive attitudes, beliefs, feelings, and faith in politics. With regard to incorporation, elected officials and their representatives promote efforts to mobilize different constituent groups in society by considering the timing and degree of nonparticipation within a group or population (e.g., youth voting age, ineligible non-citizens, formerly incarcerated members, and lack of interest in politics).

Disadvantaged SES typically translates into the concerning political profile that was sketched out in Chapter 3, where it was noted that Latino political participation and representation has been historically low in America with the exception of Cuban Americans, and that the majority of Latinos have been ineligible to vote because they are either too young or are non-citizens. However, it is imperative to highlight that far too many *eligible* Latinos, citizens as well as documented immigrants, are neither registered to vote nor naturalized and thus remain the focus of increasingly successful voter registration and naturalization campaigns. For example, while over 27 million Latinos were eligible to vote in the 2016 presidential election, only about half actually did so (Gonzalez-Barrera, 2017). With regard to the largest Latinx population, only 42% of the 3.5 million eligible Mexican immigrants applied for or were naturalized in 2015, a legal process that bestows full citizen rights including voting in federal elections. While over 90% of these legal permanent residents claimed to be interested in applying for naturalization (i.e., tested for English and civic knowledge), obstacles cited include lack of English and lack of money to cover application costs (about $700 at the time of the Gonzalez-Barrera publication).

The net effect of such mixed political participation is a Latino electorate that remains about half of what it could be given the steady growth of Latinos, now at 62.1 million or 19% of the population and composing a significant 12% of the electorate. While Latino political power continues on a slow but steady incline, the pervasive historical lack of political participation has meant little Latino political representation in politics, or a minimal role in social policy development, which is the path to consequent benefits. This long-standing predicament, however, is beginning to change thanks to continued community-based efforts and recent unprecedented election wins and appointments at local, state, and federal levels.

Getting Out the Latino Vote

While the rapidly growing Latino population translates to increasing in voting power, service providers and community organizations and initiatives can significantly expedite this process by advocating and supporting the following four major approaches to increasing voter registration and voting.

Register Eligible Latinos
While the number of eligible Latinos registered to vote in California increased from 52% in 1990 to 62% in 1996, data show that of the over *four and a half million* eligible Latino citizens, only about *half* are registered (Fraga

& Ramirez, 2003). Thus, making Latino clients and community groups aware of such sobering numbers, and of their considerable potential influence on local, state, and national elections, is a persistent need. The Center for American Progress (Root & Kennedy, 2018) describes a number of ways to expedite voter registration despite the recent rise in structural barriers, including recent voter suppression tactics:

- The state of Oregon automatically registers eligible residents to vote, using information from driver's license or identification card applications. Residents are notified by post card with the option to opt-out if they wish. California and other states have followed suit.
- Same (election) day voter registration is now occurring in about one-third of the United States and demonstrating improved voting rates.
- Pre-registrations of 16- and 17-year-old citizens allows such youth to be automatically ready to vote upon turning 18, and has increased voting in this age group by about 5% where practiced (e.g., Florida). Teens need to be made aware that most states now practice some form of pre-registration for those nearing 18 years of age.
- Online voter registration: Between 2014 and 2016, Georgia's online registrations system enrolled over 350,000 primarily young, 18 to 34, voters, 42% of whom were first time registrants. Other states such as California and Arizona show higher turnout for online registered voters as compared to those registered through traditional methods, and almost 40 states currently provide online registration.
- Early voting: Up to 14 days before Election Day, including weekends, helps to counteract recent reductions in voting places, days, and hours.
- No-excuse absentee voting and at-home voting allows absentee voting in about 24 states *for any reason* rather than just for those in the military, permanently disabled, living in isolated rural residences, or to avoid pandemic-related infection. Ballots are mailed to all registered voters, who have more time to review and mail in ballots with the option to drop them off at voting centers (practiced in only three states). Former President Trump, who routinely votes by mail, claimed that voting by mail is "horrible" and a "terrible thing" subject to corruption, even though no evidence exists to support his persistent, disquieting, and baseless claims.
- Restore rights to formerly incarcerated Americans: More than 25,000 formerly incarcerated people in Virginia participated in the 2016 elections after their rights were restored by former Governor Terry

McAuliffe (D). While these enfranchised voters are a tiny fraction of the over six million formerly incarcerated still barred from voting, this is an overdue remedy to help mitigate the excessive punishment of people who have served their time yet remain excluded from the democratic process. States vary tremendously on this recommendation—from Rhode Island, where the formerly incarcerated are automatically registered upon release, to Iowa, where the formerly incarcerated are banned for life. The latter's excessive punishment stands in stark contrast to countries in Europe that not only allow incarcerated folks to vote, but where political candidates running for office actually hold televised debates from inside prisons.

- Enhance civics education in schools so that students understand the rights and duties of citizenship that help to ensure a functioning democracy, versus apathy among our youth.
- Promote integrated voter engagement (IVE), or registering voters by combining advocacy and organizing for relevant issues with voter mobilization. For example, in New York, *Make the Road* has registered more than 30,000 voters since 2011 by advocating for immigration rights, including passage of an anti–wage theft law to protect immigrant workers from exploitation. IVE motivates registration by making voting directly relevant to important local issues in real time.

Integrate Latinx Youth into the Political Process

According to the Pew Research Center, by 2016 millennials were 42% and the main driver of the steady increase in eligible Latinx voters nationwide (Krogstad, 2016). In fact, between 2012 and 2016, 3.2 million Latinxs turned 18, accounting for 80% of the growth in Latino voters nationally. History and government classes represent school-based sites for integrating such a relevant lesson into the general curriculum. Service providers working with system-impacted juveniles and gang-affiliated Latinxs could integrate prosocial political involvement as a way of redirecting misdirected time and energy to relevant youth and community issues.

Increase Naturalization and Voting among Documented Latinxs

Even documented immigrants cannot vote unless they apply for citizenship through the process of *naturalization*. Garcia (2003b) reports that less than half of all permanent residents in the United States are naturalized, and that rates for Latinos have been the lowest of all immigrant groups, especially for Mexicans. For instance, while the percent of documented Mexicans that became naturalized rose from 20% to 42% between 1995 and 2015, the increase for all other documented immigrants rose from 47% to 67% for this same time period (Gonzalez-Barrera, 2017). Thus, service providers should be familiar with the criteria for naturalization to motivate eligible Latino immigrants to apply: 18 years of age or older; living as a legal permanent resident (i.e., green card holder) for at least five years; able to read, write, speak, and understand basic English; and demonstrate a basic knowledge of U.S. history and government. Fraga and Ramirez (2003) note that adult education and English classes are ideal sites for teaching immigrants about the naturalization process and its link to voting, citizenship, and civic duty. Mexicans, who comprise the majority of all U.S. immigrants, should also be informed that naturalization no longer means losing Mexican citizenship, because Mexico honors dual citizenship. While there will always be a few immigrants unwilling to pursue citizenship, surveys indicate high interest in the vast majority of eligible Latinx immigrants.

Assisting Undocumented Latinxs with Citizenship Applications

While this is tricky business, given that failed applications risk detection and deportation, undocumented migrants with several years and investments in the United States, as well as those with *non-economic* hardships, may qualify (Chavez, 1998). Such hardship refers to a compelling need to remain in the United States other than losing one's job or not being able to attain comparable earnings in country of origin. Non-economic examples might include family members with pressing health problems (e.g., children or elderly with disabilities or chronic illnesses requiring services) that would suffer in country of origin due to inadequate services. Undocumented Central Americans in particular can be urged to request sponsorship from employers to whom they are close. However, requests for political asylum still depend on providing proof of political persecution, not to mention the Trump administration's efforts to forestall and severely limit asylum applications to about 10% of what they were before his presidency.

While initially blocked by lower federal courts, the Supreme Court allowed Trump's change in asylum policy to stand, requiring those seeking asylum on the southern border to first seek asylum in Mexico. Casting a dissenting vote, Justice Sonia Sotomayor said, "Once again, the Executive Branch has issued a rule that seeks to upend longstanding practices regarding refugees who seek shelter from persecution" (Sherman, 2019). The Biden administration promises humanitarian reform of the asylum process as well as immigration reform more broadly. For example, asylum seekers are no longer required to seek asylum in Mexico.

2020 Census Participation

Relatedly, organized outreach to undocumented Latinos by trusted Latino organizations represents a collective response to the Trump administration's yearlong effort to impose a question about citizenship status on the 2020 Census. Politically neutral census counts need to be as accurate as possible regarding state population sizes in order to best allocate federal funds to key social institutions, and to determine each state's needed number of congressional districts and corresponding state assembly and senate seats. Critics of Trump's effort, including officials at the Census Bureau, assert that such questioning would inhibit the participation of undocumented residents, as well as mixed-status families, and result in population undercounts in heavily immigrant states that tend to be pro-immigration and Democrat. While the Supreme Court blocked Trump's attempt, critics fear that his boisterous efforts may have succeeded in having a chilling effect on census participation and its purpose to be as accurate as possible in counting *all* U.S. residents regardless of citizenship status.

Hence, Latino-focused organizations launched major efforts to mitigate potentially chilling effects on Latino census participation. For instance, California's Latino Community Foundation (LCF) launched its "To resist we must exist" campaign to promote a fair and accurate count of Latinos in California. As the lead organization selected by the state to conduct outreach and education, the LCF partnered with the NALEO's (National Alliance of Latino Elected Officials) Educational Fund to host the nation's first gathering of Latino leaders to strategize ways to properly count Latinxs. LCF also used Spanish-language radio, television, and social media to promote participation by allaying fears, communicating what's at stake, and partnering with community-based small businesses, health centers, and nonprofit organizations to encourage Latino resistance to the administration's effort to dampen their participation, which was needed to secure their state's fair share of federal funding and political power.

Political Representation

While all of the above efforts enhance the Latino electorate in America, it remains imperative to develop social policies designed to support and empower Latino voters by reducing institutionalized barriers to political representation. For example, in their study of political incorporation in California, Fraga and Ramirez (2003) note impressive trends in the election of Latino state officials directly attributable to Latino registration percentages of 40% and above in Latino-majority districts, created by the legislature to help Latinos elect candidates of their choice. Given the partisan nature of Democrat and Republican legislators negotiating the creation of voting districts after each new census, the process in California has been changed to allow appointed councils of citizens (5 Democrat, 5 Republican, and 4 Other parties) to propose redistricting upon which legislators vote. The result is greater control and representation at the local community level.

In California, for example, Fraga and Ramirez (2003) note that all nine Latino-majority districts elected Latino state officials in 1998. Further, between 1990 and 1998, the number of Latino state assemblypersons increased from four to 17, while Latino senators increased from three to seven. Fraga and Ramirez further note that the majority of these Latino state officials are Democrats, thereby concentrating partisan political power, and a significant proportion have also been women (e.g., almost a third of Latino assembly and over half of senators in 2000). Today, the California Latino Legislative Caucus (CLLC) numbers an astounding 29 members: seven senators, 22 assembly members, and five constitutional officers, such as lieutenant governor, attorney general, and secretary of state, that are either elected or appointed positions. When Kamala Harris vacated her seat in the U.S. Senate upon her election as vice president of the United States, California governor Gavin Newsom was able to appoint long-time legislator Alex Padilla as the state's first Latino U.S. Senator by filling Harris' seat, where he continues to enact policies beneficial to Latino needs.

The Embattled Voting Rights Act

Latino-majority districts not only guarantee electing Latino officials but also the long-term *institutionalization* of Latino political leadership in evidence today. As such, the practice of using census data to create voting districts, allowable under the Voting Rights Act (VRA), needs to be defended, whether by a bipartisan committee of elected legislators or by new citizens' councils as currently practiced in California. The VRA was enacted in 1965 to enhance and protect the embattled voting rights of African Americans who, like other ethnic minorities, historically have been unable to elect local officials in white-majority districts. Indeed, where Blacks and Latinos have been historically numerous (e.g., the South and Southwest, respectively), voting districts were purposefully drawn to disallow racial and ethnic minority voting blocks in what became known as *gerrymandering*. This odd term derives from 18th-century Massachusetts Governor *Gerry*'s extreme efforts to maintain a majority of white voters by drawing a district that worked around concentrations of Black voters, resulting in a sala*mander*-shaped voting district.

The success of the VRA was expanded in the early 1970s to include language minorities and has accelerated Latino political representation and benefit ever since. For example, Garcia (2003c) notes that there were only five Latinos elected to the U.S. Congress before this VRA amendment; the number quadrupled to 21 by the 1990s and stands at around 30 presently. Garcia also notes that the VRA's largest impact on Latino representation has been at the local level, where over 10,000 such officials have been elected to school boards, city councils, and county boards of supervisors.

Gutting the VRA

With regard to safeguarding minority voting, for decades the VRA required federal *preclearance* from states with egregious histories of voter suppression wishing to change any voting law or practice. Such states needed to clear any planned changes to voting with the U.S. Department of Justice. However, in *Shelby County v. Holder* (2013), the preclearance provision was challenged and eventually struck down by the U.S. Supreme Court in a five to four vote, with Chief Justice John Roberts declaring that, "Things have changed dramatically" with regard to past discriminatory voting practices, and that, "while any racial discrimination in voting is too much, Congress must ensure that the legislation it passes to remedy that problem speaks to current conditions." However, immediately following this ruling, states previously needing preclearance rapidly began to suppress voting by closing voting places in predominately African American counties, limiting early voting and voting hours, purging voter rolls, and imposing stricter voter ID laws.

Sullivan (2019) recently reported that Republican-led southern states have now closed over 12,000 polling places. While civil rights organizations are calling for the restoration of preclearance at the national level, a more immediate solution is for states to implement their own versions. For example, state law in South Carolina requires multiple official sign-offs to approve any change in voting practices. As a result, this state has actually added 45 new polling places since 2012. With dozens of states currently implementing multiple forms of voter suppression laws, this pernicious problem will loom large over future midterm and presidential elections, with major implications for Latino political power within the larger crisis of democracy under threat in America.

In spite of continuing minority political disadvantage, backlash against the VRA continues in such states such as Texas, Louisiana, Georgia, North Carolina, New York, Illinois, and Florida, where it is frequently disparaged as "reverse gerrymandering." This term is reminiscent of the term "reverse racism" aggressively used to discredit and dismantle affirmative action. There is, however, a major difference between racist laws deliberately designed to disempower and oppress minorities and anti-racist laws designed to empower and liberate them for a more just society.

Backlash in the Golden State

While Latinos continue to make gains in political participation, they still comprise a minority of voters in most states, a historically vulnerable position. In California, for example, the non-Latino white (NLW) population still represents 58% of voters even though it has decreased in population size from a two-thirds majority of the state in 1980 to a minority at less than 50% in 2000 (PPIC, 2019). Historically, white block votes in California passed contentious anti-immigrant, anti-bilingual, and anti-affirmative action statewide referenda during the 1990s (see Table 11.2). The combined agenda of these backlash referenda can be viewed as a combination of displacement anxiety on the part of white voters and racial resentment stoked by politicians scapegoating Latinos in California.

However, it should also be noted that such polarizing propositions also resulted in the greatest surge of Latino voter registration and turnout, including immigrant applications for naturalization, ever witnessed in the history of California (García, 2003c; Fraga & Ramirez, 2003). A parallel

Table 11.2. Anti-immigrant, Anti-bilingual Education, and Anti-affirmative Action Referenda in California

Latino-Relevant Referendum in California	Purpose and Outcome
Proposition 187	The so-called "Save Our State " proposition, passed in 1994, to deny undocumented people access to publicly funded health, education, and social services, and to deny even legal permanent residents access to social welfare programs. Proposition 187 was immediately challenged and ruled unconstitutional in 1997 for its multiple violations of federal and state laws governing basic human rights.
Proposition 227	The "English Language Initiative for Immigrant Children," passed in 1998, replaced bilingual education programs in public schools (K–12) with one-year English immersion programs. 227 was essentially repealed in 2016 with the passage of Proposition 58 that restored the right of California public schools to implement bilingual education as needed. Prop 58 reflects the growing political power of Latinos as discussed below.
Proposition 209	Removed state affirmative action provisions for diversifying both employment and higher education in 1996. While the California Assembly passed Assembly Constitutional Amendment 5 that would give voters the option to repeal 209's ban on affirmative action, it was withdrawn due to opposition by former UC regent Ward Connerly, as well as some Chinese American organizations.
Proposition 54	The so-called "Racial Privacy Act", defeated in 2003, *would have prohibited* the collection by state and local government of information that includes reference to race and ethnicity.

enhancement of Latino civic engagement appears to be underway in response to the Trump administration's relentless attacks on Latino immigrants and hyper-criminalization of the undocumented, addressed next in Chapter 12.

To some degree, problematic state propositions have also alerted racial and ethnic minorities in California, and progressive NLWs, of their common interests, which probably helped to defeat Proposition 54 in 2003, the so-called "Racial Privacy Initiative" designed to amend the California constitution by disallowing state and local government from collecting and using race and ethnic identifiers (e.g., in public health, schools, crime prevention, civil rights enforcement). While Proposition 54's author (also author of Proposition 209), former University of California regent Ward Connerly, viewed it as a step toward a colorblind California, such a proposition would make it nearly impossible to address deep and numerous health and racial disparities that come from an overly color-conscious society. Such quick and misguided efforts to address entrenched structural racial problems in America are naively premature at best, and downright regressive at worst.

Fraga and Ramirez (2003) proactively urge elected Latinos to practice more inclusive politics by building coalitions and addressing issues that include but go beyond Latino benefits. For example, California's 1998 Healthy Families Initiative extends the availability of low-cost health insurance to the state's millions of uninsured residents, about half of whom are Latino. Healthy Families is an example of a policy that is beneficial to the poor and working class in general and Latinos in particular (Burciaga Valdez, 2003), a winning strategy increasingly spearheaded by today's CLLC.

Policy Benefit

Policy Done *to* Latinxs

Nearly 30 years ago, Hero (1992) developed a durable model for Latinos in the U.S. political system, which he refers to as "two-tiered pluralism" designed to capture the condition of Latinx citizens as characterized by equal legal rights to participate in the political process, coupled with lower SES and limited political power due to historical social stratification and subordination. Thus, while conventional pluralism presumes equal opportunity for different groups in society to compete for resources and power through political participation, two-tiered pluralism acknowledges historical conditions of racism and discrimination that have marginalized many populations, setting in motion entrenched legacies of unequal power, opportunity, and limited political clout.

As can be seen in Figure 11.1, a large diamond, divided into a first and second tier, is used to illustrate the relatively healthier distribution of wealth and political power for NLW Americans located in the first tier, with a smaller proportion in the second tier. In sharp contrast, Latinos are concentrated predominantly in the less powerful second tier due to historical subordination and continuing informal and institutionalized discrimination. The unhealthy triangular shaped distribution of Latino wealth conveys that only a minority have achieved middle class status. The positionality of Latinos as predominantly occupying the second tier underscores the connection

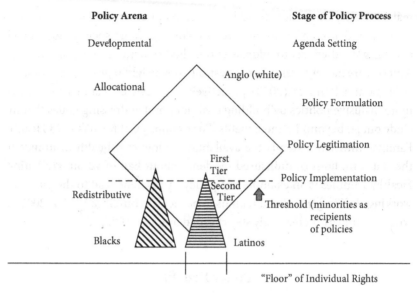

Figure 11.1. Two-tiered political participation for Latinos and African Americans.

From Hero (1992). Latinos and the political system: Two-tiered pluralism. In R. Hero, *Latinos and the U.S. political system: Two-tiered pluralism* (pp. 189–206). Philadelphia: Temple University. With permission.

between low SES and low political clout. In a recent personal conversation with Hero (2020), he shared that while the space between tiers has closed somewhat over the past 30 years (i.e., growth in Latino political representation, high school and college graduation rates, increasing number of professionals), social inequality continues and has even worsened in many ways (e.g., rates of poverty, lack of health insurance, accelerating gap in wealth).

One result of the political predicament of Latinos is that their political needs and demands have historically been those of a disadvantaged ethnic minority group striving for equity and primarily responded to by mediating institutions, such as meager government assistance programs, welfare bureaucracies, political tasks forces charged with studying minority groups' problems, and nonprofit organizations trying to address entrenched problems with few resources. Consistent with social stratification theory, the demands of ethnic minorities have also largely been viewed as undeserving complaints because it is widely presumed that equality already exists, which is technically but not actually true.

In contrast, the "demands" of first tier occupants are rarely viewed as complaints, because the politically powerful can more easily meet their needs through direct access to the political system with little need to resist and demand equality. Most importantly for the current discussion, it should also be noted in Figure 11.1 that being concentrated in the second tier means that Latinxs have little power to set agenda, formulate, and legitimate policy, and thus receive the prize of policy benefits. As a result, top-down public policy has generally been *done to* Latinxs because they have rarely been its creators despite being in an excellent position to articulate and remedy social problems over-affecting their communities.

Only through increased political participation and representation are Latinos becoming more centrally involved with agenda-setting and policy formation, legitimation and implementation, as depicted in Figure 11.1. Understanding the links between the dynamics of Latino voting and political representation capable of influencing social policy helps service providers to more clearly imagine different places in the political incorporation process in which they can participate to advance Latino well-being at the macro-level while supporting such endeavors at the micro-individual and meso-community levels.

Using California as perhaps the best example of Latino political incorporation and power, Fraga and Ramirez (2003) provide a framework and a decade's worth of data to illuminate the complex dynamics of growing political power and lingering problems. They begin by noting that between 1992 and 2000, Latinos doubled their percentage of the California electorate from 7% to 14% of state voters, significantly affecting state politics:

> From 1990 to 2000, 11 elections were held [in California] for governor, U.S. senator, and president. Democrats have won nine of these races. In seven of these nine (78 percent) Latino voters were significant contributors to the winning Democratic candidates. Three of these nine successful Democratic candidates (i.e., one-third) would not have won without the Latino vote. . . . Latino voters utilized their growing percentage of the California electorate to vote consistently as a majority block in favor of Democratic candidates (p. 316).

By 2016, Latino voters in California had doubled again to 28% with increased influence on local, statewide, and national elections. However, Fraga and Ramirez (2003) also underscore that influencing policy benefit for Latinos is not simply a function of the increasing Latino electorate or voters, but requires increasing the number of Latinos elected to office (i.e., Latino representation) and depends on whether such Latino representation influences policymaking by playing key roles within local government and state legislature. Such key roles range from seats on local city councils and school boards to becoming party leaders, committee chairs, and assembly speakers at the state level, who are second to the governor in power.

For example, John A. Perez, who served as the 68th Speaker of the California State Assembly from March 1, 2010 to May 12, 2014, introduced AB 1602 to facilitate implementation of President Obama's signature Affordable Care Act (ACA, 2012). Called *Covered California*, this bill created the nation's first-ever health benefit exchange program that provides individuals and small businesses with access to a broad range of insurance products and cost-saving options. Covered California became a model used by states across the nation to amplify health insurance coverage as intended by the Affordable Care Act. Subsequently, through AB1X1, Perez expanded Medi-Cal coverage to an additional 1,000,000 Californians earning at or below 120% of the federal poverty limit. Such policies generally benefit California's low-income and working class people, small businesses, and the state's rapidly growing Latino population in particular.

Policy Done *for* Latinxs

Is Latino policy benefit, especially in high priority areas such as employment and economic development, health, education, immigration, and prison reform, beginning to occur in ways that would be predicted by the political gains outlined above? While the answer to this question is less clear at the national level, it seems to be a resounding *yes* for the state of California. For example, by 1998, Latino Democrats constituted a 54% majority in both the assembly and senate, necessary to elect party leaders that included Antonio Villaraigosa as the *second* Latino Speaker of the Assembly, the first being Cruz Bustamante, who subsequently was elected as lieutenant governor and the first Latino statewide elected official in over 100 years. Today's California Latino Legislative Caucus (CLLC) exemplifies the hard-won accrual of Latino political power, particularly over the past three decades, as a result of persistent grass-roots and community organizing, statewide redistricting, and the election of Latino representation committed to policy benefit for working-class Californians.

The California Latino Legislative Caucus: A Blueprint for Latino Power

California's "Chicano" Legislative Caucus was formed in 1973 when elected Latino legislators numbered five for the first time in the state's history. Prior to this, only four Latinos had been elected to the California legislature be-tween 1962 and 1970. The pioneer of this story is Edward Roybal (see Figure 11.2), the first Latino to be elected to the Los Angeles School Board in 1949 through 1962, after which he was elected to the California state assembly for 30 years (1963 to 1993).

Roybal was a founder of the U.S. Congressional Hispanic Caucus (CHC) in 1976, currently composed of 38 Democratic members of the U.S. Congress. While originally a bipartisan caucus, Republicans abandoned the CHC in the late 1990s due to political differences and founded their own CHC in 2003. While the mission of the CHC is to advocate for Latinos nationally through the legislative process, it is unclear how much policy benefit they have achieved at the national level. Examples of current CHC policy efforts include advocating for financial assistance and protection for farmworkers

Figure 11.2. The Honorable Edward Roybal (U.S. Government).

(over half of whom are undocumented) and essential laborers, vital to our nation's food supply during the Covid-19 pandemic, and urging the U.S. Department of Homeland Security (DHS) to automatically extend employment authorization for all immigrants whose work authorization documents about to expire, given their need to shelter in place. The CHC is also encouraging the nation's three top manufacturers of insulin to lower prices during the pandemic, which has eliminated both work and health care for millions of Americans with diabetes, a chronic illness rendering them more vulnerable to harmful effects of Covid-19. While admirable, it remains to be seen if any of these recommendations will translate into national policy given the impact of the Trump administration's anti-immigrant agenda, backed then by a Republican-majority Senate and Supreme Court.

In contrast, the CLLC continues to exemplify Latino political power with regard to multiple policy benefits in high priority areas for the state's huge and overlapping Latino and working-class populations. The significance of the CLLC is that for the first time, an agenda was formulated and legislative priorities developed to protect and preserve the rights of Latinos throughout California. Today's CLLC hold strategic leadership positions and also chair committees developing and working to pass policies beneficial to all Californians.

A review of the CLLC website (https://latinocaucus.legislature.ca.gov/) describes a long list of passed and in-progress bills authored by members to achieve policy priorities in the areas of civic engagement, SES enhancement, health, immigration support and protection, and prison reform. As described below, examples of bills—proposed, implemented, and pending, and aligned with the CLLC policy priorities—illustrate policy benefit and a blueprint for Latino political power at the state level, with implications for national-level political power. Also illustrated in Figure 11.3 is the annual CLLC *Latinos Leading California* poster from 2016.

Civic Engagement and Census Participation

To enhance civic participation in the 2020 census, AB 1666 (Gómez Reyes) *2020 Census—Providing Information at Schools* was a bill designed to increase participation rates by requiring state officials to provide census information to students and parents at school. This bill was partly intended to counter the

Figure 11.3. California Latino Legislative Caucus.
From CLLC website photo gallery, with permission.

inhibiting effect of the Trump administration's failed yet chilling efforts to ask participants about their citizenship status during the 2020 census. Because of the 2020 Covid-19 pandemics' rapid acceleration during the April 1st census start date, the deadline was extended four and a half months to give states, local agencies, and institutions more time to urge *all* Latinos to participate for the financial and political health of the state.

AB 49 (Cervantes) *CA Voter Protection Act of 2019* is designed to strengthen the vote-by-mail process utilized by a growing majority of Californians by requiring county registrars to finish sending all vote-by-mail ballots within five days of the existing threshold of 29 days before Election Day. This is one of many strategies to both boost voting as well as mitigate voter suppression, despite former president Trump's unfounded claims that voting by mail is rife with voter fraud.

Policy Benefit to Enhance Latinx Social Positionality

Economic Development and Reform

Historically, the ebb and flow of Latino political power has bumped up against powerful and well-orchestrated backlashes. For instance, while the Chicano and Puerto Rican movements of the 1960s and 1070s produced substantial gains for their communities, partly by building upon the federal government's War on Poverty during the 1960s, CBOs serving Latino communities soon lost needed funding. In their early economic analysis of Chicano communities in Southern California, Moore and Vigil (1993) concluded that despite significant federal funding of CBOs, responsible for improvements in education, health and mental health care, community relations with the police, the criminal justice system, and the INS, funding rapidly dried up during the 1970s and 1980s partly due to an economic recession but mainly because of rising neoliberal political and economic momentum to deregulate capitalism and shrink the federal welfare state.

The loss of Latino-focused CBOs left hundreds of thousands of community members without adequate safety nets for coping with the rapid disappearance of core sector jobs in unionized industrial plants, referred to as *economic restructuring*. Since then, there has been little alternative for most Latinos but to join the ranks of the working poor within the expanding service sector economy, characterized by a lack of benefits and opportunities for advancement (Moore & Vigil, 1993). Thus, while working-class Americans have increasingly been hurt by economic restructuring during the latter half of the 20th century (e.g., downsizing industry, corporate outsourcing of jobs to Mexico and China), Latinos have been especially vulnerable given their overrepresentation among the working class with few policy protections.

President Reagan, Champion of Neoliberalism

The election of President Reagan for two terms during the 1980s, and his administration's *New Federalism* legislation, drastically slashed federal government spending on programs for the poor and working class, partly in response to the lack of tax revenue from corporations given huge tax breaks and credits in the name of remaining competitive in the world. However, New Federalism was really old federalism in that it reinforced the United States' historical condemnation of the poor and conviction that poverty is a moral failure, not to be subsidized by government but rather shouldered by families, churches, charity, and self-help groups and organizations, if at all. Yet by the end of Reagan's second term as president, instead of the "trickle-down economics" promised to all Americans, the national debt doubled, the stock market plummeted, and homelessness began to surge. Despite the failure of "Reaganomics," subsequent presidents continue to repeat the pattern of major corporate tax breaks—most recently former president Trump's multi-trillion-dollar tax break for corporations and wealthy Americans—resulting again in lost revenue for government safety net and support programs, while amplifying the tax burden on a shrinking middle class.

As noted by De La Rosa (2000), "Reaganomics" was further solidified in the 1990s with huge Republican wins in the 1994 congressional election and passage of the 1996 Personal Responsibility and Work Opportunity Act, signed into law by Democrat president Bill Clinton, whose "if you can't beat 'em, join 'em" platform further strengthened neoliberalism. The fact that neoliberalism's penchant for outsourcing living-wage manufacturing jobs contributes to the rise of the working poor somehow eludes conservatives determined to shrink "big government" (including its safety nets for the poor) and deregulate corporations while embracing *corporate welfare* (i.e., the use of taxpayer money to supplement the expenses and losses of big business in ways that often do not result in net gains for the government and its citizens).

The result has been unprecedented wealth inequality paid for primarily by an overtaxed and shrinking middle class, as noted earlier. If the average American knew how little tax money goes to safety nets for the poor and basic public infrastructure (public schools, roads and bridges, parks and recreation, water works, etc.), and how trillions in taxes continue to subsidize profitable corporations that frequently return little to the public (e.g., living-wage jobs, cheaper products and services) or to the government in tax revenue, there would be greater motivation to lift all Americans out of poverty while stemming the kind of corporate greed that resulted in the great recession of 2008–2009.

While beyond the scope of this book, Rothman (2002) wrote two decades ago that welfare for the wealthy and corporate business class has been estimated at $60 billion in industry-specific annual tax breaks, and another $75 billion in government spending directly benefiting business. For example, Rothman notes that the government contributes about $100 million every year to help major U.S. corporations advertise their products abroad. Major corporate welfare recipients such as McDonalds, Mars Candy, Campbell's Soup, Miller Beer, and Gallo defend government subsidies as enabling them to remain competitive in the global economy and better able to provide cheaper products and job opportunities—which is true, but to what degree?

In a Forbes magazine article, *Why Amazon Pays No Corporate Taxes*, Denning (2019) explains that tax break incentives motivate corporations to stimulate economic activity, job creation, and innovation. They underscore that Amazon spent an average of $20 billion annually over the past five years, as well as over $22 billion in research and development, to spearhead innovation. Denning then concludes that not providing tax breaks would disincentivize such essential business-related activity. However, while the estimated $42 billion in expenses for Amazon is a huge amount, Denning fails to share that Amazon's annual earnings for 2019 were an astounding 280.5 billion dollars! It turns out that Amazon paid $162 million in taxes in 2019 based on a miniscule tax rate of 1.2%. Compare this to the average middle-class family tax rate of about 32% to get a sense of the immense corporate welfare in the form of tax breaks and credits.

These contributions to wealth inequality mean that tax revenue is being diverted from the major essential domains of public infrastructure that continue to deteriorate and undermine the quality of life for *most* Americans, but especially the working class. According to Nader (2000), well over 20 years ago:

- A third of schools need extensive repair or replacement ($113 billion needed over three years to remedy). For example, a quarter of schools in Cleveland need replacement. Yet the city phased out athletic programs to save money while $300 million in taxpayer money was used to build professional basketball and baseball arenas for multi-millionaire team owners who do little to make tickets affordable to the city residents whose tax dollars subsidized their stadiums.
- About $9 billion in services are needed to restore and upgrade public parks in the United States.
- The U.S. Department of Transportation estimates that almost $10 billion is needed to maintain public transportation at its current mediocre level. Another $4 billion would result in an upgrade of the public transportation system to "good."

Uphill Climb toward SES Policy Benefit

For a brief moment in the 1960s and 1970s, it seemed as though the educational crisis of Latinos, as well as their anemic political engagement, would be partially remedied when the U.S. Congress adopted the Bilingual Education Act of 1968, and when the VRA was extended to language minorities in the 1970s, eliminating linguistic barriers to voting (e.g., bilingual ballots). But as early as 1981, backlash campaigns to make English the *official language* were introduced to Congress every year until they finally began to succeed in as many as 17 states by 1990, either through initiative or legislative action.

However, in California, Latino persistence in securing policy benefit has recently resulted in bills that have largely repealed anti-bilingual education laws and thereby serve to enhance SES. For instance, a recent snapshot of the CLLC website reveals that SB 594 (Rubio) *English Language Learner Roadmap Initiative*, aimed at public elementary and secondary schools, forges new state partnerships to implement instructional programs to develop bilingual/biliterate proficiency to help close the gap in academic achievement for English language learners. Similarly, Proposition 58 gives state public schools the power to implement bilingual education for Latino students, now the majority in California public schools, as well as other language minority students. Both of these bills work to essentially mitigate the negative effects of past anti-bilingual education and English-only state initiatives such as Proposition 227. Other educational bills have aimed to support and enhance the ailing public education pipeline in California, as described below.

At the high school level, AB 331 (Medina) *Ethnic Studies*, requires, starting in the 2024–2025 school year, the completion of an inclusive ethnic studies course to meet high school graduation requirements. Not only will this bill better engage Latino students by teaching relevant history, but it also appears to respond to the state of Arizona's 2010 reactionary banning of high school Mexican American art and history courses, accused of stirring up ethnic solidarity and resentment in students. This pernicious Arizona law was overturned in 2017 by a U.S. federal judge ruling that anti-Latino racism and political gain motivated this law.

With regard to junior college, AB 2 (Santiago) *Two Years Free Community College* now expands upon the *California College Promise* by providing a second year of free tuition for community college regardless of financial background. Latinos are currently overrepresented among community college students in California yet underrepresented among graduates. AB 1307 (Rubio) *College Opportunity Act—Cal Grant Expansion Program* is designed to expand college affordability to students choosing to attend private, nonprofit colleges and universities. California's private nonprofit college sector serves 354,000 students, including 22% of undergraduates and 53% of graduate students, and nearly half (48%) of this educational sector's Cal Grant recipients are Latino. Hence, more generous Cal Grants not only expand educational choice but may actually save money, because private colleges are more successful than public colleges in graduating students in four years.

Several bills listed in the website are aimed at economic development and work enhancement. Signed into law by Governor Newsom, AB 378 (Limón) *Building a Better Early Care and Education Act* helps professionalize the child care workforce by increasing training opportunities for workers and granting them the right to collectively bargain as providers of needed child care for working parents. AB 539 (Limón) *Fair Access to Credit Act of 2019* expands access to credit and affordable capital by limiting interest rates on certain consumer loans. This bill intends to mitigate predatory lending that played a major role in the great recession of 2008–2009.

AB 16 (L. Rivas), *Statewide Homeless Coordinators & Local Technical Assistance Centers* addresses the growing homeless crisis for families with children by increasing the number of homelessness coordinators and establishing new navigation centers to provide regional support services. This bill would partly mitigate rising displacement because of gentrification in California's urban centers, including Latino anchor communities.

AB 1783 (R. Rivas) *Farmworker Housing—Streamlining the Development Process* addresses the historical and severe shortage of quality and affordable housing for hundreds of thousands of farmworkers by streamlining the process for farm owners and operators to develop new employee housing on their property. Developed by Assemblyperson Rivas, the son of migrant farmworkers, AB 1783 intends to partially mitigate the shameful history of farmworkers in America lacking adequate housing. The perennial neglect of farmworkers surfaced again during the Covid-19 pandemic when they were recognized as "essential workers" helping to feed the nation while marginally housed, inadequately paid, and over half of the state's farmworkers who are undocumented were denied entitlement to stimulus funds.

Health Care Benefits

Given the high percentage of Latinos that lack health insurance due to lack of employer benefits in the service sector, as well as undocumented status, the following bills on the CLLC website were designed to address this entrenched problem:

- AB 1759 (Salas), *Increasing Health Care Workforce in Underserved Communities*, appropriates $50 million in state funding to support programs that develop the health care workforce in areas facing severe shortages, particularly underserved, rural, and ethnically/linguistically diverse communities. This win–win bill is intended to increase health care services to underserved communities by funding job development, training, and opportunities in the California health care workforce.
- SB 29 (Durazo) *Health for All Adults—Access to Medi-Cal for the Undocumented* is a bill that expands access to quality medical care by extending full scope Medi-Cal benefits to undocumented adults, who would otherwise be eligible but for their immigration status. As the Covid-19 pandemic has revealed, bills such as these not only protect the health of undocumented residents but the interrelated health of all Californians, and all U.S. residents. SB 29 is scheduled to go into effect in January of 2024.

Immigration Support and Protection

Immigration and Entitlements

Latino and other immigrant populations remain vulnerable to policies restricting their access to public services and benefits. For instance, legal permanent residents (LPRs) who had not yet naturalized their citizenship were impacted by the 1996 Personal Responsibility and Work Opportunity Reconciliation Act (PRWORA), which slashed cash benefits to impoverished LPR elderly, blind, and disabled immigrants, needed to purchase food, clothing, and shelter. Sponsors of immigrants (e.g., family members) were also made legally responsible for those LPR immigrants unable to support themselves. To facilitate deporting undocumented immigrants, PRWORA also mandated verification of eligibility in applications for public benefits.

Criticism of PRWORA influenced how the subsequent Balanced Budget Act of 1997 restored SSI and Medicaid benefits to pre-PRWORA eligible immigrants whose benefits had been terminated, and also to those in the country as of 1996 who had become disabled. Further, the Agricultural

Research Act of 1998 restored food stamp benefits to pre-PRWORA qualified immigrant children, the elderly, and disabled (Kilty & Vidal de Haymes,
2000). Despite such small gains, policy benefits for immigrants, both
documented and undocumented, continue to be vulnerable. Once again, the
Covid-19 pandemic reveals the unjust lack of policy benefit for immigrants
who have higher work participation rates than citizens, typically as essential
workers benefiting the country and promoting its economic recovery.

Essential Workers

A recent report by the Center for Migration Studies (Kerwin et al.,
2020) conveys that almost 20 million immigrants work in "essential critical
infrastructure" jobs, according to DHS, that meet the health, infrastructure,
manufacturing, service, food, safety, and other needs of all Americans. While
about half of these immigrant workers are naturalized citizens, 4.6 million
are legal non-citizens (mostly LPRs), and 5.5 million are undocumented. As
compared to 65% of native-born workers, 69% of all immigrants are in the
labor force, and 74 % of undocumented workers are essential infrastructure
workers. Regarding the latter, Kerwin et al. (2020) assert:

> Undocumented immigrants comprise 54 percent of foreign-born workers
> in agriculture and farms, and 40 percent in disinfection. These workers
> contribute to the nation's food security and health. Undocumented
> immigrants also comprise 50 percent of foreign-born workers in construc-
> tion, including plumbers and electricians, and the plurality of immigrant
> workers in tire, rubber, cement, and household appliance manufacturing.
> These workers will also be vital to the ability of the Americans and the US
> economy to rebound from the pandemic. (p. 5).

Despite being deemed by the DHS as essential workers during the pandemic, undocumented workers were not eligible for federal stimulus checks.
Surprisingly, stimulus checks are also currently denied to needy mixed-status
families in which a working, taxpaying, undocumented family member uses
an Individual Taxpayer Identification Number to file taxes (Kapur, 2020).
Such family ineligibility affects two million families in which a U.S. citizen
or green card holder files taxes jointly with an undocumented spouse. The
result is denial of up to $1,200 per family, and $500 per child. Democrats
in the national Assembly have advocated changing this clause, within the
Coronavirus Aid, Relief, and Economic Security Act or CARES Act of 2020,

but without success. Such a practice extends the punishment of undocumented workers to their citizen spouses and children struggling economically during the pandemic. However, such punishment does not compare with how undocumented people are now criminalized and persecuted.

Militarizing the Border and Criminalizing the Undocumented

With the passage of the Illegal Immigration Reform and Immigrant Responsibility Act (IIRIRA) of 1996, increased militarization of the U.S.-Mexico border became a very high policy priority to curb undocumented immigration. IIRIRA built upon 1994's *Operation Gatekeeper* by erecting a 14-mile steel fence and increasing the number of border patrol agents, providing them with para-military gear and training (Kilty and Vidal de Haymes, 2000). In the same year, President Clinton signed NAFTA (North American Free Trade Agreement) into law, claiming that undocumented immigration would cease as Mexico became a more prosperous trading partner. While neither of those things happened, extreme border security did. A tragic outcome of these combined policies has been the continuously mounting deaths of desperate migrants attempting to cross in less guarded but more treacherous border areas characterized by harsh deserts and precarious mountains (e.g., the Sonora desert).

A report by Soto and Martínez (2018) conservatively estimates that 6,751 such deaths occurred between 1998 and 2015 as a result of deterrents that simply make it more dangerous to cross the border rather than address the structural source of the problem through comprehensive immigration reform. The following photographs show but a few gravesites of unknown souls that have perished while desperately attempting to cross the southern border

Figure 11.4. Paupers' graves of those who died crossing the U.S.-Mexico border.

in treacherous terrain (see Figure 11.4). Note how locals adorn these pauper's graves with *ofrendas* [offerings] of water jugs and holy crosses, asserting that these unidentified are not forgotten or *No Olvidado*.

Building upon the 1996 laws, subsequent laws, policies, and presidents—Democrat as well as Republican—have made life harsh and punishing for undocumented people and their mixed-status families and communities, rather than passing urgently needed, sensible, comprehensive immigration reform, as was last done with the 1986 Immigration Reform and Control Act. While anti-immigrant laws and sentiments ramped up during the George W. Bush presidencies (2001 to 2009), spurred by the national shock and trauma of 9/11, they continued to accelerate under President Obama only to become even more extreme and pernicious under President Trump. With such federal-level assaults on undocumented people, many cities, counties, and states have implemented their own local protections for immigrants, often in the form of Christianity inspired sanctuary ordinances.

California: Rise of the Sanctuary State

In California, where undocumented workers now compose 10% of the work-force, a variety of supports and protections have been legislated on behalf of undocumented residents and their families, vital to the state's annual $3.4 tril-lion economy. Assembly and senate bills that have been pending discussion, modifications, and voting include AB 1747 (Gonzalez) *Protecting Californians' Right to Privacy—DMV Driver's Licenses* is a proposed bill that enhances pri-vacy protections for Californians by prohibiting state law enforcement agencies from making certain databases available for federal immigration enforcement purposes. This bill builds upon a set of recent bills designed to support and protect California's 2.5 million undocumented immigrants, including AB 60, *Safe and Responsible Drivers Act* of 2016, that allows Californians to obtain a driver's license regardless of citizenship status. Until 1994, all immigrants had the right to obtain driver's licenses in California. However, once the law was changed to deny undocumented residents, the state saw a predictable increase in uninsured and unlicensed drivers. Hence, the goal of this act is to sensibly protect *all* drivers in the state by decreasing the number of uninsured drivers, car accidents, and unlicensed drivers, a position supported by the California Highway Patrol at the time of its passage.

In addition to protection at the DMV, SB 456 (Archuleta) *Privacy Protection for Faith Based Organization Volunteers* is designed to prohibit faith-based organizations from divulging volunteer information to third parties, such as federal immigration officials, without a subpoena, warrant, or order. The above proposed bills exemplify states' rights to support all California residents regardless of citizenship, given the U.S. Congress' chronic lack of political will to advance urgently needed comprehensive federal immigration reform over the past three decades. Because of such national legislative gridlock, and the harsh criminalization and persecution of undocumented immigrants, California has successfully passed landmark legislation to improve and support the lives of immigrants regardless of citizenship status. Perhaps most notable is AB 4, or the TRUST Act, signed into law on January 1, 2014, to limit local and county jails from holding people longer than their sentences dictate simply so that ICE can intercept and evaluate them for deportation. Contrary to popular belief, exceptions are made for the very few with violent and other serious felony convictions or excessive misdemeanor convictions within the past five years.

The TRUST Act ensures that people with low-level, nonviolent offenses (misdemeanors) pay fines and serve their sentence but are not held beyond that for deportation purposes (i.e., when ICE asks that they be detained). This act is intended to repair damage done to police–community relations during California law enforcement's participation in IIRIRA's Secure Communities Program (2008–2011), which resulted in the deportation of an estimated 90,000 residents. Despite widespread criticism of Secure Communities, even on the part of law enforcement, former President Trump reinstated Secure Communities in 2017, although California does not participate because of AB 4, declaring California a sanctuary state.

Relatedly, SB 1064, the *Reuniting Immigrant Families Act* enacted September 30, 2012, is the nation's first law addressing the unique reunification barriers faced by many immigrant families experiencing parental deportation and involvement with the child welfare system. Under California and federal law, courts must ensure that reasonable efforts are made by the Department of Social Services to prevent removal of children and to reach permanency if children are removed from the home. The law requires an individualized case plan, customized to the unique needs of each family, designed to reunite children in the child welfare system due to parental deportation, with family members, regardless of their immigration status.

California DREAM Act

In view of the U.S. Congress' repeated failure to pass a national Dream Act, California's own version of the Dream Act, passed in 2011, allows children brought to the United States under the age of 16 without documentation, and who have attended school on a regular basis, to be eligible for in-state tuition and GPA requirements for student financial aid benefits. In a sense, California leads the nation in policy benefit to undocumented residents through a series of laws that attempt to mitigate federal laws designed to persecute undocumented people and make them suffer rather than remedy the chronic and entrenched problem of absent comprehensive immigration reform.

Conclusion

Today, California exemplifies a hard-won and long overdue accrual of Latino political power that, while minus a Latino governor to date, represents Latino constituencies while providing unprecedented policy benefit alignment with an agenda of priority areas that support all working-class families in California. Despite over a century and a half of conflict, exclusion, and political disempowerment, Latinos in California consistently resisted, organized, and mobilized grass-roots and community movements, as well as waged legal challenges, culminating in today's CLLC. Backlashes past and present require resiliency and persistence in securing and enhancing political power, with California fresh from a four-year collision course with the Trump administration and his Republican enablers in Congress. Movements, past and present, are the subject of the next chapter, with an emphasis on immigration rights as one of the major civil rights issues of our time, currently over-affecting Latino populations in the United States.

Haynes and Mickelson (2019) remind us that service providers can volunteer to provide testimony, either alone or with clients, as an essential and influential part of legislative deliberation on pressing senate bills. Such testimony can include presentations of case studies and relevant agency data, as well as speculation on the consequences of policy implementation. Such actions can be taken by individual service providers locally, and by their professional organizations (e.g., NASW, APA, AMA) at regional, statewide, and national levels. Ultimately, race-linked ethnic dilemmas prompt multiple responses from professionals working with clients overly affected by harmful social policies. From a multilevel practice perspective (i.e., micro-individual through macro-social policy), it is beneficial for practitioners to understand the basics of Latino political empowerment and to find various roles and activities with such macro-level efforts to raise Latino social positionality, and psychosocial and health profiles in the process.

References

Burciaga Valdez, R. (2003). Access to illness care and health insurance. In D. Lopez and A. Jimenez (Eds.), *Latinos and public policy in California: An agenda for opportunity* (pp. 189–215). Berkeley, CA: Institute of Governmental Studies, University of California, Berkeley.

De La Rosa, M. (2000). An analysis of Latino poverty and a plan of action. *Journal of Poverty*, 4(1/2), 27–62.

Denning, S. (2019). Why Amazon pays no corporate tax. *Forbes*, February 22, online: https://www.forbes.com/sites/stephaniedenning/2019/02/22/why-amazon-pays-no-corporate-taxes/#5b998a2054d5

Fraga, L. R., & Ramirez, R. (2003). Latino political incorporation in California, 1990-2000. In D. Lopez & A. Jimenez (Eds.), *Latinos and public policy in California: An agenda for opportunity* (pp. 301–335). Berkeley, CA: Institute of Governmental Studies, University of California, Berkeley.

Garcia, J. A. (2003a). Culture and demographics. In J. A. Garcia (Ed.), *Latino politics in America: Community, culture, and interests* (pp. 31–51). New York: Rowan and Littlefield.

Garcia, J. A. (2003b). Immigration and Latino immigrants. In J. A. Garcia, *Latino politics in America: Community, culture, and interests* (pp. 166–186). New York: Rowan and Littlefield.

Garcia, J. A. (2003c). Education and voting rights. In J. A. Garcia, *Latino politics in America: Community, culture, and interests* (pp. 187–215). New York: Rowan and Littlefield.

Gonzalez-Barrera, A. (2017). Mexican lawful immigrants among the least likely to become U.S. citizens, 1995–2015. Pew Research Center, June.

Haynes, K. S., & Mickelson, J. S. (2019). *Affecting change: Social workers in the political arena* (7th ed.). New York: Longman.

Hero, R. (1992). Latinos and the political system: Two-tiered pluralism. In R. Hero (Ed.), *Latinos and the U.S. political system: Two-tiered pluralism* (pp. 189–206). Philadelphia: Temple University.

Hero, R. (2020). Personal communication with author.

Kapur, S. (2020). Democrats demand stimulus money for Americans married to immigrants. NBC News, May 1, online:. https://www.nbcnews.com/politics/politics-news/democrats-demand-stimulus-money-americans-who-are-married-immigrants-n1198176

Kerwin, D., Nicholson, Alulema, D., & Warren, R. (2020). US foreign-born essential workers by status and state, and the global pandemic. Center for Migration Studies.

Kilty, K., & Vidal de Haymes, M. (2000). Latino poverty in the new century: Challenges and barriers. *Journal of Poverty*, 4(1/2), 1–22.

Moore, J., & Vigil, J. D. (1993). Barrios in transition. In J. Moore & R. Pinderhughes (Eds.), *In the barrio: Latinos and the underclass debate* (p. 27–49). New York: Russell Sage.

Nader, R. (2000). *Cutting corporate welfare.* New York: Seven Stories Press.

Rothman, R. A. (2002). The dynamics of economic inequality. In R. A. Rothman (Ed.), *Inequality and stratification: Race, class and gender* (4th ed., pp. 92–113). Upper Saddle River, NJ: Prentice-Hall.

Sherman, V. (2019). Supreme Court allows broad enforcement of Trump asylum rule. Associated Press News, September 12. https://apnews.com/a817cf3affb04f3d8ad3c 4940366a5fe

Soto, G., & Martínez, D. E. (2018). The geography of migrant death: Implications for policy and forensic science. In K. Latham & A. O'Daniel (Eds.), *Sociopolitics of Migrant Death and Repatriation* (pp. 67–82). Bioarchaeology and Social Theory. Springer, Cham. https://doi.org/10.1007/978-3-319-61866-1_6

Sullivan, A. (2019). Southern U.S. states have closed 1,200 polling places in recent years: Rights group. Reuters (September, 9). https://www.reuters.com/article/us-usa-election-locations/southern-u-s-states-have-closed-1200-polling-places-in-recent-years-rights-group-idUSKCN1VV09J

12

Latino Resistance, Activism, and Social Movements Past, Present, and Future

> We will not be dragged back into the past. We will lead the resistance
> to any effort that would shred our social fabric or our Constitution.
> California was not a part of this nation when its history began, but
> we are clearly now the keeper of its future.
>
> —Anthony Rendon, Speaker, California Legislative Assembly
> (2016 to present)
> —Kevin de Leon, President pro tempore,
> California State Senate (2014 to 2018)

Implicit in Chapter 11's primer on Latinx political power is a legacy of resistance, community activism, and social movements with the twin goals of responding to racism and discrimination (e.g., segregation, exploitation, and scapegoating) while advancing human and civil rights. This final chapter not only builds upon Chapter 11 by explicating salient Latinx movements past, present, and future, but also brings this textbook full circle with Chapter 1 and 2's analyses of the acculturation histories of major U.S. Latinx populations. Thus, Chapter 12 describes the persistence of Latinx resistance and movements that have steadily improved Latinx social positionality, with an emphasis on the current immigration rights movement including rejecting the criminalization of undocumented people, their families, and communities. Enhanced awareness of Latinx activist history is foundational to the understanding of practitioners, researchers, and policymakers regarding what cultural communities do, under dehumanizing conditions, to protect and advance humanity, their social positionality, and well-being.

Solving Latino Psychosocial and Health Problems. Kurt C. Organista, Oxford University Press.
© Oxford University Press 2023. DOI: 10.1093/oso/9780190059637.003.0012

Historical Resistance to Anti-Latinx Racism and Discrimination

Mexican Americans in Early California

In his illuminating book *El Nuevo California: From Pioneers to Post-millennials*, Hayes-Bautista (2017) details the consistent resistance of the original Mexican residents of California in response to mounting anti-Mexican racism and discrimination on the part of white settlers who, following the lead of the Texas revolt, claimed California as their own. As soon as California was ceded to the United States by a defeated Mexico in 1848, an onslaught of white supremacist organizations quickly began excluding and persecuting Mexicans despite their status as citizens, conferred by the treaty of Guadalupe Hidalgo that ended the war with Mexico. Interestingly, Hayes-Bautista notes that these new Americans of Mexican descent were generally open to U.S. citizenship, constitutional rights, and the aspiration of American democracy extending to the west coast.

However, as soon as California was admitted to the union in 1850, white settler leaders promoted white-only voting to disempower Mexican Americans. Francisco Ramirez, editor of Los Angeles' *El Clamor*, regularly defended California Latinos, including calling out New York's racist Know Nothing Party that had inserted itself into the state and was winning local elections on anti-immigrant, anti-Catholic, and anti-Mexican platforms. From the late 1870s through the 1880s, Reginaldo del Valle, lawyer and only Latino legislator from Los Angeles, protested the California Convention of 1879 for excluding Latinos and ending bilingual state laws, as advocated by white supremacist Denis Kearny of the Working Man's Party. Equal rights would be a steady uphill struggle for Mexican Americans, perceived not as equal citizens but as defeated mixed-blood Catholics from a failed mongrel republic, and the descendants of Spaniards, long maligned as inferior Europeans afflicted by the Black Legend (see Sidebar 12.1).

Sidebar 12.1. Spanish Black Legend

It is worth noting that the racist framing of early Mexican American, and all persons of Spanish descent in the United States, is rooted in the Black Legend of Spain, a demonizing portrait of Spain historicized and perpetuated by colonial rivals England and the Netherlands. In hindsight, accusations that Spanish colonists were crueler and more barbaric than Northern European colonists toward colonized populations is absurd. In reality, the Black Legend was propaganda in retaliation for the anti-Protestant policies of Spain's King Phillip the II (1556–1598) that included not accommodating Protestants in Spain, and a failed attempt to conquer England and make it Catholic country. However, transported to America by English colonists, legacy of the Spanish Black Legend survived through the centuries and was conveniently used to justify the war with Mexico in 1856 as well as the war with Spain in 1898, which yielded the United States possession of the Caribbean and Philippines. How much Black Legend thinking continues to underscore today's anti-Latinx racism is a fair question.

Source: Encyclopedia Britannica (2020).

Lemon Grove Incident

A few decades later in California, and well before *Brown v. Board of Education* (1954), the first successful school desegregation case was won by Mexican immigrant parents in 1931 by legally challenging the Lemon Grove School District Board of Trustees' decision to build a separate school for the 74 Mexican students attending the town's only grammar school (Alvarez, 1986). Typical of the day, exclusionary planning by the all-white school board avoided notifying Mexican parents. On the designated day, Mexican students at Lemon Grove Grammar School were denied entrance by the principal and redirected to a rundown two-room makeshift school near the Olive street *barrio* settled by immigrants from Baja California. Furious parents protested by striking, keeping their children home, and organizing *El Comité de Vecinos de Lemon Grove* [Lemon Grove Neighbors Committee] to plan legal strategies that included community organizing on both sides of the border, raising funds for legal fees, and receiving newspaper coverage by *La Opinión* weighing in on their side (see Figure 12.1).

The Lemon Grove Incident
Alvarez vs. the Board of Trustees Lemon Grove School District

1928. Robert Alvarez, plaintiff in "The Lemon Grove Incident," is in the third row at far left. Lemon Grove Grammar School

- **Mexican students formed close to 50% of the student body at Lemon Grove Elementary**

- **School expected Mexican parents to obey orders but parents organized, fought back, boycotted the school, & sought legal counsel**

- **Evidence presented in court disproved Trustees' allegations and judge ruled in favor of Plaintiff, Roberto Alvarez**

- **A decade later, schools desegregated throughout California with Mendez v. Westminster**

- **First successful school desegregation case in U.S.**

- **1930-31 - Lemon Grove, CA**
- **Jan. 5, 1931: Principal admits all children except Mexicans. Mexican students are sent to an old, 2-room building ("la caballeriza')**

- **Trustees argued decision was based on Mexican children's intellectual inferiority, English language skills, & sanitary issues**

Lemon Grove Grammar School in 1905

"This was the first situation when a group of immigrants had gotten together, challenged a school board and won." - Robert Alvarez, historian

Figure 12.1. Lemon Grove Incident Flyer.
With permission from Lemon Grove Academy Middle School (Principal Vanessá Ruiz).

Although the Mexican school idea was supported by the PTA and Chamber of Commerce, the Superior Court of San Diego ruled that such discriminatory segregation violated California state law. Up until this time, about 80% of Mexican children in California public schools were segregated in separate schools while the other 20% were segregated within school mainstream classrooms. Stereotypes at the time included viewing the children as suffering from a *language handicap* and needing training for *Mexican jobs* rather than education. Lemon Grove was a typical rural California town with a citrus industry and need for essential farmworker labor. Unfortunately, the pattern of segregating Mexican students in California would persist in different parts of the state until 1947, when Mexican mothers and fathers in Santa Ana, California, won a statewide ruling prohibiting racial segregation in schools.

From early *familias activistas* to more recent *madres activistas*, Pardo (1998) documents the community activism of the Mothers of East Los Angeles (MELA; see Figure 12.2), formed in the mid-1980s to defeat the first California state prison planned for an urban setting. The prison proposal infuriated Gloria Molina (Figure 12.3), the state's first Latina assemblywoman, because 75% of Los Angeles County prisons were already located in her East Los Angeles district. But when her objections were dismissed by the California Department of Corrections and then-governor Deukmejian, Molina, a seasoned Chicana feminist, took the fight to the grass-roots level where eight years of marches, rallies, and litigation by MELA defeated the state's prison plan.

Molina went on to become the first Latina elected to the Los Angeles City Council (1987–1991) and the first woman *and* first Mexican American elected to the Los Angeles Board of Supervisors, which oversaw an annual budget of $13 billion (Pardo, 1998). Molina's vacated assembly seat was won in 1986 by fellow Latina community activist Lucille Roybal-Allard (Figure 12.4), who also worked to defeat the prison plan and was later elected the first Mexican American U.S. congressperson in 1992 (Garcia, 2003a). There, she continues to champion immigration reform, including coauthoring the latest version of the yet to be passed DREAM Act, the DREAM and Promise

Figure 12.2. The Mothers of East Los Angeles (MELA).
National Parks Service.

Figure 12.3. Honorable Gloria Molina.
Wikimedia Commons (Author: Zulma Aguiar).

Act of 2021 that aims to provide various protections from deportation, in-cluding legal permanent residency, for over 4.4 million DREAMers.

Subsequent MELA activism prevented the construction of a toxic waste in-cinerator, also planned for East Los Angeles, and a branch of MELA that in-corporated itself in 1990 as a nonprofit organization has promoted water conservation, lead poisoning abatement, immunization awareness, and scholarships for college. Thus, Pardo's research contributes to the larger story of Latino activism by focusing on local community mothers sparked to action by locally elected Latina representatives and supported by Catholic parish priests, who challenge powerful state officials and corporations to protect their com-munity. The fact that the pioneering elections of Molina and Roybal-Allard resulted from Latino-majority voting districts, created under the Voting Rights Amendment and expanded to include Latinos as a result of litigation on the part of the Mexican American Legal Defense Fund (MALDEF), helps us connect the dots of Latino activism, growing political power, and community benefit.

One particularly amusing MELA story is when *las madres* helped to defeat a proposal by oil companies to construct a shallow oil pipeline from offshore

Figure 12.4. Honorable Lucille Roybal-Allard.
United States Government.

rigs in Santa Barbara to Long Beach through the heart of East LA in order to bypass affluent and predominantly white coastal cities such as Pacific Palisades. At one hearing, community members asked oil representatives why not simply run the pipeline along the coast from Santa Barbara to Long Beach, to which one official replied "Oh no! If it burst, it would endanger the marine life!" (Pardo, 1998; p.132).

Gendered Politics

As Pardo underscores, MELA is the story of ordinary women doing extraordinary political things because they view their activism not as a deviation but as an expansion of their traditional Mexican gender role to protect their families. Given this perspective, and extra measures to meet traditional family responsibilities (e.g., early cooking and cleaning to free up time for meetings and marches), were complemented by husbands that supported and drove their wives to political activities and occasionally participated themselves. As such, Pardo's analysis mitigates the commonly presumed

Sidebar 12.2. Two Latino Thumbs Up for *Salt of the Earth*

The 1953 movie *Salt of the Earth* provides a dramatic reenactment of the Empire Zinc mining strike in New Mexico during the 1950s, in which the wives of Mexican miners replaced their husbands on the picket line when legal harassment and intimidation prevented the men from continuing their union-supported strike. Far ahead of its time, the film depicts how these strong Mexican women contested subordination by their husbands who were initially unsupportive of their political involvement. That this film includes lead Mexican actors in inspiring roles and was the only blacklisted film in America, with director Herbert J, Biberman sent to federal prison by the House on Un-American Activities as part of the red scare of the 1950s, makes it a remarkable testament to the agency of those oppressed on the basis of social class, race, gender, and culture against powerfully oppressive corporate and legal systems. Such past and ongoing stories should inspire service providers and others not to underestimate the history and potential of Latinas to care for their families and communities by successfully blending political activism and Latino culture.

boundary between public political and private domestic work for Latinas, and centers women in the long history of Latinx resistance, activism, and social movements (e.g., see Sidebar 12.2).

Catholic Church-based Activism

As exemplified by MELA, a reinvigorated Catholic Church as a culture-based space for community activism continues to unfold in the aftermath of criticism of the Church from Latino activists during the 1960s and 1970s for under-responding to Latino social justice issues. Also, the fact that Latino immigration continues to revitalize and expand Catholic congregations throughout the United States has raised the Church's accountability to its Latino parishioners. Thus, service providers working with Latinos benefit from familiarizing themselves with local Church activism in order to support ongoing campaigns and programs such as immigration rights, to encourage client involvement where appropriate, and to introduce new issues to Church coalitions.

The Resurrection Project

Another example of Catholic Church–driven community organizing and social justice work comes from the predominantly Mexican Latino community of the Pilsen community in Chicago's lower west side. For over 25 years, the Resurrection Project (TRP) has offered leadership training to empower community residents to pursue central needs in nonpartisan ways. As reported by Grossman et al. (2000), TRP emerged in 1994 after years of coalition building among eight local Catholic churches, community organizations, businesses, and city government, and its bylaws require two-thirds community residents on the Board of Directors to promote accountability.

With a budget of $25 million, four major programs are directed at some of the most pressing community needs: (1) *community organizing* attempts to institutionalize local power by identifying and training local community leaders to advocate for local issues (e.g., community policing, voter registration); (2) *family support services* ranging from Head Start, daycare, and parenting skills to housing programs for homeless women and children; (3) *homeownership and financial services* that develop low-income housing to replace inadequate housing, increase savings and loan options for residents; and (4) *real estate and assets management* for developing and renovating community-owned real estate in order to increase sustainability and affordability, increase tenant management of church-owned properties, and support a cooperative of minority-owned construction companies.

TRP's United Power for Justice coalition of churches, residents, and nonprofit organizations aims to hold elected officials accountable to the Latino community. General training classes offered to parishioners emphasize "the prophetic teachings of Jesus, the role of the church in seeking justice, and the importance of building people power for justice" (Grossman et al., 2000, p. 141). While there has been occasional controversy regrading developing housing units and gentrification in the Pilsen, TRP promotes transparency in its website by explaining the details and rationales for complex decision-making. Recently TRP, the mayor, and Societyfoundations announced a $5 million cash assistance fund to help mitigate Covid-19-related losses for 300,000 residents not eligible for federal government stimulus funds despite being especially vulnerable to the pandemic.

Puerto Ricans versus Hurricane Maria and President Trump

We are dying here. If we don't get the food and the water into the people's hands, we are going to see something close to a genocide.
—Maria Yulín Cruz, Mayor, San Juan,
Puerto Rico, 9 days after landfall

Every death is a horror, but if you look at a real catastrophe like Katrina, and you look at the tremendous hundreds and hundreds and hundreds of people that died, and you look at what happened here and what is your death count? Sixteen people, versus in the thousands.
—President Donald Trump, visiting Puerto Rico
13 days after landfall

Hurricane Katrina was a "real catastrophe" that claimed the lives of 1,833 people, left hundreds of thousands homeless, and caused over $100 billion in damage to the Gulf coast of New Orleans in 2005. Katrina also exposed the racialized vulnerability of African Americans in NOLA that bore the brunt of this natural disaster, exacerbated by the federal government's inept emergency response to weeks of flooding that left the city 80% underwater because of breached levees and floodwalls previously constructed and neglected by the federal government. An investigation by the U.S. House of Representatives documented failure at all levels of government and initiated reforms such as reorganizing FEMA (Federal Emergency Management Agency), fortifying the levees, and grants for evacuation plans to mitigate such future disasters. Why, then, did Hurricane Maria claim 2,975 lives in Puerto Rico, destroy tens of thousands of homes, and reveal the racialized vulnerability of a Latino population to a slow and inadequate federal emergency response exacerbated by a lack of island preparedness, bring an inadequate response from Puerto Rico's Governor Ricardo Roselló and insults from President Trump?

Maria, a Category 4 Hurricane, landed a direct hit on the U.S. territory of Puerto Rico on September 20, 2017, knocking out the island's antiquated electrical infrastructure and eliminating power and communication to the entire island, along with access to clean water for about half the population. The slow federal response included President Trump waiting almost a week to call a Situation Room meeting to address the disaster, waiting two weeks to send in military assistance, and 11 days for the hospital naval ship *USNS*

Comfort to arrive (Meyer, 2017). An increasingly frustrated Carmen Yulín Cruz, the mayor of San Juan, described to the media people forced to drink from creeks, needing to be rescued from destroyed buildings, the chronically ill going without medication, and infants without formula and baby food. Trump's many politicized responses to Cruz included:

> The Mayor of San Juan, who was very complimentary only a few days ago, has now been told by the Democrats that you must be nasty to Trump.
>
> Such poor leadership ability by the Mayor of San Juan, and others in Puerto Rico, who are not able to get their workers to help. They want everything to be done for them when it should be a community effort. 10,000 Federal workers now on Island doing a fantastic job.

Despite the president's subsequent flurry of high praise for relief efforts and insults to Cruz, reports of people dying from lack of insulin and oxygen began to appear. With a year's distance from the disaster, researchers at the Milken Institute of Public Health, George Washington School of Public Health, published the results of its rigorous analysis of Maria's death toll of 2,975. Void of empathy, Trump insisted that "3000 people did not die," that the report was the results of "bad politics" and Democrats trying to smear his reputation. In addition to condemnations of Trump's insults, from senators on both sides of the aisle, Mayor Cruz continued tangling with Trump on Twitter calling him "delusional, paranoid, and unhinged from any sense of reality," while Governor Rosselló offered to walk him through the scientific process of the study and requested that the president show empathy for the dead (Wikipedia, 2020).

Amidst a devastated island, and months without power, Puerto Ricans eventually took to the streets to protest Governor Rosselló, who was eventually forced to resign, as well as FEMA's slow response, mired down by botched contracts that failed to deliver food, tarp, and other needed resources (Pinchin, 2019). Some protesters painted the number of the dead on their faces, displayed the shoes of those lost across the beach, and *Calle 13*, the Puerto Rican hip-hop band, recorded a song protesting the governor that went viral. Part of the outrage was in response to intercepted messages by Rosselló's leadership team that heartlessly mocked victims. Protesters, jubilant about Rosselló's resignation, included Puerto Rican youth disenchanted with old-school elite politics and the perpetual vulnerability of colonial status laid bare by Hurricane Maria. Many Puerto Ricans in the United States also protested in solidarity with their island counterparts (Chotiner, 2019).

Protest would return to the streets of Puerto Rico in 2020, this time calling for the resignation of Governor Wanda Vazquez (2019–2021) after huge stock piles of unused emergency disaster relief aid (water, food, tarps, stoves, etc.), some dating back to Hurricane Maria, were discovered (Rosa & Mazzei, 2020). Hundreds of outraged residents had been sleeping in the streets, their homes damaged and unsafe as series of earthquakes assailed the vulnerable island. Such protests, past through present day, have frequently culminated in the development of formal Latino political organizations continuing to elevate the well-being of Latinos at local and larger levels.

Formal Latino Political Organizations

The history of Latino political organization is as old as Latino resistance to anti-Latino discrimination, including community movements designed to promote survival, civil and human rights, and political power, despite frequently hostile conditions outlined in Chapters 1 and 2. Many of the organizations profiled below continue to thrive and enhance Latino social justice and well-being in America. As such, they offer a wide variety of sites and specialized activities with which service providers can promote Latino social positionality at the macro-level by lending their professional skills, making financial contributions, and working with Latinx communities to promote beneficial policies at local and larger levels. Organizations profiled below in Table 12.1 come partly from the work of Garcia (1993a) and feature some of the major historical as well as currently active political organizations, now spanning three centuries.

As can be seen above, national Latino political organizations such as NALEO promote networking among *all* elected Latino politicians and appointed representatives, with the objective of addressing Latinx-wide priorities (e.g., naturalizing immigrants as citizens, language rights), building coalitions, and consolidating nationwide Latino political power and impact. While the CHC aims to do the same at the U.S. congressional level, it's telling that Republican Latino congresspersons refuse to participate in this predominantly Mexican American and Democrat organization. Huge historical differences on Fidel Castro and the ongoing Cuban blockade make the inclusion of Cuban Republican congresspersons in the CHC highly unlikely, again underscoring major political differences between Latino populations based on their unique acculturation histories covered in Chapters 1 and 2.

Table 12.1. Overview of Latino Political Organizations, Past & Present

Latino Political Organization	History and Scope
La Alianza Hispano Americano [Hispanic American Alliance]; *Orden de Los Hijos de América* [Order of the Children of America]	19th-century mutual aid societies that combated segregation and discrimination by providing basic survival-oriented resources such as credit, burial insurance, and social services, especially to immigrants.
Mexican American Legal Defense Fund (MALDEF)	Los Angeles-based MALDEF, founded in San Antonio, TX, in 1968, is a litigation organization modeled after the NAACP. MALDEF has a $6.5 million annual budget, with offices in San Antonio, Atlanta, Chicago, Houston, Sacramento, and Washington DC. Its staff of 75 employees includes 22 attorneys, 10 legislative and policy analysts, and outreach staff to promote community education and leadership. MALDEF focuses on the central Latino program areas of education, employment, immigrants' rights, political participation, fair share of government services, and access to justice. MALDEF was instrumental in litigation that expanded the VRA to include Latinos and other language minorities, securing free access to public education for undocumented children, and recently filing a suit to prevent a for-profit children's detention center from being built in San Antonio, TX.
League of United Latin American Citizens (LULAC)	While founded in Texas in 1927 as a nonpartisan organization of Latino citizens designed to promote assimilation, LULAC eventually fought the segregation of Mexican students in Texas and California. It is now a DC-based, inclusive multi-Latino-issue membership organization.
Puerto Rican Legal Defense and Education Fund (PRLDEF)	Like MALDEF, a litigation organization founded in the 1970s that assisted with expansion of the VRA to language minorities. In *Aspira v. New York*, PRLDEF litigated for bilingual education and service rights for Puerto Rican and other language minority students. PRLDEF has rebranded itself, Social Justice.
Cuban American National Foundation (CANF)	Founded in 1981 as an anti-Castro, anti-communist exile organization, CANF has been successful in winning asylum status for Cuban refugees and support for their adaptation, and promoting foreign policy that isolates Cuba (e.g., trade blockade).
Southwest and Midwestern Voter Registration Projects (SVRP & MVRP)	SVRP and MVRP have conducted campaigns to register eligible Latinos to vote for over 25 years, often timing their efforts to coincide with local elections.
Dominican American National Roundtable (DANR)	Example of a more recent civic organization, serving as an umbrella for over 60 local Dominican groups to promote adaptation in the United States.

(continued)

Table 12.1. Continued

Latino Political Organization	History and Scope
Congressional Hispanic Congress (CHC)	From five Latino Congress members in 1976 to currently over 20, the CHC is designed to promote a collective Latino agenda at the federal level (e.g., developing a pool of Latino candidates for Supreme Court vacancies). CHC efforts are limited by its generally Mexican American membership and Democrat politics, avoided by the few Latino Republicans in congress.
National Association of Latino Elected and Appointed Officials (NALEO)	Nonprofit, nonpartisan organization founded in 1976 to enhance the effectiveness of all Latino representatives through assistance and training, networking, research reports, assistance with policy matters, and establishing Latino-wide priorities (e.g., its major campaign beginning in 1985 was to promote naturalization of Latino immigrants in order to vote).

Garcia (2003b) advances a pan-Latino political scenario that depicts Cuban Americans as an "outlier" whose predominant conservative Republican political agenda and higher SES has historically distinguished them from the majority of U.S. Latinos. But even among the remaining groups, Garcia underscores the challenges of pan-Latino politics beyond a *symbolic* form in which different Latinx populations pursue their own group-specific agenda while occasionally invoking the term *Hispanic* or *Latino* as a strategy for greater recognition at the national level. Garcia does conceive of gradually growing pan-Latino political power based on a "community of interests" rooted in commonalities in culture, language, and history (including minority status, discrimination, and negative public image) as the basis for addressing Latinx subgroup and cross-cutting concerns such as immigration rights, scapegoating, and other issues surfaced below.

Immigration Rights as a New Civil Rights Issue in America

25th Anniversary of California Proposition 187

In celebration of MALDEF and the ACLU (American Civil Liberties Union) legally challenging California's Proposition 187 the day after it was passed in 1994, resulting in its blockage and eventually being declared unconstitutional in 1999, the Latino Community Foundation (LCF) of California proudly posted a short essay by University of Southern California professor of sociology Manuel Pastor on its website, succinctly capturing the significance of Proposition 187 regarding Latinx resistance then and now:

> Proposition 187 sought to ban undocumented immigrants from schools, hospitals, and access to public assistance. It sought to turn teachers and doctors into immigration officers. It shaped a narrative of immigrants and Latinos as "welfare queens" and "super predator gang members." Pitting Californians against each other, politicians fear-mongered and managed to pass Prop. 187 with 59% of votes in California. It was the epitome of hate-driven public policy rooted in nativism and xenophobia.
>
> But California's fall from grace was turned back around by a wave of leaders that organized, mobilized, and reinstated a moral code in the state's political engine. Latino leaders joined forces with Black, Asian, and concerned White leaders to propel the state out of the dark period that had begun to consume it. Students organized walk-outs, health centers filed lawsuits, and community organizations demanded and sought justice. Through the combined efforts of the people, California didn't just rise from the ashes. The Anti-Prop 187 movement reshaped the political landscape of the state. Today, California is one of the most pro-immigrant states in the Union. And, while we have yet to fully live up to our progressive ideals, California has led the way in becoming the first Sanctuary State, extended drivers licenses to the undocumented and health insurance to their children. All common sense laws that 25 years ago would have been considered criminal (Latino Community Foundation, 2019).

The LCF conducted interviews with community, student, and a legal team leaders of the Anti-187 movement to document lessons learned that can be implemented today: (1) short-term losses can be transformed into long-term gains; (2) turning out the vote matters (i.e., increased naturalization and voting resulted in many elected members of the California Latino Legislative Caucus [CLLC] members); (3) anti-immigrant nativist rhetoric can be a losing proposition for candidates; and, perhaps most important today, (4) broad-based and inclusive coalitions are increasingly necessary to achieve sustained political success (community organizers, clergy, lawyers, school teachers and college professors, foundations funding nonprofit organizations and initiatives).

Many powerful members of today's CLLC emerged from the Anti-187 movement (e.g., Kevin de Leon, Maria Elena Durazo, and Antonia Hernandez), and organizations such as the Coalition for Human Immigrant Rights of Los Angeles were battle tested and emerged stronger in their mission to organize families, churches, and communities on behalf of immigrant rights. Lessons learned are currently being implemented with the goal of advancing immigrant rights, decriminalizing undocumented people, and preserving democracy in America.

Immigration Rights and DREAMers Movements

In the excellent book *The DREAMers: How the Undocumented Youth Movement Transformed the Immigrant Rights Debate*, Walter Nicholls (2013) not only documents the post-Proposition 187 rise of the immigration rights movement, spearheaded by regional and national organizations and networks, but also how courageous undocumented youth transformed the narrative while assuming leadership of the movement. As described below, the movement's initial goal was to pass national comprehensive immigration reform (CIR), including the DREAM Act for youth brought into the country without authorization. However, the movement needed to devolve to local state, county, and city levels after repeated failures to pass CIR at the national level given Congress' long-standing lack of political will in this area. Disentangled below are some highlights from this complex and ongoing civil rights struggle.

Comprehensive Immigration Reform
As the 21st century got underway, seasoned immigration rights organizations and coalitions across the nation pressed Congress to fix our nation's broken immigration system by passing some kind of CIR. While there have been multiple versions of CIR since 2001, essentially such a federal policy would confer legality and a path to citizenship for the estimated 10.5 million undocumented people in exchange for even greater border enforcement. Culminating with the failed Secure Borders, Economic Opportunity and Immigration Reform Act of 2007, previous failed versions of CIR included the Secure American and Orderly Immigration Act proposed in May 2005;

the Comprehensive Enforcement and Immigration Reform Act proposed in July 2005, which was passed in the Senate in May 2006, only to be defeated in the House of Representatives.

Despite our nation's chronic need to fix a badly broken immigration system, all versions of CIR over the past two decades have engendered intense partisan divide, heated debate, and proposed amendments that ultimately sank any chance of passage. Thus, immigration rights coalitions and allies in Congress have shifted their efforts and energies to the DREAM Act as a stand-alone policy that had been previously packaged within various CIR and other bills since 2001. Essentially, the DREAM Act would provide undocumented youth the legal right to remain and work in the country based on the following criteria: (1) must have entered the country before the age of 16; (2) must graduate high school or obtain a GED; (3) have no criminal record; and (4) have at least five years of continuous presence in the United States.

However, even the DREAM Act, with its strategic appeal to cultural assimilation and sympathy for youth, failed to pass in both 2007 and 2010, frustrating a decade of activism and organizing that attempted to secure just a sliver of immigrant rights at the national level. Such disillusionment was experienced most profoundly by undocumented youth, living under the radar during the early years of the movement but quickly emerging to center stage. By 2010, undocumented youth began outing themselves in public and asserting their rights as a nascent political group as reflected in their courageous rallying cry, "Undocumented, unapologetic and unafraid!" Local and national immigrant rights organizations had been convening and supporting these youth throughout the country, mitigating their isolation and mentoring them in community organizing, political activism, and crafting persuasive political arguments for the public and elected officials during an increasingly hostile political climate toward undocumented immigrants. These resilient youth made adaptive meaning of their so-called illegality, rejected stigma, and asserted their civil and human rights on college campuses, in social media, street rallies, and high-risk demonstrations such as occupying the offices of U.S. senators and even the Department of Homeland Security (DHS)! In a sense, these young people were implementing all that they had learned from the movement by making the movement uniquely their own, even while engendering pushback from older immigration rights networks bracing for how these new and bold civil rights activists would be received (Nicholls, 2013).

Burciaga and Martinez (2017) theorize that undocumented youth are primed for civil activism because of their early social inclusion through high school, followed by harsh social exclusion upon graduation. That is, the stigma experienced through their youth is viewed as a trigger for eliciting resistance on the part of undocumented youth, including a reactive challenging identity easily transferable to political activism. Such theorizing promotes understanding of why undocumented youth eventually transcended immigration rights organizations and rejected the politically strategic yet divisive "good versus bad" immigrant dichotomy. They could no longer tolerate throwing their parents under the bus for bringing them to the United States without documentation, and began referring to their mothers and fathers as the *original dreamers*. These youth also assuaged their guilt over fighting only for the rights of immigrant youth, or about 10% of the 10.5 million or so undocumented people in the United States. Inspired by the massive national protest for immigrant rights in 2006, undocumented youth strategically targeted change at local city, county, and state governments. A choice quote from Burciaga and Martinez's study of these activists captures the frustration with national level politics and the urgent need to return home to effect meaningful local change:

> I want to really affect people . . . in a more personal way, not just through politics because that doesn't help anyone at all. It's a fucking game, you know? (p. 461).

Intersectionality

Expanding upon Nicholl's (2013) study of the outspoken DREAMers movement, Terriquez et al. (2018) also analyze how this movement, led mainly by Latinx college students and graduates, embraced the concerns of lesbian, gay, bisexual, transgender, queer (LGBTQ), nonbinary and gendernonconforming members. Based on semistructured interviews with 24 sexual minority and 30 sexual majority young adult activists, Terriquez and colleagues conclude that deploying "intersectionality as a collective action frame" helps activists make better sense of their own multiply marginalized identities; increases motivation to act; and supports building more inclusive organizations and social movements. The advantages of such *bonding* within the immigration rights movement, as well as *bridging* between the immigration and LGBTQ movements, is reflected in the following choice quote:

> Both communities face laws that treat us like we are less human. We both are very vocal about society's problems, we both are afraid for the security of our families, we both feel vulnerable and unsafe because of policies,

institutions, and attitudes that keep us on the margins. We are frequently ignored, misrepresented, or made fun of by the dominant culture! (p. 271)

The undocumented-led immigration rights movement illustrates implementation of the above lessons learned and need for more robust and impactful social movements by way of more broadly based coalitions in which the needs and rights of multiple constituent groups intersect. As described in the final section of this chapter, such coalition building needs to be broad and inclusive enough to bridge race and social class in America. For example, there is currently ample Latinx support of the Black Lives Matter (BLM) movement in the wake of the horrendous murder of George Floyd, a 46-year-old African American man killed by Minneapolis police officer Derek Chauvin, after a convenience store employee reported to police that Floyd had attempted to purchased cigarettes with a counterfeit $20 bill. Captured on cellphone video by various bystanders urging Chauvin to stop, the officer crushed the life out of Floyd by pressing his knee down upon his neck, for a full nine and a half minutes, as Floyd pleaded that he could not breathe and eventually called out his mother's name before expiring. In an unusually swift move, Chauvin and the three other officers who stood passively by were fired and charged—Chauvin for 2nd degree murder and the others for aiding and abetting 2nd degree murder. In an unprecedented result, jurors at Derek Chauvin's trial found him guilty on all three counts: 2nd degree murder, 3rd degree murder, and 2nd degree manslaughter.

Las Vidas Negras Importan [Black Lives Matter]

In an op-ed published in *La Opinión* entitled, " 'Black Lives Matter' *merece todo nuestro apoyo*" [deserves all of our support], Professor Cristina Mora of UC Berkeley and professors Claudia Sandoval and Sylvia Zamora of Loyola Marymount explain why it is in the best interest of Latinxs and immigrants to support the BLM movement and related protests across the nation (La Opinión, 2020). These three Latinx professors elaborated during an interview by Univisión (2020) as summarized below, along with additional facts to bolster their recommendations:

- Second to African Americans, Latinos also experience disproportionate over-policing, police brutality, and killings (Figure 12.5). For instance, using data from the National Violent Death Reporting System, which

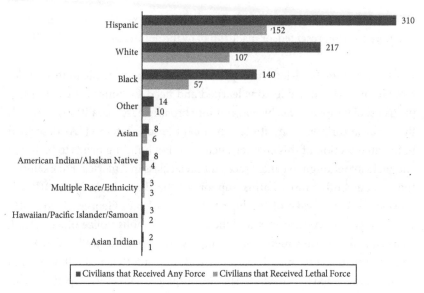

Figure 12.5. Lethal and all types of police force against civilians by race/ethnicity in California, 2017.

From Racial and Identity Profiling Advisory Board (2019). Annual Report 2019. California Department of Justice.

captures nearly all lethal police shootings in participating states, Wertz et al. (2020) report that while Latinx are 17.1% of the U.S. population, they are 23% of unarmed victims presenting no threat to police. In California where Latinxs are 39% of the population, they are 44% of violent police encounters, including 47% of fatalities in such encounters. California data are from the 2019 Annual Report of the Racial & Identity Profiling Advisory Board, using 2017 data from law enforcement throughout the state required by the 2015 Racial Profiling Act to report all violent encounters (RIPAB, 2019). Data from LA County's Homicide Report reveal that Latinxs compose 49% of the county but 53% of 886 police killings since 2000 (Los Angeles Times Staff, 2020). For this same time period, whites made up 26% of the county and 19% of police killings, while these percentages for African Americans are 8% and 25%, respectively.

- African American leadership has consistently supported immigration rights. From public figures such as Jesse Jackson, Cornell West, and Al Sharpton speaking out early against the persecution of undocumented residents, to the NAACP, which joined the University of California in challenging former president Trump's executive order to end DACA, African Americans continue to stand against anti-immigrant and anti-Latinx racism and discrimination.

- It is important to underscore that many Black people targeted by police are Latinx. While Latinxs are racialized in America, they are an ethnic group from many racial backgrounds, including African. Such individuals bridge the Black and Latinx experience in America, for better and for worse.
- Anti-Black, anti-Latinx, and anti-immigrant racism and discrimination all derive from white supremacy that is harmful to all groups of color, as evident in the separation of children from their families detained on the southwestern border in 2018.

Professors Mora, Sandoval, and Zamora would be pleased to know the results of the Survey of U.S. Adults, conducted June 4–10, 2020, show that the majority of Americans express support for BLM (Pew, 2020). As can be seen in Figure 12.6, 77% of Latinxs support current BLM protests (42% strongly and 35% somewhat), second to African Americans (71% and 15%, respectively), and more so than non-Latino whites (NLWs) (31% and 30%, respectively). Recommendations for continued support include Latinx family members taking up hard conversations about BLM, colorism within Latinx culture, recognizing that silence or not speaking up against anti-Black violence contributes to its lethality, and that in addition to joining protests, Latinxs should also donate what they can in terms of volunteer time and money.

Criminalizing Undocumented People through Federal Laws and Policies

Given the enormity of ongoing issues to highlight in today's resistance to the criminalization of Latinx and other undocumented people, featured below is a review of key federal laws that lay the foundation for criminalizing immigrants, and especially undocumented immigrants, over the past 25 years. Also listed are some of the Trump administration's executive orders (EOs) and efforts designed not to advance urgently needed CIR, but to strip immigrants of legal rights and protections and to persecute undocumented immigrants in ways intended to make their lives miserable. This complex

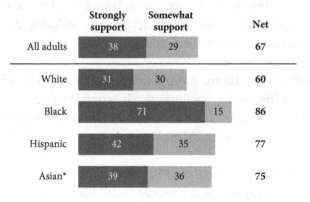

Most Americans express support for the Black Lives Matter movement

% saying they ___ the Black Lives Matter movement

*Asian adults were interviewed in English only.
Note: Figures may not add to subtotals due to rounding. White, black and Asian adults include those who report being only one race and are non-Hispanic. Hispanics are of any race.
Source: Survey of U.S. adults conducted June 4–10, 2020.
"Amid Protests, Majorities Across Racial and Ethnic Groups Express Support for the Black Lives Matter Movement"

PEW RESEARCH CENTER

Figure 12.6. Support for Black Lives Matter in adults by race/ethnicity. From Parker, Menasce Horowitz, & Anderson (2020). Amid protests, majorities across racial and ethnic groups express support for the Black Lives Matter movement. Washington DC: Pew Research Center (2020). With permission.

web of federal policies, and relentless EOs from the Trump administration, represent an unprecedented and deliberate conflation of crime and immigration despite research consistently demonstrating no such relationship, or even an inverse relationship indicating that as immigration increases, crime decreases.

For instance, a 2017 report by yhe Sentencing Project, *Immigration and Public Safety*, concludes: (1) immigrants, regardless of legal status, commit crimes at lower rates than native-born citizens; (2) higher levels of immigration in recent decades may have contributed to the historic drop in crime rates; (3) many police chiefs believe that intensifying immigration law enforcement undermines their work and public safety; and (4) immigrants are underrepresented in U.S. prisons (Ghandoosh & Rover, 2017). For example overall, non-citizens are underrepresented in the U.S. prison system (6% versus 7% of U.S. population) while citizens are overrepresented (94% versus 93% of U.S. population). Further, while immigrants are now overrepresented in federal prisons at 22%, the Sentencing Project reveals that only 2% of these cases are for violent crimes, while the vast majority are for immigration violations or new expanded felony charges affixed to what used to be an administrative rather than a criminal violation. It's as if immigrants commit so few crimes that our government needs to invent new crimes with which to charge them, in order to support its false claims that immigrants are criminals that endanger the public. A striking figure from the above report clearly illustrates the pronounced inverse relationship between immigration and serious crime in America:

Figure 12.7 illustrates the dramatic decline in violent crime in America between 1990 and 2014, from just under 750 crimes per 100,000 residents to about half, or 375 per 100,000. Equally dramatic for this same time period is the simultaneous increase in immigration from just under 30 million in 1990 to double, or just over 60 million, in 2014, including undocumented immigration that increased from about three million to 11 million. While

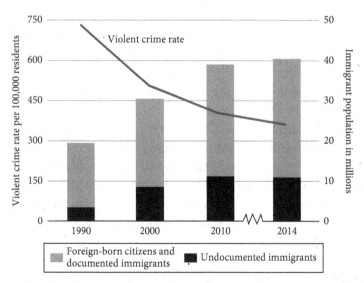

Figure 12.7. The inverse relation between immigration and violent crime, 1990 to 2014.

From Ghandnoosh & Rovner (2017). Immigration and public safety. The Sentencing Project. Washington DC. With permission.

correlational data do not imply causality, they clearly do not support repeated false accusations by former president Trump and the right that immigration threatens public safety with dangerous crime. The authors of the Sentencing Project report conclude:

> Before and after his election, Donald Trump has raised concerns about increasing crime and immigration in the United States. Indeed, he has signed an executive order and made regular statements alleging that curbs to unauthorized immigration and dismantling sanctuary cities would reduce U.S. crime rates. The evidence presented here concludes otherwise (p. 14).

Even stronger evidence is provided by Ousey and Kubrin (2018), who conducted a quantitative systematic meta-analysis of the literature entitled *Immigration and Crime: Assessing a Contentious Issue*. Regarding methods, these researchers focused on the recent generation (1994 to 2014) of immigration crime research based on large geographical areas captured by census data to synthesize 543 effect sizes from 51 publications comparing before and after increases in immigrants, or between locations differing in immigration populations. Two-thirds of the studies reviewed show *no relationship between immigration and crime*, while the remaining one-third of studies reviewed show that inverse relationships were 2.5 times more likely than positive relationships (i.e., as the number of immigrants goes up, crime goes down). The majority of the studies reviewed made sure to focus on violent crimes, including homicide, in order to dispute racist lies about immigrants as an existential threat to the public.

The above research is so conclusive that it begs the question, why does the former U.S. president and his base, including so many Republican members of Congress, perpetuate alarmist falsehoods designed to portray immigrants as dangerous criminals that should be feared by the public? Why perpetuate racial fear and animosity to justify persecuting immigrants for non-criminal reasons while blocking their entrance into the United States? Answers to such vital questions have powerful implications for the direction of current and future strategies of resistance, activism, social movements, and coalition building on the part of Latinxs and others. Table 12.1 summarizes two of the 1996 federal laws, and related programs, that have conflated U.S. immigration and criminal systems of government.

Crimmigration

This term is increasingly used in the literature to capture how laws like those in Table 12.2 conflate crime and immigration by merging the criminal legal system, charged with punishing crimes harmful to society, with the former Immigration and Naturalization Service (INS), charged with regulating ports of entry and processing immigration applications (i.e., green cards, naturalization) based on federal immigration policy. However, the INS was disbanded in 2003 and its function subsumed under the Department of Homeland Security (DHS), newly established in 2002 in response to the 9/11 terrorist attacks of 2001. DHS subdivisions assuming INS functions, now with unprecedented reach and power, include CBP (Customs and Border Protection), ICE (Immigration and Customs Enforcement in the interior United States), and the Citizenship and Immigration Services (immigration application processing).

Given the central purpose of the DHS to combat terrorism, antiterrorism is now the lens through which immigration and border regulation are viewed and operationalized. With a budget of approximately $50 billion and nearly a quarter of a million employees, DHS is a massive federal cabinet with immense power and resources to label as felons, detain, imprison, and deport predominately undocumented Latino people at the southwest border and throughout the interior United States.

Intolerance on the Southern Border

Introduced by DHS in 2005, *Operation Streamline* began charging undocumented border crossers with federal-level crimes in criminal courts, a radical departure from the previous practice of civil deportation proceedings in immigration courts that used their discretion to allow many to leave the country voluntarily. Since 2005, those caught for the first time are charged with a misdemeanor and up to six months in federal prison, while reentry is now labeled an "aggravated felony" punishable with up to two years in federal prison followed by deportation (Macias-Rojas, 2016). Such immigration violations now constitute the majority of "crimes" for which people are sent to federal prison in a *New Jim Crow* scenario for Latinx immigrants.

Given the creation of new and severe immigration crimes and penalties, processing apprehended undocumented people is now done in criminal courts en masse, or groups ranging from a dozen to as many as 100 people a day, in order to streamline the process (Kerwin & McCabe, 2010). Macias-Rojas (2016), who witnessed many such criminal hearings as part of her

Table 12.2. Crimmigration: Merging the Immigration and Criminal Systems through 1996 Federal Laws

The Illegal Immigration Reform & Immigrant Responsibility Act (IIRIRA) (1996)	• IRRIRA's 287(g) program expanded federal immigration enforcement throughout the interior United States by deputizing local law enforcement and granting them authority to police the immigration status of anyone encountered during routine stops or arrests.
	• Although 287(g) was eliminated during the Obama administration, it was revived in 2018 by President Trump.
	• Bars reentry of undocumented people for three years upon first apprehension, and 10 years upon second apprehension.
	• Eliminates option to adjust immigration status while in the United States by requiring the undocumented to return to country of origin to apply for documentation status, thereby triggering the three-year ban.
The Antiterrorism & Effective Death Penalty Act (AEDPA) (1996)	• Ironically, AEDPA was partly motivated by the 1995 Oklahoma City bombing of the Alfred P. Murrah federal building by American terrorist Timothy McVeigh, which killed 168 people including 19 children and wounded hundreds more.
	• While McVeigh was a white male citizen, veteran, and white supremacist with a grudge against the government, this law expanded the number of immigrants, undocumented and documented, eligible for detention, deportation, and expedited removal via bypassing regular immigration court discretion.
	• For immigrants, AEDPA elevated minor and nonviolent crimes such as not paying taxes or minor drug and burglary offenses by now labeling them "aggravated felonies" despite such crimes not constituting felonies, aggravated or otherwise, on the basis of criminal law.
	• While McVeigh received the "effective death penalty" for his heinous crime, immigrants became the primary target of this law's enhanced criminalization and expedited removal policies.
	• McVeigh's horrible crime would never be blamed on his race or citizenship, yet very rare and isolated crimes committed by undocumented people were weaponized by Trump to slander undocumented immigrants and perpetuate racial fear, animosity, and resentment against the government for supposedly caring more about immigrants and people of color than citizens people.
	• Hence the rage of McVeigh, and others like him, now dangerously target the government because of strategically divisive political rhetoric designed to obtain power on false pretenses.

ethnographic study of the deportation-to-prison pipeline, observes that the vast majority of these shackled Spanish (and indigenous dialect) speaking captives have little to no understanding of the proceedings or the charges to which they are being advised to plead guilty.

Furthermore, while the DHS during the Obama administration insisted that its number one priority was arresting undocumented terrorists and dangerous criminals, the vast majority of detainees had no criminal records, unless you count the new crime of being undocumented in America. In fact, the highest rates of deportations occurred under the Obama administration (see Figure 12.8) partly because of the congressional "bed mandate" that made DHS (CPB and ICE) funding contingent upon keeping 31,000 detention beds filled at all times (Macias-Rojas, 2016). The mandate to keep that many beds filled explains how mass deportation has been achieved during the past two decades, and how necessary it is to forego criminal priorities and rather deport anyone that is undocumented.

In fact, the Trump administration eliminated DHS criminal priorities by making all undocumented people subject to criminal charges and prosecution, imprisonment, and deportation. In one of the cruelest examples

U.S. deportations of immigrants decline for second year in a row
In thousands, by fiscal year

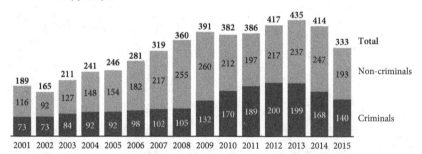

Source: Data for 2001–2004 come from U.S. Department of Homeland Security, *Yearbook of Immigration Statistics: 2010*. Data for 2005 to 2014 come from U.S. Department of Homeland Security, *Yearbook of Immigration Statistics: 2014*. Data for 2015 come from U.S. Department of Homeland Security, *Yearbook of Immigration Statistics: 2015*.

PEW RESEARCH CENTER

Figure 12.8. Mass deportation of non-criminal and criminalized undocumented people.

From Gonzalez-Barrera & Hugo Lopez (2016). U.S. immigrant deportations fall to lowest level since 2007. Washington DC: Pew Research Center. With permission.

of persecuting unauthorized border crossers to date, the DHS and CBP in particular were charged with implementing Trump's 2018 "Zero Tolerance" policy that separated as many as 3,000 children from their parents in an effort to deter families without authorization intercepted on the border (see Figure 12.9).

At the inception of Zero Tolerance, then Attorney General and longtime anti-immigrant senator from Alabama Jeff Sessions threatened, "If you are smuggling a child then we will prosecute you, and that child will be separated from you as required by law." And, "If you don't like that, then don't smuggle children over our border." Consequently, children were ripped from their mothers' arms, placed in detention cages wailing in shock while their parents, shackled in federal criminal courts, went without notification that their children were being disbursed to shelters throughout the country. Domestic and international outrage and condemnation of such state-sponsored violence was so immediate and immense, as were hundreds of spontaneous demonstrations across the country, that within a mere six weeks, Trump issued an EO canceling his Zero Tolerance policy. Even the Pope and former first lady Barbara Bush publicly denounced the cruelty of Zero Tolerance (Burnett, 2019).

Figure 12.9. Iconic photo of cruel zero tolerance policy on the U.S./Mexico border, 2018.
John Moore/Getty Images.

Intolerance in the Interior United States

With a budget of nearly $4 billion and about 8,000 employees, ICE was charged under the Trump administration with targeting *all* undocumented people within the interior United States, a departure from Obama's failed efforts to focus on "felons not families," as he frequently stated (Nixon & Qiu, 2018). Terrifying tactics by ICE have included separating families at schools and churches, as well as raiding businesses such as meatpacking plants, leading to public outcries by immigrant rights organizations to abolish ICE. Even special agents within DHS have complained that the entanglement of ICE in immigration politics interferes with anti-terrorist work by incurring community resentment and reluctance to cooperate. ICE and its orders reinforce the Trump administration's framing of all undocumented people as criminals that should be prosecuted, imprisoned, and deported despite being propelled to the United States by poverty, violence, and our broken immigration system that fails to regulate immigrant labor upon which the United States depends. Other, mainly Latino-focused anti-immigration executive orders and related policies are summarized in Table 12.3.

Table 12.3. Anti-immigrant Policies during the Trump Administration (2016–2020)

| Campaign Promise to Build the Wall | • Despite unprecedented globalization or the interaction and integration of people, business, governments, and technologies, including free trade agreements between the United States and Mexico, a U.S. neighbor and third, sometimes fourth largest trading partner, President Trump ran on the campaign promise to build a wall along the nearly 2,000-mile U.S.-Mexico border and to make Mexico pay for it.
• During his administration he was relentless in this pursuit espite multiple failed attempts to secure funding from Congress. In an effort to seize privately owned land along the Texas-Mexico border to build his wall, Trump filed dozens of cases in federal court during 2020 alone (Renshaw, 2020).
  • Such cases force private landowners, including native American reservation residents, to sell and vacate their homes, even during the Covid-19 pandemic.
  • Trump used the Covid-19 pandemic as an excuse for fortifying the border and attempting to temporarily halt all immigration into the United States.
  • In February 2019, Trump declared the border to be a national emergency and sent army troops to an already heavily militarized region.
• Multiple millions of dollars were diverted from the Pentagon to secure funding for the wall despite a lack of support from the military and congress.
  • While successful as a xenophobic symbol to unite and mobilize his supporters, Trump's failed, breached, and partial rusty wall is one of the most useless and expensive infrastructure projects in American history. |

(continued)

Table 12.3. Continued

EO to Terminate DACA	• In addition to removing the immediate threat of deportation, DACA recipients are entitled to employment, in-state tuition when attending college, a driver's license, and other benefits based on President Obama's executive order (EO) from 2012.
	• In 2017, President Trump followed through on his campaign promise overturn Obama's EO with his own.
	  • However, several federal lawsuits challenged Trump, resulting in a preliminary injunction allowing DACA to stand while winding its way to the Supreme Court.
	• While estimates vary, the fate of between 650,000 to over 800,000 predominately Latinx recipients of Deferred Action for Childhood Arrivals rested in the hands of the Supreme Court, which ruled against the merit of Trump's EO in June of 2020 referring to it as "arbitrary and capricious" because it provided no rationale and as such was an unconstitutional exercise of authority by the executive branch.
	  • Trump vowed to try again but did not follow through.

EO to Terminate Temporary Protective Status (TPS)	• The fate of over 300,000 immigrants, primarily from El Salvador (195,000), Honduras (57,000) and Haiti (46,000), or what President Trump refers to as "shithole countries" as compared to Norway, stood to lose their TPS, between 2020–2021, given the former president's 2018 EO to end it rather than accommodate these long-term U.S. residents who, among other things, have an estimated 273,000 U.S.-born children. • Because of multiple lawsuits filed by recipients of TPS and their U.S. citizen family members, the DHS extended TPS through January 2021 while it decided whether or not to end the program and give recipients 120 days to return to their impoverished and violent countries of origin. As of 2022, TPS benefits remain in effect.

Public Charge Rule	• Many non-citizens, both undocumented and those applying for legal permanent residency, have been avoiding testing for COVID-19 or any health or social service for fear that doing so will result in denial to change their immigration status and even deportation.
	  • Despite multiple federal injunctions to prevent this short-sighted EO from taking effect, former president Trump asked the Supreme Court to allow his 2018 executive order to stand while it made its way through the lower courts.
	• In February 2020, the Supreme Court enabled Trump by lifting all injunctions in a partisan five Republican to four Democrats vote among Supreme Court judges.
	  • Supreme Court Justice Sonia Sotomayor issued a scathing dissent castigating the president's administration for repeatedly crying emergency and asking the Supreme Court to allow controversial policies to go into effect, accusing her conservative Supreme Court colleagues of being too eager to please Trump and interfering with the appellate process of the lower courts, which would normally handle such cases (de Vogue, 2020).

Table 12.3. Continued

	• Before President Biden rescinded Public Charge in March 2021, applications for citizenship needed to include a public charge questionnaire to determine inadmissibility based on the *likeliness* of becoming dependent on the government (e.g., including using vital services such as health care and nutrition programs such as federallyfunded Medicaid, SNAP benefits, formerly known as food stamps, and Section 8 housing).
	  • While some immigrants (i.e., asylees, refugees, those with U-Visas), immigration processes (naturalization), and types of services (Medicaid received by applicants while under age 21, or while pregnant and up to 60 days after a pregnancy, or during an emergency) were exempt, such convoluted exceptions evaded most non-citizens who feared that any use of public services or benefits would derail their hopes of obtaining a green card.
	  • Adding to this predicament is the fact that immigrants have been overrepresented in what is now being called *essential* work with greater risk of exposure to Covid-19 than non-essential work.

Defunding Sanctuary Ordinances	• In 2020, the U.S. Court of Appeals for the 2nd Circuit in Manhattan sided with President Trump's EO to withhold millions of dollars in crime prevention grant money to sanctuary states that refuse to allow their local law enforcement to assist ICE with immigration control by turning over information about undocumented people in their custody, or detaining such individuals beyond their sentences in order to allow ICE into jails and prisons to determine their citizenship status.
	  • Many cities and states appealed the decision, and the EO was eventually repealed by the Department of Justice in 2021.
	  • The ironies are many and include the fact that sanctuary cities and counties are safer than non-sanctuary counties despite the Trump administration's false claims to the contrary.
	  • Also, withholding funds for law enforcement and crime prevention programs directly reduces a state's resources for addressing crime.
	• Interestingly, in June 2020, the Supreme Court refused to hear the Trump administration's appeal of a lower court rulings that upheld a California law barring its local law enforcement from notifying ICE when immigrants are about to be released after completing sentences for local crimes.
	  • The latter is a win for sanctuary ordinances that essentially eliminates any rationale for Trump's defunding of sanctuary states.

Sanctuary Promotes Public Safety

While defunding sanctuary states actually make them less safe by with-holding millions of dollars in crime prevention grants, it creates the illusion of punishing states for refusing to allow their local law enforcement to co-operate with the federal government's mass deportation efforts. However, sanctuary should not be confused with lack of cooperation with immigration control, given that its goal is to maintain public safety by not contaminating the role of local law enforcement by engaging in immigration control—a responsibility of the federal government. Local policing depends upon the trust of community residents, many of whom are disinclined to call or coop-erate with police for fear of their own detention or that of family members, neighbors, friends, or coworkers lacking authorization.

Sanctuary states also do not support holding undocumented arrestees in their jails or prisons 48 hours beyond their release time in response to ICE issuing detainers to determine their deportability. However, anti-sanctuary forces fail to acknowledge that sanctuary states do use their discretion to turn over the very few undocumented arrestees that commit violent or se-rious felonies. Thus, propaganda claiming that sanctuary cities endanger the public by shielding criminals, whether from the mouth of the former president or his attorney general, contributes to the contentious divide in America regarding the role of local and state government in protecting im-migrant civil rights.

The primary purpose of sanctuary ordinances is to protect the civil and legal rights of *all* residents, regardless of citizenship, in order to foster trustful interactions with local law enforcement and hence safer communities—a principled position supported by research on the topic. Not surprisingly, a re-view of the literature examining the relationship between sanctuary policies and crime finds either no relationship or a negative relationship between sanctuary and crime in America (Martinez, Martínez-Schuldt, & Cantor, 2017). The authors also note that sanctuary ordinances now operate in four states, 364 counties, and 39 cities, all targets of the former administration's defamation campaign.

A particularly revealing study by Wong (2017) compares rates of se-rious crime in 608 sanctuary counties to carefully matched non-sanctuary counties (i.e., on the basis of population size, rural versus urban, number of immigrants, etc.) throughout the country. These sanctuary data were obtained directly from ICE through the Freedom of Information Act, and crime data were obtained from the most recent FBI Uniform Crime Reporting database. Serious crimes compared in this study were the total number of violent (i.e., murders, rapes, robberies, and assaults) and property crimes (i.e., burglaries, larceny, motor vehicle thefts, and arsons) per 10,000 county residents. Wong also compared economic indicators, using the 2015 American Community Survey five-year estimates, which is part of the U.S. Census.

As can be seen in Table 12.4, results from Wong's comparisons reveal significantly less crime in sanctuary counties, whether large central metro counties, small metro counties, micropolitan counties, or noncore, rural counties. More specifically, there are 36 fewer serious crimes per 10,000 residents in sanctuary counties overall, and 65.4 fewer crimes in large central metro sanctuary counties versus non-sanctuary counterparts. Further, as compared to non-sanctuary counties, sanctuary counties had household

Table 12.4. Comparison of 608 Sanctuary Counties and 608 Matched[1] Non-Sanctuary Counties Regarding Serious Crime and Other Social Indicators

Serious Crimes[2]	36 less per 100,000 Residents
	• 66 less in Large Central Metropolitan Areas
Median Household Income	$4,353 Higher on Average
Poverty Rate	1.4% Lower
	• 2.3% Lower for Whites and 2.9% Lower for Latinos
Labor Force Participation	2.5% Higher
Employment	3.1% Higher
Unemployment	1.1% Lower
Public Assistance	2.6% Less SNAP
	1.0% Less SSI
	4.9% Less Children Receiving Assistance

Notes: [1]Counties compared matched for population size, percent of immigrants, rural or urban locations, etc.; to ensure proper comparisons; and [2] Serious crimes are number of violent crimes (murders, rapes, robberies, and assaults) and property crimes (burglaries, larceny, motor vehicle thefts, and arsons) per 100,000 residents.

Adapted from Wong's (2017) analysis of ICE dataset obtained through Freedom of Information Act filed by the Immigrant Legal Resource Center of California.

annual incomes $4,353 higher on average, a poverty rate 2.3% lower, 1.1% less unemployment, higher rates of work participation rates, and lower use of public assistance. Wong (2017) concludes:

> Altogether, the data suggest that when local law enforcement focuses on keeping communities safe, rather than becoming entangled in federal immigration enforcement efforts, communities are safer and community members stay more engaged in the local economy. This in turn brings benefits to individual households, communities, counties, and the economy as a whole (p. 11).

The above research provides ample reasons for continued and increased Latinx resistance, activism, and social movements beginning to diversify in intersectional directions. One overarching direction is the ambitious goal of fusing race and class to mitigate the politics of racial division in the United States addressed next.

Fusing Racial and Economic Justice to Defeat the Politics of Racial Division

The best response to divide and conquer is unite and build. (p. xxiii)
—Ian Haney Lopez (2019)

> Regardless of where we come from, what our color is, or how we worship, every family wants the best for their children. But today, certain politicians and their greedy lobbyists are putting all of our families at risk. They rig the rules to enrich themselves and avoid paying their fair share of taxes, while they defund our schools and threaten seniors with cuts to Medicare and Social Security. Then they turn around and point the finger for our hard times at new immigrants—even tearing families apart and losing children. When we reject their scapegoating and come together across racial differences, we can make this a nation we're proud to leave all of our kinds—whether we're white, Black, or brown, from down the street or across the globe (p. 206).

The above paragraph, a carefully worded narrative about immigration, is the culmination of years of ongoing research by Ian Haney Lopez (2019) and his Race-Class Narrative Project (RCNP). The RCNP conducts exten-sive focus group and survey testing, with people from across the nation and political spectrum, to assess the persuasiveness of what Haney Lopez calls *race-class narratives* as compared to the *racial fear narratives* of right-wing conservatives, as well as the *colorblind economic narratives* of center-left Democrat politicians that avoid addressing racial justice. Example of racial fear narratives include the former president's scapegoating of Mexicans and Central Americans as dangerous threats to American citizens, as reviewed earlier. Interestingly, racial fear messages not only pander to racism but also provoke cries of racism by the left, so that the right can counterpunch by la-beling such accusations as racist. Next, the right infuriates its base by telling members that *they* are accused of being racists simply because they favor *se-cure borders* and deporting *criminal illegal aliens* in order to keep *our* country safe—all coded messages, as explained by Haney Lopez.

Such language exemplifies what Haney Lopez calls *dog whistle politics* or the deliberate use of coded messages to tap racism without mentioning race per se. As a result, candidates on the left find themselves in a bind: either incur the wrath of the right and be labeled racist, or say nothing and incur the wrath of the left and people of color within their own base. However, the bind for Democratic politicians is even more complicated.

As Haney Lopez documents, over the past five decades, Democrat politicians have felt forced to either copy the right by becoming *tough on crime* (President Clinton's support of mass incarceration), or *tough on immigration* (President Obama's support of mass deportation), or advocate colorblind ec-onomic policies that avoid mentioning racial justice for fear of losing con-servative voters. While center-left politicians rationalize that improving work, education, and health care will benefit all working and middle-class Americans, fear of prioritizing racial justice is rooted in the right's narra-tive that government is being used by the left to support underserving racial and ethnic minorities *at the expense* of hardworking white people. Thus, the right's solution to "big government" is to weaken government by starving it of the tax revenue needed for safety net and public support programs, and by eliminating government regulation of business so that untethered free market capitalism can fix society's economic and related social problems.

However, since the Reagan administrations of the 1980s, this failed ex-periment in neoliberal economics has exacerbated today's toxic wealth in-equality via immense tax breaks for corporations and the wealthy, slashed programs for the poor, fueled the loss of living wage jobs for the working class now largely outsourced to foreign countries, and deregulated business practices that contributed to the Great Recession of 2008. Ironically, despite the right's condemnation of government assistance for the poor, Congress responded to the Great Recession by allocating multiple billions of dollars to bail out failing businesses including banks and financial institutions responsible for the near collapse of our economy in the first place. However, bailing out major American business has done nothing to mitigate rising wealth inequality in America.

Toxic Wealth Inequality

In his sobering book *Our Kids: The American Dream in Crisis*, distinguished Harvard professor of public policy Robert Putnam (2016), combines economic data and close-up portraits of rich, middle class, and poor families to convey the rapidly growing "opportunity gap" over the past 30 years. After unprecedented access to the American Dream for most Americans between 1945 and 1980—enabled by the New Déal protections, post-WWII prosperity and the GI Bill, the War on Poverty, and both the Civil Rights and Women's Rights movements—a sharp reversal has occurred for concerning reasons, including recessions and the expansion of global capitalism and related neoliberal economic policies (e.g., downsizing, outsourcing) that have hollowed out the industrial sector of America, upon which thousands of towns and millions of workers depended.

Putnam illustrates accelerated wealth inequality since 1980 by conveying that per capita income has grown by only $900 for those within the bottom one-fifth or lowest quintile of society, just under $9,000 for the middle quintile, and an astounding $745,000 for the top 20% of society. Further, between 2009 and 2012, income grew 31% for the top 1% of Americans versus only 0.5% for the remaining 99%. Such data signal the abrupt end of those 35 years prior to 1980 when working-class families had access to local industrial employment that afforded them a home, car, annual vacations, and children destined to exceed their parents' social mobility. Putnam even uses his own family and generation to illustrate such past opportunities in his hometown of Port Clinton, Ohio, a once prosperous town now reduced to a few haves and many have nots, mirroring thousands of such towns across America populated mainly by working-class whites who justifiably feel left behind by the government. In a warning that has come to pass, Putnam cautions that such a neglected and politically marginal population is vulnerable to manipulation by volatile extremist fascists that scapegoat minorities, exacerbate racial division, but also stoke their bitterness toward the government falsely portrayed as favoring minorities over whites in a zero-sum game.

A recent analysis of the percentage of adults within social class income brackets further supports Putnam's analysis of growing wealth inequality in America (Parker, et al., 2020). As can be seen in Figure 12.10, between 1971 and 2015 adults in the lowest income bracket grew from 16% to 20%, while adults in the highest income bracket grew from 4% to 9%, and middle class–income adults shrunk from 80% to 71%. Hence, we continue witnessing a shrinking middle class in America (61% to 50% for solidly middle class), precisely in the direction opposite a healthy distribution of wealth in the United States.

Putman mainly analyzes the advantages of the rising one-third of *neo-traditional* families with the similarly rising bottom one-third of *fragile*

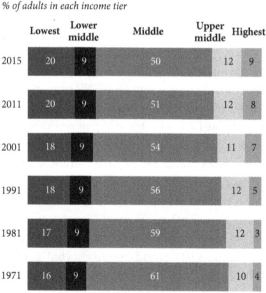

% of adults in each income tier

	Lowest	Lower middle	Middle	Upper middle	Highest
2015	20	9	50	12	9
2011	20	9	51	12	8
2001	18	9	54	11	7
1991	18	9	56	12	5
1981	17	9	59	12	3
1971	16	9	61	10	4

Note: Adults are assigned to income tiers based on thier size-adjusted household income in the calendar year prior to the survey year. Figures may not add to 100% due to rounding.

Figure 12.10. Expanding poorest and richest, and shrinking middle class Americans, 1971–2015.

With permission from Pew Research Center.

families. In a data-rich series of graphs, brought to life with detailed vignettes, Putnam illustrates fragile families' lack of opportunity resulting in a cascade of poverty-linked disadvantages including rapidly declining neighborhoods, family stability, child rearing, civic unity, and educational attainment, with most families impacted by mass incarceration and the recent opiate addiction crisis. Putnam makes sure to assert that while the above portrait of fragile families is framed by the right as the result of government nurturing dependency among the poor and in communities of color, fragile families are actually now more common in politically red versus blues states, with no correlation to welfare dependency. Putnam also underscores that while the diminishing opportunity gap is more pronounced for Latino and African American families, such families also manifest parallel disparities between their own neo-traditional and fragile families. Hence, racial and economic justice are intertwined and must be addressed simultaneously, as addressed below.

While this chapter cannot do justice to Haney Lopez's analysis of politically propagated economic and racial injustice, shared here are his insightful conclusions with implications for movement-building designed to remedy the real threat to America: accelerating wealth inequality, strategically obscured by stoking racial fear, animosity, and division; and the undermining of democracy by fomenting rage against the government falsely accused of prioritizing people of color and the poor over non-Latino whites and the affluent in America. Major findings from his RCNP support Haney Lopez' insightful yet at times counterintuitive conclusions:

First, a majority of non-Latino whites hold progressive views on racial justice, but also hold reactionary views, and switch back and forth as influenced by political rhetoric, news media and popular culture, internet chatter, and current events. Thus, the task is to help the majority of whites realize the profoundly deep connection between their antiracist values and their economic self-interest and overall well-being.

Second, a majority of African American and Latino voters find large parts of the right's narrative of racial fear and resentment convincing. That is, while the majority of Blacks and Latinos are liberal leaning Democrats, most also buy into racialized fear of people of color, including the fear of being economically replaced by immigrants. Thus, neutralizing the right's narrative is key to coalescing people of color around political action in their racial and economic self-interest.

Third, when exposed to race-class, racial fear, colorblind economic, and social justice narratives, about 20% of the extreme right strongly endorse racial fear and anti-government narratives. Similarly, about 20% of the extreme left strongly adhere racial justice narratives. Thus, Haney Lopez concludes that while these 40% are unpersuadable, approximately 60% of people in the middle of the political spectrum are persuadable, and more so by race-class fusion narratives as opposed to the other three types of narratives, regardless of respondent race or party affiliation.

Intriguingly, the third conclusion above suggests that while political ideologies and related voting patterns are resistant to change at both extremes of the political spectrum, they are flexible and amenable to change for the majority of people in the middle, or what Haney Lopez calls *persuadables*. Therefore, the overarching task is to fuse race-class consciousness, coalitions, and voting patterns using narratives that convey how most people, across race and class, benefit from advancing racial-economic justice. Examples from the RCNP supporting the above conclusions are plentiful, with a few key findings briefly summarized to underscore the empirical basis for Haney Lopez' sobering yet hopeful conclusions:

An unexpected early test of RCNP research findings occurred in 2017 when Haney Lopez was approached by the SEIU Health Care Minnesota and Faith in Minnesota, both hoping to elect Democrat Tim Waltz as governor. Until then, the RCNP's auspicious findings had not been tested in an actual major political campaign. Thus, in collaboration with the RCNP, the two Minnesota organizations compared the appeal of three political flyers by canvassing 800 households (400 non-Latino white and 400 racial and ethnic minority homes): 1) a Republican racial fear flyer displaying an American flag, stressing safer communities, and claiming that opponents will raise taxes and demand more sanctuary cities for criminal and illegal aliens; 2) a Democrat colorblind economic flyer displaying a large white family, stressing better pay for hard working Minnesotans deserving a better life, noting that special interests monopolize wealth, and the need for quality education, health care, environment, and infrastructure; and finally 3) a Democrat race-class fusion flyer displaying a mix of black and white people standing shoulder to shoulder, and stating that "Minnesotans work hard to provide for our families. Whether white, black or brown, 5th generation or newcomer, we all want to build a better future for our children." and "My opponent says some families have value while others don't count. He wants to pit us against each other in order to gain power for himself and kickbacks for his donors"; and finally, "It's time for Minnesotans to join together and rewrite the rules so that all our families have the opportunity to pursue their dreams." (Haney Lopez, 2019; pp. 47–49).

Minnesota respondents were asked to rate how convincing they found the Republican racial fear flyer on a 5-point scale from Strongly agree to Strongly disagree with a neutral mid-point. Among white respondents, 7% strongly agreed, 38% agreed, 24% disagreed or strongly disagreed, with the remainder neutral.

Next, respondents were asked which of the candidates would they vote for if the election was held tomorrow, the Democrat or Republican? Focusing only on results for the 38% of white respondents that agreed with the Republican racial fear flyer, the Republican candidate beat the Democrat by only 11% (55% to 44%) when these respondents were next shown the Democratic colorblind economic flyer. However, when next shown the Democratic race-class fusion flyer, the Democrat candidate beat the Republican by 14% (57% to 43%)! Among the 7% of whites strongly agreeing with the racial fear flyer, subsequent exposure to either colorblind or racial justice flyers had much effect on their preference for the Republican candidate. Not surprisingly, the superiority of the race-class fusion narrative was also found for respondents of color.

Looking only at the 35% of people of color that agreed with the Republican racial fear flyer, exposure to the colorblind flyer increased their intention to vote Democrat by 15% while exposure to the race-class fusion flyer increased it by 34%. Thus, while more influential for people of color, for respondents overall the race-class unity message was more persuasive than either the racial fear or colorblind economic messages. Tim Walz went on to defeat his Republican opponent by the largest margin for a Democrat candidate since 1986, and received more votes than any candidate for governor in Minnesota's history.

Clearly the RCNP has much to apply in real time. One invaluable lesson is that the effectiveness of a race-class unity approach lies in its ability to tap preexisting progressive values on racial justice held by *most* people while also appealing to their economic self-interest. Thus, Haney Lopez concludes that it is more strategic to lead with race-class unity rather than racial justice, which typically emphasizes white supremacy or white over people of color racism and discrimination. While the latter is imperative and has its place, findings from the RCNP demonstrates that it can also be counterproductive

by triggering *white fragility* (Diangelo, 2018) characterized by feeling accused, defensive, and guilty, and reinforces the misperception that that
helping minorities is a zero-sum game in which any gain for minorities is
a loss for white people. While the latter is not supported by research, such
white resistance is better transcended by leading with race-class unity, with
its explicit convergence of self-interest.

Another equally compelling argument for supporting race-class unity
approaches is that such a value and practice is also preferred by most Latinos
and African Americans over racial justice narratives that many misperceive
as complaining, playing the race card, promoting dependence on the government, blaming white people for the problems of people of color, and
dismissing individual responsibility. Thus, while racial justice narratives resonate with approximately 20% of the base on the extreme left of the political
spectrum, RCNP findings show that such narratives miss *persuadables* that
compose the middle 60%—essential to political influence and victories, intersectional movement building, and ultimately greater equity for the vast
majority of Americans.

Conclusions

> We've got to recreate the Obama coalition to win. And that means
> about women, that's people of color, that's our LGBTQ community,
> that's working people, that's our labor unions.
> —Kamala Harris, 2019 November Vice Presidential Debate

While Harris' plea is congruent with race-class fusion, the legendary Obama
coalition of 2008 and 2012 appears to have splintered in 2016, given that
about six million members switched to Trump, 4.4 million didn't vote, and
2.3 million backed third-party candidates (Larsen & Simonson, 2019).
Almost 1.6 million of nonvoters were African American; about five million Obama-to-Trump voters were white, and a majority of women voted
for Trump rather than Hilary Clinton, who also had 5% less of youngest
voters (18- to 29-year-olds), as compared to Obama in 2012. However, the
challenge of building a progressive coalition could be enhanced by taking a
few pages from the RCNP playbook. That is, political campaigns should be
aimed at the majority of middle-spectrum voters by appealing to their racial justice values, and mitigating their reactionary values by conveying that

fighting for racial and economic justice is in their self-interest regardless of political party, social class, or racial and ethnic background.

The above strategies will benefit Latino social positionality and well-being in view of the formidable federal laws and policies and the flurry of executive orders and initiatives aimed at stripping immigrants of supports and protections while criminalizing undocumented Latinos in cruel and violent ways. The unprecedented criminalization and persecution of undocumented people stands in stark and ironic contrast to Trump pardoning so many of his loyal colleagues convicted of multiple serious crimes, including criminal felonies.

The predominantly Latinx immigrant rights movement will continue building upon a consistent history of Latinx resistance to racism and discrimination, ranging from grass-roots community movements to enacting legislative policy at local, state, and national levels. Continued diversification of Latinx movements is strategically necessary to more effectively counter *strategic racism* used by the Trump administration, and too many on the right today, to stoke racial fear and division as a distraction from toxic wealth inequality and economic injustice for the majority of Americans.

Greater diversity in Latinx movements is already apparent in what Terriquez et al. (2016) call the *intersectional collective action framework* currently embraced by undocumented LGBTQ youth activists and allies. This framework aims to enhance understanding of their own intersectional identities, build greater solidarity within and between social justice movements, and motivate political activism to produce sustained change. Over the past two decades, undocumented youth activists have courageously modeled for the Latino family, community, and culture, the need to embrace intersectionality in order to transform oppression within mainstream society and Latinx culture and to continue liberating our unlimited human potential. By raising up Latino resistance, activism, and movements past, present, and future, this chapter underscores ways in which a dynamic conceptualization of Latino culture works to support collective humanity while encountering, enduring, and transcending dehumanization and advancing our aspiring yet challenged democracy. Such knowledge is foundational to practitioners and agencies working Latino clients, families, and communities in order to better understand, support, and integrate Latino strengths and assets into needed services.

References

Alvarez, R. (1986). The Lemon Grove Incident: The Nation's First Successful Desegregation Court Case. *The Journal of San Diego History, 32*(2), 116–135.

Burciaga, E. M., & Martinez, L. M. (2017). How do political contexts shape undocumented youth movements? Evidence from three immigrant destinations. *Mobilization: An International Quarterly. 22*(4), 451–471. https://doi.org/10.17813/1086-671X-20-4-451.

Burnett, J. (2019). How the Trump administration's 'zero tolerance' policy changed the immigration debate. All Things Considered, National Public Radio (June 20). https://www.npr.org/2019/06/20/734496862/how-the-trump-administrations-zero-tolerance-policy-changed-the-immigration-deba

Chotiner, I. (2019). The frustration behind Puerto Rico's popular movement. *The New Yorker*, July 26. https://www.newyorker.com/news/q-and-a/the-frustration-behind-puerto-ricos-popular-movement

de Vogue, A. (2020). Sotomayor issues scathing dissent in Supreme Court order that could reshape legal immigration. CNN Politics. https://www.cnn.com/2020/02/23/politics/sotomayor-dissent-supreme-court/index.html

Encyclopedia Britannica (2020). Black Legend: Spanish History. https://www.britannica.com/topic/Black-Legend

Garcia, J. A. (2003a). Building political alliances. In J. A. Garcia (Ed.), *Latino politics in America: Community, culture, and interests* (pp. 216–249). New York: Rowan and Littlefield.

Garcia, J. A. (2003b). The Latino community: Building recognition politics. In J. A. Garcia (Ed.), *Latino politics in America: Community, culture, and interests* (pp. 241–257). New York: Rowan and Littlefield.

Ghandnoosh, N., & Rovner, J. (2017). Immigration and public safety. The Sentencing Project. Washington DC. https://www.sentencingproject.org/reports/immigration-and-public-safety/

Gonzalez-Barrera, A., & Hugo Lopez, M. (2016). U.S. immigrant deportations fall to lowest level since 2007. Washington DC: Pew Research Center.

Grossman, S. F., Cardoso, R. M., Belanger, g. G., Belski, J., Corethers, T. C., Pettinelli, M. E., & Redd, M. A. (2000). Pilsen and the Resurrection Project: Community organization in a Latino community. *Journal of Poverty, 4*(1/2), 131–149.

Haney Lopez, I. (2019). Merge left: Fusing race and class, winning elections, and saving America. New York: The New Press.

Hayes-Bautista, D. (2017). La Nueva California: Latinos from pioneers to post-millennials (2nd ed.). Oakland, CA: University of California Press.

Kerwin, K., & McCabe, K. (2010). Arrested on entry: Operation Streamline and the prosecution of immigration crimes. Washington DC: Migration Policy Institute. https://www.migrationpolicy.org/article/arrested-entry-operation-streamline-and-prosecution-immigration-crimes

Los Angeles Times Staff (2020). Police have killed 886 civilians in L.A. County since 2000. June 9. https://www.latimes.com/projects/los-angeles-police-killings-database/#nt=00000172-6be6-d818-a7fb-6bfe448e0001-liE0promoSmall-7030col1-main

La Opinión (2020). 'Black Lives Matter' merece todo nuestro apoyo [deserve all of our support]. June 5. https://laopinion.com/2020/06/05/black-lives-matter-merece-todo-nuestro-apoyo/

Larsen, C., & Simonson, J. (2019). 2020 Democrats chase mirage of Obama coalition. *Washington Examiner* (December 5). https://www.washingtonexaminer.com/news/2020-democrats-chase-mirage-of-obama-coalition

Latino Community Foundation (2019). Latino political power in California: 25 years after Proposition 187. https://latinocf.org/

Martinez, D. E., Martinez-Schuldt, R. D., & Cantor, G. (2017). Providing sanctuary or fostering crime? A review of the research on "Sanctuary Cities" and crime. *Sociological Compass, 12*(1), e12547. https://doi.org/10.1111/soc4.12547

Meyer, R. (2017). What's happening with the relief effort in Puerto Rico? A timeline of the unprecedented catastrophe of Hurricane Maria. *The Atlantic*, October 4. https://www.theatlantic.com/science/archive/2017/10/what-happened-in-puerto-rico-a-timeline-of-hurricane-maria/541956/

Nicholls, W. (2013). The DREAMers: How the undocumented youth movement transformed the immigrant rights debate. Stanford, CA: Stanford University Press.

Nixon, R., & Qiu, L. (2018). What Is ICE and why do critics want to abolish it? *New York Times* (July 3). https://www.nytimes.com/2018/07/03/us/politics/fact-check-ice-immigration-abolish.html

Ousey, G. C., & Kubrin E. C. (2018). Immigration and crime: Assessing a contentious issue. *Annual Review of Criminology, 1*, 63–84.

Pardo, M. S. (1998). Mexican American women activists: Identity and resistance in two Los Angeles communities. Philadelphia: Temple University Press.

Parker, K., Menasce Horowitz, J., & Anderson, M. (2020). Amid Protests, majorities across racial and ethnic groups express support for the Black Lives Matter movement. Washington D.C.: Pew Research Center (2020).

Pinchin, K. (2019). How Hurricane Maria fueled Puerto Rico's resistance. Frontline, August 2. https://www.pbs.org/wgbh/frontline/article/how-hurricane-maria-fueled-puerto-ricos-resistance/

Putnam, R. (2016). Our kids: The American dream in crisis. New York: Simon and Shuster.

Racial and Identity Profiling Advisory Board (2019). Annual Report 2019. California Department of Justice. https://oag.ca.gov/sites/all/files/agweb/pdfs/ripa/ripa-board-report-2019.pdf

Renshaw, J. (2020). Exclusive: as the U.S. shut down, Trump's legal fight to build wall ramped up. *Reuters*, April 16. https://www.reuters.com/article/us-usa-election-trump-wall-exclusive/exclusive-as-the-u-s-shut-down-trumps-legal-fight-to-build-wall-ramped-up-idUSKCN21Y2DR

Rosa, A., & Mazzei, P. (2020). Video reveals unused earthquake aid in Puerto Rico: 'We are outraged'. *The New York Times*, January 20. https://www.nytimes.com/2020/01/20/us/puerto-rico-protests-emergency-supplies.html

Terriquez, V., Brenes, T., & Lopez, A. (2018). Intersectionality as a multipurpose collective action frame: The case of the undocumented youth movement. *Ethnicities, 18*(2), 260–276.

Univisión (2020). ¿Por qué los hispanos deben apoyar el movimiento Black Lives Matter? [Why Hispanics should support the Black Lives Matter movement]. (June 6). https://www.univision.com/local/los-angeles-kmex/elecciones-estados-unidos-2020/por-que-los-hispanos-deben-apoyar-el-movimiento-black-lives-matter-video

Wertz, J., Azrael, D., Berrigan, J., Barber, C. Nelson, E., Hemenway, D., Salhi, C. & Miller, M. 2(2020). A typology of civilians shot and killed by US Police: a latent class analysis of firearm legal intervention homicide in the 2014–2015 national violent death reporting system. *Journal of Urban Health*, *97*, 317–328. https://doi.org/10.1007/s11 524-020-00430-0

Wikipedia (2020). Hurricane Maria death toll controversy. https://en.wikipedia.org/wiki/ Hurricane_Maria_death_toll_controversy

Wong, T. (2017). The effects of sanctuary policies on crime and the economy. Center for American Progress (January 26), 1–24. https://www.americanprogress.org/article/the-effects-of-sanctuary-policies-on-crime-and-the-economy/

Epilogue

Context and Synthesis

In the 2007 epilogue to the first edition of this book, I underscored the historical and sociocultural embeddedness of *nonrandom* patterns of psychosocial and health problems over-affecting Latino populations in the United States. The current edition expands upon disparities in health insurance and health literacy rather than disease prevalence per se. These disparities result in deferred detection and care, and disparities in preventable morbidity and mortality that are too frequently built into the Latino experience.

Pressing national crises such as increasing rates of suicide and gun violence, substance abuse and overdoses, mental illness and homelessness, all during a politicized global pandemic, are but a few of the social crises erasing the lines between psychological, social, and health problems. These render more visible the larger contexts of individual, family, community, and population-wide problem patterns requiring *multilevel practice* that integrates micro-individual and family, meso-network and community, and macro-social and political interventions.

Our Democratic and Fascist Impulses

Today's derisive-by-design politics, pandering to our worst impulses and increasingly on the basis of non-truths, betray our greed for excessive power which, when left unchecked, creates corruption, conflict, and imbalance. If you think the protracted struggle for equity has been difficult within our aspiring democracy, imagine the challenge should we succumb to fascism void of freedom. Fortunately, today's ends-justify-the-means politics also engage our deeper impulses to upend oppression.

Welcome to My Positionality

Thus, the goal of this book to advance *sociocultural competence* with Latino populations necessarily integrates *la política* [politics] in ways that align with the author's social positionality, shared in the "About the Author" section, to provide insight into the values driving this book project as well as my assets and blind spots. *¡Bienvenido!*

Accrual of Latino Scholarship

In the 2007 epilogue, I expressed commitment to ongoing learning and looking forward to the next (now this) edition *con mucho gusto*. Since then, I've been awestruck by the steady accrual of Latino-focused scholarship advancing the helping professions. Indeed, it was challenging to selectively integrate over 15 years of research since the first edition. The revisiting and amplification of book sections were many, as were insertions of new chapters, topics, and fresh data, frequently compelled by the onslaught of anti-Latino and anti-immigrant rhetoric, policies, as well as the many hopeful forms of individual and community pushback.

Expanding Representation

While *Dominicanos* and several *Centro Americano* populations are now represented in this second edition, alongside Mexican Americans, Puerto Ricans, and Cuban Americans that predominated the first edition, more Latino populations and intersectional experiences deserve attention to continue advancing the helping professions. Greater inclusion of the complementary and alternative practices of diverse communities and networks promise to do the same. For instance, mounting evidence reviewed in this edition regarding the effective integration of *promotores de salud* into professional community-based care inspires expanding such hybrid approaches to health care by and for Latino populations.

The Rising

In closing, whether or not a third edition of this book is advanced, the enormity of the topic area will continue accelerating, as will the informative and directive scholarship of Latino-focused researchers and practitioners, including parallel community-based practices. In concert with the resistance and agency lifted up in this second edition, Latino social mobility and well-being will continue rising regardless of regressive social forces beckoning our resolve. *¡Adelante!*

Index

For the benefit of digital users, indexed terms that span two pages (e.g., 52-53) may, on occasion, appear on only one of those pages.

Tables, figures, and boxes are indicated by *t*, *f*, and *b* following the page number